ESSAYS PRESENTED TO
RUDOLF WITTKOWER

PHAIDON

ESSAYS PRESENTED TO

RUDOLF WITTKOWER

ON HIS SIXTY-FIFTH BIRTHDAY

=====

IN TWO PARTS

ESSAYS IN

THE HISTORY OF ARCHITECTURE

WITH TWENTY-SIX CONTRIBUTIONS

ESSAYS IN

THE HISTORY OF ART

WITH THIRTY-NINE CONTRIBUTIONS

=====

ESSAYS IN THE HISTORY
OF ARCHITECTURE
PRESENTED TO
RUDOLF WITTKOWER

EDITED BY DOUGLAS FRASER
HOWARD HIBBARD & MILTON J·LEWINE

PHAIDON

PHAIDON PUBLISHERS INC · NEW YORK
DISTRIBUTORS IN THE UNITED STATES: FREDERICK A. PRAEGER · INC
111 FOURTH AVENUE · NEW YORK · N.Y. 10003
LIBRARY OF CONGRESS CATALOG CARD NUMBER: 69–20280

THE FIRST PRINTING OF THIS VOLUME WAS PUBLISHED IN 1967

WITH THE GENEROUS SUPPORT OF THE INDIVIDUALS AND INSTITUTIONS

LISTED IN THE PREFACE

SBN 7148 1300 1

MADE IN GREAT BRITAIN
PRINTED BY THE PITMAN PRESS · BATH

RUDOLF WITTKOWER, FBA

Photo by Walter Bird,
FIBP, FRPS

PREFACE

THE idea of honoring Professor Rudolf Wittkower with a collection of essays on the occasion of his sixty-fifth birthday was greeted with such enthusiasm by his apparently innumerable friends that, had we not maintained a rigorous schedule of deadlines, we would have been forced to launch a periodical rather than just two volumes of essays. The warmth of the replies in response to our query was eloquent witness to the friendship and respect that Professor Wittkower has always engendered—from his university days in Munich and Berlin and his years at the Bibliotheca Hertziana in Rome (1923–1933) through what art historians might call his 'English' and 'American' periods (from 1934 to 1956 at University College, London, as Durning-Lawrence Professor of the History of Art and at the Warburg Institute, and from 1955 to the present at Columbia University, first as Visiting Professor and then as Professor and Chairman of the Department of Art History and Archaeology). During these years he accumulated impressive knowledge and developed theories of far-reaching consequence. But his thoughts have never remained sterile arcana or precious bits of private property: his titanic capacity for work is matched by characteristic generosity, and his information and ideas have always been made available to students, friends, colleagues, and the public in consultations, letters, lectures, and a staggering number of publications.

In order to reflect Professor Wittkower's own contributions to scholarship, these essays are designed to deal with subjects in each of the overlapping categories into which most of his published work falls: the migration and interpretation of symbols, problems of proportion and perspective, the iconographic interpretation of art, Italian Renaissance sculpture and architecture, Baroque art in all its manifestations, Palladio and Palladianism, and English architecture. Many of these essays expand our knowledge in these various fields; others refine ideas or explore new aspects of material Wittkower has worked on. But it is safe to say that a majority of these essays could never have been written without his pioneering work in such fields as the Italian Baroque, which opened the way to modern interest and scholarship.

The generosity and scholarly dedication of many friends made this volume possible. We owe an inestimable debt to each of the authors for their efforts to contribute essays of solid value. And we owe our warmest and sincerest thanks to those who underwrote the major costs of publication: The Edgar J. Kaufmann Charitable Foundation; The Graham Foundation for Advanced Studies in the Fine Arts; The Samuel H. Kress Foundation; an anonymous donor; Mr Philip Johnson; The J. M. Kaplan Fund, Inc., through the interest of Mrs Alice M. Kaplan; Mr Frank P. Leslie; Mr Edwin C. Vogel; Mr and Mrs John de Menil; The Luis A. Ferré Foundation, Inc., through the interest of Mr Luis A. Ferré; Mr Henry Ittleson, jr.; Mr Myron S. Falk, jr.; Mr and Mrs Henry H. Weldon; Mr Max Abramovitz; Mrs Anthony A. Bliss; Mr Armand G. Erpf; Mr Willard B. Golovin; Mrs David M. Heyman; The Four Oaks Foundation through the interest of the late Mr Donald F. Hyde; Miss Dorothy Miner; Mr Nathan Ratkin; Mr Hanns Schaeffer; and Mrs David Shiverick Smith. Additional contributions have been made by Mr Paul H. Ganz, Mr and Mrs Bernard J. Lasker, Professor James Grote Van Derpool, Mr Alfred H. Barr, jr., Mr and Mrs Robert Delson, Dr Frederick J. Dockstader, Mr René d'Harnoncourt, Mr and Mrs Howard E. Houston, Mrs Elisabeth Blair MacDougall, Mr and Mrs Leo Najda, Commander and Mrs Marsden J. Perry, Mrs Jeanne Siegel, Messrs Stephen Spector and Peter Josten, and Mrs Morton Baum.

At different stages of planning this work many friends gave helpful advice and encouragement. From the very beginning Miss Mary M. Davis, Mr H. I. Miller, and Mr Desmond Zwemmer encouraged our efforts. Professor H. W. Janson and Mr Edgar J. Kaufmann, jr., offered constant support and help throughout the entire evolution of the project in ways too numerous to mention. For the volume of studies in architectural history we owe particular thanks to the helpfulness of Mr Philip Johnson, and we are also indebted to Mr Arthur Drexler and Mr John D. Entenza. Special thanks for their aid are also due to Miss Sarah Faunce, Mrs Alice M. Kaplan, Mr Frank P. Leslie, and Mrs Henry H. Weldon. At Columbia, Miss Etta Arntzen corrected the bibliography of Professor Wittkower's published work; Mr Stanley Salmen handled the burden of all contractual obligations; and Miss Konstanze Bachmann, Mrs Russell Edgerton, Miss Helene Farrow, and Mrs Glenn Kohlmeyer cheerfully carried out the major part of the secretarial work involved. Dr I. Grafe saw the book through production, and we should like to thank the Phaidon Press for their cooperation throughout. We thank all of these ladies and gentlemen most gratefully, and finally, with particular warmth, we wish to express our heartfelt thanks to Mrs Margot Wittkower, who has helped and supported us from the beginning.

All of us join together in dedicating this book to Rudolf Wittkower with thanks, respect, and affection. May he enjoy these essays as fruits of his own labor, and may they inspire him to still more prodigious achievements.

DOUGLAS FRASER

HOWARD HIBBARD

Columbia University   MILTON J. LEWINE

22 June 1966

CONTENTS

EDITH PORADA

Battlements in the Military Architecture and in the Symbolism of the Ancient Near East

In the *Journal of the Warburg Institute*, II (1938–1939), Rudolf Wittkower published an article 'Eagle and Serpent; A Study in the Migration of Symbols'. His stated aim was the demonstration of a method by which the diffusionists' concern with a migration of symbols would be combined with 'the "functional" method: that is, the attempt to understand the significance of a particular symbol in a given context' (*op. cit.*, p. 293).

Only a scholar with the encyclopedic knowledge, the insight, judgment and organizing ability of Rudolf Wittkower, as well as his working power, could have succeeded in such an undertaking, which led him from the origins of the symbol in Western Asia to its manifestations in nineteenth-century Europe with asides on the arts of the Pacific and of ancient America. Today, almost two decades after the article was written, the main points of the section on the ancient Near East are still valid. This is remarkable in a field in which successive discoveries have resulted in the elimination of many earlier theories. Wittkower's article remains even now a source of inspiration, both for its insights and for the method which it demonstrates. Although the present article on battlements is limited in scope and deals with only one aspect of the problem posed by that architectural element, the fact that it was sparked by Wittkower's 'Eagle and Serpent' may nevertheless be mentioned.

The battlement as a symbol of military protection is still understood, especially because it was brought back into use for the armories built in the United States in the last decade of the nineteenth century or the first decade of the twentieth (Fig. 1).[1] Before that, battlements had been eliminated from the rooftops of British and continental castles only about the middle of the sixteenth century, to reappear again with incipient Romanticism in the eighteenth century.

To trace the earlier history of battlements throughout the world and to determine their military and symbolic significance at the places of their occurrence is far beyond this writer's competence. Here an attempt will be made only to define more precisely than has been done heretofore the history of battlements in the ancient Near East and to gain thereby additional insight into their architectural function and symbolic meaning.

According to Webster's *New International Dictionary* (2nd edition), a battlement is 'a parapet, consisting of alternate solid parts and open spaces, surmounting the walls of ancient fortified buildings. . . .' Such parapets first appeared in Egypt. A small ivory tower, probably a gaming piece of ivory, found at Abydos in the royal graves of the First Dynasty has on its top a strongly projecting circular platform which rests on round beams and has a parapet with rounded merlons.[2] Their rounded shape was probably derived from that of the shields carried by the Egyptian warriors, which may have formed the earliest protective enclosures.[3] The shape remained characteristic of Egyptian battlements as is shown by renderings of fortresses in reliefs and paintings[4] and by the remains of Ramesses' fortified palace and temple at Medinet Habu (Fig. 2). It may be noted that in an Egyptian relief representing a model of a fortified temple complex of the type of Medinet Habu the temple itself has a cavetto cornice.[5] This shows that battlements were used in Egypt for practical, perhaps partly also for decorative, purposes

1. R. Koch, 'The Medieval Castle Revival: New York Armories', *Journal of the Society of Architectural Historians*, XIV/3, 1955, pp. 23–29.

2. A. Scharff, *Die Altertümer der Vor- und Frühzeit Ägyptens* (Staatliche Museen zu Berlin: Mitteilungen aus der ägyptischen Sammlung, IV, v), vol. II, Berlin, 1929, pl. 33: 279; text pp. 147–8. Scharff was inclined to consider this and related representations as silos for grain rather than as fortification towers, whereas U. Hölscher, *Das hohe Tor von Medinet Habu* (12. Wissenschaftliche Veröffentlichung der Deutschen Orient-Gesellschaft), Leipzig, 1910, p. 56, Fig. 52, used the little ivory tower to document the earliest occurrence of battlements.

3. The suggestion that the shape of the Egyptian merlons was derived from that of shields was made by A. R. Schulman, who referred me to shield walls which the Egyptian armies erected when in the field as represented in the reliefs of the battle of Kadesh, W. Wreszinski, *Atlas zur altaegyptischen Kulturgeschichte*, pt. II, 1935, pls. 82, 92, 170. Schulman discussed these temporary fortified camps in his M.A. thesis, *The Military Establishment of the Egyptian Empire*, Chicago, 1958, p. 61.

4. The best known among these reliefs and paintings have been collected by Hölscher, *Das hohe Tor von Medinet Habu*, pp. 56–62; more material was assembled by A. Badawy, *Le Dessin architectural chez les anciens Égyptiens* (Service des antiquités du Caire), Cairo, 1948, pp. 139–58 (*l'architecture militaire*).

5. The model of a fortified temple was reproduced by Hölscher, *Das hohe Tor von Medinet Habu*, p. 60, Fig. 56, after a paper imprint of a relief on the Chons temple at Karnak.

but that they did not partake of the religious meaning of a temple.

Egyptian battlements seem to have had a decisive influence on battlement forms in Hittite Asia Minor, Syria and Palestine. For the last two countries reliefs portraying wars fought by the Egyptian pharaohs Seti I (1308–1291 B.C.) and Ramesses II (1290–1224 B.C.) provide us with views of battlemented fortresses,[6] the accuracy of which is probably greater than has been assumed in the past. Evidence from Imperial Hittite sources in the form of the headgear of the goddesses in the rock sanctuary of Yazilikaya shows them wearing turreted crowns, each tower having two rounded merlons.[7] Such merlons are also seen on the fragmentary models of vases in the form of fortified towers found at Boghazköy, one of which is reproduced here (Fig. 3).[8] Similar merlons also lined the walls below the towers. Evidence for survival into the Late Hittite period of rounded merlons on major walls comes from Carchemish, where several stones were found in front of the long wall of sculpture, 'dating well back in the Late Hittite period; some of these were oblong blocks 0.20 m high, the tops rounded from back to front: the others were similar, but in the middle rose a tall round-topped crocket 0.25 m in height; these would seem to have stood along the top of the wall'.[9]

Battlements with stepped merlons, which have often been indicated in reconstructions of Late Hittite architecture, have been found but in a size so small that their use could have been only for decoration.[10] Such

stepped battlement decoration was also found on an altar top from Carchemish (Fig. 4), as well as in the enameled wall decoration of an altar at Tell Halaf.[11] The appearance of these stepped battlements in North Syria and their use for religious structures and furnishings point toward the influence of Mesopotamian battlements, to which we may now turn.

The defensive architecture of Mesopotamia has yielded only one certain instance of utilitarian battlements: in one place on the low exterior rampart of Assur, raised in Late Assyrian times, probably shortly before the destruction of the Empire (Fig. 11). Otherwise we are dependent on representations in art for the history of Mesopotamian battlements. There is no evidence for them before the early second millennium B.C.,[12] a fact which also seems to be supported in the language by the absence of early terms which can be identified as referring to battlements. From that time, that is, from the early second millennium, dates a single, partly damaged clay plaque from Larsa which shows a deity stepping on a fallen warrior who lies above a battlemented wall and city gate.[13] The shape of the merlons

6. Wreszinski, *Atlas*, II, pls. 34 ff., *passim*.

7. Drawings of the headgear of two goddesses from Yazilikaya were reproduced and discussed by Bittel in K. Bittel, R. Naumann, H. Otto, *Yazilikaya* (61. Wissenschaftliche Veröffentlichung der Deutschen Orient-Gesellschaft), Berlin-Leipzig, 1941, p. 116, Fig. 46.

8. The second battlemented vase from Boghazkoy has the head and forelegs of an animal, identified by Bittel as a wolf, above the inception of each of the three ribbon handles. Bittel left open the question of whether these zoomorphic decorations of the handles merely conform to a fairly common Hittite practice or whether in this case the protomes should be taken as being in some relation to the towers; K. Bittel in *Mitteilungen der Deutschen Orient-Gesellschaft*, no. 91, 1958, pp. 32–34, Figs. 36, 37. Both vessels were published by F. Fischer, *Die hethitische Keramik von Bogazköy* (75. Wissenschaftliche Veröffentlichung der Deutschen Orient-Gesellschaft), Berlin, 1963, pl. 123: 1080, 1082.

9. C. L. Woolley, *Carchemish, Report on the Excavations at Jerablus on Behalf of the British Museum*, pt. II, *The Town Defences*, the British Museum, 1921, p. 151.

10. Small decorative terracotta battlements only about 20 cm long and covered with glaze, probably originally blue, were found at Zincirli, F. von Luschan and W. Andrae, *Ausgrabungen in Sendschirli V* (Staatliche Museen zu Berlin, Mitteilungen aus den orientalischen Sammlungen, Heft XV), Berlin, 1943, pl. 31, a–c. The suggestion was made that these battlements were used inside the building, perhaps in the decoration of an altar, *op. cit.*, p. 61 and R. Naumann, *Architektur Kleinasiens* (Deutsches archäologisches Institut), Tübingen, 1955, p. 154.

11. Glazed stepped merlons were used at Tell Halaf on a structure described as a '*Postament*' or altar, located before the eastern lion portal (F. Langenegger, K. Müller, R. Naumann, *Max Freiherr von Oppenheim, Tell Halaf*, vol. 2, *Die Bauwerke*, Berlin, 1950, pl. 13; plan 11: NS– Schnitt 5–6; text pp. 71–78).
There were merlons in two sizes; the larger merlons, probably alternately white and green (perhaps originally blue), may have crowned the structure, the smaller in the same colors may have been applied as a frieze below the top.

12. Renderings of Mesopotamian buildings dated before the early second millennium B.C. fail to show battlemented parapets. This becomes obvious from the text figures of E. Heinrich, *Bauwerke in der altsumerischen Bildkunst* (Schriften der Max Freiherr von Oppenheim—Stiftung 2), Wiesbaden, 1957, and from an examination of the architectural renderings in cylinder seals and other works of art dating from the Akkad to the early Isin Larsa period, from the twenty-fourth to the nineteenth centuries B.C. Possible examples in a steatite vase from Adab (reproduced by P. Delougaz, 'Architectural Representations on Steatite Vases', *Iraq*, XXII, 1960, pl. IX: c) and in fragments of another steatite vase in the Iraq Museum, IM 27889 and 27233 (F. Basmachi, 'Sculptured Stone Vases in the Iraq Museum', *Sumer*, VI, 1950, pt. 1, pl. 2: 5, 6 [Arabic section], pt. 2, p. 172; also reproduced by Heinrich, *op. cit.*, p. 88, Fig. 112, and in *The Illustrated London News*, Sept. 12, 1936, p. 134, Figs. 10, 12) have non-Mesopotamian, eastern connections. These are exemplified by the humped bull on one of the fragments. Further support for the eastern derivation of a decorative frieze resembling stepped battlements is supplied by the frieze of upright and reversed stepped 'merlons' above the colonnade of the northern façade of the palace at Mundigak east of Kandahar in Afghanistan, tentatively dated in the second quarter of the third millennium B.C. by J.-M. Casal, *Fouilles de Mundigak* (Mémoires de la délégation archéologique française en Afghanistan), t. XVII, Paris, 1961, vol. II, Fig. 22, pl. XII: B; vol. I, text, pp. 49–50.

13. A. Parrot, who reproduced the plaque in *Sumer* (The Arts of Mankind), New York, 1961, Fig. 358 (C), kindly informed me that it is not in the Louvre as stated *loc. cit.* but in the Iraq Museum in Baghdad. Moreover he noted that the relief

rendered in the plaque cannot be recognized; they may be stepped or rounded. Of a different nature are the projecting rectangular plaques observed in a house-shaped offering stand found in Temple F at Nuzi,[14] probably dated about 1700–1500 B.C. Though these plaques were called battlements by the excavator[15] who noted their appearance between the first and second stories of the house, they cannot have been anything else but parts of a cornice without the military value of battlements. All other representations of battlemented walls are later, beginning about the middle of the second millennium B.C. A cylinder seal impression from Assur dated in the thirteenth or twelfth century B.C. (Fig. 5), shows defenders of a city under attack standing behind the battlemented parapets of walls or towers. The merlons of the parapet are drawn as if they were rounded in the Egyptian and Syrian manner. While the town portrayed was probably not Assyrian, since the Assyrians always showed themselves in their art as the attackers, never as the defenders of a town, they nevertheless usually pictured foreign towns much like their own, paying attention only rarely to the individual features of walls and buildings.[16] In view of the occurrence of battlements of Egyptian type in Fig. 5, it seems very likely that the Assyrians took over from Egypt not only the idea of having battlements but also their rounded shape. The transformation into a stepped form, which was easier to produce with bricks and which may have also had ancient religious connotations in Mesopotamia and Iran,[17] probably occurred only secondarily and gradu-

ally. A cult vessel from Nuzi, near Kirkuk in northern Iraq (ancient Mesopotamia), dated in the fifteenth or fourteenth century B.C., in the shape of a house or a fortress still seems to have merlons which are rounded on top (Fig. 6). One would like to know whether there was a figure of a bird perched on each of the four corner merlons, which were vertically pierced to a depth of 5 mm.[18] References to birds sitting on battlements are occasionally encountered in texts.[19] From the same period as the offering stand may date the painting in the palace at Nuzi (Fig. 7), which seems to be composed of architectural elements such as city gates, walls and towers and which may have abbreviated renderings of stepped battlements in its borders of triangles.

An intermediary form between Egyptian rounded and Mesopotamian stepped battlements seems to be represented in the tower-like structure borne by a horned animal forming one of the cult vessels found at Bazmusian, a site in northeastern Iraq.[20] Such vessels representing fortified buildings seem to have been a widespread fashion in Western Asia between about 1500 and 1200 B.C. Perhaps this fashion for rendering architectural forms, which is further exemplified by the battlemented walls and towers on a boundary stone from Susa of about the twelfth century B.C.[21] and also on cylinder seal impressions with temples from Assur,[22]

has been chipped off at the lower right corner, thus giving an unusual appearance to the design.

A recent study of the fortifications in Mesopotamia at the beginning of the second millennium B.C. by Ruth Opificius, 'Befestigungen des Zweistromlandes im Beginn des zweiten Jahrtausends', *Baghdader Mitteilungen*, 3, 1964, pp. 78–90, does not add evidence for early battlements.

14. The offering stand reproduced by R. F. S. Starr, *Nuzi*, vol. II, Cambridge, 1937, pl. 61: B, was found in temple F which was transitional between the Akkad to Old Babylonian levels of GA.SUR and the Mitannian levels of Nuzi. The date of temple F may therefore be placed approximately in the second quarter of the second millennium B.C.

15. These battlements were mentioned by Starr, *Nuzi*, vol. I, p. 374, who considered them part of an ancient tradition in Mesopotamia. Since he gave no specific references, one may wonder what he had in mind in view of the absence of such early battlements from Mesopotamian representations; see above, note 12.

16. The reliefs of king Sargon (721–705 B.C.) differ from those of other rulers in showing considerable variation among the fortified towns portrayed. The most distinctive of these is Musasir; P. E. Botta and E. Flandin, *Monument de Ninive*, vol. II, Paris, 1849, pl. 141.

17. The most obvious antecedents of the stepped battlements in the form of decorative architectural elements with possible religious connotations have been collected by G. Garbini, 'The Stepped Pinnacle in the Ancient Near East', *East and West*, 9, 1958, pp. 85–91. See also note 12 above.

18. Starr, *Nuzi*, pp. 439–40; such birds are rendered on the 'two-part trough', probably an offering vessel, *op. cit.*, pl. 113: B.

19. A text mentions that a falcon appeared sitting on the top of the *samītu* of a wall, cf. *Cuneiform Texts from Babylonian Tablets in the British Museum*, pt. XXXIX, 1926, pl. 30: 58 (cf. pt. II of this article, s.v. *samītu*).

20. The vessel from Bazmusian was described in the catalogue of the exhibition *Schätze aus dem Irak*, Rautenstrauch-Joest Museum der Stadt Köln, 1964, 86, no. 121. A photograph is published in the Iraq Museum Guide [in Arabic], pl. 75, IM 60294.

21. *Encyclopédie photographique de l'art*, vol. I, 1935, pls. 266, 267.

22. That the buildings represented are indeed temples is indicated in unequivocal manner by the dog, symbol of the goddess Gula, on an altar in the opening of the gate in Fig. 8a. There is evidence for such an altar before the main gate of the sanctuary from the central court of the Nabu temple, eight meters from the portal, cf. G. Loud, *Khorsabad* (Chicago University, Oriental Institute Publications, vol. 40), pt. II, Chicago, 1938, pl. 22 C–F; text p. 42. The altar at Tell Halaf, mentioned in note 11 above, seems to have stood in a similar position before the lion portal of the 'temple palace' of that site. Proof that a temple was rendered in Fig. 8a is further supplied by the representation of a goddess herself, seated within the gate of a similar temple, in one of the scenes of an obelisk ascribed by E. Unger to Ashurnasirpal I (1050–1032 B.C.). (The date for Ashurnasirpal I cited here and all other regnal dates of Assyrian and Babylonian kings given in the present paper are taken from J. A. Brinkman, 'Mesopotamian Chronology of the Historical Period', Appendix to A. L. Oppenheim, *Mesopotamia, Portrait of a Dead Civilization*, Chicago, 1964, pp. 335–52.) The scene of the obelisk was reproduced by Unger in *Mitteilungen der altorientalischen Gesellschaft*, VI/1, 2, 1932, pl. III, below.

likewise of twelfth-century date (Fig. 8a, b), was not unconnected with the visual interest stimulated by actual battlemented parapets.

The appearance of the stepped battlement in art follows by a few centuries the introduction of the battering ram against which sloping glacis were built in the Hyksos fortifications of Palestine.[23] It may be suggested that tall towers such as those appearing in the representations cited here also would have been useful in enabling the defenders to shower missiles upon the personnel operating the war machines. Battlements may therefore have been more urgently needed at this time than before.

A practical, decorative and probably also a propitious value thus assured the ultimate success of the stepped battlement in Mesopotamia, where, as we have seen, it was used not only in fortification walls but also on the towers and walls of temples. The use of these battlements in the military, temple and palace architecture of Assyria and Babylonia continued in the early first millennium B.C. as is shown by the reliefs of the Assyrian kings from Ashurnasirpal II (883–859 B.C.) to Ashurbanipal (668–627 B.C.). Battlements thought by the excavators to have been used decoratively rather than for defence were found at Khorsabad, the short-lived residence of king Sargon II (721–705 B.C.). There the masonry of the palace terrace was apparently topped by blocks of limestone cut with stepped crenelations.[24] Some represent complete battlements, others merely halves intended for use on the many angles caused by the buttresses. Their thickness was about 28 cm, and they ranged from a height of 1.20 m to 1 m. Battlements also made of limestone, of slightly lesser height, about 70 cm, but otherwise similar in proportion, were considered by the excavators of Assur to be part of the parapet walk on top of a low rampart of Late Assyrian times.[25] At both sites the excavators noted the lack of uniformity in the single merlons.[26] In view of the regularity in other elements of Assyrian architecture one would like to find an explanation for this variety. Most probably the reason lies in the working methods of the Assyrian stone cutters. Regardless of such irregularities in actual battlements, however,

contemporary representations in art show that uniformity in the shape of the merlons was taken for granted. The example given here (Fig. 9) is a fragment of bone inlay from Ziwiyeh in northwest Iran, probably dated in the end of the eighth century B.C., in or about the time of Sargon's reign.

In the renderings of the large brick-built battlements of fortification walls the steps of the battlements were usually simplified to a triangular outline. This is true even of a statue base from Susa, the ancient capital of Elam, located in southwest Iran near modern Ahwaz. The base is now in the Louvre and is published here with the kind permission of MM. Parrot and Amiet, *Conservateur en Chef* and *Conservateur* of the *Département des antiquités orientales*.

The base (Figs. 10a–d) is made of soft greenish-black stone, badly burnt. The object is approximately square, each side measuring about 7.5 cm at the top. Since the base is damaged its measurements cannot be given. The height is 4.7 mm. On its four sides it is decorated by a turreted wall, and on its top rest the nude feet of a statuette the rest of which is not preserved. On the front of the base (which is indicated by the position of the feet) is the gate of a town or its citadel, flanked by two tall towers. The gate is surrounded by an irregularly rectangular double frame, the inner part of which curves in from the top and from both sides while the outer frame echoes these curves very slightly. Over the top of the frame stretches a horizontal strip of battlemented wall, joining the two gate towers; in this strip are seen triangular or roughly rectangular loopholes, openings through which the defenders could observe and shoot at the enemy at the foot of the wall. Each tower is topped by a superstructure also pierced by loopholes, square in the upper row and roughly triangular in the intervals below. Tall towers similar to those flanking the gate stand at the corners. Between them and the gate towers are what appear to be shorter ones—actually probably merely bastions—which are slightly narrower than the tall towers. On either side of the superstructure of the small towers are seen the merlons of a wall, while no such traces are visible beside the tall towers. The remaining sides of the base are similar to the front except for the gate, which is replaced on three sides by a single tall tower. At each corner of the base there is a groove where the tall towers would meet. The most likely explanation for this feature, which is unparalleled, is that the carver thought of each side as a separate unit and then combined them in such a way as not to change the proportions of the towers.

A few signs of an inscription are recognizable on top of the base and probably name the donor or the person represented.

Lastly, the goatfish, symbols of the god Ea, which flank the turreted gate in the seal impression Fig. 8b, confirm the character of that building as a sanctuary.

23. Y. Yadin, 'Hyksos Fortifications and the Battering-Ram', *Bulletin of the American Schools of Oriental Research*, no. 137, 1955, pp. 23–32, and *The Art of Warfare in Biblical Lands*, New York, 1963, pp. 69–71.

24. Stepped limestone blocks found at Khorsabad were reproduced by Loud in *Khorsabad*, pt. II, pl. 8: C, text p. 40.

25. The German excavators referred to this low rampart as the 'Niederwall'; W. Andrae, *Die Festungswerke von Assur* (23. Wissenschaftliche Veröffentlichung der Deutschen Orient-Gesellschaft), Leipzig, 1913, *passim*.

26. Andrae, *Festungswerke*, p. 91; Loud, *Khorsabad*, pt. II, p. 40.

The little statue base renders in simplified manner the main features of ancient Near Eastern fortifications: walls and towers with battlemented parapets. Such fortifications were planned to offset the disadvantage inherent in the limited number of the defenders by placing them in a superior position in relation to the theoretically unlimited masses of attackers. This was done by giving the defenders the possibility of attaining with their missiles, slingshots and arrows, the attackers at any point before the walls. The defences were more effective the higher the point from which the missile was hurled for its impact would have been all the stronger. Furthermore, the wider a platform projected over a wall or tower, the easier it was for an archer to see what was going on at the foot of the walls. Loopholes with embrasures placed at different angles further facilitated the task of the archers who could shoot in all directions. The finest example of ancient military architecture in which installations for these needs could be observed, was the fortress of Buhen in Nubia.[27] This and other Middle Kingdom fortresses of Egypt probably served as models for the military architecture of Western Asia although at present only the form of the battlements suggests the path of such Egyptian influences.

Wherever possible the foundations were made of stone. The upper structures were made of mud brick over which reeds were laid crosswise as binders after every seven to ten courses.[28] The walls at Buhen and Khorsabad showed that they had been covered with white plaster.[29] We may therefore imagine the fortresses visible from afar as a gleaming white mass from which the battlemented towers rose sharply against the sky.

Assyrian fortress walls were straight to judge by those of Khorsabad, except for a lower portion of about 3 m which was battered on its outer face. At periodic intervals bastions provided structural and defensive strength for the walls.[30] On these bastions often rose a super-structure in the form of a tower on top of which was a projecting platform usually built on beams. These beams are clearly recognizable on the statue base in the Louvre but are not indicated in Assyrian reliefs. To judge by medieval practices, archers often shot at the attackers at the foot of the walls through holes in the floors of these platforms.

We know some details of the defensive platform or parapet walk because the German excavators of Assur were able to reconstruct the top of the low exterior rampart where they found the fragmentary stepped mud-brick battlement mentioned above (Fig. 11). We may assume that the installations of this parapet walk resembled the installations in the superstructure of other walls.

The total width at the top of the rampart was 2.85 m; of this width, 2 m was used as a walk that included the bank on which the archers stepped to shoot. This bank was three bricks high and one brick wide. The size of the Neo-Assyrian bricks was about 35–39 cm square and 12–15 cm thick.[31] The outer half of the parapet with its merlons was about 43 cm wide; behind the merlons at a height of about 1 m was a flat surface from which descended the loopholes. At the top of each loophole two bricks formed a roof-like protection for the rest of the hole. The resulting form resembled an arrow. This form subsequently became an integral part of the merlons, as is shown by examples of the Achaemenid period from Susa (Fig. 12) and by stucco patterns of Late Parthian or Sasanian times.[32] Channels about 14 cm square that pierced the parapet wall about 1.50 m from the floor of the walk and about 3.50 m distant from one another, could not be explained by the excavator, W. Andrae. Despite the fact that Andrae denied the use of wood,[33] one wonders whether these channels were not intended for wooden bars. If they were empty, however, they could have been occasionally used to hold magical figures meant to be hidden in the parapet although the preferred place for such figures seems to have been the shaft of the narrow terracotta drains which ran through the parapet, carrying off the rainwater. Texts mentioning this procedure may be exemplified by the complaint of a man who believed that he had been bewitched by means of

27. Preliminary reports on Buhen have been published by W. B. Emery in *The Illustrated London News*, June 2, 1958, pp. 1048–51, and Sept. 12, 1959, pp. 249–51. More detailed reports were published in *Kush*, VII, 1959, pp. 7–14; VIII, 1960, pp. 7–10; IX, 1961, pp. 81–86; X, 1962, pp. 106–8; XI, 1963, pp. 116–20; XII, 1964, pp. 43–46.

28. Loud stated in *Khorsabad*, pt. II, p. 18, that after every nine courses of brick matting appears to have been used as a binder whereas the German excavators claimed that in Assyria, reeds were merely laid crosswise in contrast to the matting employed in Babylonia (Andrae, *Festungswerke*, p. 15).

29. Loud reported that both faces of the fortification wall were covered with white lime-plaster; *Khorsabad*, pt. II, p. 18, col. I. Emery stated that the main wall of the xviiith Dynasty fortifications at Buhen was faced with white painted gypsum plaster, cf. *Kush*, VII, 1959, p. 9.

30. The distance between the bastions was determined by the safe range of the archers as suggested by A. Billerbeck, 'Der Festungsbau im alten Orient', *Der Alte Orient*, I/4, 1900, p. 13; the safe range of the archers did not exceed 30 m, cf. *op. cit.*, p. 5.

31. The height of Late Assyrian bricks given by Andrae, *Festungswerke*, p. 14, as 13–15 cm agrees with the 13 cm indicated by D. Oates, for Fort Shalmaneser, 'The Excavations at Nimrud (Kalhu), 1961', *Iraq*, XXIV, 1962, p. 7.

32. E.g. the patterns of the stucco decoration from Kuh-i Kwadja, reproduced in R. Ghirshman, *Persian Art* (The Arts of Mankind), New York, 1962, Fig. 54. Also A. U. Pope, *A Survey of Persian Art*, vol. I, London-New York, 1938, p. 415, Fig. 93.

33. For Andrae's statement that he had no explanation for the horizontal channels, cf. Andrae, *Festungswerke*, p. 116; for the absence of wood in the wall, cf. *op. cit.*, p. 15.

magical figures hidden in the parapet. '[My image] in the samētu of the wall they have imprisoned, in the drainshaft of the wall they have . . . ed it.'[34]

The main features of the walls just described probably changed little in the course of the Neo-Assyrian period, but the proportions seem to have undergone some modifications. Since, especially in height and width, the superstructures on the towers changed, this development will permit us to date the base from Susa. Reliefs of Ashurnasirpal II show in general a relatively low and wide superstructure with upward of four merlons on the parapets.[35] The bronze gates of Shalmaneser III have very abbreviated renderings of fortifications but the proportions of the superstructures on the towers are still rather low and wide, although there are usually three merlons, two half-merlons at the corners and one triangular one in the center.[36] Different proportions were introduced, however, in the time of king Tiglathpileser III (745–727 B.C.) (Fig. 13); superstructures on the towers are now higher and narrower than before. It is possible, of course, that these changes were determined by stylistic predilections; Ashurnasirpal's wide, low shapes conform to the static massive impression created—and surely desired —by his artists. But the pronounced horizontality of the earlier style gives way to a tendency toward verticality in the reliefs of Tiglathpileser III and his successors. The actual height of the towers in Tiglathpileser's reliefs is less than that of Ashurnasirpal's, but the taller superstructure gives the impression of a vertical stress. Since the proportions of the statue base are closer to those of Tiglathpileser III than to those of Ashurnasirpal, we may assume that it belongs to the time of the Late Assyrian rulers in the late eighth or in the seventh century B.C. Support for such a date for the base is given by the apparent similarity to models of towns brought as tribute to Sargon (Figs. 14a, b).

Differences which exist between the statue base from Susa and renderings of the models in Sargon's reliefs concern the widening of the towers toward the bottom of the base in contrast to the straight towers of the models. The latter also have a greater width in the superstructures than the towers of the base. Perhaps

these differences are due to the fact that the statue base renders a specific Elamite town, conceivably Susa itself,[37] whereas the models may portray different localities. The reason for assuming that they may refer to certain towns rather than symbolize a general concept is that they vary among each other, so that some intentional characterization is not excluded. This would conform to a tendency in the reliefs of Sargon noted above (see note 16).

To about the same period as the models pictured in the reliefs of Sargon belongs a bronze model of a tower (Fig. 15) from the site of Toprak Kale near Van in eastern Turkey, which was once the capital of the kingdom of Urartu. Unlike the Assyrian renderings but similar to the statue base from Susa, the Urartian model shows the beams on which the platforms of the towers rest.

There is no parallel known, however, for a figure on top of a model of a town. One may cite as a distant parallel only the god from a painting in Khorsabad who stands upon an architecturally decorated dais, perhaps meant to represent his temple.[38] But it is also possible that the base from Susa bore the dedicatory image of the ruler, who had himself portrayed standing on his fortified town.

The sacred and protective character of the battlement pattern may be documented by its survival in Persepolis, where it ubiquitously forms the parapets of stairways and probably originally also crowned the tops of buildings. As mentioned above, Susa yielded merlons of the Achaemenid period which have in their center an arrow-shaped hollow derived from the utilitarian form of the loophole in Assyrian fortifications.[39] By Achaemenid and later times the arrow-shaped mark inside the merlon was surely considered an integral element of the propitious form which survived in later times.

In the West the Greeks seem to have used battlements consisting of rectangular merlons separated by similarly shaped crenels. These could have been independently devised, but they recall the battlements on the

34. S. Langdon, *Sumerian Liturgical Texts* (Publication of the Babylonian Section of the University Museum, University of Pennsylvania, Philadelphia, 1917, 18: 29, cf. pt. II of this article, s.v. *samītu*).

35. For renderings of fortified towns in the reliefs of Ashurnasirpal II, cf. R. D. Barnett, *Assyrian Palace Reliefs*, London, n.d., pls. 10–12, 22, 23, 25.

36. The bronze gates are reproduced in L. W. King, *The Bronze Reliefs from the Gates of Shalmaneser . . .*, London, 1925, *passim*, and Barnett, *Assyrian Palace Reliefs*, pls. 137–73. The two towers of the model pictured on the throne dais of Shalmaneser (*Iraq*, XXV, 1963, pl. va) resemble the Middle Assyrian type of Fig. 8a in having stepped merlons and these only at the corners.

37. Evidence that an Elamite town is rendered is given by the shape of the gate, with a horizontal, perhaps dipping, lintel, for which there is no precise parallel in the Assyrian reliefs, though a gate with a straight lintel, narrowed above on either side, is seen in the rendering of the royal Elamite city of Khamanu as represented in a relief of Ashurbanipal (cf. E. Strommenger and M. Hirmer, *5000 Years of the Art of Mesopotamia*, New York, 1964, pl. 237). In contrast, Syrian and Babylonian towns have gates with a rounded top indicating an arched opening. Remains of an actual gate of this type were found in Fort Shalmaneser, cf. Oates, *Iraq*, XXIV, 1962, p. 4.

38. *Khorsabad*, pt. II, pl. 89.

39. The transformation of the 'arrow-slot' of the Assyrian battlements into a decorative motif of the Achaemenid period at Susa and its survival in Parthian stucco was discussed by N. C. Debevoise, 'The Origin of Decorative Stucco', *American Journal*

buildings of the Urartian town of Musasir.[40] An Urartian legacy to Greece by way of the Black Sea is not completely impossible. Greek battlement forms subsequently prevailed in Europe. It is all the more interesting to find that in the Phoenician enclaves of Sicily, Eryx and Motya, the builders with a North African heritage employed the most ancient form of battlement, the rounded merlons of Egyptian origin.[41]

of Archaeology, XLV, 1941, p. 51. Stepped merlons enclosing arrow-shaped designs are also seen on a terracotta bucket of Achaemenid or later date, cf. G. Perrot and C. Chipiez, *A History of Art in Chaldea and Assyria*, vol. II, 1884, p. 300, fig. 169. For remarks on the bucket by this writer see *Artibus Asiae*, XIII, 1/2, 1959, p. 127, note 5.
40. See the reference in note 16 for the relief depicting Musasir. In that relief two of the towers (at the right) have triangular battlements as does the wall rendered in the lower left. The rest of the battlements seem to have rectangular merlons and crenels.
41. Cf. F. Krischen, *Die Stadtmauern von Pompeji und griechische Festungsbaukunst in Unteritalien und Sizilien (Archäo-*

The survival of battlements of various forms over centuries and millennia in the Near East and Europe is surely due to the visual impact made by these light and articulated parapets which must have contrasted effectively with the solid towers and stretches of wall. At the same time the battlemented parapets proclaimed the protective power and probably often the sanctity of the buildings which they crowned. Today the sober, plain forms of modern buildings leave no room for meaningful parapets. However, in modern Iraq, which once was ancient Assyria and Babylonia, where stepped battlements may have been used first in defensive architecture, the lonely traveler may still be reassured by the distant sight of the battlements on the roof of a military outpost.

logisches Institut des Deutschen Reiches: die hellenistische Kunst in Pompeji, VII), Berlin, 1941, Figs. 33–35, pp. 34–36.

PART II

Akkadian Terms Possibly Associated with Battlements

In the correlation of the archaeological evidence assembled in the foregoing paper with the Akkadian terms which may be associated with battlements I have had the friendly help of Dr. A. L. Oppenheim, who delegated to Miss Joyce Bartels the collection of relevant material from the files of the Assyrian Dictionary of the Oriental Institute of the University of Chicago, abbreviated CAD. For this part, Miss Bartels supplied the *List of Abbreviations* (found at the end of this paper on pp. 11–12) and selected textual references, from which I have further selected those that I consider most pertinent. Some of the remarks concerning the meaning of the terms discussed here were made by Miss Bartels, and these will be cited in quotation marks to set them off from my text, for which I alone am responsible.

The terms under consideration are *gabadibbû*, *samītu*, *pašqu*, *naburru* and, in a different category, *kilīlu*. Before discussing them, however, the nature of the written documentation should be stressed. The words cited here are largely taken from historical or religious texts or dedicatory inscriptions. Collective terms for parts of buildings or of a city wall are more likely to occur in such texts than terms of the technical language of masons or stone cutters who would have had to refer to single merlons and other specific

parts of the wall. Furthermore, the principles of classification in Sumer, Assyria and Babylonia differed from those prevailing today. In our visually directed culture we make differentiations of shape as between a parapet and the battlements upon it, whereas an Akkadian might have called the entire battlemented parapet by one name because it was built of the same type of bricks. We will return to this point at the end of the discussion of the terms.

gabadibbû

The word is discussed in CAD 'G' p. 1 where it is translated as parapet. In lexical texts it occurs in a group with *dūru* (wall) and *samītu* (parapet, see below). 'The word is composed of two Sumerian words, gaba "breast" plus dib "fasten".'
This suggests to me that the word meant not only a parapet but a platform as well which projected from a wall as if it had been fastened to it in the order of a balcony. If such a projecting platform with a parapet was built on top of a wall it would have had the character of a chemin de ronde or parapet walk. On top of a building such a construction would appear to the viewer as a cornice.
'The majority of the texts mentioning the word

gabadibbû do so in a formula which, with few variations, in speaking of building or rebuilding a temple, etc. (and less often of destroying it), runs as follows: *ištu uššēšu adi g. arṣip ušaklil* from its foundations to its g. I erected, I completed (it).'

This formula occurs as early as a text of the Assyrian king Aššur-bēl-nišēšu (1419–1411 B.C.) (AOB I p. 34:10 var.) and as late as a text of the last king of Babylon, Nabonidus (555–539 B.C.) (VAB 4 p. 222:9). These kings applied the formula to whole cities (e.g. Aššurnaṣirpal II, 883–859 B.C., to Calah, AKA p. 186:17; p. 245:10; p. 387:136), to a certain part of a city (e.g. Aššur-bēl-nišēšu to the wall of the New City, part of Assur, *loc. cit.*), to temples (e.g. Shalmaneser I, 1274–1245 B.C., to the Aššur temple, AOB I p. 124:25 and p. 132:9), to parts of the temple buildings (e.g. Adad-nīrārī I, 1307–1275 B.C., to the *abūsātu*, literally 'storehouse', part of the temple complex in Assur, AOB I p. 96:7), to palaces (e.g. Aššurnaṣirpal II to the city wall in Tušha, AKA p. 296:4) or special halls (e.g. Sargon II, 721–705 B.C., to the 'juniper' hall [*ekal* giš*duprānī*] of Calah, Winckler Sar. 48:17).

On the basis of the various architectural units with which the formula is used, 'a more general meaning, "I rebuilt from top to bottom" or something similar', was suggested. While such a phrase surely renders the sense of the formula, I would prefer to translate it by a more concrete phrase: from the foundations to the superstructure. This would imply that under g. could be subsumed all the installations from the floor of the parapet walk up. The parapet walk was at the same time the top of the solid mud-brick wall. From there to the top not only of the parapet but perhaps even to that of the bastions and towers—all of which must have been accessible from the parapet walk or chemin de ronde of the fortification wall—would form a logical unit. By such an assumption one could explain Sargon's reference to 21 cities girt with walls whose g. had 120 courses of brick (located on Mt. Arzabia) (TCL 3 line 240, *120. TA. ÀM tipkī gaba-dib-ú lānišunu lamū*, cf. ZA 34 pp. 113–22 and AfO 12 144–8).

The material of the g., which was mentioned specifically by Tiglathpileser I (1115–1077 B.C.) as burnt brick (*gaba-dib-bi-šu ina agurrī urekkis* I constructed its [the Anu Adad Temple's] 'parapet' with kiln-fired bricks, AKA p. 98:103), would not mitigate against an interpretation of the term as meaning the superstructure since the king was obviously speaking of the visible part which would be the parapet, not of the g. for which wooden beams would have been needed. References to wood in the buildings mentioned in the formulas are not likely to have included

the structural beams of the g. Probably such references merely alluded to the valuable materials with which the rooms in the interior were paneled and from which the building sometimes derived its name (e.g. the 'juniper hall' of Sargon II at Calah mentioned above).

A text which names g. in a different context than the formulas tends to support my contention that it could have been something like a balcony. The text mentions a g. of 15 brick courses reaching to the (roof) beams of the building (AKA p. 21:10). This is about 1.95 m which would be a comfortable height for a balcony or a walk (see the calculations by Oates for the height of a fighting platform in the reconstruction of the west gate at Fort Shalmaneser, *Iraq*, XXIV, p. 8).

Probably the use of g. was not precise and the word could refer to a projecting parapeted platform and occasionally to its superstructure but also to a parapet alone. This would explain a g. of pots or rails on private houses (*gaba-dib-bu šá DUG.MEŠ; g. šá ÙR* (read <GIŠ>ÙR?), CT 38 13:84, 85). The various meanings probably implied by g. also account for the various opinions concerning the translation of the word (Baumgartner in ZA 36 219–25 believed it to be a 'Zinnenkranz', Weidhaas in ZA 45 127 stated with assurance that the word meant 'Gesimse, Brustwehr', cornice and breastwork, although the two terms are by no means identical!).

samītu

The word has not yet been published in the CAD; I therefore give here the textual references that were sent to me from the CAD and will discuss below correlations with the archaeological material.

LEXICAL TEXTS

7. (BÀ)D.gi	*du-ú-ru*	wall
8. (BÀ)D.gi.si	*sa-mi-tu*	
9. (BÀD).gi-ri.a	*gaba-dib-bu*	

Erimhuš III

13. ki.sag.gál.la	*a-šar sa-ma-ti*
14. ki.sag.gál.la	*a-šar di-ma-a-ti*

Izi C iii

193. dar₄.bar.lá.lá	ZA-*mi-tum*
194. zag.è	ZA-*mu-ú ša* BÀD (see

Nabnītu I   CAD *zamû*)

RITUAL, INCANTATION, OMEN
AND LITERARY TEXTS

epir sa-mit dūri ŠUB-ti   dust of a fallen s. of a
(ritual for a woman in   wall.
labor)
KAR 196 rev. right col. l. 7

ana dūri ù sa-me-ti tap-qi-da-in-ni
Meier, *Maqlu* IV:24

to the wall and to the s. you have delivered me.

dūri ù sa-me-ti la tab-ba-lak-ki-ta-ni
Meier, *Maqlu* V:134

you shall not climb over wall and s.

ᵈBēlet dūri ù sa-me-i-ti
Reiner, *Šurpu* III:81

the Lady of the wall and of the s.

[enūma] lu igār bīt ili lu . . . lu sa-me-et dūri imqutu
Ebeling, Handerhebung, p. 100:26

(if) either the wall of the house of the god or the (. . .) or the s. of the wall has collapsed.

. . . ina muḫḫi sa-mit dūri a-šib-ma
CT XXXIX pl. 30:58 (Alu)

(Supposed: . . . a falcon appeared sitting on the top of) the s. of the wall.

ina sa-mit dūri ipḫû ina bi-'i ša dūri i-te-pu-ú
Lambert, AfO 18, p. 292 1. 29

(my image) in the s. of the wall they have imprisoned and . . . ed it in the drain-shaft of the wall.

for *samīt dūri* a place where one buries magical figures cf. Ungnad in Or. n.s. 12, p. 305.

ina sa-mīt BÀ[D teqebber]
Lassøe, *Bît rimki*, p. 59:98

You bury (the figurine) in the s. of the wall.

i-tap(!)-la-as sa-me-ta-šu šá la ú-maš-šá-lu man-ma
Said of Uruk in Thompson, Gilgamesh Tablet I. i. 12.

Look upon its s. which none can equal!

HISTORICAL TEXTS

nāmerī nibiḫi sa-me-tu (var. ti) *u sikkāti šūt abni iptiqma ušalmâ siḫir[tišu]*
Said of the temple of Aššur Eḫursagkurkurra by Sargon II. AfO III 1:5.

He decorated(?) with glazed (bricks) the towers, the friezes, the s. and the pegs on all sides (of the temple).

bītu šuātu igārātišu iqūpumu uptaṭṭiru riksūšu(m) sa-mit-su ussarriḫumu uḫtammimu temenšu
Said of the Eanna temple at Uruk by Sargon II. YOS 1. 38. i. 22.

That house, its brick walls had buckled, its courses had become disintegrated, its s. was in ruin, and its foundation was despoiled.

igār Eanna kīdānu ša kisalli šaplî sa-mit-su issuḫma unammir temenšu
Said of the Eanna temple at Uruk by Sargon II. YOS 1. 38. i. 36.

The outer wall of Eanna's lower courtyard, its s. he tore out and exposed its foundation.

nibiḫi sa-mit É-šár-ra
OIP 2, p. 148. No. IV. 4

(Sennacherib, 704–681 B.C., beautified) the frieze? cornice? of the s. of Ešarra (with burnt brick blocks).

[sa]-mit-su iḫ-ḫar-mi-mu-ma itūru arbuššu
Said of the Eanna temple and the temple of Ningiš-zida within it at Uruk (text found at Nimrud). Marduk-apla-iddina II (703 B.C.) barrel cylinder. Iraq XV 123:6 (p. 131).

Its s. which had become decayed and had turned to ruin.

sa-mit-su is-suḫ-ma ú-nam-mir te-me-en-[šú]
See references just above. Iraq XV 124:26

He tore down its 'inner wall' and let light upon its foundation deposit.

DISCUSSION

In AfO 7 274 Weidner says the s. is 'part of a wall'. Zimmern, Fremdw. p. 31 also says it is part of a wall, probably related to the Aramaic zāwītā 'corner' and later, Arabic zāwijat and probably late Hebrew (plural) zāwijjūt. Perles, OLZ 29 (1926), p. 194, refers to Psalm 144:12 which the King James version translates as 'corner stone'. The word also occurs in Talmudic writing (Levy I 522) with the meaning 'corner'. Perles treats these instances as probable loan words from Akkadian *samītu, zamītu.*

The lexical texts indicate that the *samītu* was intimately connected with a wall, specifically with its upper part, and suggest that it had an angular shape. The fact that birds could sit on the s. confirms that it was to be found on top of a wall. Except for two texts, one of Sargon II referring to the s. of the temple of Assur, Ehursagkurkurra (AfO III 1:5), the other of Sennacherib referring to the Ešarra (OIP 2, p. 148. No. LV. 4), which indicate that the s. was made of glazed and burnt brick respectively, it seems to have been built of mud brick, easily ruined or turned to dust. These indications point to a parapet such as was reconstructed for the parapet walk on the low rampart at Assur, see Fig. 11. The most important features, for identification with the *samītu* in that parapet, are the narrow terracotta drains which ran through the wall and in which objects like magical figures could have been immured. Only an already existing cavity could have served for such a purpose. Making a new hole in the city wall would have surely drawn attention to the reprehensible action and been severely punished. For this reason these drain shafts in the mud-brick parapet of the city wall, which was accessible to everyone, must have been a favorite hiding place for magical figures, to judge by the texts cited above.

If I am right in assuming that the drain shaft of the wall belonged to the *samītu*, then there was no division made between the parapet wall and its crowning battlements. Built of the same material, the battlemented parapet seems to have formed a unit in the minds of the Assyrians. It is nevertheless conceivable that the stepped shape was considered propitious, since there is no indication that walls in general were so regarded. Possibly for this reason dust from a fallen *samītu* of a wall was used in a ritual for a woman in labor. Perhaps we may mention in this connection the curious practice noted by C. F. Nims, *Thebes of the Pharaohs*, New York, 1965, p. 80, who mentioned a type of defacement on the walls of the Theban temples in the form of 'vertical gouges often covering large areas. These were made by persons collecting the stone dust from sacred buildings for magical potions and charms. This superstitious practice began as early as the end of the Twentieth Dynasty. Similar gouges appear on the outer walls of medieval cathedrals in Europe.'

The suggestion made in the first part of this paper that the stepped form of the battlements rendered them propitious may be confirmed by this use of the dust of the *samītu* as well as by the frequent appearance of the *samītu* on temples. In a few instances the pair of words *samītu—temennu* seems to have been used in a formula paralleling *gabadibbû—uššu* (YOS I. 38. i. 22; Iraq XV, p. 124:26).

The most frequent use and probably the principal meaning of the *samītu*, however, seems to have been the battlemented parapet of a fortification wall such as the one over which strides the deity seen on the plaque from Larsa mentioned above (see note 13). This rendering makes one think of 'the Lady of the wall and of the *samītu*'.

pašqu

The following references were given for this word not yet published in the CAD:

e-la-niš a-di pa-aš-qí-šu i-na pi-i-li rabûti	above, up to its p. (I carefully built it) of great limestone (blocks).

Said of the outer wall (probably of Nineveh)
Bàd.níg.erím.ḫu.luḫ.ḫa (Wall that terrifies the enemy)
This wall was built from under water up to the p. by Sennacherib. OIP 2, p. 113:11.

si-el-lum nibiḫi ù gi-mir pa-aš-qí-ši-in Said by Sennacherib of the walls of his palace. OIP 2, p. 107:44 and p. 120:30–32.	the arch, the friezes(?) and all their p.

ni-bi-ḫu pa-áš-qu ša ṣurri uqnî ú-še-piš-ma Borger, Esarh. p. 62:24	I made a frieze and a p. of red stone and lapis lazuli (actually red and blue glazed or enameled bricks).

DISCUSSION

These references show that *pašqu* was found on top of the wall, that it could be made of stone or a related material such as red or blue glazed terracotta (the probable meaning of the red and blue stones mentioned by Esarhaddon), and that it frequently occurred with *nībiḫu* for which the interpretation 'frieze' was given by Weidhaas, Bauer and Baumgartner (cf. ZA. 45, p. 127). In view of the invariable occurrence of a frieze below the battlements in the surviving examples of glazed battlements (see the altar from Tell Halaf mentioned in note 11 above, and the reconstructions attempted of the glazed brick battlements of Shalmaneser III (858–824 B.C.) in Andrae, *Festungswerke*, Pl. LXXXIII), often abbreviated to no more than one or two horizontal lines in the Assyrian reliefs (see Fig. 10a–c and Fig. 11), it seems likely that *nībiḫu* and *pašqu* refer to just this combination of decorative features.

The difference between *samītu* and *pašqu* would be that the first word includes the parapet wall, whereas *pašqu* would only refer to the battlements on top. Such an interpretation would not disagree with the evidence provided by the texts of Sargon II (721–705 B.C.) in which *pašqu* is paired with *aṣītu* (bastion?) and delivered up to the battering rams (Weidhaas, ZA 45, p. 127 n. 6).

naburru

The word is mentioned in the CAD 'E' under *epēšu* v. 5a 1; other references are given below.

a-di na-bur-ri-ša ar-ṣip ú-šak-lil Said of a palace by Sennacherib; OIP 2, p. 130:72	up to its n. I constructed, I finished it.

bīta ša-a-tú ul-tu na-bur-ri-šu Borger, Esarh. p. 4:17	that temple from its 'turrets' (to its foundation walls I tore down).

na-bur-ri-šu-un eš-šiš ú-še-piš Said of Esagila, its shrines, Babylon and the walls of Babylon, Imgur-Enlil and Nimitti-Enlil by Esarhaddon; Borger, Esarh. p. 21: 22	(I built) anew their 'turrets'.

bi-rit apsasâte ul-ziz na-bur-riš ú-še-me-ma Referring to the *bit kutalli* (armory) in Nineveh by Sennacherib; OIP 2, p. 133:81 (CAD 'E' p. 415a s.v. *ewû* 3a)	. . . set them (or it) between the female genii and made them into (or reach up to) a *naburru*.

DISCUSSION

The last reference is so obscure that the meaning of the word cannot with certainty be given as turrets as has been suggested in the quotations above. All that can be said here is that *naburru* is elsewhere mentioned as the highest point of a structure in formulas paralleling those with *gabadibbû* to express a meaning such as 'from top to bottom'.

kilīlu

Of all the terms discussed the one which is most interesting for the symbolism of the stepped battlements is *kilīlu* the basic meaning of which is something like circlet or garland, see von Soden, AHw p. 476, *kilīlu*.

On the basis of Nebuchadnezzar's inscriptions, *kilīlu* can be identified with the battlements of stepped merlons, made of blue glazed brick, surrounding the top of his buildings at Babylon. The *kilīlu* could also be painted with black bitumen and as precious a material as fine gold was claimed in a hymn to have adorned the *kilīlu* of the Ezida temple at Borsippa. The valuable material and the fact that the *kilīlu* was used as a decoration of temples and palaces indicates the distinctive character of this type of battlement.

The difference between the *kilīlu* and the *samītu* probably consisted more in the materials used for the *kilīlu* than in the fact that the *samītu* seems to have been a parapet wall plus battlement, the *kilīlu* probably the decorative battlement alone.

The difference between *kilīlu* and *pašqu*, a term which also seems to refer only to the battlement' is that the

former expresses the concept of a battlement as a crowning member (Lambert, BWL p. 166. K. 8413. Pl. 44 12), whereas *pašqu* seems to refer collectively to the merlons. Moreover, the practical use of the *pašqu* is implied by the connection with defensive bastions mentioned in the texts of Sargon II whereas there is no such practical, defensive use known to me for *kilīlu*.

While some of the interpretations of the terms here discussed on the basis of the archaeological evidence will surely be subject to revision, I nevertheless hope to have shown that each term refers to a specific part of the superstructure of the wall. Some very slender evidence may exist, moreover, for a connection of the term *kilīlu* with sanctuary.[42] Such a connection would confirm the suggestions made in the first part of this paper for the sacred—and implicitly—protective symbolism of stepped battlements in Mesopotamia and probably also in other parts of the ancient Near East.

42. von Soden, *loc. cit.*, quotes the equation *kilīlu* = [*ešertu*] from RA XIV 168. iii. 7, an Assur synonym list now republished by Anne D. Kilmer, JAOS 83 (1963), pp. 442 ff., as Explicit *malku* = *šarru* Tablet II, Source A (the pertinent section appears on p. 444, lines 166–74, with the restoration [*i-ši-ir-tum*] from *malku* = *šarru* Tablet I line 278 (*ibid.*, p. 429). Another Assur fragment of Explicit *malku* = *šarru*, Kilmer's Source B, cited *ibid.*, p. 443, equates a similar group of terms, in which however *kilīlu* is not included, with *bītu* in lines 107–18. It is possible that sources A and B treat of the same subject matter and should be considered as duplicates, and thus the right column of source A should be restored as *bītu*, as suggested CAD 'E' p. 137 s.v. *emāšu*, and not as *ešertu*. However, if we accept Kilmer's reconstruction we would have evidence for the above equation of *kilīlu* with sanctuary.
I owe this note to Professor Erica Reiner. She and Professor A. L. Oppenheim generously gave of their time to cooperate in the present attempt at coordinating the archaeological and philological evidence concerning battlements in ancient Mesopotamia.

ABBREVIATIONS FOR PART II

All abbreviations used are those found in CAD 'A' pp. xxiv ff. as follows:

AfO	Archiv für Orientforschung
AHw	W. von Soden, Akkadisches Handwörterbuch
AKA	E. A. W. Budge and L. W. King, The Annals of the Kings of Assyria
AOB	Altorientalische Bibliothek
Borger, Esarh.	R. Borger, Die Inschriften Asarhaddons, Königs von Assyrien (= AfO Beiheft 9)
CT	Cuneiform Texts from Babylonian Tablets (in the British Museum)
Ebeling, Handerhebung	E. Ebeling, Die akkadische Gebetsserie Šu-ila 'Handerhebung' (=Veröffentlichungen des Instituts für Orientforschung, Berlin, 20)
Erimhuš	lexical series erimhuš = *anantu*
JAOS	Journal of the American Oriental Society
KAH	Keilschrifttexte aus Assur historischen Inhalts

KAR	Keilschrifttexte aus Assur religiösen Inhalts	RA	Revue d'Assyriologie
Lassøe, *Bît Rimki*	J. Lassøe, Studies on the Assyrian Ritual *Bît Rimki*	Reiner, *Šurpu*	E. Reiner, Šurpu (=AfO Beiheft 11)
Lambert, BWL	W. G. Lambert, Babylonian Wisdom Literature	TCL	Textes cunéiformes du Louvre
Meier, *Maqlu*	G. Meier, Maqlu (= AfO Beiheft 2)	Thompson Gilg.	R. C. Thompson, The Epic of Gilgamish
Nabnītu	lexical series SIG$_7$ plus ALAM =nabnītu	VAB	Vorderasiatische Bibliothek
		Winckler Sar.	H. Winckler, Die Keilschrifttexte Sargons . . .
OIP	Oriental Institute Publications	YOS	Yale Oriental Series, Babylonian Texts
OLZ	Orientalistische Literaturzeitung	ZA	Zeitschrift für Assyriologie
Or.	Orientalia	Zimmern Fremdw.	H. Zimmern, Akkadische Fremdwörter . . ., 2nd ed.

ROBERT BRANNER

The Montjoies of Saint Louis

When Saint Louis died in Tunis in 1270, his bones and heart were brought back to France for burial. His son, Philip III, personally helped to carry the box containing them from the cathedral of Notre-Dame in Paris to the traditional resting-place of the kings at St.-Denis. The bearers paused periodically to repose themselves en route, and at each spot where they lowered the litter to the ground Philip later erected great stone crosses.

So runs the tale of the origin of Saint Louis' Montjoies. Although mentioned by almost no contemporary writer,[1] the crosses were famous from the very start, and their reputation persisted into early modern times. They were freely imitated in the Eleanor Crosses of England, and they also seem to have inspired a number of monuments in the International Style of the late fourteenth and fifteenth centuries. Despite such prestige, however, they were portrayed only a few times before their destruction during the French Revo-

lution, and these images have remained scattered or unpublished. The original purpose of the monuments has also never been explained. Their general form and meaning therefore merit a moment of attention.

The nine Montjoies are shown in two anonymous etchings from the first half of the eighteenth century, in the Cabinet des Estampes in Paris (Figs. 1, 2).[2] The artist seems to have simplified and standardized the monuments, for like the Eleanor Crosses they probably were not all of the same shape or size.[3] Some were hexagonal, others seem to have been octagonal, and one may even have been square. The general liberty of the etchings is confirmed by two other views of the crosses standing in front of St.-Lazare (Fig. 3) and

1. The only medieval mention seems to be Le Nain de Tillemont's 'Chronique qui finit en l'an 1319' (*Vie de saint Louis*, ed. J. de Gaulle, v, Paris, 1849, p. 202). The nearly total absence of contemporary documents led Dom Brial to doubt whether the crosses were really from the time of Saint Louis ('Recherches sur l'origine et l'antiquité des colonnes ou croix qu'on voyait de nos jours sur le chemin de Paris à Saint-Denis', *Histoire et mémoires de l'institut royal de France, classe d'histoire*, III, 1818, pp. 71–76 [read in 1809]); his conclusion that they were really property markers set up by Abbot Suger is erroneous, for Suger's markers ran east to west, from Aubervillers to St.-Ouen, forming a perimeter *between* St.-Denis and Paris (see A. Molinier, ed., *Vie de Louis le Gros*, Paris, 1887, p. 105, note 1). When the kings' bodies were later transported to St.-Denis for burial (e.g., Charles VI, Charles VII and Henri IV), the bearers (called Hanouards, or Officers of Salt) walked only from St.-Lazare, where the bodies were kept overnight and prepared, to the Croix Penchante, where the monks took over the convoy (H. Sauval, *Histoire et recherches des antiquités de la ville de Paris*, Paris, 1724, II, p. 350; P. Hurtaut and Magny, *Dictionnaire historique de la ville de Paris*, Paris, 1779, III, pp. 206 and 392); this cross marked the intersection of the two files and was probably the sixth of the Montjoies (see note 2 below).

The next mentions of the Montjoies seem to be those of Guillebert de Metz (1407–34; A. Leroux de Lincy, *Paris et ses historiens*, Paris, 1867, p. 230) and G. Corrozet (*Les antiquitez de Paris*, Paris, 1561, f. 91); the modern legend can be said to begin with the latter. Most recently, see L. Lambeau, *Histoire des communes annexées à Paris en 1859* (Seine, Département. Direction des affaires départementales), Paris, 1923, pp. 151–200, with bibliography. The Montjoies must not be confused with the 'stations' of Saint Denis (see S. McK. Crosby, *The Abbey of St.-Denis*, New Haven, 1942, p. 46), an error made, *inter alia*, by H.-F. Delaborde (*Mémoires, Société de l'histoire de Paris*, XI, 1884, pp. 368–9 and note 1).

2. Paris, Bibl. Nat., Est., Vx 16, p. 115 (Coll. Lallemand de Betz). The numbers have been added in ink in a nineteenth-century hand. In both cases the sheet measures about 210 × 305 cm, the image about 165 × 245 cm. They were made before 1753, when the collection was given to the royal library; I have not found an identical watermark (three linked circles in a shield framed by olive leaves tied below by a ribbon and bearing a heart, with the initials PF below), although a similar one was used in 1677 by Pierre du Val, *Diverses cartes et tables* (E. Heawood, *Watermarks*, Hilversum, 1950, no. 701). A date after the 1720s is suggested by the dilapidated state of the crosses (see note 6 below), which was probably the result of neglect after the new and straight royal road to St.-Denis (begun in 1731) had, as it were, shunted them to the side. The etchings were used for the imaginary view by Gailhabaud in Leroux de Lincy, p. 230.

The right half of Fig. 1 shows the tympanum of the church of La Chapelle which lay on the route to St.-Denis; the building occupied the traditional site of Saint Genevieve's 'retreat' when on her way to pray at the tomb of Saint Denis, and the tympanum contained scenes of her life; Guilhermy was familiar with the iconography, perhaps through this etching (for the bibliography, see M. Dumolin and G. Outardel, *Paris et la Seine* [Les églises de France], Paris, 1937, pp. 45–47). The number of Montjoies was quite clearly nine (as Dom Brial wrote in 1809) and not seven, a number which dates only from the time of La Caille (*Description de la ville et des faubourgs de Paris*, Paris, 1714, f. 13 v); but this later description probably omitted the one between La Chapelle and St.-Lazare (which La Caille said was at St.-Chaumont, although this was actually a few hundred yards north of the leprosery) as well as the one at St.-Denis itself. On the Inselin plan of 1704–6 (Paris, Arch. Nat., N III [Seine] 737) and on the Nicolas de Fer view of 1717 (Bibl. Nat., Est., Va 198.1), nine can easily be counted. For another analysis, see J. Lair's communication to the bulletin of the *Société de l'histoire de Paris*, XXIII, 1896, pp. 97–116.

3. For the Eleanor Crosses, see most recently: J. Evans, 'A Prototype of the Eleanor Crosses', *Burlington Magazine*, XCI, 1949, pp. 96, 99; M. Hastings, *St. Stephen's Chapel*, Cambridge, 1955, pp. 20–27; L. Stone, *Sculpture in Britain. The Middle Ages*, Baltimore, 1955, pp. 143–5.

La Chapelle (Fig. 4)[4] (cf. Fig. 1, nos. 1 and 3 respectively), which suggest that the pedestals had two stories above a steplike plinth, the upper perhaps with gabled arcading like that of the Eleanor Crosses. The etchings seem to be fairly reliable in details, however. Variations in gables and arches are carefully delineated, and five of the angels atop the pinnacles of one cross stand out clearly (Fig. 2, no. 1; the central angel is enclosed by the shaft of the cross). Each Montjoie also held three or four statues of kings[5] that are probably drawn accurately, if their resemblance to the figures of Queen Eleanor is a criterion: like the Eleanors, the kings stood in relaxed positions, the hands holding the cloak or a strap, a pair of gloves or a scepter. There is some doubt as to whether the traditional description of the figures as Louis VIII, Louis IX and Philip III (or Philip II, Louis VIII and his son) should be accepted; probably all represented the sainted king, a form of multiple image intended to make Louis visible and accessible from every side. The crowned monograms in the Estampes views indicate that some of the monuments were restored under the Bourbons—probably Louis XIII, to judge from the state of disrepair into which they seem to have fallen by the 1740s.[6]

Crosses, like ancient hermai, were often erected as property boundaries in the Middle Ages, and the term, *montjoie*, may even have come from an Old High German root with this meaning.[7] Sometimes a large cross signified the presence of a wayside oratory or topped a lantern of the dead, and one was often placed upon a height, whence the learned but inaccurate etymology from *montem gaudii*, the hill from which the pilgrim first or last saw a holy site.[8] The Spinnerinnen of Vienna and Vienna-Neustadt, the Haimburg lantern, and the monument marking the meeting of the Magi in Jean de Berry's *Très Riches Heures*, fall into these categories.[9] But the Saint Louis Montjoies and the Eleanor Crosses seem to have differed from the above. They had images of rulers instead of saints or scenes from the Passion, and this gave them a distinctly temporal flavor. Moreover the Montjoies also seem to have differed somewhat from the Eleanor Crosses, at least in their original intention.

Eleanor of Castille, consort of Edward I, died at Hardby near Lincoln in 1290, and her body was borne to London for burial. As with Saint Louis, crosses were erected at the places where the procession stopped. But the route taken was not the normal one from Lincoln to London; it passed instead through the more populous regions and near some of the greater religious houses such as Woburn.[10] The suggestion that the procession and the crosses were carefully planned in advance is confirmed by the story of what happened at Dunstable: when the procession came to the town, the bier was stopped in the market place; the chancellor, assisted by a group of nobles, chose the site where it was to rest, the prior of the convent sprinkled the ground with holy water, and only then was the casket dismounted for the night.[11] There a monumental cross was later erected. Edward's purpose in such elaborate arrangements, according to a chronicler at St. Albans who wrote only a decade after the event, was the stimulation of prayers in behalf of the queen.[12] The images of the consort on the monuments, the phrase, 'Orate pro anima', on the pedestals,[13] and the aspersion of the sites, indicate that the Eleanor Crosses were in fact a set of cenotaphs.

A similar purpose undoubtedly nourished the program of the Montjoies, but it was joined to another aim of quite different character. In order to understand this, we must take into account the traditions of the French monarchy. No educated Frenchman in the thirteenth century could have been ignorant of the story of Saint Remi, the Apostle of the Franks who had baptized

4. Fig. 3 is from J. de Saint-Victor, *Tableau historique et pittoresque de Paris*, Paris (*c.* 1808), II, p. 308, copied from a drawing said to have been made before the corps de logis was added to St.-Lazare (*c.* 1719–20). Fig. 4 is from L. P. Prudhomme, *Revolutions de Paris*, no. 3, p. 116, Paris, 1791. John Evelyn noted the presence of fleurs de lys on the monuments in 1643 (*The Diary*, ed. E. S. de Beer, II, Oxford, 1955, p. 90), and Viollet-le-Duc said fragments of one socle remained on the Quai de la Briche (*Dictionnaire*, IV, p. 438, note 1), which has unfortunately since been filled in.

5. Three, according to Corrozet and all historians through S.-J. Morand, *Histoire de la sainte chapelle royale du palais*, Paris, 1790, p. 75; the number four is first mentioned by A. Lenoir, *Musée des monuments français*, I, Paris, 1800, p. 197.

6. The Montjoies are said to have been attacked by the Huguenots in 1567 (J. du Breul, *Le théâtre des antiquitez de Paris*, Paris, 1639, p. 829; Sauval, II, p. 350; see *Bulletin, Société de l'histoire de Paris*, XXXVII, 1910, p. 203, for the date). For other Bourbon uses of the crowned 'L' in medieval monuments, see the description of the west portal of Royaumont (H. Duclos, *Histoire de Royaumont*, Paris, 1867, p. 165); the 1634 spire of the Ste.-Chapelle (H. Stein, *Le palais de justice et la Sainte-Chapelle*, Paris, 1912, pp. 123–5); and the 1688 choir screen at Orléans Cathedral (G. Chenesseau, *Ste.-Croix d'Orléans*, Paris, 1921, Fig. 101).

7. Cf. G. Thaumas de la Thaumassière, *Coutumes locales du Berry*, Bourges, 1679, pp. 72–74 and 86–88; see also R. Louis, *A propos des Montjoies autour de Vézelay. Sens successifs et évolution du nom 'Montjoie'* (Société des fouilles archéologiques . . . de l'Yonne, monographies et fouilles IV), Auxerre, 1939.

8. P. Irigoin, 'Montjoies et oratoires', *Bulletin monumental*, XCIV, 1935, pp. 145–70, citing Hugh de St.-Cher (p. 146).

9. Cf. Stone, p. 255, note 38.

10. J. Hunter, 'On the death of Eleanor of Castile, consort of King Edward the first, and the honours paid to her memory', *Archaeologia*, XXIX, 1842, pp. 167–91.

11. W. Lovell, 'Queen Eleanor's Crosses', *Archaeological Journal*, XLIX, 1892, pp. 17–43, esp. p. 32.

12. O. Lehmann-Brockhaus, *Schriftquellen zur Kunst in England*, no. 5895.

13. Hunter, p. 180.

King Clovis in the Merovingian period.[14] Before he died, Remi expressed the desire to be buried in the church of SS. Timothy and Apollinaris outside the walls of Reims; as his coffin was being borne thither, it grew as heavy as lead and had to be put down—a not infrequent occurrence in Merovingian times[15]— and it could be moved again only after another resting-place had been decided upon; a cross was erected where the coffin touched the ground, and miracles were performed there through the intervention of the saint. The story bears a striking resemblance to the procession of Louis IX, and if miracles are not recorded as having been performed at the nine sites between Paris and St.-Denis, they did take place when the king's remains, borne on a litter, entered the city from the south.[16]

The Montjoies were unquestionably meant to liken Louis to the saint who had Christianized the kings of Gaul and instituted the unction, possibly the most important single act in the French coronation cere-mony. In a way Louis thus became Clovis and Remi rolled into one. This suggestion may be supported by the fact that similar Montjoies, with a similar aim, had already been erected for his grandfather, Philip II, who died at Mantes in 1223. Philip's coffin was carried to Paris and thence to St.-Denis, and, according to the Minstrel of Reims, writing about 1260–1263, 'à chascune reposée faisoit on une croix où l'image est figurée...'[17] Guillaume le Breton called one of these outside Mantes a 'crux Philippi' and said that miracles shortly began to take place there.[18] The image of the king again suggests a cenotaph,[19] while the miracles were a measure of his saintliness in the eyes of the populace. There are, however, some indications that this was not so much a popular movement as a care-fully calculated political one.

Few French kings had a less saintly character or career than Philip II. But to insist upon such a realistic point of view is to reckon without the needs of the Capetian dynasty.[20] Two European kings had been sainted in the 1160s—Edward the Confessor in England and Charlemagne in Germany—and this naturally put pressure on France to attain the same dignity. Philip's father, Louis VII, was intrinsically a better candidate than Philip himself, and at the old king's death in 1180 the possibility of his canonization was probably raised. This may explain why he was buried in a Cistercian abbey rather than a Benedictine one, break-ing with tradition and also engaging the prayers and support of the young, strong Cistercian order on the king's behalf. No overt steps seem to have been taken, however, and no results were forthcoming. During Philip's long reign (1180–1223), the temporal power of the French crown increased enormously, and the theory of kingship was developed into an instrument of international policy.[21] Philip II carried on an elaborate pretense to the suzerainty of Europe, assum-ing the imperial epithet of Augustus, marrying a Carolingian heiress to complete the legitimization of his dynasty, and generally indulging himself in a cult of Carolism. 1223, then, must have seemed a natural and propitious moment for a promotion through Rome. Describing the death and burial of Philip, an English chronicler noted as miraculous only the fact that, at the time, there was a conclave of bishops and barons in Paris, all of whom were able to attend the funeral which thereby became an extraordinarily splendid affair.[22] But French chroniclers told how a vision of Saint Denis appeared to the cardinal of Sta. Sabina on the night of the king's death, instructing him to inform the pope of the event—a vision, incidentally, in which the king himself appeared carry-ing the Holy Lance; and how the crippled and the blind sought relief at his tomb in the abbey of St.-Denis and were cured.[23] Even the king's epitaph suggested the factual attainment of heavenly bliss.[24] Clearly the movement to canonize Philip was loud and strong, and it included emblematic devices like the Montjoies.

The use of a Merovingian precedent at the death of Philip II was not unusual, for there are suggestions

---

14. Cf., *inter alia*, Flodoard, *Vita sancti Remigii* (*Patr. Lat.*, CXXXV, cc. 59–60).

15. E.g., *Vita sancti Eligii*, II, xxxvi (*Patr. Lat.*, LXXXVII, cc. 567–568).

16. Guillaume de Saint-Pathus, *Les miracles de saint Louis*, ed. P. B. Fay, Paris, 1932, pp. 173–5.

17. N. de Wailly, ed., *Récits d'un ménestrel de Reims*, Paris, 1876, no. 307 (p. 160).

18. Guillaume le Breton, *Philippides*, XII, 11. 606–17 (*Recueil des historiens des Gaules*, XVII, p. 281). The priory of St.-Julien-la-Croix-le-Roi was later founded on the site and in the six-teenth century the commune of Mantes was apparently still maintaining the cross (L. Cottineau, *Répertoire topobibligra-phique des abbayes et prieurés*, Mâcon, 1938, c. 2749; A. Durand and L. Graves, *La chronique de Mantes*, Mantes, 1883, pp. 160–1 and 427).

19. It is significant in this respect that, on the spot where Saint Albert of Liége was murdered outside Reims in 1192, there was erected a cross on four columns, but without an image (*Mon. Ger. Hist., Scriptores*, XXV, p. 165).

20. See P. E. Schramm, *Der König von Frankreich*, Weimar, 1939, p. 185; R. Fawtier, *The Capetian Kings of France*, London, 1960, p. 59.

21. Schramm, pp. 178 ff; Fawtier, pp. 55–57.

22. Ralph of Coggeshall, *Chronicon Anglicanum*, ed. J. Steven-son (*Rer. Brit. Script.*), London, 1875, p. 196.

23. Anonymous of Tours, *Rec. Hist. Gaules*, XVIII, p. 304; Guil-laume le Breton, *ibid.*, XVII, p. 283; *Gesta Philipi Augusti* in F. Duchesne, *Historiae Francorum Scriptores*, V, 1649, p. 260.

24. *Rec. Hist. Gaules*, XVII, p. 116. I am informed by Dr. Georgia Sommers that the idea of burying the king in Charles the Bald's tomb at St.-Denis is a modern misinterpretation; see B. de Montesquiou-Fezensac, communication, in *Bulletin, Société nationale des Antiquaires de France*, 1963, p. 86.

that from his Charles-cult there gradually emerged a Clovis-cult that was to bloom during the short reign of his son, Louis VIII (1223–1226).[25] At this time the tomb of Clovis, which lay in the abbey of Ste.-Geneviève in Paris, was provided with a new stone *gisant* and a new inscription that began, 'Hic est illustrissimus Rex Ludovicus qui et Clodoveus ante Baptismum est dictus', linking Louis and Clovis in the best Isidorean manner.[26] This must have attracted considerable attention, since the abbey had been founded by Clovis and dedicated by Saint Remi himself. It may even have sparked the monks of St.-Denis, who shortly began to rebuild their church and to confect new tombs for the kings of France who were buried there.

The attempt to gain sainthood for Philip II was unsuccessful, and it was not repeated for Louis VIII. Louis IX, on the other hand, was a natural candidate, combining as he did the aspirations of the dynasty with the qualities most revered in a Christian prince, and it is small wonder that Philip III and Philip IV did their utmost to bring about his canonization. In this they had widespread popular support. Louis' relics were first kept with the army in Tunis as a talisman to protect it from defeat by the Arabs; when a portion of the remains was buried at Monreale, miracles occurred at once; and we have seen that miracles also took place when the casket containing his bones neared Paris.[27] Far from being mere cenotaphs like the Eleanor Crosses, however, the stone monuments studding the route from Paris to St.-Denis also were signboards promoting the saintliness of the Capetian king, as well as guides leading to his tomb. They were a public statement, a proud counterpart to the secret inquiry into Louis' miracles that the pope instituted as early as 1273.[28] And both were ultimately successful, for in 1297, after many delays, the king's name was finally entered on the roster of saints.

25. Schramm, pp. 178 and 183–4, notes that the legend of the unction by Saint Remi became part of the canon of the French theory of kingship only about 1200.
26. Corrozet, *op. cit.*, ed. N. Bonfons, Paris, 1586, II, ff. 7 v–8 r; for the tomb, see C. Giteau, 'Les sculptures de l'abbaye de Ste.-Genevieve de Paris', *Paris et l'Île-de-France*, XII, 1961, pp. 7–55, esp. 40–41.

27. Le Nain, pp. 173–6.
28. H.-F. Delaborde, 'Fragments de l'enquête faite à Saint-Denis en 1282 en vue de la canonisation de saint Louis', *Mémoires, Société de l'histoire de Paris*, XXIII, 1896, pp. 2–3. I should like to express my thanks to Mmes F. Bercé, F. Buge, L. Damiron, C. Giteau, C. Gauchery-Grodecki and N. Villa, and to MM. William Hinkle and Robert Glénisson, for their assistance during my research on this paper.

I. Q. VAN REGTEREN ALTENA

Hidden Records of the Holy Sepulchre

More than forty years have passed since Rudolf Wittkower, a gifted student of the history of architecture especially, and I met and joined in walks through Baroque Rome. I could not think of a better tribute to the scholar and the friend he has since proved to be than to choose a subject which stresses a gap between a world-famous building and its tiny shadow like that which now exists between Wittkower's knowledge of architecture and mine.

The tiny shadow came to hand in an object of very small dimensions[1] which I happened to come across in The Hague Communal Museum (Gemeente-museum) several years ago; since then the problem it seemed to contain has not lost its fascination for me. What fascinated me was the fact that not exclusively great works of art appear to be relevant for major art-historical situations but that remote derivates may also sometimes be considered even better stimulants to sharpen one's heuristic capacities.

In a show-case containing a diversity of medieval works of art of minor dimensions the poor, fragmentary object in corroded lead was labelled: 'a bird's-food-container' (vogel-voederbakje). Though lacking one side, it seemed to be shaped in the form of a small building consisting of one square room, on one side completed by a circular wall, provided with seven windows which are circular on top, and crowned by a low circular turret on its flat roof (Fig. 1). Three enlarged, excellent photographs provided by the museum enabled me to verify my first impression, that, rather than serving a profane use, it might reflect the forms of a sacred building. What else than those of the Holy Sepulchre to which, exceptional as they were, it seemed to be related? And I still believe that first impression was right. From the photographs its walls, though small, appeared to be decorated in low relief by a pattern of lozenges alternated by horizontal bands, with the exception of the 'apsis', which shows the coat-of-arms with three lilies, apparently of one of the kings of France (Fig. 2). The same pattern of oblique intersecting lines covers the walls between the windows and the flat rim above them, behind which the roof stretches at a slightly lower level. This pattern also runs along the tambour and covers the cupola, which has been obtained by curving the pointed sec-

tions inwards, so that fissures remain in between them. These seemed to sustain my idea, as the Burial Chamber had to have openings to the sky to let escape the dense smoke produced by candles burning day and night around the holy site, so as to prevent the pilgrims from being suffocated when entering it.

This was the limit of my knowledge when I was informed that, according to the files of the museum, the object had been labelled previously as follows: 'Très ancienne *Ecritoire* qui date du 13e ou 14e S., retirée de la Seine lors des Travaux faits dans son lit en 1850 près du . . . Palais.' This provided a clue, for it is known that between the years 1848 and 1860 a great number of objects in lead were found during excavations around the Île de la Cité in Paris, most of which at the time were bought piece by piece by M. Arthur Forgeais who gave the entire collection to the Musée Cluny, in 1861. The main discovery spots corresponded with the nearby bridges, such as the Pont S. Charles, the Pont S. Michel, the Pont Notre Dame and the Pont au Change, about which it is known that many shops of the goldsmiths and silversmiths and of the merchants in objects of ordinary metal were formerly located. Even some of the moulds of hard stone from which the leads had been cast were included in the finds.

All of them have been enumerated in the last part of E. du Sommérard's Catalogue of 1883 and among them a number of supposed inkstands,[2] similar in shape to the bird's-food-container. The Cluny collection, now mainly kept in store, was shown to me in 1963 by M. Salet, keeper of the Museum, who kindly had three of the objects photographed for comparison (Fig. 3). Moreover, when coats-of-arms occur, M. Salet identified them as belonging to Louis XII and to Charles IX, which dates them exclusively to the sixteenth century. Not believing in the theory of the 'écritoires', he added, conjecturally, that they might have been small lights ('*quinquets*') to be used when a king made his 'entrée' in a town. That they may have been lights does seem probable, and the two slabs from the front side (the side lacking in The Hague), bent downwards (shown in the middle of Fig. 3), suggest that after having been lit, they could be hung on a

---

1. Height 7.6 cm, breadth 3.2 cm, length 4.7 cm.

2. E. du Sommérard, *Musée des thermes et de l'hôtel de Cluny: Catalogue et description des objets d'art, etc.*, Paris, 1883, nos. 9234 to 9306 and 10041 to 10046.

horizontal border in the same way as a scabbard is fastened to a belt. The turning off, then, of the only side capable of possessing a larger opening when the object was used excluded definitely that any bird could have reached the hypothetical food in it and the quill pens dipping in the hypothetical ink through the very small windows.

On the other hand, a great number of the leads found at the same spots have been proved to be pilgrims' ensigns. The variety of the places of worship to which their emblems refer is demonstrated by a systematically arranged set on exhibition in the Musée Cluny. When consulting Forgeais' 'Plombs historiés'[3] and du Sommérard's Catalogue we are filled with admiration for what the first, or perhaps not quite the first, generation of 'Antiquaires de France' achieved by identifying almost all the 'lieux de pélerinage' they were meant for, not only the more obvious ones but also churches like Saint Maur-des-Fossés, Saint Jean-en-Grève, Saint André-de-Chartres, Saint Hubert-d'Eu, Roquemadour, etc. . . . . All of them must have been produced at Paris and we wonder, when coming across the *coquille de St. Jacques* and the coupled images of St. Peter and St. Paul, which mean respectively Compostella and Rome, that the production did not stop at the limits of the realm of the Kings of France. Besides bringing them back from the final goal when it was reached, as do the mountaineers nowadays, the pilgrims could obtain all of them at the Pont au Change, and, when the mountain was too high, even abstain from the contracted journey by buying it elsewhere. The inference concerning the 'quinquets' to be drawn from these co-finds in the Seine seems to be that they are the only comparable objects likely to be connected with one of the most ambitious pilgrimages, one of the most expensive too, still practised in the days of Louis XII and his immediate successors.

Moreover, the idea of a portable model symbolizing, as it were, a pious end of the pilgrimage which is human life may have lived more in the sixteenth century than we are inclined to think when reading Erasmus' ridiculing the habits of the travellers.[4] We may cite a variant to be found in the cult of St. Sebaldus at Nürnberg, which is well expressed in Hans Sebald Beham's engraving[5] (Fig. 4) showing the legendary pilgrim, recognizable as such from the two

ensigns on his cap, sitting in the wood where he died and bearing on his right hand a model of the church to be erected over his grave. It had been his will that he be buried in the Peter's Chapel which was to become his shrine and was afterwards visited by innumerable pilgrims. This was a minor cult when compared with the general one of the Sepulchre of the Lord, which was endowed with the power of plenary indulgence, hardly ever conferred upon the sanctuaries which replaced it in the west.[6]

On such grounds the solution would be easy if the small structure were really an exact rendering of the building as it existed at the time of the French kings to whom the coats-of-arms refer. This is not the case: originally it had nine windows instead of seven if indeed there were windows at all and not only blind arched walls, the exterior decoration, if there was any left after the damage it had suffered, did not contain intersecting lines; and the turret consisted of an onion-shaped dome that stood not on a tambour but on free-standing columns. Yet the whole aspect of the lead model lacks any connection at all with the architecture of the time of Louis XII and the Valois kings. We ought to go back before Gothic forms were introduced and perhaps even before the flowering of Romanesque architecture to find analogous forms.

Two features of it deserve closer inspection because they are not met with in the monuments constructed out of the wish to copy or to evoke the Jerusalem monument, *viz.* the decoration by oblique intersection and the coats-of-arms. Quadrangles used as lozenges in or on walls are not uncommon in medieval architecture, both in the Near East and in Western Europe. If we exclude one single lozenge decorating the field of a tall wall ended by an arch,[7] we may distinguish

3. A. Forgeais, *Collection de plombs historiés trouvés dans la Seine: 2. ser.: Enseignes de pélerinages*, Paris, 1863.
4. In the Colloquium 'Peregrinatio Religionis erga': '—Sed quid istuc ornatus es? Absitus es conchis imbricatis, stanneis ac plumbeis imaginibus oppletus undique, culmeis ornatus torquibus, brachium habet ova Serpentum.'—'Visi divum Jacob Compostellanum. . . .' And what follows.
5. Pauli, *Hans Sebald Beham: ein Kritisches Verzeichnis seiner Kupferstiche, Radierungen und Holzschnitte*, Strassburg, 1901, p. 81, no. 69. A related drawing is reproduced in E. H. Zimmer-

mann, *Neuerwerbungen des Germ. Mus., 1921–1924*, Nürnberg, 1925, pl. 115.
6. G. Dalman, *Das Grab Christi in Deutschland*, Leipzig, 1922, pp. 19–21.
7. Such as occur in the eleventh-century churches of Southern Italy and Pisa, and before, in the Cairo Mosque of El Hakim, the very ruler who was guilty of the most complete destruction the Church of the Sepulchre ever underwent. On one of the Monza ampullae (A. Grabar, *Les ampoules de Terre Sainte*, Paris, 1958, p. 22; *ampoule 5 revers*, pl. XI, 2) a lozenge is produced on the field formed by the arched door of the Sepulchre, so as to form the exact likeness of such panels. It symbolizes the grave and is a simplification of its image seen in perspective. This way of falling back on to a decorative formula from an illusionistic model is not surprising in the fifth century after Christ. A similar abbreviation in the flat may have been misinterpreted afterwards and have been interpreted as the very symbol of the place of worship and, but this remains pure conjecture, may have been inserted by El Hakim as a trophy in the walls of his major construction. The Sepulchre was destroyed shortly before 1009, the mosque completed in 1010. Kuehnel ('Das Rautenmotiv', *Gedenkschrift Redslob*, 1954, pp. 83–89) interpreted the lozenge as a purely Islamic motive, though leaving its origin unsolved.

three main types: (a) *opus reticulatum*, in which the individual stones constitute the lozenges, in use all over the former Roman world; (b) any pattern executed in relief independent of the shape of the stones; and (c) transennae based on the intersection of lines parallel to the diagonals or at an angle of 90 degrees.

The alternation of *opus reticulatum* with bands of stone laid horizontally was popular in Roman Imperial and Early Christian architecture, but it served also in pilgrimage ensigns of the later Gothic ages to designate churches of a considerably later time, maybe even Romanesque ones. We may cite one such ensign found recently under a house in the oldest parts of Amsterdam,[8] the church on top of which shows this kind of masonry in its walls as well as oblique intersections on the roof and the helms of the towers (Fig. 5). It is clear that the lead founders had but few variations at their disposal to express the qualities of material.[9] The designer of the 'quinquets', however, instead of continuing the system of alternating flat bands and *reticula*, as did the worker of the ensign, separated the windows by tall rectangles covered by *reticula* (Figs. 1 and 2). Now in the vertical direction the arrangement with lozenges is much less common than in horizontal sequences. One example of an overall vertical use may be cited from Hampshire, where the priory church of Christchurch[10] has an early Romanesque round turret at the northeast angle of its north transept decorated after the second method noted above (Fig. 7). The type seems to be of considerably earlier origin and is no fresh invention, but it is a fresh way of application.[11] The same is the case with several of the elements

that compose the wonderful apse-exterior of Nôtre-Dame-de-Rioux (Charente Maritime), which, among others, contains colonettes decorated in the same way (Fig. 8). Indeed, the reticulated fields of the 'quinquets' do prove to derive from colonettes[12] when we compare them to one example bearing the coat-of-arms of Louis XII on its side. In this one the windows are divided by short columns from whose flat capitals the arches spread (Fig. 3 on the right). The Holy Sepulchre was surrounded by colonettes standing against the walls in between the windows. 'Lilies' are likely to have played a part in the early decoration. They are mentioned in connection with the earlier columns of the building, and their presence may have encouraged a preference for applying lilies to imitation Holy Sepulchres, especially to the one in the Capella Rucellai.[13] In this way the lilies of the king were welcome ornaments on the tiny reductions.

Assuming that the sixteenth-century 'quinquets' were meant to evoke the forms of the Holy Grave at an earlier moment, we shall have to ask: 'What time, then, did the first makers have in mind?' The question implies another one: 'And what could they have known about it?' At first sight the vertical reticulated field reminds one of a similar trellis which figures on several of the ampullae of Monza (Fig. 6).[14] There, however, they have been identified with the 'claustra', belonging to our third type. One explanation is that, at the time of Louis XII, the man who replaced the column on the 'quinquet' by the element in question meant to correct it, while misinterpreting one of the earliest testimonies which had come to his knowledge.[15] The groundplan of the 'quinquets' is an obvious simplification of the one known.[16] The rest of the

8. It has not been localized so far, but the costume of the kneeling person dates it in the second half of the fourteenth century. On top of it we see a church whose pillars inside the nave are shown, as well as the exterior of the apse and of the two western towers, with their tall spires. In that form it may have been an early Romanesque building. Comp. H. H. van Regteren Altena in *Stadskernonderzoek in Amsterdam*, edited by the same, Groningen, 1966, pp. 44–49.

9. A contribution to the knowledge of their fabrication is in: L. Maxe-Werly, *Bulletin de la Société nationale des antiquaires de France*, 1885, p. 194. The fourteenth-century models reproduced follow the same system as the one quoted in the foregoing note.

10. A drawing by Sir Thomas Graham Jackson, Bart., reproduced in his *Byzantine and Romanesque Architecture*, Cambridge, 1920, I, pl. CLIII, renders it well. We use it in our Fig. 7.

11. From one period only do we know monuments the ornament of which was entirely based on a system of diagonal intersecting lines: the period around the year A.D. 700. We may cite the sides and the lids of the majestic tomb of Saint Aguilberte in the crypts of Jouarre (Fig. 9) and the casket of Teudericus in the treasury of St. Maurice d'Agaume, both of which show different solutions, all of them based on the same geometrical principle. That its origin was related to the idea of resurrection is shown by the short sides of certain early Christian sarcophagi found in the Provence, where they symbolize the doors of Paradise (F. Benoit, *Sarcophages paléochrétiens d'Arles et de Marseille*, Paris, 1954, pp. 27, 83 et pl. XXXVI, 4).

12. In what manner the diapered pattern was applied originally on columns does not appear from such reductions. We may think of painted diapers or of those in intaglio or in relief.

13. L. H. Heydenreich, 'Die Capella Rucellai', in *Essays in Honor of Erwin Panofsky*, New York, 1961, pp. 224 f., which contributed in a general way to my insight into the kind of problems contained in the subject.

14. A. Grabar, *op. cit.*, *passim*. The same applies to other ampullae and to the painting from the Sancta Sanctorum, well reproduced in H. Grisar, *Die Römische Cappella Sancta Sanctorum . . .*, Freiburg, 1908, p. 115, pl. 59. The illumination on the page following the canon tables in the Adysh Gospels (Georgia, A.D. 897) seems to reflect it too (C. Nordenfalk, *Die Spätantiken Kanontafeln*, Göteborg, 1938, Fig. 5 on p. 115, comp. pp. 107, 108).

15. It cannot be overlooked, though, that on the miniature in the Sacramentary of Henry II (Munich, cod. Lat. 4456, fol. 14) the large columns before the entrance of the church are similarly decorated; cf. R. Krautheimer in the *Journal of the Warburg and Courtauld Institutes*, vol. v, 1942, pl. 2 e.

16. There is much to be said about this, but that would lead too far. In the chapel at Görlitz (consecration in 1504; Dalman, *op. cit.*, pp. 81–87), the outside colonettes have been reduced to seven, which means one in the middle of the 'apse'; note the occurrence of the same thing in Nôtre-Dame-de-Rioux, quoted

masonry was done in the usual way of the ensigns, after an alternating system such as could be found in several early medieval buildings still existing in France. The balustrade along the roof found in the twelfth-century copy at Eichstädt, though, may be linked indirectly to the rim of the 'quinquet' and speaks in favor of an example from the time of the crusades.[17] One more object points in that direction: the twelfth-century seal of the Chanoines-du-Saint-Sépulchre.[18] Here the cupola rests on a low tambour, pierced by circular windows (Fig. 10).

Most enlightening is one of the sides of the Stuttgart ivory shrine, a kind of contraction of the façade of Sepulchre and Church, with a cupola on a tambour pierced by arched windows, crowning an inside-outside synopsis of the Sepulchre with winding columns, consisting of alternating light and dark shafts, and with reversed lilies in the spandrels, the whole being flanked by vertical reticulated fields. Similar combinations occur in the mosaics on the north wall of the basilica of the Nativity in Bethlehem.

Such is the thin chain of evidence which our sources seem to allow. We shall have to wait for new arguments before suggesting that the marble revetment of the walls of the Jerusalem building during the kingdom of Jerusalem contained lozenges and lilies in *opus sectile*.[19] Neither do we have any proof that the lamps were shaped after a prototype from the time of the Crusaders. Yet what seems factually impossible need not be so theoretically. Lamps in the form of a church already existed in late Roman times,[20] and a small lamp, thought to be lit from oil brought home in small quantities, would remind the medieval believer of the heavenly lit fire burning before the tomb of Christ.[21] Nor can the relation between the Kings of France and the Holy Sepulchre be overlooked. It is true that after a long interval it was only reasserted after the treaty of 1535 between Francis I and Suleiman the Magnificent had brought under the King's protection the Francis-

cans who performed the church services. But their claim had existed since Louis XII had cherished the idea of another Crusade and, on November 11, 1500, had concluded a secret treaty with the King of Spain envisaging a partition of the kingdom of Naples and Sicily: besides the lands to be acquired, Louis would get the titles of 'Roi de France, duc de Milan, roi de Naples et de Jérusalem', all of them verbatim recognized as 'fiefs de l'eglise Romaine'. His pretensions were to be fulfilled by his successor. Hence the lights in the form of the Holy Sepulchre must have been newly made shortly after the year 1500, with a political aim[22] under the mantle of piety. Not for nothing were palms[23] added to the coats-of-arms of the Kings of France (Fig. 2).

Among the hidden records of the Holy Sepulchre which escaped the notice of J. Formigé when he composed his useful survey of the sources of our knowledge, we may finish by mentioning some other pieces in Dutch possession. The first Dutch artist to evoke one of the holy sites concentrated on the inside of the Nativity Chapel at Bethlehem, when he introduced it in the painting commemorating the journey to Jerusalem of a group of four Amsterdam citizens of distinction, who are seen kneeling before it.[24] They had visited the Holy City in 1519, a year before Jan van Scorel entered it near Christmas to remain there till Easter of 1521. The months spent in the Holy Land must have provided ample occasion for him to fill his sketchbooks, from which so far only one leaf has been identified.[25] Among them more than one general view of Jerusalem must have occurred since one of them was used by the master in his triptych for the Lockhorst family (about

before. The Holy Sepulchre at Leutesdorf (seventeenth century; Dalman, pp. 112–14) and others possess seven arches between eight columns.

17. L. H. Heydenreich, *op. cit.*, p. 224, n. 24, where Dalman is cited.

18. J. Formigé, 'Un Plan du Saint Sépulchre', Académie des inscriptions et belles-lettres, Fondation Piot, *Monuments et mémoires*, vol. XLVIII, 1954, p. 125, Fig. 37.

19. Shortly before, the abbot Daniel, who travelled from 1113–1115, described it as 'from fine marble, like an ambo'.

20. The 'lamp Basilewsky' at Leningrad was found near Orléans-ville (Algérie) about 1850; *vide* Cabrol-Leclercq, *Dictionnaire d'archéologie chrétienne et de liturgie*, vol. II, col. 580–4; and VIII, col. 1213–14.

21. J. Morgenstern, *The Fire upon the Altar*, Leiden, 1963, pp. 114 f., describes the Easter rites by which the holy lamps, after having been spent, were to be lit everywhere from the one light let down into the Holy Sepulchre and considered to be their unique source.

22. That is to say in an economical sense. Unless they were free engagements the pilgrimages produced revenues, to the church as well as to the towns. The ensigns brought home or bought from the ecclesiastical office looking after the penalties (according to the authors I was able to consult) originally served as a receipt to be produced to its civil counterpart. It seems likely that, the strict applications having become obsolete, the authorities finished by selling them on behalf of the mission, just as collections are held today.

23. So, at least, they do look. The interpretation may be questioned; their placement, however, could be compared to one of two rose-twigs flanking the crowned *armes-de-France* on a medal (1454) struck for Charles VII, the reverse of which bears a cross and the fifth strophe of the 'Horae Canonica Salvatoris' (*Trésor de numismatique*, Paris, 1836, vol. X, 1, pl. 1, n. 5); F. Mazerolle, *Les médailleurs français du XVe siècle au milieu du XVIIIe*, Paris, 1902, vol. II, p. 2, n. 3.

24. Description with literature appended in the *Catalogue of Paintings in the Utrecht Museum*, 1933, p. 238, sub. n. 501.

25. A. E. Popham in *Old Master Drawings*, vol. III, March, 1929, pp. 65–66, pl. 56. Hans Bol possessed a general view of Jerusalem which Scorel had drawn while seated on the Mount of Olives (Christianus Adrichomias [van Adrichem], *Urbis Hierosolymae Descriptio*, Cologne, 1597, cited by Popham). A view of Jerusalem, seen from that side, was on exhibition at Utrecht (*Jan van Scorel*, 3 Aug.–30 Oct., 1955, n. 98, pl. 81; but listed as anonymous).

1525–1527, now in the Central Museum, Utrecht) and another one by an anonymous woodcutter who executed the main theme of this triptych, *viz.* Christ's entrance into Jerusalem, in a different arrangement, in a print edited by Herman van Borculo in 1538 at Utrecht.[26] A close-up of this print (Fig. 11) shows the outside of the Holy Sepulchre as Scorel drew it at the spot, thus providing us with the best evidence of the difference between the 'quinquets' and the almost coëval state of the building *in situ*. The number of colonettes left there, however, seems to have corresponded between them.[27]

One veritable 'simile', executed in wood, bone and inlaid mother-of-pearl, has, so far, not been taken into consideration. It belongs to the Van de Poll — Wolters — Quina — Foundation, now entrusted to Jonkheer Ir. A. N. J. van de Poll at Zeist (prov. Utrecht), to whom I owe the information about it, as well as the photographs here reproduced (Fig. 12). It consists of a model of the entire church in the inside containing a proportionally reduced one of the Sepulchre which, however, can be removed from it (Fig. 12, right side), whereas a separate enlarged one of the Sepulchre, as being its principal part, has been added to it (Fig. 12, left side), so as to show the exterior decoration. The complete set was obtained by its first owner, Carlos Quina, at Jerusalem from a monk attached to the sanctuary. Quina belonged to a family of Amsterdam merchants and arrived at Jerusalem on April 7, 1669, in the company of Rochus Stubbe of Hamburg and a young Englishman called Samuel Terrey. By a document bearing Quina's name and the oral tradition that the model

had been kept for three days in the Holy Sepulchre before being presented to him, its origin is authentically dated to not later than 1669; this is in contrast with several others of the same kind, but not dated, which have been preserved at different places.[28]

One aspect of the entire simile is that it has been executed on scale. Another is the decoration in alabaster and mother-of-pearl inlaid in the olive-wood from which the simile has been built up, a decoration which differs in the two parts shown in Fig. 12. Thus, for instance, the roof of the smaller one shows white squares divided by black diagonals, whereas the larger version has a more lavish ornament in the same place. As the absence of decoration on the exterior of the walls seems to agree with Scorel's image, the smaller type is likely to be the architectural portrait of the chapel as it appeared at the time. The separate one proves that on the outside it was decorated in the flat by opus sectile with regularly placed diapers, each of them containing a quatrefoil lily. The difference of colour may have been less obvious than the substituting material suggests, and for this reason Scorel may have suppressed it in his drawing.

In conclusion I may say that by itself the fragmentary object in The Hague Museum, analyzed here, is no more than a trifle. There is an advantage in this: if some deductions will find no support, I shall, at least, not have hurt susceptible aestheticism. To others, as it did to me, interrogating records of the Holy Sepulchre may mean another journey through the ages and the chance that one day will bring more evidence demanding that even trifles may have to be weighed.

---

26. Reproduced in its entirety by W. Nijhoff, *Nederlandsche Houtsneden, 1500–1550*, The Hague, 1933–6, p. 22 and pl. 114–115.

27. A similar image in a frame was introduced by Jan van Scorel into his group of members of the Noble Confraternity of the Holy Land at Haarlem, in which each of them bears a palm; it is held up before the group by the clerk Thijs Thomasz. A drawing after the last-mentioned detail by Cornelis van Noorde (1731–1795) is in the possession of the author.

28. Several of them have been dealt with by Dalman in the *Palästina-Jahrbuch*, vol. XIII, 1917, pp. 22 f.: 'Die Modelle der Grabeskirche in Jeruzalem als Quelle ihrer ältesten Gestalt', when, apart from others, this model was still unknown.

Carlos Quina described his journey from Amsterdam to Jerusalem in a beautifully executed MS. now belonging to the Koninklijk Oudheidkundig Genootschap at Amsterdam. It may have constituted one out of two volumes, for it, unhappily, ends at the moment when the Holy City came in sight.

RUTH OLITSKY RUBINSTEIN

Pius II's Piazza S. Pietro and St. Andrew's Head

Standing today among the cars in the vast sweep of Bernini's colonnade, no one could doubt that he had reached the very centre of Christendom. But the sublime assurance of the piazza and façade of St. Peter's makes it hard to imagine how they must have looked when Aeneus Sylvius Piccolomini was elected Pope Pius II in September, 1458. The uneven slope and decaying façades on top of the treacherous steps were all victims of a long neglect which Nicholas V's new doors and possible restorations of the campanile, and Calixtus III's paving of the piazza, could do little to relieve.[1] Pius himself describes the condition of the steps which he believed were built by Constantine, and which in the time of Calixtus III had fallen into decay: 'the marble itself was corroded with age and worn away by the trampling of many feet'.[2] Could this have seemed an echo of the fall of Constantinople, a symbol of the position of Christianity itself, made more precarious daily by Turkish advances in the Aegean?

Intensely aware of the 'unhappy calamities' of his time, Pius's goal was to drive the Turks out of Europe. As soon as he was elected Pope, he planned the Congress of Mantua (June, 1459–January, 1460), but it failed to stimulate the support of the princes of Europe for a crusade. Having spent eighteen months away from the Vatican in Mantua and Siena, Pius came back to Rome in October, 1460.[3] It was on his return that a new opportunity to win public support for the crusade presented itself and I hope to show that it also provided the spur to his building activity on the Piazza S. Pietro. This was the plan to bring the exiled head of St. Andrew the apostle to Rome.

When the Turks invaded the Peloponnesus in May, 1460, Thomas Paleologus, the Despot of Morea, rescued the relic from Patras and took it, together with his family, to Corfu. Pope Pius, on hearing that the head was likely to go to the highest bidder, wrote Thomas asking him to bring it to Rome, 'the citadel of the Faith', to rest beside the bones of its brother St. Peter. The Pope promised to receive both the Despot and the head as long as the danger lasted, and until, as he said, it might one day be restored to its own throne with the help of its brother.[4]

Thomas landed at Ancona on November 16, 1460,[5] and arrived in Rome on March 7, 1461,[6] but the head of St. Andrew was deposited in the citadel of Narni until Pius could control the civil wars that had been raging in and around Rome on his return. When peace was restored, he sent out proclamations to the chief cities of Italy promising indulgences 'since the more people were present the more magnificent would be its welcome'.[7]

'In the meantime at Rome,' Pius wrote, 'all the preparations were made that were thought fitting for the solemn and magnificent reception of the holy apostle. The Pope was afraid of seeming niggardly in the honors paid to so great an apostle and thought nothing good enough.' Pius only mentions a plan that failed, to bring the heads of the apostles Peter and Paul out to greet the head of St. Andrew, but they were so weighed down with lead and silver that they

1. T. Alfarano, *De Basilicae Vaticanae antiquissima et nova structura*, ed. D. M. Cerrati (Documenti e ricerche per la storia dell'antica basilica Vaticana, Studi e Testi 26), Vatican City, 1914, p. 19, n. 1; E. Müntz, *Les arts à la cour des papes pendant le XVᵉ et le XVIᵉ siècle: Recueil de documents inédits*, I, Bibliothèque des Écoles Françaises d'Athènes et de Rome, IV, 1878, p. 120, n. 3; H. Egger, 'Turris campanaria Sancti Petri', *Mededeelingen van het Nederlandsch Historisch Instituut te Rome*, Tweede Reeks, V, 1935, p. 67; R. Lanciani, *Storia degli scavi di Roma*, I, Rome, 1902, p. 63. For the topography of the piazza, see C. Thoenes, 'Studien zur Geschichte des Petersplatzes', *Zeitschrift für Kunstgeschichte*, 26, 1963, pp. 97–145.
2. *The Commentaries of Pius II*, bk. V, translated by F. A. Gragg, historical notes by L. C. Gabel, *Smith College Studies in History*, Northampton, Mass., 1947, vol. XXX, p. 380; *Pii Secundi Pont. Max. Commentarii rerum memorabilium, quae temporibus suis contigerunt*, edited by Francesco Bandini Piccolomini, Frankfort, 1614, p. 131. Pius II's *Commentaries* have never been completely published in Latin, having been edited during the Counter-Reformation by Francesco Bandini Piccolomini (first edition, Rome, 1584). The missing passages have been published by J. Cugnoni, 'Aeneae Silvii Piccolomini Senensis qui postea fuit Pius II P. M., Opera inedita descripsit ex Codicibus Chisianis, L. VII. 253' in *Atti e memorie dell'Accademia dei Lincei (scienze morali)*, Rome, 1883, ser. III, VIII, pp. 495–549. An English translation of the whole text based on the original MS. in the Vatican Library, Reginensis lat. 1995, has been published by Professors Gragg and Gabel in the *Smith College Studies in History* (hereafter referred to as S. C. tr.): bk. I in vol. XXII, 1–2 (1936–7); bks. II and III in vol. XXV, 1–4 (1939–40); bks. IV and V in vol. XXX (1947); bks. VI–IX in vol. XXXV (1951); bks. X–XIII in vol. XLIII (1957). A critical edition of the complete Latin text (Reg. lat. 1995) is being prepared by Professor Remo Ceserani of the University of Milan.

3. *Commentaries*, bks. II–IV.
4. *Ibid.*, bk. VIII, S. C. tr., p. 524; Frankfort ed., pp. 192 f.
5. G. F. Herzberg, *Geschichte Griechenlands*, II, Gotha, 1877, p. 578, n. 1.
6. L. Pastor, *Geschichte der Päpste*, 3rd and 4th ed., vol. II, Freiburg im Breisgau, 1904, appendix 42, p. 728.
7. *Commentaries*, VIII, p. 525; Frankfort ed., p. 193.

had to be left on view at the Lateran.[8] What then were the preparations actually made for the reception of the head?

It must have been clear to everyone concerned with the planning of the ceremony that something had to be done above all to improve the approach to the basilica of St. Peter. Such unprecedented crowds as Pius hoped to gather could not be expected to struggle up worn-out steps, nor could the decaying condition of the piazza and façades inspire anyone, least of all St. Andrew himself, with confidence in the eventual Christian triumph over the Turks, a triumph which Flavio Biondo so fervently reflected the hope for in his preface of *Roma Triumphans* dedicated to Pius.[9]

There is no record of any written program which Pius planned for the piazza, and although he must have been familiar with Nicholas V's plans, described by Gianozzo Manetti,[10] such ideas as the porphyry and emerald-colored marble steps, and the four colossal bronze evangelists supporting the obelisk on which was to stand a bronze figure of Christ in the middle of the piazza, clearly were not likely to appeal to a pope with limited resources and with no time to spare. The papal account books, incomplete as they are, do partially provide in some detail the material for a reconstruction of Pius's projects on the piazza.[11]

The records of payments as published by Müntz and briefly interpreted by him in a manner which sometimes suggests a taste for the Gothic Revival[12] do not present any clear picture of Pius's work at the Vatican. Although Zippel was the first to grasp the importance of Pius's contribution on the basis of additional documents which he published,[13] Pius's patronage of the arts at the Vatican has received only limited attention

from art historians who have preferred to concentrate on Pienza as Pius's greatest architectural achievement.[14] Therefore before focusing on the piazza projects, a brief outline might help to show the extent of Pius's work in the Vatican which falls into three main periods dependent upon his presence in Rome.

The first has to do with short-lived projects inside the palace of which nothing survives except a doorway of 1460 in the Cortile del Maresciallo.[15] This covers the time in Rome after Pius's election on September 3, 1458, and during his absence from January, 1459, until October, 1460, when his rooms were repaired and decorated, and some which had burned were restored.[16] The second period is dedicated to work on a larger scale which began with Pius's return to Rome in October, 1460. The main focus of activity was the Piazza S. Pietro, in preparation, as I shall suggest, for the ceremony of St. Andrew's head which took place during Easter week, 1462. This included clearing the piazza of houses, and the rebuilding of the steps with two colossal statues of St. Peter and St. Paul at their foot[17] and the area on top of the steps to make room for the new Loggia of Benediction which could only be begun as a token in time for the ceremony. Inside the basilica, work before the ceremony consisted in clearing away tombs of medieval popes and cardinals and other encumbrances in the middle of the nave and aisles and placing them in order along the walls.[18] It was only after the ceremony that Pius published a bull to protect the ruins of Rome from pillagers of marble, thus cutting himself off from quick and convenient supplies.[19]

8. *Commentaries, loc. cit.*

9. First edition, Mantua, 1472 (?). See B. Nogara, *Scritti inediti e rari di Biondo Flavio*, Studi e Testi 48, Vatican City, 1927, pp. CLI–CLV.

10. See T. Magnuson, *Studies in Roman Quattrocento Architecture*, Figura, Studies edited by the Institute of Art History, University of Uppsala, IX, Rome, 1958, pp. 356–7 (Manetti, 85–88).

11. The bulk of these payments have been published by Müntz, *op. cit.* They are supplemented by the following articles bearing on Pius's patronage: A. Rossi, 'Spoglia Vaticana', *Giornale di erudizione de d'arte*, VI, Perugia, 1877, pp. 129–60; 196–228; 262–87; A. Bertolotti, 'Urkundliche Beiträge zur Biographie des Bildhauers Paolo di Mariano', *Repertorium für Kunstwissenschaft*, VI, 1, 1880, pp. 426–42; V. Leonardi, 'Paolo di Mariano Marmoraro', *L'Arte*, III, 1900, pp. 86–106; 259–74; Lanciani, *Scavi*, I, *cit.* pp. 64–70; G. Zippel, 'Paolo II e l'arte. IV', *L'Arte*, XIV, 1911, pp. 181–97; Zippel, 'Piero della Francesca in Roma', *Rassegna d'Arte*, 1919, pp. 86–94; E. Casanova, 'Un anno della vita privata di Pio II', *Bullettino Senese di storia patria*, N.S., II, 1931, pp. 19–34. Some unpublished payments from the Libro delle Fabbriche (1460–4) in the State Archives in Rome will hereafter be referred to as F. 1460–4.

12. Müntz, I, p. 279.

13. Zippel, *L'Arte*, 1911, *cit.*

14. For Pienza, see now Enzo Carli, *Pienza: la città di Pio II*, Monte dei Paschi di Siena, 1966.

15. Phot. Anderson 2229; E. Steinmann, *Rom in der Renaissance*, Leipzig, 1908, p. 21.

16. Zippel, *Rassegna d'Arte*, *cit.*, pp. 87 and 88; Müntz, I, pp. 272–5, 277, 286, and 308. (See below, note 26.)

17. The statues remained at the foot of the steps until 1847 when they were taken to the entrance of the Sacristy. See G. Vasari, 'Le Vite di Paolo Romano e Maestro Mino', *Le Vite de' più eccellenti pittori scultori ed architettori*, II, ed. G. Milanesi, Florence, 1878, p. 648 n. From there they were taken to the Museo Petriano, and later were placed at the entrance of the Grotte Vaticane. Pope Paul VI has recently had them brought to the Papal Apartments.

18. 'M° Galaxo di contra de avere duc. 63 d. c. sono per suo laboro . . . e molte altre opere sue a levare le sepulture dele pontifici in San Piero e riporle neli luoghi deputati e simile a levare dicti edifitii e marmi nel coro vecchio in San Piero e farle riporre in somma—Duc. lxiii.' (F. 1460–4, f. 60: n.d., 1462.) Cf. *Liber Anniversariorum* (1464): ' . . . corpus templi totum expolivit, sepulchra veterum pontificum media in aede perturbate posita in ordinem reducta parieti coaptavit' (in Müntz, I, p. 278, n. 1). See also Giovanni Antonio Campano, 'Vita Pii II', ed. G. C. Zimolo in Muratori, *Rerum Italicarum Scriptores*, III, 3, rev. ed., Bologna, 1964, p. 67: ' . . . quo reddita est facies interior Templi augustior et patentior'; and Bartolomeo Platina, *Vita Pii II*, in Muratori, *ibid.*, p. 118.

19. Müntz, I, appendix IV, pp. 352 f. The bull is dated April 28, 1462.

The final phase of activity, implemented by the discovery of alum at Tolfa which increased the papal revenue,[20] begins with Pius's return to Rome after a seven-month absence, as soon after the ceremony of St. Andrew's head, he left for Viterbo, Monte Amiata, and Pienza, and did not come back to Rome before December, 1462.[21] This last period begins in January, 1463, and seems to continue until his death in August, 1464, and again is mainly concerned with projects visible from the piazza: the great Pulpit or Loggia of Benediction, the statue of St. Paul by Paolo Romano for the top of the steps,[22] the new tower entrance to the lower Vatican palace,[23] and the restoration of the pyramidal campanile to which a gilded copper globe and cross were fixed on top, with four iron torch-holders at the base of the pyramidal spire, and gilded *banderiae* from which the arms of the Pope and the Church were flown when Pius left for the crusade on June 18, 1464.[24] To commemorate the ceremony of St. Andrew's head, a marble tabernacle was erected on the spot where Pius received the relic near the Ponte Molle, with a statue of St. Andrew by Paolo Romano, and a Latin inscription (Fig. 11).[25] Inside the basilica, a chapel was dedicated to St. Andrew and contained a tabernacle supporting a ciborium with gilded marble reliefs of the apostle's head by Paolo Romano and Isaia da Pisa, with the silver-gilt reliquary by Simone da Firenze inside. Pius also restored the chapel of S. Petronella to the south of the basilica.[26]

My plan is to concentrate on the projects of the second period which seem to have led up to the ceremony of St. Andrew's head, and to limit myself to illustrating a few of the projects from the last period which concern the commemoration of the ceremony.

THE PIAZZA S. PIETRO

'...stravitque aream amplissimam.'
Campano, *Vita Pii II.*

When Pius returned to Rome early in October, 1460, work began on the piazza with the tearing down of houses which interfered with Pius's idea of its limits.[27] The payments for digging stone, marble and earth from the piazza seem to indicate that the purpose of the excavations was to make a smooth, though sloping, surface prior to pounding it down.[28] But where did the excess rubble go? The parapet to the north of the steps which is visible in the sixteenth-century views seems to be the logical recipient of the shifted terrain for which payments continue throughout Pius's pontificate.[29]

Campano's statement quoted above, and Platina's 'Aream pro templi foribus ruderibus purgatam sternere parabat'[30] may refer to the area on top of the steps which, according to Alfarano, Pius extended 45 palmi to the north,[31] evidently to make room for the new Pulpit of Benediction which was to be begun within the span of the steps, but to be built from the north so as not to interfere with the new doors of the atrium contributed by Nicholas V. A payment to the stonemason Manfredo da Como 'per muratura de

20. Apparently discovered in the spring of 1462; see *Commentaries*, VII, S. C. tr., pp. 505 ff., Frankfort ed., pp. 185–6, and Pastor, *Geschichte der Päpste*, II, Freiburg im Breisgau, 1904, p. 236, n. 1.
21. *Commentaries*, bks. VIII, IX, and X.
22. Placed on the Ponte Sant'Angelo by Clement VII, and is still there. See Vasari, Milanesi, II, *cit.*, p. 649, and IV, p. 580; also F. Antal, 'Observations on Girolamo da Carpi', *Art Bulletin*, XXX, 1948, p. 97 and Fig. 13. For payments, see Müntz, I, p. 280; Leonardi, *L'Arte*, 1900, *cit.*, pp. 259 ff.; Bertolotti, *Rep. f. Kunstwiss.*, 1880, p. 431; Lanciani, *Scavi*, I, p. 67. Phot. Anderson, 4918.
23. All that remains of the tower entrance, which was absorbed immediately into Paul II's lower palace, is the marble bust of Pius by Paolo Romano now in the Appartamenti Borgia. Phot. Anderson 5099, and profile, Archivio Fotografico Gall. Mus. Vaticani neg. XIX. 16.2. See Müntz, I, p. 276.
24. Egger, *Mededeelingen*, 1935, *cit.*, pp. 66 ff.
25. The tabernacle was destroyed by lightning and rebuilt in the nineteenth century. See A. v. Reumont, *Geschichte der Stadt Rom*, III, Berlin, 1868, p. 145. For inscription, see V. Forcella, *Iscrizioni delle chiese e d'altri edificii di Roma*, XII, Rome, 1878, p. 213, no. 245. The statue and inscription are still in the cemetery of the Pellegrini, which has been isolated in the middle of the traffic of the Piazzale Cardinal Consalvi. For a reconstruction of the original tabernacle, see G. A. Guattani, *Memorie enciclopediche romane sulle belle arti, antichità, etc.*, I, Rome, 1806, pp. 8–10. For payments, see Müntz, I, pp. 267 and 297; Leonardi, *L'Arte*, 1900, p. 265; and F. 1460–4, ff. 68 v, 80, 81 v, 84, and 93. Phot. Alinari 26782 b.
26. This rotunda, forming a pair with S. Maria della Febbre, was reroofed, whitewashed, and painted by Pietro Giovenale with blue and gold paint, and eight windows were made for it. See Müntz, I, pp. 289 ff., 262, n. 5; Zippel, *L'Arte*, 1911, p. 187; Rossi, *Giorn. di erud*, 1877, pp. 148 and 263. Mosaics from the time of Paul I were visible in the chapel in June, 1458, shortly before Pius's accession, and were thought to depict 'tutta la storia di Constantino molto antiqua'. According to Armellini, the pictures were destroyed when Pius restored the chapel as no description of them after that time is known. They would have still been visible in any case when Piero della Francesca (if Zippel's identification of Pietro dal Borgho with him is correct: see *Rassegna d'Arte*, 1919, *cit.*), came to Rome to paint the Pope's rooms in the Vatican in the spring of 1459, and it is possible that they may have offered some inspiration to him for the Constantine cycle which he painted in San Francesco in Arezzo. For the mosaics see Pastor, I (ed. *cit.*, 1901), p. 558; M. Armellini, *Le chiese di Roma dal secolo IV al XIX*, ed. C. Cecchelli, Rome, 1942, vol. II, p. 936; Lanciani, *Scavi*, I, p. 70.
27. '...a ro(m)pare et ruinare case p. la piazza de sampiero.' Lanciani, *Scavi*, I, p. 65.
28. *Loc. cit.*, and p. 69; Müntz, I, p. 292; Zippel, *L'Arte*, 1911, p. 184; F. 1460–4, ff. 64 v and 85 v.
29. There is also mention of a fountain on the Piazza which may have already existed at the site of Innocent VIII's fountain, begun in 1490. (24 October 1460, 6 ducats to Domenico d'Antonio for work on the 'fontana ala piazza', F. 1460–4, f. 85 v; cf. f. 60 v (n.d.) for 'condocto dela fontana dela piazza'.)
30. Platina, ed. *cit.*, p. 118; see also Müntz, I, pp. 278 f., n. 1, for quotations of early descriptions of Pius's patronage.
31. Alfarano, *op. cit.*, p. 22.

li travertini ala piazza de le scale' indicates the way in which this piazza on top of the steps was paved.[32] A later payment to Pagno da Settignano, the stonecutter, for travertine tiles which he cut for the 'piazza de le scale' and for recutting many travertine tiles for this piazza which had been badly cut,[33] shows perhaps that this area on top of the steps had been paved quickly to be ready in time for the ceremony, and that it had to be done more carefully afterwards.

Pius evidently extended the area on top of the steps beyond the point at which the Benediction was to be begun and the steps ended, to the north to the new door of the lower palace, thus creating a level passage along the front of the façades.[34]

The new marble Pulpit of Benediction was too enormous an undertaking to be ready in time for the ceremony, once the area on top of the steps had been prepared for it. However, what seems from the payments to be the first of the columns for the later marble Benediction had already been set up on top of the steps as soon as a place had been prepared for them, in February, 1462.[35] The *edifitio* for hauling up the columns at Sant' Angelo in Pescheria (the Portico of Octavia) had already been designed by Fra Antonio da Gaeta during the summer of 1461.[36] That these columns, their number is unspecified, were no more than symbols of the future Benediction is clear from the payment made on April 6, shortly before the ceremony, for the 'pulpito per la benedictione de legname' made of 300 elm planks, nails, and brick, and costing no more than 35 ducats.[37] This platform, from which Pius showed the apostle's head, must have been hung with tapestries for the occasion and was probably dismantled after the ceremony, as the Pope left Rome in

May, and came back in December, 1462. Soon afterwards the work on the marble pulpit began.[38]

THE STEPS

'scalas ipsas commodiores pulchrioresque reddidit.'
Pius II, *Commentarii*, bk. V.[39]

The restoration of the steps also began in October, 1460, the first payments being to the sculptor Isaia da Pisa for over 300 braccia of marble which he worked 'per le scale' in December.[40] Although most of the payments for the steps themselves continue until the time of the ceremony for St. Andrew's head, Flavio Biondo describes them in a letter of September, 1461 as nearly finished: 'pulcherrimas et dignissimas Pio pontificere auctore scalas prope absolutas'.[41]

Francesco dal Borgo, an apostolic secretary who supervised the work done in the palace while Pius was away from Rome, was also in charge of the steps ('operi curando praefectus', according to Biondo).[42] The various activities in turn were managed by others. Fra Jacopo da Gaeta was 'soprastante ala fabrica dele scale',[43] while Giovanni da Verona, the sculptor, was in charge of the work of the scarpellini.[44] According to the payments, two more of Pius's best sculptors are paid for carving marble for the steps: Paolo Romano for 204 braccia,[45] and Pagno da Settignano for 80 braccia of a marble cornice for the side walls of the steps ('parapecti desse scale').[46] Two long unpublished payments outline the work of the stonemason, Manfredo da Como, for the steps.[47] He was paid for building their sub-structure and side walls, as well as for the foundation of the area on top. He was also responsible for putting the treads, after they had been worked by the sculptors and stonecutters, into place on the prepared foundations. Although the payments give

32. 1462, n.d., F. 1460–4, f. 59.

33. 1463, n.d., 'Pagno dev avere . . . ducati 47 sono per braccie vᵒxx di pianj lavorati in trevertinj per la piazza de le scale . . . e duc xv per piu opere ad aconciare e di rifare molti travertini dessa piazza mal tagliati . . .' F. 1460–4, f. 65.

34. 1463, 27 February. Manfredo 'dev avere flor. 30 per paxi 80 di muro facto nel fondamento dela prima costa dela benedictione e del muro che va ala porta del palazzo. Cioe il fondo desse per costra [sic] alto paxi iij. largo [paxi] ii palmi octo, longo paxo uno, palmi viiij. Quello muro alto paxi uno palmi viii, longo paxi 4 palmi 9 e grosso palmi 4. flor 30.' F. 1460–4, f. 89.

35. Lanciani, *Scavi*, I, p. 68.

36. Lanciani, *loc. cit.*

37. 1462, 6 April. 'Pulpito per la benedictione facto di legname de dare a di vi daprile duc. trentaquatro bol. xxxiii auri d. c. cioe duc. viiii o. xxvii per antonio di cola di lamatrice per taule [tavole] CCCᵒ dolmo e ducatj iii b. xxxvj a paluzzo marmoraro per costo di legni secte per de socto e ducati liij b. xlii ad antonio ferazolo per mazzoni xlii e ducati v ad antonio damiano per liberi lxxxx di chiodi e mazzoni viii e ducati xxii d. c. a mᵒ stenzo e li conpagni legniaoli per la factura desso in tucto ducati xxxiiii b, 33.' F. 1460–4, f. 71 v. It was this kind of temporary pulpit or raised platform which was recorded in witness accounts of ceremonies from the time of Martin V and Nicholas V. See Alfarano, *op. cit.*, pp. 20 f., n. 3.

38. For the marble pulpit, see below, note 104.

39. S. C. tr., p. 380; Frankfort ed., p. 131.

40. 'Marmi che si lavorono per le scale di Sampiero con travertini devono dare adj 23 octobre ducatj auri d. c. ventocto b. viii contati a mᵒ Isaja scultore sono per costo di braccio CL de marmo lavorati a quadro per le scale di sampiero.' F. 1460–4, f. 3 v. 1460, 23 December: 'Ducati ventitre a mᵒ Isaye scultore pro braccia 157 di marmi.' *Loc. cit.*

41. Nogara, *Biondo, cit.*, p. 202.

42. *Loc. cit.* Cf. (1460, 7 April): 'Franciscus de Burgo. Litterarum apostolicarum scriptor sanctissimi domini nostri papae familiaris . . . pro dm. Jacobo de Mucciarette de Bononia domini nostri papae Thesauriarei Locotenente viceregens . . .' from Mandati Camerali 1460, f. 11. See also Magnuson, *Studies, cit.*, p. 295, and the essential review by Elisabeth Macdougall, *The Art Bulletin*, XLIV, 1962, p. 70.

43. Müntz, I, p. 244, n. 2.

44. *Ibid.*, p. 260, n. 1.

45. Leonardi, *L'Arte*, 1900, p. 99.

46. 1462, n.d. (Pagno de avere) 'ducati clx per braccie lxxx di cornice di marmo poste neli parapecti desse scale', F. 1460–4, f. 65.

47. F. 1460–4, ff. 16 and 59.

detailed measurements of the foundations, it is hard to form from them an idea of the dimensions of the steps themselves, which Alfarano does indirectly and partially provide.

By comparing descriptions before and after Pius built the new steps, it is clear that he added seven more steps to the original count of 28.[48] Alfarano not only describes the steps by saying that they were in five flights of seven steps each with a small landing above each flight,[49] but gives the measurements. According to his original drawing of the groundplan of the basilica of 1571, the steps were 245 palmi across from north to south, but even in the drawing he erased the 45-palmi extension to the north which was in fact made by Pius to accommodate the pulpit within the span of the steps.[50] Alfarano's reason for confining the span of the steps to 200 palmi is because he saw the groundplan of the basilica symbolically as a symmetrical cross, the base of which (the steps) had to be narrower than the shaft (the nave and atrium) in order to be planted into the ground.[51] The steps running an extra 45 palmi to the north of the centre axis disturbed the basic symmetry of the groundplan of the whole basilica.[52] It is clear that Pius did not consider them in relation to the whole groundplan but only in relation to the pulpit on top of the steps as seen from the Piazza.

The 'major ambitus'[53] of the steps not only allowed for the pulpit to be seen within their span, but for many more people to use them at one time, while the new spacing made for a nobler and more dignified progress for those who walked up and down them.

The beauty of the steps themselves which impressed Biondo must have been in their simplicity and proportions. None of the views show elaborate mouldings.[54]

Their only ornaments were the colossal statues of St. Peter and St. Paul on high pedestals at their base.

THE COLOSSAL APOSTLES

> '...scalas...statuis adornavit marmoribus candissimis...'
> Pius II, *Commentarii*, bk. V.[55]

The first payment for the statues was made on March 11, 1461, a few days after the arrival of the Despot of Morea in Rome. It was for a 'petra de marmo per fare due figure cioe s. petro et s. paulo per le scale'.[56] The payments of April, 1461, to Paolo Romano only refer to the two pedestals with the figures of *spiritelli* (Figs. 1 and 2) holding the Pope's arms,[57] but when Flavio Biondo visited the new steps on September 18, 1461, he reported that the statue of St. Paul was not yet on its pedestal and was still being finished, while the statue of St. Peter had not yet been begun.[58] Early in December, to judge from the payments, St. Paul may have been hoisted on to its two bases, the one with the papal arms, and the second forming part of the steps themselves, in an elaborate manœuvre involving 'mastri e manuali a tirare e porre suso larmatura per la figura di san paulo su la sua base'.[59]

While the armature for this was being constructed, the marble for the figure of St. Peter was being excavated in Rome, as evidently the original piece of marble meant for both statues was only enough for one. The payments for the marble began early in November, 1461.[60]

Paolo Romano's work on the statue of St. Peter must have proceeded remarkably quickly if one can trust what the payments show, as by March 8, 1462, St. Peter was already in place at the foot of the steps.[61]

48. See N. Muffel, *Beschreibung der Stadt Rom*, ed. W. Vogt, Bibliothek des Litterarischen Vereins in Stuttgart, Tübingen, 1876, p. 18: 28 steps; and J. Capgrave, *Ye solace of pilgrimes*, ed. by C. A. Mills, London, 1911, p. 62: 29 steps (the difference is due to the method of counting either treads or risers); compare with Ritter Arnold von Harff, 'Viaggio in Italia nel MCDXCVII', ed. by A. v. Reumont, *Archivio Veneto*, VI, Venice, 1876, p. 137: 36 steps; and Alfarano, *op. cit.*, p. 22: 35 steps.

49. Alfarano, *loc cit.* Cf. *ibid.*, p. 129. See L. B. Alberti on the subject of steps, *De re aedificatoria*, Florence, 1485, bk. I, 13, f. ciii verso.

50. Alfarano, *op. cit.*, cf. tav. I and tav. II. In tav. I (the engraving of the plan of the basilica, 1589–90), see key *ll*: 'Pars gradinis a Pio II amplificata' to the north of the steps.

51. Alfarano, *ibid.*, p. 22.

52. Cf. Thoenes, *Zeitschrift f. Kunstg.*, 1963, *cit.*, p. 100, and note 31. Thoenes measures Pius's steps 79 palmi to the south of the central axis and 163 to the north.

53. P. Egidi, *Liber Anniversariorum della Basilica Vaticana*, Fonti per la storia d'Italia, Rome, 1908, pp. 240 ff.; also quoted by Müntz (I, pp. 278 f.) from another MS.

54. The clearest view of the steps is the Heemskerck panorama of the Vatican, C. Hülsen and H. Egger, *Die römischen Skizzen-*

bücher von Marten van Heemskerck, vol. II, Berlin, 1916, pl. 130 (1534/5).

55. S. C. tr., p. 380; Frankfort ed., p. 131.

56. Lanciani, *Scavi*, I, p. 67; see also Müntz, I, p. 279, and Leonardi, *L'Arte*, 1900, p. 101.

57. 1461, 3 April. 'M° paulo marmoraro de avere duc. 6 a lui con[ti] per parte de lavoro fa nelle base de le figure per la scala de San Piero.' F. 1460–4, f. 38 v. (Leonardi, *loc. cit.*, gives date of 1462 wrongly.) Two other payments to Paolo for this work are on the same page (38 v), one for 29 ducats on April 30, and one for 33 ducats on June 1 (1461). On November 15, 1461, Paolo was paid for finishing 'li spiritelli che tengono larmi di n. s....' and was given 146 ducats for his work until then on the bases of SS. Peter and Paul. F. 1460–4, f. 52 v; see Leonardi, *loc. cit.*

58. Nogara, *op. cit.*, pp. 202 and 204; letter to Gregorio Lolli Piccolomini in Tivoli: '...et Pauli...quae nunc expolitur... de marmorea beati Petri statua nondum inchoata.'

59. 1461, 5 December. F. 1460–4, f. 53 v; cf. Leonardi, *ibid.*, p. 102.

60. See Lanciani, *Scavi*, I, p. 67.

61. Payment of 2 ducats to M° Bartolotto 'per tirare et componere la figura de sanpiero a pro le scale'. F. 1460–4, f. 81 v. See Leonardi, *loc. cit.*

This haste is reflected in further payments for marble and for lead supports for both the figures which must have been adjusted *in situ*, but it is clear that both statues were in place at the time of the St. Andrew's head ceremony.[62]

Paolo Romano's figures, nearly ten feet tall, not counting their bases, carried gilded attributes, sword, keys and halos made for them by Meo the goldsmith in December, 1461.[63]

Their relative position at the foot of the steps was the object of considerable discussion at the time and eventually led to an official formulation of left and right in relation to the altar cross.[64] Biondo in his two letters to Gregorio Lolli during the summer of 1461[65] describes his astonishment at being told by Francesco dal Borgo that the Pope ordered St. Paul to be placed to the right of the visitor approaching the basilica, when the position of honour was certainly St. Peter's. He defended his point of view with reference to antique and Early Christian practices which put, in important matters, left and right in relation to the observer.[66] But Pius's Sienese cousins, the jurists Gregorio Lolli and Jacopo Tolomei, who were with the Pope that summer in Tivoli, upheld the view of Bartolo da Sassoferrato who claimed that the important insignia on shields should be worn so as to be held on the wearer's right.[67] Pius himself might have given

Biondo a more relevant argument than his cousins, if he had read Manetti's description of Nicholas V's plans for St. Peter in which the basilica was considered as a human form with arms outstretched,[68] and therefore the statue of St. Peter would have had to be placed to the right of the symbolic microcosm. In any case the statues were set up as Pius first ordered, with St. Peter to the left of the visitor arriving at the Vatican, and St. Paul to the right.[69]

The unpublished drawing in the collection of Sir Anthony Blunt (Fig. 3) seems to illustrate the two statues more accurately than any other view, in spite of evident spatial misunderstandings elsewhere.[70] Apart from slight differences in drapery folds and the position of the head of St. Peter, it shows them as they must have been before St. Paul's upraised arm and sword broke off, possibly in 1586 when the obelisk was moved to the piazza. The present restoration of the figure's right arm and sword hanging down spoils its original forceful posture, and this should always be taken into account in considering the significance and impact of its pose.

Both these statues have been criticized by Müntz who himself published the documents to prove they were by Paolo Romano. At first, however, he found them to be 'd'une facture trop grossière pour qu'on puisse les attribuer à Paul Romain', a judgment of the 'due mostrosi apostoli' shared by Gnoli and others in the nineteenth and twentieth centuries.[71] They were more appreciated in their own day. Porcellio de' Pandoni provides a contemporary approach to them in his rhetorical poem praising Pius's contributions to the

62. F. 1460–4, ff. 67 v. On May 27, 1462, Guglielmo da Siena was paid 36 bolognini for work done 'far harma di N. S. che ponesi socto le figure di Sanpiero et S. paulo [Fig. 1] di marmo alescale'. This may account for the unusually clumsy hands of the angels holding the *stemma*. (Leonardi, *ibid.*, p. 102.)

63 Müntz, I, p. 316. December 22, 1461.

64. This was formulated in 1488 by Agostino Patrizi, who had been Pius's amanuensis, in a ceremonial in his *Rituum Ecclesiasticorum Libri III*, Venice, 1516, pp. 137 v f. and 124. (See R. Avesani, 'Per la biblioteca di Agostino Patrizi Piccolomini Vescovo di Pienza', in *Mélanges Eugène Tisserant*, vol. IV, Studi e Testi 236, Vatican City, 1964, pp. 1–87.)

65. Nogara, *op. cit.* Letter 19: 18 September, 1461, pp. 202–4; Letter 20: 30 September, 1461, pp. 205–7.

66. *Loc. cit.* Letter 19. Biondo quotes Varro on the 'sky temple' in which birds fly to the left or right from the point of view of the augurs (*De Lingua Latina*, VII, 2, 5–8); he also quotes Livy, *Hist.*, II, 49, and Virgil, *Aeneid*, III, 420. Biondo points out furthermore that on the altar of St. Peter's and in the seals of the apostolic bull, Peter was on the right, and Paul on the left.

67. Nogara, *ibid.*, Letter 20, and note 1. See Bartolo da Sassoferrato, *De insigniis et armis*, Altdorf, 1727, p. 189, paragraph 28. Biondo (p. 207) criticizes Bartolo's unfamiliarity with philosophy and Hebrew, and with the histories of the Greek and Roman authors which Biondo uses to support his argument. Cf. Lorenzo Valla's attack on *De insigniis et armis* in a letter of 1433 accusing the jurists of adhering too closely to scholastic medieval traditions and contrasting the jurists with the humanists who respected the practices of ancient Rome. (Lorenzo Valla, *Ad Candidum contra Bartoli libellum quem de insigniis et armis scripsit*, Vienna, 1516; see V. Rossi, *Il Quattrocento*, Storia Letteraria d'Italia, Milan, 1945, p. 82.) For Jacopo Tolomei, see C. Dionisotti, 'Jacopo Tolomei fra umanisti e rimatori', *Italia medioevale e umanistica*, VI, 1963, pp. 137–76.

68. Magnuson, *op. cit.*, pp. 206–8, Manetti 135, 136. For the significance and adaptations of this interpretation, see R. Wittkower, *Architectural Principles in the Age of Humanism*, London, 1962, pp. 13 ff.

69. P. Egidi, *op. cit.*, pp. 242–3. The *Liber Anniversariorum* states that Pius erected 'Petro a dextra, Paulo a sinistra', the wording evidently following the concept expressed later by Agostino Patrizi (see above, note 64). The earliest view to show an apostle at the foot of the steps is by Jacopo Foresti da Bergamo (*Cronicha de tuto el mondo vulgare*, Venice, 1491, f. 60 r) with St. Paul on our right.

70. Cf. the view in Dresden of St. Peter's from the southeast attributed to Pirro Ligorio (H. Egger, *Römischen Veduten*, I, Taf. 21, and p. 26). There are, however, many differences which show that the Blunt drawing could not be a copy of the Dresden view which shows St. Peter only, and the pentimenti of a St. Paul on the far right, misplaced, and almost invisible. The two drawings seem to have been made, from topographical evidence, at about the same time and from a similar position, and share the odd device of representing the Campanile, which would not fit on the page, in two sections, side by side, but otherwise, they depend very little upon each other. The fairly careful drawing of the apostles shows that if the artist had not seen them himself, at least he had seen a far more detailed representation of them than the Dresden view provides. I am grateful to Sir Anthony Blunt for kindly giving me his permission to reproduce this drawing.

71. Müntz, I, p. 247. See Alfarano, *op. cit.*, pp. 22 f., n. 4.

arts and his times. He describes the statues without a word of praise or exaggeration, rare for him:

> At the foot of them [the steps] on either side the twin colossi stand
> One holding in his hand a sword, the other keys.

He adds as an afterthought praises of the works of the famous Greek artists, and concludes:

> But Paolo alone [?] who grew up in the midst of Rome, was in our times the first in the world.[72]

The Roman background of Paolo Romano's sculpture is what makes it significant in the context of the St. Andrew's head ceremony. How much of Paolo's sculpture was his own individual style deriving from the still-living medieval tradition in which a certain antique influence never died out; how much came from a deliberate choice of prototypes perhaps pointed out to him by Pius himself or members of his circle?[73] While unable to point to exact prototypes for Paolo's apostles, I can only indicate some evidence of interest in Early Christian practices in Pius's time which may be of help in seeing the statues as they were intended to be seen by the crowds who were summoned to Rome for the ceremony of St. Andrew's head.[74]

72. 'Ad divum Pium II. de rebus a se gestis et ab aliis suo tempore', Vat. lat. 1670, f. 38 r and v. Müntz (I, pp. 228 ff.) publishes an extract, but does not even refer to this passage. The relevant lines are:

Hic delubra vides centum fundata columnis,   Templum divi
   Et totidem sculpto cernis in aere fores.   Petri columnae
Quo te mille gradus duro de marmore ducent,   centum.
   Qualia migdonio permare vecta sinu.   Fores aereae
In quorum extrema gemini stant fronte colossi.   centum.
   Hic ensem, claves detinet ille manu.   Gradus mille
Haec Pius ille suo fabricaverat aere secundus,   marmorei.
   Quae sunt Phidiaca marmora facta manu.   Colossi duo
Mira suis manibus Policletes, mira Lysippus,   Petri et Pauli.
   Finxit, Praxiteles mira suis manibus;
Sed unicus [?] Paulus media nutritus in urbe
   Temporibus nostris primus in orbe fuit.

The correct reading of the fourth lines is probably:

     Quae a migdonio per mare vecta sinu.

The last four lines were written hastily in the margin with an indication that they should be included in the text.
73. See L. Filippini, *La scultura nel Trecento in Roma*, Turin, 1908. When seen against the background of this rigid sculpture, Paolo's work, stiff and clumsy as it may seem in comparison with contemporary Florentine sculpture, seems to · be dramatically charged with a fresh approach to late antique or Early Christian sculpture.
74. An interest in Early Christian art, architecture and ritual seems always to have been present in Rome. For a Trecento example of it, see C. Mitchell, 'The Lateran fresco of Boniface VIII', *Journal of the Warburg and Courtauld Institutes*, XIV, 1951, pp. 1–6; for examples in the Quattrocento, see R. Krautheimer, 'S. Pietro in Vincoli and the tripartite transept in the Early Christian basilica', *Proceedings of the American Philosophical Society*, LXXXIV, 3, 1941, pp. 353–429; and L. D. Ettlinger, *The Sistine Chapel before Michelangelo, religious imagery and papal primacy*, Oxford, 1965.

Pius's eagerness to see again 'the sacred bones of the martyrs and apostles, the soil watered by holy blood' which he expressed on his way back to Rome in 1460[75] is an echo of Flavio Biondo's words in *Roma Instaurata* (III, 93), and his longing to see relics was soon to be fulfilled significantly with the arrival of St. Andrew's head. The reason for his intense interest in the early saints of the Church can be found in a speech to his cardinals which he made in a secret consistory on September 23, 1463.[76] Here he recapitulates the events of his pontificate in terms of his preparations for the crusade. ('Before attacking the Turks we must bring about peace at home.... We were attacking the Turks when we battered Sigismondo's lands.') Indeed the preparations for the crusade included the reform of the Curia, for, he argued, who would give financial support for the crusade when the Curia is known to be greedy and luxurious and without credit? His plan to restore the dignity of the clergy he felt was untried in his times. It was to imitate the virtues of the martyrs and saints who founded the Church: 'Abstinence, purity, innocence, zeal for the faith, religious fervour, scorn of death, and eagerness of martyrdom.' These are the virtues which 'have set the Church of Rome over the whole world. Peter and Paul were the first to dedicate it by the glory of martyrdom.' Then came the confessors. 'We must', Pius urged his cardinals, 'draw near to those earlier saints.' It is probable that Pius's desire to follow the examples of the early saints of the Roman church led him to select Early Christian prototypes for Paolo Romano. Before working for Pius, Paolo seems not to have done any religious sculpture, and after Pius's death the majestic and militant quality seen in the four large statues of the apostles, particularly in the St. Paul for the top of the steps, does not occur again in his work.[77] It is as though he looked at the Early Christian

In Pius's own circle, before he became pope, a humanist actively interested in the archaeology of the Early Christian Church was Maffeo Vegio ('De rebus antiquis memorabilibus Basilicae S. Petri Romae', in *Acta Sanctorum Junii vol. vii*, Paris, 1867, appendix, pp. 56–76); see also the letter about the sources for his life of S. Potitus which Alberti wrote to Leonardo Dati in c. 1434, in *Opuscoli inediti di Leon Battista Alberti*, 'Musca', 'Vita S. Potiti', ed. C. Grayson, Florence, 1954, pp. 86 f. For Alberti's interest in the Early Christian Church in connection with architecture, see Wittkower, *Architectural Principles, cit.*, part one, and particularly p. 5; S. Lang, 'The programme of the SS. Annunciata', *JWCI*, XVII, 1954, pp. 288–300.
75. *Commentaries*, bk. IV, S. C. tr., pp. 342 f.; Frankfort ed., p. 114.
76. *Commentaries*, bk. XII, S. C. tr., pp. 817–27, for whole speech; Frankfort ed., pp. 336–41.
77. For literature on Paolo Romano's role in the triumphal arch for Alfonso of Aragon in Naples, c. 1455–8, see J. Pope-Hennessy, *Italian Renaissance Sculpture*, London, 1958, pp. 329–31. See also A. Venturi, *Storia dell'Arte Italiana*, VI, Milan, 1908, pp. 1110–20.

sarcophagi and statues, even at Byzantine portable works of art which may have been brought to Rome by such Greek exiles as Bessarion or by Thomas Paleologus, in order to bring them to life for this purpose. The St. Peter is the least successful, with his fin-like left leg and over-complicated drapery (Fig. 2), but the St. Paul (Fig. 1) for the foot of the steps is more grandly conceived, and while the carving is close to that of the late antique or Early Christian statues, the original upraised arm and turn of the head and body free it from the kind of rigidity found in earlier Quattrocento works in Rome such as Filarete's relief of St. Paul for Eugenius IV's bronze doors.[78]

Whatever Paolo Romano's prototypes were, and whatever he was looking for in them, the quality in his statues at the foot of the steps unique in his work is the emotion in the faces of both the apostles (Fig. 4). Can it be that they were intended to be seen not only as dignified ornaments for the new steps, and as the virtuous founders of the Roman Church, but also as actual participants in the ceremony to receive the exiled head of St. Andrew? I shall return to this point in describing the ceremony.

THE CEREMONY OF ST. ANDREW'S HEAD

'. . . la Santità con le sue mano la portò a San Pietro con la magna processione e grandissimi trionfi e tutte le strade coperte e moltissimi lumi di cera e moltissima moltitudine di gente.'
Paolo di Benedetto di Cola dello Mastro dello Rione di Ponte.[79]

Six weeks before the ceremony, Pius called together his six most trusted cardinals and confided to them his anguish about the Turkish situation which was continually getting worse. Part of his distress seems to have been his fear of losing public support because of his silence on this matter since his return from the unsuccessful congress in Mantua, a silence, he explained, not of indifference but of a kind of despair. He told them of his restless nights turning 'the eye of the mind in all directions' to find various solutions, all of which he felt would be criticized. Finally a plan occurred to him. He would hold Philip, Duke of Burgundy, to his forgotten vow which he made when Constantinople was lost, that when another great prince would follow him, he would wage war against the Turks. Now Philip could not go back on his word when the Pope himself was ready to risk his own life

for the Catholic Faith. Nor could any of the other Christian nations then fail to follow the crusade. It remained only to secure the approval of the Venetians, who found the plan to be divinely inspired, just as the amazed cardinals had done, and Lorenzo Roverella, Bishop of Ferrara, was sent to France to persuade the King and the Duke to follow the Pope's wishes.[80]

Pius then concludes Book VII saying that it was now the Holy Week when he had decided to transfer the head of St. Andrew to Rome from the citadel of Narni.

The importance of the ceremony for Pius at this particular time is clear from the speeches and from his description of it in the *Commentaries*.[81] It was as though Pius, having failed to capture the imagination of the self-interested princes at the Congress of Mantua, was now making an effort to win their support for the crusade through the mass appeal of the ceremony for St. Andrew's head. He was using the ceremony, not only to honour and welcome the apostle's head, but to ask St. Andrew's help through St. Peter and St. Paul so that by defeating the Turks, it would be possible for the head to return in glory to Greece. In stressing this recurrent theme in his speeches Pius hoped that the people as well as the leaders of

78. Pope-Hennessy, *cit.*, pl. 108, and pp. 77 f.
79. M. Pelaez, 'Il memoriale di Paolo di Benedetto', etc., *Archivio della R. Società Romana di Storia Patria*, XVI, 1893, p. 71. For the ceremony, see Pastor, ed. *cit.*, II, pp. 233–6, and Campano, ed. *cit.*, p. 74.

80. *Commentaries*, bk. VII, S. C. tr., pp. 515–19. Frankfort ed., pp. 189–91.
81. *Commentaries*, bk. VIII, S. C. tr., pp. 523–41; Frankfort ed., pp. 192–202. See the observations, in the course of being developed further, by R. Ceserani at the end of his careful review of R. J. Mitchell, *The Laurels and the Tiara*, London, 1962, and B. Widmer, *Enea Silvio Piccolomini*, Basle, 1960, in *Giornale storico della letteratura italiana*, CXLI, 1964, pp. 265–82. Ceserani (who is editing the Latin text of the *Commentaries* from Reg. Lat. 1995) points out (pp. 279–81) that in the MS., the description of the St. Andrew's head ceremony forms a *sesternio* in the regular handwriting of a copyist bound in with the pages written by Agostino Patrizi to Pius's dictation, and by Pius himself. In fact, the *Andreis* is a separate work which exists in other MSS. (e.g. Vat. lat. 5667; see S. P. Lampros in *Neos Ellenomenon*, X, 1913, pp. 80–112, who edits the *Andreis* based on this MS. and on Reg. Lat. 1995 which is almost identical; I am grateful to Professor Ceserani for this information). Ceserani follows G. Bernetti ('Richerche e problemi nei Commentari di Enea Silvio Piccolomini', *La Rinascita*, II, 7, 1939, pp. 450 f.) in thinking that the *Andreis* was the original essay of the *Commentaries* which itself was begun by Pius (according to Ceserani who extends slightly the time limits for the writing of the *Commentaries* suggested by Bernetti) in the summer of 1462, and was finished in the spring of 1464 as the original MS. was being copied (Cod. Corsinianus 147). If this is true, then the *Commentaries* was not a work written day by day as a diary, as many students of Pius have supposed, but was a compilation of notes, speeches, reports and memories connected retrospectively with various themes in mind, the increasingly dominant one being that of the crusade.
Although Ceserani sees a break between the end of bk. VII and the beginning of bk. VIII (the description of the ceremony), it seems to me that in the *Commentaries*, the ceremony follows most logically upon Pius's speech to the six cardinals, as in fact it provided an ideal opportunity for Pius to move a great gathering of people with the fresh conviction gained from his recent decision to lead the crusade himself.

Christendom would be stirred to support the crusade. It is also clear, by the way in which he organized the procession, that he wanted to demonstrate to the people the piety and reverence of his Curia, no doubt in view of the criticisms that were levelled against it.

Pius's beautiful description of the ceremony brings to life the gay spring season, the miraculous behaviour of the uncertain weather, and the sounds of the music and voices, the fragrances of flowers and herbs, incense and burning shrubs, the spectacle of the crowds, and the procession with its candles, the clergy in their ceremonial robes, and the decoration of houses along the route with sculpture, paintings and tapestries, carpets and canopies, exhibited outside. On the walls of Roderigo Borgia's house were poems 'recently composed by great geniuses which set forth in large letters praises of the divine Apostle and eulogies of Pope Pius'.

On the first day of the ceremony, Palm Sunday, April 12, 1462, on a large wooden tribune built in the meadows near the Ponte Molle (Fig. 5),[82] Pius, very moved, received the head from the weeping Bessarion. After Pius's speech of welcome and a short prayer that by the apostle's intercession, the insolence of the faithless Turk might be crushed, the choir sang a hymn in sapphics composed for Pius by Agapito di Cencio dei Rustici in which the Pope's recently developed plans which had been entrusted to the Venetians in secrecy are suggested apparently for the first time to the public.[83]

That night Pius and the head stayed at S. Maria del Popolo, and the storms threatened to disappoint a larger crowd of foreigners and Italians than had been gathered even for Nicholas V's jubilee year. The next day was radiant, which Pius attributed to St. Andrew's intercession, evidently with the intention of having it interpreted by the people as a good omen for the crusade.

The head of the two-mile procession through the centre of Rome reached St. Peter's before the Pope, carried in his golden chair and holding St. Andrew's head sheltered from the sun by a golden baldachino, could start from S. Maria del Popolo. Pius insisted that everyone in the procession should go on foot to do honour to the sacred head, but those who were really too old and ill could go on horseback by another route and wait on the steps of St. Peter's, while others who could only manage part of the way could start at a point from which they judged their feet would carry them to St. Peter's. Pius was pleased that some of the bishops who had been 'reared in luxury and scarcely been able to go a hundred feet except on horseback, on that day, weighed down as they were with their sacred robes, easily accomplished two miles through mud and water'. He was greatly reassured by the dignity and humility of the clergy and that there was 'not a single unseemly gesture'.

Pius describes the festive route in considerable detail, and particularly the cardinals' magnificent decorations in the squares near their houses. The climax of the procession was the arrival at St. Peter's. 'Thus the Pope was carried through so many wonders, himself carrying the sacred head, and came finally to the great broad square before the basilica of the Prince of the Apostles, which was already filled with a crowd of strangers.' These were mostly people from north of the Alps and from other parts of Italy, evidently used to watching mystery plays in the squares of medieval towns, for from them 'arose a great noise of voices like the murmur of many waters, since at the sight of the apostle's head all fell to beating their breasts and with groans and wailings commended themselves to it'. This must have been most gratifying to the Pope. Pius then climbed the steps 'which he himself had recently built at great expense', and on the top step turned to the crowd, blessed them, and showed them the sacred head.

'On entering the atrium the Pope turned his eyes towards the statue of St. Peter[84] which sits before the vestibule and fancying that the statue wept with joy at the coming of his brother, he himself burst into tears as he reflected on the meeting and embrace between two brothers who had been so long separated.' It is disappointing at this juncture that Pius had nothing to say about the new colossal statues of St. Peter and St. Paul at the foot of the steps, but his reaction to the late antique statue in the atrium shows that the new statues were intended to play a similar role, and

82. Florence, Museo Horne, no. 5876 (the Horne drawings are deposited in the Uffizi). Pen and brown ink with reddish wash. 27 × 12 cm in a long lunette shape. Inscribed 'Salimbeni'. It could be that this drawing is a rejected preliminary sketch for a fresco in the Chapel of Sant'Elena in the Grotte, commissioned by Francesco Bandini Piccolomini, Cardinal of Siena, who in 1584 edited Pius's *Commentaries* (see above, note 2). The actual fresco which I have only seen obliquely through a grille, is in a differently shaped frame and is quite another composition of the same scene, and has been so overpainted towards 1800 that it is impossible to attribute it to the original hand. For a description of the fresco as it must have been painted originally, see F. Torrigio, *Le Sacre Grotte Vaticane*, Rome, 1639, pp. 222–31. Although the drawing is topographically confused (the tribune appears to the north of the Tiber in order to show the city of Rome in the background, and the inscription is in fact in Latin (Fig. 11), not in Greek as suggested), it is, like the original fresco in the chapel, an attempt well over 100 years after the event to illustrate this passage from the *Commentaries*.

83. See also *Commentaries*, bk. XII, S. C. tr., p. 825; Frankfort ed., p. 340.

84. Alfarano, *op. cit.*, pp. 18, n. 2, and 116

by their intense upward looks, and with St. Paul's brandished sword, to stimulate the people to an awareness of the drama they were witnessing, of the plea of the apostles on behalf of St. Andrew for divine help against the Turks. Their Early Christian appearance, which may also have been intended to help St. Andrew recognize his brother apostles, could only emphasize this impression.

Inside the basilica, which had recently been cleared of medieval tombs and encumbrances,[85] it 'seemed one blaze of lights' as almost all the people were holding lighted candles, and 'there was a glow of innumerable lamps and candelabra and all this was made still more marvellous by the music of the organ[86] and the singing of the clergy'. The Pope's carriers struggled with great difficulty through the crowds to the high altar under which, he believed, 'lie the bodies of the two apostles, Peter and Paul which are objects of worship the world over'. It was on the altar that the head of St. Andrew was set down, and Bessarion, on behalf of St. Andrew, addressed St. Peter, and finally Pius, urging him not to stop exhorting Christian princes to support the crusade through which one day they will win everlasting fame.

All that the ceremony meant to Pius and what he hoped it would mean to others was summed up at last in his reply to 'St. Andrew's' long speech. He tells St. Andrew that the souls of St. Peter and St. Paul are evoking divine aid to restore his head to its own throne, and that Pius himself promised all the aid in his power, 'for nothing is closer to our heart than the defence of the Christian religion and the orthodox faith which your enemies and ours, the Turks, are trying to trample under foot. But if Christian princes and people will hear our voice and follow their shepherd, all the Church will see and be glad that we have not neglected the duties of our office and that you will not come here in vain to get your brother's help.'

Finally Pius 'went to a place where he could be seen by all and blessed the multitude'. This was the new wooden pulpit by the columns of the future marble pulpit on top of the steps. On Easter Sunday, the head was exhibited again with another great relic in the basilica, the veil of Veronica, the Volto Santo.

At the end of the ceremonies, the head was deposited in the Castel' Sant' Angelo until a proper receptacle (loculus idoneus) could be prepared for it.

This was not done until the following year, when not only a new reliquary was made, but also a tabernacle on four columns[87] supporting, according to the Early

Christian and Romanesque formula, an aedicule or ciborium containing the reliquary.[88] This was placed in the southeast corner of the basilica, near the entrance, which Pius made into a chapel dedicated to St. Andrew.[89] The white and gilded marble ciborium[89] lighted by new windows[90] could not be missed by those entering the church. It was in the first bay to the left framed by the low arch and first two columns of the south aisle, and was to be seen as a pendant to the tabernacle of the Volto Santo on the extreme right. The space of the chapel which was enclosed by the entrance wall and the south wall was further defined by a painted vaulted roof[91] built beneath the sloping beams of the side aisle, a tile pavement,[92] and the ciborium was enclosed by an iron grille which had two doors (to the north and west) and was ornamented by four gilded palle.[93]

Three marble reliefs from the lunettes of the ciborium survive in the Vatican Grotte, and were begun by Isaia da Pisa and Paolo Romano, according to the payments, in March, 1463.[94] They each show two angels supporting the frontal head of St. Andrew on a swag of drapery. From what is known of Isaia's elegant carving of parallel drapery folds,[95] apparently based upon Byzantine prototypes, it is clear that the relief with the angels not unlike those of fourth-century

85. See above, note 18.
86. For the organ built for Calixtus III, see Müntz, I, p. 197.
87. Lanciani, Scavi, I, p. 69; Müntz, I, p. 287.

88. Pius placed the ciborium over the tomb of St. Gregory the Great which he had moved to his new chapel in the course of reorganizing the tombs in the basilica. The statue of St. Andrew (Phot. Anderson 20574) which stood on St. Gregory's tomb was not by Paolo Romano as many historians have supposed, but was placed there by Francesco Bandini Piccolomini in 1570 (see C. von Fabriczy, 'La statua di S. Andrea all'ingresso della Sagrestia de S. Pietro', L'Arte, IV, 1901, pp. 67 ff.). For an illustration of the tabernacle from Cod. Barb. lat. 4410, f. 6, see W. R. Valentiner, 'The Florentine Master of the Tomb of Pius II', in The Art Quarterly, XXI, 1958, Fig. 25. The statue does not appear in the Grimani view of the interior of Old St. Peter's (Barb. lat. 2733, PI, f. 104), but the ciborium is shown and the vaulted ceiling of the St. Andrew chapel is suggested by the low arch over the entrance end of the south aisle, which is missing on the north side of the basilica.
89. See Müntz, I, p. 278, n. 1 (cf. Liber Anniversariorum) for a contemporary description, and Alfarano, op. cit., p. 87.
90. Müntz, I, p. 288.
91. Müntz, I, pp. 286 ff.: 1463, 23 May, 17 December; 1464, 4 February, and esp. (p. 289) 29 May. For paintings by Pietro Giovenale, see p. 288, and payments for colours and gold, 1464, 27 and 30 April, 5 and 21 May.
92. Müntz, I, p. 289: 1464, two payments for 29 May.
93. Müntz, I, pp. 287 f.: 1463, 16 September, 24 December; 1464, 8 May. See also Cerrati in Alfarano, op. cit., p. 87 n., who reports from Grimaldi (Barb. lat. 2733, f. 45 v) that the chapel was enclosed by a marble balustrade one and a half metres high which extended for several bays to the west and had to be removed for the Jubilee of 1575.
94. Müntz, I, pp. 286, 287, 289: 1463, 8 March, 16 May, 25 June, 28 June, 11 August; 1464, 29 August (retrospective). The marble for the reliefs may have been chosen by Paolo Romano in Carrara (Müntz, I, p. 276).
95. For examples, see Pope-Hennessy, op. cit., p. 334, pl. 109, and fig. 108.

sarcophagi[96] and the delicately linear head of St. Andrew is his work (Fig. 6). In ·the other two reliefs by Paolo Romano (Figs. 7 and 8), the angels are handled with more competence than those so quickly made for the base of the statue of St. Paul at the foot of the steps (partly visible in Fig. 1); they have a committed and energetic air, their tunics slipping off their shoulders in their exertions (Fig. 8). The forward lunge, curving wings, fluttering drapery and cloud-supported back feet conform to the space of the lunette more realistically than Isaia's detached and almost disembodied angels do. The massive unseeing head of St. Andrew (Fig. 8), on the other hand, while characteristic of Paolo's recessed and dome-like eyelids and drooping mouths, is appropriately without the urgency peculiar to his statues of the apostles and the portrait bust of Pius II in the Vatican palace.

Although the heads in the three reliefs make no reference to the reliquary head from Patras brought by Thomas Paleologus (Fig. 9),[97] the new silver gilt reliquary, 77 cm high, for the head of St. Andrew to which the payments made late in 1463 to Simone di Giovanni da Firenze must refer[98] might be expected to be even more like the reliefs than it is. It seems to have been begun some months after Isaia and Paolo started their reliefs, but as it introduces a new kind of divided beard to these images, it seems instead to reflect Paolo Romano's treatment of hair and beard in his statue of St. Andrew at the Ponte Molle (Fig. 11) for which payments were made in June, 1463.[99]

The significance of the St. Andrew chapel in the history of St. Peter's is not small. It could be said that it was the first time that a Renaissance pope cleared a prominent place in the basilica not only for certain saints, but for himself. When Pius ordered that he should be buried in this chapel,[100] he was once more identifying his cause with that of St. Andrew: the crusade against the infidels which led to Pius's disappointment and death. He died in Ancona on August 14, 1464 as the crusaders dispersed. The marble relief on his tomb (Fig. 12) portraying his reception of St. Andrew's head in Rome, shows how well Cardinal Francesco Todeschini Piccolomini understood the way in which his uncle valued the relic.[101]

Against a background of classical architecture which recalls the smaller arches of the Arch of Constantine and the background architecture in one of its reliefs, with the symbols of Christianity triumphant over paganism: the obelisk surmounted by a globe on which stands a cross,[102] and the crucifix obscuring a river god in a spandrel of the triumphal arch, Pius receives St. Andrew's head from Bessarion, surrounded by his Curia and friends. The altar, a Roman sarcophagus, is probably intended to be the tomb of St. Peter. In this relief, made within a few years of Pius's death, Pius's Rome of uncertain supremacy in a threatened world is approaching the triumphant Rome of Sixtus IV.[103]

Pius's own efforts to achieve a more monumental architectural impression of the Vatican, both for the ceremony of St. Andrew's head and for posterity, were not insignificant. Although nothing now remains of his piazza, it is immortalized in the sixteenth-century views, in which the dignified and elegant Loggia of Benediction which he began, presides over the steps and apostles.[104]

96. See G. Wilpert, *I sarcofagi cristiani antichi*, III, Vatican City, 1936, pl. 299, 1 and 2.

97. This reliquary was sent to Pienza when the new one was made to contain the head in Rome. For a detailed description of the old reliquary, see the inventory of 1784 of the Opera dell'Duomo in Pienza, published by G. B. Mannucci in *Pienza: L'Arte e Storia*, 3rd ed., Siena, 1937, p. 170; see below note 106.

98. Müntz, I, pp. 287 and 317: 1463, 5 October and 10 December. For a detailed study of Simone's reliquary see Carli, *Pienza*, *op. cit.*, pp. 115–17 and pls. XXII, 62 and 63.

99. The forked beard of Simone's reliquary (Fig. 10) appears again in the tomb relief (Fig. 12). For St. Andrew at the Ponte Molle, see Müntz, I, 297 and above note 25.

100. Campano, in Muratori, ed. *cit.*, p. 67.

101. This tomb was commissioned by Francesco Piccolomini, later Pope Pius III (1503), whose own tomb, which he also commissioned, was placed below his uncle's on the entrance wall of St. Peter's in the chapel of St. Andrew (Alfarano, *op. cit.*, tav. I, 84). For the subsequent history of the tombs after the destruction of the chapel in the time of Paul V, see A. Boni, *La Chiesa di S. Andrea della Valle* (Conferenza letta all'Associazione Archaeologica Romana, 8 dicembre, 1907), Rome, 1908; quoted in C. M. Ady, *Pius II*, London, 1913, pp. 339–41). For important documents for the tomb of Pius III, see E. Piccolomini, 'Alcuni documenti inediti intorno a Pio II e a Pio III', in *Atti e memorie della sezione letteraria e di storia patria municipale della R. Accademia dei Rozzi di Siena*, N.S., I, Siena, 1871. (This is extremely rare. There is a copy in the Biblioteca Comunale in Siena, and a photo-copy in the Warburg Institute, London.) For documents which indicate that the commission for Pius's tomb was given to Paolo Romano who left it unfinished at his death, see Bertolotti, *Rep. f. Kunstw.*, 1881, *cit.*, 433 and 441. Paolo Romano seems to have died in 1470, the year in which he signed his will. For a discussion of the style of the tomb relief (Fig. 11), largely conjectural, see Valentiner, *The Art Quarterly*, 1958, *cit.*, pp. 117–50, who reproduces the whole tomb and details.

102. Cf. Pius's campanile, see above, p. 24, and Manetti, 86–8, in Magnuson, *op. cit.*, pp. 356 f.

103. Ettlinger, *op. cit.*, ch. VI, and esp. pp. 112–13.

104. Pius's original plan for the Pulpit of Benediction and the construction of it in his time are problems too complicated to discuss at length in these pages, but as the Pulpit plays such a major role in Pius's piazza, his contribution to it must be suggested, however briefly. Of the four-bay triple portico seen in the sixteenth-century views, nearly all the four ground-floor bays with their corresponding blind arches against the inside wall seem to have been built by the end of Pius's pontificate. Paul II continued it, adding the second-story 'secundum quod est in parte inferiore' (G. Gatti, 'Alcuni atti camerali rogati dal notaro Gaspare Blondo', *Studi e documenti di storia e diritto*, VII, 1886, pp. 82 f.; Zippel, *L'Arte*, 1911, p. 188). Alexander VI contributed the third story (Müntz, IV, pp. 194 f.). In spite of a

Pius relied very little on the Manetti plan[105] for inspiration. Although it touched upon many of the same areas on which Pius worked, the steps, the area on top of the steps, the Benediction, the campanile, the entrance to the palace, and the rearrangement of the tombs in the basilica, all problems needing urgent

attention, he seemed to proceed independently and realistically.

It would be difficult, however, for anyone familiar with Leone Battista Alberti's architectural theory to miss entirely his influence on Pius's contributions to the piazza. What Alberti has to say in his *De Re Aedificatoria* on the desirability of few statues of white marble to inspire reverence (VII, 17), on flights of seven or nine steps with landings (I, 13), on the elegant proportions of porticoes in squares (VIII, 6), on the unimpeded circulation of the congregation in basilicas (VII, 14), and above all, on the importance of the pope appearing to his people (VII, 13), and the functions of festivals in Roman times (VIII, 7) to arouse the feelings of the masses, is worthy of consideration in this connection.

As for the head of St. Andrew, Pius's prayers were answered five hundred years after his death in a way which he could not have foreseen, when Pope Paul VI ceremoniously returned the relic by air to Patras on September 26, 1964.[106]

project only begun to continue the Loggia across the top of the steps (Pius's original plan?) in Julius II's time (cf. the Bramante Loggie of the upper Vatican Palace, a monumental screen to hide medieval clutter), it remained with only four bays until its destruction in the time of Paul V. (See Hülsen and Egger, *Heemskerck*, II, pl. 130, and notes pp. 69 f.; R. Krautheimer, review of H. Egger's *Römische Veduten* in *Zeitschrift für Kunstwissenschaft*, II, 1933, pp. 120 f.) For a succinct building history of the Benediction, see Cerrati in Alfarano, *op. cit.*, pp. 20–22, n. 3. More recently P. Tomei (*L'architettura a Roma nel Quattrocento*, R. Istituto d'archeologia e storia dell'arte, Rome, 1942, pp. 109–12) discusses the authorship of the Benediction, which is continued by Magnuson (*Studies, op. cit.*, p. 291) and Macdougall (review of Magnuson, *Studies*, in *Art Bull.*, 1963, *cit.*, p. 71) who believes it is not necessary to look further than Alberti, for whom, however, biographical documentation during this period is even scarcer than usual. No one has thought of connecting Bernardo Rossellino (who died in the summer of 1464 in Florence: M. Tyszkiewiczowa, *Bernardo Rossellino*, Florence, 1928, p. 133) with the wooden model which Pagno di Antonio da Settignano went to Florence to get in June or July, 1464 (Zippel, *ibid.*, p. 187), and no one has properly assessed the role of the best documented of all the sculptors and stonecutters who worked on the Pulpit in Pius's time: Pagno da Settignano. From the payments in Müntz and Zippel it appears that he received twice the amount of all the others for his work on the bases for columns, pilasters, arches, architraves, cornices and friezes, and for cutting marble for the Pulpit in Porto during the summer of 1463. Could he have had a working relationship to Alberti such as Luca Fancelli had to him in Mantua? Unpublished material on Pagno's later work on the cupola of the Duomo in Florence is to be found in the Deliberazioni of the Archivio dell'Opera del Duomo; see Müntz, I, pp. 254 f. For Pagno's place among the Florentine architects of the late Quattrocento, see C. Botto, 'L'edificazione della chiesa di Santo Spirito', *Rivista d'Arte*, XIV, 1932, pp. 34 ff.

105. Manetti in Magnuson, *Studies, op. cit.*, pp. 351–62.

106. See the Brief of Pope Paul VI quoting Pius II's words, when he received the head at the Ponte Molle, praying that one day, God willing, it should be restored to its throne in glory, and that one day it will say: 'O felix exilium quod tale repetit auxilium.' The Brief continues: 'Id ipsum, ex divina Providentiae consilio, opportune hac aetate evenire videtur, qua bonae voluntatis homines annituntur, ut post discidii acerbitatem tandem spes pacis et concordiae inter christianas communitates effulgeat.' *L'Osservatore Romano*, CIV, n. 224, 2nd ed., Sunday, September 27, 1964, p. 1. For the recent history of the reliquaries, see Don Aldo Franci, 'Pienza e la reliquia di Sant'Andrea Apostolo', *Terra di Siena*, XVIII, 4, 1964, pp. 29–30, and Carli, *op. cit.*, p. 137. I am grateful to Monsignor Franci and to Professor Carli for kindly sending me photographs of Simone's reliquary which is now in the Museum at Pienza, sent by Pope Paul VI to replace the Byzantine one which was returned to Patras.

GIUSEPPE FIOCCO

Alvise Cornaro e il Teatro

Benedetto Croce ha solennemente distinto la "storia dell'arte" dalla "storia della cultura"; ma oggi ci accorgiamo che non vi può essere l'una senza l'altra; perché i due tessuti sono inscindibilmente connessi; come non vi può essere poesia senza letteratura, e, in un certo senso logico, nemmeno letteratura senza poesia. A voler parlare dell'arte, senza la cultura, si va a rischio di uccidere entrambi.

La prova patente della colleganza dei tanti vasi comunicanti dello spirito umano è offerta, per quanto riguarda i primordi rinascimentali del teatro e della scenografia nel Veneto, dai contributi e dalla antiveggenza singolarissima di Alvise Cornaro, che non fu nè scultore, nè pittore, nè architetto.

Alvise Cornaro capeggiò uno dei più imponenti capitoli del suo Cinquecento artistico, che, una volta ancora, come nel Quattrocento con Donatello e con Mantegna, gravita attorno a Padova.

Il panorama che dobbiamo premettere nei riguardi di Alvise Cornaro, non è però quello pacifico e quasi idillico prospettato dai commentatori ultimi della famosa *Vita sobria*, che lo ha reso celebre, scritto da Pompeo Molmenti, in primo luogo, quando la ripubblicò dottamente nel 1902; poi da Pietro Pancrazi, che ce ne diede la più recente edizione, nel 1942.[1]

Nessuno sospettava, prima della pubblicazione del mio saggio, scritto in onore di Roberto Cessi nel 1958, e dedicato alla casa di Alvise Cornaro a Padova (divenuta tale, però, soltanto nel 1514, perché prima Alvise abitava in via delle Alberelle, l'odierna via Antonio Locatelli, come solo di recente ho potuto constatare), che il nucleo fondamentale dei suoi beni, a cominciare da questa casa di via del Bersaglio, oggi via Melchiorre Cesarotti, 21, ma che nei documenti antichi si vede talvolta definita via del Santo, per la vicinanza alla Basilica nota a tutti, proveniva dallo zio Don Alvise Angelieri, fratello della madre; uomo su cui le mie ricerche, e quelle recenti di Emilio Menegazzo, hanno gettato ombre poco edificanti.[2]

Alvise Cornaro, che doveva essere da poco entrato in possesso dell'eredità dell' "emace" parente, con cui evidentemente non aveva voluto abitare, denunciando questi beni ai X Savi, per avere lo sgravio delle tasse provocato dai danni delle soldatesche della famigerata Lega di Cambrai, l'agosto 1514, se ne valse per proporre, se non proprio un ricatto, un baratto fra il suo trasferimento a Venezia, e la sua residenza definitiva a Padova, condizionandolo al riconoscimento di quella nobiltà dogale che egli vantava, e che, rimettendolo nel Libro d'Oro, gli avrebbe aperte le porte del Gran Consiglio e del governo geloso della Serenissima.[3]

"Felix culpa" d'altronde, se proprio colpa vi fu, il che non credo, nella mancata concessione; perché senza di essa noi non avremmo avuto il grande mecenate padovano Cornaro, con quello che ne segui.

Alvise Cornaro era nato, per la verità, a Venezia, a San Bartolomio, da Antonio e da Angeliera nel 1475, come oggi sappiamo appieno, e quando nel 1514 si fissò a Padova era sulla via dei quaranta anni, e doveva già possedere una forte personalità; per aver osato di porla sulla bilancia, nell' "aut aut" proposto al governo della sua Venezia.

Personalità rivelatasi poi nel famoso proponimento di lasciare la vita dissipata della giovinezza, per quella regola che lo risanò, e gli fece varcare i 90 anni. Ma più di questi fatti e divisamenti personali, doveva essersi imposto nella sua Città per altezza d'ingegno e per quell'amore che, sin d'allora, aveva dimostrato per il Teatro.

Alvise Cornaro, infatti, era stato di quella famosa Compagnia della Calza, che aveva introdotto a Venezia l'uso di recitar commedie. I suoi regolamenti, tanto bene studiati dal Molmenti, e da Lionello Venturi anche più, nel tempo della sua dimora veneziana, cioè nel 1909, accanto al Monticolo, sono ben noti, e

1. L'opera di *Pompeo Molmenti* fu edita a Milano—Treves; quella di *Pietro Pancrazi* a Firenze—1919—Le Monnier—1942.
2. Di Alvise Cornaro richiamo qui gli studi più recenti:
a. *Giuseppe Fiocco*—"Alvise Cornaro e i suoi trattati di architettura", in "Memorie dell'Accademia dei Lincei"—Roma, 1932.
b. Id. "La casa di Alvise Cornaro", in "Miscellanea in onore di Roberto Cessi". Roma, 1958—Ed. di Storia e Letteratura.
c. *Emilio Menegazzo*—"Ricordo intorno alla vita e all'ambiente del Ruzante e di Alvise Cornaro", in "Italia medioevale e umanistica"—Padova 1963.

d. *Giovanni Lorenzoni*—"Lorenzo da Bologna"—Neri Pozza ed. 1963—Ivi si pubblica, su mia indicazione, il documento trovato dal p. Antonio Sartori, che condanna Alvise Angelieri alla costruzione della nuova arcipretale di Codevigo: Arch. di Stato di Padova (A.S.P.) Notarile, t. 3392, c. 414.
A chiarimento della condanna del vescovo Pietro Barozzi, alfine avvertito delle malefatte dell'Angelieri, risulta dagli atti che egli aveva incassato per suo conto le rendite della chiesa, prima amministrate dai locali.
3. L'abitazione di Alvise Cornaro non fu quella di via Melchiorre Cesarotti, 21, prima del 1514. Sino al 1513 lo vediamo risiedere in via Alberelle, non lontano dal Santo—A.S.P., notaio Antonio Giusti, t. 3257, cc. 367—377—380.

si riflettono clamorosamente nella pittura, come dimostrano le raffigurazioni dedicate ad essa da Vittore
Carpaccio, da Cesare Vecellio e da tanti altri, che
giovano a farcene conoscere gli sgargianti vestiti, dalle
brache rigate a colori. Era una Compagnia gaia, che
organizzava, in variatissime sezioni (26 per il Sanudo,
43 per Francesco Sansovino) i carnevali, e ingaggiava
il meglio della gioventù nobile della città. Alvise
Cornaro doveva avervi avuto gran parte negli anni
della vita gaia. Lo testimonia il nipote Giacomo
Cornaro, nel famoso Necrologio conservato a Vienna,
pubblicato dal Cicogna, ma in parte rettificato dal
Mortier, che andrebbe ormai riveduto di sul testo
originale.[4]

E' in questo sbrigliato periodo che sospetto sia da
assegnare a lui, ancora legato ai gaudenti, quella
Veneziana che si distingue dalle produzioni anchilosate
che le stanno intorno, per una libertà alquanto
sbarazzina di eloquio, preludio della modernità veneta
in questo campo. Le assegnazioni perciò al Cadmo,
tanto manierato, o al Fracastoro, totalmente incognito
per queste imprese, o a Maffeo Venier, deve cedere il
campo piuttosto a quella da me avanzata, non da
oggi, al Cornaro giovane. Bene si comprende che,
imboccata la via dell'austerità, non gli convenisse
rivendicarla.

Leggiamo quanto dice di lui il Necrologio del nipote:
"Ei fu posto ad imparare lettere, e nell'età di 15 anni
ne sapeva assai bene. Ed era molto piacevole, arguto,
e, come si suol dire, buon compagno. Per questo
deliberò di fare una compagnia come si costuma a
Venezia, della calza, la quale fu molto bella e piacevole, e fu la prima che vi recitasse commedie (lasciando
da parte quindi le quasi medioevali "momarie")
allestite da loro compagni con grazioso modo, e
gl'intermezzi erano similmente fatti da loro con
musiche e canti molto belli e piacevoli, ed egli com-
poneva tali canzoni e le parole" e, quel che più conta,
le commedie stesse, le quali erano "piene di un onesto
ridere". Frase evidentemente medicata secondo le
direttive della vita sobria. E il nipote conclude: "tanto
che in questi sollazzi la città fu tenuta gaia per quattro
anni".[5]

Ciò dovette avvenire prima dei 22 anni, quando si
trasferì a Padova per gli studi della legge. Vi sarebbe
quindi giunto nel 1497.

Ma il difendere cause non gli piaceva, e forse non gli
piaceva nemmeno dipendere dallo zio trafficante,
sempre più scandalosamente ricco.

Egli dovette assistere ai suoi trionfi pecuniari, ma
anche alla sua giusta disgrazia presso la Curia, che
determinò la crisi del processo vescovile, con la condanna di fabbricare a tutte sue spese, nel 1505/6 la
chiesa di Codevigo; la decadenza dal fruttuoso retto-
rato del Collegio Pratense, e dai benefici ecclesiastici.[6]
Il vero Alvise Cornaro, quello che ha valore di fermento
indimenticabile nella storia dello spirito umano,
sbocciò dunque intorno al 40 anni, quando egli, nel
1514, non solo prese possesso della casa famosa di via
del Bersaglio (oggi, come si è detto, Melchiorre
Cesarotti in fianco del Santo, ma decise di farne la
sua dimora definitiva, dato il rifiuto del Governo
veneziano, d'inserirlo nel Libro d'Oro.[7]

Egli ne prese definitivo possesso, e, da uomo geniale,
vi forgiò il programma del suo avvenire, mettendosi a
capo, per intenderci, di una specie di "partito della
Terraferma", che sboccò nelle famose bonifiche, le
quali attrassero, con l'ausilio delle "ville rustiche", da
lui proposte, realizzate dal Falconetto, ed esaltate dal
Palladio, i capitali inerti della Dominante, suscitando
la "Magistratura delle Terre incolte" (figg. 1–2).[8]

Ma a noi interessa il Teatro. Vero inventore di uomini,
nel senso etimologico della parola, egli dovette divinare
in Angelo Beolco, detto Ruzante, che già nel 1518
circa ci aveva dato, non ancora ventenne, "la Pas-
toral", il suo uomo: un attore straordinario, ma anche
più un poeta, di stupendo e libero genio, il quale,
giovandosi del linguaggio, rustico, cioè dell'icastico
dialetto "pavano", proprio dei contadini, di cui il
Cornaro aveva (seppure sempre avveduto nei suoi
affari) riconosciuto le miserie, poteva fare un quadro
pungente, parlando dei loro bisogni e delle loro tri-
stezze, facete e tragiche insieme, come doveva dettarlo
a della povera gente l'orrore delle guerre recenti, dei
saccheggi, dei soprusi; a cui tenne dietro quella
terribile carestia del 1528 che il Ruzante eterna nel
Ménego, terzo dialogo teatrale scritto e recitato da lui.
Ivi, seppure forse con alquanto danno della qualità
dell'opera, si esalta il Cornaro, come quello che con le
sue sagge provvidenze, aveva difeso i suoi protetti

4. Per la Compagnia della Calza sono da vedere: *P. Molmenti*—
"La storia di Venezia nella vita privata", v^ ed., Bergamo 1920,
pp. 257 e segg.; e massimamente *Lionello Venturi*—"La compagnia della Calza" (sec. xv e xvi) in "Nuovo Archivio Veneto",
xvi, ii^, 1909.
Per *Marin Sanudo*, vedi i "Diarii"—Visentini, Venezia, 1879–
1902, e *Francesco Sansovino*—"Venetia città nobilissima et
singolare". Venezia, 1581, i^ ed.
Il Necrologio tanto ricco di notizie su Alvise Cornaro, pronuncia-
to dal nipote Giacomo Cornaro Piscopia, è, con ampie notizie,
edito in *A. Emanuele Cicogna*—"Delle iscrizioni veneziane"—
T. vi, S. Giobbe—1857, pp. 687-98.
5. Cfr. *A. E. Cicogna*, cit.

6. Cfr. *E. Menegazzo*, cit. e *G. Lorenzoni*, pure cit.
7. Cfr. "La casa di Alvise Cornaro" in "Miscellanea R. Cessi"
cit.
8. A questa rivoluzione economica della Terraferma ho dedicato
una lezione nell'Istituto palladiano di Vicenza, intitolata "La
lezione di Alvise Cornaro", che apparirà nel "Bollettino del
Centro Internazionale di Architettura Andrea Palladio"—1963
—Vicenza.

dalla fame. Ben sapeva, e lo rivelano pur fra le lodi, i malumori del Sanudo, che quelle commedie dovevano spesso far rizzare le orecchie ai Veneziani.[9]

Tutte le commedie del Ruzante devettero essere scritte nella casa di Padova, o nelle ville del suo patrono. Ed è, a proposito di questa casa di Padova che bisogna rettificare quanto si è finora ripetuto.

Il Ruzante, come tutti gli altri ospiti abituali di Alvise, e innanzi tutto il Falconetto, oltre alla figlia Chiara col marito Giacomo Cornaro Piscopia, che restituiva l'ambita nobiltà al casato, non abitavano propriamente nella casa padronale, divenuta un complesso cospicuo, che ci è possibile rievocare, attraverso a quanto diremo; abitava invece in fondo ai Giardini che il Necrologio descrive ed esalta. "Sei beli giardini de diverse forme, et ognuno adornato di diversi adornamenti, fra li quali corre un largo fiume", ora ridotto in miserabile Businello, ma allora un ramo del Bacchiglione, che conduceva a Venezia.[10] Essi non hanno nulla a che vedere con il Cortile di cui si parlerà, sebbene ancora il "von Fabriczy" lo descriva come un giardino; ma stavano al di là della strada, e vi si giungeva agevolmente attraverso un ampio sotterraneo, o corridoio, adorno di grottesche, ritrovato nei recenti lavori stradali (fig. 1).[11]

E' in fondo a questi giardini che stava la Foresteria, destinata a tutti gli ospiti abituali, compresi i familiari, naturalmente eccetto lui Alvise, e la moglie Veronica Spilimbergo; ed ivi infatti si redasse l'elenco dei pochi beni lasciati nel 1535, dal Falconetto, come ci hanno detto le carte scoperte dal Lovarini (fig. 3).[12]

A Padova, a Este, a Codevigo, a Fosson, cioè sempre in ville e case di Alvise Cornaro, Ruzante aveva amato stendere tutte le sue opere, prima della presta morte, tanto deplorata e pianta da Alvise, avvenuta nel 1542.[13]

Ed ecco l'altra divinazione del Cornaro, che fu messa a beneficio del Teatro dal grande Padovano: quella della "seconda edizione artistica" di Giammaria Falconetto, cioè del Falconetto non più povero pittore senza gloria, come dimostrano le sue opere in tal campo, e mi basti ricordare i tre momenti successivi, esemplati dall'Augusto e la Sibilla del Museo di Verona e ivi ancora dall'affresco di San Giorgetto, presso S. Anastasia, del 1514 circa, e la serie infine dei dodici scomparti con scene dello Zodiaco, da me individuati nel Palazzo d'Arco a Mantova, spettanti al 1520.[14]

E' dopo questa data che nasce il vero Falconetto, cioè il Falconetto che si dedica all'architettura e agli stucchi.

Alvise lo aveva accolto sotto la sua protezione, per incitamento di Pietro Bembo; e fra il 1521 e il 1524, data della Loggia famosa che fa da fondale al Cortile di Palazzo Cornaro (fig. 4), era andato con lui a Roma, per studiare le antichità; e fu là che gli si rivelò la sua vera vocazione; non fatta per il dipingere, ma per il costruire. Avvenne cioè al Falconetto l'opposto di quanto era avvenuto a Donatello, che, andato col Brunelleschi a Roma, aveva capito di non poter fare l'architetto ma lo scultore; come del resto il Brunelleschi stesso si era persuaso, sebbene orefice e scultore dotato, che era meglio si dedicasse all'architettura.

Dopo questo viaggio o dopo questi viaggi a Roma, Falconetto, stabilitosi definitivamente a Padova, fu un altro; non solo perchè fece architetture e decorazioni, non più pitture; e perchè il suo gusto si destreggia ormai fra Peruzzi, Antonio Sangallo il Giovane, e specialmente fra Raffaello e fra Giocondo; ma anche perchè non fu più arcaizzante e rozzo, come abbiamo detto, ma artista aggiornatissimo e raffinatissimo. Basti prospettarlo col mezzo di un'opera tarda, del 1533: il soffitto della cappella del Santo (fig. 5), la più esemplare, per vedere che egli è ormai nell'orbita di Raffaello e di Giovanni da Udine, l'inventore delle grottesche e dello "stucco bianco" o stucco forte, checchè ne pensi il Berliner, come ha ben chiarito il mio discepolo Riccardo Averini.[15] Si potrebbe dire una trascrizione delle decorazioni del Salone dei Pontefici nell'Appartamento Borgia del Vaticano. Ed ecco

9. Cfr. *Emilio Lovarini*—"Ruzzante a Venezia", in "Archivio Veneto", 1943—v⁴ serie; voll. 32–33, N. 63–66. Il malumore raggiunse il massimo, dopo la burla del gallo sanguinante, sulla tavola a cui sedeva l'ambasciatore di Francia.

10. Per le questioni idrauliche riguardanti il Cornaro, cfr. *Roberto Cessi*—"Antichi scrittori di Idraulica Veneta", vol. II, p. II, edito dal Magistrato delle Acque di Venezia—1941.

11. *E. von Fabriczy*. "Die Gartenhäuser des Palazzo Giustiniani in Padua", in "Zeitschrift für bildende Kunst", 1888.

12. Lo provano i documenti, a cominciare dall'inventario dei pochi beni lasciati dal Falconetto. Cfr. *E. Lovarini*—"L'eredità di Gianmaria Falconetto"—in "Bollettino del Museo Civico di Padova", 1925, redatto "in Contrata Ponticurvi' ". Ivi abitavano anche Giovanni Cornaro Piscopia con la moglie Chiara—A.S.P., Notaio Gaspare Villani—Notarile, T. 4836, c. 718; e gli artisti operosi per Alvise, come Tiziano Minio; e gli attori, che recitavano col Ruzante.

13. Per la morte del Ruzante, vedi il compianto del Cornaro, nella lettera diretta a Sperone Speroni, del 2 aprile 1542, in "Opere di Sperone Speroni"—Venezia, D. Occhi, 1740—T. v, pp. 329–31.

14. Per tutto ciò si veda il mio articolo in "Dedalo", 1930–1, pp. 1202–41; confermato in pieno, e me ne rallegro, anche per i contatti col Pinturicchio, da *Tilmann Buddensieg*—"Jahrbuch der Berliner Museen"—vol. v, 1963—fasc. 2; pp. 121–50: "Die Ziege Amalthea von Riccio und Falconetto". Si ricordi che fino al 1524, non abbiamo alcuna prova di un'effettiva attività del Falconetto a Padova. Ancora nel 1523 egli operava in pittura a Verona, come indica il dipinto citato nella sua Guida dal *De Persico* (1820, p. i, p. 90), e ancora da *Cesare Bernasconi*—"Studi sopra la storia della pittura italiana", Venezia, 1864, p. 258. I Viaggi a Roma col Cornaro dovettero avvenire, in ogni modo, fra il 1520 e il 1524.

15. Cfr. *Riccardo Averini*, in "Studi Romani", 1957, n. 10, pp. 29–38; e *D. Redig de Campos* in "Palazzo Baldassini"—Bollettino del Centro per la Storia dell'Architettura—1956, n. 10.

spiegata la frase che il Falconetto vi si giovasse di "carte di Raffaello", detta non senza profonda ragione dall'Anonimo Morelliano, una volta ancora bene informato; come quando accenna a relazioni del giovane veronese con Melozzo.[16]

Viene certo di là il gusto dello stucco bianco, ripreso dall'antico, a cui si dedicarono i figli Provolo e Ottaviano, e in cui eccelse il genero Bartolomeo Ridolfi, trapiantatosi in Polonia. Con essi vi si dedicarono sollecitamente anche i padovani, guidati da Tiziano Minio: quello stucco che ebbe tanta fortuna nel Veneto col Vittoria e, nel Veneto e a Roma, con Camillo Mariani; perchè il "ductus" più proprio alla loro visione pittorica.[17]

E' col nuovo stile che il Falconetto fece a Padova tutte le sue architetture, creandovi una scuola in cui eccelle Andrea da Valle; e, nella casa del Cornaro la celebre Loggia e il non meno famoso, e ancor più realizzato, squisito Odeo (fig. 6), primo esemplare di un'architettura pittorica veneta, che gli sta a fianco.

Fu questo Falconetto rinnovato che ebbe il compito di dar corpo ai Teatri; come il Cornaro li veniva ideando, per Fosson (se non fu soltanto un palco, come pare convenisse a un luogo rustico, da caccia grossa, vicino alla Mesola degli Estensi), e non dovette mancare certo nemmeno a Codevigo, dove il Ruzante scrisse il più delle sue commedie; ma che certo esistette ad Este, tanto più invitante con le sue colline e con i molti beni e le molte bonifiche ivi realizzate dal Cornaro, per un teatro stabile. Ha ragione, credo, il Menegazzo nel dire che forse il nipote Giacomo confuse nel suo necrologio le due località.

Ad Este esiste infatti, e non si saprebbe davvero a che cosa dovesse servire, quella stupenda porta (fig. 7), esemplata sull'Arco di Giano a Roma, visto che non è in diretta direzione con Ca' Farsetti, che ha preso il luogo di Casa Cornaro, se non avesse condotto, come bene indica una stampa del Coronelli (fig. 8), a quel teatro, piazzato stupendamente in vetta alla scala che conduceva ad esso, di cui il Brunelli ricorda il basamento, citato nella relazione degli scavi archeologici che vi si erano condotti, quando scrisse delle Ville del Brenta e del Padovano.[18]

Dovunque il Cornaro ebbe una sua sede, o estiva o agricola, dovette provvedere a far posto a un teatro per

il suo Ruzante, che ospitava in fondo ai Giardini, nella casa prospettante via Pontecorvo, dove furono pure raccolti, con il Falconetto, i maggiori attori che coadiuvavano il Beolco, cioè il Menato (Marcantonio Alvarotto), e il Bilora (Battista Castagnola); non so il Vezzo (Gerolamo Zanetti). Ma è per la sua casa, la casa padronale, la casa di rappresentanza di via del Bersaglio che il Cornaro ideò il principale e certo il più attivo teatro per il suo Ruzante, e per le recite in genere. E questo fu il cortile, come ancora lo vediamo intatto nella stampa del Valle (fig. 9), incisa nel 1784, e come ancora lo vide l'abate Moschini, che nella sua Guida del 1817, rimpiange, prima la distruzione della facciata lombardesca, che vediamo in qualche modo nel disegno del 1735 (figg. 1–2), del perito Lorenzo Mazzi e poi, avvenuta sotto i suoi occhi, quella dell'agile Loggia di sinistra (fig. 9), che stimo costrutta da don Alvise Angelieri, dopo il suo incontro con Lorenzo da Bologna, suggerito dalla costruzione della chiesa di Codevigo, e dalle ultime trasformazioni della Loggia esterna del Collegio Pratense, in cui operò lo stesso capomastro Zanetto "de Pisonis" da Cremona (fig. 9).[19]

Ma che cos'era in effetti questo luogo che il von Fabriczy considerava Giardino, e che appare ancora un semplice cortile, senza né alberi, né aiole néla stampa del Valle? Era un vero e proprio teatro, in cui la Loggia di sinistra, fatta dallo zio Angelieri poteva fungere da quinta; chiusa dalla nuova fabbrica costruita nel fondo, perpendicolarmente ad essa, e dall'Odeo di fronte; edifici congiunti da lievi mura archeggiate, proprio come nei scenari del Peruzzi e del Serlio.[20] Uno splendido teatro, che statue, vasi arborati e parche scenografie del Falconetto, potevano animare a seconda dei bisogni teatrali.

Che così fosse, dichiara in modo esplicito il secondo preludio della Vaccaria, recitata il 17.2.1533, al Santo, come ci ricorda Marin Sanudo, da cui si deduce che, non solo il cortile era il palcoscenico, ma che volta a volta, allorquando vi si recitavano commedie, e ne conosciamo tante, oltre alle opere del Ruzante, dalla "Canace" di Sperone Speroni, messa in scena dopo la morte del Ruzante, alla "fabula" dell'Anguillara, che ci ricorda il Ramusio. Ma leggiamolo, traducendolo in italiano, il periodo esplicito del preludio secondo della Vaccaria, tanto malinteso dalla Böhm, che prima si interessò dei teatri padovani nell' "Ateneo Veneto" del 1899, e da Bruno Brunelli, che ad essi dedicò un

16. *Notizie di opere di disegno*—(Anonimo Morelliano)—Ed. di *Gustavo Frizzoni*, Bologna, Zanichelli, 1884, pp. 22–27.
17. Cfr. *Wolfgang Wolters*—"Tiziano Minio als Stukkator"—in "Pantheon", 1963, pp. 20–28 e 222–30.
18. Cfr. *E. Menegazzo* cit. e *Bruno Brunelli*—*Adolfo Callegari*—"Le ville del Brenta e degli Euganei"—Treves, Milano, 1930, pp. 254–7. "La villa in Este di Alvise Cornaro"—*Vincenzo Maria Coronelli*—La Brenta, III—Venezia, Accademia degli Argonauti, 1709, tav. 150, riproduce la "Scala Farsetti", come ancora esistente.

19. Sul De Pisonis, oltre al documento edito da *G. Lorenzoni*, cit., vedi *E. Menegazzo*, pure cit., p. 11 dell'estratto.
20. Non solo i teatri dovette eseguire il Falconetto per il Ruzante, ma anche gli scenari; cfr. *Cristoforo da Menisburgo*—Banchetti (alla corte di Ferrara)—Neri Pozza ed. Venezia, 1960 e *Ludovico Zorzi*—"La Vaccaria", Randi ed., Padova, VIII—1954.

ottimo libro.[21] Eccolo: "Non dico per voi donne, perché siete lassù in alto; che non è mal fatto mettervi la sopra; in quanto siete tanti angioletti e arcangioletti, e perciò state bene in alto; e potete bene anche starvi sicure, perché ci sono tanti sostegni, e tanti puntelli di sotto, tra grossi, corti e lunghi, che non vi lasceranno certo cadere a terra. E il dabben uomo, che fa fare questa festa (cioè il Cornaro), ha fatto fare anche questi "palchi" alti e sicuri, affinché tutti ci stiano senza pensiero, tanto da pigliar piacere da questa storia compiutamente."

Come tutto questo po' po' di attrezzatura si potesse elevare nel "Casino", cioè nell'Odeo, come commenta anche il Brunelli, proprio non si comprende. Ma allora non si poteva forse capire, specie da un letterato che si interessava dell'arte, più da dilettante che da conoscitore, che il Cortile della casa di Alvise Cornaro, aveva realizzato gli scenari del Peruzzi e del Serlio; ed era lui il Teatro; il vero stupendo primo teatro di Padova e del Settentrione d'Italia.

Tutto va a posto però quando ci si riferisca all'ampio e adorno cortile, al suo fondale e alle sue quinte di bellissima architettura, che avevano tratto vantaggio anche dalla Loggia di sinistra, già fatta erigere, come si è detto da don Alvise Angelieri intorno al 1506, e che venivano animate da elementi scenografici, certo eseguiti dal Falconetto, come si dirà.

Non vorrei si obbiettasse che la voce della Vaccaria, testé riportata non è sufficientemente esplicita, perché si possa concludere a favore di uno spettacolo all'aperto, specie se si consideri che esso era avvenuto il 17 febbraio, ed era durato sino alle ore 9 o 10 della sera (si badi che il "fino alle ore 4 del mattino" riferito dal preciso Sanudo, va inteso nei modi di contar le ore dei veneziani, e non nel modo nostro). In quei tempi, sia che la stagione fosse favorevole, sia che non lo fosse, non si aveva paura del freddo, da cui ci si riparava con pellicce e opportuni vestiti; anche nelle case, di rado e sempre mal riscaldate.

Che si fosse all'aperto convalida del resto un'altra frase del preludio della Vaccaria, a mio parere non ancora ben compreso, il quale accenna alla visione che vi si godeva delle cupole del Santo. Nel prologo, come lo leggiamo nella eccellente edizione di Ludovico Zorzi, il Ruzante, dopo aver parlato del palco per gli spettatori, ove troneggiavano le donne, accenna proprio che di là, penso specie nei fianchi, se questo palco era elittico o semicircolare, si vedeva Padova con le cupole del Santo.[22]

Ecco il testo: "A no ve staré gran a dire che questa che è chialò sea Pava, ché a la dii cognoscire a sta Giesia". Cioè, non starò a dirvi, o spettatori, che questa che è qui davanti a voi (o dietro a voi, anche, si potrebbe aggiungere) è Padova, perché la dovete riconoscere dalla sua chiesa del Santo. Il Colosseo invece, a cui fa subito appello dopo, specifica il preludio, che era stato fatto di nuovo; figurato quindi, come doveva essere stato in antico, da uno scenario ("a l'aom fato de nuovo"). Bene già lo Zorzi si appella al Falconetto, notando il suo amore per le antichità, davvero strepitoso nelle scene dello Zodiaco del Palazzo d'Arco di Mantova, che gli ho rivendicato.[23]

Il riflesso del Teatro all'aperto di Casa Cornaro, fu raccolto dallo stesso Palladio il quale nell'Olimpico, per quanto fatto per un'Accademia, e quindi chiuso, aveva richiamato con la pittura nel soffitto questo cielo aperto; memore certo del cortile del Cornaro.[24]

La "simbiosi artistica" nei riguardi dei più cospicui maestri, che il Cornaro via via ospitava fu tale talvolta, che la superba conversione di Giovanni Maria Falconetto, da modesto arretrato pittore, ad architetto insigne, moderno e precorritore, apparve, per suggestione del Lovarini a molti studiosi, dal Molmenti, al mio maestro Adolfo Venturi, identità, e si confusero addirittura l'illuminato e illuminante patrono con l'artista, a proposito delle sue fabbriche, quasi fossero opera eseguita in collaborazione.[25] Ciò che è negato dalle tante esplicite firme, e dai documenti, che lo sanzionano, anche là dove non ci sono scritte; come per il Monte di Pietà, o per il contributo dato dal Falconetto alla Loggia dei Signori di Padova; oltre che, beninteso, dalla esplicita parola del Trattato sull'architettura, da me pubblicato nelle Memorie dei Lincei del 1952.[26]

Altrettanto si dovrebbe dire allora (ma chi oserebbe farlo) per le stupende commedie del Ruzante.

21. Cfr. per la "Vaccaria", il testo nell'edizione citata di L. Zorzi—Per i teatri a Padova vedi: A. Böhm—"Notizie sulla storia del teatro a Padova nel sec. XV", etc., in "Ateneo Veneto", 1899, v. II, fasc. I, p. 102; ma soprattutto Bruno Brunelli, nel suo ottimo lavoro su "I Teatri di Padova", Padova—Draghi ed., 1921, p. 30 e segg.
22. L. Zorzi, cit.

23. Giuseppe Campori, in "Notizie per la vita di Ludovico Ariosto", Modena, 1871, pubblica una lettera del Ruzante in cui si affida a lui per le scene di Ferrara; certo eseguite dal Falconetto.
24. Ciò non è stato ancora detto. Si cfr. Lionello Puppi "Il Teatro Olimpico"—N. Pozza ed., Venezia—1963.
25. Per il Monte di Pietà di Padova, si veda Erice Rigoni—"Un rilievo di Silvio Cosini", in "Rivista d'Arte"—1930—4. La facciata del Falconetto è del 1532.
Per la Loggia della Piazza dei Signori cfr. Rusconi, in "Padova" Aprile 1935, p. 40. Falconetto assume la direzione, dopo A. Bassano e il Bigoio (Biagio da Ferrara; non Rossetti), nel 1532.
26. Le influenze decisive di Roma e delle "carte del Raffaello", sono testimoniate anche dall'ignoto monumento, citato nelle schede del Brandolese al De Lazzara, che si trova nella chiesa di Arzergrande presso Codenigo (Arch. vescovile di Padova). L'ho scovata nella vecchia abside, ora ridotta a cappella separata; e si compone di un'arca a mezzo rilievo, "in stucco", con ornamenti attorno. Vi manca l'epigrafe, che data l'opera 1553, e la riferisce giovane, rapita dalla peste, sorella del Rettore della chiesa, Camilla Tedolda; ma si legge in J. J. Salomonio, "Agri patarini inscriptiones", Padova, 1696, p. 313 (fig. 10).

Ma che l'opera di questo sommo sia forse, se non proprio creata, accompagnata, carezzata, imposta da Alvise Cornaro, dovrebbe apparire chiaro a tutti gli specialisti. Lo proclamano del resto le rime del riconoscente Maganza (Giambattista Maganza il Vecchio) detto in "pavano" Magagnò, pittore e poeta, che, dopo aver ricordato con Pierio Valeriano e tanti altri, la favolosa generosità del Cornaro (d'altra parte avvedutissimo nella pratica), al di fuori della quale non aveva trovato chi gli donasse "una rapa", scrivendo nelle sue Rime in pavano, ci dice questo che si può considerare il sigillo di quanto ho detto:

Se Ruzante, che fò
Bon cantarin, e così gran Bovaro
No s'imbattea cattar quel Cornolaro
Donde el se fé un zugiaro
E 'n bon baston da pontarseghe sù.
Mi so che Pava non l'harae sentù
Cantar co a fagon nu
E la so bella Trese, e la Fiorina
N'harae mè passò Lezaffusina.[27]

27. "La terza parte de la Rime di Magagnò, Menon e Begotto" Venezia, 1569, p. 17.

FRANZ GRAF WOLFF METTERNICH

Über die Massgrundlagen des Kuppelentwurfes Bramantes für die Peterskirche in Rom

I

Das Gespräch über die Baugeschichte der neuen Peterskirche in Rom, welches durch das Monumentalwerk Heinrichs von Geymüller auf breiter Grundlage eröffnet worden war, ist noch in vollem Gang. Nachdem die Reaktion auf diesen mit genialischem Schwung unternommenen Versuch lange Jahre hindurch praktisch ausgeblieben war, hat Dagobert Frey[1] vor nunmehr einem halben Jahrhundert unter voller Anerkennung der Leistung Geymüllers eine kritische Nachprüfung seiner Ergebnisse vollzogen mit dem Ziele, die entscheidende Frage nach dem Ausführungsplan Bramantes, die Geymüller von dem Ende seiner Laufbahn nicht mehr hatte beantworten können, der Lösung näher zu bringen. Ihm kam die kurz zuvor erschienene Publikation der Baurechnungen der "fabbrica di S. Pietro" Karl Freys zunutze,[2] die Geymüller, obzwar er in dieses umfangreiche Material Teileinblicke gewonnen zu haben scheint, in ihrer Gesamtheit als unentbehrliche Forschungsgrundlage noch nicht ausgewertet hatte. Die Veröffentlichung der Veduten durch Egger und Hülsen lieferten weiteres Quellenmaterial. Es folgte in den letzten vierzig Jahren eine schier unübersehbare Anzahl weiterer Untersuchungen über die Baugeschichte von St. Peter von unterschiedlicher Zielsetzung und unterschiedlichem Wert, die z.T. beachtliche Ergebnisse zeitigten, teilweise auch zur Vermehrung der nicht ohne Verschulden Geymüllers entstandenen Verwirrung beitrugen. Keiner hat die grossen Verdienste aber auch die gefährlichen methodischen Irrwege dieses enthusiastischen Forschers so objektiv gewürdigt wie Dagobert Frey. Aber auch er hatte sich nicht ganz aus den Netzen dieser Irrwege befreien können. In zahlreichen fruchtbaren Gesprächen, die der Verfasser dieses Aufsatzes wenige Jahre vor dem Tode des grossen österreichischen Kunstforschers das Glück hatte, mit ihm führen zu dürfen und wofür er ihm zu tiefem Danke verpflichtet ist, gelang es, neben der Klärung von Einzelfragen die Gedanken über die Fortsetzung der St. Peter-Studien und ihre methodischen Verfahrensgrundlagen zu ordnen.

Als wichtigstes Korrelat zu den erwähnten Quellenpublikationen erscheint die Bearbeitung und die Veröffentlichung des gesamten Planmaterials. Dieser Aufgabe hat sich der Verfasser, als er zum Leiter der Bibliotheca Hertziana berufen ward, gewidmet. Er plante, damit den bedeutenden Grundlagenforschungen und Quellenpublikationen, wie die Michelangelobibliographie 1510–1926 von Steinmann-Wittkower (1927) oder die Zeichnungen des Gian Lorenzo Bernini von Brauer-Wittkower (1931) einen weiteren Beitrag in Gestalt eines Korpus der St. Peter-Entwürfe hinzuzufügen.

Aus dem ersten Abschnitt dieses Unternehmens, welcher die Zeit von den Anfängen der Planung bis zur Unterbrechung durch den sacco di Roma im Jahre 1527 umfassen soll, haben der Verfasser und mehrere Angehörige des Institutes bereits eine Anzahl von Teilergebnissen veröffentlicht, in der Absicht, sie baldmöglichst bekanntzugeben—nicht erst bei Erscheinen des Korpus, das in erster Linie als Quellenpublikation geplant ist.

Der vorliegende Aufsatz ist gedacht als Huldigung und Dank an Rudolf Wittkower, der in der Frühzeit der Geschichte des Institutes, das der Verfasser während zehn Jahren zu leiten berufen war, zusammen mit dem ersten Direktor, Ernst Steinmann, Ludwig Schudt und anderen ausgezeichneten Gelehrten die wissenschaftlichen Grundlagen dieser Forschungsstätte gelegt hat. Er soll weiterhin ein persönliches Zeichen der Dankbarkeit sein für viele fruchtbare Aussprachen über gemeinsame wissenschaftliche Anliegen und

---

1. *Dagobert Frey*, Bramantes St. Peter-Entwurf und seine Apokryphen, Wien 1915, zitiert: "*D. Frey, St. Peter-Entw.*"
2. *Karl Frey*, Zur Baugeschichte des St. Peter, Jahrb. d.K. preuss. Kunstsammlungen XXXI (1910) u. XXXIII (1915), Beiheft.

zugleich dem vor kurzem erschienenen, als Muster methodischer Architekturforschung hoch zu preisenden Buch Wittkowers "La cupola di San Pietro di Michelangelo" einen bescheidenen "Grundlagenbeitrag" liefern.

II

Die Aussenansichten von St. Peter auf den Münzen Caradossos zeigen einen Kuppelaufbau, dessen Einzelheiten des kleinen Masstabes wegen schwer erkennbar sind. Über den Grundgedanken lassen sie indessen keine Zweifel. Es handelt sich um einen säulenreichen Tholos, der eine Attika trägt, aus der über mehrfachen Abtreppungen eine Kuppelschale herauswächst. Das Ganze bekrönt eine Laterne, die auf den verschiedenen Versionen, in denen das Münzbild Caradossos bis zum Pontifikat Leos X. erscheint, ungleich wiedergegeben wird. Trotzdem darf als sicher gelten, dass die von Carodosso dargestellte Kuppel identisch ist mit der von Serlio im 3.Buch in Grundriss, Aufriss und Schnitt abgebildeten.[3] Auch der Holzschnitt Serlios ist nicht frei von Ungenauigkeiten, die jedoch bei einiger Überlegung unschwer nachgewiesen und korrigiert werden können. Unbeschadet dieser Mängel gestatten die Angaben Serlios in Verbindung mit dem Münzbild, die Absichten Bramantes für seine St. Peterkuppel bis in die Einzelheiten zuverlässig zu rekonstruieren.

Dieser Kuppelentwurf behielt seine Gültigkeit auch nachdem der erste Plan für St. Peter abgelehnt worden war. Auf der Rückseite der Rötelzeichnung Uff. 20 A ist die winzige Skizze einer Kuppel zu sehen, die, wie die vier über den grossen Spiralrampen der Kuppelpfeiler emporwachsenden Türmchen erkennen lassen, zum Grundriss auf der Vorderseite gehört. Selbst der kleine Masstab lässt erkennen, dass es sich um keine andere als die Kuppel des ersten Entwurfes handelt. Einige Studien, die vor der Fixierung des Ausführungsplanes, aber nach Uff. 1 A, aus dem Sangallokreis hervorgegangen sind, scheinen allerdings dem Florentiner Typus eher als dem bramantesken zu folgen. Nachdem aber der endgültige Entschluss über die für die Ausführung gültigen Masse gefallen war, scheint die Form der Kuppel nicht mehr erörtert worden zu sein, wie Zeichnungen aus dem Skizzenbuch des Menicantonio[4] und Studien B. Peruzzis beweisen.[5] Erst als die Vorarbeiten Antonios da Sangallo für das Modell einsetzten, wurde Bramantes Plan verlassen.

*   *   *

3. *Sebastiano Serlio*, Tutte le opere d'architettura etc. Venetia 1619, Libro terzo, Fol. 65 v, 66 r u. v. *D. Frey, St. Peter-Entw.*, S. 58.

4. *Otto H. Förster*, Bramante, Wien—München 1956, Abb. 116 u. S. 281. Zitiert: *"Förster"*.

5. Uff. 24 A, 26 A r, 27 A r u. v.

Der heutige Durchmesser der Kuppel, also der von Michelangelo über den vier Bogen Bramantes bis zur Höhe des Tamburgesimses errichteten, beträgt nach Letarouilly im Tambur gemessen 188$\frac{4}{10}$ palmi (= 42,088 m), während die Breite des unteren Kuppelraumes[6] zwischen den Pfeilern 185$\frac{4}{10}$ palmi (= 41,44 m) beträgt. Der Tambur ist also nur etwa 1½ palmi (= rd. 0,34 m) vom Kuppelfussring zurückgesetzt.[7] Die Breite des unteren Kuppelraumes erscheint zunächst ungewöhnlich und in keiner rechten Beziehung zu den anderen Abmessungen des Gebäudes zu stehen. Sie ist in der Tat das Ergebnis einer komplizierten Evolution, die, bei Uff. 1 A ansetzend, erst bei der Fundamentlegung ihren Abschluss fand. Zwei massbestimmende Konstanten sind von den Anfängen der Planung an nachweisbar: erstens technischer Art: die von der konstantinischen Basilika abgeleitete und über das Chorfundament Nikolaus V. verbindliche Breite der navata grande und der cappella maggiore (Langhaus, bzw. Kreuzarme) mit 106 palmi (= 23,68 m),[8] zweitens stilistischer Art: durch die gesamte Planung lässt sich die Befolgung einer die Höhe der Räume, Arkaden und Wandnischen determinierenden einfachen Proportionsregel nachweisen, von der die gesamte Hierarchie der Grössenwerte abgeleitet ist und die als einzige trotz mannigfaltiger Wandlungen der Konfiguration des Grundrisses unverändert ihre Geltung behielt. Erst die Eingriffe Antonios da Sangallo und der Barockmeister haben später fühlbare Verschiebungen gebracht.

Die Lage der Gewölbe—bzw. Bogenansätze—wurde durch das Verhältnis der lichten Breite zur Höhe gleich 2:3 und die Höhe der Scheitel nach dem Verhältnis 2:4 (sesquialtera) fixiert.[9] Zwangsläufig führt die Analyse des Evolutionsprozesses, aus dem der endgültige Plan Bramantes hervorgegangen ist, zu einer systematischen Ordnung aller jener Entwürfe, die eine Etappe der Entwicklung markieren. Der

6. Der Terminus "Vierung" sollte als ungenau und irreführend vermieden werden. Vierung ist ein nur im Grundrissbild wahrnehmbares, zweidimensionales Gebilde, in der dritten Dimension ist es jedoch faktisch nicht existent. Erst in der Gewölbezone wird dieser aus der Durchdringung zweier kubischer Körper gebildete ideelle Raum auf die eine oder die andere Weise "realisiert".

Der durch die breiten Schrägseiten der Kuppelpfeiler verfestigte Zentralraum von St. Peter ist dagegen ein reales, autonomes Individuum, von dem die Kreuzarme emanieren. Ihn der Gattung "Vierung" zu subsumieren, würde eine Schmälerung seines spezifischen Wertes bedeuten (vergleiche etwa die Vierungen von Speyer, Mainz, Worms, dagegen Siena, S. Petronio in Bologna, Eley, Loreto, Pavia Dom).

7. *Paul Létarouilly* et Alfonse Simil, Le Vatican et la Basilique de Saint-Pierre de Rome, Paris 1882, pl. 2 u. 22.

8. Die Lage der Apostelmemorie ist topographisch zwar ein Fixpunkt, nicht aber kompositionell. Bei keinem der St. Peter-Entwürfe bildet sie ein Symmetriezentrum.

9. *D. Frey, St. Peter-Entw.*, S. 68.

Verfasser ist, auf experimentell-empirischem Wege,[10] zu Ergebnissen gekommen, die grundlegend von den Auffassungen vieler früherer Autoren abweichen.[11] Die wichtigsten Punkte sind *erstens* die Erkenntnis, dass Uff. 1 A nicht nur der erste Entwurf Bramantes für den Neubau von St. Peter ist, sondern auch chronologisch an der Spitze aller überkommenen Pläne von St. Peter steht, keiner von diesen kann als eine genetische Vorstufe des ersten Bramanteplanes nachgewiesen werden. Von den "infiniti disegni," aus denen Bramante nach Vasaris Bericht einen ausgewählt und von Caradosso im Münzbild habe festhalten lassen, ist bisher noch kein Exemplar aufgetaucht. Es liegt nahe anzunehmen, dass diese Vorstudien, nachdem einmal die Entscheidung gefallen war, vernichtet worden sind, *zweitens* dass die Rötelzeichnung Uff. 8 A verso eine Transparentpause von Uff. 8 recto und die grosse Zeichnung Uff. 20 A massgleich mit den vorgenannten ist.[12] O. H. Förster hatte schon die späte Datierung dieser Zeichnung durch Dagobert Frey widerlegt und ihre für die Baugeschichte von St. Peter erhebliche Bedeutung erkannt.[13] Die drei genannten Zeichnungen sind also Glieder einer Entwicklungsreihe, die mit Uff. 8 A r beginnt. Die zu lösende Aufgabe besteht nun darin, den Anschluss dieser Reihe nach unten, d.h. zu Uff. 1 A, und nach oben, d.h. zum Ausführungsplan, zu finden.

A

Der *Pergamentplan Uff. 1 A* gewährt, allein als planimetrische Konfiguration betrachtet, ein Bild vollendeter Symmetrie und Harmonie von hohem ästhetischem Reiz; unschwer erkennt das Auge das Obwalten ausgewogener Proportionsgesetze. Im Lauf der Zeit sind viele und erfolgreiche, wenn auch methodisch unterschiedliche, Versuche unternommen worden, auf mathematischem Wege die Beschaffenheit dieser Gesetze zu ergründen, die einen ausgehend vom Kreis, die anderen von der Geraden, dem Quadrat oder dem Dreieck.[14] Ohne Zweifel sind diese Untersuchungen als Beiträge zur Erkenntnis der Architekturtheorie der Renaissance, weil an einem paradigmatischen Objekt unternommen, von hohem Wert; als heuristisches Mittel für die Beantwortung der uns bewegenden Frage nach den massbestimmenden Fakten der Urplanung des Neubaus von St. Peter erwiesen sie sich jedoch als wenig förderlich. Wenn auch normales Augenmass genügt, z.B. zu erkennen, dass die Durchmesser der Nebenkuppeln dem Radius der Hauptkuppel entsprechen und allein dadurch das Vorhandensein einer Grössenhierarchie, d.h. geregelter Massabstufungen von den zentralen, zu den peripheren Elementen der Komposition erkennbar wird, so geben weder Proportionslehre noch Augenschein eine Erklärung für das mathematisch nicht erfassbare Problem des massstäblichen Verhältnisses zwischen Kuppelraum und Kreuzarmen. Das Rätsel, welches uns Bramante hinterlassen hat, indem er davon absah, seinen Plan mit Massangaben auszustatten, erweist sich demnach als mit theoretischen Mitteln nicht lösbar.

10. Die zuverlässige Ausdeutung des Planmaterials und die Klärung des entwicklungsgeschichtlichen Ablaufes des Planungsprozesses sowie der wechselseitigen Abhängigkeitsverhältnisse der verschiedenen Entwürfe, d.h. die Herstellung einer systematischen Ordnung, ist eine in erster Linie empirisch auf dem Wege des praktischen Experimentes zu lösende Aufgabe, 1. durch Konfrontierung der einzelnen Entwürfe mit den topographischen Fixpunkten (alte Basilika, Fundament Nikolaus V., Apostelmemorie, nach 1506 vollendete Teile), 2. durch den Versuch, die Absichten über die Planimetrie der Grundrisse hinaus in bezug auf Raumbild und Aussenarchitektur zu rekonstituieren auf der Grundlage gesicherter Masse und nachweisbarer Proportionsgesetze unter Beschränkung auf das aus gegebenen Anhaltspunkten erkennbare und unter Berücksichtigung der historischen Daten. Ein solches flexibles Verfahren wird sich aber für die gestellte heuristische Aufgabe nur unter der Voraussetzung als brauchbar erweisen, dass es auf das gesamte Material angewandt wird.
D. Frey, St. Peter-Entw., S. 4, *Gustavo Giovannoni*, Antonio da Sangallo il giovane, Roma 1959, VIII–X.
Franz Wolff Metternich, Le premier projet pour St.-Pierre de Rome, Bramante et Michel-Ange, Studies in Western Art, acts of the twentieth International Congress of the History of Art, vol. II, Princeton 1963, pp. 72–73, zitiert: *"Metternich, Kongress"*.
11. Der Verfasser möchte sich auf diese Bemerkung beschränken und auf eine Polemik über die von den verschiedenen Autoren vertretenen Ansichten verzichten.
12. *Franz Graf Wolff Metternich*, San Lorenzo in Mailand, St. Peter in Rom, Vortrag auf dem neunten Deutschen Kunsthistorikertag, Regensburg 1962, Kunstchronik, 15. 1962, Heft 10, S. 285 ff., zitiert: *"Metternich, Regensburg"*.
13. *Förster*, S. 279 ff., *D. Frey, St. Peter-Entwurf*, S. 11 ff. Die von D. Frey ausgesprochene grundsätzliche Ablehnung einer systematischen Ordnung zugunsten einer auf stilkritischer Analyse der einzelnen Zeichnungen beruhenden musste unweigerlich auf Abwege führen. Übrigens hat D. Frey bei vielen anregenden Gesprächen mit dem Verfasser sowie in daran anschliessendem Schriftwechsel seine auf das Jahr 1914 zurückgehende These nicht mehr aufrechterhalten.

14. Über die Proportionen bei Bramante: *Rudolf Wittkower*, Architectural Principles in the Age of Humanism, London 1962, S. 13, Anmerkung 1, zitiert: *"Wittkower"*, *Günter Hellmann*, Proportionsverfahren des Francesco di Giorgio Martini, Miscellanea Bibliothecae Hertzianae, Römische Forschungen der Bibl. Hertz. Bd. XVI, München/Wien, 1960, S. 157 ff., für den St.-Peter-Plan Uff. A 20, S. 165/166, Abb. 114, *Gerda Soergel*, Untersuchungen über den theoretischen Architekturentwurf von 1450–1550 in Italien, Dissert. Köln 1958, S. 108 ff., *Förster*, S. 225, Abb. 96.
Die methodischen Schattenseiten einer Architekturbetrachtung einseitig vom Standpunkt des Proportionsnachweises hat *Günter Bandmann*, Ikonologie des Ornaments und der Dekoration, Jahrbuch für Ästhetik, IV, 1958/59, S. 239/240, gekennzeichnet. Bei den Proportionsgesetzen, die aus den Architekturen Giulianos da Sangallo und Bramantes abzulesen sind, scheinen sich empirische Erkenntnis aus langjähriger Praxis sowie aus der Beobachtung antiker *und* mittelalterlicher Denkmale einerseits und theoretische Studienresultate andererseits die Waage zu halten.

Geymüller hat sich auf der Suche nach der Lösung eines methodisch nicht vertretbaren Mittels bedient, indem er, sei es aus Voreingenommenheit, sei es aus Unachtsamkeit, den Durchmesser der heutigen Kuppel als konstant annehmend, auf dieser Grundlage die Skala errechnete.[15] Damit begab er sich in ein ausweghloses Labyrinth und verlegte sich den Weg zu seinem wichtigsten Ziel, die Rekonstruktion des endgültigen Planes Bramantes für St. Peter.

Gehen wir zunächst von der Arbeitshypothese aus, dass die Breite der Kreuzarme auf dem Pergamentplan mit der des Chorfundamentes Nikolaus V. und über dieses mit der Breite der Konstantinischen Basilika identisch ist (106 palmi = 23,68 m), so entschlüsselt sich das Problem. Die von diesem Grundmass aus zu ermittelnde Skala[16] erlaubt den Durchmesser der Zentralkuppel auf 160 palmi (= 35,74 m) und die lichte Länge der Kreuzarme auf 228½ palmi zu berechnen. Trägt man das Fundament Nikolaus V. im gleichen Masstab in den Grundriss Uff. 1 A ein (Abb. 1), so werden die Zusammenhänge deutlich: die lichte Länge der Kreuzarme entspricht etwa der Entfernung der Apostelmemorie vom Chorhaupt des nikolasischen Fundamentes; sie steht mit dem päpstlichen Altar also mitten unter dem Chorbogen. Auf die Wichtigkeit dieser Entdeckung für die Würdigung der Einstellung Bramantes zur humanistischen Architekturtheorie[17] sowie auf die szenographische Bedeutung dieser Anordnung[18] einzugehen, ist hier nicht der Ort.

Bramante hatte das Zentrum seiner Kuppel mitten unter dem Triumphbogen am Langhaus fixiert. Ihr Radius entspricht mit 80 palmi der Entfernung der Apostelmemorie von der östlichen Querhauswand der alten Basilika, oder der Breite ihres Querschiffs, oder der Spannweite des Triumphbogens am Langhaus, oder dem Durchmesser der konstantinischen Tribuna. Alle diese Beobachtungen ergänzen und bestätigen sich gegenseitig, sie schliessen mit der Sicherheit eines mathematischen Beweises jede andere Möglichkeit der Massfindung und der Lokalisierung des ersten Bramanteentwurfes aus und erleichtern dadurch die Auslegung der Bemerkungen des Egidio da Viterbo über die geplante Freilegung eines Vorplatzes an der Südseite der Basilika und der Stellung des Obelisken; sie beweisen ferner, dass der Entwurf Bramantes keineswegs ein nur von Regeln der schönen Proportion bestimmtes, gewissermassen in den leeren Raum auf dem Reissbrett konzipiertes Idealprojekt, sondern ein konkreter, den technischen, topographischen, liturgischen und künstlerischen Forderungen gleichermassen gerecht werdender Plan gewesen ist. Er konnte seine Entstehung nicht einem genialen Wurf sondern gründlichen Vorstudien verdanken. Man wird sie in den von Vasari erwähnten "infiniti disegni" erblicken dürfen.

Die der Hauptkuppel diagonal zugeordneten kleineren Kuppeln—Zentralelemente der Nebengruppen— haben einen Durchmesser von 80 palmi, der also dem Radius der Hauptkuppel entspricht. Die Flächeninhalte stehen demnach in einem Verhältnis von 1:4. Dieser Hinweis allein genügt zur Erkenntnis des Weges, den der Meister beschritten hat, um seiner von heterogenen Vorbedingungen eingeengten Komposition eine eurhythmische Ordnung zu geben.

B

Nachdem dieser erste Vorschlag Bramantes sein Ziel nicht erreicht hatte, "non ebbe effetto",[19] scheint Giuliano da Sangallo, der alte Vertrauensmann Julius II. in künstlerischen Dingen, den in der ersten Planungsphase gesunkenen Einfluss wieder gewonnen zu haben.[20] Der im Zusammenhang unserer Untersuchung zunächst zu betrachtende Plan Uff. 8 A r ist als Werk Giulianos anzusehen[21] (Abb. 2). Die Eintragung am Blattrand von seiner Hand "In tutto canne 70" ist entscheidend. Siebzig canne (= 700 palmi = 157 m) ist die approximative lichte Länge der konstantinischen Basilika einschliesslich des Chores

15. *Heinrich von Geymüller*, Die ursprünglichen Entwürfe für St. Peter, Paris und Wien 1875, Tafelband, Bl. 4, zitiert: *"Geymüller"*.
D. Frey, Ein unbekannter Entwurf Giulianos da Sangallo für die Peterskirche in Rom, Miscellanea Francesco Ehrle, Roma 1924, II, S. 438/439.
16. *Günter Urban*, Zum Neubau-Projekt von St. Peter unter Papst Nikolaus V., Festschrift für Harald Keller, Darmstadt 1963, S. 138/139, Abb. 4, Anm. 45, zitiert: *"Urban"*. *Metternich, Krongress*, S. 74.
Man bedient sich zur Ermittelung der Skala am einfachsten des Durchmessers des Tribunafundamentes Nikolaus V., das auf Uff. 20 A wie auf allen Grundrissen des von Bramante über diesem Fundament errichteten Chores mit 100 palmi (= 22,34 Meter) angegeben wird.
17. *Wittkower*, S. 12 u. S. 12 Anm. 5.
18. *Metternich, Kongress*, S. 74.

19. *Metternich, Kongress*, S. 78.
20. *Vasari*, Le Monier, Firenze 1851, VII, S. 221, zitiert: *"Vasari"*.
21. Der Zeichenstil bestätigt es (vergl. die anderen Blätter Giulianos, z.B. Uff. 7 A, 9 A und die des taccuino senese). *Rodolfo Falb*, Il taccuino senese di Giuliano da Sangallo, Siena 1902, Fol. VIII, X, XIX, XXII, XXVII, XXX, XXXI. Die von Degenhart Antonio dem Älteren zugeschriebene Aufschrift, "sagrestia co. campanilo" würde die historisch nicht bedeutungslose Zusammenarbeit der Brüder Antonio und Giuliano beweisen. Sie könnte aber in diesem Falle nur brieflich erfolgt sein, da Antonio in den Jahren 1505/1506 als Festungsingenieur der Florentinischen Republik im Raum Pisa—Livorno tätig war. Zeichenstil, Kausalnexus und Chronologie verbieten die Zuschreibung der Zeichnung an Antonio den Älteren. *Bernhard Degenhart*, Dante, Leonardo und Sangallo, Römisches Jahrbuch für Kunstgeschichte, VII, S. 199–201, Abb. 241 a, b, c.

Nikolaus V.[22] Wenn auch die Zeichnung mit einer Skala versehen ist und alle Masse unschwer abgegriffen werden können, so legte der Meister ohne Zweifel durch seinen ausdrücklichen Hinweis Wert darauf, zu beweisen, dass einer bestimmten Forderung des Bauprogrammes Genüge getan sei.[23] Spätestens seit dem Machtspruch Julius II., er fordere—wie wir durch Egidio da Viterbo erfahren—Respekt vor den geweihten Stätten, zu denen selbstverständlich auch das konsekrierte und durch Altäre, Gräber und Monumente ehrwürdige Areal gehörte, war die Einbeziehung der gesamten Grundfläche in den Neubau ein fester Programmpunkt, dessen Erfüllung, wie bekannt, sich trotz vorübergehender Preisgabe noch in letzter Stunde durchgesetzt hat.

Das Mass von 70 canne ist demnach eine ausdrückliche Korrektur des Pergamentplanes, der in dieser Hinsicht nicht befriedigt hatte.

Eine andere Forderung von nicht geringerer Wichtigkeit, die zentrale Stellung des Apostelgrabes, welche Julius II., wie ebenfalls aus der Chronik des Egidio geschlossen werden darf, war auf dem durch Giuliano eingeschlagenen Weg der Massdehnung nicht erreicht worden. Bedient man sich wiederum der bei Uff. 1 A befolgten, experimentell-empirischen Methode, so lösen sich die weiteren Probleme. Das Presbyterium ist ebenfalls in das Chorfundament Nikolaus V. eingefügt, es ist 215 palmi lang; das Apostelgrab steht mitten unter dem Kreuzbogen, der mit 80 palmi die Breite der alten Tribuna grande hat. Im Gegensatz zu Uff. 1 A ist der Mittelpunkt des Kuppelraumes unabhängig von der topographischen Lage der Apostelmemorie fixiert. Er ergibt sich vielmehr aus der Quadratur der Mittelgruppe, deren Seitenlänge 300 palmi beträgt. Von diesen entfallen je 100 auf die Seiten der Kuppelpfeiler und 100 auf die Querschnitte der Kreuzarme, die der besseren Darstellbarkeit halber von dem unbequemen Mass von 106 auf das bequemere Dezimalmass von 100 palmi gebracht sind. In das Massiv des Mittelkörpers ist der gleichmässig oktagonale prismatische Zentralraum von 200 palmi (= 44,70 m) Durchmesser eingeschnitten. Der Verfasser neigt zu der Ansicht, dass der Florentiner Giuliano in Erinnerung an S. Maria del Fiore und an die von ihm soeben vollendete Bekrönung der Wallfahrtskirche von Loreto den Raum mit einem achteckigen Klostergewölbe zu überspannen gedachte, statt der ihm weniger geläufigen Kuppel.[24] Selbstverständlich sind die eingezeichneten Säulen an den Innenseiten der Kuppelpfeiler nicht als Kolossalsäulen zu deuten, wie etwa bei Uff. 20 A, sondern als Giebelträger von Ädikuln, welche die 40-Palmennischen der Pfeilerschrägen einzufassen bestimmt waren.[25]

Von Wichtigkeit für unsere Schlussfolgerung ist die Spannweite der Schiffarkaden von 60 palmi. Der Übergang von den 50 palmi des Bramanteplanes zu diesem Mass bedeutete, wie wir sehen werden, einen entscheidenden Schritt in der Richtung auf die definitive Ordnung. Er ist eine Folge des Ersatzes der kleinen Ordnung und der zweigeschossigen Gliederung der inneren Aufrisse des Bramanteplanes[26] durch die eingeschossige Kolossalordnung (Abb. 6). Die Ausweitung der Arkaden und die dadurch bewirkte Verlängerung der Joche hatte die Komprimierung und im weiteren Zuge der Entwicklung die Eliminierung der äusseren Traveen, die im Bramanteplan noch gleichwertig mit den innern gewesen waren, und schliesslich eine gesteigerte Konzentration der Raumeinheiten auf das Mittelelement hin zur Folge.

Während der Grundriss der Mittelblocks in ein Quadratnetz von 100 palmi Seitenlänge eingetragen ist, lässt sich für die Nebengruppen eine solche Ordnung nicht nachweisen. Das Mass 60 ist bestimmend. Die Nebengruppen sind nicht wie bei Uff. 1 A Repliken der Zentralfigur im Reduktionsverhältnis 1:4, sondern autonome, d.h. von der Mittelgruppe differenzierte Gebilde auf der Grundlage des griechischen Kreuzes, deren Arme 100 palmi in die Länge und 60 in die Breite messen. Ihre Durchschneidungen sind durch kantige Eckpfeiler, die der Meister mit Nachdruck in den Grundriss eingezeichnet hat, als echte Vierungen gekennzeichnet. Die scharfen Absetzungen der Raumkompartimente voneinander im Gegensatz zu den Kantenverschleifungen des Bramanteplanes geben ihnen ein toskanisches Gepräge, das an die Madonna dei Carceri in Prato erinnert und in die eigentliche Welt Giulianos führt, wie ebenfalls, wenn die Vermutung des Verfassers zutrifft, die oktagonale Form des Zentralraumes und seiner Überwölbung. Florentinisch ist auch die Gestalt der Sakristeiräume in den

22. Die nicht mehr exakt zu ermittelnden Masse schwanken je nach den verschiedenen Grundrissen und Messverfahren zwischen 692,5 und 710 palmi. Nach Uff. 8 A 700, nach Uff. 20 A 710, nach *Urban* S. 138, Abb. 4: 692,5.

23. *Franz Wolff Metternich*, Der Entwurf Fra Giocondos für St. Peter, Festschrift für Kurt Bauch, München Berlin 1957, S. 156/157, zitiert: *"Metternich, Festschr. Bauch"*. *Ludwig Freiherr von Pastor*, Geschichte der Päpste im Zeitalter der Renaissance, III, 2, 5-7. Aufl. Freiburg i.B. 1924, S. 929, Anhang 135.

24. Eine sphärische Kuppel wäre allerdings wegen der bei gleichmässig oktagonaler Gestalt der Basis relativ kleinen Pendentifs technisch leichter zu bewältigen gewesen als die 14 Palmen kleinere, heutige Kuppel mit ihren weit ausladenden Pendentifs.

25. Die Durchschnitte der flüchtig einskizzierten Säulen schwanken zwischen 4 und 6 palmi, ihr richtiges Mass lässt sich aber über die Höhe der Nischen (2 × 40 = 80 palmi) errechnen. Das Horizontalgesims der Giebel erreicht die Höhe der Kämpfergesimse der Schiffarkaden, wodurch sich die Ädikuln in den Schematismus der grossen Pilasterordnung eingliedern (Abb. 6).

26. *Metternich, Kongress*, S. 74-76.

Ecktürmen, die Bramante, antik-römischen Vorbildern (z.B. Caracallathermen, Villa Hadrians in Tivoli oder Seitenkapellen von S. Lorenzo in Mailand) folgend, als Achteckräume mit alternierenden Halbrund- und Flachnischen geformt hatte, während Giuliano sie der Chorkapelle der sagrestia vecchia von San Lorenzo in Florenz nachbildete.

So stellt sich der Plan Giulianos da Sangallo als eine Art von florentinischer Überarbeitung des aus der byzantinisch-romanischen Welt des adriatischen Küstengebietes von Bramante über Mailand nach Rom importierten tetrastylen Anlagemotivs von Uff. 1 A und trotz Abbreviatur und Vergröberung als ein Derivat von diesem dar. Darin liegt zugleich die Begründung für die Einbeziehung des ersten Bramanteplans in unsere Untersuchung.

C

Eingangs hatte der Verfasser bereits seine Entdeckung erwähnt, dass die *Rötelskizze Uff. 8 A v* (Abb. 3) eine Transparentpause des Giulianoplanes auf der Vorderseite sei.[27] In der Tat ist zu erkennen, dass die Konturen der wichtigsten Elemente mit leichter Hand und weichem Stift flüchtig nachgezogen sind. Einige markante Punkte der Komposition werden durch kräftigeren Druck des Stiftes markiert. Dieses Verfahren beschränkt sich auf die Mittelgruppe, die vier Kuppelpfeiler und die westlich, südlich und nördlich angrenzenden 60 Palmen-Arkaden. Von den östlich der Kerngruppe gelegenen Bestandteilen des Giulianoplanes ist nichts übernommen. Die gleiche Hand und derselbe Stift haben die Apsiden und Umgänge ohne Unterbrechung des Zeichenvorganges, natürlich auf fester Unterlage, angefügt. Von ihr stammt auch, wie die Zeichenweise der Bogenlinien erkennen lässt, der Grundriss am oberen Blattrand. Während die östlichen Partien (Langhaus) und die verschiedenen Eingriffe an der rechten Bildhälfte sich durch kräftigeren Druck und dunklere Farbe abheben. Anderseits stimmen gewisse Charakteristika der Handschrift, wie die erwähnte Art, die Halbkreise zu zeichnen, nicht in flüssiger Linienführung sondern durch zwei gegenständig ansetzende und sich überschneidende, in nervösem Griff hingeworfene Kurven mit den obengenannten Teilen überein.

Die Konstatierung des Zusammenhangs der beiden Pläne beinhaltet keine Aussage über zwei entscheidende Punkte, erstens über den Autor oder den Zeichner, zweitens über die Ubikation der Apostelmemorie. Über beides geben jedoch die Darstellungen selber mehr oder minder zuverlässige Auskunft. Am

oberen und am unteren, leider beschnittenen, Blattrand sind zwei Mailänder Grundrisse, oben von S. Lorenzo, unten, weniger genau aber einwandfrei erkennbar, des Domes einskizziert.[28] Es können also nur Künstler in Betracht kommen, welche die lombardische Hauptstadt kannten; das waren Bramante und Giuliano da Sangallo. Mag auch das Grundmotiv der Kerngruppe dem Pergamentplan Bramantes entlehnt sein, so ist es in seiner spezifischen Ausprägung jedoch als Werk Giulianos anzusehen, vorausgesetzt, dass die naheliegende Annahme zutrifft, der Plan auf der Vorderseite des Blattes sei ohne unmittelbare Einwirkung Bramantes entstanden, wofür neben der Kausalität der Entstehung manche Züge, u.a. die toskanischen Elemente, sprechen dürften. In diesem Falle würde dem Florentiner auch das überragende Verdienst zufallen, die Kolossalordnung in die St. Peter-Planung eingeführt zu haben. Ob die Aufnahme des altchristlich-byzantinischen Bereichen, in diesem Falle unmittelbar von S. Lorenzo in Mailand entnommenen Motivs des Umgangchores erneut sich geltend machendem Einfluss Bramantes zugeschrieben werden muss, oder ebenfalls ein Gedanke des weitgereisten, auch mit südfranzösischen Bauten vertrauten Giuliano war, wird dahingestellt bleiben.[29]

An der linken Bildseite wird das Thema des fünfschiffigen Langhauses durch den Grundriss des Mailänder Domes dem Verständnis näher gebracht. Anschliessend an den linken Kuppelpfeiler werden die beiden im Abstand von 60 palmi verlaufenden Stützenreihen durch zwei parallele Linienpaare gekennzeichnet. Im Abstand von weiteren 60 palmi, anschliessend an die Vierung der südöstlichen Nebengruppe, bzw. an dem Eckturm bezeichnet ein weiteres Linienpaar die Aussenwand. Es entsteht also ein fünfschiffiger Querschnitt, dessen Proportionen und Abmessungen aus dem Masschematismus des Giulianoplanes abgeleitet sind.[30] Aber das besagt, so wichtig dieses Ergebnis ist, wiederum nichts über den Zeichner oder den Autor der Langhausidee.

Die Einzeichnungen auf der rechten Bildseite verfolgen zwei Ziele, erstens die Gliederung des Langhauses,

---

27. Vergl. Anm. 12.

28. Der Sinn dieser Grundrisse auf dem Plan für St. Peter ist einleuchtend: es sollen die historischen Quellen der beiden Grundmotive des in der Terminologie der humanistischen Architekturtheorie als "Kompositbau" zu kennzeichnenden Neubaus an bekannten Denkmalen illustriert werden.
Franz Wolff Metternich, St. Maria im Kapitol, St. Peter in Rom und S. Lorenzo in Mailand, Festschrift für Willi Weyers, Köln, 1963, S 172, 173, Anm. 4, Abb. 6.
29. Vergleiche Giulianos Massaufnahmen im *Libro di Giuliano da Sangallo*, Cod. Barb. lat. 4424, fol. 24 v, 25 r, 40 r, 64 r und im taccuino senese XIX, XXII, XXIII, XXVII, XXX, XXXV.
30. Ein vergleichbares fünfschiffiges Langhaus zeigt unter allen Entwürfen für St. Peter einzig der im *Codex Coner (Ashby, 17)* abgebildete Grundriss eines Anonimus.

zweitens die Umgestaltung der Nebengruppen.[31] Um die Monotonie einer ununterbrochenen Pilaster-Bogenreihe zu vermeiden, wird der Versuch unternommen, eine rhythmische Ordnung za schaffen.

Von grösserer Wichtigkeit ist dagegen das andere Problem, welches wieder näher an Bramante heranführt. Die Proportionierung der Nebenräume des Giulianoplanes konnten ästhetisch nicht befriedigen. Einer Länge von 100 palmi der Kreuzarme stand ein Kuppeldurchmesser von nur 60 palmi gegenüber, ausserdem widersprach das kontrapunktische Grössenverhältnis zwischen Haupt- und Nebenkuppelräumen dem koordinierenden Kompositionsprinzip der Uridee des Bramanteplanes, die auch für die Umdeutung im Entwurf Giulianos Gültigkeit behalten sollte.[32] Die nordwestliche Nebenkuppel ist durch "Ausklinken" und Verkröpfen der Vierungspfeiler, die Giuliano durch die rechtwinkelig aneinanderstossenden Pilasterflächen betont "geschärft" hatte, ausgeweitet und auf einen Durchmesser von 100 palmi gebracht worden. Später ist die immer noch bestehende Härte der rechtwinkeligen Pfeilerkanten durch Abschrägung gemildert worden (vergl. Uff. 1 A).

Indem auch die nordöstliche Nebenkuppel durch das gleiche Verfahren auf 100 palmi gebracht wurde, stellte man das Verhältnis von 1:4 des Urplanes wieder her.[33]

Die Annäherung an die Prinzipien des ersten Bramanteplanes, welche die Korrekturen an den Nebengruppen erkennen liessen, scheinen auf Eingreifen des Urbinaten hinzudeuten, während andererseits die indirekte Einwirkung Giulianos da Sangallo durch die Tatsache der Kongruenz der Kerngruppen in den Grundrissen auf den beiden Seiten des Blattes Uff. 8 A jedem Zweifel entrückt ist. Ob darüber hinaus vor dem Objekt ein persönlicher Gedankenaustausch stattgefunden hat, mit anderen Worten, ob der Entwurf das Resultat einer echten Gemeinschaftsarbeit gewesen ist, kann aus der Analyse der Zeichnung nicht bewiesen werden. Der Bericht Vasaris, dass Giuliano kurz nach der Grundsteinlegung im April 1506 Rom enttäuscht verlassen habe, nachdem der Papst ihn mit Trostgeschenken ausgestattet hatte, legt den Gedanken nahe, dass es in der Tat bei der Zusammenarbeit beider Meister nicht mit rechten Dingen zugegangen sei. Offenbar argwöhnte er—die historischen Fakten scheinen es ja zu bestätigen—dass

Bramante sich seines geistigen Eigentums, oder wesentlicher Teile desselben bemächtigt habe. Andererseits spricht gegen eine solche Vermutung die Tatsache seiner Rückkehr nach Rom, allerdings erst als sich Bramante bereits in extremis befand, und dass er von dann ab wesentlich an der Vollendung der nicht in allen Punkten ausgereiften Pläne des Urbinaten mitgewirkt hat.

Die Rötelskizze auf der Rückseite des Giulianoplanes ist, wie wir erkannten, abgesehen von den besprochenen Korrekturen, zügig von einem mit der Materie und den Absichten des (oder der) Erfinder des Entwurfes vertrauten Zeichners ausgeführt. Dass sie von einem dritten, jüngeren Gehilfen, sozusagen nach Diktat angefertigt worden wäre, schliesst sich damit von selber aus. Der Zeichenstil verrät weder die Hand eines jungen Künstlers, noch ausgesprochenen Altersstil, sie ist die eines auf der Höhe der Arbeitskraft Stehenden, eines Gereiften, dessen noch sichere Hand einen charakteristischen Eigenstil entwickelt hat. Wer war es?

Der Umstand, dass bisher noch nicht eine einzige authentische Handzeichnung Bramantes hat nachgewiesen werden können, verbietet kategorisch die Zuschreibung der Zeichnung, also des graphischen Werkes, nicht der Idee oder einzelner Teile derselben, an Bramante.

Die Pläne Uff. 1 A und Uff. 8 A r waren so orientiert, dass sich die Apostelmemorie auf der Peripherie der Kuppelprojektion unter dem Choreingangsbogen befand. Diese vom Standpunkt der Architekturtheorie wie aus liturgischen Gründen gleichermassen vertretbare Anordnung scheint Julius II., wie aus dem Bericht des Egidio da Viterbo indirekt deduziert werden muss, nicht gebilligt zu haben.[34] Der Giulianoentwurf erfüllte zwar die beiden Programmpunkte, Inkorporation des nikolasischen Fundamentes und Einbeziehung des geweihten Areals in den Neubau, das dritte, dem Rang nach wohl wichtigste Postulat der zentralen Stellung des Apostelgrabes war aber nicht berücksichtigt worden. Die Gründe mochten zunächst auf statischen Erwägungen beruhen. Wie die Abb. 2 zeigt, sind die westlichen Kuppelpfeiler so weit nach Osten gerückt, dass sie fast ausserhalb des Bereiches des alten Fundamentes, also auf unberührtem Boden, stehen würden, damit eine asymetrische, "einhüftige" und dadurch statisch bedenkliche Belastung des Baugrundes vermieden werde. Man befand sich also auf einem circulus vitiosus, in dem sich die Erfüllung aller Programmvorschriften auf der Basis des Zentralbaues wechselseitig ausschloss.

Nehmen wir nun als Arbeitshypothese an, dass auf

---

31. *Förster*, S. 246/247.

32. Bei der Analyse von Uff. 8 A r war schon auf die Indizien hingewiesen worden (z.B. Abschnürung der Kreuzarme durch Pfeilervorlagen an den Kuppelarkaden).

33. Im Zusammenhang mit der Erweiterung der Kuppelräume steht die Gruppierung der Langhauspfeiler. Die in die Arkaden gesetzten Säulen nehmen einen Gedanken von Uff. 1 A wieder auf. *Metternich, Kongress*, S. 80/81.

34. *Metternich, Kongress*, S. 78/79.

dem Grundriss Uff. 8 A v die Kuppelpfeiler in Beziehung zur Apostelmemorie so weit nach Westen versetzt worden seien, dass sie symmetrisch auf das alte Fundament zu stehen kämen (Abb. 3)[35] so hätte eine feste Fundamentplatte hergestellt werden können. Aber auch auf diese Weise wäre es nicht gelungen, den topographischen Punkt der Apostelmemorie mit dem geometrischen Zentrum des Kuppelraumes zu kombinieren. Dieser Wunsch sollte niemals in Erfüllung gehen. Auch im Plan Nikolaus V. konnte die Apostelmemorie nicht den mathematischen Mittelpunkt der Vierung einnehmen, der sich 27 palmi weiter östlich in einer Entfernung von 53 palmi vom Triumphbogen des Langhauses befand. Der Grund lag bekanntlich in der Absicht, die Seiten der projektierten Vierung der Breite des Langhauses der in substantia zu erhaltenden konstantinischen Basilika anzupassen (106 palmi). Die im Mittelpunkt der alten Tribuna auf der Fluchtlinie der Westwände des Querhauses lokalisierte memoria Sancti Petri mit dem darüber befindlichen Papstaltar befand sich, der Breite des Querschiffs entsprechend, 80 palmi westlich des Triumphbogens des Langhauses, woraus sich die oben angegebene Entfernung zwischen der Apostelmemorie und der Mitte der Vierung erklärt.[36]

Die Verschiebung der Kuppelpfeiler auf dem Grundriss Uff. 8 A v musste zwei für den weiteren Ablauf der Planung bedeutsame Wirkungen haben: erstens rückten die Mittelpunkte der Kuppel und der Vierung Nikolaus V. zusammen. Damit war das Zentrum der Anlage nicht nur zeichnerisch, sondern auch topographisch fixiert.

Zweitens setzte sich die Ostgrenze der Zentralanlage merklich von der Eingangswand der alten Basilika nach Westen ab. Dadurch wäre die wichtigste Errungenschaft des Giulianoplanes, nämlich die Überbauung des konsekrierten Areals, vereitelt worden. Bei den Erwägungen, welche der Formulierung des Planes Uff. 8 A v vorausgingen, muss man sich der inneren Widersprüche zwischen der in der Natur der Sache begründeten Unabänderlichkeit des Bauprogramms und dem Ideal des Zentralbaues bewusst geworden sein, und dass auch die masstäbliche Ausweitung im Sinne des Giulianoplanes keine Lösung des Dilemmas bringen konnte. Die unausbleibliche Folge dieser Einsicht war der Übergang zum Longitudinalbau gewesen, dessen erste Ausprobung in unserer Rötelzeichnung zu erkennen war. Zwar sollte die

Lösung nicht durch einen Rückgriff auf die mittelalterliche Pfeilerbasilika gefunden werden, sondern durch die Ergänzung des Zentralbaues zu einer "kompositen" Anlage, etwa im Sinne der Ss. Annunziata in Florenz oder von S. Francesco in Rimini. Auf der linken Seite der Zeichnung hatten wir die erste Fassung der Langhausidee als fünfschiffige Pfeileranlage kennen gelernt.

Nachdem durch die Ubikation der Apostelmemorie das eigentliche Anliegen der Studie sichtbar geworden ist, werden die weiteren Einzelheiten verständlich. Die Korrekturen auf der rechten Seite, welche in erster Linie die Nebengruppen betrafen, mussten sich auch auf das Langhaus auswirken und zwar zunächst auf die Seitenschiffe. Das innere derselben wurde beinahe auf die Breite der Nische im Kuppelpfeiler (40 palmi) komprimiert. Es erscheint, ähnlich wie bei dem Pergamentplan Bramantes, als kurzer Kreuzarm der Nebengruppe. Über die Gestalt des äusseren Seitenschiffes gibt die Korrektur keine Auskunft. Dagegen sind die Anhaltspunkte für die Gestaltung des Mittelschiffes aufschlussreich. Es lässt sich folgendermassen rekonstruieren: das Ziel, die additive Gruppierung gleicher Raumkompartimente durch einen alternierenden Rhythmus (b—a—b) zu ersetzen, wird erreicht, indem die beiden kurzen Joche mit ihren 60 palmi weiten Bogen je an die Kuppelpfeiler und die östliche Abschlusswand angelehnt werden; dazwischen ist das Mittelschiff zu einer Vierung von etwa 130 palmi Seitenlänge ausgeweitet, die Langhausjoche und die beiderseits querschiffartig ausgebildeten Nebenräume, die von ihr ausstrahlen, bilden eine auf die Hauptgruppe vorbereitende kreuzförmige Raumkombination. Die Vierung dürfte man sich mit einer Flachkuppel überdeckt vorzustellen haben. Der Gedanke, das Langhaus dergestalt aufzugliedern und die Längsrichtung durch ein die Raumachsen sammelndes Motiv zu unterbrechen, ist in der späteren Planung, besonders seit der Einführung des langen Mittelschiffes zu fünf Traveen wiederholt ausgeprobt worden.[37]

Während die linke Variante zuverlässig rekonstruiert werden kann, führen auf der rechten Seite die durch hastig hingeworfene Linien angedeuteten Versuche nicht zu einem schlüssigen Ergebnis. Die Analyse der Rötelzeichnung Uff. 8 A v führte zu der wichtigen Entdeckung, dass bei den Varianten zu beiden Seiten der Mittelachse des Langhauses die östliche Raumgrenze sich mit der Eingangswand der konstantinischen

---

35. *Förster*, S. 247.

36. Bei den Neubauplänen des 16. Jahrh. waren Masse und Mittelpunkt der Kuppel nicht unmittelbar von der konstantinischen Basilika abgeleitet worden wie bei den Projekten Nikolaus V., sondern im umgekehrten Verfahren mittelbar über das Fundament des Chores.

37. Vergleiche die Entwürfe, A. d. Sangallo d. J. im Anschluss an sein Memoriale, in dem er die Nachteile des langen Mittelschiffes gerügt hatte, z.B. Uff. 36 A r und 37 A. Das Langhaus Madernos verwirklicht in reduziertem Masstab und unter veränderten Umständen verwandte Gedanken.

Basilika deckt (Abb. 4). Damit ist unsere Arbeitshypothese bewiesen. Die Zeichnung, welche unter unscheinbarer Gestalt Grosses verbirgt, ist nur dann sinnvoll, wenn sie verstanden wird als Versuch, die Forderungen des Bauprogrammes mit den künstlerischen Zielen in Einklang zu bringen. Zwei dieser Forderungen sind der Erfüllung so nahe gebracht worden, wie die Voraussetzungen technischer und topographischer Art es gestatteten: die Stellung der Apostelmemorie im Kuppelraum und die Einbeziehung des geweihten Areals der konstantinischen Basilika in den Neubau.

D

Schon ein flüchtiger Blick führt zur Erkenntnis, dass die *Rötelzeichnung Uff. 20 A* (Abb. 5) ein Derivat der vorher betrachteten Zeichnung Uff. 8 A v[38] ist. Das Grundmotiv der Verbindung einer zentralisierten Anlage im Westen mit einem sich nach Osten erstreckenden Langhaus ist das gleiche;[39] dem entsprechen Einzelheiten wie die Umgänge und die in Anlehnung an die Korrekturen auf der rechten Bildseite des genannten Planes ausgebildeten Nebenkuppelräume. Auch die Grundmasse sind übernommen, 200 palmi als Durchmesser des Hauptkuppelraumes, 100 palmi für die Nebenkuppelräume; das Verhältnis 1:4, welches über die Versuche von Uff. 8 A v zu dem ersten Bramanteplan zurückgeführt hatte, ist gewahrt, ferner das Mass von 100 palmi für die Seitenlänge der Quadrate, in welche die Grundrisse der Kuppelpfeiler eingetragen sind. Die Hauptschiffe sind mit Rücksicht auf das Quadratnetz des Blattes in einer Breite von 110 palmi eingezeichnet statt im konstantinischen Mass von 106 palmi. Offenbar wurden 108 palmi als das richtige Mass angesehen. Die Scheitelhöhe von 216 palmi, welche der nachfolgenden Aufrissplanung zu Grunde lag, erscheint nur so sinnvoll.[40]
Wer war der Urheber dieses innerhalb des Planungsprozesses von St. Peter eine Schlüsselstellung einnehmenden Entwurfes? Trat der Rückgriff auf Urgedanken Bramantes bei dem vorigen Plan bereits deutlich in Erscheinung, so darf der Einfluss des

Urbinaten bei Uff. 20 A als prädominierend gelten. Die bereits erwähnten Grundlagen werden durch Einzelheiten ergänzt, so die Einführung der vom Pergamentplan entnommenen Eingangsloggien zwischen den Ecktürmen und den Apsidenumgängen, ferner die Rückkehr zu den antiken Vorbildern entlehnten Oktagonalräumen in den Türmen an der Stelle der florentinischen des Giulianoplanes. Aber diese Fakten reichen für eine positive Zuschreibung nicht aus.
Der Zeichenstil ist ein anderer als bei Uff. 8 A v, die Linienführung, soweit nicht mit Lineal oder Zirkel gearbeitet wurde, langsamer, ängstlicher, weniger nervös, selbst bei den freihändig eingezeichneten Perspektiven am oberen Bildrand; die Bogenlinien sind durchweg zügig ohne Stocken mit sicherer Hand und trefflichem Augenmass geführt. Die Präzision dieser Zeichenweise ist nicht nur auf die Anlehnung an die Hilfslinien des Quadratnetzes zurückzuführen, sie ist vielmehr ein individuelles Charakteristikum der Handschrift des Meisters. Die vielfältigen Rückgriffe auf Elemente des Pergamentplanes legen den Gedanken an Bramante nahe.
Eine Zuschreibung der Zeichnung an ihn ist, solange das tertium comparationis, eine gesicherte Handzeichnung des Meisters, fehlt, ebensowenig vertretbar wie bei Uff. 8 A v.[41]
Die geistige Urheberschaft des Entwurfes gehört ohne Zweifel dem Urbinaten und dem Florentiner gemeinsam an, das tetrastyle Grundmotiv der Westgruppe dem ersteren, der grosse Masstab, die Kolossalordnung und die aus ihr abgeleitete Spannweite der Arkaden von 60 palmi dem letzteren. Wie der Giulianoplan Uff. 8 A r sich als eine Umdeutung des Urentwurfs Bramantes herausstellte, so könnte Uff. 20 A als eine Umdeutung des Giulianoplanes im bramantesken Sinne bezeichnet werden. Bramante gebührt auf jeden Fall das Lob, mit dem auf dem Pergamentblatt Uff. 1 A niedergeschriebenen Gedanken das Samenkorn gelegt zu haben, aus dem die weitere Planung bis zur Vollendung gewachsen ist.

III

Die abschliessende Frage nach der Findung der

38. Der Grundriss ist in ein Quadratnetz eingetragen, das, wie der Verfasser glaubt, aufgedruckt und nicht mit der Hand gezeichnet ist. Die Quadrate entsprechen einer Skala von 5 palmi.
39. Der Gedanke der Rhythmisierung des Langhauses wird nicht weiter verfolgt. Welche Bedeutung der Eintragung eines Kuppelpfeilergrundrisses auf der rechten Seite des Langhauses, der eine gewisse Ähnlichkeit mit dem von Uff. 1 A aufweist, beizumessen ist, bleibt unklar. Die Einzeichnung dürfte nicht mehr als theoretische Bedeutung haben.
40. Die Massberechnungen werden bestätigt durch die Eintragungen auf dem St. Peter—Grundriss im *Libro di Sangallo*, fol. 64 v. Vergl. *Geymüller*, Bl. 28, fig. 3 und Bl. 29.

41. Aus dem Sangallokreis kämen nur Giuliano, Antonio d. Ältere oder d. Jüngere in Betracht, andere Mitglieder scheiden aus chronologischen Gründen aus, Antonio d. Ä war nicht anwesend (Anm. 21). Das in Bezug auf Uff. 8 A v vorgebrachte Argument, es könne nur ein mit den Gedanken und ihren Quellen (z.B. S. Lorenzo) Vertrauter berücksichtigt werden, ist nicht auf Uff. 20 A anwendbar, nachdem Uff. 8 v alle nötigen Informationen geliefert hatte. Eine Entscheidung für einen der beiden Sangallo, die bei einer Federzeichnung ohne Bedenken möglich wäre, wird bei einer Rötelzeichnung aus einem so engen Arbeitskreis kaum gewagt werden dürfen. Die Frage bleibt offen.

endgültigen Masse *des Kuppelraumes* und aller weiterer Masse, welche die mathematischen Grundlagen *des Ausführungsplanes* bilden, ist jetzt reif zur Beantwortung. Den wichtigsten Forderungen des Bauprogrammes, Stellung der Apostelmemorie im Kuppelraum, Einbeziehung des geweihten Areals der alten Basilika in den Neubau, möglichst zahlreiche Nebenräume zur Unterbringung von alten und noch zu errichtenden neuen Denkmälern, Heiltümern, Stätten privater Andacht u.s.w. war in den beiden zuletzt betrachteten Entwürfen Genüge getan. Dagegen war die Vorschrift, das Fundament Nikolaus V. dem Neubau zu inkorporieren, welche die ersten Pläne Bramantes und Giulianos erfüllt hatten, in den Entwürfen Uff. 8 A v und 20 A unbeachtet geblieben. Bei dem ersteren war das Chorhaupt um 30 und bei den letzteren gar um 50 palmi über die Apsis Nikolaus V. nach Westen verschoben. Jene Forderung des Bauprogramms aber war kategorisch. Welche Gründe die Bauherren bestimmt haben können, ökonomischer, technischer oder gottesdienstlicher Art, das zu untersuchen ist ebenfalls nicht Aufgabe dieses Aufsatzes.

Es muss als feststehend gelten, dass die Entscheidung schon vor Baubeginn gefallen war. Die beiden westlichen Kuppelpfeiler wurden zusammen mit dem Chor in einem kontinuierlichen Arbeitsprozess hochgeführt, im Herbst 1510 ward das Gewölbe geschlossen, die wichtigsten Teile des Bauschmuckes, das Kranzgesims, die Pilasterkapitelle, die Kassettierung des Gewölbes, die dorische Kolossalordnung des Äussern bis auf die oberen Glieder des Triglyphengebälkes und die Profile der Pilastersockel vollendet.[42] Dieser Vorgang setzt eine intensive, die bisher befolgten Grundsätze in wichtigen Punkten durchbrechende Planungstätigkeit voraus. Gerade für den der Entscheidung unmittelbar vorausgehenden Zeitabschnitt fehlen die zeichnerischen und archivalischen Dokumente, jedoch lassen sich die Vorgänge in den Grundzügen rekonstruieren.

Die Wirkungen jenes für die Planung folgenschweren Machtspruches waren:

(1) *Aussen* wurde die Symmetrie der Westgruppe zerstört. Auf die Ecktürme, die Nebenkuppeln einschliesslich der Querarme und den Chorumgang wurde verzichtet. Die Frage, ob und inwieweit diese Massnahme von den Zeitgenossen, den Laien wie den Künstlern, namentlich den unmittelbaren Nachfolgern Bramantes als mehr oder minder langfristiges Provisorium betrachtet wurde, ob und welche Hoffnungen für seine Beseitigung gehegt, und welche

Möglichkeiten zur Wiederherstellung des Gleichgewichtes, wenn auch nur auf dem Wege eines Kompromisses theoretisch ausgeprobt wurden, ist hier nicht zu untersuchen.[43] Es ist indessen wichtig, daran festzuhalten, dass Bramante, vor der harten Realität des unabänderlichen Gebotes stehend, alle Folgerungen zu ziehen und alle Folgen auf sich zu nehmen hatte. Für ihn konnte es kein Provisorium geben. Alle Versuche, diese aus der Analyse der Pläne zu ziehende Lehre ausser Acht zu lassen, führen auf unentrinnbare Abwege.

(2) Während das Ebenmass des Äussern durch die Amputation wichtiger Teile der Westgruppe zerstört werden musste, sollte *innen* durch illusionistische Kunstgriffe der Eindruck der Symmetrie des Raumbildes gerettet werden.[44] Das wirksamste Mittel, diesem Ziel nahe zu kommen, bestand in der optischen Angleichung der Kreuzarme im Süden, Norden und Westen. Der westliche Kreuzarm, die tribuna grande, musste dementsprechend mit Arkaden in den gleichen Dimensionen versehen werden, wie die beiden andern (60 palmi Spannweite). Da die Apsis des Neubaues auf das Tribunafundament Nikolaus V. gesetzt wurde, d.h. 50 palmi weiter nach Osten als im Entwurf Uff 20 A vorgesehen war, hätten sich die Arkaden bis in das Massiv der Kuppelpfeiler vorgeschoben. Ein Ausgleich war nur durch entsprechende Komprimierung des Volumens derselben zu erreichen, und zwar durch zentripetales Vorrücken der äusseren Grenzflächen (Abb. 5).

(3) Hierdurch wurden die *Nebengruppen* an der Ostseite—die westlichen mussten ja verschwinden— näher an das Mittellot der Hauptkuppel herangezogen, die Kreuzarme verkürzt und die Nebenkuppelräume wieder zu Vierungen, wie im Giulianoplan, und ihr Durchmesser von 100 auf 66 palmi verringert. Durch das Zusammenrücken der Aussenflächen der Pfeiler wurden die Kantenabschrägungen auf schmale, zwischen die Pfeilervorlagen der Vierungsbögen eingezwängte Streifen von 1½ palmi Breite reduziert.[45]

(4) Die Massreduktion der Kuppelpfeiler führte zwangsläufig zur Einengung der den Kreuzarmen zugewandten *Seitenflächen*. Im Entwurf Uff. 20 A waren sie, wie vermutlich schon bei Uff. 8 A v, durch die charakteristischen Pilasterpaare der Kolossalordnung im Rhythmus 15—20—15 palmi gegliedert.

42. *Franz Graf Wolff Metternich*, Bramantes Chor der Peterskirche zu Rom, Römische Quartalschrift, 58, 1–4, Freiburg i.B. 1963, S. 274–6, zitiert: "*Metternich, Bramantechor.*"

43. Vergl. die Studien Giulianos und Antonios da Sangallo und Baldassare Peruzzis. Erst die Genehmigung des Modells Antonios unter dem Pontifikate Pauls III. führte zur Wiederherstellung der Symmetrie im Sinne des Bramante-Entwurfes.

44. *Vasari, VII*, S. 136 *Christof Thoenes*, Studien zur Geschichte des Petersplatzes, Zeitschrift für Kunstgeschichte, München Berlin, 1963, S. 105, *Metternich, Bramantechor*, S. 281/282.

45. Das ist der Ursprung jenes von Antonio da Sangallo regelmässig angewandten Vierungspfeilertypus, der im Barock zur Regel wird.

Rechnet man die Vorlagen für die Archivolten der
Arkaden mit 5 palmi dazu, so ergibt sich ein Breitenmass von 55 palmi. Durch das Vorrücken der
Arkaden nach Osten wurde diese Fläche auf 36 palmi
verringert. Das verbleibende Spatium reichte also für
Pilasterpaare in den genannten Dimensionen nicht
mehr aus; andererseits würde eine Verbreiterung in
Richtung auf das Mittellot des Kuppelraumes mit
dem Ziele, die erforderliche Fläche zu gewinnen, eine
unerwünschte Verkleinerung des Zentralelementes be-
wirkt haben. Ausschlaggebend für die weiteren Ent-
schlüsse musste die Stellung der Apostelmemorie sein.
Die Situation des ersten Bramanteentwurfes und des
Giulianoplanes, aus der man sich durch schwierige
Manipulationen gelöst hatte, wäre wieder eingetreten,
wenn der Kuppelraum merklich eingeengt worden
wäre.[46]

Andererseits waren die Pilasterpaare mit den in die
Intervalle eingeschnittenen Nischen als Vorstufe zur
"rhythmischen Travee" des Ausführungsplanes ein
unentbehrliches Requisit geworden. Auf der Rötelzeichnung Uff. 20 A war das Motiv auf die Schmalseiten der Kuppelpfeiler beschränkt geblieben. Erst
nachdem es im Ausführungsplan auch am Ende der
Querarme als Flankierung der Arkaden auftrat, kam
die rhythmische Travee zur vollen Entfaltung. Sie
blieb zunächst noch, an den Querhäusern zwischen
Kuppelpfeilern und Apsiden eingezwängt, isoliert.
Indem sich aber der Integrationsprozess der Westgruppe mit dem Langhause vollzog, und die
rhythmische Travee aus dem Kuppelraum in kon-
tinuierlicher Kettenbewegung auf die Innenseiten des
Mittelschiffes überflutete, wurde sie, aus der Isolierung
befreit, zum Leitmotiv des den gesamten Innenraum
umspannenden architektonischen Systems,[47] welches
der an sich amorphen und indifferenten Flächen-
struktur der tragenden Glieder spezifische Ausdrucks-
kraft verlieh. Der genetische Prozess dieser Ordnung,
die auch heute noch weitgehend das Bild der Peterskirche bestimmt, setzte just an dem Punkt an, topographisch und entwickelungsgeschichtlich gesehen,
den unsere Untersuchung nun erreicht hat. Es ist der
Augenblick, in welchem sich das künstlerische
Schicksal der neuen Peterskirche entschied. Der ent-
werfende Künstler stand am Scheideweg: entweder
war das Motiv der gekoppelten Pilaster, mithin auch
der rhythmischen Travee, beizubehalten und der
aufgezwungenen neuen Situation anzupassen oder es
war darauf zu verzichten und eine andersartige Lösung
zu ersinnen. Er entschied sich für das erstere.

Durch die Fixierung des Kuppelzentrums und die
damit kausal verknüpfte Einbeziehung der Apostelmemorie in den planimetrischen und stereometrischen
Schematismus der Gesamtanlage war das Problem
erster Ordnung, das der Neubau von St. Peter stellte,
gelöst worden. Das Problem zweiter Ordnung, das der
baukünstlerischen Artikulation des Gesamtorganismus,
wurde durch die genannte Entscheidung in den
Grundlagen ebenfalls gelöst.[48]

Um das Verständnis der nun folgenden Beschreibung
des genetischen Vorgangs zu erleichtern, sei daran
erinnert, dass die Höhenmasse der Räume und der
Arkaden grundsätzlich festlagen, d.h. 216 palmi für
die Hauptschiffe und 120 palmi für die Arkaden; die
Kämpfer lagen also bei 162, beziehungsweise bei 90
palmi. Zunächst muss versucht werden, die Entstehung des Motivs der gekoppelten Pilaster zu klären.
Die Entdeckung eines antiken Vorbildes würde zwar
die Quelle der Idee aufzeigen, keinesfalls aber die
spezifische Ausbildung erklären, noch würde der
naheliegende Hinweis auf das Beispiel von St. Andrea
in Mantua genügen. Wir werden daher zu dem ersten
nachweisbaren Auftreten des Motivs bei der Planung
von St. Peter in den Entwürfen Uff. 8 A v und Uff.
20 A zurückkehren müssen.

Die Abmessungen der Schmalseiten der Kuppelpfeiler
wurde bei Uff. 20 A aus dem Grundmass von 100
palmi im Quadrat abgeleitet. Von den äusseren
Kanten wurden zunächst 5 palmi als Vorlagen für die
Arkaden abgezogen; bis zu den Innenkanten der gross-
en Kuppelarkaden verblieben sodann als Breitenmass
noch 50 palmi. Der Flächenraum, der für die grosse
Pilasterordnung zur Verfügung stand, betrug demnach
50 × 162 palmi. Er wurde der Breite nach im Rhythmus 15 (Pilaster)—20 (Intervalle)—15 (Pilaster)
gleich 3—4—3 aufgeteilt (Abb. 5 und 6).

Die Höhenverhältnisse der Kolossalordnung sind in
einem umständlichen Kompromissverfahren aus-
gemittelt. Als Grundmasse gelten seit dem Giulianoplan, wie bekannt, Spannweite und Höhe der Arkaden
(60 zu 120 palmi), dazu kommt die den Arkadenvor-
lagen entsprechende Breite der Archivolten von 5
palmi; die äussere Scheitelhöhe der Arkaden erreicht
somit 125 palmi. In die durch dieses Mass nach unten
und die auf 162 liegende Kämpferlinie der Gewölbe

---

46. Die Apostelmemorie wäre wieder in die Nähe der Peripherie geraten.
47. *Vasari, III*, S. 136, Grundrisse Giulianos da Sangallo, Uff.
7 A und 9 A.

48. Die Hierarchie des ordo architectonicus, die Verflechtung
der Motive, der Pilaster, Bogen, Nischen u.s.w., der Rhythmus
ihrer Abfolge und ihre Proportionen, alles wird von der rhythmischen Travee, jener Verbindung der Kolossalordnung und der
Arkade in ihrer spezifischen Ausprägung determiniert. Die in
dem Ausführungsplan verwirklichte Konkordanz zwischen der
Innen- und Aussenarchitektur, d.h. die Projektion der Innen-
gliederung auf die Aussenwandflächen, also jene Folgerichtigkeit
des gesamten inneren und äusseren Schematismus mag Michelangelo mit dem berühmten Ausspruch von der "verità" haben
kennzeichnen wollen. (Vergl. Uff. 7 A, 9 A.)

nach oben begrenzte Zone von 37 palmi ist das Gebälk einzufügen, dessen Höhe der für die korinthische Ordnung gebräuchlichen Norm entsprechend zweimal die Pilasterbreite, gleich 30 palmi, ausmacht. Die verbleibenden 7 palmi sind auf den Abstand zwischen Archivolte und Architrav mit 3 palmi und mit 4 palmi auf die Stelzung der Gewölbe und Gurtbogen zu verteilen.[49] Demnach beträgt die Höhe der Pilaster 128 palmi, und zwar nicht nur für den Entwurf Uff. 20 A, sondern auch für die beiden vorherbetrachteten Uff. 8 A r und v.[50] Das für die korinthische Ordnung kanonische Massverhältnis von Breite zu Höhe konnte nicht eingehalten werden.

Wir können nunmehr zu dem Kernproblem der Genesis der heutigen architektonischen Ordnung des Inneren der Peterskirche zurückkehren. Die Errichtung der tribuna grande und des Chores auf dem Fundament Nikolaus V. hatte, wie wir erkannten, eine Reduktion der Schmalseiten der Kuppelpfeiler auf eine Breite von 36 palmi mit sich gebracht; die von jeher festliegende obere Grenze lag an der Kämpferlinie der Gewölbe in der Höhe von 162 palmi. Diese gegenüber dem Entwurf Uff. 20 A erhebliche Komprimierung des Flächenraumes erzwang eine masstäbliche Neuordnung des in den Grundlagen zu erhaltenden Motivs der gekoppelten Pilaster. Das erwies sich als segensreich, insofern die für die relative Enge der Räume überdimensionierten und plumpen Glieder auf, zwar immer noch bedeutende, aber sowohl den Räumen als auch den einzelnen Elementen der Komposition adäquatere Masse zurückgeführt werden mussten. In der Horizontalen wurden den drei Zonen der vorhergehenden Entwürfe—Gewölbe, Gebälk, Pilasterreihe—als vierte der Sockelstreifen hinzugefügt.[51]

Von den vertikalen Gliedern wurden die Pfeilervorlagen der Archivolten auf eine Breite von 4 palmi gebracht; die Pilastergruppe erhielt den neuen Rhythmus 12:15:12 palmi (= 4:5:4), im Ganzen also 43 palmi, sodass die verfügbare Fläche um 7 palmi überschritten wurde. Die Höhe der Pilaster wurde, immer noch unter der Norm, auf 9 × die Breite

gleich 108 palmi festgesetzt, das Gebälk dagegen nicht im gleichen Verhältnis verkleinert, es blieb bei einer Stärke von 27 palmi über der Norm, welche 2 × die Pilasterstärke gleich 24 palmi erfordert haben würde.[52] Die Höhe der Pilasterordnung war somit im Ganzen auf 152 palmi gekommen (10 palmi unter dem Gewölbeansatz). Die Gurtbogen und Gewölbe erhielten dadurch die der Ausladung des Kranzgesimses entsprechende Stelzung.[53]

(5) Die bis an die Grenzen des Möglichen getriebene Neuordnung der Massverhältnisse hatte zu einer geringfügigen Ausweitung der Schmalseiten der Kuppelpfeiler von 7 palmi in der Richtung auf das Innere des Kuppelraumes geführt. Dementsprechend kontrahierten sich die Schrägseiten des oktagonalen Raumprismas und wurden zugleich zentripetal vorgeschoben. Der Durchmesser des Raumes wurde um 14 palmi verringert und auf das Mass von 186 palmi gebracht.

Bei den vorhergehenden Plänen hatte die Spannweite der Kuppelarkaden 100 palmi betragen und dementsprechend die Ausladung der Pilaster 3–5 palmi. Der geringere Umfang der Pilaster des Ausführungsplanes zog die Reduktion ihrer Ausladung auf 2 palmi nach sich. Demgemäss mussten die Fluchtlinien der Pilasterfronten um 1 palmo zurückgenommen und dadurch die Breite der Kuppelarkaden auf 102 palmi und die Schiffe auf das Mass der konstantinischen Basilika von 106 palmi zurückgeführt werden (Abb. 5).

Eine planimetrische Gegenprobe bestätigt den gefundenen Durchmesser von 186 palmi für den Kuppelraum: Durch den geschilderten Vorgang hatten die Grundquadrate der Pfeiler eine Seitenlänge von 85 palmi erhalten und die den Querarmen zugekehrten Schmalseiten eine Breite von 43 palmi. Die kurzen Seiten der gleichschenkeligen rechtwinkeligen Dreiecke, welche dem Pfeilergrundriss abgeschnitten worden waren, messen also 42 palmi. Die Addition 42 + 102 + 42 gleich 186 bestätigt das ermittelte Mass von 186 palmi.[54]

49. Bezüglich der Stelzung der Bogen siehe unten Anm. 53.
50. Die Pilasterbreite von 15 palmi ist im Wiener Plan des Sangallo-Kreises, Albertina XXIV, II a/1, n. 791 angegeben. Die Breite der Kreuzarme und der Seitenschiffe beträgt 60 palmi. Daraus ergeben sich die gleichen Dimensionen der Kolossalordnung wie bei den Entwürfen 8 A recto und verso und 20 A. Das Höhenverhältnis der Pilaster beträgt 8,5 × die Breite gegenüber rund 9⅞ × die Breite bei den Innenpilastern des Pantheon, deren Einzelformen bekanntlich für St. Peter vorbildlich waren.
51. Über die Höhe der Sockel siehe *Metternich, Kongress*, S. 81, pl. XXI, 7, 8. *Ders.* zur Aufstellung des Juliusgrabes nach dem Entwurf von 1513, Festschrift für Heinrich Lützeler, Düsseldorf 1962, S. 448.
Metternich, Bramantechor, Taf. 29.

52. Die Differenz zwischen diesem Mass und dem für Uff. 20 A vermuteten erklärt sich wahrscheinlich durch das Weglassen der Sima. Die hier errechneten Masse entsprechen der Ausführung. Vergleiche auch die Eintragungen auf dem Grundriss der Peterskirche im Libro di Giuliano da Sangallo (Anm. 29), und den Aufriss von Antonio da Sangallo, Uff. 60 A recto.
53. Siehe Anmerkung 49. Die Stelzung war bei Uff. 20 A mit 3 palmi zu gering, in St. Peter ist sie ungefähr so bemessen, dass sich die Vorderkante des Kranzgesimses von den gegenüberliegenden Wänden aus gesehen mit der Kämpferlinie der Gewölbe deckt. Durch die Höherlegung des Bodens unter Antonio da Sangallo hat sich diese Anordnung ungünstig verschoben. Die schmucklosen Streifen unter der Kassettierung sind trotz des später aufgebrachten Mäanderbandes allenthalben sichtbar.
54. Die Ursache der geringen Unterschiede gegenüber der Messung Letarouillys, Tf. 2 von 0,4 palmi = rund 0,09

Die auf dem Kuppelgrundriss Serlios eingezeichnete Skala ist irreführend, sie ergibt nur einen Durchmesser von 147 palmi. Legt man jedoch das obige Mass von 186 palmi zu Grunde, d.h. passt man den Masstab der Kuppel den Resultaten der vorhergehenden Berechnungen an, wie das der Text Serlios fordert,[55] so erhält der Kuppelfussring eine Stärke von 39 palmi, und diese entspricht der Breite der vier

Meter, fällt nicht ins Gewicht. Auf der grundlegenden Massaufnahme Antonios da Sangallo, Uff. A 44 des Bramantechores und des südwestlichen Kuppelpfeilers, ist die Arkadenspannung mit 104 palmi angegeben. Der Irrtum erklärt sich durch eine Ungenauigkeit der im übrigen zuverlässigen Messung. Die Westseite des Pfeilers ist mit 84 palmi angenommen statt, wie an der Südseite richtig eingetragen, mit 85 palmi. Daraus ergibt sich ein oblonger Grundriss, der Durchmesser der Kuppel wäre in der Ost-Westachse 42 + 104 + 42 = 188, in der Nord-Südachse 41 + 104 + 41 = 186. Dieser scheinbar geringfügige Fehler ist nicht ohne Folgen für spätere Pläne und Publikationen geblieben.

55. *Serlio, III*, Fol. 65 v, bemerkt, dass die von Bramante zu Lebzeiten entworfene, auf Fol. 66 r und 66 v dargestellte Kuppel auf die vollendeten Pfeiler und Bogen gesetzt werden sollte. Da, wie eingangs bemerkt wurde, der Kuppelentwurf sowohl Uff. 1 A als auch den anderen Plänen anpassungsfähig ist, lassen sich die Masse aller Teile auf der Grundlage einer aus dem Durchmesser ermittelten Skala errechnen. In unserem Text ist der Durchmesser des Ausführungsplanes (186 palmi) zu Grunde gelegt. Serlio hat das irrige Mass A. d. Sangallos von 188 palmi übernommen.

den Tambur tragenden Gurtbogen. In der Ausführung Michelangelos ist der Fussring gleich breit.

Die äussere Höhe des Tamburs bis zur Oberkante des Hauptgesimses des Säulenkranzes beträgt bei der Bramantekuppel 95 palmi, bei der Michelangelos 82,5 palmi, dagegen ist die Attika bei der ersteren nur 20 palmi hoch, gegen 25 bei der letzteren. Die durch die Fussringe teilweise verdeckte Kuppelschale erhebt sich nur um 61 palmi über die Attika. Die Absichten Bramantes sind also weniger auf die Aussenerscheinung der Kuppel als solcher gerichtet als auf den Tambur, dessen tragender Zylinder von 48 korinthischen Säulen umkreist wird.

Aus der näheren Umgebung der Kirche würde die Kuppel hinter dem weit ausladenden Gesims des Tholos fast ganz verschwunden sein, dagegen hätte sich die Laterne als ein zweiter Rundbau erheblichen Ausmasses (der Durchmesser gleich ein Drittel des Gesamtdurchmessers des Tamburs) optisch unmittelbar auf die Stufenringe gesetzt. Erst aus grosser Entfernung, namentlich von den umgebenden Höhen aus betrachtet, wäre die eigentliche Silhouette zur Geltung gekommen (Abb. 7).

Die Höhe darf erst von der Oberkante des Fussringes aus gemessen werden (die darunter befindliche Zone wird durch die Gewölbe und ihre Dächer teilweise verdeckt).

PETER MURRAY

Observations on Bramante's St. Peter's

The meaning of Bramante's plan for the rebuilding of St. Peter's can be interpreted on several different levels, of which the two most important are those of the perfection of architectural form and of liturgical symbolism. Such an interpretation is in keeping with the medieval exegesis by which Scripture was interpreted on four separate levels—literal, allegorical, tropological and anagogical. Both Bramante's aims were pursued together, and at the same time there can be no doubt that he was consciously attempting to create a building completely in the idiom of Imperial Roman architecture, but at the same time on a grander scale than any domed building which could possibly have been known to him at first hand. These three desires interact so that at any given moment it is impossible to say which is dominant in the architect's mind, and the problem is made far more difficult by the fact that we have only ambiguous evidence for Bramante's actual projects.

The problem starts from the large drawing known as the Parchment Plan, or Uffizi no. 1, which is probably the only surviving drawing that can be attributed with any confidence to Bramante himself. It belonged to Vasari and bears an inscription in the hand of Antonio da Sangallo to the effect that it is the plan for St. Peter's by Bramante which was never executed. We have, therefore, reasonable evidence for assuming that this represents Bramante's intention at some stage between about 1505, when the first plans were being drawn up, and 1514, when Bramante died. The Parchment Plan appears to represent half of a centrally planned Greek cross church; so that it may be regarded as a half-plan which was intended to be doubled and executed as a perfect central plan, or it may well be regarded as a design for a tribune to be added to an existing basilica, just as Bramante had done a few years earlier in Milan. In this case it can be thought of either as an addition to an existing building, or as a design for a building later to be completed in the traditional Latin cross shape.

To take the first alternative, there can be no doubt that, at some point, Bramante intended a pure Greek cross plan. The incontrovertible evidence for this is the considerable number of Greek cross plans which clearly derive from the Parchment Plan and which can be dated in the early sixteenth century. The collection in the Uffizi contains several such drawings of which

nos. 8 and 19 are typical in that they are based upon the same shape for the piers, which were intended to support the dome rising above the Greek cross. These drawings, and others like them, make it almost impossible to ascertain the official plan for new St. Peter's since they seem to have been produced more or less as design exercises, and the accidents of survival have probably preserved some of them at the expense of other drawings which may have been intended for execution. In fact, however, one of the most surprising things about the early history of St. Peter's is the extraordinarily haphazard method of office procedure. So far as we can now judge, no definitive plan, model, or even memorandum was made by Bramante or under his supervision, so that some forty years after his death, when Michelangelo took over, it can hardly have been possible for him to have known with certainty what Bramante intended to do. This is not to say that he did not have a fairly clear idea of Bramante's general plans since his famous letter of 1555 praises Bramante's design and it is quite evident that Michelangelo's own designs were based, rather freely, on Bramante's.

We have some further evidence for a Greek cross plan in the celebrated account by Egidius of Viterbo which was published by Pastor. This records a disagreement between Bramante and Pope Julius II over the question of the main entrance and the alignment of the Vatican obelisk. According to Egidius, this would have involved moving the tomb of St. Peter, and this Julius flatly forbade. The difficulties of alignment seem to indicate a Greek cross plan, but what is far more important about this story is the fact that Julius, at any rate, was sure that the new basilica, like the old, must be centred on the spot which was traditionally the grave of St. Peter. In the first year or two of the new basilica it seems that the projects were kept deliberately vague since no-one had made up his mind about the exact amount of rebuilding involved (and still less about how it was to be paid for) and it seems clear that the old basilica was the cause of much anxiety. For at least fifty years the Constantinian structure, which was then more than eleven hundred years old, had been in a ruinous condition and there seems to be some reason to believe that by about 1503, when Julius II was elected, the whole structure was visibly tottering. Nobody wished to take the responsibility of demolishing one of the most hallowed buildings in Christendom, the more so as the advance of the Turks in the fifteenth century had made the Holy Land and the Church of Santa Sophia in Constantinople equally inaccessible. At the beginning of his reign Julius must have decided that action of some kind could no longer be postponed and the Foundation Medal, commemorating the laying of the first pier of the new basilica on the 18th April, 1506, is evidence of the speed and determination with which he acted. It seems that this decision must have been made in the spring of 1505, since in March 1505 Bramante was not being asked to do more than provide a suitable chapel to contain Julius's own tomb, then being commissioned from Michelangelo. Within a few weeks, however, the completion of the work begun half a century earlier was being contemplated and on the 11th April, 1505, it was decided to complete these repair works; yet by the summer of the same year, perhaps as a result of a report by Bramante, the decision seems to have been made to use only those parts of the Constantinian basilica which could be safely incorporated in a new building. This explains the inscription on the Foundation Medal where the word 'Instauracio' is used and can make sense only in connection with the older building since it seems to mean not a replacement but a renewal, almost a summing up of the older building.[1] Such a completion of the new building as something based firmly on its fourth-century predecessor yet at the same time modern in execution and on a scale of Imperial amplitude, and far larger than any building erected for centuries past, would be entirely in keeping both with the character of Julius II and the architectural ambitions of Bramante.

Julius II, in the commissions already given to Michelangelo and later to be given to Michelangelo and to Raphael, proved himself the most grandiose patron of the sixteenth century; but the enormous undertaking of the new St. Peter's was far greater than any of these and, as he must have realized, was likely to be cripplingly expensive. It seems that the ruinous condition of the old church made it essential to rebuild, but there seems also to be good reason to believe that Julius II wanted the new building to provide the most tangible evidence of the Papal supremacy. Throughout all his somewhat tortuous diplomacy, he maintained the traditional principle of the supremacy of the spiritual over the temporal power, and there are paintings in the Stanze which relate to this, just as the Sistine

Chapel was decorated with the Arch of Constantine as a symbol of the Donation of Constantine, at the command of Julius II's uncle, Sixtus IV. The urgency of some of these political claims lies probably in the Turkish conquest of Constantinople in 1453, when it seemed that the Eastern Roman Empire lapsed to Julius as the successor to the Western Roman Empire. Julius became, therefore, both successor to St. Peter, whose tomb had been covered by the old basilica erected by the Emperor Constantine, and to Constantine himself in his Imperial capacity.

Bramante's task must thus have been conditioned by a number of factors of a non-architectural kind which imposed upon him the need to provide a building grand enough to commemorate the tomb of the Apostle and the heritage of ancient Rome, together with the need to provide a building which had two distinct liturgical functions. The basilica type evolved by Constantine himself was known from the Lateran and old St. Peter's in Rome and was, of course, something entirely new in Christian church building. After 313 it became necessary to provide large halls for a congregation and the Imperial building-type was therefore adapted to this purpose. In this sense Constantine played a very real part in the design of old St. Peter's. Even more important, however, was the fact that Constantine erected the building to commemorate the spot where he believed St. Peter was buried; and there is a far older tradition of Christian church building connected with martyria, which themselves derived their form from ancient mausolea. These martyria were centrally planned buildings, often quite small, which commemorated some sacred place, or contained some particular relic; unlike basilicas, they were not intended for congregational use. Constantine himself built one such centrally planned church in Rome, Santa Costanza, of about 324–326, but he also built two important churches in the Holy Land itself soon after the Eastern Empire fell to him in 324. These, the Church of the Nativity in Bethlehem and the Church of the Holy Sepulchre in Jerusalem, are both referred to in early sources as martyria, but the essential thing is that, because of the attraction of these places for pilgrims, it became necessary to make them large enough to contain crowds and to organize liturgical functions. These two buildings have, therefore, the same architectural form as old St. Peter's in that they consist of a combination of a basilica with a centrally planned martyrium, and the recent excavations under St. Peter's have shown conclusively that there was a very marked break between the nave and the transept of old St. Peter's, sharply distinguishing the martyrium part from the congregational part. Contrary to general belief, old

---

1. Compare the usage in the Epistle for the fourth Sunday after Epiphany (Romans 13:8–10): in hoc verbo instauratur: Diliges proximum tuum. The Authorized Version translates as 'comprehended'.

St. Peter's was not the general model for Early Christian churches, because of this unique feature. These three churches, the two in the Holy Land and old St. Peter's, can therefore be regarded as a special type which one might call an extended central plan, and it would seem that at the very beginning of Christianity as a state religion there were pure basilicas, pure central plans, and these combined versions, of which the first was old St. Peter's. Later, a somewhat similar extended central plan was to be used by Justinian for Santa Sophia in Constantinople, but this may have been due to the antecedent building by Constantine himself, and it certainly seems that Santa Sophia was not a martyrium in the accepted sense of the word. The plan may have been adopted for convenience in housing a large congregation, because the fourth-century church at Tebessa in North Africa also consisted of two parts with a centrally planned martyrium, in this case juxtaposed to a basilica. The type of central plan at Tebessa is, however, relevant since it is practically identical with the small church of St. Martin which now lies beneath one of the piers of new St. Peter's; and both these designs are very close in type to the Greek cross plan obtained by duplicating the Parchment Plan. Another very close approximation is provided by the plan of the Church of the Apostles at Ani in the Caucasus, which was destroyed in 1031.

It seems inconceivable that Bramante's Greek cross plan could have been directly influenced by a church in North Africa or a church that had already been a ruin for five centuries in the Caucasus. The extremely close approximation of forms can best be explained as the persistence of a type developed by Roman and Byzantine architects, deliberately re-used by Bramante as the expression of more than a thousand years of tradition.

The direct Byzantine influence in Italy came, as far as Bramante was concerned, from three sources. In the first place, in Bramante's day, there were a great many churches in Milan itself which must have been semi-Byzantine in their design and decoration, although none now exists in its original form. Most of the seventh- and eighth-century churches have either been destroyed completely or were so rebuilt in the late sixteenth and seventeenth centuries that they are now unrecognizable, but there is at least one building, the basilica of San Lorenzo, which still exists in a form not too distant from that in which Bramante knew it. This, however, is not Byzantine in the strict sense of the word since it dates, in all probability, from the fourth century. It is therefore a building which Bramante would, quite properly, have considered to be Imperial Roman, and he would have contrasted this with the Eastern Byzantine types which, he must have realized, were considerably later. The second source of Byzantine influence in Italy is the complex of buildings in Ravenna, which have remained almost unchanged. So far as we know, however, the buildings of Ravenna were not famous in the sixteenth century, and there is no direct evidence that Bramante ever went there. Neither is there any evidence that he ever visited Venice, but St. Mark's is by far the largest and most splendid Byzantine building in Italy and it seems likely that Bramante may have known it at first hand or at least knew it by repute. The building derives from the Church of the Apostles in Constantinople which is now lost, but is known to have been built by Justinian in the sixth century. From the point of view of St. Peter's, the importance of St. Mark's lies in the fact that it was large, famous, and venerable—and it consisted of a Greek cross plan surmounted by domes. There is also a narthex at the west end which gives the church an axial direction. The domes, it is true, are five in number though unequal in size, but the general impression of the church is that of a domical building, and there seems no reason to suppose that this domical tradition was not present to Bramante's mind, the more so as his own design approximates much more closely to the Church of Sta Sophia itself. There are two ways in which Bramante could have known with a considerable degree of accuracy what Sta Sophia looked like. The first of these, which there is every reason to assume he knew, is the sketch-book (the Barberini Codex) by Giuliano da Sangallo which is now in the Vatican. This contains two reasonably accurate representations of Sta Sophia, with a plan and a section of the church made presumably from drawings imported by somebody like Ciriaco d'Ancona (who was in Constantinople in 1444). Giuliano da Sangallo certainly never went to Constantinople, but his sketch-book contains drawings of a number of classical buildings, most of which he had seen himself, while others, such as Sta Sophia, seem to have been copied from earlier drawings. So far as we know, Giuliano's sketch-book has always been in Rome and it is possible to assume, therefore, that Bramante knew these two drawings or the drawings on which they were based. There is excellent evidence for an interest in Sta Sophia at this time, not only as a symbol of the Christian Eastern Empire, but also as a building since it is specifically mentioned by the *operai* of Pavia Cathedral in August 1487, when they wrote to Cardinal Sforza in Rome specifically declaring that they hoped to rebuild Pavia Cathedral in the same form as those of the most famous Roman churches, or Sta Sophia at Constantinople: '. . . conferre possit cum aliis pulcherrimis Romae Sacris Aedibus atque vel in primis cum illo Sanctae Sophiae Constantinopolis celeberrimo omnium Templo cujus instar illud figuratum invenire posse speramus . . .' In the following year, Bramante was officially consulted about a revision of this project, which would indicate that he must have been aware of their desires, and, therefore, of the general shape of Sta Sophia itself. Apart from these two drawings and any others that he might have known, there is the famous quotation from *The Buildings of Justinian* by Procopius, which was written about 560 or very shortly afterwards.

> . . . A structure of masonry is built up from the ground so that it forms the shape of half a circle, which those who are skilled in such matters call a half-cylinder. . . . The upper part of this structure rises, fitted to the adjoining parts of the building, marvellous in its grace, but by reason of the seeming insecurity of its composition altogether terrifying. For it seems somehow to float in the air on no firm basis, but to be poised aloft to the peril of those inside it. . . . And in the centre of the church stand four piers, two on the North side and two on the South, opposite and equal to each other, each pair having between them just four columns. The piers are composed of huge stones joined together . . . and rising to a great height. . . . From these spring four arches which rise over the four sides of a square, and their ends come together in pairs and are made fast to each other on top of these piers, while the other portions rise and soar to an infinite height. Upon the crowns of the arches rests a circular structure, cylindrical in shape. . . . And upon this circle rests the huge spherical dome which makes the structure exceptionally beautiful. Yet it seems not to rest upon solid masonry, but to cover the space with its golden dome suspended from Heaven. . . . The whole ceiling is overlaid with pure gold, which adds glory to the beauty, yet the light reflected from the stones prevails, shining out in rivalry with the gold. And there are two stoa-like colonnades, one on each side, not separated in any way from the structure of the church itself, but actually making the effect of its width greater . . . while in height they are less than the interior of the building . . . they have nothing to distinguish them, nor do they differ from one another in any way, but their very equality serves to beautify the church, and their similarity to adorn it.

The description is comparatively detailed; that is to say, it represents an attempt by a man who had no knowledge of architecture to give a clear account of a complicated building. In fact, it is probable that no-one, not even Bramante, could have made a convincing reconstruction on Procopius's description alone. Yet if this description is read in conjunction with the two drawings in the Sangallo Codex a very fair idea can be obtained of the church as it was; and, above all, the enthusiasm of Procopius's description makes it seem a different kind of building from anything which would have been familiar in the west. On top of this enthusiasm for the fame of the building and its great antiquity there was the fact that Julius II must have been fully aware of the importance of Sta Sophia as a symbol of the Orthodox Church and of its tradition going back to the beginnings of the Eastern Roman Empire.

The Eastern Empire was, however, only one element, since the tradition of the Western church was paramount in the mind of Julius II, and the tradition of Western Roman architecture was the only one available to Bramante. From sheer force of circumstances he had to base himself upon Western Roman constructional methods in so far as he could interpret them from the existing remains, but there is also every reason to suppose that the combination of Eastern and Western elements was deliberate and symbolical. There is a persistent tradition that Bramante expressed the desire to rebuild St. Peter's in the form of 'the dome of the Pantheon over the vaults of the Temple of Peace'. In essence this story may well be true, once more on two levels. Firstly, the Pantheon had, since the seventh century, been a Christian church under the name of Sta Maria ad Martyres. The symbolism would thus be basically that of a dome—the symbol of Heaven—based on the martyrs, and standing on a substructure formed by the Pax Romana. The Temple of Peace is, of course, what is known to us as the Basilica of Maxentius, which was completed by Constantine immediately after his victory over Maxentius; and in fact it seems to have had no connection with the genuine Temple of Peace, although this identification was certainly normal in the sixteenth century (as may be seen in Serlio) and seems to have persisted until the nineteenth century.

On another level, the Pantheon was the only surviving classical building in perfect preservation—this had been ensured by its consecration as a church in 609—but of the other remains of antiquity the Basilica of Maxentius was one of the most impressive, along with the Baths of Diocletian and the remains of the Baths of Caracalla. Judging from the illustrations given by Serlio and Palladio, and the engravings made in the sixteenth century by Dupérac and others, the Basilica of Maxentius was one of the best preserved of Roman antiquities. If the scale of these two prototypes is also taken into account, it will be seen that Bramante's ambition was very great. In actual fact, the dome of the Pantheon is 140 feet in diameter, some three feet more than St. Peter's as built. San Lorenzo in Milan was again a model but on a smaller scale, the width of the dome of San Lorenzo in Bramante's day being less than 100 feet. The architectural or formal elements of New St. Peter's were thus intended to be basically Roman, whether of the Western or Eastern Empires, and it is perfectly licit to argue that Sta Sophia, completed in 537, was itself a Roman building; even though the architects are known to have been Anthemius of Tralles and Isidore of Miletus.

The exact importance of the Roman and Lombard buildings which Bramante had known and studied before 1500 can perhaps never be completely evaluated, since San Lorenzo is one of the few remaining in anything like its original state. Nevertheless, the St. Peter's medal of 1506 shows strong Milanese influence, particularly in the two minaret-like towers which can be paralleled in Milanese buildings such as the Portinari Chapel, as well as in the designs by Filarete for the Hospital, or in the theoretical drawings by Leonardo. Leonardo's drawings are, indeed, of primary importance since it is likely that his theoretical expositions of the Greek cross plan and of a section built up of half-domes clustered round a dome over a drum may well reach back to Florence Cathedral and forward to Bramante's early designs for St. Peter's.

It seems likely that, at some stage, perhaps even before 1506, Bramante made a wooden model of one of the early projects for St. Peter's following the precedent of Pavia. This model may have been used by Caradosso for his Foundation Medal, and it underlies the drawing in the recently-discovered sketch-book by Bramante's assistant Menicantonio. The sketch-book has an inscription including the date 1513, the year before Bramante's death, but it was evidently continued for several years after that. It is likely, therefore, that the highly detailed drawing of the west end and the section records, with some accuracy, the lost wooden model. Further light on the shape of the plan and the directional emphasis given by the two campanili can perhaps be obtained from the church of San Biagio at Montepulciano. This was the masterpiece of Antonio da Sangallo the Elder and was built between 1518 and 1545 to mark the site of a miracle: in other words, it was a martyrium. The church has an extremely interesting plan which is internally that of a Greek cross with a dome over the centre, but externally has an apse at the east end and two detached campanili at the west end giving an external orientation opposed to the complete symmetry of the interior. Both the actual shapes and the subtlety of this contrast in the dispositions recall Bramante and

we know nothing else by Antonio the Elder comparable with this as a design. There is at the same time a connection with the model for St. Peter's made by Antonio the Younger long after Bramante's death, but which probably contains some at least of the original forms intended by Bramante.

At some point, therefore, the project for St. Peter's was for a building with an internal Greek cross plan without any orientation, an external orientation with two campanili at the entrance and a dome as the dominating feature. This was essentially a Lombard type of building, though expressed in terms which were almost equally Eastern and Western Roman. We do not know how extensive Bramante's knowledge of Roman Imperial architecture was, particularly in the first five or six years of his stay in Rome, but to judge from the Memorandum presented to Pope Leo X almost immediately after Bramante's death, it may have been surprisingly precise. It seems very likely that Bramante provided the greater part of the background knowledge which underlies this Memorandum, whether or not it was actually written by Raphael or Castiglione. The assumption that by 1505–1506 Bramante had a considerable knowledge of Late Roman architecture makes it particularly important to regard such buildings as the Romanesque church of San Fedele at Como, or the Church of the Holy Sepulchre at Milan, with some caution. We do, however, know that both these buildings with their trilobate eastern ends had some influence on the early designs for St. Peter's and that Bramante must have considered them as buildings which, however remotely, had a connection with earlier and more important works. We know, for example, that the Church of the Holy Sepulchre in Milan was a copy of its famous prototype in Jerusalem,[2] and that Leonardo da Vinci regarded it as a building of sufficient importance for him to make a recognizable plan, inscribed with its name. This copying of an actual building is very rare indeed in Leonardo's architectural designs.

Leonardo's MS. B contains several designs based on the type of church with a centrally planned east end and a long nave which derives, on the one hand from Florence Cathedral, and on the other from the Holy Sepulchre type. These theoretical drawings have, therefore, great importance in the genesis of St. Peter's and, at the same time, they would seem to show that the plans sometimes attributed to Peruzzi and Raphael are to be found in Leonardo about 1489, and must therefore have been introduced into St. Peter's by Bramante rather than by Peruzzi or Raphael acting on their own.

2. Itself known (approximately) from fifteenth-century woodcuts in e.g. Breydenbach's *Reise ins Heilige Land*, Mainz, 1486.

Some further deductions can reasonably be made from the Tempietto built by Bramante in the courtyard of S. Pietro in Montorio, on a spot which traditionally marks the site of the crucifixion of St. Peter. The dedicatory inscription gives the date of the building as 1502, and, by comparison with the Doric cloister in Milan of the 1490's it is clear that, in some three years, Bramante's style had become even more classical and that he had made an intensive study of ancient Roman buildings, as well as absorbing the peculiar qualities of travertine, which does not lend itself to the decorative style so prevalent in the North. Unfortunately, the full design for San Pietro in Montorio was never completed, but we have the Tempietto itself in almost perfect condition, and the original layout is known to us from the plan reproduced by Serlio. The essential point is made at once by the fact that the church is a martyrium in the strictest sense. It is far too small for congregational use, since it holds about four or five people at most, and in any case the large church of San Pietro is no more than twenty feet away. Because it is a martyrium, we would expect to find it based on early Christian centrally planned churches; and it is in fact a combination of the design for a part of San Satiro in Milan (which was itself based on San Lorenzo), with the original peristyle form of Constantine's Sta Costanza of c. 324. There are also deliberate reminiscences, in the elevation, of pagan Roman temples such as the one near the Tiber ('Mater Matuta'), or even the Temple of the Sibyl at Tivoli.

In the years immediately following 1506 Bramante and his assistants seem to have designed several churches which can reasonably be regarded as experiments directed towards the solution either of formal or of static problems, the results of which could be applied on the grand scale of St. Peter's itself. These experiments include S. Eligio, SS. Celso e Giuliano, and S. Biagio, all in Rome; the church at Todi, which was certainly built after Bramante's death, but may nevertheless be a practical application of one of his ideas; and, in addition to these buildings, we can probably include the architectural backgrounds in Raphael's *School of Athens* and *Heliodorus*. Obviously, the conclusions to be drawn from these buildings and paintings must be tentative, but features which can be shown to be common to all or most of them have a presumptive claim to be regarded as features current in Bramante's immediate circle in the last ten years of his life.

Unfortunately, the two most important buildings, SS. Celso e Giuliano and S. Biagio, have been lost, in the sense that one has been destroyed and the other so much rebuilt that it is almost impossible to regard it in its present form as having anything to do with Bramante. We have, however, a certain amount of evidence which allowed Giovannoni to reconstruct the plan and section of both churches with some accuracy. Since Giovannoni, one very important new piece of evidence has come to light—the Menicantonio sketchbook. The drawings by Menicantonio show that Giovannoni's reconstruction of SS. Celso e Giuliano is probably wrong in two important points: the Menicantonio drawing shows that the plan consisted of a salient curve emerging from the flat plane of the walls, whereas the Giovannoni restoration had only parallel flat planes. Thus, the Giovannoni restoration resembles the Parchment Plan, whereas Menicantonio's version is closer to the shape of St. Peter's as given by Menicantonio himself in his two-scale plan, the form with the salient curve being that once associated with Peruzzi's design. Secondly, the Menicantonio drawing shows a narthex which converts the design once more into an extended central plan. We should not, however, necessarily conclude from this that Giovannoni was wrong and is simply to be corrected in the light of the information now available. It is, in fact, highly probable that these two points were the very points at issue, and that the presence of the rounded side and the narthex in some of the projects for St. Peter's may have come about as a modification of the original designs for SS. Celso e Giuliano. In other words, it would seem as though the tentative nature of the St. Peter's drawings may well be paralleled by equally tentative designs for the experimental churches. In the section of SS. Celso e Giuliano it can be seen quite clearly that the basic form is very similar to the idea of the Basilica of Constantine, with a Pantheon dome above it. Giovannoni's reconstruction of S. Biagio shows rather similar ideas. It is, however, sharply distinguished from SS. Celso e Giuliano in that the weight of the dome is carried on an octagon very reminiscent of Florence Cathedral; and it may well be that this arose from the difficulty experienced, even on the small scale of SS. Celso e Giuliano, in carrying a solid dome on four rather feeble supports. Apart from this basic difficulty, the type of dome is similar to that at SS. Celso e Giuliano, and the vaulted bays of the main part of the church are again close to the traditional Roman coffered type known to us in the Basilica of Constantine and in more recent times in Bramante's own work in Milan.

One of the drawings for St. Peter's (Uffizi A. 23), perhaps by the hand of Peruzzi, shows a remarkable similarity to this type of plan. It certainly does not represent S. Biagio as it is much too long, yet, on the other hand, the narthex columns would have presented great problems on the scale of St. Peter's. The essential fact is that both churches and sectional drawing represent an extended central plan with a narthex at the entrance and a dome clearly based on that of the Pantheon. Put in other terms, this would represent the dome of a martyrium, Sta Maria ad Martyres, supported on the substructure of the Temple of Peace, and it would then be necessary to reconstruct the early sixteenth-century view, both of the Pantheon and of the Basilica of Constantine, and to see them in terms of a martyrium and the pagan, antique, Temple of Peace. The Serlio plate of the Templum Pacis is particularly important because it represents the plan of the Basilica of Constantine as a triconchos with a nave at one end. We know from excavation that this is wrong, but the significant fact is that the sixteenth-century version is far closer to the projects for St. Peter's or S. Biagio, and even resembles the type of central plan represented by the destroyed church of S. Martino below New St. Peter's. Furthermore, the Pantheon itself seems, early in the sixteenth century, to have retained some of the remains of the Baths of Agrippa, nothing of which is now visible.

There is, however, a drawing by Palladio in the Royal Institute of British Architects showing his reconstruction of the whole area. It is very probable that this drawing went beyond the evidence available to Palladio and was probably altogether too optimistic as a reconstruction, but it is certainly worth noting that Palladio shows halls of a type similar to Sta Sophia with half-domes abutting against flat walls, as well as a large central space with an extended central plan which has similarities to some, at any rate, of the drawings connected with St. Peter's.

*   *   *

The Memorandum on Ancient Rome speaks of Bramante as the restorer of the antique style, but he was more than that. Grabar has called Old St. Peter's 'the first martyrium' and the Foundation Medal of the new basilica has the inscription—which was Bramante's brief—*Templi Petri Instauracio*. He was trying to do several things at once, for his designs were intended to be interpreted on the Iconographical level as expressing the two main types of Early Christian church building, united in a unique way to form the Basilica-Martyrium of the Prince of the Apostles; on the Historical level, as the Temple of Peace crowned by the dome of the Martyrs, just as Christianity had grown out of paganism, and as a Classical Revival, using the same forms as the Pantheon and the Temple of Peace and to be judged by the rules of Latinity, just as he was also to be judged on purely Formal grounds —on the beauty of his forms considered in themselves. He was also concerned with structural problems, which no-one else of his generation could even begin to face; problems of designing a building in the Eastern Roman manner with only the Western Imperial tradition before his eyes. Finally, the building had a Political significance, like the Stanze, as an anti-conciliar gesture of the Papal supremacy and an assertion of the succession to Constantine (it is significant that there are two representations of the Two Swords, the Spiritual and Temporal Powers, in the Stanze).

The idea that New St. Peter's can be anything but 'pagan, proud and unholy' may still be strange to some people, but Durandus in the thirteenth century, and Krautheimer and Wittkower in the twentieth should have convinced everybody that there is such a thing as architectural symbolism. This essay can best be concluded by two quotations from the scholar to whom it is dedicated; they come from his seminal *Principles*:

> In retrospect, it would almost seem an historical necessity that the mother church of Christianity, St. Peter's, was planned by Bramante, and planned as a centralized building. One might even go so far as to say that in the year 1505 the holiness and singularity of this church could not have been expressed by any other type of plan. . . .

> Renaissance architecture, like every great style of the past, was based on a hierarchy of values culminating in the absolute values of sacred architecture. We maintain, in other words, that the forms of the Renaissance church have symbolical value or, at least, that they are charged with a particular meaning which the pure forms as such do not contain.

LUDWIG H. HEYDENREICH

Bramante's "Ultima Maniera"

Die St. Peter-Studien Uff. arch. 8 v und 20

Lange Zeit haben—im Anschluß an Geymüllers epochales St. Peter-Werk und seine Kontroversen mit Jovanovic und Redtenbacher—die beiden Rötelstudien Uff. arch. 8 verso und 20 (Abb. 1, 5) als eigenhändige Entwürfe Bramante's gegolten.[1] Als vorbereitende Studien für dessen sogenannten zweiten Plan, der dem Baubeginn im April 1506 unmittelbar voranging, sind beide Zeichnungen als eindrucksvolle Zeugnisse der "ultima maniera" des Meisters gewürdigt worden, bis Dagobert Frey in seinen "Bramante-Studien" (1915) erneut und mit subtiler Argumentation die Autorschaft Bramante's anzweifelte[2]; er setzte die Entstehung beider Zeichnungen aus stilistischen Gründen um ein Jahrzehnt später, d.h. um 1514/15 an und wies sie dem Sohn des Giuliano da Sangallo Francesco (geb. 1494) zu. Eine starke Stütze seiner Zuschreibung sah Frey dabei darin, daß bekanntlich auf der Gegenseite von Uff. arch. 8 (Abb. 2) ein St. Peterentwurf von der Hand Giuliano's gezeichnet ist, den Frey in dieser Untersuchung in die gleiche Zeit datiert, d.h. in die kurze Spanne, in der Giuliano 1514 Mit-Bauleiter von St. Peter war: so bietet sich nach Frey eine zwanglose Erklärung dafür, daß der Sohn Francesco, damals als Zwanzigjähriger in der Werkstatt des Vaters tätig, die Rötelskizze auf der Gegenseite ausgeführt habe.

Seitdem sind über Entstehungszeit und Autorschaft beider Blätter viele Meinungen geäußert worden, die sich im wesentlichen nach den Anhängern Geymüller's oder Frey's scheiden lassen; hierbei ist jedoch die wichtige Selbstberichtigung, die Dagobert Frey 1924 mit seiner Studie über Giuliano da Sangallo's St. Peter-Pläne in dieser Frage vornahm,[3] u.E. nicht genügend beachtet worden. Wir kommen sogleich darauf zurück.

Gegenüber dieser ersten, bereits eine Generation zurückliegenden Diskussionsphase[4] ist in den letzten zehn Jahren das Problem erneut aufgegriffen und unter verschiedenen Aspekten behandelt worden.[5] Die in diesen Studien vorgebrachten Einzelargumente und -fakten fordern nun u.E. förmlich zu einer subsumierenden Prüfung auf, da sie bei rechter Bezugsetzung und kritischer Auswertung eine gleichsam logische Schlußfolgerung zulassen. Auf sie hinzuführen soll im Folgenden versucht werden.

Unsere "Revision" muß ihren Ausgang von der Argumentation Dagobert Frey's nehmen. Der Schreiber dieser Zeilen gesteht, daß er sich bei aller Bewunderung, die er sonst den "Bramante-Studien"—noch heute eine Propädeutik architekturgeschichtlicher Methode—entgegenbringt, gerade von den Beweisführungen zu den uns hier beschäftigenden Blättern Uff. 8 und 20 nie hat überzeugen lassen können. Gehindert haben ihn zunächst zwei Überlegungen grundsätzlicher Art: 1) daß es unmöglich erscheint, Zeichnungen von so überragender Qualität und so starker Individualität wie Uff. 8 v—und in ihrer Zugehörigkeit auch Uff. 20—einem eben Zwanzigjährigen zuzutrauen, der noch in den Anfängen seiner Berufsausbildung stand, und dessen sonstige von Frey herangezogenen Zeichnungen keineswegs die Zuschreibung von Uff. 8 und 20 an ihn rechtfertigen; und 2) daß die Thematik beider Blätter in ihrer eminenten Bedeutung für die Entwicklung des St. Peter-Plans in der Bramante'schen Ära von Frey verkannt, bzw. mißinterpretiert wurde.

Angesichts dieser Zweifel bleibt nur der Weg, das ganze Problem noch einmal soweit aufzurollen, wie es erforderlich ist, um andere Schlüsse vorzubereiten.[6]

1. H. von Geymüller, Die ursprünglichen Entwürfe für St. Peter in Rom. 2 Bde. Paris und Wien 1875, 1880.—L. A. Jovanovits, Forschungen über den Bau der Peterskirche. Wien 1877.—R. Redtenbacher, Baugeschichtl. Mitteilungen an der Handzeichnungensammlung in den Uffizien. In: Z.f. bildende Kunst IX (1874), 261 ff.—Ders. Rezension des Geymüller-Werks in Z.f. bildende Kunst XIX (1884), S. 163.
2. D. Frey, Bramantes St. Peter-Entwurf und seine Apokryphen. Bramante-Studien. Hrsg. v. H. Egger. Bd. I, Wien 1915, S. 11 ff.
3. D. Frey, Ein unbekannter Entwurf Giuliano da Sangallo's für die Peterskirche in Rom. In: "Studi e Testi", 38, Roma 1924. Miscellanea Francesco Ehrle vol. II, p. 432–48.

4. H. Wölfflin, Renaissance und Barock. Bearb. u. Kommentar von Hans Rose. München 1926[4], p. 254 u. 257, Anm.—Theobald Hofmann, Entstehungsgeschichte des St. Peter in Rom. Zittau 1928.—Hans Kauffmann, Rezension v. Th. Hofmann in Repert. f. Kunstwiss. 50, 1929, p. 170–4.—A. Venturi, Storia dell'Arte Italiana. Vol. XI, I, Milano 1938, p. 105 ff.
5. F. Graf Wolff Metternich, Gedanken z. Baugeschichte der Peterskirche im 15. u. 16. Jhdt. Festschrift f. Otto Hahn z. 8. März 1954. II, S. 6/7.—Ders., San Lorenzo in Mailand, Sankt Peter in Rom. "Kunstchronik" 15, 1962, p. 285 f.—O. H. Förster, Bramante. Wien-München (1956) passim, bes. p. 279 ff.
6. Dabei beschränken wir uns mit voller Absicht auf die Blätter 8 und 20, weil uns ein Wiederaufgreifen der Diskussion

Merkwürdigerweise scheint allgemein übersehen worden zu sein, daß uns die erste kritische Handhabe Dagobert Frey selbst bietet, der in seinem bereits erwähnten, 1924 erschienenen Beitrag zur Ehrle-Festschrift den sicheren Beweis erbringt, daß die Zeichnung des Giuliano di Sangallo auf Uff. 8 r nicht erst 1514, sondern bereits 9 Jahre früher entstanden ist. Sangallos Plan schließt sich stilistisch und motivisch auf das engste mit zwei weiteren Entwürfen seiner Hand, die sich heute in der Wiener Albertina befinden,[7] zu einer Gruppe zusammen. Diese drei Pläne können nicht erst in der (kurzen) Phase der offiziellen Amtspartnerschaft Giulianos mit Bramante (1514) entworfen worden sein, sondern lassen erkennen, daß sie—aus Anregungen von Uff. 1 (Abb. 6) entwickelt— in der Übergangsphase zwischen Bramante's erstem und zweitem Projekt, d.h. also genauer zwischen August 1505 und April 1506 ausgearbeitet worden sein müssen. Sangallos Anwesenheit in Rom für diesen Zeitraum ist mehrfach belegt.[8] Alle Umstände sprechen dafür, daß Sangallo und Bramante—konkurrierend oder in gegenseitigem Einvernehmen—von ihren Plänen Kenntnis hatten und sie mutmaßlich sogar miteinander besprachen.[9]

Unter diesem Aspekt muß konsequenter Weise auch die Frage nach der zeitlichen Bestimmung von Uff. 8 verso neu gestellt werden.[10] Es ist ein großes Verdienst von Otto H. Förster, darauf hingewiesen zu haben, daß Uff. 8 verso aus dem einfachen Grunde nicht erst 1514—also 9 Jahre nach Entstehung des Sangalloplans—angefertigt sein kann, weil um diese Zeit ja der St. Peterbau bereits in vollem Gang war und die Form der Vierungspfeiler—die auf 8 verso erst erarbeitet wird, schon feststand. Um 1514 wäre also das Hauptthema von 8 verso völlig sinnlos.[11]

Weiterhin ist Graf Wolff Metternich die Feststellung zu danken, daß Uff. 8 verso eine Transparenz-Pause von recto ist, dergestalt, daß die Rötelskizze auf recto unter Nützung der bei einem Gegen-das-Licht-Halten des Blattes durchscheinenden Zeichnung von recto angelegt wurde.[12] Wir haben nun auf Grund der gleichen Beobachtung zwei Transparenz-Photoaufnahmen des Blattes (Abb. 3, 4) herstellen lassen, die es ermöglichen, die Variationen genau zu determinieren, die der Zeichner der Rötelskizze vorgenommen hat.[13] Sangallos Plan auf 8 recto hält sich eng an seinen, ganz ähnlich bereits in den zwei Albertina-Zeichnungen entwickelten "Quadrat-Typus"—d.h. die Einbindung der Außenfront in ein geschlossenes Viereck. Innerhalb der 3 Varianten ist die auf Uff. 8 recto entwickelte—wie aus der Bildung der vier starken Vierungspfeiler ersichtlich wird—die reifste Form.[14]

Dieser Concetto Sangallos wurde von dem Zeichner der Rötelskizze auf verso in genialer Weise umgeformt und weitergeführt. Die hier auftretenden wesentlichen Neuerungen erscheinen nun auch—mutatis mutandis —auf der Zeichnung Uff. arch. 20 und sind vor allem —wieder mutatis mutandis—bei der tatsächlichen Aufführung des Baus berücksichtigt: es sind die drei Hauptmotive, die den zweiten Plan Bramantes charakterisieren: (1) die "Modellierung" der verstärkten Vierungspfeiler, (2) die hieraus resultierende Einführung der Pseudo-Umgänge nebst Vereinfachung und Vergrößerung der Nebenzentren, sowie (3) die Andeutung einer Erweiterung des Zentralbaus zum Langhaus.

Mehrere dieser Varianten auf 8 verso sind nur durch absichtsvolles Ändern von Formen auf recto motiviert (während sie im umgekehrten Falle unerklärbar blieben): z.B. die wiederholte, freihändig gezeichnete, gleichsam experimentierende Modifizierung der Nebenkuppeln (besonders rechts oben und unten); ferner die Alternativlösungen an den Vierungspfeilern zum Langhaus hin; die oberen Pfeiler zum Chor hin bewahren im wesentlichen die Form von recto. Überhaupt lassen die kraftvoll dezidiert geführten Linien spezielle "Interessenzentren" des Zeichners erkennen —etwa an den Nischen der unteren Vierungspfeiler

über die übrigen von Geymüller (und seinen Anhängern) diesen zwei Zeichnungen zugeordneten Studien—Uff. arch. 3 r/ v, 104 und 7945 r/v—erst möglich, d.h. nutzbringend zu sein scheint, wenn Uff. 8 und 20 zeitlich und stilistisch eindeutig bestimmt sind.
7. Die besten Abbildungen bei O. H. Förster a.a.O.: Albertina, ehem xxx, Nr. 791 (Abb. 93), Nr. 790 (Abb. 102). Dazu Exkurs v, S. 278.
8. 1505, April, ist Giuliano (nach Condivi) bei der Beratung über die Aufstellung des Juliusgrabes beteiligt.—1505, 30. Mai, Zahlung für Arbeiten an der Engelsburg.—Das Datum MDV trägt Giulianos Entwurf für die Loggia der päpstlichen Bläser (Uff. arch. Nr. 203).—1506, 14. Januar: Besuch am Fundort des Laokoon. 1506, 2. Mai, Brief Michelangelos aus Florenz an Giul. da Sangallo in Rom. Quellennachweis bei G. Marchini, Giul. da Sangallo. Firenze 1943, p. 110.
9. So auch D. Frey (Miscellanea Ehrle, l.c., p. 443/4).
10. D. Frey übergeht oder verschleiert sie gleichsam, indem er einerseits (Misc. Ehrle, p. 443) zwar andeutet, daß recto und verso gleichzeitig, d.h. in unmittelbarer Abfolge entstanden sein müssen, es aber andererseits unterläßt, die sich hieraus ergebende Konsequenz auszusprechen, nämlich daß dann Francesco da Sangallo—damals elfjährig—als möglicher Autor ausscheidet.
11. O. H. Förster, Bramante l.c., p. 279 f.

12. Vgl. "Kunstchronik" 15 (1962), p. 285.—Auch Metternich kommt damit zu der "logischen" Datierung von 8 verso auf 1505/6.
13. Es ist mir ein Bedürfnis, der Leiterin des Handzeichnungskabinetts der Uffizien, Dott. ssa Anna Forlani sowie dem Photographen meinen aufrichtigen Dank für die große Bereitwilligkeit zu sagen, mit der sie auf meine Bitte eingegangen sind und sie in vollkommener Weise erfüllt haben.
14. Dieser engste Zusammenhang mit den Albertina-Entwürfen schließt auch die—wenngleich nur theoretisch bestehende— Möglichkeit aus, daß 8 recto nach verso entstanden ist. Außerdem hätte sich der mit Lineal und Zirkel sorgfältig als Reinzeichnung angelegte Entwurf schon rein technisch-praktisch gar nicht im Pausverfahren herstellen lassen.

oder den Kuppel-Kreisen—die nur als Variationen des mit Zirkel und Lineal konstruierten Sangallo-Plans verständlich werden.

Hauptthema der Studie 8 verso ist die Erweiterung des Zentralbaus zur Langkirche. Die Aufgabe, einen organischen Anschluß der fünf Schiffe an die Pfeiler des tetrastylen Baukörpers zu finden, wird mit der kühnen Lösung der Konchen-Umgänge bewältigt. In diesem Zusammenhang gewinnen nun die beiden Grundrisse, die wie Erinnerungsskizzen flüchtig auf das Blatt geworfen sind, entscheidende Bedeutung: es ist (oben) ein schematischer Plan von S. Lorenzo in Mailand,[15] der ganz in der gleichen "geometrisierten" Weise gezeichnet ist, wie wir dies aus mehreren Studien Leonardos kennen,[16] während (unten) der Mailänder Dom skizziert ist, auch dieser in der Zeichenweise (dünne durchgehende Linien als Unterzeichnung und darüber liegende Eintragung der Pfeiler und Mauerzüge) Leonardos Skizze im Codex SKM III, 55 v sehr verwandt.[17] Es ist evident, daß sich der Zeichner gerade diese beiden Bauten gleichsam "vergegenwärtigte", weil sie sich ihm als speziell geeignete Vorbilder für seine geplanten Bauerweiterungen anboten: San Lorenzo für die Konchen-Umgänge, der Dom für den Anschluß eines fünfschiffigen Langhauses an eine überkuppelte Vierung.[18]

Unsere Untersuchungen ergaben bisher, daß auf den

Blättern 8 recto und verso zwei Entwürfe für St. Peter vereinigt sind, die thematisch so eng aufeinander bezogen sind, daß sie beide *einer* Zeitphase, und zwar der um 1505/6 angehören müssen; für die Zeit um 1514 wären alle hier angestellten Erwägungen verspätet bezw. überholt.

Als nächstverwandte Studie muß nunmehr das Blatt Uff. arch. 20 (Abb. 5) herangezogen werden. Es hat die gleichen Themen zum Gegenstand wie 8 verso, indem die dort aufscheinenden Hauptgedanken auf einem maßgerechten Grundriß unter Berücksichtigung des gegebenen älteren Baubestandes weitergeführt und auf ihre praktische Realisierbarkeit hin "getestet" werden.[19] Form und Maße von Vierungspfeilern und Umgangsmauern werden aufeinander abzustimmen gesucht; die hieraus sich ergebende Vereinfachung der Nebenzentren wird detaillierter durchgestaltet (einschließlich der äußeren Eckräume). Für den Anschluß des Langhauses sind noch zwei Alternativlösungen erwogen: rechts ist das Bestreben ersichtlich, die fünf Schiffe der alten Basilika im neuen Raumbild zu erhalten; links wird hierauf verzichtet, und die Zeichnung läßt erkennen, daß dieser Lösung der Vorzug gegeben wird.

Wir können es in diesem Zusammenhang nicht auf uns nehmen, das Verhältnis von 8 verso zu 20 exakter zu bestimmen,[20] und müssen uns mit der Feststellung ihres engen Aufeinanderbezogenseins begnügen. Damit steht aber auch ihre zeitliche Zusammengehörigkeit ausser Zweifel: auch Uff. 20 muß wie Uff. 8 verso um 1505/6 entstanden sein. Vor allem spricht hierfür die Übereinstimmung des graphischen Stils, der sich—wo vergleichbar—im Duktus der freigezeichneten Linien zu erkennen gibt. Hierbei ist freilich einschränkend zu sagen, daß u.E. auf Uff. 20 zwei Hände unterschieden werden müssen und daß nur der Zeichner der kraftvolleren Strichführung mit dem von 8 verso identisch ist.[21]

Was die Thematik von Uff. 20 betrifft, möchten wir nochmals auf das u.E. zu Recht bestehende Argument Försters verweisen, daß Pfeilerstudien, wie sie in 8 v

---

15. Daß es sich, wie Graf Wolff-Metternich darlegt (Kunstchronik *l.c.*, p. 286) um die Grundrisse von S. Lorenzo und des Domes von Mailand handelt, steht auch für uns seit langem außer Frage.—Förster irrt, wenn er die Skizze auf S. Biagio bestimmt, dessen Plan weder tetrastyl angelegt ist noch Umgangs-Konchen aufzeigt. (Die Schriftzeile "Biagio vista col dattajio" muß einen anderen, noch zu ergründenden Sinn haben.)

16. Besonders zum Vergleich geeignet sind die Skizzen von S. Lorenzo auf fol. 271 v-d und 7 v-d (mit verblaßtem, kaum sichtbaren Grundriß zwischen dem perspektivischen Schnitt und dem quadratischen Plan r.o.) des Codex Atlanticus; desgl. Leonardos Entwurf für ein teatro da predicar (Ms. B. 55 recto), der aus dem Typus von S. Lorenzo entwickelt ist; schließlich die blasse Silberstift-Studie Ms. B. 57 verso, die genauso gezeichnet ist wie noch Antonio da Sangallo d.J. den St. Peterplan skizziert (Uff. arch. 824).—Vgl. auch C. Pedretti, A Chronology of Leonardo da Vinci's architectural studies after 1500, Genève 1962, p. 87/88 u. 93/94, der die Zeichnungen auf Codex Atlanticus 271 v-d aus technisch-graphologischen Gründen erst in die Zeit des römischen Aufenthalts Leonardos (1513/14) verweist.

17. Abbildung in der Facsimile-Edition der R. Commissione Vinciana, Il Codice Forster nel Victoria and Albert Museum (Roma 1930 ff., vol. III, p. fol. 55 verso; ferner in J. P. Richter-H. v. Geymüller, The Literary Work of Leonardo, 1939², II, pl. XCIX, 2 und in L. Firpo, Leonardo architetto ed urbanista. Torino 1963, p. 22.—H. Kauffmann (*l.c.*, p. 172) hielt den Grundriß auf 8 verso für eine toskanische Anlage in der Gattung von S. Spirito in Florenz, doch steht die Identifizierung mit dem Mailänder Dom außer Diskussion.

18. U.E. ist es kein Zufall, daß der Grundriß der Mailänder Doms auf 8 verso gerade in der Übergangszone zwischen Zentral- und Laufbau skizziert ist, während der Plan von S. Lorenzo am oberen Rand—also im Bereich der Konchen-Umgänge steht.

19. So auch G. Urban, Zum Neubau-Projekt von St. Peter unter Papst Nikolaus V. in: Festschrift für Harald Keller, Darmstadt 1963, p. 135 und 163, Anm. 22.

20. Unserer Überzeugung nach ist 20 die Fortführung von 8 verso, während Förster (*l.c.*, p. 243–8) das umgekehrte Verhältnis annimmt.—Eine Beweisführung würde nur unter Einbeziehung und genauer Auswertung der übrigen Zeichnungen der Gruppe (vgl. unsere Anm. 5) möglich sein, die wir uns für eine gesonderte Arbeit vorbehalten.

21. Die Angabe D. Frey's (Bramante-Studien *l.c.*, p. 11), daß auf Uff. 20 beim südöstlichen Pfeiler "unter den stark deckenden Strichen der Schlußfassung in zarten Strichen der ausgeführte Pfeiler Bramantes notiert ist", hält einer Nachprüfung am Original nicht stand. Förster (*l.c.*, p. 280) macht dieselbe Feststellung; auch dieses Argument erweist sich also für eine Spätdatierung (auf 1514) als nicht stichhaltig.

und 20 betrieben werden, für 1514—als die realen Kuppelpfeiler bereits in der Aufführung waren—jeden Sinn verlören; dagegen gewinnen sie ihre klare Geltung als vorbereitende Studien für die Wandlung von Plan 1 zu Plan 2 und sind hier von höchster Bedeutung.[22]

Da somit die Datierung von Uff. arch. 8 verso und 20 feststeht—sie ist nicht nur, wie wir wiederholen möchten, von Graf Wolff Metternich und Förster, sondern auch von Dagobert Frey selbst (1924) erwiesen—müssen wir in rein logischer Konsequenz anerkennen, daß auch der zeichnerische Stil beider Blätter für 1505/6 ein gegebenes Faktum ist.

Die Bemühungen Frey's, in den "Bramante-Studien" eine so weiche, zügig-modellierende Strichführung, wie sie in 8 verso zum Ausdruck kommt, als dem "Zeitstil" von 1505 widersprechend abzulehnen, basieren letztlich auf dem vorgefassten Bestreben, seine Zuweisung an Francesco da Sangallo zu begründen, die er—ex silentio—in seinem Aufsatz von 1924 dann selbst widerlegt.—Der Bestand an erhaltenen Zeichnungen zwischen 1495 und 1505 läßt es ohne weiteres zu, den graphischen Stil von 8 verso (und damit auch 20) in diese Zeitspanne einzubereichen. Leonardo's Giebelstudien in Rötel im Cod. SKM II, 22 r (um 1495), seine Skizzen der Cappella del Perdono in Urbino (Ms. L, fol. 73/74—1502), seine Villen-Fassade im Deckel-Vorsatzblatt des Vogelflugtraktats (1505) und schließlich die Entwürfe für den Sockel des Trivulziomonuments (Windsor 12353 und 12355, 1506/7) zeigen ganz ähnliche Tendenzen des Duktus, und auch Giuliano da Sangallo's Zeichenweise in diesem Zeitraum darf nicht auf die "harte, trockene, schematische", des stofflich-substanzielle nicht differenzierende Linienführung beschränkt werden, wie dies Dagobert Frey in seiner methodisch allzu antithetischen Argumentation als spezifische Eigenheit des Bramante-Stils um 1500 darstellt.[23]

Graf Wolff Metternich hat die Frage, wem 8 verso zuzuschreiben sei, offen gelassen, wiewohl er durch den Hinweis, Giuliano da Sangallo seien San Lorenzo und der Dom von seinem Aufenthalt in Mailand her vertraut gewesen, andeutet, daß er auch der Autor der Rötelstudie sein könne. Wir dagegen vertreten die Ansicht, daß der ganze Ideenkomplex von S. Peter, wie ihn Bramante zunächst in Uff. 1 und dann im veränderten zweiten Plan der Aufführung (1506) entwickelt, nur aus einer grandiosen Synthese lombardischer, toskanischer und römischer Bautraditionen entstehen konnte,[24] wobei u.E. gerade Uff. 8 verso die

entscheidendenden Elemente des Übergangs vom ersten zum zweiten Plan enthält und daher nicht sangalleske sondern bramanteske Charakteristica aufweist. Hinzu tritt die einzigartige künstlerische Potenz, die in der Zeichnung 8 verso spürbar wird: die geniale architektonische Konzeption und die überlegene, energiegeladene Sicherheit der Strichführung. Sangallo's St. Peter-Pläne bis 1514 lassen es u.E. nicht zu, ihm diese spontane Kraft zuzutrauen, die aus jeder Linie von 8 verso spricht.[25] Sein Partner in dieser, für den unmittelbar bevorstehenden Baubeginn entscheidenden Planungsphase war Bramante. Nachdem die zeitliche Ansetzung der Zeichnung um 1505/6 feststeht und nachdem alle in ihr—und Uff. 20—in Erscheinung tretenden Überlegungen in der späteren Aufführung des Baus Berücksichtigung finden, bleibt unserer Überzeugung nach keine andere und "schönere" Konsequenz, als zu Geymüllers Ansicht zurückzukehren und in diesen zwei Zeichnungen die Hand Bramantes zu erkennen.

Freilich, die in diesem zweiten Projekt für St. Peter erwogene kühne Idee blieb als Ganzheit am realen Bau unverwirklicht. Bramantes Plan, durch Einführung der Konchenumgänge den zentralen Chor als dominierende Raumgruppe des Gesamtbaues zu erhalten, scheiterte an der dezidierten Haltung des Papstes, der die Aufführung der Tribuna grande in der modifizierten Form bestimmte, wie sie in den anschliessenden Jahren auch gebaut wurde.[26] Graf Wolff Metternich hat eindringlich dargelegt, wie hart Bramante der Verzicht auf sein souveränes Projekt getroffen haben muß, über welch ungebrochene Kraft er aber dennoch verfügte, indem er imstande war, selbst die rigoros einschränkenden Vorschriften seines Bauherrn noch zu einem schöpferischen Kompromiss zu gestalten und dies in der unfaßlich knappen Zeitspanne von wenigen Monaten zwischen der Ablehnung des ersten Entwurfs und dem Baubeginn im April 1506.[27] In diese dramatische Phase gehören auch Uff. 8[r] und 20;[28] Beide Blätter spiegeln das Ringen um die Erhaltung einer großen Konzeption wieder und bezeugen damit die geistige Spannweite der "ultima maniera" des Meisters.

22. O. H. Förster, l.c., p. 280.
23. D. Frey, Bramante-Studien, l.c., p. 9, 12/13.—S.a. unsere Anm. 25.
24. L. H. Heydenreich, Zur Genesis des St. Peter-Plans von Bramante. "Forschungen und Fortschritte", x, 1934, S. 365 ff.

25. Wir kennen keine Zeichnung Giuliano's, die sich für einen stilistischen Vergleich mit Uff. 8 verso und 20 eignet. Zwar weisen die skizzenhaften Partien im Entwurf für die Loggia der päpstlichen Blässer (Uff. arch. 203) und manche Einzelheit seiner Strichführung besonders im Taccuino Senese (etwa fol. 7, fol. 8, fol. 33) entschieden über die von Dag. Frey etwas apodiktisch determinierte "Zeichenweise um 1505" hinaus, andererseits fehlt jedoch die Energiegeladenheit, die 8 verso kennzeichnet und auszeichnet.
26. Franz Graf Wolff Metternich, Bramantes Chor der Peterskirche zu Rom. "Römische Quartalschrift" 58 (1963), S. 271 ff.
27. Idem, l.c., p. 286.
28. Dies bestätigt auch wieder erneut Graf Wolff Metternich, l.c., p. 273, note 9.

NICOLAI RUBINSTEIN

Vasari's Painting of *The Foundation of Florence* in the Palazzo Vecchio

On 3 March 1563, Vasari presented Duke Cosimo de' Medici with his first scheme for the decoration of the ceiling of the Salone del Cinquecento in the Palazzo Vecchio: he had been asked by him to begin work *questo anno presente*, which according to the Florentine calendar was ending three weeks later, so he was just in time.[1] In January, he had informed the duke that he and Vincenzo Borghini were busy preparing the *inventione del palco*, and would have it ready soon.[2] Throughout the work for the ceiling, as well as for the walls, Borghini remained chiefly responsible for the programme of the decoration,[3] although he consulted other learned men, such as Giovan Battista Adriani; and the duke himself took an active part in the discussions.[4] Borghini states in his testament of 1574 that Cosimo had commissioned from him 'la pittura della gran sala del Palazzo',[5] and Borghini's literary executors, who edited his *Discorsi* after his death, affirmed, in 1584, that 'aveva d'ordine del Duca divisato tutta la pittura'.[6]

The scheme for the paintings of the ceiling which Vasari sent to Cosimo on 3 March (Fig. 1)[7] combined descriptions of signal events in the history of Florence with representations of its districts, i.e. its *Quartieri* and *Gonfaloni*, and of its guilds. The original plan for the decoration of the Salone, devised soon after its completion in 1496, had been to cover its walls with paintings representing famous Florentine victories.[8]

These were not executed at the time, and their purpose, like that of the Great Hall itself, ceased to exist with the fall of the republican régime in 1512. The restoration of that régime in 1527, while once more bringing into its own the original function of the Hall, was too brief to affect its pictorial decoration, whose execution had to wait until Cosimo transferred his residence to the ancient Palace of the Signoria. But if his decision to choose subjects from Florence's history for the decoration followed the original plan, it did so on a much more ambitious scale, and with a different purpose. The representations of the battles of Cascina and Anghiari, in illustrating the victories of republican Florence over the Pisans and the Visconti,[9] would have aimed at arousing the patriotic sentiments of the members of the Great Council assembled in its Hall. No such response was any longer required, and it was therefore fitting that, in its final form, the decoration of the ceiling culminated, in its central panel, in the glorification of Duke Cosimo being crowned by a figure representing Florence.

This glorification of Cosimo did not, however, form part of the programme as presented to the duke in March 1563. According to this programme, the central panel was to contain 'Fiorenza in una Gloria celeste in somma Felicita'. Much space was allotted to representations of the *Gonfaloni*, which were derived from the ancient civic militia, and of the guilds. As Gunther Thiem has convincingly pointed out in his study of the various schemes for the ceiling, these survivals from Florence's republican past were not to Cosimo's taste; and in view of his criticisms, the first programme was revised.[10] Vasari may have presented the new version to the duke in the following month.[11] In the revised programme, the central panel is still meant to

1. *Der literarische Nachlass Giorgio Vasaris*, ed. K. Frey, (Munich, 1923–30), I, cccxcvii, p. 722.
2. *Ibid.*, I, ccclxxxix, p. 696 (20 January).
3. Cf. Frey, *ibid.*, p. 729. M. Barbi, 'Degli studi di Vincenzo Borghini sopra la storia e la lingua di Firenze', *Il Propugnatore*, nuova serie, II, 112 (1889), p. 13.
4. Frey, II, cdlxix, p. 123 (Vasari to Cosimo, 5 November 1564); cdlxxiv, p. 131 (Vasari to Don Giusti, 27 November 1564); cf. Frey, *ibid.*, p. 120. Borghini to Girolamo Mei, January (?) 1566, in Borghini, *Carteggio artistico inedito*, ed. A. Lorenzoni, I (Florence, 1912), pp. 55–56: 'dove infra gli altri ... [Cosimo] si degnò ch'intervenissi anch'io ... et sene tenne più volte lunghi ragionamenti et alla presentia di S.E. et indisparte fra noi'. See also below, pp. 65–66.
5. G. Gaye, *Carteggio degli artisti*, I (Florence, 1899), p. 386. Cf. A. Legrenzi, *Vincenzo Borghini* ... (Udine, 1910), p. 45.
6. Vincenzo Borghini, *Discorsi* (Florence, 1584–5), I, preface. See also below, p. 72.
7. Ed. Frey, I, p. 728.
8. See J. Wilde, 'The Hall of the Great Council of Florence', *Journal of the Warburg and Courtauld Institutes*, VII (1944),

pp. 78–81, and now Ch. A. Isermeyer, 'Die Arbeiten Leonardos und Michelangelos für den grossen Ratssaal in Florenz', in *Studien zur toskanischen Kunst, Festschrift für Ludwig Heinrich Heydenreich* (Munich, 1964), pp. 83–130. Cf. Borghini to Mei, *loc. cit.*: Cosimo wanted that 'una parte [of the *pittura*] servisse a quello che fino nel tempo de' nostri Padri si era determinato, ciò era la Guerra di Pisa', etc.
9. Wilde, p. 80.
10. 'Vasaris Entwürfe für die Gemälde in der Sala Grande des Palazzo Vecchio zu Florenz', *Zeitschrift für Kunstgeschichte*, XXIII (1960), pp. 97–135, see p. 100.
11. Frey, I, p. 742, n. 3.

depict Florence in her glory, but the space reserved for the guilds and for the *Gonfaloni* is much reduced. In the final programme the guilds have disappeared altogether, and the glorification of Florence is replaced by that of Duke Cosimo, 'trionfante e glorioso, coronato da una Firenze'.[12]

In the first programme, the two largest rectangular panels of the middle band, on either side of the *tondo* containing Florence in glory, were devoted to representations of the foundation and of the rebuilding of Florence. These two subjects were taken over unchanged into the second programme,[13] and appear in a drawing which is now in the Fogg Museum (Fig. 3).[14] However, while the former subject is described in both schemes as *Edificatione prima* of Florence by the Romans, and in the drawing simply as *Edificazione*, the latter appears first as *Restauratione et anplificatione*, then as *Redificatione et anplificatione*, and, in the drawing, as *Restauratione o alplificatione* of Florence. These apparently negligible differences in the wording of the titles reflect hesitations about what remained a major problem of early Florentine history. Was Florence destroyed by Attila or Totila, and refounded by Charlemagne and the Romans, as Florentine medieval tradition had it?[15] Or had the city, as Leonardo Bruni and other humanists after him had argued, never suffered total destruction, so that its 'restoration' under Charlemagne was much less complete than had been believed?[16] In either case, did this 'restoration' entail an increase, or a reduction, in its size?[17] In spite of Bruni's historical criticisms, the belief that Charlemagne was the second founder of Florence was widely accepted in Florence during the fifteenth century, when it also served the political purpose of flattering the French kings, and was defended

by humanists like Poggio.[18] The most recent work on the history of Florence, which had been commissioned by Cosimo himself in 1547, Benedetto Varchi's *Storia fiorentina*, followed Giovanni Villani in assuming the total destruction of the city, and its rebuilding on Charlemagne's order, and the Malispini chronicle in believing that this was done on a larger scale.[19] This was not Borghini's view. In his letters to Girolamo Mei, written in 1566, to which we shall presently return, as well as in his later *Discorsi*, he proclaims his disbelief in the tradition 'che Fiorenza fussi disfatta et rifatta', and points out that he had not allowed the 'Reedificatione per Carlomagno' to be put 'in pittura in sala'.[20] This did not mean that he did not appreciate what Charlemagne had done for Florence: having defeated the Longobards, he says in the *Discorsi*, he had restored it to its pristine freedom and prosperity; and although the old chroniclers mistakenly assumed that this restoration had been preceded by the destruction of the city, 'è veramente quella restaurazione e rifacimento della patria nostra che e' vollero dire'.[21] A third scheme, drawn up by Vasari and revised by Borghini, reflects these criticisms (Fig. 2).[22] Charlemagne is banished to one of the smaller panels, which had been allotted to a representation of Charles IV giving privileges to the city, and he appears only as effecting its *restauratione*; while in the space which had originally been reserved for the rebuilding of Florence, the title 'Terze mura et ultime' is substituted for 'Anplificatione di Fiorenza per Carlo Magno'. In the end, this was the subject that was chosen to form the pendant to the foundation of Florence.

This decision was reached after the intervention of Duke Cosimo in autumn 1564, when most of the paintings for the ceiling had been completed and when of the final designs for the central band only the one devoted to Charlemagne was missing.[23] On November 12, Cosimo was evidently still thinking in terms of the original plan of having the city's rebuilding by

12. Vasari, 'Ragionamenti', in *Opere*, ed. G. Milanesi, VIII (Florence, 1882), p. 221.

13. Uffizi 7979 A, reproduced by Thiem, Fig. 1.

14. Reproduced by A. Mongan and P. J. Sachs, *Drawings in the Fogg Museum of Art*, Cambridge, Mass., 1940, II, Fig. 105, and by Thiem, Fig. 6. It is here reproduced again by courtesy of the Fogg Art Museum, Harvard University, Bequest of Charles A. Loeser.

15. See my article, 'The beginnings of political thought in Florence . . .', *Journal of the Warburg and Courtauld Institutes*, V (1942), pp. 215 sqq.

16. Bruni, *Historiarum florentini populi libri XII*, ed. E. Santini, in Muratori, *Rer. Ital. Script.*, new ed., XIX, 3 (Città di Castello, 1914–16), p. 24: 'urbem . . . reparatam magis quam rursus conditam existimo'.

17. Giovanni Villani, *Cronica*, III, 2 (ed. F. G. Dragomanni [Florence, 1845], I, p. 126): Florence was refounded 'di piccolo sito e giro'; Ricordano Malispini, *Storia fiorentina*, 44 (ed. V. Follini [Florence, 1830], I, p. 93): 'fu di maggiore cerchio ovvero giro che la prima'. (On the question of the authenticity of the Malispini chronicle, see Ch. T. Davis, *Dante and the Idea of Rome* [Florence, 1957], pp. 244–62, and G. Aquilecchia, 'Dante and the Florentine chroniclers', *Bulletin of the John Rylands Library*, XLVIII [1965], pp. 53–55.)

18. See H. Baron, *The Crisis of the Early Italian Renaissance* (Princeton, 1955), p. 478.

19. Ed. L. Arbib (Florence, 1838–41), II, pp. 63–67.

20. Florence, Biblioteca Nazionale, Carte Rinuccini, 25. This *filza* contains many drafts of letters by Borghini to Mei of 1566. They are not paginated and are mostly undated; the first passage quoted is from the letter of 12 April. See also below, p. 72, n. 113.

21. *Discorsi*, II, pp. 290–300 ('Se Firenze fu spianata da Atila e riedificata da Carlo Magno').

22. Florence, Archivio di Stato, Carte Strozziane, 1a serie, CXXXIII, fol. 141; the titles are ed. by Paola Barocchi, *Mostra di disegni del Vasari e della sua cerchia* (Florence, 1964), pp. 31–35. I would place the composition of this scheme after, and not before, that of the programme contained in Uffizi 7979 A. It is not discussed by Thiem (see above, p. 64, n. 10).

23. Frey, *Nachlass*, II, cdlxviii, p. 116.

Charlemagne depicted, for he wrote to Borghini that 'trattandosi di dipignere la sua reedificatione', it should be made clear that 'non era mai stata desolata'.[24] But, as Borghini informed Mei in 1566, the duke 'non volse cose che si potessino tener d'alcuno per dubio, nonchè riconoscere false manifestamente',[25] and this was probably the reason why he was won over to Borghini's viewpoint. Thus the construction of the third *cerchio* of walls, as initiated 'circa l'anno 1284' (Fig. 4),[26] was put in the place of the restoration by Charlemagne, the concept of the *reedificazione* having thus altogether been supplanted by that of the *amplificazione* of Florence.[27] As for the duke's desire to demonstrate that Florence had never been devastated (*desolata*), Borghini had at first understood him to mean that it had never been subdued (*soggiogata*);[28] and being at a loss as to how to suggest a programme for so elusive a subject, he proposed to represent instead a miraculous event connected with the siege of Florence by the Ostrogoths. Since, he writes in 1566, 'per le pitture da farsi in Palazzo in un quadro la restaurazione per Carlomagno non soddisfaceva', he was wondering whether 'non vi starebbe forse male il caso di Radagasi Re de' Gotti, rotto sotto Fiorenza mentre che e' l'assediava, e dove non fu piccola ... l'opera de' nostri cittadini'; accordingly, he began to research into the origins of the church of San Lorenzo, which he believed to have first been called the *Basilica Ambrosiana*, having been founded by none other than St. Ambrose.[29] In a letter to Duke Cosimo of 4 November 1565,[30] he expounded the results of his researches: St. Ambrose had appeared to the Florentines in a vision during the siege, and had encouraged them to resist. But there may have been doubts about the reliability of Borghini's theory; at any rate, it was the

uncontroversial subject of the defeat of Radagiasus in 405 which was accepted and incorporated in the final programme, where it found a place in one of the two rectangular panels next to that of the foundation of Florence.[31]

While the original plan to depict the *restauratione et anplificatione* of Florence had created so many difficulties as to have to be finally abandoned, that for the painting of the foundation of the city remained substantially unchanged. From the start, Borghini and Vasari had discarded the legendary tradition, transmitted by Villani and other fourteenth-century authors, that Florence had been founded on the order of Julius Caesar.[32] They had probably not even seriously considered Leonardo Bruni's view that it had been founded by Sulla.[33] For Poliziano's theory, that Florence had been a colony established by the second triumvirate of 43 B.C., which he had based on the newly discovered *Libri regionum* or *coloniarum*, had achieved all but unanimous acceptance among the Italian humanists and historians.[34] Nor was it the first time that this theory had been used for a pictorial representation of the city's foundation. The theatre on the Capitol, which was erected in 1513 for the festivities on the occasion of the conferment of the Roman citizenship on Giuliano de' Medici, contained a series of historical paintings that were designed to extol the close relationship between Etruscans and Romans.[35] One of these paintings represented the foundation of Florence by the Triumvirs Octavius, Antonius and Lepidus, precisely on the basis of the evidence of the

---

24. *Ibid.*, cdlxx, p. 124.
25. Filze Rinuccini, *cit.*
26. Vasari, 'Ragionamenti', in *Opere*, ed. Milanesi, VIII, p. 210. The painting shows the building of one of its gates, that of San Frediano. According to Villani, *Cronica*, VII, 99 (vol. I, p. 431), the building of the new gates was begun in February 1284 (Florentine style), the walls being erected in the early fourteenth century (*ibid.*, IX, 256; vol. II, pp. 301–2).
27. This final development appears to be prepared in the Fogg Museum drawing, where the sketch corresponding to that of the foundation of Florence is still meant to depict its rebuilding or aggrandizement by Charlemagne. However, the site of the wide ring of walls surrounding the city, which is enclosed in its first walls, does not fit any extant account of the Charlemagne episode, including those by Malispini and Varchi, who thought that Florence had been rebuilt 'di maggiore cerchio' (see above, p. 65). It bears, on the other hand, some resemblance to Villani's account of the building of the second *cerchio* towards the end of the eleventh century, when the *borgo* on the left bank of the Arno was included in the new walls (*Cronica*, IV, 8; vol. I, pp. 146–8).
28. Frey, *Nachlass*, II, cdlxviii, cdlxx, pp. 116, 124.
29. To Girolamo Mei, Filze Rinuccini *cit.*
30. Frey, II, cdlxviii, pp. 116–17.

31. In the Carte Strozziane scheme (Fig. 3), this panel had been reserved for Clement IV conferring his coat-of-arms to the Guelph party (cf. 'Ragionamenti', *op. cit.*, pp. 209–10), the panel on the other side being devoted to the 'restauratione per Carlo Magno'. This subject having been eliminated in the final programme, Clement IV was painted in its place, while the space originally reserved for him was used for the defeat of Radagiasus.
32. See my article, 'The beginnings of political thought' *cit.*, pp. 201, 208–9, 215.
33. *Historiae florentini populi*, p. 5; see my article *cit.*, p. 225, and 'Il Poliziano e la questione delle origini di Firenze', in *Il Poliziano e il suo tempo* (Florence, 1957), pp. 101–5.
34. *Ibid.*, pp. 109–10. Bartolomeo Scala was exceptional in being non-committal: see my article, 'Bartolomeo Scala's *Historia Florentinorum*', in *Studi di bibliografia e di storia in onore di Tammaro de Marinis* (Verona, 1964), IV, p. 52.
35. '...dinotando che fra etrusci e Romani non solo il vincolo d'amicitia ma ancora coniuntione di sangue intervenisse (Antonio Altieri, *Giuliano de' Medici eletto Cittadino Romano ovvero Il Natale di Roma nel 1513*, ed. L. Pasqualucci [Rome 1881], p. 30). There are a number of accounts of the festivities, and of the theatre which was much admired; cf. H. Janitschek, 'Das Capitolinische Theater vom Jahre 1513', *Repertorium für Kunstwissenschaft*, V (1882), pp. 259–70; E. Rodocanachi, *Rome au temps de Jules II et Léon X* (Paris, 1912), pp. 321–324; E. Flechsig, *Die Dekoration der modernen Bühne in Italien* ... (Dresden, 1894), pp. 51–60; H. Siebenhüner, *Das Kapitol in Rom* (Munich, 1954), p. 48.

Libri coloniarum. It included two Latin inscriptions recording this event, which were copied from one of the manuscripts of that work which were then in Rome.[36] This painting, as described in some detail by Paolo Palliolo,[37] must have been a remarkable product of contemporary antiquarian studies; Borghini, who refers to it in the *Discorsi*, states that 'fu da' dotti d'allora, che erano molti e da molto, approvata'.[38] He may, in fact, have derived some of the subject matter for the painting of the foundation of Florence in the Palazzo Vecchio from one of the accounts of the theatre on the Capitol.[39] However, while in that theatre also the distribution of land among the colonists had been depicted,[40] Vasari's painting solely represents the foundation and the initial building of the city. It could certainly have vied with its Roman predecessor in its concern with archaeological and historical accuracy.

In the foreground of the painting (Figs. 5 and 6) we see the triumvirs, Octavianus, Antonius and Lepidus, completing the foundation of the colony with the conferment of its standard. They are identified by the crests on their helmets. The triumvir nearest to the onlooker, and thus occupying a prominent place, is Octavianus, identified by the capricorn with globe and rudder which appears on many of Augustus' coins.[41] The capricorn was Augustus' horoscopic sign,[42] but it was also that of Duke Cosimo, who had equally used

it as an emblem for one of his medals.[43] Octavianus' prominent position is evidently intended to reflect his leading role in the founding of the colony, which had already been pointed out by Poliziano, and which was emphasized by Borghini to the extent of describing Augustus as the real founder of Florence.[44] This astrological relationship between Augustus and Cosimo has significant political overtones: for while Augustus thus appeared, in the decoration of the Salone, as the founder of Florence, Cosimo did so as the creator of the greater Tuscan state—an achievement which was celebrated in the panels devoted to the conquest of Siena.[45] The small statue on the next triumvir's helmet identifies him as Antonius, who claimed to be descended from Hercules;[46] but that just this emblem was chosen for him may have also been partly due to other considerations. Hercules figures on early seals of the Florentine commune, as well as on a seal used by Duke Cosimo and on one of his medals; in fact, the representation of Hercules on Cosimo's seal bears some resemblance to that in Vasari's painting.[47] Antonius hands over the new colony's *vexillum* to one of the colonists; following medieval tradition, it has a white lily on a red ground.[48] The third triumvir's helmet carries an equestrian figure as its crest; some of the coins struck by Lepidus show a horseman as his genethliatic sign.[49] There seems to have been some attempt at portraiture, based on coins: thus Antonius' aquiline nose, on which also Plutarch remarks, is clearly discernible.[50]

36. The first inscription as copied by Paolo Palliolo (see next note) reads: 'M. ANTONIVS/M. AIMIL. LEPIDVS III VIRI/C. CAESAR OCTAVIAN. R.P.S.', the second 'FLOREN-TIA COLONIA PO. RO./A III VIRIS DEDVCTA'. The reading of these passages shows that the MS. from which these inscriptions were derived was not the Laur. 29, 32, which had been used by Poliziano (see my article *cit.*, pp. 105 sqq.), and which was in Rome between 1508 and 1522. On other MSS. of that work available in Rome, see C. Thulin, 'Die Handschriften des Corpus agrimensorum Romanorum', *Abhandlungen der Preuss. Akad. d. Wissenschaften*, 1911, Phil.-histor. Klasse, pp. 32–36, 75–77, and 'Humanistische Handschriften des Corpus agrimensorum Romanorum', *Rheinisches Museum*, Neue Folge, 66 (1911), pp. 417–51; and G. Mercati, *M. Tulli Ciceronis De republica libri*, Prolegomena (Città del Vaticano, 1934), pp. 95–96.
37. Paolo Palliolo Fanese, *Le Feste pel conferimento del Patriziato Romano a Giuliano e Lorenzo de' Medici*, ed. O. Guerrini (Bologna, 1885), pp. 49–50.
38. I, p. 10.
39. There are some parallels between that painting and Palliolo's account: '...è ritratta Fiorenza, et gran numero di muratori con suoi instrumenti se affaticano in rinovarla et augumentarla ... Antonio, Lepido et Ottaviano con suoi militi intorno, sedeno sopra certi gradi, tutti tre al pare ...' (see Fig. 5).
40. *Ibid.*: 'Questi Trionviri, havendo constituita Fiorenza colonia de' Romani, assegnano a' nuovi coloni le suoe portioni del terreno ...'
41. See H. A. Grueber, *Coins of the Roman Republic in the British Museum* (London, 1910), II, p. 19. Normally the capricorn carries a cornucopia on its back; but this is not always the case: cf. p. 433.
42. Suetonius, *Augustus*, 94.

43. See I. B. Supino, *Il Medagliere Mediceo nel R. Museo Nazionale di Firenze* (Florence, 1899), p. 100, no. 262. (According to the beginning of Cosimo's rule.) Borghini refers to it in a letter to Francesco I (ed. in *Raccolta di prose fiorentine*, IV [Florence, 1734–45], iv, p. 200, and Lorenzoni, *Carteggio*, p. 78. Lorenzoni wrongly believed that it was addressed to Cosimo.)
44. Poliziano, letter to Piero di Lorenzo de' Medici, in *Opera* (Basel, 1553), p. 3: 'praecipuus vestrae urbis conditor Augustus'. Borghini, letter to Girolamo Mei, *cit.* above, p. 66, n. 25: 'la guidicamo Colonia iulia dedutta da Augusto' (*Carteggio*, p. 56).
45. See e.g. Thiem, *op. cit.*, pp. 100–1, 106.
46. Plutarch, *Antony*, 4; Appian, *Roman History. The Civil Wars*, III, 16. Cf. S. W. Stevenson, *A Dictionary of Roman Coins ...* (London, 1889), pp. 58–59. See also Andrea Fulvio, *Illustrium imagines* (Rome, 1517), fol. 12 r.
47. On the Florentine Hercules seal, see Villani, *Cronica*, VIII, 95 (vol. II, p. 128); L. Passerini, 'Il sigillo fiorentino con l'Ercole', *Periodico di Numismatica e Sfragistica*, I (1868), pp. 276–85; D. Marzi, *La cancelleria della repubblica fiorentina* (Rocca S. Casciano, 1910, pp. 378–85. On Cosimo's Hercules seal, see Passerini, *op. cit.*; it is now preserved in the Museo degli Argenti in the Palazzo Pitti, where it is attributed to Domenico di Polo, evidently on the authority of Milanesi (cf. Vasari-Milanesi, v, p. 384, n. 2). On Cosimo's Hercules medal, see Supino, *op. cit.*, p. 100, no. 263, and Borghini's letter to Panvinio of 18 Feb. 1567, in *Raccolta di prose fiorentine cit.*, p. 68.
48. Villani, *Cronica*, I, 40 (vol. I, p. 63).
49. The horseman probably refers to the statue on the Capitol with which his ancestor, M. Aemilius Lepidus, consul in 187 B.C., had been rewarded; see Grueber, *op. cit.*, I, p. 447, n. 1.
50. Plutarch, *loc. cit.* For Augustus, cf. Grueber, III, Fig. LX, 11 (with the capricorn on the reverse).

The central section of the painting is occupied by the new colony in process of construction, with its walls partly standing and some of its public buildings nearing completion. On its left, we see the veterans in military order, *sub vexillo*, proceeding to their new home; while in its foreground the commissioner in charge of supervising the establishment (*deductio*) of the colony, his head covered by his toga, is marking the boundaries of the new town with a plough drawn by two oxen. Apart from telescoping two successive stages in the foundation of a Roman colony, the tracing of its boundaries and the building of it, the painting follows the accounts of the *deductio* of colonies provided by classical authors.[51] One of the city gates is already *in situ*. It is meant to correspond to the northern gate of Florence which in the middle ages was called *Porta Episcopi* or *Porta contra Aquilonem*; in Roman times, it was fortified by two round towers.[52] Vasari situates it too far to the east (it should have been to the left of the temple of Mars)[53] and represents it as a tall rectangular structure, perhaps in imitation of one of the gates of the Aurelian walls.[54] In contrast, the towers of the town walls are round. Villani states that such had been the towers of the Roman walls of Florence;[55] and his statement could have been corroborated by Vitruvius' advice to construct wall towers in a round or polygonal form.[56]

The layout of the city itself is clearly based on careful study, and is meant to provide the onlooker with a faithful picture of Roman Florence at the time of its foundation. If the results are not always satisfactory, this may partly be due to pictorial requirements rather than archaeological errors. Some of the streets appear traced in the rectangular manner characteristic of Roman colonies, and four buildings are either already erected, or in the process of construction. In the north, just inside the walls, we see the temple of Mars, in the west, the aqueduct leading to a reservoir, and in the east, outside the walls, the amphitheatre. These buildings had been singled out by Villani as the principal monuments erected by the Romans at the time of, or soon after, the city's foundation,[57] and their real or alleged remains had provided the Florentine humanists with conclusive evidence not only of Florence's Roman origins, but also of the splendour of the Roman city.[58] In fact, humanist interest in archaeology had served, in this case, to corroborate medieval traditions. Vasari's painting reflects this development. Nothing could show its scholarly inspiration better than a comparison with the clumsy and entirely imaginary representation of Caesar's Florence in the so-called Florentine picture chronicle attributed to Maso Finiguerra.[59]

Let us briefly examine the single monuments. According to medieval tradition, the amphitheatre was originally called *parlatorio* or *parlagio*, and was built by Caesar's soldiers during the siege of Fiesole which preceded the foundation of Florence, 'per potere in quello fare suo parlamento'.[60] Bruni rejected this explanation, and considered the Florentine amphitheatre the counterpart of the Roman Colosseum.[61] Some of its foundations and arches were still visible in the days of Villani, who comments on its vast size,[62] and Bruni speaks of the 'reliquiae . . . theatri ingentis'.[63] Giovanni da Prato uses topographical evidence to show that it was 'di circunferenzia amplissima'.[64] From both archaeological and topographical evidence it was natural to assume that it was built on the model of the Colosseum—the more so as one could still see such provincial 'colosseums' outside Florence.[65] Borghini found further confirmation of this view when,

51. Cf. Cicero, *Philippics*, II, 102; Servius *in Aen.*, v, 755: 'conditores enim civitatis taurum in dexteram, vaccam intrinsecus iungebant, et incincti ritu Gabino, id est togae parte caput velati, parte succincti, tenebant stivam incurvam, ut glebae omnes intrinsecus caderent, et in sulco ducto loca murorum designabant . . .' Cf. Varro, *De lingua latina*, v, 143.

52. G. Maetzke, *Florentia* (Rome, 1941), p. · 26; M. Lopes Pegna, *Firenze dalle origini al Medioevo* (Florence, 1962), p. 66.

53. Borghini, following Villani and the Malispini chronicle, placed it correctly at the entrance of Borgo San Lorenzo: *Discorsi*, I, p. 293. Cf. the map of Roman Florence in Maetzke, Fig. 1.

54. Cf. e.g. the drawing of the Porta Ostiensis in the *Codex Escurialensis*, ed. H. Egger (Vienna, 1905), fol. 45 v.

55. *Cronica*, I, 38 (p. 61). Around 1400 remnants of round towers were still visible: Coluccio Salutati, *Invectiva in Antonium Luschum*, ed. D. Moreni (Florence, 1826), p. 28: 'Extant adhuc rotundae turres . . .'. On present archaeological remains, see Lopes Pegna, pp. 66–68.

56. *De architectura*, I, v, 5. Barbaro's translation, Venice, 1556, p. 32, contains an illustration of such a tower by Palladio.

57. *Cronica*, I, 38, 42 (pp. 60–61, 65–66). The *Liber de origine civitatis* (in O. Hartwig, *Quellen und Forschungen zur ältesten Geschichte der Stadt Florenz*, I [Marburg, 1875], p. 55) does not include the Baptistery, which it assumed to have been built after the alleged destruction of Florence. This tradition is also followed by the Malispini chronicle (*Storia*, 38; vol. I, pp. 82–83).

58. Cf. Salutati, *Invectiva*, pp. 26–28; Bruni, *Historiae populi florentini*, p. 6; Giovanni da Prato, *Il Paradiso degli Alberti*, ed. A. Wesselofski (Bologna, 1867), III, p. 232: 'le quali cose non furono fabricate se non per grande potenzia e grandissimo spendio' (cf. also pp. 241–2).

59. *A Florentine Picture Chronicle . . . by Maso Finiguerra*, ed. S. Colvin (London, 1898), pls. 91–92.

60. *Cronica*, I, 36 (pp. 58–59). Cf. Malispini, 27 (p. 60).

61. *Loc. cit.* By the sixteenth century, it came naturally to a Florentine who had resided in Rome to call the Florentine amphitheatre 'collosseo': see Cellini, *Vita*, ed. O. Bacci (Florence, 1901), p. 4.

62. *Loc. cit.*: ' . . . ancora a' nostri di si ritrovano i fondamenti, e parte delle volte presso alla chiesa di San Simone . . .', etc. Villani believed that its height was over sixty *braccia*.

63. *Loc. cit.*

64. *Op. cit.*, III, p. 233.

65. Cf. e.g. Fazio degli Uberti, *Il Dittamondo*, III, 3, ed. G. Corsi, I (Bari, 1952), p. 191, on Verona: 'Vidi l'Arena, ch'è in forma come a Roma il Culiseo . . .'

during the excavations for the conduits of the Fountain of Neptune, which were begun in June 1565, foundations of the amphitheatre came to light.[66] In contrast to Villani, who considered it to have been round, Borghini concluded from the layout of the streets on its site, as well as from the teachings of Vitruvius on the building of theatres, that it had been of oval shape rather than *tondo perfetto*.[67] It is, accordingly, in this shape that the amphitheatre appears in Vasari's painting. The façade is a fairly close replica of that of the Roman Colosseum; however, it has one storey less, and only one order of columns, as against the Colosseum's four. The height of the building would thus have come close to that indicated by Villani,[68] and this may have been thought to be in keeping with the inferior status of a provincial city, however splendid and prosperous. As for the columns, it is not without interest that, as Serlio informs us, many people were wondering why the Romans had adopted four orders of columns for the Colosseum, 'e non lo fecero di un solo ordine come gli altri, cioè quello di Verona ... e quello di Pola'.[69]

The aqueduct had been, according to Villani, one of the principal building projects carried out at the time of Florence's foundation: it was intended to bring water to the new town from the foot of the Monte Morello,[70] over a distance of seven *miglia*. Its remains, like those of the amphitheatre, were subsequently used to prove the Roman origins of the city.[71] In Borghini's youth, ten or twelve arches of the aqueduct were still standing outside the Porta a Faenza; of these, only three had survived in about 1570.[72] Villani states that

the aqueduct terminated inside the city walls, in 'uno grande palagio che si chiamava termine *caput aquae*, ma poi in volgare si chiamò Capaccia, e ancora in Terma si vede dell'anticaglia'.[73] Borghini considers Villani's account of the site of the aqueduct and its reservoir *tutto vero*; as for the baths, remains of them came to light when part of the Palace of the Guelf Party was rebuilt, 'è già molti anni'.[74] He thus implicitly ignores, in the light of local evidence, Vitruvius' statement that the principal reservoir (*castellum*) of an aqueduct should be built 'cumque venerit ad moenia'.[75] Vasari's painting accordingly shows the reservoir roughly on the site of the later Via delle Terme. Eight arches of the aqueduct are already completed. Outside the walls, it makes a turn in the direction of Quinto and Sesto, at the foot of the Monte Morello.

The building which, in Vasari's painting, dominates the entire colony, is the temple of Mars (Fig. 6). According to Villani, it was built by the Florentines under the reign of Augustus, in honour of their first patron, Mars, and was later rededicated to St. John the Baptist.[76] That the Baptistery had originally been a temple of Mars was accepted by the humanists and used by them as further evidence of the city's Roman origins.[77] But while of the other Roman monuments only few remains survived, the Baptistery constituted, in their eyes, a complete Roman building, only superficially altered during the middle ages. Not surprisingly, they could hardly contain their enthusiasm about its beauty and splendour, which testified to the greatness of Roman Florence.[78] Their opinion was also accepted

66. *Discorsi*, I, p. 169: 'E già intorno a sei anni fa, fondandosi i condotti dell'acqua per la nuova, e bellissima fontana di piazza ... si scopersero ... il fondamento vero intero, e reale, con le sue scale, con le sue volte, con que' contrafforti, e mura a uso di conio, come si veggono appunto in quello di Roma, e altrove in Italia.' Work on the conduits for the Fountain of Neptune was begun on 30 June 1565: Francesco Settimanni, *Memorie fiorentine*, MS. Florence, Archivio di Stato, Manoscritti, 128, fol. 326 v: 'Addì XXX di giugno 1565 sabato si principiò in Firenze a murare il condotto dell'acqua che ... passa sul Ponte a Rubaconte, e sotto la Loggia de' Peruzzi, e poi alla Fonte di Piazza....' (On the foundations for the Fountain, see B. H. Wiles, *The Fountains of Florentine Sculptors* ... [Cambridge, Mass., 1933], p. 119.)
67. *Discorsi*, I, p. 168. Vitruvius, *De architectura*, V, 3 sqq. (which, however, does not concern amphitheatres). Borghini's opinion has been confirmed by modern archaeological research: see Maetzke, *op. cit.*, p. 61; Lopes Pegna, *op. cit.*, pp. 115–17. A groundplan of the amphitheatre by Borghini is in MS. Florence, Bibl. Naz., Magl. xxv, 551, fol. 29 r (Fig. 8). It has been reproduced by D. M. Manni, *Notizie istoriche intorno al parlagio ovvero anfiteatro di Firenze* (Bologna, 1746), p. ii.
68. See above, p. 68, n. 62.
69. *Libri d'architettura*, bk. III (Venice, 1544), p. 68.
70. *Cronica*, I, 38 (p. 60).
71. Salutati, *Invectiva*, pp. 27–28; Giovanni da Prato, *Paradiso degli Alberti*, III, pp. 234–5.
72. *Discorsi*, I, pp. 130–1.

73. *Cronica*, I, 38 (pp. 60–61).
74. *Discorsi*, I, p. 132.
75. *De architectura*, VIII, vi, 1 (ed. F. Krohn [Leipzig, 1930], p. 190). On the authority of Vitruvius, Giovanni Lami thought that the Florentine *castellum aquae* was situated outside the walls (*Lezioni di antichità toscane* [Florence, 1766], pp. LXXXII, 391–2). In fact, in Roman antiquity the *castellum* could be built on the town walls: see Th. Ashby, *The Aqueducts of Ancient Rome* (Oxford, 1935), p. 46. It could, however, be argued that in ancient Rome aqueducts entered the city, and that there were reservoirs on some of its hills: cf. Frontinus, *De aquaeductu urbis*, 18–21; Poggio, *De varietate fortunae*, in *Codice Topografico della città di Roma*, ed. R. Valentini and G. Zucchetti, IV (Rome, 1953), p. 238; Andrea Fulvio, *Antiquitates urbis* (Rome, 1527), fol. 32 r.
76. *Cronica*, I, 42, 60 (vol. I, pp. 66, 82). Cf. Dante, *Inferno*, XIII, 143–4: 'Io fui della città che nel Batista/Mutò il primo padrone ...'; Boccaccio, *Commento alla Divina Commedia*, ed. D. Guerri, III (Bari, 1918), pp. 150–1. According to a different medieval tradition, the Baptistery was built much later, when Florence was rebuilt after her destruction by Totila or Attila (see above, n. 57): *Liber de origine civitatis*, in Hartwig, *op. cit.*, pp. 59–60. See also W. Horn, 'Das Florentiner Baptisterium', *Mitteilungen des Kunsthistorischen Institutes in Florenz*, V (1937–40), p. 100, n. 1.
77. Cf. Salutati, *Invectiva*, pp. 26–27. Bruni, *Historiae populi florentini*, p. 6.
78. Giovanni da Prato, *Paradiso degli Alberti*, III, pp. 232–3. Poggio, *Historia florentina* (Venice, 1715), p. 3. Poliziano to

by Borghini, who in his *Discorsi* defends it at length against criticisms that were made after the ceiling of the Salone had been completed.[79] He believed that the octagonal shape of San Giovanni came close to that of the temple of Mars Ultor erected by Augustus on his forum, as could be seen from those medals of Augustus which on their reverse showed the temple of Mars, supported by columns, of 'forma ritonda, o quasi ritonda, che tale si riputa l'ottangulare'.[80] And he pointed out to his critic in 1566 that Leonardo Bruni may already have thought that the Florentine temple of Mars was 'molto più simile al tempio di Marte Ultore, per quello che rappresentano anchor hoggi le medaglie d'Augusto'.[81] From Borghini's description of these medals,[82] it would appear that he was referring to the gold and silver coins of Augustus that have on their reverse, standing on a base with three steps, a round domed temple, six of whose columns are visible, with an *aquila* between the two central columns and military insignia on either side of them (Fig. 9b).[83] However, the temple of Mars Ultor was not the only model for the Florentine temple. The other was the Pantheon —Borghini thought it might even have been built by the same architects, 'mutate alcune poche cose, come fanno i maestri, per mostrar pur di non copiare affatto, e di sapere variare'.[84] Vasari's picture of the temple of Mars constitutes an attempt to combine architectural elements derived from these two Roman temples with the extant structure of the Baptistery. The result may not have struck the onlooker as entirely convincing, but it should be added that Borghini, no doubt in view of criticisms, disclaims, in the *Discorsi*, any pretence at complete accuracy.[85] The temple, of which the

ground storey only appears completed, stands, like the temple of Mars Ultor on Augustan coins, on a base.[86] On each of its three visible sides it shows two columns, or six in all, like the Baptistery and the Mars temple with six columns on Augustan coins.[87] On the other hand, the contrasting colours of marble of the Baptistery are reproduced in the corner pillars. In the centre of the temple, and projecting above the cornice of the ground storey, we see an equestrian statue of Mars. In the design for the second programme (Fig. 3) the temple appears roofed, with one storey only: had this sketch been fully executed, it would not only have shown the temple as differing substantially from the Baptistery, but would also have prevented the statue of Mars being depicted. But this statue formed so important a part of Florentine popular tradition that it could hardly have been excluded from a representation of the temple of Mars. Villani writes that the Florentines, having dedicated it to the god, placed an equestrian marble statue of him 'sopra una colonna di marmo in mezzo di quello tempio', where it remained until the rededication to St. John the Baptist when it was removed to a tower near the Arno.[88] Borghini may well have originally intended to exclude this statue from the painting, the more so as he affirms explicitly that it was not Roman custom to represent Mars on horseback: anyone with even the slightest knowledge of Roman medals would not make such a *ridiculo errore*.[89] At this point, Borghini's classical scholarship had clearly to give way to popular beliefs.

In the background of the painting, towering over the new colony, we see Fiesole on its hill—a large city with temples and a fortress on its highest point, on the site where now the convent of San Francesco stands (Fig. 7). In contrast to what Borghini and Vasari attempted in the representation of Roman Florence, that of Fiesole is patently imaginary. The reason for this is obvious: Borghini himself admits that no vestiges of ancient public buildings existed in that town which could still testify, as in Florence, to 'quella pura e vera ... grandezza romana'.[90] True, he says, Cicero

Piero de' Medici, *loc. cit.*: 'Unum antiquitatis in ea vestigium pulcherrimum extat adhuc, templum hoc mirifica structura olim Martis, nunc Praecursoris titulum gerens.'
79. I, pp. 145 sqq; see also below, p. 72.
80. *Ibid.*, pp. 153–4. Poliziano had already referred to this temple in connection with Augustus, whom he considered the principal founder of Florence (*loc. cit.*). See above, p. 67.
81. Filze Rinuccini, *cit.*: than the Lateran Baptistery.
82. *Discorsi*, I, p. 153: '... nelle medaglie, che hanno per rovescio questo Tempio, si vede fra le colonne ripieno d'insegne militari'.
83. See H. Mattingly, *Coins of the Roman Empire in the British Museum*, I (London, 1923), p. 66, pl. VIII, 2–5. Cf. p. 114, pl. XVII, 12 (Fig. 9a).
84. *Discorsi*, I, pp. 162–3. As early as the fourteenth century, Villani had pointed to the resemblance between the Florentine 'temple of Mars' and the Pantheon, in so much as both had been 'scoperto al cielo' (*Cronica*, I, 60; vol. I, p. 83).
85. *Discorsi*, I, p. 154: 'Che non saranno già così fastidiose le persone che e' lo vogliano in tutto, e per tutto, e nelle misure, e nel numero delle colonne, ed in cotali altre minuzie, pari a quello, per chiamarlo simile ...' He believed that 'la incrostatura di fuori' and the 'cornice che rigira intorno ... furon fatte parecchi ... centinaia d'anni doppo la prima edificatione' (to Girolamo Mei, 1566, Filze Rinuccini, *cit.*; cf. also *Discorsi*, I, pp. 158–9) and that also other medieval additions had deprived the temple of much of its original beauty (*ibid.*, pp. 159–61).

86. As early as the end of the fifteenth century, Bartolomeo Scala had stated that originally 'per decoros ascendebatur gradus' to the Baptistery (*Historia Florentinorum*, in J. Graevius, *Thesaurus Antiquitatum Italiae*, VIII, I [Leyden, 1723], col. 18).
87. See Mattingly, *loc. cit.*, and Fig. 9a.
88. *Cronica*, I, 42, 60 (vol. I, pp. 66, 82). The illuminated manuscript of Giovanni Villani's chronicle, Chigiano L. VIII, 296 (ed. L. Magnani, *La cronaca figurata di Giovanni Villani* ... [Città del Vaticano, 1936], pl. 9), shows Mars in the costume of a medieval knight, with his horse precariously balancing on one side of the opening in the roof of the Baptistery (see above, n. 84).
89. *Discorsi*, I, p. 202.
90. *Ibid.*, p. 218 (actually 329).

speaks of the extravagant living and sumptuous build-ing of the Fiesolans;[91] but he believes that Cicero had in mind private palaces in the town and villas in the countryside. As for public buildings, he says, Fiesole would have possessed no theatres or amphitheatres at the time of Florence's foundation; and the fact that no remains whatever of such buildings existed may indi-cate the town's subsequent decline.[92] Vasari's picture of Fiesole corresponds fairly well to this theory; and on the slopes of Fiesole's hill we may see a few of the 'ville piene di delicatezze' of the luxury-loving Fie-solans mentioned by Borghini.

Above the hill of Fiesole, surrounded by a cloud and dominating the entire panel, a ram indicates the sign of the zodiac under which Florence was believed to have been founded. This belief does not appear in the medieval chronicles of the origins of that city;[93] as for Giovanni Villani, he only mentions the refounding of Florence by Charlemagne under the sign of the Ram.[94] However, the author of the *Ottimo Commento* of the *Divine Comedy* records, around 1335, that he had heard Dante say 'che li antichi ebbero opinione, che la città di Firenze fosse fondata essendo ascendente Ariete, e Marte signore dell'ora'; an opinion which he considers to be false.[95] We find the same belief further developed, towards the end of the fourteenth century, in Filippo Villani's work on the origins of Florence, and, shortly afterwards, in Cino Rinuccini's reply to Antonio Loschi's invective against Florence; it is also briefly mentioned by the Malispini chronicle. Accord-ing to Filippo Villani, Caesar laid the first stone of the new city 'saliente arietis singno super lineam circu-larem nostri orizzontis quo . . . tunc Mars atque Mer-curius benignissimis aliorum siderum aspectibus pariter ferebantur';[96] and Rinuccini states even more precisely that the Romans founded the city 'ascendente l'Ariete

sei gradi sotto il dominio di Marte'.[97] Filippo Villani and Cino Rinuccini reflect astrological speculations which not only linked the sign of the Ram with Mars, the city's first patron, but also lent additional signifi-cance to the tradition on Charlemagne: 'est miraculo proximum', exclaims Filippo Villani, that he rebuilt Florence 'eodem ascendente singno hisdem comitan-tibus planetis'. This 'miraculous' repetition of events, which was so characteristic a theme of Florentine historical legends,[98] could no longer be represented in the ceiling panels, as had been originally planned,[99] once the subject of the refounding of the city by Charlemagne had been discarded. Nevertheless, the astrological theory of the foundation of Florence under the Ram pervades the foundation panel. Borghini knew the reference to it in the Malispini chronicle.[100] How-ever, he felt that the city's birth date could be identified with even greater precision: a number of Roman colonies, he says in the *Discorsi*, used, in their domestic affairs, to count the years from the day of their founda-tion, as is borne out by inscriptions. Some people believe that this is the reason why the Florentines, 'fuor del più comune uso', have chosen the 25th of March as the beginning of the year.[101] Now March 25 was the birthday of Francesco de' Medici. It was a happy coincidence indeed, which was clearly not lost on the Florentines who crowded the Salone for his wedding festivities, that both their future duke and their city should have been born under the same sign of the zodiac. Borghini himself points out this fortu-nate connection when discussing, a few years later, the *impresa* of a medal for Francesco.[102] As he puts it in a letter to Vasari: by combining the sign of the Ram and the city of Florence in the same emblem, 'si cerca di esprimere che già due volte ci è stato favorevole et

91. *Ibid.*, pp. 208 v–9 (actually 312–13). Borghini was thinking of the passage in *In Catil.*, II, 20, which, however, refers to Sulla's Etrurian colonies in general: '. . . homines ex iis coloniis, quas Sulla constituit . . . hi sunt coloni, qui se in insperatis ac repentinis pecuniis sumptuosius insolentiusque iactarunt. Hi . . . aedificant tamquam beati . . .'
92. *Discorsi*, I, pp. 218–21 (actually 329–33).
93. Cf. Hartwig, *op. cit.*, pp. 54–56.
94. *Cronica*, III, 1 (vol. I, p. 125). Cf. Fig. 2.
95. Ed. A. Torri (Pisa, 1827–9), I, p. 225. The *Ottimo Com-mento* has been attributed to the Florentine notary Andrea Lancia: see L. Rocca, *Di alcuni commenti della Divina Com-media* . . . (Florence, 1891), p. 326, and G. Folena, "Über-lieferungsgeschichte der altitalienischen Literatur', in *Geschichte der Textüberlieferung der antiken und mittelalterlichen Litera-tur*, II (Zürich, 1964), p. 456.
96. *De origine civitatis Florentiae*, MS. Florence, Biblioteca Laurenziana, Ashb. 942, fol. 10 v. This is the first version of his work, composed in 1381–2; cf. A. Massèra, 'Le più antiche biografie del Boccaccio', *Zeitschr. für roman. Philologie*, XXVII (1903), pp. 299–320.

97. *Risponsiva alla Invettiva di Messer Antonio Lusco*, in Salu-tati, *op. cit.*, pp. 206–7. Cf. Malispini, *Istoria*, 101 (vol. I, p. 229): 'E notate qui che la nostra città è stata fondata la prima e la seconda volta sotto il pianeta d'Ariete e di Marte . . .'
98. See my article, 'The origins of political thought' *cit.*, pp. 202, 203, 214–15.
99. See above, p. 65, and Fig. 3: both the designs of the founda-tion of Florence by the triumvirs and of its refounding by Charlemagne show the ram hovering over the city.
100. He refers to it in an undated letter on the foundation of Florence (MS. Florence, Bibl. Naz., Magl. xxv, 551, fols. 21 v–22 r), and adds: 'Questo è quanto ho trovato fino ad hora di questa materia et come V.S. vede tutti concorrono in questo Aries e Marte.'
101. I, pp. 105–6. See also the following note.
102. To Francesco de' Medici, in *Raccolta di prose fiorentine*, IV, iv, p. 201, and Lorenzoni, *op. cit.*, p. 79 (who erroneously believed that the addressee was Cosimo; see above, p. 67, n. 43): 'Dal caso si può dire che il medesimo sia stato ascendente di V.A. et della patria sua insieme: la quale, secondo l'uso delle Colonie Romane di far capo d'anno il dì della fondatione, ha ritenuto sempre l'antico suo costume di cominciarlo a 25 di Marzo . . .' Cf. Supino, *op. cit.*, p. 181, no. 581.

benigno il cielo in questo segno, prima nella fondatione della patria et hora nel darle sì caro et amorevole et prudente Signore'.[103]

The ceiling was completed in time for Francesco's wedding to Joanna of Austria in December 1565.[104] On Christmas Day, a comedy was performed in the Salone as part of the wedding festivities.[105] About the same time, a treatise came to Borghini's knowledge which had recently been composed by a Florentine resident in Rome, Girolamo Mei, who radically disagreed with the historical thesis on which the painting of the foundation of Florence was based.[106] Florence, Mei argued, although a Roman colony, had not been founded by the triumvirs; nor had that colony occupied the same site as the present city; it was probably situated in the vicinity of Signa or further west towards the sea. This colony having been destroyed, the Longobard king Desiderius refounded Florence near Fiesole, and consequently none of the alleged Roman remains of Florence were Roman in fact.[107] Mei did not accept the authority of the *Liber coloniarum*, which he believed could not have been written by Frontinus: otherwise Frontinus would have been 'o huomo negligentissimo, o sommamente ignorante'. Instead he accepts that of Ptolemy, according to whom the distance between Florence and Fiesole was, in his days, several times as great as that between the present Florence and Fiesole. The modern translators of his work, says Mei, had amended this passage in the belief that it was the present Florence which Ptolemy had in mind; but the printed edition of the Greek text, as well as the manuscripts, especially that of the Vatican library, showed that this was not the case.[108] As for the foundation of Florence by the Longobards, Mei relied on the 'evidence' of an alleged decree of King Desiderius, inscribed on an alabaster tablet preserved at Viterbo, in which the king recorded the Tuscan towns which he had either restored or built anew. Among the latter were Viterbo and Florence, 'Fesulanum oppidum Munionis', in which he had gathered 'palantes Fluentinos'. That Florence was originally called Fluentia was a widely held view based

on Pliny;[109] and according to Mei, the *palantes Fluentini* were none other than the homeless Florentines of old, whom Desiderius resettled near the river Mugnone. The so-called *Decretum Desiderii*, which in fact was a forgery by Annius of Viterbo, had been known in Florence since its fabrication at the end of the fifteenth century;[110] but this was apparently the first time that it was used to reinterpret the early history of that city.

If Mei was right, one of the principal paintings of the ceiling was based on false historical premises. After all the erudition that had been lavished on it, this would have been a dismal failure for which the learned *Spedalingo* would have been held primarily responsible; a failure which would have been the more embarrassing as the duke had, as we have seen, given specific orders that only subjects that were demonstrably true should be painted.[111] Mei's treatise appears to have caused quite a sensation in Florence, although his opinion was not accepted by the *più intendenti*, and Cosimo himself ordered Borghini to defend the programme of the ceiling picture against Mei's criticisms.[112] A lengthy correspondence between Borghini and Mei followed, which lasted from January 1566 until January 1567.[113] Borghini's *Discorsi* on the early history of Florence, which were published after his death, originate in this controversy; many of the arguments contained in them can already be found in his letters to Mei and in the *discorsi* accompanying them. As he admits himself in a marginal note to one of his many drafts: 'Invero la diligentia del Mei, et l'occasione che mi ha dato del ricercare, non si può negare che mi ha giovato non poco.'[114]

By the time the correspondence was concluded, Borghini was fairly confident that he had demolished his opponent's views; the more so as his earlier doubts about the 'Decree of Desiderius' had just been more than confirmed by the learned Onofrio Panvinio in Rome, from whom he had sought enlightenment on

103. Lorenzoni, p. 80.

104. Borghini to Vasari, 17 June 1565 (Frey, *Nachlass*, II, dii; p. 188): 'La sala, il palco si finì.'

105. See A. M. Nagler, *Theatre Festivals of the Medici 1539–1637* (New Haven, Conn., 1964), pp. 15–21.

106. *Alcuni pezzi della storia di Firenze di Mei*, MS. Florence, Bibl. Naz., Magl. xxv, 390. This is a copy of extracts from Mei's work, with autograph marginal notes by Borghini. See also Mei's letters to Borghini of 1566, in *Raccolta di prose fiorentine*, IV, ii, pp. 69–72, 77–173 (on the extracts, p. 84). Mei had originally sent his treatise to Piero Vettori (p. 76).

107. Cf. *ibid.*, pp. 101–2, 143 ('non credo che si debba mai credere che la chiesa di San Giovanni fusse mai Tempio di Marte'), 146.

108. *Alcuni pezzi cit.*

109. See my article 'Il Poliziano e la questione delle origini di Firenze', pp. 107–8.

110. See R. Weiss, 'An unknown epigraphic tract by Annius of Viterbo', in *Italian Studies presented to E. R. Vincent* (Cambridge, 1962), p. 119, and my article, 'Bartolomeo Scala's *Historia Florentinorum*', pp. 49–50.

111. See above, p. 66.

112. The editors' preface to the *Discorsi*: '...la quale [opinione] con tutto che da' più intendenti non fusse approvata, diede nondimeno molto da ragionare, e al nostro D. Vincenzio Borghini, che haveva d'ordine del Duca divisato tutta la Pittura, impose necessità di difenderla, oltreche il Duca glielo comandò...' Cf. Borghini's testament in Gaye, *op. cit.*, pp. 386–7.

113. Copies of Mei's letters and drafts and copies of Borghini's letters and 'discorsi' are preserved in Filze Rinuccini, 25 *cit*. Mei's letters are ed. in *Raccolta di prose fiorentine*, IV, ii, pp. 69–72, 77–173.

114. Filze Rinuccini *cit.*

this as well as on other disputed points.[115] For while in his letters to Mei he had still accepted the 'Decretum' as genuine, he now learned that Panvinio considered it a forgery. 'I cannot tell you how contented I was about what you wrote to me about the *Alabastro* of Viterbo', he replies enthusiastically, and adds somewhat weakly that he too had been of that opinion, but had not dared to express it openly.[116] He has no such

qualms in the *Discorsi*.[117] Unfinished as these were at the time of his death, they constitute the end product of the researches Borghini began for the programme of the paintings in the Salone. Like the painting of the foundation of Florence itself, they illustrate the impact of humanist erudition and antiquarian studies on Florentine theories concerning the city's origins and provide a far better commentary on that painting than Vasari's *Ragionamenti*. In its turn, the picture of the foundation of the Roman colony of Florence by the triumvirs could be read as a pictorial representation of a historical theory which originated in Poliziano's interpretation of a passage in the *Libri coloniarum*.

115. *Raccolta di prose fiorentine*, IV, iv, pp. 58–59.
116. *Ibid.*, p. 62 (11 January 1567). Panvinio was no doubt familiar, as Borghini was not, with the treatise against Annius by G. Barreiros, published in Rome in 1565, and perhaps also with Melchior Cano's devastating criticisms, published at Louvain the year before. To the latter Borghini refers later in the *Discorsi* (I, p. 26). See A. Momigliano, review of H. J. Erasmus, *The origins of Rome . . .*, *Rivista storica italiana*, LXXV (1963), pp. 392–3.

117. I, p. 27; cf. pp. 24 sqq.

ANDRÉ CHASTEL

L'Escalier de la Cour Ovale à Fontainebleau

En France, l'escalier à rampe droite était employé, au moins dans certaines provinces, dés le XIIIe siècle. Il était rarement mis en évidence. C'est le perron, symbole du pouvoir que l'on valorise. Par exemple au Palais de Justice de Paris, il avait une curieuse forme à trois pans; au château de Montargis, on trouve trois rampes convergeant vers un palier prolongé par une arche, selon une curieuse disposition qui mérite peut-être l'attention.[1] L'escalier en vis, disposition pratique et générale pour assurer la communication entre les étages, se trouvait normalement pris dans une tourelle engagée, et cette tourelle fournissait un motif d'angle intéressant, ou pouvait accentuer une façade.[2]

À l'hôtel Jacques Cœur, au milieu du XVe siècle, les escaliers en tourelle d'angle se multiplient. Mais longtemps la vis reste un membre modeste. Une seule exception, d'ailleurs spectaculaire: la grande vis du Louvre de Charles V. L'escalier traité en hors d'œuvre se développe en un véritable corps annexe; il est remarquable par sa hauteur: 124 marches, sa clarté due à l'éclairage zénithal, le décor des statues, et l'amusante disposition "télescopique" qui introduit une petite vis au tiers supérieur de la structure, au-dessus du vide du noyau central. Cette virtuosité dans la disposition des accès au château royal, reste exceptionnelle; mais le développement de l'escalier en élément ostentatoire annonce ce qui se passera dans tout le pays un siècle et un siècle et demi plus tard.[3]

Sur la fin du XVe siècle, le phénomène prend en effet une ampleur considérable. Le fait n'a pas échappé à Viollet le Duc: "*c'était à qui dans les résidences seigneuriales, les hôtels et les couvents même, élèverait les plus belles vis et les plus surprenantes.*"[4] L'auteur du Dictionnaire a raison de rappeler que le plus bel exemple d'architecture imaginaire correspondant à l'esprit de la première Renaissance, l'abbaye de Thélème, comportera "*un bastiment . . . en figure exagone en telle façon que a chascun angle estoit*

bastie une grosse tour ronde . . . cent fois plus magnifique que n'est Bonivet ne Chambourg ne Chantilly . . .*", et "*au milieu une merveilleuse viz delaquelle l'entrée estoit par le dehors du logis en un arceau large de six toizes*", c'est à dire une vis monumentale en hors d'œuvre.[5] La croissance et l'accentuation de l'escalier est générale; celui-ci devient l'un des éléments privilégiés de l'ostentation monumentale. Elle porte à des effets de plus en plus poussés: à Gaillon la *grant' vis* en hors d'œuvre reçoit en couronnement la statue de Saint Georges en cuivre doré.[6] A Chateaudun trois escaliers successifs démontrent par leurs dispositions de plus en plus spectaculaires en loggia les progrès du nouveau style, tout en accusant les difficultés techniques auxquelles on se heurte, quand on installe la vis dans une cage d'escalier carrée qui s'amplifie et demande un éclairage plus complet.[7] La vis de Blois construite peu après 1520 est le dernier mot de cette évolution et la promotion définitive de l'escalier en élément d'honneur: le parti octogonal et engagé est conservé, mais la vis devient la pièce centrale de la façade. Elle assure la liaison entre les étages, la galerie du rez-de-chaussée et celle de la balustrade, et en même temps, traitée à claire-voie et dotée de tous les ornements modernes elle rappelle le chef d'œuvre de Raymond du Temple.[8] L'escalier est alors en France la pièce la plus représentative de l'édifice royal, et la plus évoluée de l'architecture civile.

Ces observations permettent de préciser combien l'architecture civile française, et surtout celle qui était de caractère aristocratique, était en cours de renouvellement pendant la période 1480/1490 à 1540 environ, où eurent lieu les premiers contacts sérieux avec la Renaissance méridionale, c'est-à-dire avec les exemples italiens;[9] Il n'est guère possible d'enfermer dans la

1. Pour Montargis, on s'appuie avant tout sur la gravure de J. Androuet Du Cerceau, dans *Les Plus Excellents Bâtiments de France*, 1576–9.
2. Sur l'emploi de l'escalier à vis: Viollet Le Duc, *Dictionnaire de l'Architecture au Moyen-Age*, tome v, Paris, article: escalier, p. 287–331.
3. Sur la vis du Louvre, on doit toujours remonter à Sauval, *Histoire et Antiquités de la Ville de Paris*, tome ii, p. 23.
L. Hautecœur, *Histoire du Louvre, des Origines à nos Jours (1200–1928)*, Paris, s.d., p. 9.
4. Viollet Le Duc, Dictionnaire, *op. cit.*, t. v, p. 308.

5. Rabelais, *Gargantua* (1534), chap. LIII; *Comment feust bastie et dotée l'abbaye des Thélémites.*
6. E. Chirol, *Un Premier Foyer de la Renaissance, le Château de Gaillon*, Paris, 1952, p. 104–5; sur le rôle de cette tourelle dans le prospect du château: A. Chastel et M. Rosci: *Un chateau Français en Italie le Portrait de Gaillon à Gaglianico*, dans "Art de France", iii, 1963.
7. Dr. Lesueur dans "Congrés Archéologique", 1930, p. 476–520; J. Taralon, *Châteaudun*, Paris, 1958.
8. François Gébelin, *Les Châteaux de la Renaissance*, Paris, 1927, p. 59.
9. Les études sur la "réception" des formes italiennes en France sont nombreuses; voir en dernier lieu L. Hautecœur, *Histoire de l'Architecture Classique en France*, vol. i, *La Formation de l'Idéal Classique*, t. i, *La Première Renaissance (1495–1545/1550)*, Paris, 1963.

notion de "gothique tardif" l'activité qui se déploie en France au cours de ce demi-siècle, où l'architecture civile acquiert une sorte de primat. Dans la conception de la demeure aristocratique et du château, on s'éloignait rapidement des partis gothiques, selon une évolution apparemment autonome aussi intéressante à suivre que la manière dont on les avait conquis. Fr. Gébelin a pu montrer comment, au Plessis-Bourré, en Anjou, dès l'époque de Louis XI, apparaît la formule du quadrilatère à tours d'angle, avec des ailes différenciées, sans machicoulis. Le type sera repris vingt ans plus tard, au Château du Verger, où le Maréchal de Gié reçoit Charles VIII en 1488. Et on la retrouve associée à un système décoratif "moderne" au château de Bury, qui s'élève de 1514 à 1524 en même temps que l'aile monumentale de Blois.

En quelques années, l'appareil militaire semble avoir été contraint de se modifier et de se convertir partiellement au décor de prestige. Les tourelles, les machicoulis, les poivrières, les châtelets, adoptent des proportions nouvelles; ils prennent un aspect emblématique. Le château français au début du règne de François premier est dans une large mesure un édifice dont l'économie et la représentation comporte un fort élément "symbolique", ou de "représentation sociale".[10] Pour des raisons diverses, qu'il ne nous appartient pas d'analyser ici, le souci de l'ostentation architecturale a pris d'autres formes en Italie. Et l'on n'est pas surpris de voir que dans la péninsule, on ne tire pas sérieusement parti de l'escalier dans la composition, avant le milieu du siècle et les recherches du "maniérisme".[11] Même l'Espagne, très précoce en matière d'escalier monumentaux, avec, par exemple, l'Hôpital de Sainte-Croix de Tolède (1504–1514) ne semble pas assurer à cet élément un développement aussi cohérent et aussi général que celui que l'on observe en France.[12]

Cette longue introduction nous a paru indispensable pour poser correctement le problème difficile de l'escalier de la cour ovale de Fontainebleau.[13] Comme chacun sait, le château de François Ier a été un lieu d'expériences, où le Roi a, si l'on peut dire, développé ses idées au fur et à mesure qu'elles se présentaient ou qu'on les éveillait en lui. On possède les contrats de Gilles Le Breton pour le début des travaux en 1528: il n'y est pas question d'escalier monumental dans la cour centrale de forme irrégulière qu'il s'agit de remanier et de moderniser et qui prendra bientôt le nom de *cour ovale*[14] (fig. 1). Le portique tel que l'on peut le voir autour de cette cour aujourd'hui, n'est pas d'origine: il est le résultat d'un remaniement qui l'a fait changer de forme et de plan. Les fouilles conduites en 1938–1939 par A. Bray ont retrouvé du côté nord la disposition première (figs. 2–4), avec les fondations anciennes qui impliquent un massif à deux rampes droites conduisant à une plate-forme d'où part, en direction du premier étage une troisième rampe formant pont[15] (fig. 5). C'est là, si l'on veut, une nouvelle version du perron de Montargis ou de celui du Palais.[16] Mais il y a deux innovations capitales: l'élément avancé prend une forme géométrique plus stricte, dont on trouve le schéma dans le second livre de Serlio (publié à Paris en 1545, mais sans allusion à Fontainebleau)[17] (fig. 6). D'autre part l'escalier est comme le déploiement en avant-corps d'un arc de triomphe à deux étages, dont la structure "à l'antique" est totalement neuve et n'a pas, semble-t-il, d'équivalent même en Italie (fig. 7). F. Gébelin dans son ouvrage de 1927, qui ne connaissait que l'arrangement actuel, a souligné l'espèce de révolution que représente le style ferme, tendu, romain, de ce morceau, et il ajoutait: "qui donc a documenté Le Breton pour l'élaboration d'une œuvre si nouvelle? Nous l'ignorons et pouvons seulement dire que ce ne fut pas Serlio dont la venue en France est postérieure d'une dizaine d'années à la construction du célèbre morceau."[18] En sommes-nous toujours à cette conclusion négative? C'est la question que nous nous sommes posée.

L'adoption des motifs, puis des formules antiques et méditerranéennes s'effectue en pleine transformations des partis en usage dans le domaine civil et religieux. Il suffit de rappeler les travaux à Sainte Cécile d'Albi par Louis II d'Amboise (1502–1511), ceux de la cathédrale de Beauvais avec Martin Chambiges (1500 et s.) et le panorama du "gothique tardif" donné par: A. de Lasteyrie, *L'Architecture religieuse à l'Epoque Gothique*, vol. II, Paris, 1926.
Sur l'évolution du château qui se déclare vers 1460–1470, sans rapport avec l'influence italienne, voir les pertinentes observations de F. Gébelin, *Les Châteaux de France*, Paris, 1962, p. 70 et suivantes.
10. Voir entre autres: F. Gébelin, *Les Châteaux de la Renaissance, op. cit.*, p. 5 et suivantes. Les remarques rapides de H. Damish, *Le Problèmes du Château*, dans "Annales, Economies, Sociétés, Civilisations", nov–déc. 1963, p. 1153–9.
11. N. Pevsner, *An Outline of European Architecture*, Londres, rééd. trad. all. Munich, 1957, p. 486.
12. Sur les escaliers de la Renaissance en Espagne: H. E. Wethey, *Escaleras del primer Renacimiento español*, dans "Archivo español de Arte", XXXVIII (1964), p. 295–305.

13. Sur l'ensemble de la question, F. Gébelin, *Les Châteaux, op. cit.*, p. 97 et suivantes.
14. Léon de Laborde, *Comptes des bâtiments du Roi (1528–1571)*, vol. I, Paris, 1878, p. 25 et suivantes.
15. A. Bray, *Le Premier Grand Escalier du Château de Fontainebleau et les Anciens Escaliers de la Cour Ovale*, dans: "Bulletin Monumental", 1940, p. 192 et suivantes.
16. A. Blunt, *Art and Architecture in France, 1500–1700*, London, 1953, p. 31, l'a judicieusement relevé:
"The form of the staircase with double flight leading to a single flight bridging an arch to the first floor of the building as in the late medieval French tradition, and follows examples at Montargis and in the Palais of Paris, but a closer model for the lower part was to be found at Bury." Je serais moins d'accord sur ce dernier point.
17. Serlio, Livre II, p. 42.
18. F. Gébelin, *Les Châteaux, op. cit.*, p. 98.

La chronologie prend ici toute son importance. Il y a deux choses à expliquer: l'érection de cet appendice d'apparat, de loin le plus majestueux et le plus "romain" qui ait paru en France, et, ensuite, sa surprenante, et apparemment rapide, transformation. L'établissement de l'escalier dans la cour coïncide avec la construction d'un escalier intérieur à rampes droites pris dans l'aile nord: l'ensemble se développait en quelque sorte de part et d'autre du portique. On a affaire à une interprétation complète du parti moderne. La conception des ordres est exceptionnellement précise: le large entablement à l'antique a été simplifié en raison du matériau de Fontainebleau, le grès, qui ne permet pas les fioritures de l'ornement. On retrouve la même ordonnance à l'abside de la chapelle Saint Saturnin[19] (fig. 8). Il s'agit donc d'une formule spécialement étudiée pour relever le décor médiocre de la cour. Mais à quelle date intervient-elle? Il n'y a que deux hypothèses possibles: ou bien l'escalier a été élevé autour de 1540, au moment de ce qu'on peut appeler la vague "classicisante" que représente Serlio. Mais alors on comprend mal qu'il ait été altéré radicalement presque aussitôt; ou bien l'escalier remonte aux premières transformations modernes de Fontainebleau, c'est-à-dire aux années 1530, et a subi quinze ou vingt ans plus tard des transformations importantes, mais alors on voit mal qui peut en avoir été l'auteur.

Les contrats de 1528—on l'a vu—ne mentionnent rien. En revanche, une pièce de 1540 mentionne "*le rechangement du grand escalier*" du château avec références à un contrat de 1531.[20] Ce serait, selon A. Bray, celui qui est venu compléter l'accord de 1528 en prévoyant la rampe et l'arc triomphal... Ce point semble acquis; dans la réédition récente de son volume sur la Renaissance, M. Hautecœur s'est demandé si cette datation est bien finalement la bonne; n'y aurait-il pas lieu d'interpréter autrement ces documents et de retarder le volumineux escalier jusqu'à la période 1540–50, date où il pourrait avoir été dessiné par Serlio?[21] L'inconvénient de cette solution est évidemment de mal rendre compte de la référence au contrat de 1531; elle oblige en outre à retarder la date de la chapelle Saint Saturnin qui est attestée plus tôt.[22] D'autre part, Serlio s'est plaint à plusieurs reprises de ne pas avoir été employé à Fontainebleau et il aurait, à coup sûr, mentionné ce bel ouvrage s'il y avait eu quelque part. Son intervention est d'autant moins probable que le style de l'escalier bellifontain, robuste

et large, n'est guère conforme à ce que Serlio concevait autour de 1545 pour Ancy-le-Franc. Il resterait enfin à savoir pourquoi un ouvrage de cette importance a été si vite altéré.

L'escalier monumental a été élevé à un moment où l'on faisait passer l'effet avant l'utilité, ce que l'on a du regretter par la suite pour être contraint de le modifier; et c'était aussi le moment où l'on cherchait à affirmer le caractère royal et moderne de l'édifice. Etabli au milieu de la cour, il l'occupait et même l'encombrait passablement.[23] Il doit a priori appartenir au moment où a été conçue la modernisation ambitieuse du château, donc autour des années 1530. C'est en tout cas ce qu'indique l'allusion au marché "*pour raison du dit grand escalier et de la chapelle dudit château datée du samedi cinquième d'août 1531*" qui confirme, au surplus, le lien entre l'édifice et la chapelle Saint Saturnin.[24] La seule difficulté tient finalement au fait que l'on n'a trouvé personne parmi les hôtes du château capable de donner à Gilles Le Breton les plans de cette structure que celui-ci était évidemment incapable de concevoir seul. Avant Serlio, le Roi avait appelé à Fontainebleau Le Rosso et Primatice, l'un en 1530, l'autre en 1532. Nous sommes accoutumés à ne voir en eux que les maîtres de la décoration sensationnelle de la galerie François Ier.[25] Mais tout nous indique qu'il fournissaient en de multiples occasions des modèles parés de l'attrait de la nouveauté. Le Primatice est arrivé à Fontainebleau en 1532, mais avant lui, le Rosso était là, dès la fin de 1530, et Vasari nous assure que "*le roi le fit directeur général de tous les bâtiments, peinture et décor de ce lieu*" (*capo generale sopra tutte le fabriche, pitture e altri ornamenti di quel luogo*).[26] Ce qui donne tout de même à réfléchir. On imagine difficilement, que Rosso n'ait pas eu son mot à dire dans toutes les initiatives de Fontainebleau, où le Roi l'accueillait comme le porteur d'une nouvelle "*maniera*".

L'activité d'architecte de Rosso est attestée plus tard, en 1540, au moment de la visite de Charles-Quint, que les circonstances rendirent si singulières, mais qui compta aussi, toujours à en croire Vasari, par la qualité des "*apparati*": "*fece quando Carlo quinto imperadore andò l'anno 1540 sotto il fede del Re Francesco in*

---

19. *Ibid.*, p. 98; ce rapport avait déjà observé par Léon Palustre, dans *la Renaissance*, Paris, 1879, p. 198.

20. Les *Comptes des Bâtiments, op. cit.*, t. I, p. 210.

21. Louis Hautecœur: *Histoire de l'Architecture Classique en France, op. cit.*, p. 243-4.

22. Voir l'Appendice I, Extrait des Comptes des Batiments du Roi, et L. Dimier, *Fontainebleau*, Paris, 1925, p. 10.

23. L'escalier original avait dans sa plus grande largeur environ dixhuit mètres, et onze mètres de profondeur.

24. F. Gébelin, *op. cit.*, p. 102, n. 14 et 15.

25. Ainsi, A. Bray, *op. cit.*, p. 203, considère comme allant de soi, que les italiens soient cantonnés dans le rôle de décorateurs, et affirme: "l'architecture de la Renaissance à Fontainebleau évoluera dans son propre sens, à peu prés comme s'ils n'avaient pas été là".

26. Vasari, *Le Vite*, ed. Milanesi, vol. v, p. 165 et suivantes. Rosso quitte l'Italie vers 1530, sur l'appel de François Ier; un rôle d'acquit de juillet 1531 constate un paiement pour son "entretenement", en nov. et dec. 1530; Arch. Nat. J. 960 r.

Francia avendo seco non più che dodici uomini, a Fontanablio la meta di tutti gl'ornamentiche fece il re fare per onorare un tanto imperadore; l'altra meta fece Francesco Primaticcio bolognese. Ma le cose che fece il Rosso d'archi, di colossi e altre cose simili, fureno, per quato di disse allora, le più stupende che da altri insino allora fussero state fatte mai."[27]

Vasari ajoute curieusement: *"ma una gran parte delle stanze che il Rosso fece al detto luogo di Fontanableo sono statte disfatte dopo la sua morte dal detto F. Primaticcio"*. Dimier a considéré avec vraisemblance que ces *"stanze"* ont pu être une galerie reliant à la chapelle la Porte Dorée; il fallut les détruire pour faire place à la Salle de Bal.[28] D'autre part, l'historien florentin mentionne la nouvelle galerie royale qui devait à jamais illustrer le château en impliquant que Rosso en a dirigé la construction comme le reste.[29] Les informations de Vasari sur Fontainebleau sont, bien sûr, de seconde main. Mais il connaissait bien le Rosso et ses aptitudes. Il l'a vu avant son départ, en 1528–29, précisément à un moment où *"fece molti disegni... per pitture e fabriche"*.[30] Si l'on songe à l'importance des années 1530–31 pour les entreprises artistiques de François Ier et au rôle pilote que joue alors Fontainebleau, si l'on tient, d'autre part, présent à l'esprit le

tableau du personnel disponible, on en vient invinciblement à attribuer un rôle plus précis au Rosso dans les innovations du château, et donc, en premier lieu, dans l'addition de l'escalier monumental. Celui-ci, en somme, n'aurait-il pas été conçu sur ses plans?

L'explication ne peut prendre corps que dans la mesure où l'on trouve dans les dessins du Rosso et dans les panneaux de la galerie François Ier des schémas d'architecture suffisamment proches de ce qui a été réalisé dans la cour ovale, en tenant compte du fait que l'escalier a été construit dans le grés dur et sévère propre au château et par un entrepreneur français.[31] On trouve dans la scène de l'*Unité de l'Etat* le schéma de l'arc, avec un fort entablement, sèchement découpé, qui répond à la silhouette de la composition de 1530–31. On le retrouve dans une gravure postérieure, la *Vieillesse*. L'hypothèse d'attribuer tout simplement au Rosso, à peine arrivé, le dessin entièrement neuf de l'escalier en arc triomphal n'est donc pas invraisemblable. Elle a l'avantage de mieux coordonner les faits, dans la période la plus active de Fontainebleau.[32] Car enfin, l'escalier de la Cour ovale est le plus ambitieux qui ait été conçu sous François Ier après ceux de Blois et de Chambord.[33] Il manquait quelque chose à celui de Fontainebleau en 1530. Le projet de 1531 comblait brillamment—et, vu la disposition des lieux, un peu abusivement—cette lacune. Raison de plus de supposer qu'il a été inspiré par celui que François Ier avait enfin réussi à attirer à sa cour pour y faire une démonstration décisive du nouveau style. Si l'on veut

27. Sur le voyage de Charles-Quint: V. L. Saulnier, *Charles Quint traversant la France, ce qu'en dirent les poètes français*, dans *Fêtes et Cérémonies au Temps de Charles Quint*, Paris, 1960, p. 207. Et sur son séjour à Fontainebleau: P. Dan, *Trésors des merveilles de la Maison Royale de Fontainebleau*, Paris, 1642, p. 229: "son entrée fut par la grande entrée de la chaussée. A la porte il y avait un arc triomphal orné de trophées et enrichi de peintures."

28. Louis Dimier, p. 289.

29. Vasari, *ibid.*: "nel quale primieramente diede il Rosso principio a una galeria sopra la bassa-corte, facendo di sopra non volta ma un palco ovvero soffitato di legname con bellissimo spartimento. Le facciate dalle bande fece tutte lavorate di stucchi, con spartimenti bizzari e stravaganti".
H. von Geymüller, *Die Baukunst der Renaissance in Frankreich*, Stuttgart, 1898, p. 159–60, rapporte, bien entendu, cette indication de Vasari à la Galerie François Ier, mais en suggérant la possibilité d'attribuer aussi à Rosso le décor extérieur de celle-ci et les lucarnes.

30. P. Barrochi, *Il Rosso Fiorentino*, Rome, 1950, n'aborde pas ces problèmes.
K. Kusenberg, *Le Rosso*, Paris, 1931, se montre trés prudent en ce qui concerne l'activité d'architecte du Rosso (p. 105) Mais Louis Dimier, *op. cit.*, 1924, p. 284 et suivantes, nous semble avoir vu plus clair que: H. von Geymüller, *op. cit.*, p. 159–60.
M. Roy, *Le Monument Funéraire d'Albert Pie de Savoie, comte de Carpi* (1531–5) dans "Artistes et Monuments de la Renaissance en France", Paris, 1928, p. 138 et suivantes, a souligné l'intérêt que présente un réglement indiqué dans un rôle d'octobre ou novembre 1531, mentionnant "ung model d'une sépulture" et a proposé avec vraisemblance d'y voir la maquette du tombeau d'Alberto Pio de Savoie, comte de Carpi (destinée aux Cordeliers).
Sur les dessins d'architecture de Rosso, de nouveaux éléments ont été récemment fournis par E. A. Carroll, *Drawings by Rosso Fiorentino*, in "Burlington Magazine", avril 1966, p. 168–70.

31. Le style bien particulier du portique apparait très nettement par comparaison avec la Porte Dorée, construite par Le Breton seul, avant l'arrivée de Rosso (elle figure dans le devis de 1528 et sa réception est datée de 1531). Le relief est beaucoup plus plat, les chapiteaux sont ornés seulement du monogramme de François Ier (fig. 9).

32. Elle permet de rendre compte de certaines affinités indiquées par A. Blunt (*op. cit.*, p. 39, n. 11) avec des ouvrages italiens où il n'est évidemment pas possible de voir des précédents et encore moins des sources de l'escaliers de la Cour Ovale, tels que: le nouvel escalier de la Niche du Belvédère (élevé par Michel-Ange en 1550–1, voir J. Ackermann, *The Architecture of Michelangelo*, Londres, 1961, p. 115–16) le Palais des Conservateurs (1528, *id.* p. 56 et suivantes) la villa Farnèse de Caprarola. La villa Lavigliano (entre 1529 et 1534) par Falconetto, ne peut guère, non plus, venir en considération directe. C'est l'expérience romaine et toscane de Rosso qui pourrait eclairer la situation; mais il n'existe pas encore d'étude sur l'escalier de la Haute Renaissance en Italie et son emploi "triomphal".

33. Sur Blois, voir en dernier lieu:
F. Gébelin, *Les Chateaux de la Loire*, Paris, 1957, chap. VI, sur Chambord, F. Lesueur, *Léonard de Vinci et Chambord*, dans "Etudes d'Art", Paris-Alger, no 8–10; 1953, p. 225–38, et les observations de F. Gébelin, *op. cit.*, p. 97 et suivantes, sur le rapprochement avec Palladio, *Quattro Libri*, 1581, p. 66.
Le thème de l'escalier "royal" trouvera son couronnement dans l'ouvrage conçu par Philibert de L'Orme aux Tuileries, le "degré le plus vaste, le plus aisé et le plus admirable qui soit au monde" (Sauval) cf.: A. Blunt, *Philibert de L'Orme*, Londres, 1958, p. 100–6.

bien considérer, à partir de cette hypothèse, l'ampleur de l'intervention du Rosso, la transformation de Fontainebleau autour de 1530 prend une dimension intéressante. Il s'agit, comme à Blois, de l'habillage d'une vieille structure, qui est brusquement décidé après 1528: le grand escalier s'articulant avec le portique, c'est la cour entière qui se trouve traitée dans un esprit monumental, la chapelle Saint Saturnin faisant saillie à l'extérieur de la cour, avec son abside qui répète sur deux étages le motif architectural du portique—escalier, accentue l'unité du nouvel ensemble, d'autant plus qu'il se prolongeait entre les chapelles et le Porte Dorée par une galerie et des appartements selon l'indication déjà citée de Vasari.[34] Dix ans plus tard, cette puissante composition était déjà modifiée, et l'on est frappé de voir avec quelle facilité le Primatice disposa des aménagements du Rosso. De ce que nous savons, en grande partie grâce à Vasari, ami du Primatice, de la rivalité entre le Florentin et le jeune Emilien, on est tenté de se demander si la transformation de l'escalier géant n'aurait pas également fait partie des initiatives de Primatice après la soudaine disparition du Rosso. Mais le contrat de 1540 qui concerne le "rechangement du grand escalier" est antérieur à la mort du "Maître Roux". Il est aussi à la venue de Charles-Quint, et

c'est peut-être pour cette visite que l'on a voulu dégager la cour en améliorant les conditions de réception. Si l'on forme l'hypothèse que l'escalier monumental de la cour a été conçu en 1531 sur les plans de Rosso, il faut admettre qu'il a été le témoin de sa transformation radicale. Vasari tend, en somme à presenter l'action du Rosso entre 1530 et 1540 comme un premier épisode, dont la direction de Primatice après 1540 constitue le second. Et son témoignage, même tendancieux, vient compléter utilement le dossier des comptes royaux. Primatice a d'abord compté comme peintre et décorateur puis comme architecte. Avec le Rosso, si notre hypothèse est exacte, ce serait l'inverse: les plans et dessins d'architecture pour la cour ovale auraient précédé l'idée de la création d'une galerie. Celle-ci allait être la nouveauté durable du château. Son succès a pu faire oublier l'effet sensationnel qu'a dû produire l'apparition du grand escalier portique. Implanté au milieu de la cour, conformément à la tradition française et au goût du règne, il marquait solennellement par un *degré* spectaculaire l'orientation nouvelle.[35]

34. Voir *supra*, n. 28; et Louis Dimier, *Le Primatice, op. cit.*, p. 284 et suivantes.

35. Nous joignons à cette étude une publication des Comptes Royaux concernant le problème, et une note sur les représentation de la cour ovale dans la gravure, pour lesquelles j'ai eu le concours de Mme. Fr. Hamon.
Nous remerçions la Direction des Monuments Historiques pour les photographies des fouilles de Bray; le dossier lui-même n'a pu être retrouvé.

APPENDICE I

Extrait des "Bâtiments du Roi" de 1528 à 1570, par Félibien des Avaux. B.N. ms fr. 11.179, f° 188–9 (Ed. Laborde et Guiffrey, p. 210)

Bastiments du Roy pour les deux années finies le dernier septembre 1550

Devis, marchés, toisés et certifications des ouvrages des Bastiments de Fontainebleau, Boullongne-les-Paris, que nos Seigneurs des Comptes ont ordonnés à la closture du dernier compte desdits bastiments rendus par le présent commis Nicolas Picart.

Maçonnerie

Gilles le Breton, maistre Maçon des Bastiments du Roy, à Fontainebleau confesse avoir fait marché et convenant (convention??) à Messire Nicolas de Neuville, chevalier Seigneur de Villeroy, conseiller du Roy et secrétaire de ses finances, et Philibert

Babou, aussi chevalier, et Seigneur de la Bourdaizière, conceiller du Roy, secrétaire de ses finances et trésorier de France, commissaires ordonnés et députés par le Roy, sur le fait de ses bastiments et ediffices de Fontainebleau, en la présence de Pierre Deshotels, varlet de chambre ordinaire du Roy, et par lui commis au contrôle des dits bastiments et ediffices, de faire et parfaire pour le Roy, en son chateau de Fontainebleau tous et chacun les ouvrages de Maçonnerie et taille qu'il convient faire pour le rechangement du grand escalier dudit chasteau et autres ouvrages contenus et déclarés au devis cy-devant escrit, et ce outre le contenu et marché fait avec lui pour raison dudit grand escalier et de la chapelle dudit chasteau daté du samedi cinquième d'aout 1531 et pour ce sera tenu le dit

Breton faire toutes les démolitions et rétablissement qu'il conviendra pour ce faire desquelles démolitions il remettra en œuvres tout ce qui pourra servir aux dits ouvrages et le reste il sera tenu serrer et mettre en tas dans la court dudit chasteau au profit du Roy, et fournir et ivrer (??) ledit Breton les autres matières de pierres de taille, de grais et liais, et autres matières qu'il conviendra pour yceux ouvrages, outre ce qui restera desdites démolitions, tant chaux, sable, eschaffaux, engins, peynes d'ouvriers et aydes et autres choses à ce necessaires touchant le fait de maçonnerie, et rendre place nette, le tout et duement suivant ledit devis devant transcrit, et au dit d'ouvriers et gens à ce connaissant, moyennant et parmy le prix de 1,800 livres qui pour ce fait lui en sera baillé, et payé par le commis au paiement desdits bastiments et ediffices de Fontainebleau au feur et ainsi qu'il aura besongné et fait besongné audits ouvrages, esquels il sera tenu de besongner et faire besongner en plus grande diligence et avec le plus gran nombre d'ouvriers que faire se pourra, promettant et obligeant, comme pour les propres affaires du Roy, renonçant fait et passé multiples, le jeudi 10° mars 1540.

Signé: "Drouin et Groussart"

De l'ordonnance de noble personne Maitre Philibert de l'Orme, abbe... ausmônier ordinnaire du Roy, architecte dudit Seigneur, commissaire ordonné et député sur le fait de ses bastiments et édiffices de Fontainebleau, nous, Charles Baillard, maitre maçon de Monseigneur le Connétable, Guillaume Chalou, Jean Chaponnet, maistres maçons à Paris, et Jean François, aussy maçon demeurant à Meuleun aprés serment par nous fait par devant ledit commissaire avons en sa présence et en la présence de Pierre Deshotels, notaire et secraitaire du Roy, et par lui commis au contrôle desdits édiffices, veu visité les ouvrages de maçonnerie et taille de l'édifice fait de neuf audit Fontainebleau, auquel il y a deus chapelles, l'une basse et l'autre haute, et aussi le grand escalier fait de neuf audit chasteau par Maitre Gilles Lebreton, maitres des œuvres de maçonnerie du Roy à savoir si ledit édiffice des dites deux chapelles et ledit grand escalier ont été et sont bien fait et parfait, ainsi que ledit Breton est tenu et obligé par deux devis et marché de ces faits.

On s'explique mal la présence du marché de 1540 dans les comptes de 1548-1550. La publication Laborde–Guiffrey est peu explicite sur ce point: les textes sont présentés à la suite les uns des autres sans commentaire.

Le second texte—la visite ordonnée par Philibert Delorme—n'est pas daté. On pourrait supposer que la reception du "rechangement" de l'escalier se situe en 1548; on aurait ainsi groupé dans les comptes l'ordre de "reception" et les contrats auquel il est fait allusion à la dernière ligne de ce texte. Félibien aurait donc trouvé les deux textes ensemble, sous la rubrique "1548-1550". Il parait pourtant bien improbable que les travaux de rechangement de l'escalier aient duré huit ans, alors que le contrat de 1540 précise qu'il faudra besongner en "plus grande diligence", et que ces travaux ne demandaient pas beaucoup de temps. Ce peut être une manœuvre tardive de Delorme pour prendre Lebreton en faute, ou tout simplement une erreur du copiste qui travaillait pour Félibien.

Le texte du marché de 1540 ne prête à aucune équivoque: le contrat de 1531 stipulait la construction du grand escalier et de la chapelle; celui de 1540 ordonne le rechangement de l'escalier en question sans qu'il soit encore question de la chapelle; or, il semble que chapelle et escalier soient contemporains (même profils trés énergiques). Le rechangement suppose donc un simple remaniement et non une reconstruction totale. Le texte indique que les matériaux des démolitions seront partiellement remis en œuvre, sans doute pour masquer les arrachements (à la corniche séparant les deux étages du portique principalement); on utilisera pour ce faire des moulurations identiques prises aux balcons ou aux rampes. Le reste, qui devait être important—degrés et rampes—sera réservé pour un usage postérieur.

Une seule question se pose: Breton devra fournir les autres pierres de taille, "grais et liais"; or, il semble que le grés seul ait servi à la construction du "portique", à l'exclusion de tout autre matériau, même pour les chapitaux (lors des restaurations de 1894-1896, on eut le plus grand mal à trouver des artisans qui acceptent de tailler dans le grés des chapitaux nouveaux pour remplacer ceux d'origine, en trés mauvais état. Signalons à cette occasion que les chapitaux du XVI⁰ siècle, déposés, ont totalement disparu).

Ces textes publiés par Laborde ont servi à André Félibien pour la rédaction de son *Mémoire pour servir à l'Histoire des Maisons Royales et Bastiments de France*, composé en 1681, et publié en 1874, ouvrage malheureusement inachevé, qui ne comporte que l'histoire des chateaux du Val de Loire.

APPENDICE II

Note sur les Représentations de l'Escalier de la Cour Ovale après 1540

Le seul document antérieur aux remaniements de Henri IV, est évidemment celui que fournit Ducerceau avec un plan et deux vues, l'une générale, l'autre de détail, qui est précisément la cour ovale (fig. 1). Il existe également un dessin de Ducerceau (British Museum) publié par Ward, donnant une vue de la cour ovale identique à la précédente. (Ce dessin donne une reproduction beaucoup moins satisfaisante que l'estampe.) Selon cette estampe, le portique est situé à peu près au centre du grand corps de logis, nettement décalé par rapport à la chapelle. L'escalier est désormais rentré à l'intérieur du corps de logis; il se présente, en plan, sous la forme de deux rampes droites, prenant leur départ sous les deux arcs latéraux du portique triomphal, le passage sous l'arc central permettant d'accéder aux salles du rez-de-chaussée. Le plan de Ducerceau ne permet pas de préciser s'il s'agit d'un escalier de type "impérial" avec une troisième rampe partant d'un palier intermédiaire, ou d'un escalier double à deux rampes parallèles.[1] La vue générale des *Plus excellents Bâtiments* laisse deviner dans la partie tournante de la cour ovale, la façade de la chapelle, façade disparue lors des remaniements de Henri IV pour régulariser le tracé de la cour (il prolonge la façade de la "salle de bal" de quatre travées). Cette vue générale est prise d'un point de vue opposé à celui de la planche de détail, c'est à dire du bourg.

Le premier document figurant le portique après les transformations de Henri IV est une vue de 1614 gravée par Alexandre Francini Fiorentini "*Portrait de la Maison Roayle de Fontainebleau*" (B.N. Cabinet des Estampes, Va 340, f° 9) assez sommaire, mais qui montre bien le nouvel alignement de la cour. Il faut attendre 1681 pour trouver un plan gravé (et non une vue) représentant avec exactitude le nouvel escalier construit dans le portique déplacé. Les deux plans manuscrits de la B.N. (Cabinet des Estampes, Va 340, f° 22 et 23) du fonds Robert de Cotte—achèvement de la cour des Fontaines montrent qu'en 1729 l'escalier n'a toujours pas été modifié (fig. 10). Le deuxième

de ces plans, figurant le premier étage montre bien qu'il s'agit ici d'un escalier impérial: partant d'un palier intermédiaire, une troisième rampe débouche sous l'arc central du portique (ce qui était sans doute très incommode, car il fallait passer par le portique, dans le froid, pour accéder aux salles de l'étage). Sur le plan de Ducerceau, l'escalier, dans son emplacement primitif, était représenté de façon identique au plan du rez-de-chaussée que donne Robert de Cotte: deux rampes parallèles très courtes (fig. 10). Ceci laisserait supposer que l'escalier de 1541 était lui aussi à trois rampes (impérial); on se serait donc contenté en déplaçant le portique, de transférer sans l'altérer l'escalier qui y était logé.

En 1767, Gabriel décide de créer un nouvel escalier plus commode pour desservir les appartements de la Reine qui occupait cette partie du château. Il le conçoit selon le même type que celui qu'il avait déjà construit pour les appartements du Roi, trois rampes perpendiculaires s'appuyant aux murs d'une cage carrée. Des problèmes pratiques interdisent de l'installer derrière le portique; on le construit donc à côté, et on installe sur l'emplacement de l'ancien escalier un vestibule à colonnes, au rez-de-chaussée, une salle pour les gardes de la Reine au premier étage (A.N.O[1] 1424 f° 17). Une coupe du nouvel escalier est reproduite dans l'ouvrage de Bottineau: *L'Art d'Ange Jacques Gabriel à Fontainebleau* (Paris, 1962, pl. 58). L'escalier est resté tel que Gabriel l'avait conçu et n'a subi que des altérations de détail.

Pour l'étude des motifs sculptés du portique de la cour ovale, il faut se reporter aux planches de la *Monographie du Palais de Fontainebleau*, recueil de gravures de Pfnor, accompagné d'un texte de Champollion-Figeac (texte très vieilli) publié en 1863, donc avant les réfections de Boitte, en 1894 (on remplaça alors les chapiteaux). Les gravures VI et VII (vol. I) donnent une bonne coupe du portique et des détails des chapiteaux. On retrouve les mêmes chapiteaux ornés de sirènes qui ont des nageoires à la place des pieds, et des ailes au lieu de bras (vol. II, pl. CXXXIX) sur les pilastres de l'abside de la chapelle Saint Saturnin, chapelle haute. La gravure n° XIV (vol. I) donne une bonne reproduction du pavillon de la Porte Dorée, qui permet une comparaison avec le portique (fig. 9).

---

[1] Selon un de nos élèves, J. Guillaume, la présence de Chambiges à Fontainebleau et les liens de cet artiste avec Dominique de Cortone permettent de supposer plutôt cette solution; c'est celle du modèle en bois de Chambord; elle est proche de celle qui sera adoptée par Chambiges à Challuau.

RENÉ TAYLOR

Architecture and Magic

Considerations on the *Idea* of the Escorial*

The vault over the raised choir of the Escorial displays one of the largest and least inspired frescoes painted during the whole of the sixteenth century. Executed by Luca Cambiaso, its theme is *La Gloria* or the Vision of Paradise, showing the Trinity presiding over the legions of the blessed.[1] Isolated within an aureole of light, God the Father and the Son are seated upon the rainbow, while the Holy Spirit hovers above them (Fig. 1). None of this would call for comment if it were not for the unusual object upon which the First and Second Persons rest their feet. It resembles a block of stone in the form of a cube jutting out diagonally from the plane of the painting.

Though curious in itself, it is even more curious to discover that this feature finds no mention in any description or analysis of Cambiaso's vault.[2] Yet, considering its prominence, it must be assumed that the painter did not introduce it into his fresco out of mere caprice. Moreover Philip II is known to have superintended the construction and decoration of the Escorial down to the smallest detail. If the cube is there, then it was introduced with the king's approval or even more likely at his express command. This being so, it must possess some kind of significance.

The cube or hexahedron is one of the basic geometrical figures. As a derivative of the square, that vital ingredient of Pythagorean mathematics, it was discussed by Plato in the *Timaeus*, in which he considered it geometrically, numerically and symbolically, equating it with earth, the heaviest and most inert of the four elements. During the Renaissance Fra Luca Paccioli

dealt with it in his *De Divina Proportione* as part of his treatment of the five regular figures. It may be argued that the cube was by no means an inappropriate symbol to introduce into this fresco, since earth is the base and foundation of the elements, the receptacle of heavenly influences and the material chosen by God from which to fashion mankind.[3] On the other hand, Piero Valeriano in his *Hieroglyphica* comes up with what in our context is rather a more convincing interpretation. For him the cube, besides being one of the five regular solids and the symbol of earth, has also a Hermetic meaning: it is a 'hieroglyph' of the SUPREMUM NUMEN.[4] As this figure is the outcome of a threefold operation[5] its presence at the foot of the Trinity would not be out of place. There is, however, a third source to be considered. Incidentally it is not wholly unrelated to the foregoing, since one of its points of departure is likewise the process of multiplication to the power of three. It is a manuscript treatise on the cube, of which two copies are preserved in the library of the Escorial itself.[6] Generally known as the *Discurso de la Figura Cúbica*, it was published some thirty years ago, being given the title, translated into English, of *A Treatise on the Cubic Figure according to the principles and opinions of the Art of Ramón Lull*.[7] Its author was none other than Juan de Herrera, Philip II's architect.[8] Probably

* The author wishes to acknowledge the assistance received in the preparation of this essay from Miss Frances Yates and Mrs. Enriqueta Frankfort of the Warburg Institute, London, from Padre Gregorio de Andrés, O.S.A., librarian of the Escorial, from Dr. Owen Gingerich of the Smithsonian Astrophysical Observatory, Cambridge, Mass., and from Mr. Eric Schroeder, curator of Islamic antiquities, the Fogg Museum of Art, Cambridge, Mass. He is also indebted to the Consejo del Patrimonio Artístico Nacional, Madrid, for permission to publish plates 1, 3, 4, 5, 6, 7, 8, 9, 10, 11, 12, 15, 16, 21, 22, 23, 24, 31, 34.

1. Fray Julián Zarco Cuevas, *Pintores italianos en San Lorenzo el Real de El Escorial*, Madrid, 1932, pp. 18 ff.
2. None of the chroniclers of the Escorial so much as mention it. Modern authors, such as Fray Julián Zarco Cuevas (*loc. cit.*) and Bertina Suida Manning and William Suida (*Luca Cambiaso*, Milan, 1958, p. 127), are likewise silent on this particular feature of the fresco.

3. Agrippa of Nettesheim, *De occulta philosophia*, Antwerp, 1533, bk. 1, chap. 5.
4. Piero Valeriano, *Hieroglyphica*, Lyon, 1594, bk. XXXIX, p. 383, DE TRINO, CUBUS. The 1556 edition of the *Hieroglyphica*, printed at Bâle, was no. 940 in the list of books given by Philip II to the Escorial in 1576 (see Appendix 1, p. 105).
5. Plato does not labor this point, whereas for Valeriano it is all-important.
6. MSS. nos. G–IV–39 and D–III–25.
7. Its abbreviated title is given as *Discurso de la Figura Cúbica*. It was published by Editorial Plutarco, Madrid, 1935, with an introduction by Julio Rey Pastor.
8. Though an attempt was made to discredit Herrera's authorship (Amancio Portabales Pichel, *Los Verdaderos Artífices de El Escorial*, Madrid, 1945, pp. 155 ff.), it is now generally accepted without question as his. There was a copy of it amongst his own books (Agustín Ruiz de Arcaute, *Juan de Herrera*, Madrid, 1936, p. 169). The main grounds for contesting Herrera's authorship were that MS. no. G–IV–39 bears a note assigning it to Juan Bautista de Toledo, the first architect of the Escorial. This, however, is in seventeenth-century handwriting and therefore of a later date. It is the only known indication that the latter might also have been a Lullist. The *Discurso* is of

then it is Herrera's cube, rather than any other, that is depicted on the vault.[9]

One of the most extraordinary characteristics of Renaissance and post-Renaissance thought is the extent of the influence exercised on it by Ramón Lull's Art.[10] We do not propose entering into the reasons for this here.[11] Suffice to say that with few exceptions there was hardly an important thinker from Nicholas of Cusa to Descartes and Leibniz who on some score or other failed to acknowledge his indebtedness to it. Nevertheless not all the works that passed for his at this time were by any means authentic. During the Renaissance there circulated a number of pseudo-Lullian writings which represented an attempt to graft on to the Art all kinds of Hermetic and occultist tendencies. They were largely accepted as genuine[12] and formed the basis of Lull's reputation as a Magus.[13] Yet he himself had largely pointed the way. His whole cosmology is astrological. Moreover the very manipulation of the figures, charts and wheels of the Art seems to have something of magic about it.

It is not known for certain when Juan de Herrera became a Lullist,[14] but he certainly became one of the country's leading adepts of Lull's doctrine. He had over one hundred Lullian works in his private library.[15] Then too, as Philip II's *aposentador mayor*[16] and a member of his inner entourage, he was in a markedly favorable position to influence the king on behalf of Lull and his writings. Nor did he neglect his opportunity. In 1580 while Philip was on his way to Lisbon to assume the Portuguese crown, Herrera who was in his suite contrived to have Juan Seguí, a canon of Palma cathedral and an enthusiastic Lullist—incidentally he also dabbled in alchemy—, give him an account of Lull and his Art. In Lisbon itself he continued his exposition with the result that Philip was wholly won over to the Lullist cause.[17] The appearance of the cube in Cambiaso's fresco, begun some four or five years after this event, must surely be interpreted as a visible but veiled token of the king's new-found allegiance to Ramón Lull and his doctrine.[18]

To judge from the *Discurso* or *Treatise on the Cubic Figure* as well as the large number of Lullian works he owned, Lullism must have been one of Herrera's consuming interests. That a coldly rational architect, described as 'a man of the square and plummet',[19] should have had this overriding concern may strike us today as somewhat odd. Yet, as already stated, it was shared by most thinkers at this time. On the other hand, it may be a little difficult to see just how his Lullism ties in with his other more practical forms of activity, such as architecture, astronomy, metallurgy and mechanics. The answer would seem to lie in what was one of the dominant characteristics of the thought and culture of the period, namely Hermetism. Only when it is realized that the common bond uniting all these apparently unconnected strands is magic,[20] do

special interest for the study of Lullism in the sixteenth century in that it is neither a digest of the Art nor a commentary upon it, but an original way of using its basic principles to produce a work of undeniable originality.

9. Herrera was directly concerned with this fresco. See Zarco Cuevas, *op. cit.*, p. 2, n. 2.

10. Publications on Lull and his influence are too numerous to be quoted. Most relevant to the theme of this study is Frances Yates, 'The Art of Ramón Lull', *Journal of the Warburg and Courtauld Institutes*, vol. XVII. nos. 1 and 2, 1954.

11. 'Un sentido esencialmente platónico informará, pues, toda la filosofía luliana.' This brief quotation from Joaquín y Tomás Carreras y Artau, *Historia de la filosofia española*, Madrid, 1939, vol. 1, p. 484, will go far towards explaining Lull's popularity during the Renaissance.

12. The list is a long one. It includes such titles as the *Ars Chemiae*, *Ars Auriferae*, *De auditu kabbalistico*, *De secretis naturae*, *De compositione gemmarum*, *De intentione alchymistarum*, *De virtutibus aquae vitae* and so on. Of the five books supposedly by Ramón Lull, which were made over by Philip II to the Escorial in 1576, only one was genuine. Over one hundred spurious works, attributed at one time to Lull, are cited in Littré-Hauréau, *Histoire littéraire de la France*, Paris, 1885, vol. XXIX, article 'Raymond Lulle'.

13. In one instance he was even equated with Hermes Trismegistus. He was thus referred to by Juan Luis Vileta in his *In Acroamaticam Aristotelis Philosophiam*, Barcelona, 1569 (quoted by J. & T. Carreras y Artau, *op. cit.*, 1943, vol. II, p. 262). In this work Vileta, a canon of the cathedral of Barcelona and a prominent Lullist, distinguishes between two main philosophies, a natural or 'open' one, to be identified chiefly with Aristotle, and a secret or 'closed' one which is that of Plato. The latter was known to the Egyptians, Chaldees, Persians, Babylonians, Assyrians and Jews. It was communicated to the Greeks by Pythagoras and transmitted in secret by Plato and to a lesser extent also by Aristotle. Later it was divinely revealed to Ramón Lull who perfected it and who is therefore the true Trismegistus.

14. The origins of Herrera's Lullism are uncertain, but he was certainly a Lullist by 1579, the date of his first will. He may conceivably have derived his interest in Lull from Juan Bautista

de Toledo who had come over to Spain from Naples, one of the great centers of Lullism in Italy. However, there is no evidence to show that Juan Bautista was ever in fact a Lullist (see note 8). Herrera was appointed assistant to the chief architect on February 18, 1563.

15. See the inventory of Herrera's books, made after his death, in Ruiz de Arcaute, *op. cit.*, pp. 166 ff. Also Joaquín Carreras y Artau, 'El Lul·lisme de Juan de Herrera', in *Miscel·lanea Puig y Cadafalch*, Barcelona, Institut d'Estudis Catalans, 1947–51, vol. I, pp. 41 ff.

16. Herrera was appointed *aposentador mayor de palacio* in 1579. This post gave him unrestricted access to the king.

17. This incident is related in the Prologue of Juan Seguí's *Vida y hechos de ... Ramón Lull*, Valencia, 1606. See also T. & J. Carreras y Artau, *Historia de la filosofia española*, Madrid, 1943, vol. II, pp. 258 and 266.

18. Expressed of course through the medium of the figure in Herrera's *Discurso*. Philip II, at this time a confirmed Lullist, would certainly have been familiar with this work. That several manuscripts of it exist may well have been due to his having it copied more than once. The autograph original was probably the one in Herrera's possession when he died (see note 8).

19. Thus described by Marcelino Menéndez y Pelayo.

20. The word 'magic' is here used in the wide sense in which Renaissance writers employed the word *magia*. The latter was

Herrera's multifarious interests begin to fall into place and create a consistent pattern.

According to a contemporary chronicler Juan de Herrera did not begin to cultivate scholarly interests 'until somewhat late'.[21] This statement, however, is hardly borne out by the facts. By 1563, the date of his official appointment as assistant to Juan Bautista de Toledo, the designer of the Escorial, Herrera had traveled widely, knew Latin, was versed in mathematics and architecture, had some knowledge of astronomy and mechanics, besides being a draughtsman of no ordinary skill. He was probably also conversant with Italian.[22] It would not seem too far-fetched to assume that he was appointed to be Toledo's assistant at least with the latter's consent; it may even have been at his express request. Moreover, it is logical to suppose that there were solid grounds for his being given the post. He remained close to Juan Bautista until the latter died in 1567, figuring among the witnesses to his will.[23]

Surprise has sometimes been expressed that Philip II did not at once promote Herrera to fill the vacancy thus created, the usual explanation given being the king's caution in selecting and advancing his servants. Nevertheless from 1567 onwards the architect's status did change. The monarch who had previously attached him to Juan Bautista de Toledo now attached him to himself. Thereafter Herrera was almost in constant attendance upon him.[24] He now usually visited the Escorial only when his master did. Yet his role must have been of some consequence, seeing that in 1571 he was granted leave to construct a lodging there for himself at royal expense.[25]

With the years a special bond of affection developed between Herrera and king Philip. The architect became 'intimately dear to him', as the Jesuit, Juan

Bautista Villalpando, his one-time pupil, expressed it.[26] The king consistently retained him about his person and advanced him in his service.[27] He must therefore have had talents above those of a mere draughtsman. The buildings he designed show that he was an architect in his own right. Yet he was also something more. He was, as already stated, an expert in mechanical contrivances, some of which were used on the Escorial,[28] and he wrote a treatise on elementary mechanics for the king.[29] He claimed to have saved the crown much money by showing up the deficiencies in many of the mechanical inventions submitted to it.[30] So too he was interested in metal mining and smelting.[31] He was consulted on problems of military and hydraulic engineering.[32] Then there is his statement that he had invented a number of useful navigational instruments.[33] Villalpando probably had things such as these in mind when he described him as *ingeniosissimus ac peritissimus vir*.[34]

To find the nearest parallel to the peculiar position occupied by Herrera at court we must turn to Velázquez who was likewise *aposentador mayor*, a very close personal friend of the king and at the same time both a painter and architect. The latter, however, differed from his predecessor in that he does not seem to have shared his interest in Hermetism and magic. That we know about this at all is due in the main to the survival of the inventory of Herrera's books made after his death in 1597. In his brief study of this library, Sánchez Cantón has drawn attention to the high number of occult works it contained.[35] Even so the list is rather longer than he seems to have imagined owing to misidentification and other reasons.

The works in question can be divided into three categories, according to their period: late antique, medieval and Renaissance. Beginning with Hermes Trismegistus, Herrera possessed most of the early Hermetic writers such as Plotinus, Porphyry, Proclus, Iamblichus, Synesius, pseudo-Pythagoras and pseudo-Dionysius, as

in no sense restricted to demoniacal magic, but embraced virtually all manifestations of Hermetism and occultism, being even extended to cover the workings of natural phenomena.

21. Luis Cabrera de Córdoba, *Historia de Felipe II*, bk. II, chap. 16. In the preamble to his *Discurso de la Figura Cúbica* Herrera himself states that he lacked 'todo género de estudios', which has been taken as confirming Cabrera's low estimate of the architect's abilities. This kind of polite deference, however, was common at this time and in this instance probably meant no more than that the author admitted being unable to write his treatise in elegant humanist Latin. The subsequent text shows him to have been acquainted with all kinds of disciplines.

22. Our main source for details of Herrera's early life is a *Memorial* which in 1584 he addressed to the royal secretary Mateo Vázquez. For the text of this document see Antonio Ponz, *Viage de España*, Madrid, 1780, vol. IX, letter 6, p. 171. Also Eugenio Llaguno y Amirola, *Noticia de los Arquitectos y Arquitectura de España*, Madrid, 1829, vol. II, pp. 332 ff.

23. Eugenio Llaguno, *op. cit.*, vol. II, p. 241.

24. *Ibid.*, p. 333.

25. See Luis Cervera Vera, *Juan de Herrera y su aposento en la Villa de El Escorial*, El Escorial, 1949, p. 15, appendix 3.

26. Jerónimo Prado and Juan Bautista Villalpando, *In Ezechielem Explanationes*, Rome, 1596–1604, tomus II (*De Postrema Ezechielis Prophetae Visione*), pars II, disc. I isagog., cap. 7, p. 18.

27. See Luis Cervera Vera, 'Semblanza de Juan de Herrera', in *El Escorial 1563–1963*, Madrid, Ediciones del Patrimonio Nacional, 1963, vol. II, pp. 16 ff.

28. Francisco Iñiguez Almech, 'Los Ingenios de Juan de Herrera', in *El Escorial 1563–1963*, vol. II, pp. 181 ff.

29. Ruiz de Arcaute, *op. cit.*, pp. 36 ff.

30. Francisco Iñiguez Almech, *op. cit.*, p. 181.

31. Mentioned in the *Memorial* to Mateo Vázquez. See Eugenio Llaguno, *op. cit.*, vol. II, pp. 336 and 334.

32. Ruiz de Arcaute, *op. cit.*, pp. 46–48 and 137–40.

33. Eugenio Llaguno, *op. cit.*, vol. II, p. 335.

34. Prado and Villalpando, *Explanationes*, Tom. I, Prologue to the Reader, p. XII.

35. Francisco Javier Sánchez Cantón, *La Librería de Juan de Herrera*, Madrid, 1941, pp. 13 ff.

also the astrological works of Ptolemy and Julius Firmicus. Among the medieval figures in his collection were Arthephius, Psellus, Cecco d'Ascoli, pseudo-Albertus Magnus, Geber, Avicenna, Arnold of Villanova and Alfonso the Wise. Prominent among those of the Renaissance were Ficino, Pico, Trithemius, Paracelsus, Cornelius Gemma, Camillo, Porta, Bruno and John Dee. In addition he had a number of pseudo-Lullian alchemical and cabalistic texts. Then too he owned manuscript treatises on cosmology, astrology, alchemy, numerology and kindred subjects, which cannot be identified with precision. Nor should it be overlooked that he would have been able to supplement his reading from the very large collection of magical texts in the library of the Escorial.[36]

In considering Herrera's occult books it must also be borne in mind that he possessed many 'borderline' works, such as those on mnemonics, music, medicine, astronomy, mechanics and mathematics, which could be related directly or indirectly to *magia*.[37] This is because at this period the dividing line between magic and strict science was by no means clearly drawn. Many of the leading mathematicians of the time were likewise Hermetists, astrologers and alchemists.[38] Even Copernicus who demonstrated the heliocentric system by the most sophisticated mathematical calculations adduces in his *De revolutionibus* the authority of Hermes Trismegistus and the *prisci magi*.[39]

This blurring of contours is particularly evident in the field of mathematics. The importance of these studies was consistently emphasized. The fact is, however, that they were at this period of two types. Side by side with 'scientific' or quantitative mathematics there existed what might be termed 'mystical' or Hermetic mathematics stemming ultimately from Pythagoras.[40]

Padre Sigüenza, the historian of the Escorial, described Juan de Herrera as 'a man of great intellect who achieved much in mathematics'.[41] He apparently wrote on this subject but unfortunately nothing has survived.[42] Then too in 1582 he took a leading part in the establishment of the Academy of Mathematics in Madrid.[43] But the real question, particularly in the light of his Lullism and the *Discurso*, is just how far Herrera was an adept of Hermetic as opposed to rational mathematics. There is certainly evidence to show that he was fascinated by the former. In his library there was *A manuscript discourse on the perfect number Ten in Italian*.[44] This must have been some kind of Pythagorean-Cabalist-Lullian exposition on the so-called 'perfect number', a theme touched upon in the *Discurso*.[45] Probably the truth is that, like other mathematicians of the period, he was aware of the difference and even maintained them on different levels of his mind, but was prepared to merge them should the occasion seem to demand it. The *Discurso* itself affords an illustration in point; he takes certain definitions of Euclid, the creator of rational geometry, as the basis of a highly mystical exposition of the cubic figure according to the principles of Lull's Art.[46]

Additional evidence of this mingling of the scientific and Hermetic strains is provided by a letter, dated January 1, 1584, which Herrera wrote to the secretary of the Spanish embassy in Venice.[47] Though he makes mention of the establishment of the Academy of Mathematics, most of it is taken up with requests for books. After listing several scientific works on mathematics, astronomy and mechanics, he adds 'every possible work by Hermes Trismegistus available in Italian'. Then he goes on: 'if Copernicus has been translated into Italian send me a copy...' Finally he comes to Lull. 'There is in circulation a book in Italian on alchemy and natural matters called *El Felix*,[48] which I believe is by Ramón Lull; if it can be obtained, I entreat you, Sir, to send it to me with the rest...'

36. See Appendix 1, p. 102.
37. They are too numerous to be listed in full. See Sánchez Cantón, *op. cit.*, *passim*.
38. Such as Nicholas of Cusa, Cardanus, Gauricus, Stadius, Porta, John Dee, Tycho Brahe and Kepler. Examples of the survival of this type of thinker well into the seventeenth century are Athanasius Kircher and Juan Caramuel. Even Leibniz and Newton had their 'Hermetic' side. See, for instance, the latter's reconstruction of the Temple of Solomon in his *Prolegomena ad lexici prophetici partem secundam, continens expositionem allusionum ad mundum mysticum populi Israelis*, MS. in the Babson Institute Library.
39. Frances Yates, *Giordano Bruno and the Hermetic Tradition*, London, 1963, pp. 153 ff.
40. In his *De coniecturis* of 1440 Nicholas of Cusa announced that he was working out a new supra-rational type of geometry, to which he gave the name of *geometria intellectualis*, transcending the Euclidian or rational variety. It would presumably have had analogies with the mystical geometry of Ramón Lull's *De Nova Geometria* (see José Maria Millás Vallicrosa, *El Libro de la 'Nova Geometria' de Ramón Lull*, Barcelona, 1953, and Santiago Caramella, 'Il problema del simbolo logico nell' umanesimo del Cusano', in *Umanesino e Simbolismo*, Padua, 1958, p. 155). This would seem to tie in with a statement made

by Lefèvre d'Etaples that the cardinal had written a book on Divine Numbers, which he hoped to publish.
41. Fray José de Sigüenza, *Tercera Parte de la Historia de la Orden de San Geronimo*, Madrid, 1605, bk. III, disc. IX.
42. Ruiz de Arcaute, *op. cit.*, p. 170.
43. Luis Cervera Vera, *Semblanza de Juan de Herrera*, p. 55. The history of this Academy has never been seriously investigated. The possibility cannot be dismissed that, like similar academies elsewhere, it was tinged with Hermetism.
44. Ruiz de Arcaute, *op. cit.*, p. 160.
45. Juan de Herrera, *Discurso de la Figura Cúbica*, Madrid, 1935, p. 42.
46. *Ibid.*, pp. 5 ff.
47. Ruiz de Arcaute, *op. cit.*, p. 99. It is possible that Herrera was also in touch with the Venetian occultist academies.
48. Lull's *Felix* or *Libre de Meravellas* contains an exposition of his astrological system. There is also a chapter on alchemy, but in this the author refutes the idea of the transmutation of metals. See Frances Yates, *The Art of Ramón Lull*, pp. 136 ff.

The juxtaposition of Hermes Trismegistus, Copernicus and Lull could hardly be more eloquent. Though he is not positively known to have subscribed to the Copernican system, he certainly seems to have been interested in it, seeing that among his books there were two copies of the original Latin version of the *De revolutionibus*.[49]

The study of the heavens must have been another of Herrera's main interests. In 1561 he had been commissioned by Honorato Juan, bishop of Osma,[50] who at that time was tutor to Philip II's son, Don Carlos, to draw the diagrams that were to illustrate a sumptuous copy of *The Books of the Science of Astronomy* by Alfonso the Wise, which is still preserved in the Escorial.[51] As for the astronomical works he owned, they included all the standard texts from Aristarchus and Ptolemy to Frascatoro and Copernicus. There were also others on the annulus and the astrolabe, on eclipses and the making of sundials and clocks of all kinds. He had the Alfonsine and Prutenic tables,[52] as

also a miscellaneous collection of almanacs and ephemerides. In addition he possessed a large number of quadrants, annula, globes, astrolabes and armillary spheres, some of them inscribed in Arabic.[53]

Although Herrera had a good selection of books on architecture, military engineering and kindred subjects, this ostensibly being his main field of activity, it was by no means as complete as that of his magical and near-magical works.[54] This makes one wonder whether architecture was in fact his chief concern. Was this the real reason why Philip II secured him about his person and made him accompany the royal household wherever it went? May not the explanation rather be that we are dealing with a Magus, a man deeply versed in Hermetism and occult lore, who by virtue of this was attached in a special way to the king? If, as the nature of an important part of his library would seem to indicate, Herrera was in fact such a person and performed certain occult services for his master, there can be little doubt that, as with all Hermetic manifestations, they were fundamentally astrological and perhaps largely concerned with medicine.[55]

49. Sánchez Cantón, *op. cit.*, p. 28. Officially, like his pupil Villalpando, Herrera probably endorsed the Ptolemaic system. There are, however, indications leading one to believe that, in common with other Hermetists, he accepted the system of Copernicus or at least its mathematical implications (see note 52). One of these pointers is the presence among the frescoes of the library of the Escorial, with which he was undoubtedly concerned (see notes 74 and 75), of Aristarchus of Samos, the leading advocate in antiquity of the heliocentric system. This fact was disclosed by Archimedes in his *De numero arenae*, a treatise included in Commandino's edition of the *Opera* (Venice, 1538), of which Herrera had a copy. Another pointer is the letter in question enquiring about translations of Copernicus and other works into Italian. Since he himself knew Latin and owned the Latin version of the *De revolutionibus*, presumably he did not want them for his own use, but for the Academy of Mathematics. As its members were not all Latinists, instruction and texts had to be in the vernacular. Italian versions would therefore have been easier for them to read as well as to translate. If this be so, then it follows that the study of the heliocentric system was on its curriculum. That Copernicus was accepted in certain circles in Spain at this time is demonstrated by Fray Diego de Zuñiga's well-known assertion in his commentary of the Book of Job (*Didaci a Stvnica Salmaticensis Eremitae Augustiniani in Iob commentaria...*, Toleti, 1584) that the verse 'Qui commovet terram de loco suo...' could only be adequately explained by supposing that the earth moved round the sun. Fray Diego dedicated his book to Philip II and in this connection it is of interest to note that the latter possessed a copy of the *De revolutionibus* as early as 1545, that is within two years of its publication in Germany (see Fray Guillermo Antolín, O.S.A., *La Liberia de Felipe II*, Madrid, 1927, p. 15).

50. He had also been tutor to Philip himself. From the reference to him in Cardanus' *De subtilitate* (Bâle, 1554, p. 453) it may be inferred that he was a Hermetist.

51. MS. no. h–1–1.

52. Ruiz de Arcaute, *op. cit.*, pp. 153 ff. Erasmus Reinhold's Prutenic tables, based on Copernicus, first came out in 1551. It has been noted (see Lynn Thorndyke, *A History of Magic and Experimental Science*, New York, 1941, vol. v, p. 44) that the *De revolutionibus* came out under astrological rather than astronomical auspices, its main attraction being that it enabled the evident errors in the Alfonsine tables to be corrected. There is no doubt that these tables were principally used for astrological

purposes. It is not surprising therefore that Hermetists and Magi such as Cardanus, Gauricus, Dee and Bruno were amongst the most enthusiastic adherents of the heliocentric system. This provides yet another argument for believing that Herrera too subscribed to it. At the same time it would explain the suspicion with which it was viewed in certain Catholic circles, seeing that, particularly in the case of Bruno, it was intimately bound up with magic (see Frances Yates, *Giordano Bruno and the Hermetic Tradition*, London, 1964, pp. 235 ff.).

53. Ruiz de Arcaute, *op. cit.*, pp. 150 ff. Of a total of 51 scientific instruments listed in the inventory of his effects most of them were astronomical.

54. Sánchez Cantón, *op. cit.*, pp. 8 ff. Herrera owned numerous editions of Vitruvius, including an MS. dedicated exclusively to bk. ix, in which the author treats of astronomy and astrology. On the other hand he apparently did not have Palladio's *Quattro Libri*, Vignola's *Cinque ordini* or Juan de Arphe's *Varia Conmensuracion*, though he was of course acquainted with them. In fact the Spanish translation of Vignola was undertaken with his active encouragement as the translator, Patricio Caxés, fully acknowledges. On these omissions see Sánchez Cantón, *loc. cit.*, p. 9.

55. Herrera had quite an extensive collection of medical books of various kinds (see Sánchez Cantón, *ibid.*, p. 13), which gives rise to the suspicion that he may have been something of a hypochondriac. From the nature of these books and other indications it transpires that the architect suffered from some kind of rheumatic disease. This was precisely the affliction that crippled Philip II, so it would not have been surprising if they had compared notes on the course of their respective ailments and discussed methods of alleviating them. Though it is not known what particular school of medicine Herrera favored, it may be assumed that he was influenced by Lull's approach to this subject, which was basically astrological. Thus he owned the three fundamental Lullian treatises on medicine, the *Liber de regionibus sanitatis*, the *Ars compendiosa medicinae* and the *Liber principiorum medicinae*. He also owned a fourth given as the *De gradibus medicinae*, but this has not been identified with precision. An intriguing question in connection with all this is just what relations Herrera maintained with Philip II's

Yet, if Herrera was in effect what we have suggested, it seems odd that there should be no specific mention of the fact in contemporary records. A partial explanation would be that the king would have taken care to ensure that it was not bruited abroad;[56] also Herrera's architectural activities, being undoubtedly genuine, provided a perfect cover. On the other hand, no one who reads the chroniclers of the Escorial can fail to be struck by the scarcity of references in their writings to Juan de Herrera. It is almost as though he were the victim of a conspiracy of silence. The fact has not passed unnoticed, but it has been put down to no more than professional jealousy.[57] This is probably true enough, but behind it all one senses an element of fear. Herrera enjoyed the almost unconditional protection of the king, as was demonstrated by the incident of the *aposentador*'s bloody altercation with the secretary of the Inquisition of Toledo, from which he escaped with nothing worse than a humiliation.[58] It is, however, precisely the records of the Toledo Holy Office that provide us with the only reference so far known to his occult proclivities. In a document relating to the examination of a visionary of the period called Lucrecia de León mention is made that Herrera had been given access to certain papers on the case as being an expert in the interpretation of dreams.[59] Activities

such as these would help to explain Fray José de Sigüenza's tirade against astrology.[60] To have impugned Herrera outright would by implication have smirched the carefully drawn 'official' portrait of Philip II, which the friar sought to perpetuate.[61]

That the king should have been interested in astrology and the occult is surely in keeping with his introspective character. Indeed at this period it would hardly have been possible for a monarch to be otherwise. Nor did such interests imply an ambivalent attitude towards religion. Lull, a *Beatus*, is full of astrology. Ficino does not seem to have found a belief in such things incompatible with his priestly calling. Moreover the latter's works were never condemned; Philip himself gave the *De Triplici Vita* to the Escorial library.[62] Herrera's knowledge of the stars therefore would have made him just the man for the king to have in his circle. The truth is that no sixteenth-century ruler could afford to ignore his horoscope, so as to exploit its favorable aspects and neutralize any others. Several horoscopes of Philip are known[63] and his own 'official' horoscope or *Prognosticon*[64] survives

chief physician, Francisco Vallés. The latter, a prolific writer, was not only the author of various books on medicine, but like most doctors at this time was interested in subjects such as cosmology, mathematics, Pythagorean numerology, astrology and so forth, in fact just the kind of thing that appealed to Herrera. Whether there was any kind of active collaboration between them on matters of this nature is not known.

56. Philip II's passion for secrecy was commented upon by the Venetian ambassador to Spain, Tommaso Contarini, in a report to the Council, dated 1593: 'He maintains in all his affairs the strictest secrecy, even to the point that certain matters which could well be divulged without the least harm being done remain buried in the deepest silence' (quoted by Ciriaco Pérez Bustamante, 'Semblanza de Felipe II' in *El Escorial 1563–1963*, vol. I, p. 92). The king would have had little difficulty in imposing the most complete discretion on members of his immediate entourage, so that matters of this kind were not noised abroad.

57. Francisco Iñiguez Almech, *op. cit.*, pp. 193 ff.

58. Padre Miguel de la Pinta, *La Inquisición española*, Madrid, 1948, pp. 197 ff.

59. *Ibid.*, p. 135. Except possibly for Synesius' *De insomniis*, Herrera himself does not seem to have owned any works on the subject of dreams. However, among the books which Philip II gave to the Escorial were several copies of Artemidorus' well-known *De somnium interpretatione* (Appendix I, p. 104). Lucrecia de León had foretold that Spain would be invaded again shortly by the Moors and fall under their sway. The cave of Sopeña near Toledo, duly fortified and made habitable by Herrera, would become a second cave of Covadonga, resulting in the ultimate deliverance of the country. The architect's connection with all this has been cited as an example of his ingenuousness, though he was by no means the only prominent person to be taken in, this being in much the same category as his preoccupation with searching for buried treasure. While no doubt naïve from our standpoint, such incidents become rather

more understandable when viewed against the highly 'magical' context of the period.

60. Fray José de Sigüenza, *op. cit.*, bk. IV, disc. X.

61. More than anyone else Fray José de Sigüenza is the creator of the 'white' legend of Philip II. This is quite as partial and misleading as the 'black' legend of the Protestant historians.

62. See Appendix I, p. 105.

63. Horoscopes of Philip II are to be found in the *Tractatus Astrologiae*, Nuremberg, 1540, p. 40, of Luca Gauricus, bishop of Civita Ducale in Capitanata, and Franciscus Iunctinus' *Speculum Astrologiae*, Lyon, 1581, p. 926. Another was made by Ioannes Stadius. John Dee is also known to have cast Philip's horoscope while the latter was in London as Mary Tudor's consort (see note 69).

64. MS. no. a–IV–21. It was erected by Matthias Hacus Sumbergius who describes himself as *medicinae doctor et mathematicus*. To judge from his name he was presumably of Danish origin. Otherwise virtually nothing is known about him except that he wrote a number of short treatises on the annulus, all of them with a marked astrological bias. They are likewise preserved in the library of the Escorial (MS. no. S–II–15). In a study of Matthias Hacus' *Prognosticon* (*La Ciudad de Dios*, vol. XCVI, p. 282 and vol. XCVII, pp. 191, 364 and 441) an attempt was made to discount Philip II's belief in astrology by adducing the authority of Baltasar Porreño who in his book of anecdotes about the king, *Dichos y hechos del señor Rey Don Phelipe segundo el Prudente* of 1628 (modern ed., Madrid, 1942, p. 84) describes how Philip was once presented by an astrologer with a horoscope of his son, later Philip III, but tore it up. Porreño, an ecclesiastic, was a nephew of Francisco de Mora, Herrera's successor as royal architect, and it is generally assumed that Mora was the source of much of his information. While the incident itself may well have taken place, the inference that Porreño draws from it, namely that the king was above superstitions of this kind, is at variance with established facts. For one thing he did not destroy his own *Prognosticon*, but kept it by him until he died. Thereafter it passed into the library of the Escorial under the terms of his will (see Padre Gregorio de Andrés, O.S.A., *Documentos para la Historia . . . de El Escorial*, VII, no. 6, *Los Libros de la testamentaria de Felipe II (1611)*, p. 397: the *Prognosticon* is no. 20 in the inventory of the be-

to this day in the library of the Escorial (Figs. 15 and 16). Born with Libra, the symbol of justice, in the ascendant, he is shown to have been under the favorable influence of a double conjunction of Jupiter, Venus and Mercury with Saturn in a beneficent aspect. Moreover it may be suspected that his well-known fondness for wearing black was also motivated by astrological considerations.[65]

To pretend then that Spain at this period was free from such superstitions is hardly in keeping with the facts.[66] She had always been a noted center of magic and magical books.[67] That such practices were discouraged by the Inquisition means very little; almost

all countries had enacted savage laws against them, but they continued to flourish. On the other hand Philip was not any more given to superstition than other princes of his time.[68] Probably he was less so. Nevertheless his relations in London with John Dee, the astrologer of his wife, Mary Tudor, are an indication of his concern for the occult.[69] As for his passion for relics he probably collected these so assiduously not only as objects of veneration, but also because they were believed to possess therapeutic properties.[70]

There is no evidence to show that Herrera was anything but a deeply religious man or that he was ever associated with *magia infernalis*. It is inconceivable to think of him as anything else than an exponent of what has been termed 'Christian Hermetism'. This in the strongly magical atmosphere of the second half of the sixteenth century represented an acceptable compromise between Christianity and the *prisca theologia*. If therefore one were to be asked just what kind of astrology Herrera practised, a reasonable answer would be that it was akin to the 'good' astrology of Ramón Lull, as expounded by him in the *Tractatus Novus de*

quest). Then again the royal secretary, Antonio Gracián, mentions in his Journal that an alchemist called Juan Fernández had written to the king claiming to have discovered the 'secret of alchemy' with a view to interesting him in it. Far from rejecting it as a vile superstition and setting the Holy Office on to him, Philip replied asking the writer to get into touch with him again as soon as he had perfected his discovery. 'A 25 (de julio, 1572) envié a consultar a su Majestad lo que se haría de un memorial de un juan Fernández, vecino de Madrid, que decía haber hallado el secreto de la Alchimia y pedía ciertas condiciones para hacer asiento con su Majestad; y me mando por su billete que yo me informase de él en que términos estaba y le respondiese que cuando lo tuviese todo acabado avisase a su Majestad' (*ibid.*, v, no. 1, 'Diurnal de Antonio Gracián, Secretario de Felipe II', p. 40).

65. Recommended in *Picatrix*, a noted magical book in circulation at this time, as a means of drawing down on the wearer the beneficent influences of Saturn. There can be no doubt but that Philip II felt himself to be particularly 'identified' with this planet. Though Matthias Hacus in his *Prognosticon* granted a pre-eminent place to Jupiter, he recognized the importance of the influence of Saturn, the 'intellectual' star, on the king's life. On several occasions he refers to his 'regia melancholia'.

According to Agrippa of Nettesheim (*op. cit.*, bk. III, chap. 38) the qualities derived through Saturn are as follows: sublime contemplation, profound intelligence, ponderation of judgment, solid reasoning, firmness and immutability of purpose. Jupiter dispenses unshakeable prudence, temperance, benignity, piety, modesty, justice, faith, grace, religion, equity, clemency and royalty. Though these two planets in ☍ or □ might be considered inimical, in the aspects of △, ✳ (as in the horoscopes of Philip's birth, Figs. 2–3) and ♂ (as in the horoscope of the church of the Escorial, Fig. 25) they are singularly propitious.

66. Even Padre Sigüenza, ostensibly a foe of all such superstitions, mentions astrological predictions, eclipses, comets and so on as though he believed that they affected human affairs (Fray José de Sigüenza, *op. cit.*, bk. III, disc. XII). Elsewhere he mentions the alleged unfavorable aspect of the heavens prior to the sailing of the Spanish Armada on its ill-fated expedition and other portents that occurred while it was on its way in order to explain its failure (*ibid.*, disc. XV). It was easy for Padre Sigüenza, as in this instance, to be wise after the event. The trouble was, however, that astrology not being an exact science, the disposition of the heavens at any given time could be interpreted in widely different ways, so that there was always room for error.

67. Spain's role during the Middle Ages and more especially that of Alfonso the Wise in transmitting classical and Arabic occult texts to the rest of Europe hardly requires stressing. It had also been the main medieval center of Cabala. To pretend that by the sixteenth century no vestige of this remained in the country is simply to be blind to the facts. Frances Yates cites a

letter, written by Agrippa d'Aubigné around 1572–5, describing how he had been shown some magical books which Henri III of France had imported from Spain. Among them was *Picatrix*, a work which Alfonso the Wise had caused to be translated into Spanish from the Arabic original (*Giordano Bruno and the Hermetic Tradition*, p. 51).

68. The Emperor Rudolph II, Philip's nephew, dabbled in alchemy, searching for the philosopher's stone; Henri III of France and his mother, Catherine de' Medici, consorted with astrologers and magicians; James I of England was an 'expert' on demonology; Pope Urban VIII practised astrological magic with Campanella. The list could be extended.

69. G. M. Horst, *Dr. John Dee*, London, 1922, p. 25. Also R. F. Calder, *John Dee studied as an English Neoplatonist*, Ph.D. thesis, London University, 1952, p. 311. Mention of John Dee prompts the reflection that Herrera and Dee must have been two very similar men in their basic outlook. While there is no evidence to show that Herrera went in for spirit-raising or that Dee practised architecture, they had many points of contact. Both were mathematicians who worked actively to promote the study of mathematics. At the same time side by side with their interest in rational mathematics went a passion for *mathesis* or 'mystical' mathematics. They also cultivated the sciences, such as astronomy, geography, mechanics, medicine and so forth. Both studied natural phenomena, such as the tides and their cause. Moreover both applied their studies to practical ends, inventing mechanical contrivances and marine instruments. Both studied the possibility of reforming the calendar. Then too they were both profoundly religious men. Both were enthusiastic Lullists. Both were likewise interested in Hermetism, astrology, mnemonics and Cabala. Both were in Flanders during the years 1548–50, at which time, so Dee relates, the Emperor Charles V sent him various emissaries with the object of persuading him to enter the imperial service. It is not known whether the two men ever met, but Herrera's admiration for Dee is attested by the existence among his books of two copies of the latter's *Monas Hieroglyphica*, one of which was a manuscript translation into Spanish. Philip II who had known Dee personally in connection with the casting of his horoscope also possessed this work, which he bought from the estate of Juan Bautista de Toledo (see Appendix I, p. 105 and Note 80).

70. Fray José de Sigüenza, *op. cit.*, bk. III, disc. XIX.

Astronomia.[71] This important work figured in the architect's library, being described in the inventory of his Lullian books as *The Astronomy in eleven copybooks in manuscript in Latin together with other loose papers.* Significantly enough the entry immediately following reads: *Of the instruments pertaining thereto.*[72] That he had not only the theoretical text but also the instructions for manipulating the 'instruments' concerned clearly shows that he put Lull's method of doing astrology into practice.

A particularly vivid illustration of the attempt to reconcile Christian orthodoxy and Hermetic lore is afforded by Tibaldi's frescoes in the library of the Escorial.[73] Padre Sigüenza claims to have supplied the program.[74] Though he was certainly consulted, it may be doubted whether his role in choosing the themes to be depicted was quite as important as he makes out. On the other hand there exists a drawing (Fig. 2) that provides irrefutable evidence to show that Herrera was directly concerned with the matter.[75] A superficial glance at these frescoes reveals that they represent nothing more innocuous than the Liberal Arts[76]—the Trivium and Quadrivium—reinforced by Philosophy and Theology, being yet one more example of those encyclopaedic cycles so typical of Mannerism. A closer examination, however, discloses two striking facts. The first is how closely their subject-matter is related to Herrera's interests as revealed by his books; the second is how many of the scenes and figures have Hermetic overtones. Most of them seem to have been selected precisely because they enshrine a dual meaning or allusion. This is in keeping with the contemporary passion for mysteries, sublime truths being veiled behind commonplace images so as to preserve them from contamination by the profane. Among the subjects depicted immediately above the bookcases are *The Egyptian priests, The Gymnosophists, Orpheus, Hercules Gallicus, Archimedes, The Tower of Babel, David exorcizing the demon in Saul by his music, The Queen of Sheba questioning Solomon, Daniel and his companions being instructed by the Chaldean Magi, King Hezekiah watching the retrogression of the sun's shadow* and *Dionysius the Areopagite* (Figs. 3 to 12).[77] Had Padre Sigüenza who seems to have felt scant sympathy for occultism really planned the program of these frescoes exclusively himself, he would surely have selected themes less pregnant with Hermetic allusions.[78]

71. Frances Yates, *The Art of Ramón Lull, passim.*
72. Ruiz de Arcaute, *op. cit.,* Appendix II, p. 169. The 'instruments' in question would have been the wheels and charts of the *Tractatus* in a form that could be easily manipulated. Possibly they included tables of some kind.
73. The execution of the *historias* immediately above the bookcases, which are the part that we shall be chiefly concerned with, is generally attributed to Bartolommeo Carducci. However, only Tibaldi's name figures in the relevant accounts (see Fray Julián Zarco Cuevas, *op. cit.,* pp. 253 ff.).
74. In his additions to the 'Memorias' of Fray Juan de San Jerónimo (Miguel Salvá and Pedro Sainz de Baranda, *Colección de Documentos inéditos para la Historia de España,* Madrid, 1845, vol. VII, p. 441) Fray José de Sigüenza states categorically that he was responsible for the program of these frescoes. In his *Historia de la Orden de San Jerónimo* (bk. IV, discs. IX, X and XI) he implies the same thing. He even goes so far as to say that the two *historias* in the bay dedicated to *Astrologia* were put there at his express suggestion. His authorship of the program of these frescoes has therefore been accepted without question. Nevertheless, a careful reading of the text of the *Historia* and the frescoes themselves reveal certain facts not altogether consistent with his claim. Thus he mentions that he is unable to explain why Melissus figures as a dialectician in the bay devoted to *Dialectica.* This is a very odd statement to make, if he did in fact plan the program of the library, since it implies that the initiative came from outside. Again, when he comes to describe the *historia* of *Orpheus and Eurydice,* while praising its execution, he is unable to conceal his distaste for mythology as such. 'Some day', he writes, 'there will be occasion to discuss this and other fables by which they [the ancients] sought to sell us at such high cost the truth of the doctrine that God communicated to mankind...' If he did not approve of classical mythology, why did he include it in his program? He could quite as easily have found another less objectionable subject than this to illustrate the bay devoted to *Musica,* drawn, for instance, from Holy Writ. Then, too, would a man so dead set against judicial astrology have included the Persian astrologer Alchabitius in his program? Would he have included quite so many astronomers—Aristarchus, Ptolemy, Sacrobosco, Regiomontanus, and Alfonso the Wise—as there are in the library? The truth would seem to be that he was certainly consulted about the program, seeing that he was the librarian of the monastery. He probably did a certain amount of research in connection with it and finished up persuading himself that he was the originator of it all. The initiative, however, must surely have come from Herrera. Moreover, as always, Philip II would have vetted every item, and the architect was in a much better position than the friar to influence the king in matters of this kind.

75. Preserved in the British Museum, Department of Prints and Drawings. It is a sketch by Tibaldi for the west side of the bay devoted to *Gramatica* with profuse comments by the hand of Herrera himself, each one of which he duly signed, thus demonstrating that he was directly concerned with the whole enterprise. There is a passable reproduction of this drawing in *El Escorial 1563–1963,* vol. II, p. 101.
76. One of the marginal notes on Tibaldi's drawing reads as follows: 'The program of these frescoes must either be in His Majesty's hands or in those of Francisco de Mora. Please, Sir, give instructions for it to be sent.' In the light of the foregoing, it is significant that amongst Herrera's books there was *A manuscript portfolio on the Liberal Arts.* This may well have been the text of the program of the library frescoes, prepared, not by Padre Sigüenza, but by Juan de Herrera. The latter also owned Bartolomé Barrientos' *Opuscula Liberalium Artium,* Salamanca, 1569, and Alfonso de la Torre's *Vision deleitable de la philosophia y artes liberales.* This second work which ran through many editions contains a section on magic and theurgy.
77. For a brief exposition of the Hermetic content of these *historias* see Appendix II, p. 106.
78. Although in his extensive remarks on these frescoes Padre Sigüenza tends to concentrate on their outward significance, it is plain that he was by no means unaware of their Hermetic implications. His silence on the latter, however, was not due to any concern for safeguarding the 'mysteries', but simply to a distaste for Hermetism as such. There is no doubt that he would

Herrera's manifest interest in the occult prompts the reflection that the Escorial itself may possibly be a Hermetic building. To this it will be objected that it was Juan Bautista de Toledo and not Herrera who was responsible for its design.[79] Nevertheless the latter was associated with it almost from the beginning, perhaps even before being officially appointed as assistant to the older man. But then to judge from his books Juan Bautista himself was more than a little interested in astrology and the occult.[80] This is hardly surprising seeing that before returning to Spain in 1559 he resided in Naples, one of the foremost centers of magic in Europe, from which sprang such notable Magi as Gauricus, Porta, Bruno and Campanella. Unfortunately little or nothing is known about this architect prior to his entering Philip II's service. Yet from what Padre Sigüenza says of him it is plain that he was exceptionally well endowed intellectually and lived up to the humanist ideal of the 'universal man'. He was, we are told, 'a person of considerable judgment, a sculptor and a fine draughtsman; he knew Latin and Greek and was deeply versed in philosophy and mathematics. To sum up in him were to be found many of the qualities which Vitruvius, prince of

architects, demands of those that aspire to practise architecture and style themselves masters of their art.'[81] Being the kind of man thus described, it is not unreasonable to suppose that he was acquainted with the notion, adumbrated by Ficino and then developed by Agrippa and others, that art is the outcome of a magical process.[82] Even such an apparently rational activity as architecture needed to have its bare bones vivified by the magic of a supra-rational *afflatus* that defies exact analysis. Vitruvius himself supplied the ideal example of this twofold approach in seeking to combine theory or innate gift and practice or acquired art, so that he deals with every facet of architecture from the commonplaces of building technics to astrological cosmology. But if there were some like Alberti and Daniele Barbaro who felt that it was necessary to discount the astrology as tending to lead into a domain of doubtful validity, it is equally plain that for men like Cardanus, Luca Gauricus and Lomazzo the Roman theorist's chief claim to immortality was as a Magus.[83] As has been noted,[84] the magical interpretation of art reaches its culmination in Lomazzo's *Trattato dell'Arte della Pittura, Scultura, et Architettura* of 1584 and his *Idea del Tempio della Pittura* of 1590, both of which are studded with unacknowledged borrowings from Cornelius Agrippa. The importance of the concept of *Idea* in the sixteenth century as the creator's inner vision or *scintilla della divinità* hardly needs to be emphasized here. Now it has generally been recognized that the point of departure of the designer or designers of the Escorial must have been some kind of *Idea*[85] which provided the building with its underlying symbolism. There has, however, been less agreement as to what precisely this *Idea* was. Some years ago the writer briefly suggested that in all probability it was nothing less than Solomon's Temple.[86] There are several pointers to this, notably the Hebrew kings on

have preferred subjects of a more purely devotional nature, such as those in the main cloister, which he strongly commends (*ibid.*, disc. IV) because of their improving content.

79. It is not proposed here to enter at length into the vexed question concerning the authorship of the original designs of the Escorial or the role played by the Italian military engineer Francesco Pacciotto da Urbino in the early stages of the planning. All that can be safely said of the latter is that the present plan of the church with its rigid four-square lines is due to him; so is the ambivalent solution given to the towers flanking the façade. Also the proportions of the *quadro* or main block of the building and those of his earlier *cittadella* at Piacenza are very similar, though not exactly alike. Philip II who had seen Pacciotto's drawings for this work may well have wanted something similar for the Escorial (see George Kubler, 'Francisco Pacciotto, arquitecto', in *Goya*, nos. 56–57, p. 86). The possible Hermetic nature of the plan, discussed on pp. 94–96, is not affected by problems of attribution. The symbolism behind the building could quite as well have come from Pacciotto as from Juan Bautista de Toledo.

80. No complete inventory of Juan Bautista de Toledo's library has yet come to light. All that we have is a list of 41 books acquired by Philip II from the architect's estate for the library of the Escorial. Of these more than one-third were books on architecture. Those which are chiefly of interest in our context as being either Hermetic or 'borderline' include the *In Somnium Scipionis* of Macrobius, the *Matheseos* of Julius Firmicus Maternus, the *Monas Hieroglyphica* of John Dee, the *Almagest* of Ptolemy, the *Sphera* of Sacrobosco, the *De triangulis* of Regiomontanus, which incorporates the *De quadratura circuli* of Nicholas of Cusa, and the *Natural History* of Pliny (see Luis Cervera Vera, 'Libros del arquitecto Juan Bautista de Toledo', in *La Ciudad de Dios*, vol. 152, pp. 583–622, and vol. 153, pp. 161–88). Several of these are works which, as stated before, while not in themselves magical, could be adapted to magical uses. A notable example is Sacrobosco's *Sphera* which prompted a number of necromantic commentaries (see Lynn Thorndyke, *The Sphere of Sacrobosco and its Commentators*, Chicago, 1949).

81. Fray José de Sigüenza, *op. cit.*, bk. III, disc. III.
82. For a full discussion of this point see Robert Klein, 'La forme et l'Intelligible' in *Umanesimo e Simbolismo*, Centro Internazionale di Studi Umanistici, Rome (Padua), 1958, pp. 133 ff.
83. On the authority of Vitruvius Cardanus states that architecture comprises 'militaris, magia, chimistica et machinatoria'. The Avery Architectural Library, Columbia University, New York, possesses Luca Gauricus' copy of Vitruvius (no. AA 2515 v 82). It is Fra Giocondo's edition of 1517 and is inscribed 'Lucae Gavrici Geophonensis Civitatensium epī' (see note 63). It is copiously annotated, but these notes are exclusively confined to the astronomical and astrological Book IX. As mentioned in note 54, Herrera had a manuscript containing nothing but this particular Book of Vitruvius.
84. Robert Klein, *op. cit.*, pp. 113 ff.
85. Even Fray José de Sigüenza draws a distinction between 'idea' and 'disegno' or 'traça' (*op. cit.*, bk. III, disc. III), the latter being the offspring or 'parto' of the first. On the discrepancy between 'idea' and reality see Robert Klein, *op. cit.*, p. 103.
86. R. C. Taylor, 'El Padre Villalpando y sus ideas estéticas', in *Academia*, Madrid, 1952 (second semester), pp. 13–14.

the façade of the church, but the strongest argument in its favor is simply that Padre Sigüenza says so. He refers to it as 'another Temple of Solomon whom our patron and founder sought to imitate in this work'.[87] Elsewhere he devotes much space to discussing what was generally thought of Philip II's building and here he makes it plain that this interpretation of it was widespread.[88]

If the Escorial was in some way a 'recreation' of the Temple, then we should logically expect to find Philip to be identified with Solomon. This is precisely what we do find. Possibly he himself sought to foster the notion. One of his many titles was that of 'King of Jerusalem', so that it was only natural for him to be equated with Solomon, particularly in view of his passion for architecture and his aspiration to be a wise, prudent and just ruler.[89] This idea was current in Spain until the end of the eighteenth century.[90]

Significantly enough among the works in Herrera's library there was one which is listed as *A copy of the treatise that was made on Solomon's Temple in manuscript*.[91] It has not survived, so there is no way of knowing who wrote it or what it contained. It may possibly have been composed prior to the draughting of the plans of the Escorial for the benefit of the architects. It is more likely, however, to have been related to the internationally famous reconstruction of the Temple, which Herrera's pupil, the Jesuit Juan Bautista Villalpando, published in Rome in 1604. It came out under the title of *De Postrema Ezechielis Prophetae Visione*, being the second part of an exhaustive three-volume commentary on the prophet in question, which Villalpando had undertaken in collaboration with a fellow-Jesuit called Jerónimo Prado.[92] By agreement

Villalpando was to limit himself to chapters 40, 41 and 42, which are those that deal with the Temple, but owing to Padre Prado's death, it fell to him to complete the undertaking.[93] Published with the help of subsidies from Philip II,[94] the work had an immediate and lasting success.[95]

The secret of this success is not difficult to explain. In the first place it gave the world the first full-scale *imago* of the divine archetype. The Temple was necessarily the perfect building, since God Himself had inspired its form and proportions. Then too Villalpando had advanced the interesting theory that the five orders of architecture ultimately stemmed from the divine order of the Temple.[96] Not only therefore did he invest his building with a classical appearance, but sought to demonstrate that all its dimensions, as given in Holy Writ, concurred with the doctrine of Vitruvius.[97] He thus converted the Temple into a kind of test-case to prove the basic compatibility of Christian revelation and the culture of classical antiquity,[98] a point very much at issue at the time.

Villalpando's reconstruction was of course based on a number of misconceptions and false assumptions. The idea that classical architecture provided the only acceptable style together with the blind cult of Vitruvius are manifestations of the same attitude of mind that led men at this period to an uncritical acceptance of Hermes Trismegistus, Zoroaster, the Chaldean oracles, the Orphic hymns, the sayings of Pythagoras and so forth as being the repositories of an ancient wisdom going back to the beginnings of time. The Jesuit was able to reconcile Vitruvius and Ezechiel in much the same spirit as others had reconciled Christianity with the *prisca theologia*. Here indeed we may have yet another reason for the vogue enjoyed by his book, namely that within its religious framework it has a markedly Hermetic flavor.[99]

87. Fray José de Sigüenza, *op. cit.*, bk. III, Prologue.
88. *Ibid.*, bk. IV, disc. XXII. In this chapter Padre Sigüenza discusses the whole question exclusively from the historical and literal standpoint, coming to the conclusion that the Escorial and Solomon's Temple are unlikely to have resembled one another either in size or appearance. At no point does he touch on the Escorial's underlying symbolism or *Idea*.
89. For example in 1582 Juan Gracián, the Madrid publisher, dedicated to Philip II a Spanish version of Vitruvius, made by Juan de Orea. 'To whom', he asks, 'should a book on architecture be dedicated but to this second Solomon and prince of architects? To him they owe their present knowledge and the restoration of their art after it had lain for many centuries forgotten, debased and even treated as an object of disdain.' Again, Arias Montano's illustrated *Humanae Salutis Monumenta*, Plantin, 1571, carries a plate (no. 24) showing Solomon in his study surrounded by all kinds of instruments. The engraver has given the Old Testament king the unmistakable features of Philip II.
90. For other literary examples see Fray Saturnino Alvarez Turienzo, O.S.A., *El Escorial en las letras españolas*, Madrid, 1963.
91. Ruiz de Arcaute, *op. cit.*, p. 157.
92. The title of the complete work is *Hieronymi Pradi et Ioannis Baptistae Villalpandi e Societate Iesu in Ezechielem Explanationes et Apparatus Vrbis ac Templi Hierosolymitani*.

93. R. C. Taylor, *op. cit.*, pp. 4 ff.
94. *Ibid.*, p. 11.
95. *Ibid.*, pp. 47 ff.
96. *Ibid.*, p. 46. See also Rudolf Wittkower, 'Federico Zuccari and John Wood of Bath' in *Journal of the Warburg and Courtauld Institutes*, London, 1943, vol. VI, p. 220.
97. R. C. Taylor, *op. cit.*, p. 10.
98. *Ibid.*, p. 9.
99. At the same time this may help to explain the hostility it aroused in other circles. It is known, for instance, that Benito Arias Montano, the librarian of the Escorial and compiler of the Antwerp Polyglot Bible of 1572, mounted a full-scale offensive against Villalpando's reconstruction even before it was published on the grounds that the building described by Ezechiel had nothing to do with the Temple built by Solomon. The upshot was that an Inquisitorial commission was appointed to examine the Jesuit's thesis. Though it ended by clearing Villalpando of all suspicion of heterodoxy (*ibid.*, pp. 10 ff.), it may be questioned whether this was the real issue at stake. The matter went very much deeper, the truth being that they were men of utterly divergent outlook. Arias Montano was a rationalist. By disposition and training he leant towards that

As Villalpando points out, the prophecy of Ezechiel is a particularly difficult one to interpret.[100] Had not

school whose interests lay in the field of textual criticism and exegesis. He set great store on linguistic and philological studies, and in his writings always strove for the greatest precision and elegance of expression. In this sense he stands close to Erasmus, whose approach to Biblical and patristic studies was largely his own. To such a man Hermetism can scarcely have been congenial. That this is no arbitrary interpretation of his position is demonstrated by his consistent refusal to accept the Granada 'relics', discovered in 1588 and 1595, as genuine, although subjected to almost overwhelming pressure to do so. Others, including Philip II himself, bemused by the atmosphere of magic and miracle-mongering prevalent at the time—this in spite of the vigilance of the Holy Office—accepted them without question (for a full account of this fantastic hoax see T. D. Kendrick, 'An example of the Theodicy-Motive in Antiquarian Thought', in Fritz Saxl, 1890–1948, A volume of Memorial Essays, London, 1957, pp. 309 ff.).

By contrast Villalpando was a mystic; hence his interest in Ezechiel. He represents that trend within the Society of Jesus, which runs through it by way of such Lullists as Diego Laínez, Jerónimo Nadal and Athanasius Kircher and which was in turn opposed within the order by Francisco Suárez and Martín del Rio. The difference in outlook between Villalpando and Arias Montano is best illustrated by their respective reconstructions of the Temple. Arias Montano published his in 1593, possibly as a preliminary counterblast to Villalpando (Antiquitatum Judaicarum libri IX, in quis praeter Judaeae, Hierosolymorum, & Templi Salomonis accuratam delineationem precipui sacri ac profanis gentis ritus describuntur, Lyon, 1593). It is sober and factual. Unlike Villalpando he is not concerned with Vitruvius nor does he seek to 'prove' a number of pre-established ideas. By contrast the Jesuit is a Hermetist and his reconstruction of the Temple is plainly the forerunner of the many recreations of ancient structures, produced by Father Athanasius Kircher later on, such as Arca Noe, Turris Babel and so on.

Now Padre Sigüenza was an unconditional adherent of Arias Montano. In his book (op. cit., bk. IV, disc. XXII) he goes to great pains to demonstrate Montano's contention that the Temple of Solmon and that described by Ezechiel are in no way connected. There is even an obvious though veiled reference to the Villalpando-Montano controversy. 'It would be well', he writes, 'if those that treat of Ezechiel were to follow him [Arias Montano] in this and many other places, and to embrace his doctrine.' On his side the Jesuit adduces the authority of his master Herrera: '. . . if he carried as much weight with others as he does with me, I could well look forward to being rid of all opposition on this score' (Explanationes, vol. II, part II, bk. I isagog., chap. 8, p. 18). When he wrote his book, Padre Sigüenza would not only have known all about the controversy between the two men, he would also have been aware of its outcome: the Jesuit had been cleared and Herrera, whose support of his pupil had never wavered, had prevailed on Philip II to subsidize the publication of his work. With Arias Montano living in retirement in Sevilla, Herrera, the all-influential Hermetist, had prevailed. Small wonder therefore that the chroniclers of the order could seldom bring themselves to mention the royal architect in their works.

100. Explanationes, tom. II, vol. I, chap. I, p. I. 'Id quod Prophetis maxime, ac psalmis peculiare est, vtpote qui parabolis, aenigmatis, tropis, schematis sermonem contegunt, atque ea, quae omnibus in promptu esse non debent, sapientibus percipienda conservant. Qua in re principem videtur locum tenere Sanctus Ezechiel; qui cum, prae ceteris, in adytis, sacrisque tenebris latuit, tum in hac extrema templi visione in magis recondita penetralia secessit; vt merito sane Beatus Hieronymus pronunciaret, occupatus in explicatione templi Ezechielis, quod opus in Scripturis sanctis vel difficilimum est. Hanc porro eandem difficultatem its attollit in maivs, vt vix veritatem intelligentiae consequi posse.'

St. Jerome called it a mysteriorum Dei labyrinthum?[101] Yet, though it had baffled greater minds than his own, plainly God had not meant to let its meaning lie hidden for ever. Now at last it was to stand revealed.[102] The Jesuit of course in no way implies that he is against mysteries. The concept of mystery forms an integral part of Christian belief, Christ Himself having concealed His Truth under the guise of parables so that it should not be profaned.[103] Villalpando's purpose then was to lift the arcana velamenta, as the Areopagite had put it, behind which Ezechiel had hidden his meaning. At this point the Jesuit discloses that the reconstruction of the Temple was already in existence at the time he first fell in with Padre Prado.[104] It was felt, however, that the whole prophecy needed a commentary because of the light which the rest of it would shed not only on the Temple itself but on Christ whom it prefigured—eo lux videtur assidue afflulgere qua quidem luce, noua subinde mysteria Deique arcana consilia perspiciantur, qua huius Templi maiestate atque amplitudine continentur.[105]

The most important part of the commentary in our context is the last section of the fifth book in which the Jesuit discusses the harmonic, cosmological and anthropomorphic aspects of the Temple (Fig. 13). Though he deals with each separately, they are all interrelated, the connecting link being astrology. He begins with music. Taking the monochord, he demonstrates upon it the intervals of the musical scale according to the doctrine of Pythagoras.[106] Next he shows how these consonances are used to bind the triglyphs and metopes together in all three parts of the Temple.[107] So too he explains the role of the three

101. Quoted by Villalpando. Ibid., Prologue to the reader, p. x.
102. Thanks mainly to the wisdom and generosity of king Philip, the second Solomon—'Salomonis celsitudinem animi ac sapientiam imitatus' (ibid., Dedication to Philip II, p. VII).
103. Ibid., Prologue to the reader, p. x. Villalpando contrasts Isaiah who prophesies clearly with Ezechiel who does so enigmatically. He quotes St. Augustine's commendation of mysteries —'sunt in Scripturis Sanctis profunda mysteria, quae ad hoc absconduntur, ne vilescant'—and ends by referring to Ezechiel as follows: 'hic vero contra sacris veluti hieroglyphicorum arcanis obsignauit; ita vt ea ne intueri quidem vlli fas sit, praeter eos, quos Christus illa oratione compellat: Vobis datum est nosse mysterium regni Dei, coeteris autem in parabolis'.
104. Ibid., Dedication to Philip II, p. V. 'Et quamquam Hierosolymitani Templi descriptio erat aliquot ante annis absoluta: vt eius tamen perfecta ratio redderetur; uniuersum fuit Ezechielis vaticinium enucleandum: quod videlicet totum propemodum, vt coetere paene omnia sacra volumina, ad hoc Templum augustissimum, refertur: cum hoc maxime Templo Christi Dei nostri ac liberatoris imago pulcherrima, eiusque Ecclesiae sacrosanctae, non adumbretur modo sed suis quasi coloribus exprimatur.'
105. Loc. cit.
106. R. C. Taylor, op. cit., pp. 22 ff.
107. Ibid., p. 30. Also Rudolf Wittkower, Architectural Principles in the Age of Humanism, London, 1949, pp. 106 ff.

mean proportionals and declares himself in favor of the harmonic mean as the one best suited to a divine building.[108] Now the connection between music and the heavenly bodies by way of the Pythagorean notion of 'the music of the spheres' hardly needs to be labored. Certain editions of Vitruvius actually show how the aspects of the horoscope, △, □ and ✳, are determined musically by the values of the angles between the zodiacal houses (Fig. 20).[109] Villalpando's *harmoniae* therefore implied an astrological connection.

The demonstration of this connection constitutes precisely the next step in the development of his argument. As the Temple is a microcosm of God's creation, it must needs enshrine within itself the harmony of the universal order as reflected in the motions of the stars and planets. The Jesuit does not, however, deal immediately with the Temple. He first enters into a lengthy consideration of the Tabernacle of Moses, the reason being that the one prefigures the other. In a diagram (Fig. 14) he shows how the tribes of Israel were disposed about the Ark of the Covenant in the form of a square, each phalanx facing one of the four points of the compass.[110] Within this there was an inner square consisting of the four camps of the Levites, grouped round the tent of the Ark. At the north-east angle of the outer square was the camp of Judah; next, facing due east, was that of Issachar, all the tribes being disposed according to the order in the Book of Numbers.[111] Next he describes the four battle standards of the Jews, one at each of the four angles of the square. That corresponding to Judah was green like the emerald and had the effigy of a lion; that of Reuben at the south-east corner was red like the carnelian and showed a human head; at the south-west that of Ephraim was golden like the chrysolite and bore the effigy of a bull; that of Dan at the fourth corner was red and white like the jasper and displayed an eagle. Now the four standards are mentioned in Numbers,[112] but there is no reference either to their color or to the motives emblazoned upon them. Just what the significance of all this is Villalpando does not state.[113] However, the four stones he mentions in this connection correspond exactly to those identified with Judah, Reuben, Ephraim and Dan among the twelve precious stones of the tribes on

the breastpiece of Aaron,[114] an object traditionally believed to have been endowed with magical properties.[115]

Being based on the Tabernacle of Moses, the Temple is shown by Villalpando to have had twelve *castella* or bastions along its perimeter exactly matching the position of the twelve tribes round the Ark (Fig. 17).[116] There were also four inner ones corresponding to the Levitical camps. These he proceeds to identify with the sub-lunar world of the four elements. The reasoning behind this is that the Temple is an image of the fabric of the Universe, created by the Supreme Architect, at the center of which is Man. But the zone of the elements is in turn encompassed by the bastions of the twelve tribes, symbolizing the manner in which the elemental world is encircled by the ring of the zodiac. The identification of the tribes of Israel with the zodiacal houses was hardly a novel idea, but his square plan enables the Jesuit to organize them very clearly in the accepted four groups of three signs each. Thus Judah is allotted the sign of Leo, Issachar that of Cancer and so forth. For each such identification the author succeeds in producing, often with considerable ingenuity, an appropriate Biblical quotation.

Just as he identifies the twelve outer bastions of the Temple with the zodiac, so he assigns the courts to the planets: the south-western one to Mars and so forth. They are not, however, disposed at random. Their place in the scheme is determined, as far as is feasible, by their proximity to the house in which they are 'enthroned': Saturn in Capricorn and Aquarius, Jupiter in Pisces, Mars in Aries and so on. By all this Villalpando no doubt sought to convey the idea in theory at least that the Temple was initiated when the planets were dignified in their own signs. Such an unwonted accumulation of beneficent astral influences would be in keeping with its divine origin.

Yet above the planets is the supercelestial world, to which the Temple also makes reference. Here, however, it is not the astral sun that shines, but the true Sun which is Christ. He is the Sun of righteousness and the Father of lights 'in whom is no variation or shadow of turning' and from whom issues 'every good endowment and every perfect gift . . . from above'.[117] Set as if in the midst of the twelve signs He blazes forth with the seven beacons of His sevenfold grace which He pours down abundantly upon us. Thus He walked in Judea surrounded by His twelve apostles; so too, like the igneous Cherubim, the four Evangelists whom he equates with the four inner bastions and

---

108. *Loc. cit.*
109. Cesariano's edition of 1521 and Caporali's of 1536.
110. *Explanationes*, tom. II, part II, bk. v, disput. II, chap. XXIX, pp. 466 ff.
111. Numbers 2:3–31.
112. Numbers 2:3, 10, 18 and 25.
113. Though he does not always quote his sources, Villalpando would seem to have derived much of his symbolism from writers like Josephus, Philo and St. Clement of Alexandria.

114. Exodus 28:17–20 and 39:10–13.
115. Josephus associated them with the signs of the zodiac.
116. *Explanationes*, chap. XXX, pp. 469 ff.
117. James 1:17.

whose symbols it will be recalled were on the four battle standards of Israel, proclaim the glory of His message to the four cardinal points.

Having dealt with the celestial and supercelestial spheres, Villalpando passes on to show that the Temple is likewise related to the elemental world and in particular to the microcosm which is Man.[118] The latter is circumscribed by the four complexions or humors and his ages are seven, being 'ruled' successively by Luna, Mercury and so on. He reaches his plenitude under Sol which once again he identifies with the true Sun, *lux vera quae illuminat omnem hominem venientem in hunc mundum*.[119] This Sun is enthroned in Leo, the 'house' of Judah, out of which was to issue the salvation of mankind.

This section leads the Jesuit logically into a discussion of the anthropomorphism of the Temple. Needless to say he subscribes to the Vitruvian principle that a building should reflect the proportions of the human body. He even provides a diagram (Fig. 18) showing how the porticoes of the Temple are based on the human figure. Yet Villalpando's approach to this whole subject plainly mirrors the contemporary tendency to associate the Vitruvian with the cosmological man. Whereas the Roman theorist had used the human frame to illustrate his concept of architectural *symmetria* without the least allusion to cosmology, the cosmological man was a traditional figure of astrological import. In this connection the similarity between Villalpando's engraving (Fig. 18) and one of the illustrations of the Codex Huygens (Fig. 19)[120] is significant. The latter shows the cosmological man encompassed by four concentric circles that enclose the four elements. These circles cut the body at virtually the same place as the Jesuit had set the supports of his portico. This is not to imply that he knew this particular drawing; such figures were commonplace. It does, however, show how the two strains could and did become crossed, a development that illustrates the growth of the Hermetic trend. At the hands of Magi like Pico, Agrippa, Giorgi and Cornelius Gemma a 'system' was evolved in which Pythagorean numerology, mystical geometry, music, astrology, Cabala and the microcosm-macrocosm were inextricably conjoined. In Agrippa the fusion of the Vitruvian and the cosmological man is already complete, seasoned with a strong admixture of

magic.[121] It is likewise implicit in Villalpando's treatment of this whole theme.

How far then did the Jesuit accept this magico-astrological cosmology? It may be doubted whether he produced all this elaborate zodiacal and planetary apparatus merely in order to draw a few commonplace numerological analogies. That he should have introduced astrology at all would seem to imply some degree of belief in the influence of the stars upon the sublunar world, a belief not inconsistent with religious Hermetism. But the gratuitous introduction of elements such as the relationship between the colors of the Jewish battle-standards and the gems on the breastpiece of judgment even hints of something more. It recalls the prescriptions of Ficino and Agrippa for drawing down beneficent influences from the heavenly bodies through the congruence of animals, colors, herbs, perfumes and precious stones with talismanic engravings.[122] Even more startling is the comparison he draws between the seven beacons of Christ, in other words the seven Sacraments, and the planets, the effusion of His grace upon mankind being equated with the manner in which astral influences descend upon the elemental world.

Villalpando's earlier statement that his reconstruction antedated the commentary that accompanies it[123] raises the question of how and when he first became interested in the Temple. He himself furnishes no clear answer to these queries. He merely states that, when Juan de Herrera first saw his drawings, he declared at once that he glimpsed the hand of God in the very form of the architecture. Even if he had not been familiar with the Biblical sources, he would have had no difficulty in concluding that such a design was beyond the scope of man's ability and could only have come from the Creator Himself.[124] All things considered, it is hard to avoid the suspicion that Herrera was the originator of the whole enterprise, even if he did leave the task of working it out in

---

118. *Explanationes*, chap. xxxi, pp. 471 ff.
119. John 1:9.
120. See E. Panofsky, *The Codex Huygens and Leonardo da Vinci's Art Theory*, London, 1940, pl. 6. The drawing is on folio 10 of the codex. According to the author 'this drawing illustrates the correspondence between microcosm and macrocosm' (p. 23). Villalpando's figure does so too.

121. Agrippa of Nettesheim, *op. cit.*, bk. ii, chap. 37. Though there are frequent allusions to cosmology in Vitruvius, the passage on anthropomorphism at the beginning of bk. iii contains no reference to it. Nor does Leonardo da Vinci mention it in connection with his well-known drawing of the Vitruvian man in the Accademia MS. Yet it is precisely in his Milanese circle that the process to which we have referred first becomes strongly manifest. Thus Cesariano's edition of Vitruvius has a markedly Hermetic slant. Just how much of this was due to Leonardo himself and how much to the influence of an outright Hermetist like Cardanus is a matter for speculation. In representations of the cosmological and cosmologico-Vitruvian man the circumference of the circle generally touches the top of the head (cf. Figs. 19 and 28).
122. See D. P. Walker, *Spiritual and Demonic Magic from Ficino to Campanella*, London, 1958, pp. 3–95 and 90–96.
123. See note 104.
124. *Explanationes*, tom. ii, part ii, bk. i isagog., chap. viii, p. 18.

detail to his pupil. On one score, however, we may rest assured: the Hermetic element at least must have stemmed from the master.

In considering the Escorial as a 'copy' of the Temple of Jerusalem it must be borne in mind that it was never meant to be a *vera imago* in the sense that Villalpando claimed his reconstruction to be. The Escorial was not a theoretical exercise; it had to fulfil a number of practical functions and this was precisely what the friars reproached Juan Bautista de Toledo for neglecting in favor of purely aesthetic considerations.[125] Whatever reference it bore to the Temple, it must have been of a predominantly symbolic nature. At no time was any attempt made to produce a literal transcription of the divine archetype. It would be idle therefore to look in the Biblical text for anything like identity of form and dimensions. Yet that there were certain parallels is quite evident; Padre Sigüenza mentions some of them. Thus stone was used for the foundations of the Escorial as it had been in the Temple.[126] Then too, when the church came to be built, Herrera suggested imitating Solomon's architect by having all the stonework dressed and finished at the quarry instead of on the site[127] as a means of lowering costs. Again the division of the Escorial into a convent, a palace and a church recalls the threefold division of the Temple: the *domus sacerdotum, domus regia* and *domus Domini*.[128]

A more evident similarity emerges from a comparison of their ground-plans (Figs. 13 and 25). If we suppress Villalpando's three front courts and overlook for the moment the Escorial's eastward projection, the resulting *quadros* or blocks are not dissimilar in disposition and proportions. In the Escorial the church is located in much the same place as the sanctuary of the Temple. Both have rectangular spaces before them, while the square courts likewise occupy similar positions. All this may be due to chance. On the other hand, in view of the circumstances the more likely explanation is that they are similar simply because both are the offspring of the same basic *Idea*, modified in the instance of the Escorial by practical considerations.

Where a building enshrines a symbolic reference, it is generally conveyed through the layout of the ground-plan, since this is what mainly determines its charac-

ter.[129] Taking once again the *quadro* or main block of the Escorial we find that its outer dimensions, as given by Padre Sigüenza, are 735 by 580 feet.[130] These measurements, however, are not reducible to simple ratios according to the prevailing theory of proportion based on Pythagorean musical numerology, as used by Villalpando in the Temple. The possibility must therefore be faced that here the plan was worked out geometrically. Furthermore, considering its Solomonic reference and Juan Bautista de Toledo's Neapolitan antecedents, it may well incorporate some kind of mystical or even magic figure.[131] The importance of such figures in *cinquecento* Hermetic thought —Agrippa, Gemma and Bruno, for instance—will hardly require stressing.[132]

To pursue this matter further admittedly involves entering into a labyrinth of speculation, since there is no irrefutable evidence to show how the plan was evolved. Nevertheless even at the risk of seeming arbitrary and unscientific, it is proposed to point out how a number of geometrical figures do seem to have a certain bearing on the question in hand.

In the library of the Escorial the last bay of the frescoed decoration, devoted to *Astrologia*, displays a representation of Euclid (Fig. 21).[133] He sustains against his knees a large white board on which there are three diagrams. On the right is a geometrical construction consisting of two squares, a circle and a triangle; in the center is a man taking a reading on two stars with a 'Jacob's staff',[134] while on the left, partly hidden by the scroll with his name, is one half of a 'seal' or 'star of Solomon'. The geometrical construction does not seem to be related to any propo-

125. Amancio Portabales Pichel, *Maestros mayores, arquitectos y aparejadores de El Escorial*, Madrid, 1952, pp. 171 and 190.

126. Fray José de Sigüenza, *op. cit.*, bk. II, disc. III.

127. *Ibid.*, disc. IX. See also Fray Juan de San Jerónimo, *Memorias*, Madrid, 1845, p. 160. The Scriptural reference is I Kings 6:7.

128. *Explanationes*, tom. II, part II, bk. V, disp. I, chap. IX, pp. 428 ff.

129. Circular churches built in allusion to the Church of the Holy Sepulchre in Jerusalem are perhaps the most obvious examples of this. In Spain Diego Siloe built the sanctuary of Granada cathedral on the plan of a rotunda in imitation of the form of the Anastasis (see Earl Rosenthal, *The Cathedral of Granada*, Princeton, 1961, pp. 148 ff.).

130. Fray José de Sigüenza, *op. cit.*, bk. III, disc. II.

131. In this connection mention has already been made of the possible influence on Renaissance thought of Lull's mystical and astrological geometry (see note 40).

132. Agrippa of Nettesheim, *op. cit.*, bk. II, chap. 22. Cornelius Gemma, *op. cit.*, *passim*. Giordano Bruno, *Articuli centum et sexaginta*, Prague, 1588. *De triplici minimo et mensura* and *De monade numero et figura*, both Frankfort, 1591, *passim*.

133. On some of the strange iconographical transpositions in these frescoes see notes 149 and 166.

134. This was a rudimentary measuring device consisting of a graduated staff-like upright with a peep-sight near one end. At the other there was a sliding cross-piece which moved along the upright. One or both ends of the cross-piece would be moved into alignment with the object or objects it was wished to observe. Then by taking the reading off the graduated upright an approximate angular value could be determined. On this instrument see Ioannes Spangeberg, *Brevis tractatio de baculo Iacob*, included as an Appendix to Gemma Frisius' *De radio astronomico et geometrico*, Paris, 1558.

sition of Euclid. Superficially it would seem to be just a simple configuration illustrating the importance in Euclidian geometry of those three basic shapes, the circle, the square and the triangle. Considering the mentality of the period, however, it may be suspected that there is rather more to these diagrams than appears on the surface. Moreover, bearing in mind that Herrera was almost certainly behind the whole program of these frescoes, it is not too far-fetched to think of them as 'hieroglyphs' by means of which he sought to convey a message and that this message is related in some way to the building. Taking the geometrical figure at which the sage points so assiduously, the significance of the square in relation to the Escorial plan is quite evident, since it determines the form of the courts, of the eastern projection and of the main part of the church.[135] In fact the emphasis on the square is what constitutes the most obvious link between this plan and that of Villalpando's Temple. The role of the circle and the triangle, however, are perhaps less readily evident. Yet, as may be seen, a circle convincingly circumscribes the whole structure (Fig. 25). Then too the apex of an equilateral triangle constructed on the line of the west front marks the position of the most hallowed part of the church. This is the Sagrario with its tabernacle, described by Herrera himself as *lugar de mucha deuocion*.[136] That its precise location was settled in accordance with the symbolism of the equilateral triangle would seem to be borne out by the presence on the vault immediately above this part of the church of a fresco representing the Trinity,[137] painted on the orders of Philip II. It is surely not plausible to ascribe all this to mere chance.

The second geometrical diagram on Euclid's board represents a *sigillum Salomonis*. Consisting of two interlinked equilateral triangles forming a star, it is a well-known figure of magic import. Incidentally it is

also a basic figure in Lull.[138] That a geometrical construction such as this with all its Solomonic and mystical associations should have been incorporated in some way into the plan of the Escorial is hardly surprising. But there was something more, namely that its use had the sanction of Vitruvius.

In Book V of his treatise the Roman theorist gives detailed prescriptions for designing a Roman theater.[139] At a glance there would seem to be scant connection between the plan of the latter (Fig. 29)[140] with its semi-circular auditorium and the uncompromising rectangularity of the Escorial. In this particular context, however, their respective shapes are beside the point. What really matters here is the basis used by Vitruvius for working out his design, the intriguing thing being that it is exclusively astrological. His point of departure is the use of four interlinked equilateral triangles, in other words a double 'star of Solomon', disposed 'after the manner of the astrologers in a figure of the twelve signs of the zodiac, when they make computations from the musical harmony of the stars'. Needless to say Juan Bautista de Toledo was perfectly familiar with this passage, as indeed he was with the rest of the work.[141] He would have been equally well acquainted with the astrological figure in question from the illustration of it in his copy of Julius Firmicus (Fig. 30).[142] He might even have known that it is to be found in Ramón Lull. The attraction of this particular figure is that it lent itself to multiple interpretations. On its own the equilateral triangle symbolized the Trinity; when doubled it yielded a Solomonic allusion, while in its quadruple form it stood for the order and harmony of the universe. A plan based on this zodiacal configuration would therefore necessarily be in tune with the *musica convenientia astrorum* of Vitruvius.[143] Hence there would be no need to have recourse to the alternative *magia* of the Pythagorean musical intervals.[144]

135. The form of the main part of the church was apparently determined by the Italian military engineer Pacciotto (see note 79), his ideas being incorporated into Juan Bautista de Toledo's master plan in 1562 in preference to the latter's own. At the beginning of 1567 the plans of the church were redrafted and sent to the Florentine Academy for comment, which was unfavorable. In 1573 fresh plans for the church were sent by a number of Italian architects, including Palladio, Vignola, Alessi and Vicenzo Danti. It would seem, however, that in the end the main lines of Pacciotto's original design were retained.

136. Juan de Herrera, *Svmario y Breve declaració de los diseños y estampas de la Fabrica de San Lorencio el Real del Escurial*, Madrid, 1589, p. 7 verso.

137. There are two frescoes representing the Trinity in the church, namely this one which shows the Coronation of the Virgin by the Father and the Son with the Holy Spirit above them and the one over the raised choir, to which reference was made at the beginning of this essay (see note 1). Both were painted by Luca Cambiaso.

138. It appears among the figures of the *Ars Brevis*, the *Ars Demonstrativa* and the *De Nova Geometria*, etc.

139. Chap. 6.

140. Our illustration (Fig. 29) is taken from Daniele Barbaro's edition of 1556. Drawn by Palladio, it is much clearer than those published in earlier editions of Vitruvius.

141. He owned at least six copies of Vitruvius in different editions. He is also known to have possessed a book containing 'las figuras de Vitruuio', drawn by hand on vellum. All these books were acquired from the architect's estate by Philip II (Luis Cervera Vera, 'Libros del Arquitecto Juan Bautista de Toledo' in *La Ciudad de Dios*, El Escorial, vol. CLXIII, pp. 583 ff. and CLXIII, pp. 161 ff.).

142. *Ibid.*, pp. 575 ff. Fig. 30 is taken from the Bâle, 1533, edition of the *Matheseos*, p. 24.

143. Bk. v, chap. 6.

144. Pythagorean numerology, the basis of which was the doctrine of the consonant intervals of the musical scale, was of course a basic ingredient of Renaissance *magia*. No less important, however, was the geometrical element, with which Pythagoras was also associated. Agrippa of Nettesheim em-

Just as the Roman had used the base of his upright equilateral triangle to establish the all-important line of the *scaena* of his theater and the apex to mark the upper limit of the semicircle enclosing the auditorium, so it may be surmised that the designer of the Escorial used them to determine the line of the main front and the position of the Sagrario, the perimeter of the *quadro* or main block being found by joining up the appropriate points in accordance with the accompanying diagrams (Figs. 26 and 27).[145]

Evidence of Philip II's interest in magical theaters and in this one in particular is afforded by the presence among his books of a copy of Giulio Camillo's *Idea del Theatro*, illustrated with 201 sketches on vellum by the hand of no less a person than the painter Titian.[146] Published in 1550, the dedication is to the king's good friend, the Spanish humanist, historian and bibliophile, Diego Hurtado de Mendoza.[147] It seems to have enjoyed quite a vogue in Spain; Herrera himself had two copies.[148] One of the key Hermetic works of the period, not only does it embody such elements as Pythagorean numerology, Cabala and Lullian mnemonics, but is itself cast in the form of an astrologically ordered 'architecture'. Its basis is of course Vitruvius' theater with the difference that it is planetary rather than zodiacal. In the light of what we know about them it will be readily appreciated how strongly such a mingling of architecture and magic must have appealed to Philip and his *aposentador*. At the same time a typical example such as this of what we have termed 'the blurring of contours'

affords an insight into the mental attitude behind some of the odd iconographical transpositions to be seen in the frescoes of the library, namely how it was that the author of the program assigned Euclid to the bay devoted to *Astrologia*, while displacing the astrologer Abdel Aziz Alchabitius (Fig. 22) to *Geometria*.[149]

To revert to the plan of the Escorial and its genesis, the magical Vitruvian figure in question does undoubtedly yield a set of proportions for the main block that is virtually identical with that given by Padre Sigüenza. Yet whether this hypothesis be valid or not is in a sense immaterial, since quite apart from this it is evident that the three basic geometrical shapes of circle, square and triangle are fundamental to the plan. Now these three figures and their derivatives, the sphere, the cube and the pyramid, are cosmological symbols going back to remotest time. Plato had discussed them at length in the *Timaeus* in relation to his theory of the elements. In Lull they are if anything even more important. 'He regarded', writes Frances Yates, 'the all important relationship between the elements and the heavens—the basic pattern of the physical structure of the universe—as expressible in terms of the three geometrical figures, the circle, the triangle and the square.'[150] Moreover, as she has pointed out, the elemental letter sequences of the Art actually describe a circular, square and triangular 'motion'.[151] This is not to suggest that the Escorial is in any way a Lullian building, even though Herrera is known to have been passionately attached to the Beatus' doctrine and the so-called 'star of Solomon' is one of the basic figures of the Art. Nor is it proposed to enter into the intriguing question, also raised by Miss Yates, of whether Lull's geometry could have influenced Renaissance architectural theory.[152] On the other hand these ideas, so widespread at the time, may provide a pointer to the sense in which the Escorial could be held to have been a 'recreation' of the Solomonic archetype. If the three geometrical figures in question inform the cosmos and at the same time

Rodder ?
Klein.

phasizes this point (*op. cit.*, bk. II, chap. 23). To maintain, however, that architectural proportioning in the Age of Humanism, particularly the sixteenth century, was based exclusively on Pythagorean numerology is surely an exaggeration (see Robert Klein, *op. cit.*, for an examination of this whole question, more concretely p. 107). It is significant that Vitruvius himself nowhere mentions the Pythagorean intervals as the 'key' to correct proportion. His silence on this point, however, would of course have been ascribed at this time to his refusal to betray the 'mysteries'. On the other hand, Vitruvius does mention the usefulness of Pythagorean geometry (bk. IX, Introduction, 6).

145. It is instructive to carry out this same operation on the astrological diagram (Fig. 30) in Julius Firmicus' *Matheseos*, a work that was in the possession of Juan Bautista de Toledo, Juan de Herrera and Philip II. From the angles at the base of the upright equilateral triangle the verticals are carried up to the relevant planetary points and then onwards to the tops of the lines marking the zodiacal divisions. The *quadro* is completed by joining the two latter points.

146. It no longer survives. Had it done so, it would have been a capital document for the study of sixteenth-century Hermetism, particularly in the circle of Titian. Camillo is believed to have been a friend of the painter.

147. *L'Idea del Theatro* . . . dedicated *All' Illustrissimo Signore il Signor Don Diego Hurtado di Mendozza, Ambasciatore appresso il Sommo Pontifice, & del Consiglio di Sua Maestà Cesarea*, Florence, 1550. On Camillo's *Theatro* see Frances Yates, *The Art of Memory*, London, 1966, pp. 129 ff.

148. Sánchez Cantón, *op. cit.*, p. 27.

149. While Euclid's presence here can be justified on the grounds that a thorough knowledge of geometry is necessary for the study of astronomy, the converse can hardly be maintained as justifying that of Alchabitius under *Geometria*. The latter, whose full name was Abdul Aziz ibn Otman ibn Ali al Qabisi, was a tenth-century Persian mathematician and astrologer. Many of his works were translated into Latin by Ioannes Hispalensis (Juan de Luna), the well-known Spanish 'converso' polymath of the twelfth century. The Escorial library contains three manuscripts and four printed works, all in Latin, by Alchabitius. Of these only one is not astrological. In the library decoration the word *Astrologia* is used as a synonym for *Astronomia*, but it would be simple-minded to imagine that the author of the program was not aware of the difference between them.

150. Frances Yates, *The Art of Ramón Lull*, p. 147.

151. *Ibid.*, p. 148.

152. *Ibid.*, p. 166.

constitute the fundamental elements in the planning of the building, then clearly the result will embody a reference to the divine order in much the same way as did the ancient Temple of Jerusalem. Reinforced by the more specifically Solomonic parallels and allusions already referred to, they would have provided a kind of symbolic armature upon which the architect could elaborate his inner *disegno* or *Idea*. Such notions were of course not new or exclusive to the Escorial. The incorporation of harmonic ratios into Renaissance structures is likewise an attempt to put earthly architecture in tune with the cosmic order.[153] The stress on anthropomorphism at this time is yet another facet of the same aspiration. This last-named principle too is enshrined in the Escorial; here again Padre Sigüenza is our authority.[154] This is implied by the very fact that the plan can be inscribed within a circle, although, if the human frame be imposed upon it (Fig. 28), the result is more akin to the cosmological man of Agrippa and Giorgi than to the authentic Vitruvian man, as drawn for instance by Leonardo. But this is what one would rather tend to expect, considering the probable Hermetic nature of the building.

Although the architect of the Escorial could claim to have the backing of Vitruvius for the use of the equilateral triangle in his plan, where its apex marks the position of the Divinity (Fig. 25), it must be admitted that the use of this figure would seem on the whole to have been foreign to Renaissance principles of architectural design. As the Roman theorist had been silent on the existence of any relationship between the human body and this particular figure, Renaissance writers on architecture likewise tended to ignore it.[155] On the other hand there was ample authority for identifying man with the triangle by way of the exemplarist geometry of St. Augustine's *De Trinitate*. Naturally enough the Saint finds the strongest analogies between them on the spiritual plane, particularly in the threefold *vestigia* of the Trinity with which man is endowed, namely *intellectus*, *voluntas* and *memoria*.[156] But this connection could be extended to take in the physical body as well, since the Second

Person had not disdained to assume a human form.[157] Traditionally regarded as being of perfect proportions, Christ's body thus supplied a tangible link with the triangle.

In Book IV of his treatise the saint specifically draws a parallel between the *aedificatio* of Christ's body and that of the Temple of Jerusalem.[158] That this link between St. Augustine and the Escorial is not wholly fanciful can be demonstrated by reference to a contemporary painting in the church. Completed in 1580 by the painter Alonso Sánchez Coello, it depicts St. Jerome and St. Augustine standing side by side.[159] The latter carries a book in his right hand, surmounted in lieu of the usual chapel by a schematic representation of the Escorial (Fig. 23).[160] It is not as actually executed, for instead of being rectangular, it is in the form of a perfect square with an inner cloister plainly recognizable as the Court of the Evangelists. The title of the book is not shown, but it has been taken as being the *Civitas Dei* in allusion to the celestial Jerusalem.[161] If so, it would be difficult to find a more telling illustration of the way in which the Escorial was equated with the Temple. At the same time Coello's idealized Escorial may be significant for another reason, since its strictly square form must have been dictated to him from above. Not only does it call to mind at once the plan of Villalpando's reconstruction (Fig. 13), but in doing so suggests that this perfect figure corresponded more closely than does its actual shape to the designer's original *Idea*.

The third diagram on Euclid's board (Fig. 21) represents a man using a 'Jacob's staff'. An allusion to the self-evident link between geometry and astronomy, on the surface its main purpose seems to be that of justifying the sage's inclusion under *Astrologia*. The quadrant he is holding serves the same end.[162] Strangely enough, however, Sacrobosco who balances Euclid on

---

153. Although we have attempted to demonstrate that the plan of the *quadro* of the Escorial was worked out geometrically, this is not to say that the Pythagorean musical consonances were not used in the building. Both Juan Bautista de Toledo and Herrera would have been quite familiar with what theorists like Alberti and Daniele Barbaro had to say on the subject. Moreover Padre Sigüenza mentions several examples of their use, but always in connection with parts of the elevation. On the obsession of Spanish architects at this time with the proportion of 2:3, which is a musical fifth, see Kubler, *op. cit.*

154. Fray José de Sigüenza, *op. cit.*, bk. III, Prologue.

155. Leonardo, however, had briefly mentioned that the outstretched legs of the Vitruvian man form an equilateral triangle.

156. *De Trinitate*, bk. XI, chap. I, 1.

157. *Ibid.*, bk. XII, chaps. 10, 18 and 19.

158. *Ibid.*, bk. v, chap. 9.

159. Now in the so-called 'capilla de los Doctores'. See Fray Julián Zarco Cuevas, *Pintores españoles de San Lorenzo el Real de El Escorial*, Madrid, 1931, pp. 155 and 158.

160. *Ibid.*, p. 155. 'In one hand the painter placed the traditional hermitage chapel which takes the form of the Monastery of the Escorial.'

161. Fray Gabriel del Estal, O.S.A., 'La Iglesia, Trento y El Escorial' in *El Escorial 1563–1963*, vol. I, p. 520.

162. Quadrants in the form of squares and rectangles do not seem to have been very common. However, a man is shown holding one in the well-known Landsberg engraving of 1635. As for the graphic design itself, it has not been possible to track its prototype down, if there was one. However, it may be related to one of the illustrations in Alfonso the Wise's *Libros del Saber de Astronomia* (facsimil. ed., Madrid, 1863, vol. II, p. 240). In the depiction of this instrument it is noticeable that the peepsights are wrongly turned round; also the graduation of the quadrant into 12 divisions seems unusual. From this and other peculiarities elsewhere, it appears that the painter who must

the other side of the central cartouche has a small board just behind him showing two stars in the very same relationship as those being observed by the man with the 'Jacob's staff'. The repetition of this motif then would seem to imply that there must be more to this apparently simple figure than might have been suspected and that the author of the program chose this method of underscoring its significance. If so, this would mean that, as with Cambiaso's cube, we are in the presence of a 'hieroglyph' alluding to something hidden behind its mere external appearance.

A clue to the riddle is furnished by Matthias Hacus' *Prognosticon*. In it he refers of course to the striking double conjunction of Venus, Jupiter and Mercury ruling at the time of Philip's birth. This would explain the three stars on Euclid's quadrant, which would otherwise be quite irrelevant. Elsewhere the astrologer provides a diagram (Fig. 31) to illustrate the relationship between the Venus-Jupiter conjunction and Saturn. They are shown to be in ✳, this star-shape being the conventional sign used to denote the favorable aspect of sextile. It was precisely this aspect which, according to Matthias Hacus, was to be the ruling influence on Philip's life.[163] Far from being a maleficent planet, Saturn was to endow him with a *gravitas* and *regia melancholia* proper to those who aspire to cultivate higher things. The star-diagram on the boards of both Euclid and Sacrobosco would therefore represent the Jupiter-Venus conjunction in ✳ with Saturn, as shown in the *Prognosticon*, so that the objects that appear to be innocuous stars are in reality a planetary aspect.[164]

This astrological interpretation is matched by yet another diagram. It is to be seen on a large display board held by the figure that directly faces Euclid on the opposite side of the same bay, thus emphasizing the connection between them. A scroll identifies him as the renowned medieval Magus, Alfonso the Wise, king of Castile (Fig. 24). His inclusion under *Astro-*

logia was of course most appropriate. It would in fact have been difficult to omit him, since he shed luster not only on Spain but on the very monarchy itself. This might even mean that he is to be identified with his no less illustrious and wise descendant, Philip the second Solomon.

Under king Alfonso's left hand there is a partially opened book showing an astronomical diagram. It is odd, however, that it has not been taken, as one would have expected, from any of his own works. Its source is the *Quadrans* of Apianus,[165] of which it is the very first illustration. In this book the author discourses at length on the many applications of his quadrant, but here it will suffice to mention that it could be employed to determine planetary positions and the divisions of the zodiac. Below, on the board itself, another diagram shows the use of the 'traveler's compass'. Not only therefore is king Alfonso not associated with any of his own works,[166] but he could not possibly have known either of the two instruments with which he is depicted. Such a glaring anachronism must have some ulterior meaning. This contention is reinforced by the other part of the diagram. The upper half of the instrument in question is trained on the pole star. Grouped round it are the circumpolar constellations of Ursa Minor, Ursa Major, Draco and Cepheus. In this instance too the design has been lifted from Apianus, this time from his *Horoscopion*.[167] Here, however, the whole thing has been shifted round in such a manner that, if the point midway along the top of the board be taken as the celestial zenith, then the constellations are seen in the positions they occupied in the sky at the time of Philip's birth, namely between three and four in the afternoon of May 21, 1527, Julian calendar. That a *genitura* or nativity was intended by all this is confirmed by a small but telling detail. On the upper right-hand corner of the king's book a geometrical figure has been introduced consisting of a triangle and a rectangle. The latter are none other than the favorable △ and ✳ aspects of the horoscope (Fig. 20). Apianus then supplied the author of the program with a handy means of putting his message across, which the books of king Alfonso presumably could not.

The bay in question then would appear to teem with

have been provided with some kind of a model to copy had only a very hazy idea of how these instruments were used. Alternatively, but less likely, these oddities may have crept in when the frescoes were restored at the beginning of the present century.

163. *Prognosticon*, p. 26 verso, 'Septima (domus) licet in ea Saturnus sit fortunata est quemadmodum ipse Saturnus sextili Jovis et Veneris.' The diagram does not of course illustrate Jupiter and Venus in actual conjunction. It is a schematic sketch used by the astrologer to illustrate the ✳ aspect. Incidentally Philip so cherished his nativity that everyone who attended Mass with him on that day was able by a Papal brief to gain a plenary indulgence (Porreño, *op. cit.*, p. 217).

164. There is even a possibility that the figure of Sacrobosco himself, depicted as a bald-headed old man with long white beard, may stand for Saturn. Moreover the man holding up the 'Jacob's staff' also resembles the conventional sign of this same planet: ♄.

165. *Quadrans Apiani Astronomicus et iam recens inventus et nunc primum editus*, Ingolstadt, 1532.

166. If, as suggested in note 162, Euclid's quadrant is based on one of king Alfonso's diagrams, then we are here in the presence of another of those curious transpositions in the library which are difficult to explain unless it be admitted that they carry a veiled meaning. In this instance it reinforces the connection between Euclid and his counterpart opposite.

167. *Horoscopion Apiani Generale*, Ingolstadt, 1533, p. 38. Herrera owned a copy of this work.

guarded allusions—they necessarily had to be so in a place like this—to Philip's sovereign destiny as enshrined in his horoscope. The events of 1588 had yet to mar the prospect. The author seems to have sought to do honor to it and to the way it had fulfilled its promise in the successful conclusion of the great royal building. No better setting for this tribute could have been found than this, the bay devoted to *Astrologia*.

We have dwelt at some length on the theme of the Escorial as marking the fulfilment of Philip's destiny because this will enable us now to consider the last two of what might be termed the 'sidereal' aspects of the building. The first is that it was astrally orientated, the second that it was begun under favorable astral auspices.

On the first of these we need hardly linger, since its east–west orientation is rooted in Christian tradition. The alignment, however, is not exact. Padre Sigüenza states that the architect shifted its north–south axis somewhat east–west, so that in winter the palatine and monastic sections facing south could enjoy the sunshine earlier in the day during the winter months. In fact, of course, the very reverse would have been the result.[168] Alternatively it has been suggested that the object was to protect the royal apartments from the north winds and to ensure that they enjoyed the winter sunshine for a longer period of the day. While practical considerations of this kind would no doubt have weighed with the architect, there is a far more cogent reason. The truth is that the building was aligned to the sunset on August 10, the feast of St. Lawrence.[169] That it cannot be observed because of the hills before it is immaterial; in fact, the secret has been better kept for this very reason. What matters is that it was in the afternoon of this very day in 1557 that Philip won his great battle over the French at Saint-Quintin, an event which marked one of the crucial stages in the fulfilment of his destiny and which the Escorial was founded to commemorate.

No less important at this period than that a building should be attuned to the celestial order in its plan and orientation was the need for it to be begun only when the stars were propitious. It would thus achieve its final 'dimension', the assurance of its perpetuation in time. Though Alberti had been sceptical about it all,[170] others were just as convinced that it was essential. No undertaking of this scope could afford to run the risk of neglecting the omens. Moreover Alberti himself would hardly have discussed the matter at such length, had not the conviction been widespread.[171]

Sapientia, so Solomon relates, *aedificavit sibi domum; excidit columnas septem*.[172] In Camillo's *Theatro* these pillars symbolize *stabilissima eternità*.[173] He identifies them with the seven Cabalistic Sephiroth on the empyrean, whose influence filters down to the elemental world by way of the Seven Governors. The prophet Zachariah had obviously had this in mind when he wrote of the seven *lucernae* whose oil is piped through seven *infusoria*. Elsewhere he refers to them as 'eyes', the seven eyes of God 'that run to and fro through the whole earth',[174] engraved on the foundation-stone of the new Temple. It now becomes clear that Villalpando's seven planets 'enthroned' in their houses (Fig. 17) should be read at least in part as signifying the Temple's *stabilissima eternità*.[175] This being so, there is no reason to think that Philip and his architects would have neglected in some such fashion

170. *De re aedificatoria*, bk. XI, chap. 13.

171. Perhaps the best known example at this period of this practice being put into effect was the laying of the foundation-stone of Tycho Brahe's Uraniborg observatory on the island of Hven on August 8, 1576, at sunrise, the most favorable moment having been calculated by the astronomer beforehand. Cardanus in his *Geniturae*, LXVII, Nuremberg, 1543, published the horoscopes of the *fundatio* of Venice on March 25, A.D. 421 (no. LX) and of the *instauratio* of Milan (no. LXI), Florence (no. LXII), etc.

172. Proverbs 9:1.

173. Giulio Camillo, *op. cit.*, p. 9: 'Salomone al nono de Proverbii dice la sapienza hauersi edificato casa, & hauerla fondata sopra sette colonne. Queste colonne significanti stabilissima eternità habbiamo da intender che siano le sette saphiroth del sopraceleste mondo, che sono le sette misure della fabrica del celeste & dell' inferiore, nelle quali sono comprese le Idee di tutte le cose al celeste, & all inferiore appartenenti.' Sephiroth are generally given as ten in number. See also Agrippa of Nettesheim, *op. cit.*, bk. III, chap. 10.

174. Zachariah 4:2 and 4:10.

175. Villalpando's Temple may also have been intended as a magic memory building—Herrera, his master, would have known all about this type of 'architecture' from his copy of Giordano Bruno's *De umbris idearum*. If so, then the astrological signs on the *castella* and in the courts could also be considered as somewhat akin to talismanic images, like those in Camillo's *Theatro*, which, by impressing themselves on the memory, drew down into it the all-unifying divine *spiritus*. So, too, the perfect proportions of the structure, in which Herrera had so readily discerned the hand of God (cf. p. 93 and Note 124), related it to the Pauline *spiritus Christi*. This idea is specifically developed by Villalpando, for whom, as for Ficino and Camillo, the true Sun is God (cf. p. 92). For a full discussion of this and related points, see Frances Yates, *op. cit.*, pp. 155 ff.

168. How Padre Sigüenza who does not seem to have had any very clear notion of the difference between east and west could have claimed that he supplied the program of the library with all its astronomical and astrological lore surpasses all understanding.

169. It has been difficult to find a plan of the Escorial giving a reliable orientation of the building, owing to the persistence of those that have surveyed the building to use a magnetic north reading without either indicating the year or the degrees of declination from true north. However, the official Spanish commemorative book, published on the occasion of the fourth centenary of the Escorial (*El Escorial 1563–1963*, Madrid, 1963, vol. II, p. 109), shows that the building has a clockwise skew from true north of about 16°. To face the sunset exactly on August 10, the skew in question would need to be 16° 6'. Since it could not have been orientated visually, the architects would probably have established the position by reference to the stars.

to infuse the virtue of permanence into their building. Padre Sigüenza actually alludes to Zachariah's seven eyes in his description of the laying of the foundation-stone of the church, though he carefully skirts round their obvious astrological implications.[176]

This event took place on August 20, 1563, beginning at five in the afternoon,[177] four months after the laying of the foundation-stone of the entire structure. The two occasions could not have been more different. On the first the act was performed by Juan Bautista de Toledo before his assistants, the workmen and a few friars. The day was April 23 and the time eleven in the morning.[178] Though Padre Sigüenza infers that it was all improvised suddenly,[179] the stone with its inscriptions, composed by Herrera himself,[180] recording the date and other details was ready.[181] Being the feast of a warrior, St. George, the day was eminently suitable on which to begin a building commemorating a military victory.

Equally suitable from a liturgical standpoint was the choice of August 20, the feast-day of St. Bernard, for laying the first stone of a monastic church. At the same time the signs in the heavens were propitious. Jupiter and Saturn were in conjunction in Cancer, the house of Jupiter's exaltation.[182] These were the very two planets most closely identified with Philip who was present in person with his court. The beneficent influence they were to exert on the events of his life was precisely the burden of Matthias Hacus' *Prognosticon*,[183] that little book, bound in black velvet, which

the king kept by him until his death. *Dominus geniturae*, it reads, *est Jupiter, particeps Saturnus*.[184] Horoscopes of the two events (Figs. 32 and 33)[185] not

Iove simul dominatum obtinuerit & uterq. bene atq. opportune collocatus suam cum authoritate dignitatem in figura retinuerit, natos ipsos ad probitatis ac modestiae studium excitabit. Qua propter inerit in illorum animis summa ac singularis tam aduersum senes natuq. maiores obseruantia, tum erga magistratus atque institutores eosque in quibus signa sapientiae virtutisq. apparuerint (*Prognosticon*, p. 26 v). Much of the horoscope is taken up with this theme. Cornelius Agrippa also considered this particular conjunction to be favorable (*op. cit.*, bk. II, chap. 29).

184. Twenty years later, once the building had been virtually completed, Herrera obtained leave from the king and the Council of Castile to have a number of views of the Escorial engraved and to offer them for sale. The plates were executed under the architect's personal supervision by the Flemish engraver Perret (Luis Cervera Vera, *Las Estampas y el Sumario de El Escorial*, Madrid, 1954). To the writer's knowledge no one has noted that on the engraving of the ground-plan the perimeter of the garden and the Casa de Oficios is identified by the signs of the planets and the zodiac, but they are so unobtrusive that it is not surprising that they have never been noticed. They may have no ulterior significance whatever, being handy symbols chosen by the architect to mark the contours of the building and provide a key to them in his explanatory booklet. On the other hand, he may have sought to imply by this means, for the benefit of those who could 'read' his meaning, that the influence of the stars on the building had not been discounted. At this time Herrera would have been 'reliving' the early history of the Escorial.

185. These horoscopes were calculated for the writer by Dr. Owen Gingerich of the Smithsonian Astrophysical Observatory, Cambridge, Massachusetts, co-author with Dr. William D. Stahlman of *Solar and planetary longitudes for the years from − 2,500 to + 2,000 by 10-day intervals*, Madison, University of Wisconsin Press, 1963. Though their interest is manifest, in no sense should they be considered as necessarily matching those that would have been cast at the time. The reasons for this caution are obvious. In the first place there is no means of knowing just what tables were favored by the architects or whether they were checked by direct observation. In this instance they have been calculated on the basis of the positions given in the *Tabulae Bergensis acqualibus et adparentis motus orbium cœlestium*, Cologne, 1560, of Ioannes Stadius, the reason being that they were among the most up to date at the time and Herrera owned a set of them. A second and more serious imponderable is that there is no way of knowing what particular system would have been adopted to determine the disposition of the houses and the spread of the quadrants. At this period, as nowadays, there were various methods in vogue, each astrologer having his own favorite system. Here the system employed is that of Ptolemy as expounded by him in the *Quadripartitum* (*Tetrabiblos*). This was the most popular and relatively the simplest of the systems extant. It was the one favored by Julius Firmicus, most of the Islamic astrologers including Albategnius and Alchabitius, Alfonso the Wise, Ioannes Campanus and so forth. (See Willy Hartner, 'The Mercury Horoscope of Marcantonio Michiel of Venice in *Vistas in Astronomy*, London & New York, 1955, pp. 93 ff.) This system would have been quite familiar to Herrera from his own copy of the *Astrologia* of Ptolemy and his knowledge of the books of Alfonso the Wise. It is significant perhaps that Ptolemy, Alchabitius and king Alfonso all appear in the Escorial library frescoes. As for the planetary positions these present no such problems; in this case the problem is that of the inevitable inaccuracies in the tables of the period. Apart from this, the aspects of the planets would broadly speaking be as shown in the charts.

176. Fray José de Sigüenza, *op. cit.*, bk. III, disc. III.

177. Fray Juan de San Jerónimo, 'Memorias', in Miguel Salvá and Pedro Sainz de Baranda, *Colección de documentos inéditos para la historia de España*, Madrid, 1845, vol. VII, p. 25.

178. *Ibid.*, p. 23. There is also a letter written by Fray Juan de Colmenar to Philip II describing the event (Amancio Portabales Pichel, *op. cit.*, p. 160). There is a discrepancy between the two as to the time of the ceremony. The latter says it took place at ten in the morning and Fray Juan de San Jerónimo at eleven. In all probability the ceremony as such began at ten and the stone was actually laid in position around eleven.

179. Fray José de Sigüenza, *loc. cit.*

180. This information comes from Herrera himself in his *Memorial* to Mateo Vázquez (Llaguno, *op. cit.*, vol. II, p. 333). The word 'escrebí' used by Herrera must surely mean that he composed it rather than that he carved it, as has sometimes been maintained. Possibly he may have done both.

181. The correct inscriptions were recorded by Fray Juan de San Jerónimo (*loc. cit.*). Padre Sigüenza did not hesitate to distort them.

182. The actual conjunction took place on August 25. It had been widely prophesied as calamitous, especially as bringing in its train widespread floods. The predictions of the astrologers gave rise to considerable alarm, but they proved to be groundless. Friends of Rheticus urged him to use the occasion to undertake a commentary on Copernicus. Cornelius Gemma also refers to the apprehension aroused by this conjunction in his *De Arte Cyclognomica* (tom. III, p. 124).

183. 'Hij duo cum in bona sint ad se inuicem configuratione liberiq. ab impedimentis, tribuunt natc eam naturam quam ex doctissimo Pontano recensibo. Qui sic inquit ubi Saturnus cum

only reveal that the planetary aspects were favorable, they even furnish evidence that they were both 'elections', which means that they were chronologically predetermined. But their implications as marking the fulfilment of Philip's destiny cannot be grasped completely unless they are read in conjunction with his *radix*.[186]

All this may help to explain the mysterious emblem on the medals[187] placed in the foundations of the taber-

nacle in the church. This tabernacle, the last major item to be completed here,[188] was designed by Herrera on a circular plan 'in imitation of the heavens'[189] and executed by Jacopo da Trezzo. Wrought of the finest materials in honor of the Sacrament, it marks the climax of Philip's vast project. The medals, signed by Trezzo,[190] show the king's profile on one side and on the other what has been described as 'a pair of hands securing the reins to a yoke surmounting the earth' (Fig. 34).[191] This has been interpreted in different ways, but never as alluding to the building and its conclusion.[192] Nor has astrology ever been mentioned as a possible key to its meaning. Yet there is no lack of pointers to this. One of these is the yoke itself, traditionally equated with Libra,[193] the house of the ascendant at Philip's birth. The sphere too is likewise a multiple symbol. With its tripartite division it is the well-known abstraction of the terrestrial circle at whose center is Jerusalem, King Philip's fief.[194] But it is also associated by way of the orb with the idea of kingship, so that dominion is symbolized by the very object over which it is exercised. As such it cannot but be identified with Jupiter, lord of the celestial cosmology and Philip's own *dominus geniturae*.[195] Moreover

186. For the following observations on the planetary aspects of the horoscopes the writer is indebted to Mr. Eric Schroeder, curator of Islamic art at the Fogg Museum, Cambridge, Mass.: 1. *Horoscope of the laying of the foundation-stone of the building* (Fig. 32). Not inappropriately in this instance Mars was the lord of the mid-heaven. He was in △ with Jupiter, in ✳ with Mercury and ∨ with Venus. Mercury, apparently posited exactly on the mid-heaven, was in ∨ with Venus and in ✳ with Jupiter. The latter, being in Cancer, the house of his exaltation, was more widely in ☐ with Venus, but this would have been reckoned as of small moment in accordance with the traditional dictum of 'Venus nemo nocet'. The only really unfavorable aspect was that of Mars in ☐ with the Moon. All other aspects were good. Saturn was in ♈ with Mercury and in ✳ with the Sun, also in the house of his exaltation. Such evil influences resulting from Saturn being in conjunction with the descending node, would have been minimized by his presence in Cancer, the sign of his dejection. To round it all off the Wheel or Part of Fortune was seemingly in the ascendant house. It is obvious that a moment was chosen when the principal happy configurations of Philip's *radix* were duplicated in the positions of transiting planets. The birth configuration consists of a double ✳ arrangement of the Moon and Saturn in relation to a double conjunction of Venus, Jupiter and Mercury, the planet Jupiter being clearly the lord of the horoscope. In the transits Mars (horoscope of the building) was on the Moon (Philip's *radix*), Mercury on Saturn, Jupiter on Mercury and Saturn on the Wheel of Fortune. It is remarkable to see how even the unlucky aspect of Mars in ☐ with the Moon in the chart of the building has its identical counterpart in Philip's nativity. The remaining aspects were without exception fortunate, though it would be prolix to enumerate them all.
2. *Horoscope of the laying of the foundation-stone of the church* (Fig. 33). In this figure the conjunction of Jupiter and Saturn is obviously the most important transiting figure, by reason both of the significance attached to these two planets by the astrologer who erected Philip's *radix* and the fact that this is the most powerful of all conjunctions, since it involves the two slowest of the planets which only conjunct once in about twenty years. Jupiter is both lord of the ascendant and the mid-heaven. The conjunction is in △ with the ascendant. Mars, Venus and the Sun are closely configured in a △ and ✳ relationship. Mercury is in ✳ with the Moon. In relation to Philip's nativity the Jupiter-Saturn conjunction is in △ with the king's rising Mars and in ∨ with his Venus-Jupiter conjunction. It is, however, in ☐ with both Saturn and the ascendant in his radical chart. As before, there is a ✳ configuration between transiting Mars who is on or in conjunction with Philip's radical Sun and transiting Venus who is on his Mercury and the transiting Sun. Transiting Mercury in the position given by Stadius, which is a few degrees out according to modern tables, is exactly in a ♈ aspect with the double conjunction of Venus, Jupiter and Mercury in Philip's *radix*. Though devoid of any strictly astrological significance, the mystical import of the presence of the Sun, the symbol of Christ, in Virgo would hardly have been overlooked.
187. Some were also placed on the cornice. They were struck in gold, silver and bronze. During the Peninsular War, however, Napoleon's troops who occupied the building proceeded to

demolish this tabernacle. They looted the gold and silver pieces, but left the others. Two of the latter are preserved in the Escorial library (see Padre Arturo García de la Fuente, O.S.A., 'La Numismática española en el reinado de Felipe II', *El Escorial*, 1927, p. 93; also Fray Damian Bermejo, *El Escorial*, Madrid, 1820, p. 52, Note 1).
188. The date of its completion was 1586.
189. Fray Francisco de los Santos, *Descripción del Real Monasterio de San Lorenzo de El Escorial*, Madrid, 1698, p. 26.
190. The two examples in the library bear the signature *Jac. Tricii F.* Jean Babelon, however, considers them to be workshop pieces (*Jacopo da Trezzo*, Paris, 1922). Considering the concealed place they were destined for, he is probably right. Armand (*Les Médailleurs Italiens*, Paris, 1883, vol. I, p. 242, no. 6) mentions a variant with the year 1588 instead of the signature. Considering the date of the completion of the tabernacle, in whose foundations the medals were placed, the Escorial examples must be several years earlier.
191. Padre Arturo García de la Fuente, *loc. cit.*
192. The design has been held to refer to the conquest of America, these dominions not having been submitted fully to the Spanish yoke until the reign of Philip II. Exactly why a medal alluding to such an event should have been placed beneath the tabernacle is difficult to understand. Another explanation, and a much more likely one, is that it was struck in anticipation of the victory of the Invincible Armada. This, however, would only apply to the medals bearing the date 1588.
193. Richard Hinckley Allen, *Star Names*, New York, 1963, pp. 270 ff.
194. St. Isidore of Seville illustrated it thus in his *Origenes*.
195. The classical symbol of Jupiter's authority is of course the thunderbolt. There is, however, no lack of examples both literary and pictorial of his association with the orb as creator and governor of 'questa gran machina del mondo' (Cartari, *Imagini, Giove*). He is shown holding the regal orb in the Salone at Padua (Antonio Bardón, *I cieli et la loro Influenza*, Padua, 1924, p. 55). But not only does he sustain the world as its *Stator*, he *is* the world: 'Et Mondo parimente poteuano chiamarlo (Giove), perche cio che si vede tutto e lui, che di sua

since to him alone of all the deities in the Roman pantheon was granted the title of *Optimus Maximus*,[196] it may even be suspected that Herrera's inscription on the upper face of the first foundation-stone—DEUS OPTIMUS MAXIMUS OPERI ASPICIAT—was intended to carry a twofold invocation. Lastly it should be borne in mind that the terrestrial orb is an attribute of Venus as well, no doubt because she too, no less indeed than Jupiter, exercises her sway over it.[197]

The fillets fluttering down from above clearly indicate that the two levels of the design should be read as being inseparably linked together. Such links are not difficult to find. Thus Homer had alluded to the scales held aloft by the Eternal Father.[198] The latter was also associated with the yoke, as he was the first to introduce it to men.[199] Then too the very word *iugum* implies *coniunctio*, a point underscored by the binding or conjunctive action of the hands. And, since these last were astrologically identified with Gemini, in whose house the conjunction of Venus and Jupiter hung at Philip's birth, the reference here to his *genitura* will be evident. At the same time his natal conjunction foreshadowed the equally happy conjunction of Jupiter and Saturn that presided over the inception of the church.

The whole design then would seem to be pregnant with astrological allusions. A final and conclusive pointer to its arcane character is provided by the four brief words—SIC ERAT IN FATIS—that encircle it.[200] Again their enigmatic nature has not passed unnoticed, even if no convincing interpretation has been forthcoming to explain their meaning. Yet the inference is clear. In this way Philip sought to acknowledge that, at least as far as the Escorial was concerned, the signs at his birth had fulfilled their promise. His trust in the *fata* had not been misplaced.

virtu propia si sostiene, & cosi era creduto essere in tutti i luoghi, & empire di se ogni cosa, come dice Vergilio. Del sommo Gioue l'vinuerso e pieno' (Cartari, *loc. cit.*).

196. 'Et lo dissero ancora Ottimo, e Massimo, con cio fosse che a tutti per la sua bonta volesse giouare, & far bene, e lo potesse anco fare per la maggioranza sua, che andaua sopra tutti gli altri' (Cartari, *loc. cit.*).

197. She is represented holding the orb in one of Cartari's illustrations. '...questa dea (Venere) appo loro statua staua dritta sopra un carro tirato da due cigni, e da altretante colombe, nuda, col capo cinto di mortine, &...nella mano destra teneua certa palla rotonda in forma del mondo' (Cartari, *Imagini, Venere*). She extended her sway very much over Jupiter himself, which would underline the concept of identifying the two deities under one single symbol.

198. *Iliad.* Bk. 22, 208–13. 'Et un' altro Poeta molto antico disse, che Gioue fa discendere la bilancia hor d'vna, hor d'altra parte, secondo che a quelli, o a questi gli piace di far bene; Che fu pur' anco fittione di Homero, percioche egli fa, che Gioue tenendo bilancia d'ora in mano, pesa i fatti de' Greci, & de' Troiani per vedere a quali doueua dare la vittoria' (Cartari, *Gioue*). Jupiter was the god most closely identified with justice.

199. 'Sed quid illud, quod ipsius Iouis symbolum est, iugum? Iugare siquidem inuentū esse veteres tradiderunt & a Iouis nomine Graeci deduxerunt. Ipsum autem aiunt primum iumenta iunxisse, vt ea in frugum fatu frugalem nobis operam praestarent' (Valeriano, *op. cit.*, p. 475).

200. '...y al rededor [of the medal] estas misteriosas palabras: *sic erat in fatis*' (Fray Damián Bermejo, *loc. cit.*). Cartari (*loc. cit.*) also identifies Jupiter with Fate: 'Gioue...si poteua dimandare Fato, come da lui dipendessero tutte le cose, & ordine delle cause, che sono l'vna sopra l'altra, tutto venisse da lui.' Considering the extraordinarily arcane nature of this emblem and the friendship existing between Jacopo da Trezzo and Herrera, the chances are that the design was evolved by Herrera himself.

APPENDIX I

The Hermetic Books of Juan de Herrera and King Philip II

The following summary of the Hermetic and occult books in Herrera's possession at the time of his death in 1597 makes no claim to be exhaustive. Its main purpose is to give some idea of their number and scope, thus showing how deeply he must have been interested in and no doubt influenced by the Hermetic ideas of his age.

Pride of place must necessarily be given to Hermes Trismegistus. Under the name of 'Mercurio trimexistro' or 'tremexistro' he is listed twice. From the first entry it transpires that Herrera had a Spanish translation of the *Asclepius*. This was probably the rendering made by Diego Guillén de Ávila in 1487, of which Philip II also gave a copy to the Escorial library. The second time he is mentioned the complete entry reads as follows: 'The Dioscorides of Matthiolus and Iamblichus and other works of Mercurius Trismegistus and other philosophers.' Very clearly we are confronted here by two quite different books bound together to form a single volume, a not infrequent occurrence. With the commentary of Matthiolus on Dioscorides we need not be concerned, this being a straightforward book on medicine. The second part of the entry, however, is of considerable interest. This is because the book in question cannot be any other than the compendium of Hermetic texts in the Latin translation of Marsilio Ficino, published by Aldus in 1516. It opens with the paraphrase of Iamblichus' *De Mysteriis* and likewise contains the works of Hermes Trismegistus and 'other philosophers', exactly as described in the inventory. The index of this book reads as follows:

Iamblichus de mysteriis Aegyptiorum, Chaldaeorum, Assyriorum.

Proclus in Platonicum Alcibiadem de anima, atque demone.

Proclus de sacrificio, & magia.

Porphyrius de diuinis, atque daemonibus.

Synesius Platonicus de somniis.

Psellus de daemonibus.

Expositio Priciani, & Marsilii in Theophrastum de sensu, phantasia & intellectu.

Alcinoi Platonici philosophi, liber de doctrina Platonis.

Speusippi Platonis discipuli, liber de Platonis definitionibus.

Pythagorae philosophi aurea uerba.

Symbola Pithagorae philosophi.

Xenocratis philosophi platonici, liber de morte.

Mercurii Trimegisti Pimander.

Eiusdem Asclepius.

Marsilii Ficini de triplici uita Lib. II.

Eiusdem liber de uoluptate.

Eiusdem de Sole & lumine libri. II.

Apologia eiusdem in librum suum de lumine.

Eiusdem libellus de magis.

Quod necessaria sit securitas, & tranquillitas animi.

Praeclarissimarum sententiarum huius operis breuis annotatio.

In this one book then Herrera would have possessed digests of an impressive number of important Hermetic works. But there is evidence to show that he had many of these self-same texts in another edition. One of the entries in the inventory reads: 'the second volume of the works of Marsilio Ficino in Italian'. Now prior to Herrera's death no version of Ficino's works had been published in Italian. Presumably therefore this was a slip on the part of the scribe, so that it should have read 'in Latin'. Sánchez Cantón assumes this to have been so and suggests that it might have been one of the Latin editions of Ficino's writings, published in Bâle in the second half of the sixteenth century. If this were so, then Herrera would have possessed duplicates of most of the works listed in the Aldus edition, but with the addition of the *Enneads* of Plotinus, the *De Mystica Theologia* of Dionysius the Areopagite and Ficino's own commentaries on the latter's *De Trinitate* and *De divinis nominibus.*

Prominent among his ancient texts was the *Matheseos* of Julius Firmicus Maternus, the fourth-century astrologer. There is likewise reason to believe that he had copies of the *Quadripartitum (Tetrabiblos)* and *Centiloquium (Karpos)* of Ptolemy. In connection with the art of memory he had the *Rhetorica ad Herennium.* It should also be mentioned that he had numerous books on astronomy, mathematics, mechanics, music and kindred subjects which, while not occult in themselves, could be related to *magia.* Examples of these were the *Almagest* and *Harmonics* of Ptolemy, the *De machinis, De spiritualibus* and *Pneumatica* of Heron of Alexandria, and the *De musica* and *Arithmetica* of Boethius.

Herrera's medieval occult books were less numerous. Nevertheless they included the *Clavis maioris sapientiae* of Arthephius, *L'Acerba* of Cecco d'Ascoli and the *Tractatus de philosophorum lapide* of Arnold of Villanova. He also had works by Geber and Avicenna, both being bracketed together as alchemists. Another of his medieval books was the *Pretiosa margarita*, a compilation from the writings of Arnold of Villanova, Michael Scot, Rhazes, pseudo-Albertus Magnus and pseudo-Lull. Yet another is listed in the inventory as 'a volume printed in Latin containing numerous works on alchemy by various authors'. This is probably to be identified with the *De alchimia opuscula complura veterum philosophorum*, a medieval compendium ascribed to a number of ancient writers. Of late medieval provenance were such pseudo-Lullian works in his possession as the *Experimenta*, the *Liber de secretis naturae sive de quinta essentia* and the *Antiquum testamentum et compendium animae transmutationis metallorum.* In Spanish he had the *Vision deleitable* of Alfonso de la Torre and a copy of *Los Libros del saber de Astronomia* of Alfonso the Wise, besides several copies of the latter's tables.

Not unnaturally the writers of his own period provided Herrera with the bulk of his Hermetic and occult books. His copy of the Aldus compendium contained among other original writings of Marsilio Ficino the *De vita cœlitus comparanda*, the basic text for Renaissance magic. In addition he had the *Heptaplus* of Pico della Mirandola, the *De auditu kabbalistico*, the *Polygraphia* of Trithemius, the *De vita longa* of Paracelsus, the *Margarita philosophica* of Gregor Reisch, two copies of the *Theatro* of Giulio Camillo, the *De arte cyclognomica* of Cornelius Gemma, the *Magia naturalis* of Porta, the *De umbris idearum* of Giordano Bruno and two copies of the *Monas Hieroglyphica* of John Dee, one the printed Latin edition and the other a Spanish translation in manuscript. Less well known but in the same vein were the *Tipocosmia* of Alessandro Citolini, the *Occultae naturae miracula* and the *De astrologia* of Lavinius Lemnius, the *Epistola astrologiae defensiva* of Ioannes Ganivetus, the *De remediis secretis* of Evonymus Philiatrus, the *De causis criticorum dierum* of Frascatoro, the *Oratio de methodo intramathematico* of Samuel Siderocrates and the *De sacra philosophia* of Franciscus Vallesius. Though, as already mentioned, Vallés was Philip II's chief doctor, this did not prevent his book being placed on the Spanish Index.

These were supplemented by numerous 'borderline' works which, as in the case of his classical texts, had Hermetic overtones or applications. Among these titles were Cartari's *Imagini*, the *Emblemata* of Alciatus, the *Hieroglyphica* of Estrada, the *Philosophia secreta* of Pedro de Moya, Agricola's *De re metallica*, Marbodius' *De gemmis*, the *Primum mobile* of Regiomontanus and his commentaries on the *Almagest* and *Astrolabium* of Ptolemy, the *De globo coelesti et terrestri* of Gemma Frisius, the *Primum mobile, Horoscopion* and *Astronomicon Caesareum* of Apianus, the *Institutiones harmoniche* of Zarlino, the *De Musica* of Francisco Salinas; the *De amore* of Leone Ebreo, Trissino's *Italia liberata* and Ludovico Dolce's treatise on mnemonics.

He had many books on the so-called 'Theoricae planetarum', including one devoted exclusively to the movements of the Sun and Mercury. As to astronomical tables and ephemerides, he had editions of these in Latin, Greek, Spanish, Italian, French and German. In addition to the foregoing Herrera owned a number of works which cannot be identified with precision. These include titles such as *A manuscript book in Latin, which is an introduction to astrology, A manuscript discourse on astrology in Italian, A discourse on meteors in Italian, A manuscript book in Spanish on the benefit of metals* and *A discourse on the perfect number Ten in Italian.*

Many notable Hermetic works not listed in the inventory of Herrera's books were to be found among those bought by Philip II for the library of the Escorial. Though the friars were put in charge of it, in no sense was it meant to be just another monastic library. It was founded for the use of scholars in general, a function it fulfils to this day. Its books would therefore have been accessible to Herrera, quite apart from any special facilities he might have been given by virtue of his being the king's *architecto general* and *aposentador mayor.*

The first gift of books, consisting of just over 4,500 titles, was formally made over to the monastery in 1576 and further consignments continued to be received throughout the king's reign. Acquisitions were not confined to theology and philosophy. Mathematics and related disciplines, for instance, constituted one of its

most important sections. Moreover, such was the list of its Hermetic and occult works that Arias Montano, the first librarian, created special divisions devoted to Astrology (as distinct from Astronomy), Divination, Alchemy and the Art of Memory.

Again the following list of such books makes no claim to be exhaustive. It has been compiled wholly from published sources, the main one being vol. VII of *Documentos para la Historia del Monasterio de San Lorenzo el Real de El Escorial*, Madrid, 1964, edited with a Prologue and Notes by Padre Gregorio de Andrés, O.S.A., which itemizes most, though by no means all, of Philip II's acquisitions for the Escorial library. Then too, since the following list is only intended to give some idea of the Hermetic and kindred works that circulated, however restrictedly, in sixteenth-century Spain and were specifically available for study at San Lorenzo, no attempt has been made to include editions and dates or to identify doubtful titles. Though the entries are generally clear, some of them are difficult to decipher. Nor has any reference been made to duplicate copies; quite a number were available in different forms and editions—for instance, there were eight examples of Macrobius' *In Somnium Scipionis* alone. Plato and Aristotle have been excluded; so have a number of minor Neoplatonists who would have swelled the list unduly. Arabic works have been included only when translated into Latin and therefore accessible to the ordinary scholar. As with Herrera's books they have been divided into four categories:

ANTIQUE. Hermes Trismegistus, *Asclepius* and *Pimander* in Latin, *Pimander* in Greek, also the *Asclepius* translated into Spanish by Diego Guillén de Ávila; Zoroaster, *Astrologica* and *Magia*; Orpheus, *Hymni*; Pythagoras, *Aurea carmina*; *Carmina Sybillina*; Cicero, *De natura deorum, De fato, De divinatione, Disputationes tusculanae, Somnium Scipionis* and *Rhetorica ad Herennium*; Quintilian, *De institutione oratoria* (Lib. XI); Diodorus Siculus, *De fabulosis Aegyptorum gestis*; Pliny, *Natural History*; Plutarch, *De Iside et Oriside*; Julian the Apostate, *Ad regem solem*; Ptolemy, *Centiloquium* (*Karpos*) and *Quadripartitum* (*Tetrabiblos*); Julius Firmicus Maternus, *Matheseos*; Marcus Manilius, *Astronomicon*; Artemidorus, *De somniorum interpretatione*; Horapollo, *Hieroglyphica*; Plotinus, *Enneads*; Porphyry, *De occasionibus, De animi ascensu et descensu, Vita Plotini*; Proclus, *In Timaeum, In Parmenidem, In Alcibiadem, De sacrificio et magia* and *In Quadripartitum Ptolomaei*; Iamblichus, *De Mysteriis, De vita pythagorica* and *De doctrina pythagorica*; Macrobius, *In Somnium Scipionis*; Diogenes Laertius,

Vita philosophorum; Lactantius, *De divinis Institutionibus*; Eusebius, *De preparatione evangelica*; Philostratus, *De vita Apollonii*, Philo Judaeus, *Opera omnia*.

MEDIEVAL. Morienus Eremita, *Super lapide philosophorum*, *Super librum Hermetis philosophi de minori et maiori opere*; Calid, *Tractatus diversi de alchimia*; Geber, *De alchemia traditio summae veritatis*; Alchindi, *Astrologia*; Abu Masar, *Flores, De magnis coniunctionibus, Astrologia*; Alchabitius, *Ad magisterium iudiciorum astrorum, De coniunctionibus, De differentia planetarum*; Albohacen Ali, *De iudiciis astrorum*; Averroes, *Astrologia*; Psellus, *De daemonibus, De animae potentiis, De lapidum virtutibus, De magno anno, De Assyriorum dogmatibus, De arte chimistica*; Arthephius, *Clavis maioris sapientiae*; Leo Imperator, *De sortibus et geomantia*; Abraham Iudaeus, *De nativitatibus*; Ioannes Hispalensis, *Epitome astrologiae*; Ioachim Abbas, *In Apocalypsim*; Michael Scotus, *Astrologia*; Peter of Abano, *Geomantia*; Guido Bonati, *Opera astrologica, De astronomia*; Cecco d'Ascoli, *L'Acerba*; Arnold of Villanova, *Testamentum novissimum, Vitae Philosophorum de retardanda senectute, De aqua vitae*; Pseudo-Ramón Lull, *Ars chemiae, Ars auriferae, Super alchimiam, De virtutibus aquae vitae, De figura elementali, Codicillus sive testamentum*; Alfonso the Wise, *El Lapidario, El Septenario, Libro de los Judicios de las estrellas*; Pseudo-Albertus Magnus, *Liber secretorum, Speculum astronomiae, De proprietatibus lapidum*. Bernardus Alverniae, *De probatione perfectae et verae transmutationis*; Christophorus Parisiensis, *Lucidarium artis transmutationis metallorum*.

RENAISSANCE. Cusanus, *De docta ignorantia, De ludo globi, De pace fidei, Idiota, De coniecturis, Transmutationes geometriae*; Pletho, *De fato*; Bessarion, *In calumniatores Platonis*; Ficino, *De triplici vita, Theologia Platonica, In Platonis Convivium, In Mercurium Trismegistum, In Plotinum, Epistolae*, etc.; Pico della Mirandola, *Conclusiones, Heptaplus, Apologia, Commento*; Franciscus Giorgius, *De harmonia mundi totius, Problemata*; *Hypnerotomachia Poliphili*; Reuchlin, *De verbo mirifico*; Paulus Riccius, *De coelesti agricultura*; Petrus Galatinus, *De arcanis catholicae veritatis*; Gulielmus Postellus, *De orbis terrae concordia*; Trithemius, *De septem intelligentiis, Polygraphia*; Gregorius Reisch, *Margarita philosophica*; Hieronymus Cardanus, *Astrologia*; Luca Gauricus, *Praedictiones, De eclipse solis miraculosa in Passione Domini observata*; Iovianus Pontanus, *In Centiloquium Ptolomaei, De prudentia, fortuna et immanitate*; Ioachim Camerarius, *Astrologia*; Augustinus Niphus, *De figuris stellarum, De auguriis*; Petrus

Pomponatius, *De incantationibus, De fato et libero arbitrio et praedestinatione*; Alciatus, *Emblemata*; Petrus Valerianus, *Hieroglyphica*; Philippus Beroaldus, *Symbola pythagorica*; Philippus Ulstadius, *Coelum philosophorum*; Evonymus Philiatrus, *De remediis secretis*; Frascatoro, *Homocentrica, De causis criticorum dierum, De sympathia et antipathia rerum*; Iulius Camillus, *Idea del Theatro*; Ioannes Dee, *Monas Hieroglyphica*; Cornelius Gemma, *De arte cyclognomica*; Ioannes Baptista Porta, *Magia naturalis*.

ANONYMOUS. *Exhortus in decanes zodiaci*; *Somniorum interpretatio secundum Indios, Persas et Aegyptos*; *Incerti auctoris de cœlesti dispositione et alia astrologica*; *Liber de alchimia seu transmutatione*; *Tractatus 'Aurora consurgens'*; *Liber diversorum experimentorum in arte alchimia*; *Compendium aureum artis*; *Modus reducendi argentum vivum*; *Quartum Platonis interpretatum 'esto miles'*; *Rosarium alchimiae*; *Hermetis libellus aureus*; *Tractatus cuiusdam philosophi de transmutatione metallorum et auro potabili*; *Linearum quae in manu sunt vulgo chiromantia*; *Interrogationes iudiciariae de exercitu et de aliis*; *De morte et aliae interrogationes iudiciariae*; *Liber Gulielmi philosophi de Monade*; *Sedacina totius artis alchimiae*; *Liber utilitatis naturae secretorum*; *Mercurii Trismegisti de terrae motibus*.

This list of close on two hundred titles will serve to illustrate just how complete was the section devoted to Hermetic and related works in the library of the Escorial. The only two major gaps in the collection are Agrippa of Nettesheim's *De occulta philosophia* and *Picatrix*. This does not mean to say that they were unknown in sixteenth-century Spain. In all likelihood they circulated there much as they did elsewhere, only with greater caution (on *Picatrix* in Spain see note 67). Giordano Bruno was probably omitted because of his consistently anti-Spanish outlook. Even so Herrera possessed the *De umbris idearum*, which means that the Nolan was not altogether without readers in the Peninsula.

By no means all the books in the foregoing lists are Hermetic or occult in the strict sense—those of Cusanus, for instance. They have been included, however, because they contributed decisively in creating the mystical and magical *ambiente* so widely prevalent in the sixteenth century.

The presence of so many books of this nature in the official library of Philip II, the champion of Catholic orthodoxy, certainly gives the lie to the oft-repeated contention that, thanks to the watchfulness of the Holy Office, Spain at this time was largely free from superstition and magic. The fact that her scholars, with the possible exception of Menéndez y Pelayo, have not yet got round to investigating the influence of Hermetism on Spanish thought and literature of the Golden Age does not necessarily mean that it does not exist. It will be surprising if it is not found to have existed there just as much as it did outside, though it may possibly be more difficult to detect. That Pacheco, Velázquez's father-in-law, included a long quotation from the Pimander in his *Tratado del Arte de la Pintura* (ed. Sánchez Cantón, Madrid, 1956, p. 189) can hardly have been an isolated instance. The widespread influence of Lullism in Spain at this time may provide a useful pointer to would-be investigators, since almost all Hermetists were likewise Lullists. And significantly enough Philip II himself ended by becoming an adept of the Lullian doctrine.

APPENDIX II

The Hermetic Content in some of the Escorial Library Frescoes

1. *'The Egyptian priests'* (*Fig. 3*), placed under *Geometria*, west side

In his description of this *historia* Padre Sigüenza limits himself to stating that the philosophers of ancient Egypt, who were also that country's priests, used geometry and geometrical methods to survey the lands bordering the Nile after the floods had subsided. By this means they ensured that property rights were maintained. This story which goes back at least as far as Herodotus was often mentioned by later writers, notably Iamblichus who alludes to it in his *De vita pythagorica* (chap. XXIX). At the same time this fresco carries with it an allusion to the arcane lore and magical practices of the Egyptian priesthood. Hermes Trismegistus, its most exalted member, had referred to these practices in his *Asclepius*, of which both Herrera and Philip II had copies (Appendix I). It is even possible that Hermes may be the venerable but anonymous Oriental figure in the central cartouche between Archimedes and Regiomontanus immediately above the *historia* concerned. The religion and theurgy of the ancient Egyptians had also been discussed by Iamblichus in his *De mysteriis*. Herrera seems to have been unusually interested in this work, since he possessed two copies of it in Marsilio Ficino's paraphrase. The Escorial library had at least four copies of it, including the full-length work, with which Herrera was therefore also no doubt acquainted.

During the Renaissance Egypt was considered to have been the great repository of arcane wisdom. Virtually all the great sages of antiquity, including Pythagoras and Plato, were believed to have gone at some time in their lives to Egypt in order to learn from her priests. This even applies to such unlikely persons as Archimedes and Dionysius the Areopagite, both of whom are the subject of one of these *historias*. Moreover, as

Cardanus points out (*Geniturae*, LXVII, Nuremberg, 1543, p. 165), had not Christ Himself been taken to Egypt as an infant and on His return, while still a child, been able to confound the most learned of the Jewish doctors with His wisdom?

2. *'The Gymnosophists'* (*Fig. 4*), under *Arithmetica*, east side

Usually associated with India, Ethiopia and other outlying regions, the Gymnosophists were believed on the authority of Aristotle and Diogenes Laertius to have been older, and therefore purer and more arcane, even than the Egyptian priests. Pythagoras, an inveterate traveler, is said to have associated with them and made their austere way of life his own. According to Philostratus, Apollonius of Tyana also learned from them. Here they are represented as the inventors of the science of numbers. Padre Sigüenza in his description of this *historia* repeats what St. Jerome had written about the Gymnosophists 'philosophizing with numbers in the sand'. The good friar was quite well aware that there was more to it than just that, but he refused to be drawn. He goes briefly into the significance of the Lambda, shown in the foreground of the painting, and in this connection mentions Pythagoras and Plato. But this, he goes on to say, 'is a lengthy subject and it would be out of place to discuss it here; suffice to say that neither the one nor the other was referring to the numbers with which we reckon; rather are they the symbol of a greater secret' (*op. cit.*, bk. IV, Disc. X).

3. *'Orpheus and Eurydice'* (*Fig. 5*), under *Musica*, east side

Although, as previously stated, Padre Sigüenza commends this *historia* most strongly from the artistic angle, he is equally emphatic in condemning the practice, so dear to the Hermetists of the period, of concealing profound truths under the fables of classical mythology. Just as the *historia* of the Egyptian priests implied a reference to Hermes Trismegistus and his writings, and that of Daniel (see no. 9) to the Chaldean oracles, so this one would have brought to mind at once the Orphic Hymns, another supposedly age-old repository of arcane wisdom. Copies of these were given by Philip II to the Escorial library (Appendix I, p. 104). Not only was Orpheus a *priscus theologus*, he was also a *priscus magus* who wrought many wonders by the power of his lyre. This was attested by another of his supposed works, the *Argonautica*, which was likewise in the library.

4. 'Hercules Gallicus' (Fig. 6), under Rhetorica, east side

This was by no means an unusual theme in the Renaissance. Piero Valeriano, for instance, alludes twice to the 'hieroglyph' of the Gallic Hercules (*DE LINGVA* and *MERCVRIVS*, p. 312, and *HERCVLES-ELOQVENTIA*, p. 568). As in Cartari's engraving, on which this fresco was undoubtedly based, he is shown as a man getting on in years, albeit still well preserved, who draws others after him by the magic of his speech. This idea is conveyed, perhaps not too subtly, by means of the golden chains that stretch from his mouth to the ears of those that are following him. On this account he is to be identified with Mercury, the god of eloquence. Oddly enough Valeriano also alludes to him as the spirit of silence (p. 268) and he is represented as such in an engraving in Achille Bocchi's *Symbolicae questiones* of 1574 (no. lxiv), so that by a fusion of two contrary attributes he could be considered as an 'Egyptian' symbol of Hermetic speech (Edgar Wind, *Pagan Mysteries in the Renaissance*, New Haven, 1958, p. 20). In his accompanying text Bocchi invokes the name of Hermes Trismegistus, a link likewise implied by Valeriano. 'Aiunt vero Aegyptij', writes the latter, 'Mercurium primum omnium verba in ordinem redigisse, multisq. rebus indidisse nomina, litteras, eius inuentum fuisse, Deorumq. cultum instituisse, quae sine magna vi eloquentiae mortalium mentibus insinuari minime potuerint'. This eloquent figure, the inventor of language and the promoter of the worship of the gods, who at the same time enjoined silence lest the divine mysteries should be profaned, seems by common consent to have been identified with Trismegistus, the Mercury who gave the Egyptians their laws and letters (see also Edgar Wind, '"Hercules" and "Orpheus": two mock designs by Dürer', *Journal of the Warburg Institute*, vol. II, p. 206).

The conviction that divine truths must be safeguarded from profanation by being concealed under the guise of myths and parables was deeply ingrained in the thought of the period. This may possibly be the explanation for the presence of Melissus in the next bay which is devoted to *Dialectica*. Padre Sigüenza was wholly at a loss to explain his inclusion here, since as far as he could see, this sage had never been outstanding as a master of dialectic (bk. IV, disc. IX). Melissus, however, like St. Augustine whose *historia* occupies the same bay, had insisted that the divine mysteries needed to be hidden behind enigmatic veils lest the profane should be blinded by their splendor. As a reader of Giulio Camillo, Herrera would have been in a position to enlighten Padre Sigüenza on his significance at this point. 'Melisso dice', reads the *Theatro*, 'che gli occhi delle anime volgari nō possono sofferire i raggi della divinità (*Idea del Theatro*, p. 7; also Frances Yates, *op. cit.*, p. 151). St. Augustine had been no less emphatic: 'Sunt in Scripturis Sanctis profunda mysteria quae ad hoc absconduntur, ne vilescant' (Note 103).

5. 'The death of Archimedes', under Geometria, east side

Along with the Egyptian, Heron of Alexandria, Archimedes was considered to have been one of the two foremost figures of antiquity in the field of mechanics. He was also known as a great mathematician. During the Renaissance mechanics, dioptrics and pneumatics were classified as *magia naturalis* and were therefore not considered to be as suspect as some other forms of *magia*. For this reason perhaps Padre Sigüenza permits himself to go at some length into the historical circumstances of the siege of Syracuse—or Çaragoça, as he would have it.

Unlike Heron, Archimedes was a Greek. However, on the authority of Diodorus Siculus (who incidentally is represented in the very next bay) Archimedes is known to have gone to Egypt to study at the fountainhead of wisdom and while there to have invented the *cochlea*. In this *historia* he is shown absorbed in a geometrical construction, while one of the Roman soldiers is about to despatch him. The figure in question is none other than Euclid I, 47, known as the theorem of Pythagoras. This would seem to be a somewhat strange proposition for the sage to be poring over at the time of his death. It might be argued that his quadrature of the circle would have been more appropriate. This theorem, however, by the mere fact of his association with a *priscus magus* such as Pythagoras, carried with it certain Hermetic and cosmological implications. This is made abundantly clear by Cornelius Gemma in his *De Arte Cyclognomica*, of which Herrera owned a copy: 'Deinde ad illam magis respexit proportionū regulā, vnde omnis locorū origo, forma & materies Dialectica, omnis naturae vis, in vniuerso, vel entibus rationu protinus elucescit: sed omniū maxime ad doctrina trianguloru, cuius inuentionē multi Pythagorae tribuerūt; arcanū certe mirabile et vere philosophis minime negligendū . . . ' (ed. Antwerp, 1569, p. 110).

To the Renaissance Hermetist who was perfectly well aware that such Neoplatonist Magi as Porphyry and Proclus had studied Euclid and even written commentaries on him, particularly Proclus, there seemed to be no possible objection to the use of rational geometry as 'mathesis', in other words *more Hermetico*. This is precisely what Herrera did in his *Discurso de la Figura Cubica*. The drift of Pico's Euclidian *Conclusiones* seems to be in this self-same direction.

6. '*The Tower of Babel*' (*Fig. 7*), under *Gramatica*,
   west side

This is the classic example of an undertaking which came to naught because it was not in tune with the universal order, being based on *impietas* and *superbia*. Cesare Ripa (*Iconologia, CONFVSIONE*) gives a succinct account of the significance of the Tower of Babel, which he identifies with Chaos. In the following century Father Athanasius Kircher was to treat this theme in detail (*Turris Babel sive Archontologia*, Amsterdam, 1679). Just as Noah's Ark, the Tabernacle of Moses and the Temple of Jerusalem foreshadowed the Celestial City, so the Towers of Nimrod, Ninus and Semiramis prefigured the infernal kingdom. (For this and related symbolism see especially the Dedication to the Emperor Leopold I and Chapter IX, 'De mystico sensu, qui sub Mosaica Turris historia continetur'.)

7. '*David exorcizing Saul by means of his music*'
   (*Fig. 8*), under *Musica*, west side

This incident is recorded in 1 Samuel 16:14–23. Here the evil spirit is actually shown issuing out of the king's mouth. According to Hermetic belief this kind of exorcism was achieved not through any 'virtue' in the sounds themselves but as a result of their connection with the harmony of the celestial spheres, which in turn reflects the harmony of the supercelestial world of God. This theme is developed at some length by Agrippa of Nettesheim: 'Musicalis etiam harmonia non est siderū muneribus viduata: est enim imitatrix omnium potentissima: quae cum corpora coelestia opportune insequitur, coelestē influxū mirifice provocat, omniumq., audientium affectus intentiones, gestus, motus, actus atq. mores imutat, & ad suas proprietates subito provocat, ut ad loetitiam vel lamentationem, ad

audaciam vel tranquillitatem & ad similia. . . . Sic David furentem Saulem cithara repressit' (*De occulta philosophia*, Lyon, bk. II, chap. 24) and again: 'Nihil praeterea pulsandis malis daemonibus musicali harmonia efficacius, ut qui ab harmonia illa coelesti collapsi, concentum aliquem verum tanquam sibi inimicum nequeunt sustinere, proculque fugiunt: sicut Saulem spiritu nequam furentem David cithara repressit' (*ibid.*, bk II, chap. 28).

8. '*The Queen of Sheba questioning Solomon*' (*Fig.
   9*), under *Arithmetica*, west side

The occult implications of this scene which represents Solomon, the Magus *par excellence*, traditionally associated with every type of arcane knowledge, answering the enigmas of the Queen of Sheba, hardly needs stressing. More specifically, however, Solomon was considered to have been a master of the Cabalist art, being an important link in the transmission of this oral wisdom, first revealed by God to Moses. In this *historia* the inscription is not in Latin, as in all the others, but in Hebrew. Written on the border of the cloth that covers the table, it is none other than the well-known quotation from Wisdom 11:20: 'Omnia in numero, pondere et mensura.' That it should have been written in Hebrew accords with the Cabalist insistence on the superior virtue of the Hebrew tongue and characters, a point emphasized by Pico della Mirandola in his *Conclusiones Cabalistae* and also in his *Heptaplus*. Herrera owned a copy of this last-named work which treats of the Creation and is markedly tinged with Cabalism (Appendix I). In addition Pythagorean numerology makes its appearance on the board to which Solomon is pointing. There is an obvious link between the Pythagorean Decad and the ten Cabalistic Sephiroth.

9. '*Daniel and his companions instructed by the
   Chaldean Magi*' (*Fig. 10*), under *Gramatica*, east
   side

Based on the account given in the first Book of Daniel, this *historia* records the education of the prophet and his three companions at Nebuchadnezzar's court and their instruction in the language and lore of the Chaldees. According to the Scriptures God granted them such wisdom and understanding in all branches of knowledge that they emerged ten times wiser than the Magi and astrologers of Babylon. Daniel in particular distinguished himself as a notable interpreter of visions and dreams. The Bible thus provided contemporary Hermetists with irrefutable proof of the existence of Chaldean *prisca magia*, just as it also demonstrated the existence of magic in ancient Egypt.

There were therefore solid grounds for believing in Zoroaster and the Chaldean oracles.

10. '*King Hezekiah watching the retrogression of the sun's shadow*' (*Fig. 11*), under *Astrologia*, east side

This *historia* and the next one correspond to the bay devoted to *Astrologia*. Padre Sigüenza claims to have had these two subjects placed here with the object of demonstrating that the power of God transcends astrological influences, in other words 'Inclinant, sed non cogunt'. This furnishes him with an opportunity of strongly denouncing astrology, thereby making it plain that belief in such things was more widespread in Counter-Reformation Spain than many care to admit. Oddly enough Agrippa of Nettesheim chose these two selfsame incidents to illustrate the identical argument advanced by Padre Sigüenza, namely that under certain circumstances God dispenses with the intermediate spheres and intelligences, and works His will directly upon the sublunar world, thereby producing miracles (*op. cit.*, bk. I, chap. 13. On the numerological significance of this *historia* see *ibid.*, bk. II, chap. 15).

11. '*Dionysius the Areopagite observing the eclipse at Christ's Passion*' (*Fig. 12*), under *Astrologia*, west side

'St.' Dionysius the Areopagite was universally believed during the Renaissance to have been the author of the *De divinis nominibus* and the *De coelesti hierarchia*, two of the most influential mystical books in the history of Christianity. The first deals with the names of God and the second with the organization of the super-celestial world, both of which were subjects of the greatest interest to Hermetists and Cabalists at this period. Dionysius and his companion Apollophanes were supposed to have been in Heliopolis in Egypt, whither they had gone to study, at the time of the Passion and Death of Christ. Here they are shown observing the phenomenon of the eclipse of the sun that took place after Christ had expired. Padre Sigüenza in his account of this *historia* mistakenly placed the scene in Athens, no doubt confused by the fact that it was in the latter city that Dionysius ran into St. Paul. But at this time, as every Hermetist would have known, he was not then in Greece but in Egypt, the fountainhead of arcane wisdom.

JAMES S. ACKERMAN

Palladio's Lost Portico Project for San Petronio in Bologna

Palladio's façade projects for San Petronio in Bologna (Fig. 2) have been known since Bertotti Scamozzi reproduced in 1786 three of the four drawings preserved in 'e Museo di San Petronio[1] and Giovanni Gaye published in 1840 the extensive correspondence relating to them in the archive of the church.[2] In a recent article, Wladimir Timofiewitsch coordinated the data of the projects and the documents to produce a convincing chronology and characterization of the style.[3] But a further important project based on a projecting portico, frequently referred to and partially described in the correspondence, could not be discussed by Dr. Timofiewitsch or his predecessors because it had not survived in the church *Fabbrica* and was presumed to be lost. In 1963 a drawing of this project (Fig. 3) was acquired by Phyllis Lambert of Chicago from the London bookseller Bernard Weinreb, who correctly identified it in his sale catalog no. 2 of that year.[4] There could be no fitter place for the

publication of a lost Palladio façade project than in a volume honoring the author of the fundamental study of Palladio's church façades.[5]

The prospect of a portico appeared first in the correspondence in a letter of January 11, 1578, from Palladio to Count Giovanni Pepoli, president of the *Fabbrica* of San Petronio.[6] At this time, the project that Palladio had presented with the Bolognese architect Francesco Terribilia in 1572 (no. 'D') still was considered final, though nothing had been done about it in the intervening years. Its attempt to superimpose a two-story classical design on the existing medieval and early *Cinquecento* lower story (Fig. 1) encountered increasing opposition, mostly pro-Gothic, which Pepoli reported to Palladio in a lost letter at the end of 1577. Palladio's lengthy answer takes up point by point the criticisms quoted by Pepoli and adds only at the close:

> As for making the portico outside, although it would break up the new façade, still, done with sound design, it would give the work grandeur and commodity, and I like the idea.[7]

The portico scheme must have been Pepoli's idea; though he did not share the views he reported,[8] they

1. O. Bertotti Scamozzi, *Le fabbriche e i disegni di A.P....*, Vicenza, 1786, IV, pp. 24 ff. and pls. 18–20 (engraved copies). They were cited earlier by Temanza, *Vita di A.P.*, Venice, 1762, pp. LVIII f. In addition to these drawings, inscribed in a sixteenth-century hand 'D' (executed by Palladio's Bolognese collaborator, Terribilia), 'E' and 'G', there is a fourth ('F') which is a variant of 'E'. Photographic copies and a description of all the façade projects preserved in the museum were published by Guido Zucchini, *Disegni antichi e moderni per la facciata di San Petronio di Bologna*, Bologna, 1933.
2. G. Gaye, *Carteggio inedito d'artisti...*, Florence, 1840, vol. III. The letters written by Palladio were published also by A. Magrini, *Memorie intorno la vita e le opere di A.P.*, Padua, 1845, vol. II.
3. 'Fassadentwürfe A.P.'s für San Petronio in Bologna', *Arte Veneta*, XVI, 1962, pp. 82–97. Timofiewitsch shows that drawing 'D', in Terribilia's hand, is the definitive project of 1572, and that it was still considered so in 1578, when it was subjected to the criticisms with which the correspondence between the chief of the *Fabbrica* and Palladio reopened. Drawings 'E' and 'F' were presented in 1578, and 'E' apparently was preferred. 'G', which proposes the removal of all preexisting parts of the façade, belongs to the 1578–80 phase but is not mentioned in the correspondence.
4. p. 60, no. 97: 'Palladio, Andrea. Original drawings for a projected façade to the Church of San Petronio (Bologna)... The question of hand or draughtsmanship is always a controversial problem in the Palladian corpus, and often one must interpret "authentic Palladio designs" in terms of execution by his "office". This may also be the case here, but attention must then be drawn to the very elegant figures which are clearly in another hand, most likely that of the master himself. Drawing in

sepia pen and wash, 570 by 380 mm. Two corners repaired for tears which did not affect the design.'
The absence of the left half of the façade on this drawing is not due to mutilation; the lines stop short of the left edge of the sheet.
The inscriptions on the columns read 'piedi 42½', 'p 4¼' (15.2 m and 1.52 m, calculating from the Vicentine foot). In the frieze, 'p. 8½'. They are not in Palladio's hand.
I am most grateful to Miss Lambert for permission to publish her drawing and for the photograph.
5. *Architectural Principles in the Age of Humanism*, London, 1949, Part III; pp. 89 ff. in the revised edition of 1962. See also his 'Sviluppo stilistico dell'architettura palladiana', *Boll. del Centro internazionale di storia dell'architettura*, I, 1959, pp. 61–65; 'Le chiese di A.P. e l'architettura veneta', *Barocco europeo e barocco veneziano*, ed. V. Branca, Florence, 1962, pp. 77–87; 'L'influenza del Palladio sullo sviluppo dell'architettura religiosa veneziana nel sei e settecento', *Boll. del Centro...*, V, 1963, pp. 61 ff.
6. Gaye, III, pp. 396–402, from Venice.
7. *Ibid.*, p. 401.
8. Pepoli already referred to the opposition in an earlier letter, of Nov. 22, 1577 (Gaye, III, pp. 395 f.), and adds 'Io sono stato fermo nel disegno vostro, sapendo quanta sia la sua intelligenza et valor, ma ancor ho voluto avisarla delle oppositioni che se gli fano.'

must have had enough support to prompt him to offer this alternative on his own initiative.

A month later, Palladio was pressed to come to Bologna to make other proposals.[9] Sometime before November, he made the trip and submitted new designs which were highly praised by Camillo Bolognino, the Bolognese ambassador in Rome, whose opinion was solicited at each step.[10] Bolognino's letter refers to a revised façade design without any portico, and asks Pepoli to proceed with construction on this basis.

On December 10, 1578, however, Bolognino answers a request of the Gonfaloniere di Giustizia in Bologna for his views on the portico proposal.[11] Though strongly opposed, he is balanced, modest, and more intelligent than Palladio in defense of his views. He begins by asking whether the church ought to be considered an isolated monument or a part of an environment. In the former case, he says, the choice of a portico would be a matter of the caprice of the architects, but in the latter, the effect on the piazza as well as on the church would have to be weighed. The portico would be ugly and inconvenient in the piazza; it would fill up the stair platform, hide the façade, and disturb the eye, which delights in ample spaces. The advantages to a portico—one being the public convenience of a shelter from the weather for pedestrians and vendors in the piazza, and the other that it observes a tradition of the ancients—do not outweigh the disadvantages. The first is a function unsuitable to a sacred building and anyway fulfilled by neighboring loggias, and the second is a tradition that survived in only a minimum of churches and was not even a rule in antiquity. The majority of recent churches, notably that of the Jesuits in Rome and all those in Venice, Florence, Siena, Padua and Ferrara, are without porticoes, and although San Pietro, San Giacomo and the Servi in Bologna do have them, the aim there was to continue the line of the street porticoes alongside, not to give the church its own portico. Bolognino obviously shares that sensitivity to the urban environment that made Bologna the most homogeneous large town in Italy, and he saw that a motive which would have disrupted continuity in the central square could reinforce it in the back streets, which all are bordered by the characteristic ground-floor porticoes.

This letter is sent by the directors of the *Fabbrica* of San Petronio to Camillo Paleotto, a proponent of the portico scheme whose official position is not stated, and he answers, on December 20, 1578,[12] that the portico would beautify the piazza, and cites Roman precedents: San Paolo, San Giovanni in Laterano, San Pietro, the Pantheon. It would not impede the space because it would be elevated; moreover, there is insufficient shelter in the piazza, and a portico would rather preserve than defile the sanctity of the basilica by harboring those who now carry on trade and create a racket inside. Bolognino's claim that medieval and modern churches elsewhere are without porticoes is irrelevant because even in cities where there are no street porticoes, the fashion is changing and 'I cannot offer you gentlemen a more timely or clearer example of this than a book printed in this very year in Milan on how to build temples, which desires and exhorts all those who are building temples to provide porticoes for them.' The reference is to Cardinal Carlo Borromeo's *Instructionum fabricae et supellectilis ecclesiasticae libri duo*, the handbook of Counter-Reformation practice in church building and decorating.[13] Borromeo's work is known to have been influential, but Paleotto's letter is the only actual document of its direct impact on architectural practice. At the close of his letter, speaking of the great saving in time and cost that a portico would permit, Paleotto shows that he had in mind a much less extravagant one than Palladio was about to propose—something light and semi-medieval, probably. The Counter-Reformation

9. A. Gatti, *La fabbrica di San Petronio*, Bologna, 1889, p. 122: documents of Feb. 28, 1578 (invitation) and Nov. 3, 1578 (payment for the trip from Venice to Bologna and for 'varii disegni' cited by Timofiewitsch, *loc. cit.*).

10. Gaye, II, pp. 406 ff., letter of 24 Nov., 1578, from Bolognino to Pepoli. References in the letter appear to be to design 'E' of the Museo di San Petronio. Design 'F', a variant, may have been sent, too (Timofiewitsch, 1962, p. 90, Figs. 98, 99; the only available photograph of design 'E', used by Timofiewitsch and by me for Fig. 2, has been cropped at the bottom so that the completely free-standing columns before the buttresses flanking the side-aisle doors are not visible). While Palladio's design 'D' of 1572 retained the whole lower floor of the then (and still) existing façade, these designs preserved only the dado.

11. Gaye, III, pp. 409 ff. On Dec. 14 (*ibid.*, pp. 412 f.) Bolognino adds that he hopes Palladio agrees with him, but if not, he is willing to cede to his decision.

12. *Ibid.*, pp. 413 ff.
13. Milan, 1577. The passage on porticoes, quoted from the Italian ed. of C. Castiglioni and C. Marcora, Milan, 1952, p. 29, reads:

L'atrio davanti della chiesa sara' proporzionato all'ampiezza e alla massa della medesima; chiuso, dietro parere dell'architetto da portici e ornato di altro conveniente lavoro architettonico. Se per la ristrettezza dello spazio o per mancanza di mezzi non si puo' costruire tutto intorno il portico, lo si costruisca almeno lungo tutta la fronte della chiesa. Questo portico con collonne di marmo o di pietra oppure con pilastri in muratura adequi esattamente la larghezza della chiesa. Sia desso poi largo ed alto in proporzione della sua lunghezza. È conveniente che di tale portico sia provvista ogni chiesa parrochiale. Se per mancanza di denaro non si può costruire neppure questo portico, si faccia in modo di costruire almeno un vestibolo davanti la porta maggiore. . . .

spirit as well as Bolognese taste encouraged elements of Gothic Revival.[14]

On January 12, 1579, Palladio writes from Vicenza[15] that he has read the letters on both sides of the portico question and believes that, while the façade solution is surely beautiful and also has the support of Vitruvius and certain ancient buildings, nevertheless most ancient buildings have porticoes not only in front but all round (e.g., peristyles), and Vitruvius devotes much attention to their design. 'Wherefore,' he continues, 'both in order to do that which has not been done in recent times and because it would surely be a beautiful thing, to say nothing of the many conveniences, the grandeur, and the marvelousness of it, I am nearly (*quasi quasi*) ready to accept the opinion of those who want the portico, and I have already started some designs which I shall send to your Lordship the moment they are finished together with a comparative estimate of the materials and labor for the portico and façade.'

A fortnight later, the portico project is ready and Palladio sends it to Bologna in a 'canone di disegni' with explanatory notes:[16]

Illmo. mio Signor
Già alquanti giorni inviai una mia lettera a V. S. Illma., dandole raguaglio ch'io haveva havuto li disegni e sue lettere, et il parere de quei Sigri, circa del fare o il portico overo la facciata, e le promisi di mandarle un disegno secondo la mente mia, ch'è questo c'hora mando; e più tosto l'haverei inviato, ma incolpasi un sfredimento, il qual certo mè stato per alquanti giorni di grandissimo travaglio, e per dire il parer mio, il portico in vero molto mi piaceria, e sarebbe cosa bellissima e non più fatta a questi nostri tempi e de grandissima commodità, e, come anco le scrissi nel altra mia, li antichi pochi tempii facevano che non si facessero li suoi portici davanti, et ad alcuni tutto a torno. Quanto alla spesa, nel portico landarano più pietre che nella facciata, essendo che per ogni colonna li seriano cinque cento e cinquanta piedi di pietra a piè quadro, onde in dieci colonne et quattro pillastri, che sono su li anguli, v'andariano in tutto piedi sette milia e ottocento, et le facie della chiessa, che sono per fianco delle capelle, seriano piedi mile e cinquecento, onde

in tutto veneria a esser piedi quatordeci mila.[17] Ho fatto il muro per testa della logia, il qual feria ledificio più forte col far spale alla chiesa, perchè incontra con el muro che divide le capelle dalle navi picciole. Et le colonne, che sono nel portico, vengono a incontrar in parte in li pillastri che dividono la nave grande dalle picciole, di modo che faria forte la facciata della logia, e faria spale alla facciata della chiesa, et andaria un volto sopra quelle colonne, come nel portico di Sta. Maria Rotonda, perchè li intercolunni di questo portico li ho fatti a ponto di quella proportione. Nelle teste della logia, dove sono quelli portoni, si potrian farli per ornamento mese colonne et nichi, come apar su la pianta, li quali portoni ligassero con la facciata della chiesa, ch'è per fianco delle capelle, e si potriano anco fare senza ornamento, e stariano bene; e facendoli pure ornati, li andaria due milia e cinque cento piedi di preda, et nella facciata senza il portico le andaria forse dodici mile e docento piedi: non intendo in conto la parte della facciata di sopra, la quale andarà, così facendo la logia, come non la facendo, quello adunque che V. Signoria Illma. delibererà che si faccia, la mi farà sapere, ch'io farò le sagome, et la provisione delle pietre; nè mando l'amontar della fattura, essendo che bisogna veder fatte le dette sagome, e col racordar che le pietre che sono condute faranno una buona parte dell'opera, per hora farò ec.

Da Vicenza a' dì 27 genaro del 79
di V. Signoria Illma.
Servitore aff. And. Palladio

As Palladio's only reference to the specific character of his portico design, this letter is the unique source for judging the authenticity of the newly found drawing. Every condition mentioned here can, in fact, be matched in the drawing, and whereas neither the letter nor the drawing by itself could be translated into a three-dimensional project, the two complement each other with so little residue of uncertainty that they allow the reconstruction of a single plan (Fig. 4) that corresponds to all the data of the two documents.[18] To authenticate the drawing and to reconstruct the plan, each specification in the letter (paraphrased in italics) must be checked against the drawing:

1. *There are ten columns and four pilasters at the corners.*

The drawing shows six freestanding columns in the

14. See R. Bernheimer, 'Gothic Survival and Revival in Bologna', *The Art Bulletin*, XXXVI, 1954, pp. 263–84; E. Panofsky, 'The First Page of Giorgio Vasari's "Libro": A Study of the Gothic Style in the Judgment of the Italian Renaissance', *Meaning in the Visual Arts*, New York, 1955, pp. 169–235; P. Frankl, *The Gothic*, Princeton, 1960, pp. 299–315.
15. Gaye, III, pp. 417 ff.
16. *Ibid.*, pp. 418 f., from Palladio in Venice to Count Giovanni Pepoli, 27 Jan., 1579. Also in Magrini, 1845, II, p. 62, no. XXIII.

17. Palladio does not say how he arrived at 14,000 feet of stone. Apparently, the expenses of the upper portion of the façade, and perhaps the facing of the lower façade within the portico, are included to arrive at this sum.
18. My original reconstruction has been much improved by the generous assistance of Prof. G. G. Zorzi.

forward row and two in a back row near the central portal. The remaining two must be hidden by the forward columns. They cannot be two of the half-columns engaged to the piers at the ends of the forward row because these are what Palladio calls the *four pilasters*.

2. *The work to be done on the 'flanks of the chapels' is called 'the facing of the church'.*
   The chapel-flanks are the two outermost bays of the façade. With the help of the drawing we can see that Palladio meant to distinguish the facing of the church (veneering) from the work to be done on and in the portico.

3. *The 'heads' or ends of the portico have walls that buttress the church at the dividing point between the side-aisles and chapels.*
   The drawing shows that there was to be a wall at the end of the portico because the profile of the tabernacle enclosing the (arched?) aperture in the wall is visible at the side of the portico. As reconstructed in the plan, this wall does buttress the façade at the point referred to by Palladio. Its thickness is arbitrarily selected in the reconstruction.

4. *Some portico columns touch the piers between the nave and the side-aisles, thus buttressing the church and strengthening the portico.*
   Fig. 4 shows the probable position of these columns. In the drawing (Fig. 3) they appear closer to the central portal, where they lose the structural function of which Palladio speaks and commit an affront to classical practice that Palladio would not have supported. Perhaps the draftsman moved them to show that there were columns within the portico.

5. *A vault is to be put over these columns as in the Pantheon portico. For this reason Palladio 'purposely made the intercolumniation of this portico to that proportion'.*
   'That proportion' refers to the Pantheon which, though roughly one-third smaller, must have been the model for the arrangement of columns (Fig. 5a). Indeed, it is the Pantheon design that suggests the ten-column arrangement of Fig. 4, fulfilling the requirement of point 1. Palladio's adherence to the Pantheon caused the portico to invade the older stairway and the piazza more than was necessary, and confirmed Bolognino's criticism. Whether the vault to which Palladio refers is the deep coffered arch over the Pantheon portal or the system of reinforcing arches between the roof trusses (Fig. 5b) is not clear. Both could have been built; the latter would explain why in point 4 Palladio claims that the columns at the rear strengthen the portico.

6. *The ends of the loggia, where the 'portals' are, may be ornamented with half-columns and niches.*
   These are the corner piers which appear in the drawing as Palladio describes them. Prof. Zorzi suggests that Palladio used the term 'portals' because he intended to put flights of stairs at the sides of the portico that do not appear on the elevation drawing.

7. *The portals join the church façade on the flanks of the chapels. If necessary they can be left without ornament.*
   The drawing corresponds; it provides as ornament a tabernacle employing the engaged half-columns of the end of the façade that carries a pediment at the attic level.

8. *The upper part of the façade would be the same with or without the portico.*
   The drawing confirms this, as the uppermost level begins above the crown of the portico. This level differs in design, however, from the concurrent projects without a portico (Fig. 2).

In sum, though the columns to the rear of the portico in the drawing are not where the letter specifies, both refer to the same project. But this conclusion cannot remove all suspicion from the drawing and reconstructed plan, which reveal affronts to classical decorum inconceivable in an original Palladio design. The difficulties are concentrated in the design of the walls at the corner and on the short end of the portico. The principle of bilateral symmetry is inviolable in Palladio's work, yet the forward walls with the engaged columns and niches are wider than the corresponding walls against the church façade, which are cut off by the side portals. Furthermore, the openings in the end walls cannot be centered in the wall and at the same time fall on the cross-axis established by the central columns. In Fig. 4, the latter alternative is adopted at the expense of the former. There is, moreover, a change in the order from the front to the side elevations of the portico that would have created chaos at the angles where the two meet: the entablature is at the scale and level of the major order at the front and of the minor order at the sides.

There also are errors in drafting: the tabernacle at the end of the portico has no basement zone and appears to rest on the basement of the chapel façade; on the upper stories the nave is projected forward from the plane of the side-aisle façade though there is no provision at the portico level for supporting the projection. Finally, the drafting and figure style is uncertain and amateurish (e.g., the side-aisle tabernacles); in fact, so far inferior to Palladio's late work that the differences are self-evident. This is true of the figures as well as of the architecture. Naturally Palladio, now over seventy, employed assistants for drawing,[19] but even they would not have been permitted to send to Bologna in Palladio's name a drawing in which there were elementary drafting errors. Fortunately, another solution appears in the documents of the *Fabbrica* archive. Among the *Mandati* of 1579, Angelo Gatti discovered a note stating that Palladio's design was copied by one Camillo Azzone in order to show the project to the Pope for his judgment.[20] The making of a copy, far from Palladio's control, by an insignificant draftsman, who may have had only the one original elevation to work from, would explain some of the unsatisfactory results. Others must be due to Palladio, who had produced his drawing in less than the fifteen days between his two letters on the subject. Finally, the size of the sheet is only a portion of that of the large façade projects presented to the *Fabbrica*, which suggests a copy. It easily could have been cast aside after its rejection, and have become separated from the corpus of Palladio's San Petronio drawings.[21] One observation, made by Carolyn Kolb, who has assisted me in this study, could be taken as implying that the drawing was not derived from Palladio's original, but was a pastiche of Palladian motives: the portico is almost identical to the central loggia of the elevation for the Rialto bridge published in the *Quattro Libri* (III, pp. 26 f.), and therefore prior to 1570. But, considering the close parallels between the letter and the drawing, it is more likely that Palladio simply re-used his earlier bridge portico in a new context.

From the moment the portico project arrived in Rome, it met unanimous opposition. Bolognino wrote again with further arguments *contra* on February 20, and said that the best architects in Rome agreed with him.[22] In March, the Cardinal San Sisto (Filippo Boncompagni of Bologna, nephew of Gregory XIII) wrote to Pepoli to say that he had spoken to the Pope who 'dice insomma che non si debba altrimente fare il portico',[23]

an ambiguous statement that on grounds of later correspondence can be interpreted as opposition. On April 25,[24] Palladio sent to Pepoli profiles for the three orders of the façade scheme, excluding the Ionic, which he had made and left in Bologna. Reference to the Ionic shows that drawing no. 'E', of the previous year (Fig. 2), was the officially accepted one, although Palladio added that he would send profiles for the portico project if they were wanted.

A further letter from Bolognino in October, 1579,[25] indicates that Palladio was still pushing for the portico, cites the Pope's opposition, and praises Palladio's façade design. This is the last record of Palladio's ill-fated participation in Bolognese architecture and politics. By June of 1580, two months before Palladio's death, the *Fabbrica* had cleaned its slate and had begun again with a study of a series of design by various architects in which the frayed issue of Gothic vs. Classic was raised once again.[26] There is no indication whether it was Palladio or the Bolognese who abandoned not only his portico but his façade project as well. Though the bare face of San Petronio today is a sad and shabby thing, it is hard to mourn the abandonment of Palladio's schemes; neither the medieval profile nor the gigantic scale of the façade could be hospitable to the fixed proportions of the ancient orders.

Though it was not Palladio who first proposed a portico for San Petronio, the solution was congenial to the direction of his late work. His last church, the tempietto at Maser (1579–1580) has a four-columned portico with perforated end walls of the kind proposed at Bologna.[27] One of the two projects for the church of San Nicola di Tolentino (1579?) has a hexastyle porch with open ends,[28] and finally, a shop drawing of 1577–1580 showing the church and cloister of San Giorgio in Venice (Fig. 6), recently published by Timofiewitsch, shows a revision of the façade model of 1565–1566 that brings the four central half-columns

19. E.g., for the drawing in Fig. 6. It has been implied that Palladio gave up drawing at the close of his life because of an unsteady hand, but the autograph drawings for San Petronio show no diminution in drafting control.

20. *La fabbrica di San Petronio*, Bologna, 1889, p. 257. A letter from Dott. Mario Fanti of the Biblioteca del Archiginnasio to Miss Carolyn Kolb, who assisted me in this study, states that Azzone is not listed in the inventories of sixteenth-century Bolognese artists.

21. The correspondence makes it clear that there was only one portico project. Lacking the drawing in Fig. 1, Zucchini (1933, p. 21, followed by Frankl, *loc. cit.*) proposed that the left half of drawing 'G' in the Museo di San Petronio (his pl. xxi) might have an extended porch, but this improbable hypothesis now is unnecessary.

22. Gaye, III, pp. 420 ff., no. CCCLX.

23. *Ibid.*, pp. 422 f., no. CCCLXI. In this letter the Pope also says that the nave may be covered in wood if there really is doubt about the strength of the piers.

24. *Ibid.*, pp. 422 f., no. CCCLXII.

25. *Ibid.*, pp. 425 f. Bolognino infers the Pope's opinion from his veto of a portico scheme for Santa Maria di Loreto. Later the Cardinal San Sisto spoke again to the Pope and got a somewhat more definite reply (*ibid.*, p. 430: letter of March 2, 1580). Probably the vagueness was due to the Pope's reluctance to intervene directly.

26. *Ibid.*, pp. 434 f.: letter of June 8, 1580 from the Cardinal to Giovanni Pepoli.

27. The chapel at Maser has an inscription of 1580, and is presumed to have been designed in the last year of Palladio's life.

28. Identified by W. Timofiewitsch, 'Ein unbekannter Kirchenentwürfe Palladios', *Arte Veneta*, XIII–XIV, 1959–60, pp. 79 ff. The date of 1579 proposed on the basis of land purchases by the monks has been accepted generally, but it may be late: the designs do not have the monumentality and mass of late Palladio works.

forward to create a freestanding portico.[29] The last example shows in retrospect how Palladio's temple-front treatment of the façade at San Francesco della Vigna, San Giorgio, and the Redentore began the evolution by separating the nave portion from the side-aisles. In his last designs, Palladio made a reality of this metaphor by drawing the central pediment and its supports out into three-dimensional space-encompassing structures inspired by the Pantheon. The change is consistent with his increased interest in mass and the play of light and shadow in his late civil works such as the Loggia del Capitaniato and Pal. Porto Breganze in Vicenza.[30]

The portico remained exceptional in later sixteenth-century Italy, in spite of Carlo Borromeo's strong advocacy. The longitudinal churches where it was used are few and not important: a number of them were designed or influenced by Pellegrino Tibaldi, who assisted Borromeo in the formulation of his theory.[31]

Porticoes appear in drawings by Alessi, Vignola and other contemporaries of Palladio,[32] but were eliminated in cases where the buildings were executed, probably to save money. The portico often appeared in projects for central-plan churches, partly because it offered a practical way to put a rectilinear front on a curved or polygonal body, and partly because of the powerful influence of the Pantheon. All the major projects for St. Peter's in the Vatican had porticoes, and the feature was kept even after the central-plan projects were abandoned. But this is already in the seventeenth century, when the attitude had changed, and porticoes, besides being features of many new designs, were added often to existing churches of earlier periods. The emergence of the Baroque portico in Rome, and most frequently on the façades of surviving Early Christian churches,[33] suggests that the church ultimately accepted Borromeo's dictum in the spirit of a revival of the earliest basilicas.

29. 'Eine Zeichnung Andrea Palladios für die Klosteranlage von S. Giorgio Maggiore', *Arte Veneta*, xvi, 1962, pp. 160–3. The model of the church was completed by 1566, but the façade was not built until 1597–1610, and followed the model rather than the revised portico project, which Palladio may not have had time to develop in detail. Dr. Timofiewitsch kindly provided the photograph for Fig. 6.

30. Also in design 'E' (Fig. 2) for San Petronio, with its free-standing columns, unfortunately cut off in this photograph.

31. E.g., Bologna, Madonna del Soccorso, Santa Maria delle Laudi, San Rocco, all attributed to Domenico Tibaldi, brother

and pupil of Pellegrino, by A. Venturi in *Storia dell'Arte italiana*, xi, 3, pp. 900–3.

32. For Vignola's designs, cf. Ackerman and Lotz, 'Vignoliana', *Essays in Memory of Karl Lehmann*, New York, 1964, pp. 7 ff., 11 ff., Figs. 5, 12. For Alessi, designs for San Vittore al Corpo, Milan (Bibl. Trivulziana, Raccolta Bianconi, vol. v, pp. 6 v, 7), in P. Mezzanotte, *Storia di Milano*, ed. Treccani, x, 4, pp. 584–586, Figs. on pp. 574, 587.

33. Santa Bibiana, 1624–6 (Bernini); S. Crisogono, 1623 (G. B. Soria); Sta Francesca Romana, 1608–15 (C. Lombardo); Sta Maria in Via Lata, 1658–62 (Pietro da Cortona). Someone should write a master's thesis on the revival of the portico.

CESARE BRANDI

Perchè il Palladio non fu neo-classico

Fra Michelangiolo e il Bernini nessun architetto fu più grande del Palladio. E come il periodo in cui visse non fu certo povero di architetti, e l'attività del Palladio cominciò a svolgersi durante il periodo tardo di Michelangiolo, nel periodo aureo del Sansovino; verrebbe da chiedersi se infine sia giusto commisurare il tempo e la grandezza del Palladio a fungere da gigante isolato in un'epoca che pullulò di insigni architetti e che sta ancora più vicino, nel tempo, al Rinascimento che al Barocco.

Portati allora a cercare più da vicino il perchè di questa spontanea antitesi, che viene fatto di istituire per il Palladio sia verso il Rinascimento sia verso il Barocco, ci si avvede allora d'un'altra singolarità, che, cioè, il Palladio, viene avvertito come fuori del proprio tempo, catalizzatore d'una architettura rivissuta sull'antico con intendimenti, almeno in apparenza, più scientifici o storicistici di quanto non si fosse fatto dal tempo del Brunelleschi e fino a Michelangiolo. Questo estraniarsi dal proprio tempo per riprendere daccapo le fila della deduzione dall'antico, sarà forse la ragione per cui il Palladio si sente porsi in antitesi sia col tempo che immediatamente lo precedé, sia con quello che lo seguì. Talchè, per trovarlo nel tempo a lui congeniale, bisognerebbe scavalcare un buon secolo e giungere alla riscoperta che ne fecero il Milizia e Goethe. Ma, a parte che la riscoperta non si produceva affatto dopo un totale oblio, dato che forse non vi è stato artista, se non Raffaello, che abbia goduto, almeno in certi settori italiani e europei, di una fama altrettanto incontrastata e continuativa, è poi giusta questa antitesi fra il Palladio e i suoi predecessori e i suoi coetanei?

Si può benissimo sostenere che non è giusta, anzi solo apparente. Non rimase estraneo il Palladio né al Falconetto, né al Serlio, né al Sansovino. E in quanto a Michelangiolo, è quasi altrettanto impossibile di rescinderlo dal Michelangiolo tardo che dall'antico.

Riguardo poi all'antico, non dipenderà forse dal caso felice che ci ha conservato i suoi disegni, e neppure uno del Brunelleschi o dell'Alberti, se ci appare tanto più studioso dei predecessori rispetto alle rovine di Roma?

Nota. Su questo argomento tenni la prolusione ai corsi Palladiani di Vicenza nell'agosto 1960, e della prolusione stessa comparí un breve riassunto nel *Bollettino del Centro internazionale di Studi d'Architettura Andrea Palladio*, II (1960), 9-13. In quanto ai riferimenti fatti nel testo ad altre mie opere teoriche, queste sono: *Eliante o dell'Architettura*, Torino, Einaudi, 1956; e *Segno e Immagine*, Milano, Mondadori, 1960.

La sua stesse fedeltà ai canoni vitruviani è molto più apparente, o per meglio dire, verbale, che reale: se perfino ai canoni suoi propri trasgredì con una disilvoltura che già fece tribolare il suo esegeta Bertotti-Scamozzi, quando, cominciato l'improbo e benemerito lavoro di misurazione dei suoi monumenti, ebbe ad accorgersi che le misure non tornavano con quelle che ne aveva dato il Palladio, anche nei casi in cui, indiscutibilmente, aveva seguito da se e non per interposta persona, le sue fabbriche famose.

Insomma sembra che, verificata in tutte le direzioni possibili, l'antitesi del Palladio col suo tempo si dissolva senza lasciar traccia. Né più fruttuosa si dimostrerà la ricerca, assai più opinabile, riguardo al barocco. Qui si ha anzi la sorpresa di scoprire, che, in un certo senso, il più grande continuatore del Palladio non fu già lo Scamozzi, ma il sommo Bernini: e il numero delle invenzioni palladiane che trapassano in lui è destinato ad accrescersi, invece che a restringersi, tanto felice era l'individuazione del Bernini in quello che, del Palladio, faceva al caso suo. Dalle orecchie del Pantheon al Colonnato di Piazza San Pietro c'è sempre il Palladio. E dunque il Palladio potrebbe dirsi pre-barocco quasi come fu preneoclassico. Ma l'assurdità di questa conclusione è tale da rimettere tutto e subito in discussione. Questa antitesi fra precedenti e susseguenti c'è nel Palladio, e solo si è sbagliato il punto di applicazione per desumerla. Quest'antitesi, forse, non è altro che l'individualità del Palladio che l'oppone alle altre individualità: e per non fare un gioco di specchi, o un circolo vizioso, dovrà interrogarsi criticamente questa sua personalità al fine di desumere nella caratterizzazione formale, la novità del Palladio rispetto ai grandi predecessori e coetanei come rispetto agli epigoni.

Forse, dunque, è questa la sola via giusta, e dovremo pertanto rinunciare a quella contrapposizione più ampia, che avevamo tentato di enucleare, quella, per intendersi, che si ha quando non solo l'individualità dell'artista mà la caratterizzazione che in esso assume tutta un'epoca, conferisce a questa la prerogativa di porsi come una svolta decisa rispetto alla precedente. Tale è l'epoca che per la pittura s'inizia col Caravaggio, ma per quanto somma, invece, sia l'arte di Piero della Francesca, in Piero non si assomma una nuova epoca che legittimamente resta quella aperta da Masaccio. Noi forse presentivamo oscuramente di potere stabilire, nella contrapposizione del Palladio fra i predessori e gli epigoni, un'apertura nuova che non investiva solo la personalità dell'artista, ma che, attraverso di lui, poteva giungere ad una proposizione nuova dell'architettura come arte. Arrivati a questo punto, si viene allora a scoprire un'altra antinomia, in quanto che, questa nuova apertura che dovrebbe rappresentare l'arte del Palladio, ci si avvede che rimase in boccio, non fiorì proprio, o semmai fiorì ad un secolo di distanza, e in modo troppo più rapido e pedissequo da quello in cui consisteva la novità e l'apertura dell'architettura del Palladio. Avveniva cioè nel senso della regola e non in quello della fantasia. Invece, era stato costante motivo di stupore e anche di biasimo, perfino negli estimatori più entusiasti, come il Milizia e Goethe, la disinvoltura con cui il Palladio infrangeva le regole che pure conosceva così bene. Ricordiamoci qualche passo: "Se egli avesse ben filosofato—scrive il Milizia—non avrebbe fatto uso (almeno sì frequente) di piedistalli sotto le colonne; non avrebbe risparmiato tanti frontespizi alle finestre e alle porte, né sul pendio di quelle avrebbe sdraiato statue.... Tuttociò dimostra che l'architetto va a tastone." Per un panegerico non c'è male. E perfino Goethe, che ha dal Palladio la rivelazione subitanea dell'architettura, arrivato a Venezia, dopo gli entusiasmi vicentini, crede d'avere imparato abbastanza da poter fare i suoi appunti: "Come deduco da un lieve accenno del suo libro, si sentiva infelice che proseguissero a costruire le chiese cristiane sul modello delle antiche basiliche, cercava di avvicinare le sue ai modelli dei templi antichi. Ne derivarono quindi certe incongruenze che nel S. Redentor mi sembrano superate felicemente, ma nel S. Giorgio mi sembrano troppo evidenti." E sebbeno di queste incongruenze pare che l'avvio fosse nel Volckmann, che Goethe si era portato dietro in Italia, sentenzia che "il Volckmann ne dice qualcosa ma non dà proprio nel segno." E' un peccato che le incongruenze notate da Goethe non fossero rese esplicite, ancorchè noi dubitiamo assai della *lettura* che, fuori della fulgorazione immediata, sarebbe stato capace di fare Goethe di un'architettura vera e propria.

*   *   *

A questo punto non ci resterebbe allora che restringere la visuale e, interrogando le opere del Palladio una per una, dedurne quelle osservazioni che possano ricostruirci, per così dire, la gravitazione estetica del Palladio come creatore di forme architettoniche.

Questa indagine, da cui nessuna premessa può esimere, ci rinvia a quanto è già stato fatto in proposito, e cioè alla delimitazione critica dell'arte del Palladio, di cui nessuna è arrivata a rivoluzionare il concetto tradizionale del Palladio secondo l'ideale neo-classico come quella che trent'anni fa ebbe a delineare G. C. Argan. La novità di questa interpretazione era in primo luogo di vedere l'architettura del Palladio in chiave dei modi pittorici che sottintende: non già come pittura, ma per quella trasposizione della visione pittorica veronesiana che conterrebbe, e che finalmente darebbe la chiave di questa *diversità* dell'architettura del Palladio rispetto a tutta quella del Rinascimento, anche dove più apparentemente consona o col Sansovino o con Michelangiolo.

L'Argan poneva un'antitesi fra l'interpretazione plastica dell'architettura antica che era nella tradizione fiorentino-romana, e l'effetto dominante di luce e d'ombra che ricercava il Palladio. Il problema veronesiano delle ombre colorate era quello che aveva intravisto il Palladio orientando la sua gamma coloristica sulla fondamentale giustapposizione cromatica di bianco e di nero. Di lì il trionfo del bianco puro, come massima intensità luminosa, come frontalità iperbolica della luce che il Palladio realizzava, ad esempio, a Masèr. "Il bianco puro, assoluta attuazione cromatica della massima intensità della luce, trasformazione completa della funzionalità architettonica in un effetto pittorico, è il punto d'arrivo, cui tende in Palladio la soluzione totale del suo problema di gusto." Fin qui Argan che in precedenza aveva sottolineato come tutti gli schemi validi per il gusto classico sono assolutamente incapaci di spiegare il gusto del Palladio, e neppure gli schemi di movimento, di luminismo, di suggerimento, i quali esprimono un'antitesi alla stasi, al plastico, all'amore per la definizione, propri del gusto classico. Osservando, infine, che Rinascimento e Barocco non fanno che risolvere in modi diversi uno stesso problema, che il Palladio, se non rinuncia del tutto a proporci, dà almeno ogni volta come risolto. Sicchè è significativo, notava ancora l'Argan, che gli elementi stilistici del Palladio non entrino negli schemi che il Wölfflin tracciò sia per il Rinascimento che per il Barocco. Col Palladio si passava da un chiaroscuro indicatore del rilievo ad una pura opposizione cromatica, attraverso la negazione dello spazio come profondità. Di qui l'antitesi posta dall'Argan fra il piano prospettico dell'Alberti, che ha in se sua piramide, e il piano come profondità assoluta del Palladio. Questa, in breve, è l'interpretazione cromatico-luminosa che dà l'Argan dell'architettura del Palladio. Ed è interpretazione d'una finezza e d'una originalità indiscutibile. Un dubbio solo fa nascere, se la contrapposizione del Palladio verso il plasticismo rinascimentale fiorentino-romano, debba veramente cercarsi nella visione cromatico-luminosa, o se gli elementi che giustificano, nelle architetture del Palladio, la contrapposizione in questi termini, non siano piuttosto la conseguenza che la causa. Se cioè gli elementi comuni di queste due architetture, quella fiorentino-romana e quella del Palladio, possano essere stati intenzionati ab origine in un modo diverso, sicchè la diversità dei resultati, più che in una ricerca figurativa radicalmente nuova, come sarebbe quella cromatico-luminosa rispetto alla visione plastica, non debba ricercarsi in una intenzionalità formale diversa di cui le caratteristiche cromatiche-luminose sarebbero una manifestazione secondaria piuttosto che la finalità principale. Il dubbio sorge, perchè, dovendo contrapporre architettura fiorentino-romana del Rinascimento e architettura del Palladio, dobbiamo inequivocabilmente risolvere il diverso comportamento verso un elemento comune, l'architettura e la precettistica classica.

Parlare del Palladio è dunque in primo luogo porre il rapporto fra il Palladio e l'architettura classica. Tanto più perchè, questo rapporto, non è precipuo del Palladio ed è il rapporto stesso da cui scaturisce tutta l'Architettura del Rinascimento. In che cosa, allora, il rapporto fra il Palladio e l'architettura classica potrà differenziarsi, per il Palladio, dal rapporto che istituiva primieramente il Brunelleschi?

Quando qualche anno fa abbiamo scritto sul Brunelleschi e sull'architettura del Rinascimento, e abbiamo anche sottolineato che, per noi, si trattava più di una nascita, che di una rinascita, nel senso che l'architettura del Rinascimento rappresenta un modo nuovo di giungere all'architettura. Ma per poter sostenere questo, che sosteniamo ancora con piena convinzione, era necessario esplicitare che valore assumono le membrature classiche, le basi, i capitelli, le colonne, le trabeazioni, nel nuovo contesto dell'architettura rinascimentale: e già da allora noi ponevamo l'antitesi fra primo Rinascimento e Neoclassicismo, che tanto più è imperativa nei riguardi del Palladio. Scoprimmo allora che nelle basi e nei capitelli nei fregi e nelle trabeazioni, in tutto insomma l'armamentario architettonico classico, il Brunelleschi e l'Alberti, isolarono delle *parole*.

La conformazione del capitello, o dorico o corinzio— scrivevamo allora—fu individuata alla stregua del gruppo sonoro che copre una determinata area semantica, ossia della parola. Il fatto di essere dorico o ionico, per un capitello o per una base, diveniva da *forma*, come era stato per l'antichità classica, *significato*, che doveva tenersi fisso perchè garantiva l'immagine, allo stesso modo che il significato di una parola è la garanzia del gruppo sonoro che l'individua. Se si perde il significato di un vocabolo, la sua sopravvivenza come aggregato fonico non farà mai recuperarlo.

Così, dicevamo, si tratta allora di determinare in che cosa consiste il significato che avrà nel Brunelleschi poniarno, un capitello corinzio. Il suo significato non sarà tanto quello generico, di essere messo a sostegno di una trabeazione, quanto quello, specifico, di essere un capitello corinzio: ossia di far ridiscendere la sua forma a conformazione, dove la conformazione varrà in quanto sostanza conoscitiva ancor più che come figuratività specifica. Tanto è vero, notavamo, che la qualità plastica dei capitelli non è eccezionale, nel Brunelleschi, proprio perchè c'è un aggio della conoscibilità sulla figuratività. Si arriva cioè a isolare, per così dire, l'elemento classico, a renderlo partecipe di una figuratività diversa da quella da cui veniva tratto, e tale figuratività altro non era che la nuova spazialità data dalla prospettiva. La differenza fra un portico corinzio classico e uno del Rinascimento è irrilevante se si cerca di coglierla sul fatto dell'esecuzione plastica dell'elemento architettonico, ma è enorme se si prende sul contesto della rappresentazione spaziale. Era la nuova organizzazione spaziale della prospettiva che permetteva una proposizione interiormente nuova dell'elemento classico: questo veniva *posto in evidenza*, o, se si vuole un'orrida parola nuova, *relazionato* all'insieme in modo diverso.

Per questo allora scrivemmo che, con questa *messa in evidenza* dell'elemento classico, il Rinascimento lo costituiva in *ideogramma* a mezzo di una spazieggiatura che non era apparentemente diversa, quanto determinante dall'interno. La trattazione del tema *spaziale* che permetteva la prospettiva, dell'*esterno come interno* era quella che permetteva anche di riassumere l'elemento classico nella sua apparente identità di conformazione e con una radicale differenza formale.

Ma ora il nostro discorso può ancora procedere appena un po' più lontano. Nella scoperta dell'uso come ideogramma dell'elemento classico noi avevamo posto il dito su una trasformazione basilare che subiva la qualità rappresentativa dell'elemento classico. L'ideogramma altro non è che un segno, un'immagine cioè, che è presa a indicare un significato. Nel caso dell'elemento classico, non è che il Rinascimento facesse precipitare l'elemento classico, come tale, in geroglifico: l'elemento classico significava ancora se stesso, ma, allo stesso modo che pittograficamento un uomo seduto significa un uomo seduto, contiene lo schema preconcettuale della parola o del gruppo di parole che designano un uomo seduto. Vi era dunque, nell'uso che veniva fatto degli elementi classici dal Rinascimento, il principio della trasmigrazione di un elemento figurativo da immagine a segno.

Ora, proprio questa trasmigrazione, che può sembrare tanto breve da non essere neppure configurata come un viaggio, ma come un lampo, un'illuminazione diversa, è quella che, una volta rilevata, permette di seguire la straordinaria parabola che porta dal Brunelleschi al Palladio dal Palladio allo Stile Impero.

La strutturazione classica, divenuta emblematica nella nuova visione spaziale consentita dalla prospettiva, seguiterà per quattro secoli a svilupparsi in un modo sempre nuovo, nella straordinaria attivazione dello spazio prospettico.

Di questo viaggio di quattro secoli il Palladio rappresenta una fase culminante. Ma è solo sul traguardo dell'emblematica classica che si può cogliere il punto critico a cui egli portò la resurrezione dell'antico.

Per quanto la messa in evidenza dell'elemento classico attraverso l'attivazione spaziale della prospettiva, finisse per isolare l'elemento stesso in modo emblematico, dal Brunelleschi all'Alberti, da Francesco di Giorgio al Peruzzi, dai Sangallo a Michelangiolo, in un secondo momento, una volta isolato dal contesto e dalla precettistica vitruviana, l'elemento classico, si trattava di riassorbirlo integralmente nel nuovo contesto spaziale, ove rimaneva nel suo valore emblematico, rimaneva nel suo significato classico inequivocabile, ma come un latinismo nel contesto linguistico del volgare. Quello che invece accade nel Palladio è la preoccupazione di mantenere a questo elemento classico un valore emblematico ancora più scoperto, una messa in evidenza ancor più esemplare, e questo apertamente dove il Palladio è più originale: non tanto dunque, nella Basilica, quanto nella Rotonda, non tanto nel Palazzo Valmarana quanto in quello Chiericati, non tanto nella facciata, quanto nel Coro del Salvatore. Si scopre allora che il nucleo essenziale di questa rivitalizzazione al limite dell'astrazione, che fa il Palladio dell'emblematica classica, è di riassumerla nel suo più ortodosso plesso figurativo, di resuscitarla in quella sua vitalità secolare; ma, una volta ottenuta questa lievitazione o fermentazione che la riscatta dal sonno del passato, gelarla all'improvviso, immobilizzarla come una statua di sale. In quel momento raggiunge, il Palladio, il supremo equilibrio fra segno e immagine, un equilibrio mai ottenuto in un modo così perfetto, su un crinale tanto sottile. Ed ecco perchè sfiora il Neoclassicismo senza mai farsi raggiungere da quella ibernazione mortale dell'emblematica classica, che si perpetrò nel neoclassicismo dello Stile Impero. Se non si ha l'occhio, e vorremmo dire l'orecchio, abbastanza sottile per intendere come il Palladio sfiori il limite di rottura di questo equilibrio fra valore d'immagine e valore di segno, non si potrà mai capire come e perchè questa architettura tocchi al tempo stesso il limite della perfezione e quello della morte.

In questo raggelarsi dell'immagine, isolata, sceverata, messa in evidenza come un segno algebrico fuori dalla parentesi, vicina a spossessarsi in un valore altro che la figuratività, ma con l'improvvisa luce bianca che, quest'affaccio sull'altra metà della coscienza, le proietta addosso come un fascio luminoso, sta l'altezza vertiginosa dell'opera del Palladio, e la ragione per cui scalda e raggela, infiamma e arresta, attira e allontana. Si sente che è un'arte che è lì lì per trasformarsi come in un ciclo genetico misterioso, da immagine che è, in una costruzione mentale così armonica e compiuta come un dialogo di Platone; e quelle colonne essere proposizioni, e quei frontoni essere periodi, e quei periodi essere un discorso muto e d'un'eloquenza inaudita né perfettibile. Ma si sente tutto ciò non come una facile e banale metafora, si sente senza poterselo spiegare, proprio perchè insensibilmente l'artista ci ha condotto su quel limite estremo, su quell'orlo periglioso oltre il quale l'immagine altro non è che un segno, il segno di un pensiero articolato. E se tanto spesso si parla per un'opera del pensiero di struttura architettonica, è giusto invece rovesciare l'immagine, perchè la coerenza, la saldezza, la consequenzialità, lo sviluppo è dell'idea e non dell'immagine: e quanto dà all'architettura del Palladio questo *non so che*, quale nessuna architettura ha mai posseduto, è proprio il fatto di proporsi come sul duplice trono della fantasia e della ragione, quasi sul punto di alienarsi dall'arte per comunicarci un messaggio cifrato. E come questa non è illusione, né sensibilizzazione a posteriori, ma si desume dal carattere stesso, davvero olimpico, con cui il Palladio ha raggiunto la convivenza, nella stessa figura, dell'immagine e del segno, è proprio l'improvvisa confluenza con cui le due strade del conoscere tornano improvvisamente ad unirsi, che produce la straordinaria pienezza e la prodigiosa sospensione con cui si impone a noi un'architettura del Palladio.

* * *

Se non siamo degli illusi, suggestionati da noi stessi—oh, la cosa càpita anche troppo spesso agli storici d'arte—ecco che ora ci troviamo ad aver dato la risposta a quelle tergiversazioni con le quali abbiamo iniziato il nostro discorso. L'antitesi che avevamo avvertito, senza riuscire a risolverla o a spiegarcela soddisfacientemente, fra l'architettura del Rinascimento fiorentino-romano e l'architettura del Palladio, è un'antitesi che si pone all'inizio e non alla fine dell'affabulazione creatrice. Ed è così che possiamo intuire la ragione della visione cromatico-luminosa che Argan vide nell'architettura del Palladio. Il modo che ha il Palladio di porre in evidenza, non già a scopo funzionale, non già per meticolosità grammaticale, l'elemento classico, e, in genere, l'elemento architettonico, lo portava a renderlo più individuo che fosse possibile, a eccettuarlo dal contesto al momento stesso che ce lo inseriva. Non era che in ciò seguisse un'intenzionalità antiplastica, anzi la colonna resta l'elemento suo basilare, ma proprio nella contrapposizione di muro e colonna accentuava la differenzazione emblematica degli elementi. Questa unione di muro e colonna non era certo eccezionale, eppure salta agli occhi nel Palladio tanto che, con quella prensilità somma che aveva Goethe, è una delle prime cose che fissa e individua. Ed ecco questa riflessione abbacinante del piano ridotto a superficie luminosa, che, osservata dall'Argan, viene da lui interpretata come elemento principe della visione cromatico-luminosa del Palladio. Ma è un effetto secondario, rispetto a quello, isolante, che, rappresenta il proporsi stesso dell'immagine emblematica. Quando il Palladio, in questo piano liscio e riflettente, taglia le finestre senza arrucchirle col trapasso plastico delle modanature, in realtà, più che stabilire due piani cromatici di bianco e di nero, proietta in avanti la facciata invece che farla risucchiare nella piramide ottica, verso il punto *focale*. E' certo che il Palladio voleva evitare, nella modanatura delle finestre, il trapasso plastico che in genere è stato sempre ricercato, perchè risponde ad un bisogno che alimenta lo schema spontaneo della percezione che tende a istituire il vuoto della finestra come *figura* rispetto al *fondo* rappresentato dalla parete. L'ambiguità che acquista con ciò una figura che in realtà è piuttosto una non-figura in quanto consistente in un vuoto, suggerisce allora il trapasso plastico della cornice. Sennonchè il Palladio intuì precisamente che, per far partecipare anche le finestre a quel particolare isolamento di cui intendeva fruissero gli elementi architettonici, doveva accentuare il carattere di vuoto della finestra invece di riassorbirlo nel piano attraverso la graduazione plastica della modanatura. Ed ecco quelle finestre tagliate come nel ghiaccio, che disturbavano il Milizia, come si è visto, ma che accentuano, nel proprio vuoto, l'isolamento nella parete. Non è dunque che cerchi in primo luogo il salto cromatico dal bianco al nero: sarà, piuttosto che un cromatismo vero e proprio, ciò che è il colore locale rispetto al tono. Inoltre, ed era questo l'assunto spaziale primo che si proponeva il Palladio, otteneva, come si è detto, di fare avanzare la parete bianca, nitidamente frontale e squadrata, verso lo spettatore, impediva alla facciata di divenire muto prospetto, cesura spaziale invece che generatrice di spazio esterno-interno, come egli intuiva.

Basta studiare le sue due facciate principali, di S. Giorgio Maggiore e del Redentore, per vedere come esalti o quasi ne esasperi il traliccio prospettico, forzando a staccarsene la parte del pronao, piuttosto che ottenendo di fare arretrare il fondo della facciata. Il trapasso dalla facciata di S. Francesco della Vigna a quella di San Giorgio è significativo. Nella prima spezza i timpani laterali senza avere il coraggio di far proseguire la trabeazione attraverso l'ordine colossale delle colonne: ma a San Giorgio questo coraggio l'ha in

pieno, e il pronao sembra emergere lentamente come si protende un mantice via via che si riempie d'aria. Nella facciata del Redentore poi la stratificazione di due piani principali non gli serve più: ben quattro divengono, nella più sapiente delle intersecazioni, i piani sovrapposti della facciata superba. Come dunque si potrebbe negare la realtà operante del piano prospettico del Palladio? Ma proprio in questo proiettarsi dell'architettura verso lo spettatore, invece che sostanziarsi nella fuga prospettica sta il nucleo della novità con cui il Palladio si propone il problema dell'esterno come interno nello spazio architettonico. Ed ecco come è inevitabile allora che dovendo ottenere questo con le lame della luce e col respingente dell'ombra più che con gli avvolgimenti del chiaroscuro, la sua architettura presenti il fianco compiacente ad un'interpretazione cromatico-luminosa piuttosto che in chiave di plasticismo. Solo che si pensi tuttavia all'interno della Chiesa del Redentore, come non sentirsi ad un passo dal Barocco, e proprio di uno dei capolavori come S. Maria in Campitelli del Rainaldi? Ma non c'è, non è ricercata quella continuità plastica che il barocco esalterà, come l'aveva coniata Michelangiolo, e che il Palladio ogni volta arresta come sulla soglia e raggela, dopo averne dato la precisa impalcatura, per mettere in evidenza, portandole al limite dell'individualità singola, come l'hanno in senso diverso le statue e la lettera alfabetica, le colonne, i pilastri, i capitelli. Non è straordinario, allora, come in questa messa in evidenza di singoli elementi, il Palladio s'incontrasse, a volte cosciente ma anche senza saperlo, con certe estrapolazioni bizantine, come nella ripresa delle cupole bizantine di San Marco o dei campanili-minareti di S. Antonio: ma soprattutto ricreando il raro partito che si vede nei Conventi rosso e bianco dell'alto Egitto, e cioè il coro forato con le colonne. Appunto perchè in questa ricerca di mettere in evidenza l'elemento, e soprattutto la colonna, amava sentirlo avvolto dallo spazio, isolato come da uno spazio rotativo. Donde la precettistica e la pratica classica non più serviva, e il Palladio, chiuso Vitruvio e le Terme romane, si ispirava al bizantino e al gotico, ricreando, senza saperlo, anche un motivo dell'architettura copta egiziana. E nella predilezione del bianco puro, più che un colorismo portato al limite estremo del tono unico, è da vedersi, secondo noi, l'espediente per togliere contiguità all'edificio inteso globalmente come unico elemento architettonico, da mettere in evidenza ed eccettuare dal resto: da quel resto a cui lo ricollegava invece la trafila prospettica spaziale.

Ma naturalmente un bianco così puro, un'ombra così nera, divenivano anche un modo di impostare il rapporto di luce e di colore quasi pre-impressionistico: donde la giustificazione del parallelo col Veronese. E tuttavia è un rapporto a posteriori. Non farà comunque meraviglia che, per tenere così in sopensione un riferimento tanto sottile e sfuggente all'architettura classica facendone scaturire un'impaginazione quasi rarefatta eppure solidissima, occorresse la ricreazione, ogni volta, di condizioni interne al monumento, tali che l'eccettuarsi dell'elemento, il suo porsi al limite estremo del segno, fosse la conseguenza di una suprema organazione di tutta la struttura formale dell'edificio.

Intesa nella sua apparente ortodossia classica, l'archi-

tettura del Palladio, non poteva che raggelarsi in quella ibernazione di cui abbiamo parlato per il Neoclassico: oppure offrire il destro per una potente rigenerazione alla stessa visione plastica, come per un Bernini o per un Rainaldi.

Ed è così che l'architettura del Palladio non chiude né apre, non continua e non inizia: meravigliosamente se stessa, quasi si apparta nella propria epoca, che illustra senza potere trascinare sulla sua strada. Quella strada che disseminava di tanti capolavori.

RENATO CEVESE

Proposta per una nuova lettura critica dell'arte palladiana

A leggere quanto alcuni decenni fa si scrisse, e si seguitò a ripetere, sul Palladio in contributi specifici o generici, stilati da studiosi veneti e non veneti, certe intuizioni critiche, sostanzialmente esatte, e quindi le "letture" delle opere che da quelle derivano, sembrerebbero possedere ancor oggi la straordinaria forza di risolvere ogni problema di interpretazione stilistica. Gli iterati inviti a considerare l'architettura del Palladio sulla base dei valori pittorici—che ne dovrebbero essere tipici e preminenti—se tuttora accettabili entro certi limiti, andrebbero in ogni caso rimeditati per attribuire ad essi una nuova dimensione.

L'indagine di non pochi creati palladiani, considerati nella loro intima logica strutturale, suggerisce infatti la necessità di seguire anche un diverso iter per considerarli alla luce di altri aspetti formali e per dare più larga e meditata giustificazione a quella stessa posizione critica. Viceversa l'esame di alcune opere del sommo architetto esclude perentoriamente la presenza del fatto chiaroscurale e atmosferico, mentre constata il risolversi dell'immagine architettonica in valori di superficie, come nel caso di Villa Pojana a Pojana, di Villa Saraceno a Finale di Agugliaro, di Villa Pisani a Montagnana nel suo prospetto su strada, di Villa Godi a Lonedo di Lugo Vicentino, di Villa Caldogno a Caldogno, di Villa Zeno a Cessalto, del prospetto meridionale della Malcontenta, ecc.

La ribadita affermazione che l'arte del Palladio nasce da una visione sostanzialmente pittorica, e che si concreta in "pagine" di vibrazione chiaroscurale e di palpiti atmosferici, sembra non aver tenuto nel debito conto la genesi di quel chiaroscuro e di quell'ariosità atmosferica, non tanto per una mancata ricerca etimologica del processo linguistico, quanto per un non immediato riferimento alla realtà formale dell'atteggiamento espressivo palladiano. Mi sembra non si sia posta sufficiente attenzione alla vitalità plastica delle membrature di certi spartiti compositivi, alla sostanza scultorea di certe trame strutturali, donde si genera e chiaroscuro e vibrazione atmosferica; si é sottaciuto, forse perché considerato implicito, ciò che veramente provoca l'aspetto ritenuto esclusivo e fondamentale dell'arte del sommo architetto. Né, d'altro canto, s'é spostato il discorso su quelle espressioni della poetica palladiana, nelle quali il messaggio architettonico é affidato all'andamento di superfici riverberanti, solo trapunte da rade finestre o aperte al centro da tre fornici, incorniciati o no dal bugnato rustico.

A giustificare quanto qui vado proponendo, si richiede un particolareggiato, anche se rapido, esame, della produzione del Palladio, nell'arco assai esteso delle sue esperienze.

PALAZZI

E mi par opportuno cominciare dalla *Loggia Bernarda* (fig. 1), nella quale la dinamica plastico-strutturale assume aspetti di insolita vivacità. In essa il gioco chiaroscurale, cui si associa la piccante bicromia della pietra bianca e del mattone scoperto, costituisce, a prima vista, il carattere più appariscente dell'opera straordinaria. Ma non é chi non veda come il fervore pittorico, qui spinto fino ad un imprevedibile orgasmo, sia raggiunto grazie ad una forte antitesi di sporgenze e di rientranze, sicché tutto l'organismo é sollecitato du una vivacissima energia plastica che determina l'aggetto delle semicolonne giganti, dei balconi rigonfi, della trabeazione obbediente alla vicenda delle strutture sottostanti. E' un plasticismo impetuoso che suscita di necessità un dramma pittorico, nel quale alle calde tonalità del cotto e al candore delle basi dei fusti fanno contrasto le ombre profonde e soffici dei tre archi e degli incassi tra le semicolonne e i balconi, tra i capitelli compositi, lussureggianti d'ornati, e le cornici delle finestre.

Il frammento su Piazza dei Signori e il fianco compiuto su Contra' del Monte non sono pareti che s'inflettano, come avverrà nell'imminente stagione barocca, o alle quali si oppongano con moto inverso elementi compositivi e decorativi, come se una forza potente agisse dal di dentro determinandone un perimetro ricurvo o sinuoso. Son pareti nelle quali risalti e incavi si attuano su piani paralleli, ora vicini ora lontani, i primi sapientemente modulati per graduali trapassi, i secondi a stacchi netti e decisi. Nei tre intercolumni su Piazza dei Signori, Palladio crea un episodio architettonico, ove la tensione plastica è generatrice di quel declamato pittoricismo, che deriva dalla trama fondamentale dell'opera e trova le sue modulate variazioni nei succosi rilievi, linfa di colore che scorre tra elemento ed elemento a mantenere una qualificazione cromatica anche nei brevissimi settori di parete, che potevano svolgere soltanto funzione di raccordo e di sostegno.

Nel medesimo spazio urbanistico si affrontano due fabbriche, dal Palladio concepite dopo un lungo intervallo di tempo: la *Basilica* e la Loggia citata. Due fabbriche che la sostanziale diversità rende isolate nella produzione palladiana e senza apprezzabili sviluppi nei successivi processi creativi del Maestro e nell'architettura del Seicento. Che la Basilica appaia come un momento poetico irripetibile per lo stesso genio che l'ha ideata, non fa meraviglia, anche perché l'Artista non avrà occasione di cimentarsi ancora in un'opera civile di altrettanta importanza; può destar sorpresa invece che la Loggia Bernarda non abbia esercitato stimolo alcuno sugli architetti dell'età barocca, costituendo essa, insieme con Palazzo Valmarana al Pozzo Rosso, un episodio larvatamente eretico nel panorama palladiano dominato da un fermo equilibrio classico. La Basilica, che profila la trama delle sue strutture di decantata purezza sull'ombra (fig. 2) del portico e della loggia superiore, nasce pur essa da una concezione squisitamente plastica: gli elementi compositivi delle sue logge sono sentiti come entità libere nello spazio (fig. 3), come trama se-portante svincolata dalla parete di fondo e creatrice essa stessa, semmai, d'una parete traforata. Il motivo della "serliana" non è più una triplice apertura di parete, una grande trifora destinata ad assicurare più abbondante volume di luce all'interno; in quella concezione palladiana essa si stacca dalla parete, si fa struttura autonoma nello spazio, corpo plastico-architettonico: da motivo lineare, cioé, diventa motivo essenzialmente scultoreo.

Non mi sembra che la Basilica Palladiana abbia ascendenze dotte nel Teatro di Marcello o nel Colosseo, tanto spesso invocati come precedenti illustri, proprio perché in essi l'arco insiste su larghi pilastri e non su colonne binate in profondità: e son proprio quei pilastri a dare il senso della parete e l'ordine a svolgere la sua unica funzione decorativa. Nella sua Basilica Palladio fa ricadere il peso dell'arco sulla duplice colonna staccata dal pilastro intermedio, che divide le cellule compositive e, al tempo stesso, le unisce scandendo gli accenti forti del discorso architettonico. Soltanto ad un architetto scultore quale era Palladio poteva apparire l'immagine di una struttura che esclude ogni raccordo di parete, perché rifiuta qualsiasi sosta nell'incalzante ripresa del "tema".

Che sia poi opportuno, anzi necessario sottolineare l'ampia vicenda chiaroscurale, la palpitante ariosità atmosferica del mirabile monumento palladiano é cosa ovvia: ma tutto questo si attua proprio per effetto di un'ossatura essenzialmente scultorea. Valori atmosferici pur esistevano nelle precedenti logge gotiche, come lo dimostrano quelle, ancor oggi esistenti, del Palazzo della Ragione di Padova: ma la loro esilità propone soprattutto valori lineari, non plastici, essendo senza spessore gli archi e senza corposo volume le colonne.

Di eccezionale forza plastica é l'incompiuto *Palazzo Da Porto Breganze* (fig. 4) a Porta Castello, nel quale, a differenza di quanto avviene nella Loggia Bernarda, l'intercolumnio si chiude e si restringe, il ritmo del tessuto s'accelera. La notevole altezza della fabbrica, che doveva costituire il superbo fondale dello spazio urbanistico, giustifica il modulo delle semicolonne e il loro zoccolo che ne accentua lo slancio. Raramente Palladio giunge ad altrettanto dinamismo plastico, che é dato dalla continua contrapposizione di sporgenze e di rientranze, queste particolarmente sensibili negli intervalli di parete tra gli zoccoli e le basi dei fusti (fig. 5). Viceversa, proprio per assolvere al compito per cui era stata concepita, la Loggia Bernarda doveva aprirsi al pianterreno in uno spazioso porticato, reso accessibile da una gradinata continua; e la risonanza atmosferica, nell'ombra vaporosa del portico, aggiunge timbri diversi a quelli donde si orchestra il colore delle colonne, della trabeazione, dei ricami scultorei. Il Palazzo da Porto Breganze non s'apre ad inspirare l'atmosfera: il suo prospetto é un involucro chiuso. Sui volumi prismatici degli zoccoli s'innalzano con prepotente vigore i fusti semicilindrici delle colonne a sostenere l'alta trabeazione che sporge e rientra, per lo sporgere dei fusti e il rientrare della parete.

L'intercolumnio é così breve che le finestre al pianterreno, affondate tra gli alti zoccoli dell'ordine, sono sprovviste di cornice e quelle del piano nobile non hanno decorazioni al loro fianco. Tuttavia Palladio realizza una fascia altamente decorativa—in termini di vera scultura—tra i timpani delle finestre e la trabeazione dell'ordine, sfruttando gli stupendi capitelli compositi e stendendo tra essi turgidi festoni di verzura. Le due macchie nere delle finestre al primo piano rendono ancor più aggressivo l'aggetto degli zoccoli dell'ordine: la concitazione plastica si mantiene anche al piano nobile, per il sollevarsi della parete di fondo dei due balconi che sopravanzano i fusti, e riprende vivissima nella cornice conclusiva a lunghe sporgenze e a brevi rientranze.

Palladio dunque parla anche qui il linguaggio dell'architetto scultore: verrebbe fatto di dire, anzi, che lo scultore prende la mano all'architetto, non perché egli si conceda alle lusinghe della decorazione, cui assegna, in verità, parte modestissima, ma perché sembra attribuire alle strutture fondamentali il significato di elementi scultorei di eccezionale dimensione e forza. A prima vista, l'ordine potrebbe non apparire come scheletro che innervi la fabbrica, come sostanza sua prima e fondamentale, forse perché lo spigolo dell'edificio, dal nitido profilo, é continuazione e termine della parete cui le semicolonne paiono addossate. Se Palladio fosse ricorso alla duplice colonna nel giro del fianco, a simiglianza di quanto aveva fatto, con magistrale bravura, nel Palazzo Barbaran Da Porto, l'ordine di Palazzo Da Porto Breganze avrebbe denunciato immediatamente, e fuori da ogni possibile equivoco, l'incontrovertibile significato di vitale ossatura: solo ad un più attento esame le semicolonne, proprio per la comune base degli zoccoli e per la comune trabeazione, che conclude anche le pareti intermedie, compongono una trama che trascende il valore d'una apparente trionfale bardatura.

Altra opera nella quale la visione del Palladio si precisa in termini scultorei é *Palazzo Chiericati* (fig. 6), ove la composizione architravata si sostituisce a quella curvilinea della Basilica. Anche in Palazzo Chiericati le colonne si isolano nello spazio, distanziate dalla parete di fondo con largo stacco. L'impulso plastico, che spingeva l'architetto a trovare pur qui soluzioni di particolare forza, genera un mirabile nodo di fusti nel punto di trapasso tra ali e settore centrale: a due colonne, che paiono compenetrarsi, se ne abbinano altre due quasi a dar vita ad un pilastro polistilo. Nell'unico settore pieno della facciata, corrispondente al salone del piano nobile, gli elementi formano una trama in altorilievo; viceversa il fianco sul Corso non assorbe l'atmosfera, ma la respinge con la sua parete liscia, solo aperta nelle grandi finestre a rigoroso contrappunto.[1] Chi si ponga sotto il portico del Palazzo e guardi la sequenza delle colonne, é spettatore di una esaltante visione plastica offerta dalle singole colonne e dai pilastri che segnano la triplice divisione spaziale del lungo vano (fig. 7).

Questo capolavoro del Palladio, assonante non con contemporanee architetture venete o del centro-Italia, ma con architetture della matura età imperiale romana —uno degli esempi più calzanti é, a mio parere, il Teatro di Sabratha—realizza più di ogni altra fabbrica del Palladio quel lungo e profondo respiro atmosferico, per il quale il maestro veneto sta solitario nel firmamento dell'arte rinascimentale italiana. Leggerezza di trama compositiva, ma al tempo stesso saldezza e forza strutturale, ampia orchestrazione chiaroscurale e straordinaria circolazione d'atmosfera, di cui la fabbrica sembra nutrirsi e vivere: questi i

valori che in sommo grado noi ammiriamo nell'opera più geniale dell'Artista.

Il senso plastico di *Palazzo Thiene* si esalta nel cortile (fig. 8), dolorosamente incompiuto, ove gli archi superiori insistono su pilastri a sezione rettangolare e a superficie liscia, che permettono la presenza di una lesena, mentre quelli del portico scaricano il loro peso su robustissimi pilastri a bugnato rustico, che escludono quindi la possibilità dell'ordine. Ma i pilastri dei due piani sono simili a corpi scultorei a tutto tondo, messi in risalto dal profondo cuscino d'ombra del portico e della loggia. Proprio aspirando l'atmosfera in così gran copia la fabbrica denuncia in modo particolarmente convincente l'uno e l'altro aspetto della poetica palladiana: una concezione plastico-strutturale al servizio di una generosissima ariosità atmosferica.

Gli impulsi plastici si attenuano all'esterno anche se esso si nutre del sanguigno bugnato rustico e, al piano nobile, s'arricchisce di finestre, ove le colonnine joniche son strette nella morsa delle forti bozze sporgenti. Ma l'architetto provoca un risentito moto plastico-strutturale nella fascia delle balustre e degli zoccoli delle lesene (fig. 9), che si succedono a stacchi netti in un rapido alternarsi di sporgenze e incassi. La parete del pianterreno é animata da una forza che la solleva nell'increspata trama del bugnato rustico, quasi agendo dall'interno della stessa muratura. Vibrato plasticismo rende concitato anche lo stupendo ingresso da Contra' S. Gaetano di Thiene, nelle colonne rustiche, nelle semicolonne addossate alle pareti, nelle bugne degli archi profilati.

Articolazione plastico-volumetrica avrebbe suscitato l'avancorpo al centro della facciata principale verso il Corso, una volta che fosse stata realizzata l'opera intera: avancorpo reso possibile dalla larghezza della strada, poiché il palazzo sarebbe stato arretrato in rapporto all'attuale linea delle case tra Contra' S. Gaetano e Contra' Porti.

Nel prospetto di *Palazzo Valmarana* al Pozzo Rosso l'Artista mortifica ogni impeto plastico, dovendo sfruttare una profondità estremamente esigua per modulare i passaggi tra la superficie delle lesene giganti e la parete retrostante. Non mancano tuttavia accenti d'una qualche vivezza plastica nello zoccolo dell'ordine, nei capitelli compositi delle lesene, nella grande trabeazione; come nell'ordine jonico del prospetto sul cortile, ove energici modiglioni, in corrispondenza dei fusti inseriti nella trabeazione e a sviluppo continuo nei fianchi, sarebbero stati il sostegno ad un ballatoio perpetuo.

Il prospetto di *Palazzo Thiene, ora Bonin Longare*, sul Corso s'eccita nei due ordini, nelle rispettive trabeazioni, nelle cornici delle finestre; un risentito, e a volte

---

1. Il lato sul Corso, eseguito alla fine del XVII secolo, subì varie alterazioni nel tardo compimento. Io credo che esso non sia il frutto di un semplice capomastro, quanto il risultato d'una non fedele esecuzione di progetto palladiano.

brusco scatto delle membrature rende particolarmente teso il plasticismo di questa facciata, concepita come un grandioso altorilievo; il prospetto sul cortile invece si risolve in una trama aerea, nella quale i fusti si staccano dalla parete di fondo, mentre l'atmosfera irrompe tra gli intercolumni del portico e della loggia.

Un vivace episodio di altorilievo architettonico é, in sostanza, l'esterno di *Palazzo Barbaran Da Porto* (fig. 10), nel quale gli ordini jonico e corinzio aggettano sensibilmente a costituire la trama della composizione, nella quale é profusa la decorazione scultorea con una dovizia del tutto insolita alle fabbriche palladiane. Strutture e sculture son qui intimamente associate nell'unità dell'organismo architettonico, di particolare effervescenza pittorica.

Nel cortile di *Palazzo Da Porto Festa* il colonnato gigante si sarebbe risolto in una mirabile sequenza di strutture scultoree, rese ancor più robuste dalla colonna parastatica, sostegno al ballatoio continuo del piano nobile. Nell'elegante prospetto su Contra' Porti un plasticismo discreto ravviva soltanto il piano nobile nelle semicolonne joniche e nei balconi delle finestre, appoggiate alla sporgenza del piano sottostante. Le teste umane qui non assumono la funzione di chiavi delle lunette, ma diventano puri elementi di decorazione: l'intonaco a finte bugne raggiate sostituisce la cornice anche del grande portone d'ingresso. Esecuzione fedele al disegno avrebbe aggiunto stole di verzura ai lati di ogni finestra al piano nobile, riducendo lo stacco dei fusti semicilindrici, ma assicurando alla parete di base un diffuso tremulo pittorico.

Non intendo portare il mio discorso sugli edifici progettati e non eseguiti o su quelli eseguiti, ma di attribuzione incerta: tralascio quindi *Casa Cogollo* sul Corso —la cosiddetta Casa del Palladio—e *Casa Angaran*, ora Vaccari a San Marco, l'autore delle quali dovrà essere ricercato nell'ambito dei palladianisti generici, essendo estremamente improbabile che per esse Palladio abbia fornito il disegno: nè è credibile che si tratti di esecuzione sciatta e maldestra di capomastro sprovveduto, incapace di interpretare rettamente un progetto autografo del sommo Artista.

TEATRO OLIMPICO

Effervescenze pittoriche determinate da una generale animazione plastica costituiscono l'aspetto precipuo del proscenio del Teatro Olimpico (fig. 11). In esso gli ordini sovrapposti scalano i loro aggetti dalla base al sommo: dalle colonne a tutto tondo, che staccano i bellissimi fusti dalla parete, alle semicolonne, addossate a largo pilastro al secondo piano, ai pilastrini dell'attico. La parete piena tra le colonne del primo ordine rientra nell'incasso della finestra cieca, sul cui timpano triangolare s'adagiano due sculture: tra le semicolonne del secondo ordine altre finestre, pur cieche, segnano una rientranza, resa anch'essa più sensibile dallo sporgere delle rispettive cornici: tra i riquadri dell'attico, frastagliati di bassorilievi, altre statue accentuano le sporgenze dei ritmici pilastri. Alla cinetica del discorso architettonico si associa il fervore delle decorazioni, specie delle tante e tante statue a tutto tondo, nelle quali sembra fissarsi il gesto dell'attore vivo: statue-attori coralmente partecipi alla scena che si svolge ai loro piedi.

L'architettura placa il dinamismo delle sue strutture nei lati del proscenio, anche se non cessa la vivace azione delle sculture.

VILLE

Palladio nella giovanile *Villa Godi a Lonedo* ricorre all'articolazione di due corpi, che includono, a guisa di grandi ali, il settore centrale arretrato e assai meno esteso. Superfici volutamente lisce e incolori rivelano i tre blocchi nella loro faticosa articolazione della facciata principale: superfici del pari lisce e incolori, nemmeno variate dalle macchie nere degli archi della loggia e dei sottopassaggi al piano terra, rendono ancor più austero e chiuso il prospetto sul parco.

Un avancorpo, che di tanto sporge di quanto rientra nell'altra fronte la loggia sormontata dall'alta parete piena, determina uno scatto volumetrico nel prospetto orientale, dal quale l'artista bandisce ogni elemento che avesse attribuito palpitazioni plastiche: sicché tutta la fabbrica si assesta nella coordinata addizione di tre grandi volumi, che la simmetria disciplina nell'unità dell'organismo: entità volumetriche, ove l'esclusione di qualsiasi elemento decorativo permette un fluire di nitidi piani, sommessamente incisi nel marmorino per l'allusa scacchiera di un bugnato gentile.

In altre volumetrie bloccate s'esprime il pensiero del Palladio: come nelle *Ville Caldogno di Caldogno, Pisani di Bagnolo, Zeno di Cessalto, Pojana di Pojana Maggiore*.

Pareti continue, solo aperte nelle finestre e nei tre fornici dei prospetti, sono il fermo involucro di *Villa Caldogno*, che pronuncia un breve aggetto nella facciata principale. Le bugne in cotto, a cornice della triade d'archi nella loggia meridionale, segnano l'unica presenza di un impulso plastico.

Nella *Villa Pisani di Bagnolo* il nodo del pronao e delle gradinate ad esso adducenti, e i lunghi porticati, a perimetro del cortile, se eseguiti avrebbero reso meno avvertibile l'impianto quadrato dell'edificio e la sua larga volumetria. Il parallelepipedo architettonico si sarebbe fortemente articolato nel prospetto sul fiume per l'innalzarsi notevole delle due torri, poi mortificate nell'esecuzione traditrice: ed esse avrebbero aggiunto una volumetria verticale a quella orizzontale della costruzione, dalla quale sorgono a guisa di membra costitutive e necessarie dell'organismo. Il pronao si sarebbe proteso nello spazio del cortile come un blocco a volumetria aperta. La loggia verso il fiume, con il trittico d'archi entro la fastosa cornice rustica tra le torri, non suscita movimento volumetrico: sta inclusa nel corpo della villa, stanza aperta sul fiume che aspira l'atmosfera e la dinamizza nelle absidi affrontate e nella volta assai alta.

La *Villa Pisani di Montagnana* ripete la volumetria chiusa nel prospetto su strada e nei due fianchi. Quella *Zeno di Cessalto* conferma un atteggiamento analogo dell'architetto; volto a realizzare volumi a profilo affilato e a superfici prevalentemente chiuse anche nella *Villa Pojana di Pojana Maggiore*, pur essa priva di ordini e di qualsiasi articolazione esterna. In quest'ultima fabbrica l'architetto si limita a variare l'episodio centrale dei prospetti, inserendovi una serliana a forma del tutto inusitata. Una quieta vicenda di pieni e di vuoti ritma le superfici riverberanti, che rinserrano gli spazi interni. Le cornici semplificate delle finestre maggiori e minori e delle serliane non sono tali da sommuovere i piani compositivi e da creare fervore plastico-pittorico. L'assenza d'ogni ornamento rende ancor più efficace la ferma fissità del prisma. Volumetria chiusa, esaltata dall'apporto plastico dell'ordine, si riscontra nel corpo centrale di *Villa Barbaro a Maser* (fig. 13). Quattro vigorose semicolonne reggenti il frontone, con inclusi vivaci rilievi, formano la fronte di un corpo bloccato, che contrasta con la cordialità delle barchesse, aperte all'atmosfera nei loro archi a pieno centro.

Villa Emo Capodilista di Fanzolo propone soluzione diversa nel pronao aperto, inglobato nel rigido parallelepipedo del corpo padronale: schema riproposto da *Villa Badoer a Fratta Polesine*, nella quale però il movimento delle gradinate e dei rustici a largo emiciclo affrontato nasce da una concezione volumetrica e plastica al tempo stesso: blocchi snodati le gradinate, corpi aperti, e divenienti nella curva del loro perimetro, i rustici.

Volumetria aperta e plasticismo balzante sono l'inatteso aspetto di *Villa Sarego a Santa Sofia di Pedemonte* in Valpolicella, ove il linguaggio del Maestro assume forma d'eroica potenza nelle colonne giganti, libere nello spazio a segnare il perimetro interno dello straordinario frammento. Le rozze bugne rustiche, donde si nutrono i fusti anche a formare il massiccio pilastro parastatico, sono l'ennesima rivelazione dell'interesse scultoreo del Palladio, che anche qui nello staccare tanto decisamente il peristilio della parete di fondo, scopertamente dimostrava la sua geniale rielaborazione

di spunti tratti dal classicismo, vuoi di ascendenza greca, vuoi di ascendenza romana.

CHIESE

Nelle chiese il linguaggio del Palladio acquista inflessioni varie, a seconda ch'egli realizzi edifici a sistema accentrato (Chiesa delle Zitelle, Tempietto di Maser) o a sistema longitudinale (San Giorgio Maggiore; Redentore). Le esperienze rinascimentali, fiorite a Venezia e in Toscana prima di lui, non gli avrebbero potuto fornire alcun insegnamento: non Brunelleschi in Toscana; a Venezia non i Lombardi, nè Mauro Coducci, nè lo Spaventa, nè Sansovino; a Vicenza e a Padova, non Lorenzo da Bologna, non l'Alberti con il suo S. Andrea, con il quale poteva forse offrire un orientamento allo spazio unitario del Redentore, che sembra tuttavia doversi ricondurre a forme dell'architettura imperiale romana. D'altro lato risalire al Bramante della Chiesa di Santa Maria presso San Satiro o a Giuliano da Majano del Duomo di Faenza o a Bernardino Zaccagni della Chiesa di San Giovanni Evangelista di Parma, o a Giulio Romano del Duomo di Mantova, e a tanti altri ancora non giova per ricercare convincenti premesse.

Palladio, per virtù di genio, sa operare una mirabile sintesi delle forme quali s'erano venute elaborando nel corso di molti secoli; e pertanto la fatica della ricerca etimologica é vana e forse, tutto sommato, insidiosa ai fini della valutazione critica dell'opera d'arte.

Proprio perché il mio assunto é volto a dimostrare la fondamentale componente plastica delle soluzioni architettoniche palladiane, mi piace esaminare anzitutto l'interno di San Giorgio Maggiore (fig. 14) e portare il discorso sui nodi di forze rappresentati dai pilastri. Questi si compongono di un fascio di lesene, separate dalle altissime semicolonne dell'ordine maggiore e, verso le navate minori, da semicolonne alte quanto le lesene, sulle quali si scaricano le volte a crociera. Un pilastro così innervato di forze multiple sembra concepito da mente che aveva tratto largo profitto dalla visione delle strutture romaniche e gotiche.

La rievocazione del classicismo, che era per Palladio non una ostentazione di accademica, inerte dottrina, ma il frutto di uno spontaneo impulso creativo, s'accompagnava ovviamente a quel profondo bisogno di chiarezza, d'ordine, di misura che ogni artista del tempo avvertiva come fatale esigenza del suo spirito.

In San Giorgio, Palladio unifica lo spazio della navata mediana, in nome evidentemente di quel rigore razionalistico che lo doveva guidare poco dopo nella concezione del Redentore. Per questo rifiuta nell'una come nell'altra chiesa la successione delle campate;

ma nelle navate minori di S. Giorgio stabilisce la sequenza delle campate, coprendole con volte a crociera. Proprio nelle navatelle balza evidente la concitata accentuazione plastica delle semicolonne a sostegno delle piccole tese crociere (fig. 12). Le lesene reggono un alto segmento di trabeazione che si snoda nella sporgenza delle semicolonne a raccogliere le spinte dall'alto: il movimento risentito dei capitelli si continua con stretto aggancio nel movimento della trabeazione, dal fregio baulato e dalla cornice assai espansa e ricca di fitte modanature.

Nell'ordine che compone la trama della navata centrale, la semicolonna s'addossa al pilastro, sporgendone con lo zoccolo assai robusto e con il fusto lucente, e provoca la sporgenza dell'alta trabeazione che s'articola proprio nella calcolata mediazione con gli spicchi della candida volta.

Concatenato moto di sporgenze, in un puntuale richiamo di strutture, esalta i valori plastici soprattutto ai vertici del rettangolo del vano, nei pilastri grandiosi su cui insiste la cupola, negli angoli del presbiterio: a fianco delle semicolonne compare la lesena forse perché il suo profilo rigido, meglio della semicilindrica colonna, continua il profilo dell'arco soprastante.

Lungo le pareti perimetrali i pilastri aggettano sensibilmente così da determinare un incavo profondo, entro cui sta l'altare dalle risentite modanature. Potremmo veramente affermare che un plasticismo dinamico contrassegni l'aspetto delle navate minori, nelle quali assume logico significato la volta a crociera, perfettamente coerente con le strutture sottostanti. La tensione plastica un po' cede nella navata centrale per effetto soprattutto del gran soffitto liscio, tenuto forse troppo depresso.

Nel Redentore plasticismo vigoroso é nelle semicolonne binate e nell'alta trabeazione che le sormonta; é nei mirabili fusti a tutto tondo dell'esedra trasparente fra presbiterio e coro dei monaci; é nelle stesse cappelle laterali, le cui absidi affrontate Palladio modella come lo scultore i piani compositivi d'una statua; é nei settori tra le cappelle; poiché le semicolonne balzano con accentuato spicco dalla parete bianca proprio per l'inverso moto delle nicchie, che rispondono alla convessità dei fusti con la concavità delle loro superfici inflesse.

Il prospetto di San Giorgio é martellato dalle quattro semicolonne giganti alte sugli zoccoli robusti e sostegno al forte timpano conclusivo, ed é animato da altri accenti plastici come dal fascio di lesene angolari e dai tabernacoli nei due settori laterali all'episodio mediano. Baldanzoso plasticismo é altresì nella più complessa e frammentaria facciata di San Francesco della Vigna, nella quale l'ordine minore é dato da colonne che si ripresentano nell'infelice riquadratura della porta di ingresso.

Il prospetto del Redentore trova pur esso vigoria plastica nelle due semicolonne centrali e nella mirabile porta d'ingresso che ne é inquadrata, nei due pilastri d'angolo, nelle lesene alle estremità, nelle cornici frangiate.

Forse l'esecuzione postuma della Chiesa delle Zitelle ha placato ogni fervore plastico per ridurre la trama compositiva esterna ed interna ad una gentile grafia, priva del consueto mordente palladiano.

Al plasticismo scattante di alcune costruzioni si contrappone il placido correre di pareti luminose in altre, fermo involucro di chiare volumetrie; il valore strutturalmente fondamentale degli ordini di talune fabbriche, nelle quali essi assumono pienezza di significato scultoreo, si tramuta in valori di precipuo significato decorativo in altre: segno della varietà perenne di un linguaggio che non ristagna in una facile ripetizione di schemi e di motivi, ma si rinnova per fatale necessità creativa. Sta di fatto tuttavia che, a ben guardare, le opere del Palladio vibrano nella maggior parte dei casi di sostanziali impulsi plastici generatori appunto di quelle vivezze chiaroscurali, tante volte sottolineate, anche per il comodo luogo comune che vuole ogni artista veneto chiamato irresistibilmente verso le facili emozioni del pittoricismo.

PAOLO PORTOGHESI

L' "Opus Architectonicum" del Borromini

L'"Opus Architectonicum" è la avvincente narrazione di un programma edilizio di un contenuto che si va formando attraverso una serie di tappe che vanno dalla concezione generale dell'organismo come innesto di tessiture dettate dalla situazione urbanistica fino alla identificazione al suo interno, secondo una precisa visione gerarchica, di alcuni episodi e sequenze spaziali che si qualificano poeticamente.

Naturalmente l' "Opus" non va scambiato per una dichiarazione di poetica che espliciti una metodologia in termini verbali. Questa potrà ricostruirsi solo dal confronto tra i programmi descritti, le idee architettoniche qua e la affioranti e l'opera realizzata, analizzata nelle sue strutture formali. Interpretarlo come un trattato, come una testimonianza teorica personale e diretta sarebbe un errore per due ragioni: prima quella che la materiale stesura del testo non è del Borromini, seconda quella che tutta l'opera borrominiana si pone come una continua esposizione di regole e di sistemi come un vero e proprio complesso di nuove istituzioni formali, facilmente deducibili e comunicabili e quindi non postula per sua natura una riduzione teorica e verbale. Si pensi in questo senso alle diverse e coerentissime soluzioni date al problema dell'angolo come innesto di superfici convergenti.

Raramente nella storia dell'architettura ci si trova di fronte a tanta chiarezza di enunciazioni sintattiche. Si possono per esempio facilmente elencare le tipiche operazioni borrominiane che sono, quando il punto di partenza è tradizionale, *la traduzione* (nella cornice dello interno di S. Carlino che deriva da quella di un frammento romano di Monte Cavallo interpretato in funzione di una nuova gradualità di trapassi tra bianco e nero, di una inedita sensibilizzazione delle superfici continuamente inflesse); *la inversione* (nelle volute arricciate all'indietro della facciata dell'Oratorio); *la semplificazione* (negli stessi capitelli in cui le volute sono l'ultimo residuo della ricca aggettivazione corinzia); *la metamorfosi* (per esempio negli ovoli trasformati in teste di cherubino a S. Carlino e a S. Ivo). Quando manca il sostegno di un esempio tradizionale altre tipiche operazioni sono: *la contrazione* (ad esempio nella cornice dei corpi laterali della facciata dell'Oratorio (tav. IV, V) che si ritrae arricciandosi a contatto con il corpo principale più alto); *la compenetrazione* (ad esempio nella finestra del secondo ordine della facciata di S. Carlino); *la deformazione elastica*

(per esempio nelle porte sporgenti del lavamano dei Filippini (tav. XXIV) o della cappella dei Re Magi).

Se l'opera borrominiana ha potuto estensivamente influenzare la cultura architettonica europea, si deve in gran parte a questa evidente didatticità delle sue strutture formali.

Riguardo al limite della non autenticità, della stesura, la questione è ben chiara. Nell'originale borrominiano, conservato nel Convento dei Filippini è contenuta una nota autografa del Padre Virgilio Spada che così si esprime a questo riguardo: "*Questo libro fu fatto da me Virgilio Spada in nome del cav.re Borromino con pensiero ch'egli facesse i disegni ma non è stato possibile e però non si vede pieno dove andarebbero e ne ho fatti fare alcuni ma poco a proposito*". L'espressione "in nome" fa supporre una collaborazione nello studio del programma ma esclude ogni partecipazione borrominiana alla stesura. Di solito si suole addurre a giustificazione dell'intervento dello Spada la poca esperienza dell'architetto nello scrivere, le sue origini artigiane, la mancanza di testimonianze epistolari e il passo contenuto nella stessa lettera di presentazione dell'"Opus" al Marchese di Castel Rodriguez dove egli dice testualmente: "la supplico ad iscusare la bassezza del mio stile, servendomi dello stile più per disegnare che per scrivere". In realtà l'esame della calligrafia borrominiana, l'esatezza con cui sono redatte alcune trascrizioni di testi latini da noi pubblicati e soprattutto la circostanza che egli possedeva un migliaio di libri nella sua casa del vicolo Orbitelli fanno pensare che non mancasse del tutto all'architetto una certa confidenza con il mondo delle lettere. D'altra parte è ben comprensibile la sua poca voglia di dedicare tempo a una attività così lontana dalla sua vocazione e può essere motivata oltretutto dalla coscienza che il contenuto di pensiero delle sue architetture filtrava da esse con sufficiente chiarezza, tanto da non render necessaria nessuna chiarificazione verbale.

Altro elemento che va ricordato a completare il quadro della "letteratura borrominiana" sono le frequentissime didascalie contenute nei suoi disegni. Nessun altro architetto forse ha così abbondantemente usato dei margini dei disegni per fissare idee, redigere appunti, precisare elementi iconologici o economici delle forme descritte. Frequentissima è per esempio la notazione: "*Questo*" a identificare la soluzione prescelta tra le molte studiate e poi scartate, quasi nel timore di dimenticare le ragioni della scelta motivata sottilmente da esigenze stilistiche non sempre riemergenti. In altri disegni le note servono a un confronto con opere studiate, come le logge del Campidoglio prese ad esempio per le navate di S. Giovanni in Laterano o un tipo di tinteggiatura la cui formula è indicata in un foglio forse riferibile al palazzo Falconieri (Berlino, 1119) o per spiegare il significato di un simbolo o per indicare una regola di proporzionamento come nel disegno (Alb; 59) per la cupola di Sant'Agnese.

Se è dunque alle note autografe dei disegni che dobbiamo chiedere la diretta testimonianza di un interesse, del resto meramente strumentale, di Borromini per il mondo delle parole, dobbiamo invece nell'Opus riconoscere non solo l'impronta di una lunga collaborazione con lo Spada nel tempo della costruzione, ma anche l'eco di conversazioni e forse di appunti appositamente redatti per dare all'estensore del testo una guida sicura.

Per chi non conosce profondamente la storia del Seicento Romano occorre specificare che lo Spada non fu solo il rappresentante dello ordine filippino con il quale il Borromini trattò durante la progettazione e la realizzazione del convento. Virgilio Spada, che forse aveva già conosciuto Borromini in occasione del restauro del palazzo Capodiferro, fu, quale elemosiniere segreto di Innocenzo X e di Alessandro VII più volte in contatto con lui e, nel caso del restauro della Basilica Lateranense, gli fu accanto come consigliere e consulente.

Il grandioso complesso di disegni architettonici appartenuti allo Spada, conservati nella biblioteca vaticana, insieme alle memorie biografiche, ci attestano un concreto interesse per l'architettura. Poiché però la sua documentata attività di dilettante architetto ha fatto supporre che il suo rapporto con Borromini possa essere stato quasi un rapporto di inspiratore e collaboratore sul piano creativo, mette conto di notare per ridimensionare la portata del suo ruolo che i disegni che possono con sicurezza attribuirglisi dimostrano niente più che una superficiale infarinatura di nozioni e non si distaccano dal repertorio manieristico, per di più in una versione provinciale e consunta.

Non è quindi pensabile che Borromini possa averne subito l'influenza dello Spada se non sul piano dei programmi liturgici delle sue opere, e anche riguardo all'"Opus" il confronto con la incertezza delle prove progettistiche fa escludere che egli possa aver scritto il testo interamente da solo, senza l'aiuto di idee e di appunti direttamente forniti dall'architetto. La frequente citazione di monumenti antichi, da Villa Adriana ai ruderi presso S. Giovanni in Fonte a un sepolcro sulla Via Flaminia, al Foro di Nerva, denunciano una competenza da antiquario che non

possiamo attribuire al prelato, e certi spontanei compiacimenti per l'andamento di soluzioni statiche o la precisione di soluzioni distributive tradiscono l'emozione diretta del costruttore che non è riducibile alla soddisfazione di un committente anche se capace di condizionare attivamente la formazione del programma edilizio.

Vi sono nell'"Opus" senza dubbio interi capitoli in cui i suggerimenti dell'architetto non furono necessari, sopratutto il primo, il secondo e parte del testo, ma spesso le disquisizioni cronistiche o religiose, evidentemente inscindibili dalla psicologia dello Spada, sono intrecciati a notazioni che ci riportano al "tavolo da disegno", che evocano il processo autocritico con una fedeltà impressionante. Dobbiamo quindi concludere che il testo oltre a rispecchiare i momenti di una stretta collaborazione tra committente ed architetto, trasmette una serie di giustificazioni e interpretazioni estranee a quella collaborazione e rivelatori di un momento precedente e più intimo della progettazione. Stabiliti i limiti della paternità borrominiana, si apre il problema del giudizio. In quale misura la struttura concettuale dell'opera contribuisce a chiarire una volontà artistica, a definire la caratteristica di una cultura? Sebbene si debba contare più su una sequenza di frammenti che su una reale struttura è indubbio che l'"Opus" può diventare strumento critico complementare anche al di là dei limiti della illustrazione dell'opera indagata. Da una attenta analisi si possono raccogliere documenti illuminanti di alcuni aspetti fondamentali del metodo borrominiano: l'atteggiamento verso la natura, l'atteggiamento verso la tradizione e la storia, il problema dell'apparenza e della sostanza, il problema dell'ornamento e della bellezza. Esaminare partitamente questi aspetti indicando conseguentemente una precisa *chiave* di lettura è tra i compiti di questa presentazione; cercheremo di svolgerlo ordinatamente.

IL PROBLEMA DEL RAPPORTO CON LA NATURA. E' oggetto di una esplicita affermazione di principio in un passo teso a giustificare la forma dei balaustri triangolari delle ringhiere della loggia dell'Oratorio. "Ne senza mistero ho fatto i balaustri triangolari, e piantatoli uno contrario all'altro, perchè sedendo i Signori Cardinali dietro a quelli sei balaustri fossero (come si usa) col suo piedestalluccio, o zoccoletto a basso, accostandosi quelli assieme, levarebbe la vista per quanto potesse l'altezza di detti zoccoli, dove nella forma datagli da me, venendo i contorni paralleli fra l'uno e l'altro da piedi fino a cima si scuopre egualmente da per tutto, e l'esser triangolari fa quello appunto, che fanno le cannoniere, quali per li sguinci che hanno danno campo, e si scuopre da per tutto, e però chi sede, vede facilmente tutto quello che si fa a basso, come se avessero avanti gl'occhi una carta forata, cosa, che non succederebbe se avessero corpo tondo, o quadrato, e per maggior intelligenza l'osservarai alla tavola al num. 43. Sapendo che molti che non sanno inventare, hanno creduto esser stato mero capriccio, ed esser improprio che una parte di essi balaustri sia più grossa di sopra, che da' piedi, non avvertendo che la natura, quale dobbiamo imitare siccome produce gl'alberi assai più grossi da' piedi che di sopra, così ha fatto l'uomo più grosso di sopra, che da' piedi".

L'architettura è secondo la tradizione imitazione della natura, ma l'esempio chiarisce che si tratta di una imitazione strutturale che non ha nulla a che fare con la riproduzione di una immagine formata. Il compito dell'architetto diventa quello di indagare le ragioni costruttive delle forme della Natura, la logica dei suoi prodotti e delle sue operazioni per trasferirne l'esperienza conoscitiva nella sua opera. La componente naturalistica delle opere di Borromini conferma questa indicazione teorica. La natura è alimento continuo nell'ampliamento lessicale e nello studio della connessione degli elementi, ma il problema non è quello di ricostruire una situazione naturale, ma di opporre ad essa e alla esperienza dello spazio non architettonico una situazione artificiale, derivata, astraendo regole metodi leggi dalla rigorosa analisi strutturale dei testi naturali. La spirale di S. Ivo deriva certamente da quella conchiglia marina, montata su un piedistallo, che Borromini teneva nel suo studio, ma non risponde nell'opera a una esigenza illusiva di paesaggio naturale; è invece una indagine inedita nel dominio di nuovi più complessi tipi di simmetria, la evocazione e la conquista di una regolarità e di una necessità che oltrepassa il repertorio delle forme elementari e attinge a quei tipi di configurazioni più direttamente connessi al mondo della vita. Concavità, convessità, spirale, articolazione mistilinea delle superfici, tutto ciò è anzi tutto imitazione della natura al di là della perfezione minerale, del cubo, della sfera, del cilindro, del prisma, verso la bellezza vegetale e animale del raccordo.

IL PROBLEMA DELLA TRADIZIONE. L'atteggiamento verso l'eredità classica espresso nelle pagine dell'"Opus" coincide con quello che può dedursi indirettamente dalle opere e dalle testimonianze storiche. Abbondano le citazioni di edifici antichi: un torrione fuori Porta del Popolo ricordato per il rivestimento in sottili mattoni arrotati, Villa Adriana, le Terme di Diocleziano e i ruderi vicino a S. Giovanni in Fonte ricordati per il dispositivo strutturale della crociera che scarica il suo peso direttamente sui sostegni, il Foro di Nerva per la non ortogonalità dell'impianto. Generica-

mente all'uso antico è riferita anche la adozione per le nicchie, di una pianta che eccede di poco il semicerchio.

La cultura archeologica però non è come nel Rinascimento un orizzonte mitico. Il problema di Borromini sembra essere quello di conoscere profondamente per contestare anzitutto la concezione restrittiva della tradizione, insaturata dalla cultura manieristica, e in secondo luogo per variare, deformare, piegare a nuove significazioni i dati lessicali analizzati. "Chi segue altri non gli va mai innanzi" è scritto nella prefazione e ancora... "non mi sarei mai posto a questa professione col fine d'esser copista". Il superamento dell'antico, dalle prime formulazioni dell'Alberti, è diventato una certezza, ma tale superamento non può effettuarsi che in virtù di una profonda totale assimilazione dei metodi e delle forme classiche, la storia e la cultura diventano indispensabile alimento del fare.

Nei riguardi della tradizione più recente l'"Opus" non fornisce elementi. Molti edifici sono ricordati come il Collegio Romano, il Palazzo Borghese, la Casa Professa dei Gesuiti come termini di confronto per l'uso di materiali costosi, dimostrando unicamente una volontà di valutare il significato della propria azione e delle proprie scelte non astrattamente ma rispetto alle convenzioni e alle abitudini di un ambiente ben determinato.

Unico legame esplicitamente riconosciuto e direi ostentato è Michelangelo, ricordato nella introduzione come esempio di architetto che ha avuto solo dopo la morte, il riconoscimento dei suoi meriti e citato come modello a proposito della scelta dell'ordine gigante, non senza ricordare il fatto che questo partito architettonico non era stato dopo l'esempio del Campidoglio mai più adoperato. Possibile che il Borromini ignorasse gli esempi palladiani? Certamente no, è da pensare piuttosto che la osservazione voglia limitarsi all'ambiente romano o che in questo caso lo Spada abbia mal ricordato i discorsi dell'architetto.

Il richiamarsi a Michelangelo è in realtà assai più di un generico riferimento culturale. Borromini trae dall'esempio michelangiolesco l'indispensabile avvio a quella radicale revisione anticlassicistica che gli permette di conquistare, nell'orizzonte barocco, una posizione autonoma. A distanza di un secolo egli si ripropone gli stessi temi in una nuova prospettiva umana: al titanismo michelangiolesco, legato a un preciso momento della cultura europea, sostituisce il culto della qualità, della intensità che pone sullo stesso piano il grandissimo e il piccolissimo; al respiro drammatico eroico sostituisce un procedimento di ricerca rigoroso, quasi tecnico ma continuamente riscattato da una azione trasfiguratrice. Le relazioni con il mondo politico e civile che determinano le contraddizioni e gli scatti della produzione michel-angiolesca non contano più nella vicenda borro-miniana, tutta assorbita in una intimità gelosa aperta verso la storia civile solo al livello della quotidiana esperienza artigianale, ma sostanzialmente assorta nella descrizione di un mondo utopico, ideale, in cui la stessa protesta cerca e raggiunge una dizione con-templativa.

Problema della apparenza e della sostanza e cioè del rapporto fra verosimile e vero. Anche in questo il metodo borrominiano si rivela chiaramente nella rela-zione. L'architettura ha il compito di migliorare la vita degli uomini e quindi di offrir loro immagine di *con-venienza* e cioè di rispondenza funzionale tra le parti e il tutto. Quando condizioni limitative impongono scelte contrastanti con questa aspirazione, conviene che essa, se non può trasferirsi in un risultato sia almeno un contenuto della sintesi architettonica. Fin dove è possibile, fin dove l'attenta valutazione dei fattori positivi e negativi della scelta lo consente, Borromini trasfigura il tema con un sottile procedi-mento di adattamento in cui la difficoltà è integral-mente rivissuta e diventa occasione di stimolazione fantastica. Più in là interviene la poetica del vero-simile: "perchè la convenienza fosse in apparenza, giacchè non poteva essere in sostanza", è scritto nel testo per giustificare la tinteggiatura in falso travertino del soffitto della biblioteca. Sarebbe stato preferibile costruire un soffitto di pietra che esprimesse nella sua materia la resistenza agli incendi. Poichè ciò non è possibile, a malincuore si sceglie la soluzione didattica della *convenienza*.

Altrove a proposito dello sfasamento tra il vano dell'Oratorio e la facciata, Borromini scrive: "mi risolsi dunque ad ingannare la vista del riguardante". E a proposito dell'effetto di correzione ottica in senso verticale, realizzato nella galleria dei Cardinali, "per ingannare per quanto potei e seppi la vista". Il pro-blema qui è quello di controllare con ogni mezzo il risultato ottico della immagine: l'inganno non è che una commisurazione del dato alla funzione psicologica. Se nel caso della non corrispondenza tra facciata e Oratorio è lecito parlare di concessione alla poetica della sorpresa, al rovesciamento delle apparenze caro alla cultura barocca nei suoi aspetti generali, altrove, quando l'inganno è il risultato di una operazione lucidamente razionale di controllo della configura-zione spaziale, può cogliersi viceversa uno degli aspetti specifici dell'apporto borrominiano.

IL PROBLEMA DELL'ORDINE COME INVARIANTE MODULARE. Frequentissimi sono gli accenni a pro-blemi di concordanza metrica. La costruzione della sagrestia, realizzata prima dell'intervento borro-

miniano e senza tener conto che avrebbe dovuto essere incorporata in una fabbrica nuova, divenne fonte di una serie di difficoltà per la concordanza nei livelli nelle altezze e nel ritmo delle aperture.

Tutte queste difficoltà come quelle sorte a proposito delle aperture della facciata o dell'ordine interno dell'Oratorio furono risolte con sottili accorgimenti e segnano un deciso scatto fra la planimetria del Marus-celli (incaricato prima di Borromini della progetta-zione del complesso) che pure aveva già individuato molte delle caratteristiche distributive adottate nella realizzazione e quella definitiva di Borromini. Mentre il Maruscelli avevadisposto la sagrestia, in refettorio, le scale, lo stesso Oratorio senza rispecchiare il partito modulare delle logge dei cortili, Borromini fa di questo elemento delle archeggiature in seguenza, la trama metrica fondamentale di tutto l'edificio. Nel disegno n. 284 dell'Albertina di Vienna, il primo redatto presumibilmente dopo l'incarico, le idee formulate dal Maruscelli sono reintegrate in una struttura straordina-riamente regolare; un unico asse di simmetria unifica i due cortili, l'Oratorio e la sagrestia in una seguenza organica. E' in questa fase che nasce la configurazione della facciata dell'Oratorio come proiezione della struttura spaziale dello interno. Più tardi esigenze distributive suggeriranno di far slittare la sala all'in-terno, verso sinistra, ma la facciata nella sua stesura rimarrà invariata. Problemi di coordinamento modu-lare sono di nuovo affrontati a proposito della difficoltà intervenuta durante il corso della costruzione per l'ostinazione del proprietario di una casetta attigua al refettorio che da occasione al Padre Spada di de-scrivere con vivacità e rigore la soluzione di un pro-blema in cui tutta una serie di parametri vincolanti sono controllati con straordinaria sicurezza.

Il problema della sagrestia può riassumersi così: questo ambiente posto ortogonalmente all'asse principale della chiesa aveva un suo ritmo di forature indipen-dente, simmetrico rispetto all'interno, ma non rispetto all'esterno, poichè in fondo e ai lati dell'ingresso vi erano dei camerini di servizio di differente lunghezza. Per questo le "tre finestre della sagrestia non corri-spondono—scrive Borromini—al mezzo delli cinque archi della loggia", "il che—aggiunge—rendeva grandissimo sconcerto". La soluzione di questo sfasa-mento di elementi è quella del raddoppio: vengon cioè replicate rispetto all'asse di simmetria del cortile tutte le finestre e riunite due a due.

Ancora più complesso è il problema della illumina-zione degli stanzini attigui alla sagrestia. O bisognava rinunciare a far girare in curva le lesene terminali del cortile o bisognava chiudere le finestre. Ecco come è raccontata dall'"Opus": "La sagrestia finita molti anni prima, ha, come si è detto, due camerini per parte, cioè due da piedi, e due per parte, cioè due da piedi e due da capo, ed essendo piccoli ne sono stati fatti sopra di quelli altri quattro, cioè due per parte. Questi quattro camerini dalla parte del primo Cortile non ponno ricevere lume, se non dal detto cortile, e se si fosse seguitato con la loggia fino alla muraglia della Sagrestia con tre archi il pilastro del cantone di detta loggia averebbe levato il lume a detti camerini. In oltre la Sagrestia ha da una parte verso il Cortile maggiore una fila di Camere, e dall'altra parte, e cioè verso il primo cortile non ha cosa alcuna, sicchè abbracciando la lunghezza della Sagrestia tre archi, e le camere uno, la porta di essa, che ha all'incontro una simile porta, che conduce in Chiesa è situata nel secondo arco dopo il primo Cortile ed essendo stato stimato necessario chiudere questo andito fra la Chiesa, e Sagrestia, sì per decenza, acciò non vi avessero a vedere dalla porta della scala i Sacerdoti apparati passare col Calice in mano, come per riparare e la Chiesa, e la Sagrestia dall'aria e venti, che dalle loggie delli due cortili sarebbe imboccata, veniva molto in isconcio, che dette due porte grandi adornate di bigio antico non fossero nel mezzo... Fu dunque pensato, che il pilastro del cantone della loggia non si facesse al fine del terzo arco contiguo alla Sagrestia, ma nel fine del secondo, ed in luogo del terzo arco si girasse nel Cortile a uso di Teatro addosso la Sagrestia, occupando dalla muraglia di essa la larghezza eguale ad un'arco, ed in quella parte arcuata si facesse un grandissimo nicchione, nel quale prendessero lume i due camerini sotto, e sopra, anzi si desse lume per mezzo di esso anche nell'andito, col quale ripiego ponendosi il cancello, al pilastro del cantone piantato al fine del secondo arco della loggia, si veniva a chiudere nell'andito fra la Chiesa, e Sagrestia un arco di più verso il primo cortile, talchè le due porte della Sagrestia, e Chiesa venivano nel terzo arco, che è in mezzo delli cinque, e così fu risoluto, e posto in esecuzione con bellissimo garbo del cortile con tutto quel lume che si poteva desiderare per i camerini e con aver messo in mezzo le porte della Sagrestia, e Chiesa con due spasseggi uno per parte di dette porte per comodità di che vuole aspettar messa riparari dal freddo, e vento con due gran cancelli di noce pieni di vetriate per dar lume al detto andito, quali cancelli però si possono aprire totalmente, o in tempo di estate, o nel ricevimento di qualche gran personaggio, nel qual caso dalla porta si vede una tirata di loggia, e andito longo poco meno di palmi 400".

Per il lettore inesperto può essere utile qualche chiarimento. Il coordinamento modulare dei due cortili e della Sagrestia determinava in realtà un problema condizionato da vari parametri come, la larghezza delle logge (predeterminata dalla distanza tra la Sagrestia e la Chiesa), l'asse della Sagrestia, i muri esterni della sagrestia, l'ampiezza dell'Oratorio e i limiti stessi del lotto. Non potendo operare su nessuno di questi parametri liberamente, l'illuminazione dei camerini rimaneva un problema insolubile e si riconnetteva al problema della omogeneità delle archeggiature. Mantenendo la larghezza indicata dal corridoio tra la chiesa e la sagrestia, uno degli archi veniva ad essere parzialmente riempito dal muro della sagrestia, oppure bisognava intermettere una pausa, e in questo caso i camerini sarebbero rimasti al buio o al massimo illuminati da fessure. L'inserimento di una nicchia disposta con il suo asse inclinati di 45° rispetto alla giacitura delle pareti e delle logge, permise di risolvere due esigenze, quella di non interrompere con una anomalia la successione delle archeggiature e quella di ricavare ampie finestre per i quattro piccoli ambienti sovrapposti. Infatti ridotte a due le arcate lateralidella loggia la nicchia stabilisce un raccordo elastico, e quindi liberamente proporzionabile, tra i vari elementi prefissati in questo punto nevralgico dell'edificio in cui l'alto numero di esigenze contrastanti rischiava di rendere inevitabile una soluzione di ripiego non filtrata attraverso una esigenza sintattica. D'altra parte l'ombra trasparente della nicchia si pone come elemento di mediazione tra la parete piena della sagrestia e l'ombra più densa del loggiato.

IL PROBLEMA DELL'ORNAMENTO E DELLA BELLEZZA. E' certamente il problema in cui più difficilmente il pensiero borrominiano può essere filtrato attraverso la stesura del Padre Spada. E tuttavia non mancano notazioni illuminanti che chiariscono il "metodo" dell'architetto. Anzitutto il passo sulle logge del cortile: "Non v'è cosa in quella Fabbrica, nella quale io resti maggiormente soddisfatto, che dall'avere con un ordine solo de' pilastri abbracciate tutte due le loggie, che sebbene fu inventato tal modo da Michel'Angelo nel Palazzo di Campidoglio, tuttavia non è stato praticato da alcuno, e veramente con mancho cose, e senza tanti pilastri, e pilastretti, e moltiplicar di basi, capitelli e cornici, riesce maggiormente maestoso, parendo li pilastri fra gl'archi tanti Giganti, che si alzino a sostenere il cornicione, che cinge li cortili, quali avendo sopra il finimento del parapetto della loggia scoperta con le piante d'agrumi, che si vedono sorgere sopra li pilastri, rendono vaghissima vista, e sebbene l'ornato pare, che ecceda la prescittami modestia dei Padri, a segno che ne fui ripreso, più d'una volta non di meno, se si considerano distintamente le parti di esso, si troverà, che il piacimento nasce più dal disegno riuscito vago, che dalla materia, o dall'ornato, essendomi contentato di fare li capitelli con cinque semplici foglie lisce senza intagli, senza volute, e senza veruna ricchezza di lavoro, ma li risalti grandi de' pilastri rispetto al muro, che chiude le logge fatte nell'estrema parte verso la loggia le ringhiere, che perciò restano fuori i vasi sopra i piedistalli in ciascuna ringhiera, fanno gran rumore, nella maniera, che un vestito ben tagliato, e ben cucito di tela sangalla comparisce molto più, che uno di drappo malfatto indosso a'un omaccio."

Probabilmente parte della vivacità di questa descrizione si deve al Padre Spada che aveva qualche confidenza con la penna, ma quel "piacimento" che nasce più dal disegno che dalla materia è una definizione che più esatta non si potrebbe desiderare, del programma borrominiano che oppone un valore lavoro a un valore materia. Altre espressioni concorrono a confermare l'idea di una stretta connessione tra il momento della forma e il momento di una effusione quasi affettiva in cui si esprime la volontà dell'architetto di offrire ai suoi simili, per virtù di ingegno e di fatica, uno spazio nobilitato dalla presenza umana. L'Oratorio è definito "capacissimo, luminoso e vago"; dove l'ordine degli aggettivi che procede dalla comodità alla bellezza suggerisce una connessione stretta tra i due momenti. "Non è stato mero capriccio—è scritto altrove—il disegno delle gelosie che si reggono in piedi impiombate nella cimasa di marmo senza appoggiarsi alli pilastri poiché la bellezza dei pilastri è ... che gli spigoli camminino senza intoppo o interrompimento". L'esigenza di una giustificazione razionale linguistica si manifesta continuamente e spesso per affermare la disposizione gerarchica delle parti. L'Oratorio è "figlio della Chiesa" e perciò meno ornato. La Sagrestia più importante dell'Oratorio è posta perciò a un livello superiore, la decorazione delle facciate è strettamente commisurata alle loro molteplici funzioni. Sulle vie comuni la parte residenziale ha finiture umilissime e si nobilita solo dove l'edificio, nella Piazza dell'Orologio, assume una precisa funzione urbanistica e perciò civile, come fondale della via dei Banchi. La facciata dell'Oratorio è in mattoni perchè meno importante di quella in travertino della chiesa e poiché sarebbe desiderabile al limite vederla troppo unita, come fabbricata di un sol pezzo di cotto, si sceglie la soluzione opposta perchè gli estremi si toccano, la minuta frammentazione delle scaglie arrotate sottilissime si assimila al blocco unito desiderato.

"Fantasticando pensai—si legge a proposito delle stanze dei cardinali—dentro la grossezza della muraglia in un cantone del camerino del letto ricavare tre quarti della pianta di una scala a lumaca". Borromini fantasticava sempre sull'appoggio di problemi concreti; autobiografia o biografia che siano queste memorie sono efficacissime: vediamo nel processo che illuminano la qualità estetica nascere come proiezione di una necessità, di un contenuto che si fa idea architettonica e quindi forma nella concretezza del testo.

Si è voluto da parte di Hans Sedlmayr artificiosamente contrapporre il Borromini delle disenteressate creazioni spaziali di S. Carlino a quello minore, meno intenso del convento dei Filippini. La contrapposizione non può essere di metodo ma solo di risultati e anche in questo senso il difetto del complesso filippino è estrinseco, sta nel non potersi offrire alla nostra osservazione, come invece il S. Carlino o il Sant'Ivo nella loro vivente funzionalità. Spenta o tragicamente ridotta, la vita della comunità che lo abitava, il grande edificio è ormai solo un insieme di frammenti rimossi dalla loro collocazione necessaria. Il passaggio del problema alla idea architettonica e da questa alla forma si ricostruisce a fatica e solo attraverso lo studio. Dobbiamo pensare per avere un giusto termine di paragone all'edificio del Bauhaus di Dessau come era dopo l'avvento del nazismo, riutilizzato per fini diversi e reintegrato in funzione di un diverso fine. L'"Opus Architectonicum" ha il pregio insostituibile di permetterci, restituendo allo stravolto organismo la sua autentica motivazione spaziale, di ritrovare una profonda continuità tra le travolgenti ed inedite visioni delle chiese borrominiane e questo ricercare minuzioso di un ritmo vitale che trasformi l'organismo edilizio senza acuti sconvolgimenti ma continuamente alimentato da una mai sopita volontà di presenza, da una tensione che nasce dalla analisi rigorosa delle funzioni e invita a una contemplazione che è nello stesso tempo riflessione e insegnamento.

"E se in qualcosa eccedei la regola prescrittami, per un pezzo udii dei brontolii, e però devo essere compatito"—scrive Borromini (o lo Spada per lui esprimendo una condizione verificata)—se non corrispondono tutte le parti a quello che per altro converrebbe". Nella aspirazione a questa "convenienza" che altro non è che la organicità della immagine, si infrappone il freno della discrezione del committente, ma di fronte a questa situazione in cui la invenzione e la forza innovatrice non possono agire direttamente la cultura di Borromini ha ancora ricchezze inesauribili da prodigare, quella dedizione, quella unità, quella fiducia nel proprio mestiere come mezzo di accrescimento della umanità che scoprono meglio di ogni altro aspetto della sua opera il legame non reciso tra la sua individualità e la società umana.

HENRY MILLON

Michelangelo Garove and the Chapel of the Beato Amedeo of Savoy in the Cathedral of Vercelli

The chapel dedicated to the Beato Amedeo of Savoy in the cathedral of Vercelli was begun on 18 September 1682 when Maria Giovanna Battista, the regent widow of Carlo Emanuele II, laid the corner-stone.[1] About this date there is no disagreement. There has been a conspicuous silence about the authorship of the design of the entire chapel. Only Carboneri has attributed the original design of the plan and over-all form to Michelangelo Garove.[2] Documents found in the Turin Archivio di Stato and here published confirm Garove as the author of the design. There are, however, conflicting attributions of the main altar (Fig. 1).[3]

Embellishments and alterations to the chapel in the eighteenth century make some attributions still hypothetical. This note has as its purpose a survey of the relevant documents, possible interpretations, dates and attributions both new and old, in order to place the chapel within late seventeenth-century Piedmontese architecture in general and within Garove's work in particular. The chapel was of particular importance for Garove since it marks his first independent work of consequence and established him as one of the possible successors to Guarini and Castellamonte who both died in 1683, the year after the chapel was begun. Garove, in the late 1680's and 90's, became the principal architect in Piedmont until Juvarra's arrival in 1714.

I

The decision to begin serious work on the chapel of the Beato Amedeo was prompted by the beatification proceedings that were begun in 1676 and successfully culminated in 1681 under Pope Innocent XI Odescalchi. At least three architects submitted designs for the chapel to be constructed in the cathedral of Vercelli.[4] Although it was not until July 1682 that the Madama Reale made her decision, plans had been prepared much earlier. In August 1680 Guarino Guarini went to Vercelli from Turin to measure and draw the plan of the cathedral and design the new

1. Dumo di Vercelli, Atti Capitolari (hereafter ACDV), 18.IX.1682, and G. Chicco, *Memorie del Vecchio Duomo di Vercelli*..., Vercelli, 1943, p. 31 (hereafter, Chicco).

2. N. Carboneri, *Mostra del Barocco Piemontese*, I, *Architettura*, Turin, 1963, p. 37, says, 'I forti accenti garoviani sono palesi nella cappella iniziata nel 1682, per incarico di Madame Reale Giovanna Battista.'

I presented a paper on this chapel at the annual meeting of the Society of Architectural Historians in Minneapolis, Minnesota, in January 1961. At that time, before finding the documents that told the story in more detail, I stated the chapel had been designed and begun by Guarini but finished by Garove.

3. The altar, attributed to Garove by A. Baudi Di Vesme (*L'arte in Piemonte dal XVI al XVIII secolo*, vol. I, Turin, 1963), A. E. Brinckmann (*Theatrum novum Pedemontii*, Dusseldorf, 1931, p. 89), A. M. Brizio (*Catalogo delle cose d'arte e di Antichità di Vercelli*, Rome, 1935, p. 66), and the TCI guide (*Piemonte*, Milan, 1961, p. 620), has also been attributed to Juvarra by L. Masini ('La vita e l'arte di Filippo Juvara', *Atti Società Piemontese di Archeologia e Belle Arti* (hereafter ASPABA), IX, 1920, A. Telluccini (*L'arte dell'architetto Filippo Juvara in Piemonte*, Turin, 1926, pp. 64–65), L. Rovere, V. Viale, and A. E. Brinckmann (*Filippo Juvarra*, Milan, 1937, p. 77) and N. Carboneri, 1963, p. 37. E. Pasteris (*Il duomo di Vercelli*, Terni-Vercelli, 1928) without attributing an author, dates the altar and *depositi* from 1739. Pasteris followed and elaborated on G. Casalis, *Dizionario storico-geografico per gli Stati Sardi*, XXIV, Turin, 1853–4, p. 67, who said, 'Il re Carlo Emanuele III la [the chapel] fece ornare con marmi nel 1739, e fece anche porre accanto le ossa dei duchi Carolo III e Vittorio Amedeo I di Savoia....' Pasteris apparently thought that if Carlo Emanuele III moved the Savoy bones he also had the tomb-niches (*depositi*) constructed. They were however already in place by 7.III.1690 when the sculptor received his final payment (see note 7). The Casalis date is probably a typographical error that has never been noticed. It was Carlo Dionisotti who wrote the entry for the Casalis *Dizionario* and he had access to the Archivio Capitolare. See C. Dionisotti, *Memorie storiche della città di Vercelli*, 2 vols., Biella, 1861, a reprint of the Casalis entry. It seems likely he wrote the accurate date, 1759, but somehow it was set in type as 1739 and the error never noticed. Documents indicate the altar was executed in 1759 by

Luigi Barberis according to the designs of Benedetto Alfieri. Only Chicco, on the basis of his close study of documents in the Archivio Capitolare, made this attribution.

4. Replacement of the ailing sixth-century cathedral was already under way in 1572–8 when a new choir, flanking chapels, and twin sacristies were constructed according to the designs of Pellegrino Tibaldi (Chicco, pp. 19–21). No other major construction was done until the Beato Amedeo Chapel was begun. Foundations for the semicircular north transept of the cathedral were also begun in the 1572–8 campaign although they were not followed in the second campaign of 1703–7. The shape and extent of the foundations may be seen in the Biblioteca Nazionale 'Turin Plan' (Q–1–64, f. 25) (Fig. 4) and although misinterpreted, on the *Theatrum Sabaudiae* bird's-eye view of Vercelli. It should be possible to reconstruct Pellegrino's plan for the transepts and crossing from these fragmentary indications. The transept on the north, according to the Biblioteca Nazionale drawing, was to be dedicated to the Beato Amedeo. Why the chapel was moved to the south transept is unknown.

chapel of the Beato Amedeo.[5] His design has been lost.

Another design, attributed to Conte Andrea Valperga, has been preserved in both plan (Fig. 2) and section (Fig. 3) in the Biblioteca Nazionale, Turin.[6] Valperga's plans were for an oval central space with a square entrance vestibule and a raised square chapel for the Beato Amedeo at opposite ends of the short axis of the oval. The oval was covered by an oval dome resting directly on the entablature. Pairs of spiral columns on single pedestals flank each of the openings. Above the entablature there is a balustrade supporting gesticulating putti, and rich relief stucco decoration in the dome segments. Light sources are four tall narrow windows in the dome on the axes, two small windows above aediculae on the oval.

A third submission (the one constructed) was that of Michelangelo Garove to be built on the south side of the cathedral at the end of the south transept. His drawings have not been preserved. The sixth-century nave was still standing when the chapel was added and there was an atrium with an oval dome built between the new chapel and cathedral. A drawing by Garove of this atrium, done when the crossing was to be begun (1703), has survived (Fig. 5). The atrium was removed when the present crossing was completed (Fig. 6).

From the exterior, the chapel appears to be a squat cubical block a bit higher than wide (ratio of 1:1.13) divided in three vertically (base, body, and attic) and in three horizontally (pairs of pilasters at each corner) (Fig. 7).

On the interior the chapel is about twice as high as wide. The plan of the chapel is based on an octagon formed from a square with the corners cut off (Fig. 8). In the four corners are doors and stairs leading to four small elevated *coretti* or choir spaces. The altar and the repository of the Beato's bones are opposite the entrance archway. On the wall there are elevated tomb-niches (*depositi*) that contain Savoy notables. The tomb-niches and the altar are each flanked by a pair of columns (six in all). There are no columns at the entrance archway.

Vertically the chapel is divided into four sections: (*a*) a lower region defined by columns, pilasters and entablature; (*b*) the pendentive region; (*c*) the attic; and (*d*) the dome (Fig. 9).

There are no windows at the lower level. In the pendentive region there are Palladian windows above the tomb-niches on the east and west (Fig. 10). The east window is blind since the chapel is built against the romanesque campanile. The window to the west is unobstructed. The bottom third of the dome has eight oval windows that are the principal light source for the chapel.

The lower region, with a polychrome marble altar and painted altarpiece, the black and white marble tomb-niches, the brown marble doorways and *coretti* in the angled corners, and the red-brown columns, contains by far the widest range of hues.

The upper regions of the chapel appear to be different in form, color (pale green and ivory) and in decorative detail from the lower portion, and in fact resemble closely mid- (or even late) eighteenth-century work (Fig. 11). Within the lower region the forms, composition and color of the tomb-niches contrast markedly with the colored marble doorways and *coretti*. The multi-colored altar appears different in both form and color from either the black and white tomb-niches or the brown doorways and *coretti*. The chapel is clearly the result of different hands at different times.

Documents indicate two major and one minor construction periods.[7] The first period (1682–1698)

---

5. Reimbursement was made to Guarini (19.XI.1680) for his trip to Vercelli 1–5.viii.1680 (Archivio di Stato, Turin (hereafter AST), Sez. Riunite, Art. 205, f. 221 verso), 'In rimborso . . . al Padre D. Guerino e suo Compagno nel Viaggio dal med.o fatto alla città di Vercelli per levare la pianta della chiesa di S. Eusebio e formar il dissegno della Cappella del Beato Amedeo che M.R. vol far edificare. . . .' Guarini and a friend left Turin for Vercelli on the 1st August. They spent the night in Cigliano and arrived in Vercelli the next day, 2nd August, and stayed until the fourth. They left on the fourth, slept in Cigliano, lunched in Chivasso and returned to Turin on the fifth. The total cost to the crown, as listed in the expense account, was 41.10 lire.

6. Q–1–64 (attributed to Andrea Valperga), Sheets 12 and 13. The intended location of the Valperga project can be seen in tentative pencil notation on the Biblioteca Nazionale plan of the Cathedral of Vercelli found in the same volume (Fig. 4). The chapel was to be placed on the north flank just to the east of the Pellegrino Tibaldi foundations for the north transept. Apparently after making the pencil sketches Valperga placed the chapel on the south side of the cathedral. The plan and section indicate an entrance on the south flank.

The volume is attributed to Conte Andrea Valperga. The wide variety of drawings indicating different hands at different periods, some perhaps later than the end of the seventeenth century, make a single attribution unlikely. The volume may indeed have been in possession of the Valperga family. Documents from the ducal archive seem to indicate the Barone Valperga, Antonio Maurizio, did more work than his father or brother, at least in the last quarter of the seventeenth century. Throughout the 80's in the account of royal stipends both the Ingegnere Valperga padre e figlio are listed (AST, Sez. 1°, Bilanci della Real Casa, 1683 in 1686; 1684; 1685; 1686).

The volume contains many drawings for work done in the 50's and 60's as well as later, for example, façade of the Palazzo Reale, Chapel of the SS. Sindone, road up to Monte Cappucino, etc. It is my, perhaps irrational, belief that the drawings in this volume and its companion are by both the father and son with the predominant part by the son Barone Antonio Maurizio. The apparent confusion will be clarified as soon as someone searches thoroughly through extant documents for material relevant to the Valpergas. See note 9.

7. The following is a summary of the pertinent construction and alteration dates for the chapel:
22.vii.1682—Decision to build the chapel, 'secondo il dissegno

produced a furnished chapel with altar, tombs, decoration, atrium, and wrought-iron gateway. Only minor alterations of the entrance wall were made as the cross-

ing of the cathedral was completed (1717). During the second period of construction (1759–1761) the original altar was removed and sold and a new marble altar

del Sig. Michel Angelo Garrove [*sic*], Ingegnere di S.A.R.', was taken after more than two years of procrastination (AST, Sez. Riunite, Art. 200: Reg. Terzo, 1682–3, f. 56 v). On 1.x.1680 the Consiglio delle fabbriche e fortificazioni set aside, at the request of the M.R., 10,000 lire for the construction of the Cappella del Beato Amedeo (AST, Sez. Riunite, Art. 200: Reg. Secondo, 1680, f. 19). A similar sum was set aside in 1682 (*ibid.*, f. 184), 1683 (AST, Sez. Primo, Bilancio Generale della Casa di S.A.R., 1683 in 1686, Mazzo 7, no. 1), and 1684 (*ibid.*, no. 2). In 1680 an unspecified quantity of brick was set aside by the fortifications contractor in Vercelli for use in the projected chapel. By May of 1681 one of the contractors, Martin Ferro, was petitioning to be allowed to use the brick since they were not being employed in the chapel (AST, Sez. Riunite, Art. 200: Reg. Secondo, 1680, f. 83), and was told that the brick must remain since a decision would be made within a few days. On 3.vi.1681 the Consiglio sent notice to Ferro that if no decision was made within the next two weeks he was free to use the brick (*ibid.*, f. 88). Bids were to be solicited immediately after the decision and were due on 3.vii.1682 (*ibid.*, Reg. Terzo, 1682–3, ff. 56 v and 59).

3.viii.1682—Bids were received but only two contractors appeared. Decision was put off three days to see if more bids might be forthcoming (*ibid.*, f. 59).

6.viii.1682—Contract signed with both of the bidders of 3 August: Giovanni Niccolao Tadeij and Sebastiano Bosso. Negotiations over unit prices, final agreements, specifications and conditions were all agreed upon on this date. Transcriptions of the contract documents follow the deliberations (*ibid.*, ff. 61 r–71 v).

12.viii.1682—400,000 bricks not needed for the construction of the fortifications of Vercelli are assigned to the contractors of the chapel (AST, Sez. Riunite, Art. 193: 1682, ff. 21–23 r).

15.viii.1682—Letter from the Duchess, M. Giovanna Baptista, to the canons of the cathedral informing them of her wish to build the chapel 'propria alla dignità delle Reliquie del Beato Amedeo' (ACDV—Cartella X, transcribed in Chicco, p. 97).

9.ix.1682—Contract for ten columns signed with Francesco and Giuseppe Salla (AST, Sez. Riunite, Art. 200: Reg. Terzo, 1682–1683, ff. 81 ff.). Four of the columns have been removed. They were on either side of the entrance opening into the cathedral. One of the pairs may be seen on the Garove drawing of 1703 (Fig. 5).

18.ix.1682—First stone laid by the Duchess Maria Giovanna Baptista (Chicco, p. 31).

31.vii.1683—Contract for the sculpting of the principal cornice signed. Giuseppe Salla to do the work (AST, Sez. Riunite, Art. 199: Reg. 1683 in 84, f. 11 v).

24.xi.1683—Trabucchi 256.3.6 of masonry construction in place by this date. The quantity represents 48.4 per cent of the Tadeij-Bosso contract (AST, Sez. Riunite, Art. 201: Reg. 1665–88, entry found on one of the last nine unpaginated folios. The entry is part of a summary of work done on the chapel with dates and quantities up to 2.v.1690).

10.vi.1684—Salla paid for placing a portion of the cornice (AST, Sez. Riunite, Art. 201: Reg. 1682 in 84, f. 154 v).

15.ix.1684—Contract documents signed according to Garove's specifications for the 'altare di marmi, Depositi, Portine, Tribune, et altri ornamenti pure di marmi . . .' giving work to Carlo Busso, Giuseppe Busso, and Francesco Busso, all *capi mastri* (AST, Sez. 1°, Materia Militare, no. 4, Mazzo 2).

6.xi.1684—Trabucchi 203.5.8 of masonry completed since 24.xi.1683 by Tadeij and Bosso representing 38.4 per cent of the contract amount. Total to this date—86.8 per cent (AST, Sez. Riunite, Art. 201: Reg. 1665–88—see entry 24.xi.1683).

6.xi.1684 (between this date and 24.x.1683)—Dome vaulted (*ibid.*).

6.xi.1684—Sometime after this date the four small cupolas were constructed (completed certainly before 10.xii.1690 but probably much earlier) (*ibid.*).

31.i.1685—Payment for the lead covering of the cupola (AST, Sez. Riunite, Art. 205: 1685–6, f. 91).

24.xi.1685—Capo Mastro Tadeij requests that Garove come and inspect the stucco work being done to see if it meets specifications and, as well, requests what he should do next (AST, Sez. Riunite, Art. 199: Reg. 1685 in 88, f. 4 v).

10.xii.1685—Trabucchi 66.3.3 of masonry completed since 6.xi.1684 by Tadeij and Bosso representing 12.5 per cent of the contract amount. Total to this date—99.3 per cent (AST—see entry dated 24.x.1683).

1.ii.1687—List of work done in 1686 cites one of the four spiral stairs and making the scaffolding for the stucco workers (*ibid.*).

1.ii.1687—Trabucchi 4.4.6 of masonry completed since 10.xii.1685 by Tadeij and Bosso representing 0.8 per cent of the contract amount. Total to this date—100 per cent (*ibid.*).

21.v.1687—Consiglio informed that the *stuccatori* were already at Vercelli to work on the chapel but their materials had not yet arrived (AST, Sez. Riunite, Art. 199: Reg. 1685 in 88, f. 118 v). This notice must refer to the stucco worker Carlo Francesco Tamino who figures shortly in the documents as the principal figure. The stucco work he did was apparently the most important (the original drum and dome?). A description indicates that there was no resemblance to the stucco work now in the chapel.

6.viii.1687—The columns made by the stone carver Busso for the large windows (the Palladian windows) arrived at Vercelli but could not be put in place because the stucco work was not finished (AST, Sez. Riunite, Art. 199: Reg. 1685 in 88, f. 154).

17.xi.1687—Tamino requests someone from the Consiglio to come and check what he has done with the stucco work at the chapel (*ibid.*, f. 179).

17.xi.1687—Roofer Francesco Caviglia paid for covering with lead the roof of the four small cupolas and the main cornice (AST, Sez. Riunite, Art. 205: Reg. 1685 in 87, f. 241 v).

18.iii.1688—Tamino requested to return to Vercelli because the season when he will be able to do stucco work is arriving (AST, Sez. Riunite, Art. 199: Reg. 1685 in 88, f. 223). Tamino arrived and began work shortly thereafter. On 23.vi.1688 he asked and received 200 lire for the work he had done and to continue working (AST, Sez. Riunite, Art. 199: Reg. 1688 in 91, f. 40 v). Tamino's name does not appear again after 1688. He apparently finished the stucco work in 1688.

23.ix.1688—A verification by Garove of work done and work in place by stone carver Carlo Busso reads as follows:

> P.mo li due capitelli sovra le due colonne del Altare con la pietra che termina il quadro dell'Incona dall'una parte all'altra
> Le pietre, che formano l'ornamento delle portine delle quattro scale
> Le dodeci colonette messe alli fenestroni [palladian windows] con basi e capitelli

Completed but not yet in place were two large statues and eight *puttini* all of white marble, two coats-of-arms (one still to finish), and 16 pieces of black marble for the completion of the altar. The only work remaining to be done were the two *depositi*. Busso was paid 3,500 lire for the work to date (AST, Sez. Riunite, Art. 199: Reg. 1688 in 91, f. 81 v).

7.iii.1690—After petitioning on 9.xii.1689 for final payment for the altar (*ibid.*, f. 198 v), Carlo Busso paid 3,600 lire (*ibid.*, f. 201).

14.viii.1692—Key for chapel was made (ACDV, Atti Capitolare, f. 31 r).

12.vii.1697—Contract signed with Carlo Busso to make the

with gilded bronze ornament was installed. In addition masonry pilasters were replaced by marble and, probably at the same time, stucco work in the pendentive and dome was redone. The third period includes the final adjustments made (1781–1783) to have the entrance conform to that of the newly completed Cappella di Sant'Eusebio at the opposite (north) end of the crossing.

Benedetto Alfieri (1700–1767) (with Luigi Barberis (1725–1798) as his assistant) was the architect for Carlo Emanuele III (1730–1773) for the construction of the cathedral and chapel. During the second period of construction of the chapel Barberis was already in charge of the execution of Alfieri's designs for the nave of the cathedral which was added in 1755–1765. Bar-

beris was also, apparently, the sole architect for the Cappella di Sant'Eusebio constructed 1763–1783 and for all other changes to the cathedral made during his lifetime.

Stucco decorations of the vault of the nave of the cathedral are similar to the decorations of the pendentives, drum, and dome of the chapel. On the basis of the documents and the close stylistic relationship to other stucco work executed under Barberis' supervision, it is possible to attribute the design and color scheme of the stucco decorations of the upper regions, from the pedentives to the lantern, to Benedetto Alfieri-Luigi Barberis. The date of these changes is not documented but it is probable they were carried out either while the new altar was being constructed or when the entrance to the Cappella del Beato Amedeo

three additional stairs that lead from the chapel floor up to the *coretti* (AST, Sez. Riunite, Art. 199: Reg. 1695 in 97, f. 159). Stair was to be completed by October 1697.
23.vii.1697—Conseglio instructs Garove to write a letter to Mons. Destrais about constructing an opening in the wall of the cathedral to gain access to the chapel (*ibid.*, f. 162 v).
27.ii.1698—Conseglio deliberates over the construction of the wrought-iron grille to separate chapel from cathedral. Contract awarded to Marco Fabio Cattelli (AST, Sez. Riunite, Art. 199: Reg. 1697 in 98, f. 116). The grille was completed in April of the same year (AST, Sez. Riunite, Art. 199: Reg. 1698 in 1700, f. 1).
23.iv.1698—The main altar painting (Beato Amedeo distributing alms to the poor) by Daniele Seyter put in place by this date. The painting was both too wide and too long and had to be cut to fit (AST, Sez. Riunite, Art. 205: Reg. 1698 in 99, f. 108). It is probable the painting was finished shortly before being sent to Vercelli. The frame was made by Cesare Neurone (*ibid.*).
27.i.1703—Work on the nave begun again (Chicco, pp. 31 and 35 ff.). Drawing and notation by Garove to permit the construction of the new crossing piers if certain adjustments were made in the atrium to make the two ends symmetrical (Fig. 5). The text accompanying the drawing signed by Garove reads as follows:

> Havendo Il sott.o representato a S.A.R. il posto, e sito, che occuparebbe il nuovo Pillastro che dessiderano far construere li SS.ri Cannonici della Cattedrale di S. Eusebio di Vercelli, nell'Atrio della Cappella del B.to Amedeo segnato con lettera 'A' nell'angolo di d.ta Atrio segnato B-B: si è compiaciuta la sud.a S.A.R. di ciò concederli; mediante che si restituischi la simetria a detto Atrio con formare a luoro spese le due piccole muraglie segnate C-C il tutto stabilito verso d.o Atrio.
>
> Torino li 27 gen. 1703

30–31.iii. to 1.iv.1719—Body of Beato Amedeo moved in solemn procession into the new chapel (ACDV—Cartella 65).
1723—G. B. Sachetti ('Catalogo dei disegni fatti dal Signor Cavaliere ed Abate don Filippo Juvara dal 1714 al 1735 compilato dal suo discepolo', published in Rovere, Viale, Brinckmann, *Filippo Juvarra*, Milan, 1937, pp. 33 ff.) reports that Juvarra designed a new altar 'a marmi lustri, con urna grande d'argento per riporre il corpo del B. Amedeo di Savoia nel Duomo di Vercelli'.
16.iii.1728—Silver urn to hold the Beato Amedeo arrived in Vercelli. Done by Carlo Guglielmo Boggetto (ACDV—Cartella —Cappella del Beato Amedeo). This urn is apparently the one designed by Juvarra. A document dated 24.III.1728 found by Di Vesme (the location of which is now lost though it is reported in Rovere, Viale, Brinckmann, *op. cit.*, p. 77) indicated the urn was made from a wood model constructed by the wood-carver Prinotto. Prinotto also made a wood model of the entire altar

which was, however, never constructed. These documents are the source of the commonly held error that the present altar is according to Juvarra's designs.
1759—Letters of Luigi Barberis (assistant to Benedetto Alfieri) about the new altar of the chapel. The old one was sold. Letters dated 15.IX.1759 and 29.X.1759 (Chicco, pp. 71 and 107).
1760—Francesco Ladatte was paid 1,000 lire for two large 'lumiere in bronzo dorato, destinate per la cappella del Beato Amedeo di Savoia a Vercelli'. (G. Claretta, 'I reali di Savoia munifici fautori delle arti', *Miscellanea Storia Italiana*, xxx, 1893, p. 140.)
23.iii.1761—Letter from Barberis to Abate Langosco di Stroppiana, Archdeacon of the Cathedral, mentions making 'le lesene della cappella del Beato Amedeo' of marble (Chicco, p. 108).
26.iv.1782—Letter from Vittorio Amedeo III to the Capitolo mentions what his father had done for the cathedral 'non solomente ordinò le necessarie riparazioni e gli opportuni riadattamenti attorno alla cappella del Beato Amedeo di Savoia, ma la fece pure adornare, oltre gli intonachi e stucchi, di un nuovo altare, a seconda dei mentovati dissegni, formato di assai preziosi marmi e decorati di non pochi ornamenti di bronzo dorato'. The letter goes on to mention the Cappella di S. Eusebio on the other side of the cathedral and mentions the cupola having been finished the year before (1781). Therefore, in order to achieve symmetry Vittorio Amedeo III suggests that the entrance to the Cappella del Beato Amedeo be altered to match that on the other side. 'Richiede ora il buon ordine, che si divenga all'amplificazione dall'arco per cui si ha accesso alla nostra cappella dedicata al Beato Amedeo di Savoija, affinchè la angustia presente di essa in confronto delle altre opere avanti enunziate non gli tolga quell'aria di magnificenza che gli conviene.' A cost estimate by Barberis appended to the letter indicates the work can be done for 3,674 lire (Chicco, p. 98, reproduces the full text of the letter). This letter confirms the change of the altar in the 1750's since Carlo Emanuele III, father of Vittorio Amedeo III, did not begin his reign until 1730 after the supposed altar of Juvarra. Also mentioned are the painting and stucco changes that are now present in the chapel. The letter also mentions gilded bronze objects with presumed reference to the bronze on the altar and the lamps made by Ladatte (see entry dated 1760). Sometime during the reign of Carlo Emanuele III the remains of Carlo III and Vittorio Amedeo I of Savoy were placed in the two *depositi* (Casalis, p. 67).
1799—Silver urn melted down by French (Casalis, p. 67, and A. M. Brizio, *Catalogo delle cose d'arte e di Antichità di Vercelli*, Rome, 1935, p. 66).
1823—New urn, designed by Prof. Fabrizio Sevesi, and made by goldsmith Giuseppe Borasio, given by King Carlo Felice (*ibid.*, p. 66). Pasteris following perhaps Casalis gives the goldsmithing to Giuseppe Borani.

was altered to match the entrance to the newly completed Cappella di Sant'Eusebio (1781).[8]

III

Until 1682 Michelangelo Garove did no independent work. Of the preceding generation Amedeo Castellamonte and Guarino Guarini outclassed him but his contemporaries proved to be weaker. His place in late seventeenth-century Piedmontese architecture can be assessed only through a survey of those who practiced at the same time as he.

On 17.IX.1683 Amedeo Castellamonte died. He had been First Architect to the duke from the early 1670's. Guarino Guarini, the only imaginative architect of the first rank in the Piedmont, had died six months earlier on 6.III.1683. There were no obvious successors for either of the architects. At his death Guarini, in Turin, was working for the regent on the Consolata, finishing the SS. Sindone, S. Lorenzo, and the Collegio dei Nobili. For the Savoy-Carignano cousins to the regent he was completing the Carignano Palace and designing the church of S. Filippo Neri. Castellamonte left unfinished the Ospedale Maggiore di S. Giovanni and the Nuova Dogana (begun 6.IV.1682). Castellamonte and Guarini were replaced by Garove, Antonio Maurizio Valperga, Francesco Baroncello, Carlo Emanuele Lanfranchi and, somewhat later, Antonio Bertola.

Valperga, the weakest architect of the group, was somewhat incongruously already serving as Primo Ingegnere from 20.III.1667. He was primarily responsible for fortification construction (Vercelli, 1665 ff.) but did an occasional small church (for example, Verrua, 1677–1681) in the Protestant valleys to the west. His influence as an architect was virtually negligible after 1680.[9]

Baroncello assumed direction of much of the work entrusted to Castellamonte,[10] primarily the Ospedale Maggiore, the Dogana Nuova, and the new enlargement of the city towards the Po. His abilities do not seem to have electrified the court, for, aside from design and supervision in 1686 of minor work done on the Bastione Verde (in the garden of the Palazzo Reale) and adjacent garden,[11] Baroncello's name became less and less frequent in the ducal accounts and disappears altogether after 1690. He did, however, continue to work elsewhere until his death in 1694. On 28.V.1684 he was appointed architect to the Prince of Carignano, replacing Guarini in that post, and held it for ten years until his death. Baroncello received payment for super-

8. See Chicco, p. 98.
9. For Valperga see Carlo Brayda, Laura Coli and Dario Sesia, 'Ingegneri e architetti del sei e settecento in Piemonte', *Atti e Rassegna Technica della Società degli Ingegneri e architetti in Torino*, XVII, 1963, pp. 66–67. Documents for the church at Verrua may be found in AST, Sez. Riunite, Art. 200: Reg. Quarto–1681, f. 8, and for the fortifications and castello at Vercelli in Art. 205: Reg. 1665 to 1671, f. 2 and Art. 205, separate volume dated 1675 devoted entirely to the fortifications at Vercelli.
There is considerable confusion surrounding the work of the Valpergas. The father, Conte Maurizio, appears to have been a contemporary of Conte Carlo Castellamonte and to have worked on S. Carlo, Turin, the Eremo dei Camaldolesi, and the Certosa at Collegno (see Brayda, Coli, Sesia, p. 67). Of the two sons, the Barone Antonio Maurizio also became primo ingegnere on 20.III.1667 (Galli della Loggia, II, pp. 258 f.), and appears to have done most of the work in the late seventeenth century. Conte Andrea, the first born, was also an engineer-architect but never more than ingegnere ordinario (25.IV.1676, Galli della Loggia, II, pp. 296 f.). The Barone Antonio Maurizio went south

with Tommaso di Savoia-Carignano on the ill-fated French-Savoy expedition to conquer the kingdom of Naples. He was captured and imprisoned there. While in prison, he wrote several military treatises, the manuscripts of which are now in the Biblioteca Nazionale of Turin. See note 6.
10. Baroncello's birth date is unknown. He died during the first quarter of 1694 (AST, Sez. 1°, Registri della casa di Emanuele Filiberto di Savoia-Carignano, Ristretto 1694: Cap. 99). He is first noted in Turin as the 'giovane' of Conte Amedeo di Castellamonte in 1673 (AST, Sez. Riunite, Patenti Controllo Finanze (hereafter PCF) 1673 in 1674, f. 92 v). He remained in this position throughout Castellamonte's lifetime. At Castellamonte's death he assumed the direction of much of the work formerly entrusted to Castellamonte. In January 1674 he was appointed supervisor of the new enlargement of the city towards the Po (AST, Sez. Riunite, Art. 201: Reg. 1673, 13.I.1674, f. 100). On the sixteenth of the same month, he was delegated to design the fortifications for the new enlargement (AST, Sez. Riunite, Art. 197: Reg. 1676 in 1677, f. 261). As Castellamonte's assistant he went everywhere with him. On 8.x.1676 he was advanced a sum of money to be used on a trip he was to take with Castellamonte into the Susa Valley.
In 1677 Baroncello was made the supervisor of construction of the new Accademia and Zecca designed by Castellamonte (AST, Sez. Riunite, Art. 205: Reg. 1679 in 1680). In 1678 Baroncello was given the job of laying out, and probably designing, Piazza Carlina (AST, Sez. Riunite, Art. 205: Reg. 1678). It was most likely Baroncello who changed the octagonal plan to the rectangle it is today. In the 1680's he began supervising work done on the Nuova Dogana as well as continuing with his former jobs. When Castellamonte began building the Ospedale Maggiore di San Giovanni in 1680, Baroncello probably received the supervision job. It is certain that at Castellamonte's death Baroncello assumed direction of the work (S. Rovere, *Relazione Storico dell'Ospedale Maggiore di San Giovanni Battista e della Città di Torino*, Turin, 1876, p. 27). The construction of the hospital was largely completed by 1689. In 1683 the Marchese Marc'Antonio Graneri della Roccia, Abbot of Entremont, began building his palace on Via Bogino in Turin. The authorship of the design is still in question. It is certain, however, that from late 1683 onwards Baroncello was in charge of the work. The design of the palace has been attributed to Castellamonte (Schede, Soprintendenza ai Monumenti del Piemonte), and to Garove (TCI Guide, *Torino e Valle d'Aosta*, Milan, 1959, p. 95). Most other authors give the design to Baroncello. G. Chevalley, 'Il Palazzo Carignano a Torino', *Bollettino della Società Piemontese di Archeologia e Belle Arti*, V, 1921, p. 13, n. 1, says that a Professor Vacchetta owned a drawing that indicated Guarini was the author of the design of the main stair. I have not been able to locate the drawing.
11. AST, Sez. Riunite, Art. 205: Reg. 1685 in 1686, f. 67 and f. 69.

vision and various designs for the Palace at Turin and the Castello at Racconigi.[12] The church of the Beata Vergine del Pilone at Moretta was built according to his designs from 1685 to 1691.[13] In 1692 Baroncello began work on the entrance, atrium, stair, and grand salone of the unfinished Palazzo di Druent (Palazzo Barolo). Final decoration was under way in 1693.[14] The Palazzo Graneri, built 1682–1683, has traditionally been given to him but there have always been other names (Guarini, Garove) associated with it also. The Provana di Druent and the Graneri, if it be by him, are his most significant works. Baroncello's architecture shows influence of both Guarini (atria of Graneri and Provana di Druent) and Castellamonte (exterior wall treatment of Graneri). Guarinesque detail predominates in both the Graneri and Provana di Druent. Baroncello left no followers.

Carlo Emanuele Lanfranchi (1632–1721), son of the architect Francesco, at Castellamonte's death took over the responsibility for work done on the Palazzo Reale. In 1684 he was the designer of the extension and widening of the east wing that was to face the new garden to the east,[15] and somewhat later of the gallery (Galleria del Daniel) connecting Palazzo Madama to the Palazzo Reale. He also did some work at the Venaria Reale in 1695 but was superseded there in 1697 by Rocco Rubatti,[16] and was also superseded at the Palazzo Reale by Garove in 1697. As a designer he drops from the accounts in the late 1690's though he continues to hold supervisory posts at the Castelli of Moncalieri and Mirafiore until his death.[17] Aside from the Galleria del Daniel, Lanfranchi did little of importance and had little influence on his contemporaries.

Antonio Bertola (1647–1719) worked on at least three of the buildings Guarini left unfinished—SS. Sindone, where he designed both the inlaid marble floor and the main altar; S. Filippo Neri;[18] and the Palazzo Carignano. His work was strongly Guarinesque in the 90's but became more sober and traditional. He did not develop a distinct individual character until the beginning of the next century.[19] At Garove's death in 1713 Bertola assumed many of his duties as he already had, in 1699, at S. Filippo Neri.

IV

Michelangelo Garove was the most creative of the architects who succeeded Guarini and Castellamonte. He took full responsibility for the Collegio dei Nobili where he had already been supervisor,[20] and, at the death of Baroncello, became architect to the Prince of Carignano.[21] In 1684 he designed the Palazzo Asinari di San Marzano and in the 1690's the Morozzo della Rocca.[22] By the turn of the century Garove was involved in virtually all major ducal construction. He was responsible for designs and work done at the

12. On 7.VIII.1679 Baroncello had been paid 58.12 lire for measuring the site of the Palazzo Carignano and the site in the Piazza Carlina where fill was to be excavated (AST, Sez. Riunite, Azienda Savoia-Carignano, Registro per la fabrica del Nuovo Palazzo). On 11.XII.1683 Baroncello was paid 300 lire for drawings relating to the new palace and the Castello at Racconigi (AST, Sez. 1°, Registri della casa di Emanuele Filiberto di Savoia-Carignano, Registro XXII, 1682 in 1683, f. 211 v). He was appointed architect to the prince at an annual stipend of 400 lire on 28.V.1684 (ibid., Reg. XXIII, 1684 in 1687, f. 13 r). Of no more than passing interest is that Baroncello had a son baptized in the fall of 1689 and the festivities that accompanied the occasion were paid for (59 lire) by the Prince of Carignano (ibid., Registro XXV, 1689 in 1692, f. 111). See also H. Millon, 'L'altare maggiore della chiesa di San Filippo Neri di Torino', Bollettino della Società Piemontese di Archeologia e Belle Arti (hereafter BSPABA), NS XIV–XV, 1960–1, p. 86.

13. See P. G. Gallizia, Istoria della prodigiosa immagine della SS. V. Maria del Pilone venerata in Moretta, first published 1718, and republished in Saluzzo, 1886, and F. G. Lardone, Il Santuario della Beata Vergine del Pilone in Moretta, Saluzzo, 1934.

14. Documents pertaining to the palace exist in the Archivio Opera Pia Barolo (Mazzi d'addizioni, volumes 115, 116, and 117). Volume 117 is divided into four sections. The first section contains a list of payments according to trades. The second lists all payments made to the general contractors and stone workers. The fourth devoted to painters is quite detailed. For the Palazzo Barolo see L. Fenoglio, Il Palazzo dei Marchese di Barolo, Turin, 1928, and G. C. Dall'Armi, Il Barocco Piemontese, Turin, 1915.

15. AST, Sez. Riunite, Art. 201: Reg. 1682 in 1684, 2°, f. 125, dated 20.III.1684, contains contracts for the 'paviglione del palazzo reale verso levante e mezzanotte...' in accord with designs of C. E. Lanfranchi. See also Art. 199: Reg. Quarto, 1683 in 1684, f. 125 v, Art. 199: Reg. 1685 in 1688, ff. 26–37, Art. 205: Reg. 1692 in 1693, f. 131 and Art. 205: Reg. 1695, f. 42.

16. AST, Sez. Riunite, Art. 199: Reg. Nono, 1694 in 1695, ff. 175–83 contains the work being done under Lanfranchi's supervision. AST, Sez. Riunite, Art. 199: Reg. Decimo, 1695 in 1697, ff. 91–94 v indicates that all work being done was under the supervision of and according to the designs of Rocco Rubatti.

17. His name is however reported in the accounts for work done on the room next to the Galleria del Daniel in 1713, see Brayda, Coli, Sesia, op. cit., p. 45.

18. See G. Chevalley, 'Vicende Costruttive della chiesa di San Filippo Neri in Torino', Bollettino del Centro di Studi Archeologici ed Artistici del Piemonte, II, 1942, and H. Millon, 'L'Altare maggiore della chiesa di San Filippo Neri di Torino', Bollettino della Società Piemontese di Archeologia e Belle Arti, N.S. XIV–XV, 1960–1.

19. See N. Carboneri, 'Antonio Bertola e la confraternità di Santa Croce in Cuneo', Boll. Società degli Studi Storici, archeologici ed artistici nella provincia di Cuneo, N.S. XXVII, 1950, and N. Carboneri, L'Architetto Franceso Gallo, Turin, 1954, pp. 42–44.

20. Scheda, Soprintendenza ai monumenti del Piemonte.

21. See notes 37 and 38.

22. For the Asinari di San Marzano palace see Guido Asinari di San Marzano, Gli Asinari di San Marzano, Alessandria, 1937. For the Palazzo Morozzo della Rocca see D. De Bernardi Ferrero, 'Il Palazzo Morozzo della Rocca', Atti e Rassegna Tecnica..., N.S. XIII, 1959, pp. 451–61, and C. Merlini, 'La Camera di Comercio', Torino, August 1932, pp. 94–103.

Palazzo Reale, Venaria Reale, and, until his death, the University.[23] More than any other single architect it was Garove who gave direction, or rather, maintained the direction set by Guarini, for the period between the death of Guarini and Castellamonte and the arrival of Juvarra (i.e., 1683–1715). The death of both Garove (1713) and Bertola (1719), when coupled with the advent of Juvarra, terminated the direct influence of Guarini and saw the beginning of a new wave of Academic Roman influence that swept up Francesco Gallo (1672–1750) and Gian Giacomo Plantery (1680–1756).

Although Garove entered ducal service in 1669 he did no independent architectural design until the Chapel of the Beato Amedeo.[24] He had served as assistant and later supervisor of the fortification at Ceva,[25] as assistant to Amedeo Castellamonte at the Venaria Reale,[26] assistant in the expansion of the city to the Po,[27] and as supervisor of construction at the Collegio dei Nobili,[28] but it was not until after his design for the Cappella del Beato Amedeo was selected that he is first specifically mentioned as designer of the fortifications at Cherasco.[29] From 1682–1683 onwards Garove appears in the documents as 'Ingegnere' and no longer as a 'sovrastante' or 'assistente'. In 1684 alone he designed the Palazzo Asinari di San Marzano (his

finest palace) in Turin,[30] new *caserme* at the Cittadella of Mondovì,[31] main altar of the Cappella del Beato Amedeo, churches of the Annunziata and S. Martino, both at La Morra.[32] S. Giovanni in Sommariva Bosco was begun in 1685 according to his designs,[33] and in 1687 he designed the main altar for S. Remigo in Carignano.[34] The following year he became prior of the Confraternità di San Luca.[35] In 1691 he was again supplying fortification designs for Cuneo.[36] The Prince of Carignano, Emanuele Filiberto, appointed Garove his architect in 1697, a post he held until 1699.[37] During his tenure he designed and began construction of the main altar of San Filippo Neri, one of the most influential altars of the end of the century.[38] In 1699 he designed a new palace being constructed in the Cittadella at Turin,[39] and a new ice house for the Palazzo Reale.[40] In 1699–1700 he began the series of designs of various rooms and pavilions at the Venaria Reale finally culminating in the Grand Gallery and terminating pavilions that were begun in 1703.[41] Before the war years he designed the provisional Corpo di Guardia at Porta Susina in 1703,[42] and during the war worked on fortifications. After the end of the war work began again at the Venaria Reale and Garove supplied designs for the new Mandria (horse-breeding farm) nearby.[43] Just before his death in 1713 Garove

23. For the Pal. Reale see 4.II.1701, AST, Sez. Riunite, Art. 199: Reg. Duodecimo, 1698 in 1700, f. 207; 14.IV.1701. Art. 205: Reg. XIII, 1701 in 1705, ff. 20 v–23 v; 23.VI.1701. Art. 205: Reg. XIII, 1701 in 1705, f. 67 v; 2.IX.1701. Art. 199: Reg. XIII, 1701 in 1705, f. 17. For the Venaria Reale see notes 41 and 43. For the University see note 44. Garove is also reported as working at the Castello di Rivoli 1711–13 (A. E. Brinckmann, *Theatrum Novum Pedemontii*, Dusseldorf, 1931, p. 88).

24. In a gift from the crown to Garove dated 5.IX.1699 mention is made of thirty years' service (AST, Sez. Riunite, Patenti del Piemonte, vol. 130, f. 172 v). Accordingly, Garove entered ducal service sometime in 1669 at the age of 19 although the first payment found is dated 25.III.1672 (AST, Sez. Riunite, Patenti Controllo Finanze (PCF), 1671 in 1672, f. 141 v). There is the possibility of exaggeration however since in a letter asking for financial assistance dated 23.x.1694 Garove mentions his more than 23 years' service, which would indicate he began working for the crown in 1671 when he was 21 (A. Baudi di Vesme, *L'Arte in Piemonte dal XVI al XVIII Secolo*, vol. I, Turin, 1963). Garove was, incidentally, captured and imprisoned by the Genoese in 1672 (AST, Sez. Riunite, PCF, 1672 in 1673, ff. 110 and 131).

25. AST, Sez. Riunite, Art. 195: Reg. 1672-3, f. 63 r; PCF, 1673 in 1674, f. 7 v; PCF, 1674 in 1675, f. 203 r; Art. 197: Reg. 1674–6, f. 11.

26. AST, Sez. Riunite, Art. 207: Venaria Reale, 1674 in 1675. A testimonial dated 30.v.1679 signed by Garove stated that in the spring of 1674 he was 'assistente' at the Venaria Reale.

27. 15.XII.1675. AST, Sez. Riunite, Art. 197: 1674 in 1676, f. 191 v.

28. 12.IX.1680 Garove begins work as 'Sovrastante' at the Collegio dei Nobili (see Scheda, Soprintendenza ai monumenti del Piemonte).

29. 8.x.1683. AST, Sez. Riunite, Art. 199: Reg. 1683 in 1684, ff. 55 ff.

30. See G. Asinari di San Marzano, *Gli Asinari di San Marzano*, Alessandria, 1937.

31. 25.v.1684. AST, Sez. Riunite, Art. 199: Reg. 1683 in 1684, ff. 164 ff.

32. G. Casalis, *Dizionario storico-geografico per gli Stati Sardi*, XI, Turin, 1850, p. 428.

33. S. B. Alasia, *Storia del Santuario della Madonna di San Giovanni in Sommariva del Bosco*, Carmagnola, 1880.

34. Brayda, Coli, Sesia, 1963, p. 39.

35. A. Baudi di Vesme, 1963.

36. 21.III.1691. AST, Sez. Riunite, Art. 199: Reg. Settimo, 1688 in 1691, f. 217 v.

37. 19.XII.1697. AST, Sez. Primo, Registri della casa di Emanuele Filiberto di Savoia-Carignano, Reg. XXVII, 1695 in 1698, f. 393.

38. H. Millon, 'L'Altare maggiore della chiesa di San Filippo Neri in Torino', BSPABA, NS XIV–XV, 1960–1.

39. 29.v.1699. AST, Sez. Riunite, Art. 199: Reg. Duodecimo, 1688 in 1700, f. 151.

40. 18.XI.1699. *Ibid.*, f. 160.

41. 28.VII.1700. AST, Sez. Riunite, Art. 810, Venaria Reale, mazzo 1–11, no. 40; 4.II.1701. Art. 205: Reg. XI, 1699 in 1700, f. 103. Tilleto dated 4.II.1703 advertising construction of the 'Grande Galleria indrittura della testa del Paviglione risguardante il luogho d'essa Venaria Reale . . .' and asking for bids (found inserted at f. 19 of Art. 199: Reg. 1711 in 1715). Contract awarded on 27.III.1703 to capi mastri Francesco Pagano, Domenico Fontana, Antonio Camerata, Giovanni Cappone, and Giuseppe Fontana (AST, Sez. Riunite, Art. 193: Reg. 1703, ff. 100–7).

42. 4.IX.1703. AST, Sez. Riunite, Art. 199: Reg. XIII, 1701 in 1705, f. 110.

43. *Venaria*: 14.XI.1708. AST, Sez. Riunite, Art. 193: Reg. 1708, ff. 117, 129; 23.XI.1708. Art. 199: Reg. xv, 1707 in 1708, f. 40. *Regia Mandria*: 15.XI.1708. *Ibid.*, f. 137. 3.XII.1708. Art. 199: Reg. xv, 1707 in 1708, ff. 44–46 v, contract was awarded on this date to Eusebio Bello, muratore.

designed the new university which was executed partially following his designs.[44]

As the first independent work leading to a productive final thirty years, the Cappella del Beato Amedeo is, for Garove, an important work. In it, as well as the works done in the 1680's, his close relationship to and admiration for Guarini are apparent.

There is little remarkable (other than its size) about the plan for the chapel. It is in the architectural detail that a debt to Guarini is most apparent, particularly in the two tomb-niches, the Palladian windows above them, and the columns.[45] Spiral fluting for the lower third of the column is probably closely related to both Guarini and Castellamonte.[46] The tomb-niches and Palladian windows (Fig. 10) are specifically Guarinesque.

The Palladian motif is common in Guarini's work from the 1660's to the end of his career and is almost a hallmark of his work.[47] The similarity between the Palladian windows in S. Gaetano Vicenza, S. Lorenzo Turin, and the chapel in Vercelli with respect to the position of the window (always under the main arches), the size of the window with respect to the arch (almost filling the lunette), and the similarity of proportions of the side spaces to the central space in each of the examples clearly demonstrate the dependence on Guarini.

Much the same can be said about the tomb-niches. Guarini often unified the three parts of a Palladian motif by joining, with a broad curve, the raised segmental pediment in the center to the reverse curved broken pediments over the horizontal entablature.[48] There is no prior example of this compositional problem or proposed solution in Garove's work.

A more inclusive idea of Garove's original design for the chapel must include windows at the attic level that are now missing. From the circular passageway at the attic level there remain four walled-up oval windows leading into the chapel. Before being closed these windows would have added light to the chapel and may have produced a different effect.

Since all the decorative stucco work, from the pendentives to the lantern of the chapel, probably dates from the remodelling in 1759–1761, it is likely that the attic windows were closed in at that period. The existence of these walled-up windows means that Barberis' alterations were extensive. The dome and drum configuration at present should not necessarily be considered to bear any resemblance to the original.

The remainder of the decoration of the lower portion of the chapel dating from Garove's tenure are the doorways and *coretti* on the diagonals of the chapel. They, like the plan itself, are more sober, more closely related to the tradition represented by Castellamonte particularly in the character of decorative detail.[49] In both plan and decorative detail the chapel shows

44. A. M. Brizio, *L'architettura Barocca in Piemonte*, Turin, 1953, pp. 3–4. Garove's drawings for the University are preserved in the Archivio di Stato, Turin (3 plans dated 9.VI, 10.VI, 15.VI.1712; two courtyard façades dated 20.II, 22.II.1713), and in the Cab. des Estampes, Paris (façade dated 3.III.1713).

45. The custom of incised fluting or reverse fluting for the lower third only of a column or pilaster was probably introduced to the Piedmont by Guarini in his design for S. Lorenzo (1666). F. Lanfranchi responded immediately (or chose it himself independently) at about the same time for the main columns of S. Rocco, Turin.

46. Spiral fluting for the lower third of the column is probably closely related to both Guarini and Castellamonte. In the Piedmont the only five known seventeenth-century instances of the use of spiral fluting for the lower third of the column are in the Cappella del Beato Amedeo, the Palazzo Asinari di S. Marzano (1684), both by Garove, the atrium of the Palazzo Provana di Druent (1692) by Baroncello, the façade of S. Giuseppe in Carignano (1677?) attributed to Castellamonte and Guarini, and the interior of Corpus Domini, Turin, date uncertain (probably 1660–70's), also attributed to A. Castellamonte (the renovations of Benedetto Alfieri done in 1753 are confined to the vaulting).

47. It makes its first appearance, in a modified form, on the main façade above the central door in Guarini's S. Anne Royale, in Paris. The Palladian window can be found in one place or another in almost every building built or projected thereafter. Of particular pertinence in this context are the windows at the Cappella del Arcivescovado in Turin, the project for S. Gaetano in Vicenza and San Lorenzo in Turin. At San Gaetano and at San Lorenzo, four Palladian windows under the main arches are the only light sources at the lower level. The windows in each of the two are very similar to those in the Beato Amedeo chapel.

48. This unification is, naturally, a perennial problem for any Baroque architect who uses a Palladian motif and in Guarini's work, in the courtyard façade of the Carignano Palace in Turin, the courtyard façade of the Castello in Govone, and on Plate XVI of Trattato III in his *Architettura Civile* several solutions are suggested. Other less well-known examples are the projects of the interior of San Gaetano in Vicenza and the façade of S. Filippo Neri in Turin. In both plan and decorative detail the chapel shows characteristics recognizably like those Garove was to employ in the later 1680's.

49. It is too simple however to say the 'Castellamonte Tradition' for Castellamonte himself had at least two definable decorative manners. His plans, spaces, structures, exterior mass forms and relationship to the surrounding environment are not particularly imaginative but his use of decorative detail was at times highly personal. In his work at the Venaria Reale and Palazzo Lascaris (1665) he displayed wilful, florid decorative detail. In both buildings Castellamonte employed detail that was full of unrelieved tensions produced principally by the sharply contrasting forms and pronounced alterations of rhythm and structure. Castellamonte's use of other sober detail is found in the façade of the Palazzo Reale (1658), the Palazzo Ferrero d'Ormea, and the Ospedale Maggiore. The existence of two 'manners' was not confined to Castellamonte alone. F. Lanfranchi (16 . . –1669) employed vigorous, florid, and even contradictory elements of detail in the church of the Eremo (pilaster capitals) at Lanzo (1663) while at S. Rocco (in spite of a new use of free-standing columns on the interior) and the Pal. Civico in Turin he employed sober, dignified, and traditional architectural detail. It was most likely A. Costaguta (16 . . –1670) who first practiced in Turin two widely divergent decorative manners. See for example the contradictory attitudes expressed in his Vigna di M. Reale (now Villa Abegg) of 1648–53 and in S. Teresa (1642). Costaguta remains a nebulous figure though his name appears frequently in ducal accounts.

characteristics recognizably like those Garove was to employ in the later 1680's.

V

The principal characteristics of Garove's architecture are already defined in the Cappella del Beato Amedeo. His plans and sections are not particularly imaginative. Neither his spaces nor his use of structure are inventive. His work does however show a developing interest in lighting. The oval windows (now closed) of the drum of the Cappella del Beato Amedeo would have increased the quantity of light at ground level and the dome-drum area would have been more open than at present. Certainly his design for the Grand Gallery at the Venaria Reale (a single long room two stories high with two ranges of windows from floor to vault on both sides) would have been remarkably open.[50]

His decorative vocabulary stems from Guarini and Castellamonte. The Guarini influence is both more pronounced and more continuous. In the Palazzo Asinari di San Marzano the primary effect derives not from the ordinary plan and staircase but from the spectacular, dramatic centralized atrium (Fig. 12), derived from the Palazzo Carignano. The atrium is vaulted by a star-shaped vault similar to that in the Carignano but with greater emphasis on the central medallion and ribs.[51] The vault is supported by the four dramatic double spiral columns that define the center and periphery of the atrium. The primary interest of the atrium derives from its close relationship to the Carignano.

---

50. The shape and dimensions of the gallery as we know it today are primarily due to Garove's design and execution. Juvarra enlarged and changed the shape of the oval windows at the second level and applied the decorative skin.

51. Stucco work in the atrium was executed by Pietro Somasso who later worked on the Carignano. See H. Millon, *Guarino Guarini and the Palazzo Carignano in Turin*, dissertation, 1963, Harvard University, Cambridge, Massachusetts, p. 217, n. 102.

Garove's decorative vocabulary did not grow substantially nor significantly change its character over his lifetime. Still he was the man who assumed most of the principal architectural responsibility for the duchy from 1684 to his death in 1713. That his abilities were limited was recognized by the duke. In 1699 the duke sent his new designs for the Venaria Reale to France for criticism by Robert Decotte, chief collaborator to J. H. Mansart, architect to Louis XIV.

In spite of Garove's limitations, in order to understand the architectural production in the Piedmont between Guarini and Castellamonte's death and the coming of Juvarra, it is to Garove that we must turn. Once Garove is recognized as the chief figure among a group of second-rate architects and his formative influences distinguished, many of the conflicting currents and influences found in his contemporaries may be seen more clearly.

Garove himself is the result of conflicting influences of Guarini and Castellamonte. From Castellamonte he took the requirement for straight-forward, no-nonsense planning and spatial organization (here the atrium of the Palazzo Asinari is an exception). From Guarini he took what occasional emphasis he places on structural form (Asinari and Galleria in the Venaria Reale), lighting, and decorative detail. From Guarini's decorative detail Garove took luxuriant non-geometric curvilinear forms and the richly contrasting use of colored marbles (dark red, black, intense yellow-ochre, rich greys, etc.) with gilded bronze and vibrant, exposed terracotta exterior surfaces. From Castellamonte he took a more restrained use of traditional architectural detail as well as license for an occasional leap backward into the world of mannerist detail.

Garove's strength, his contribution, and individuality consist in the degree to which he fused these two (or three) contradictory attitudes into a reasonably cohesive single direction that by virtue of its inclusiveness was to dominate Piedmontese architecture for thirty years.

WOLFGANG HERRMANN

Unknown Designs for the 'Temple of Jerusalem' by Claude Perrault

Louis Compiègne de Veil, a seventeenth-century Hebrew scholar of Jewish origin, was the first to embark on the formidable task of translating into Latin the Mishneh Torah or Code of Maimonides. After having published a few chapters of the Third and Fifth Books, he turned to Book Eight, the Book of the Temple Service. Its first chapter dealt with the measurements of the Temple of Jerusalem to which Veil wished to join explanatory designs. For that reason, he approached 'Monsieur Perrault, an authority in Physical Sciences, Medicine and, above all, in the Fine Arts'. Thereupon, Perrault, having studied the text, 'depicted with his own hand the shape of the Temple as described by Maimonides, arranged the [illustrations] on three plates and added also a remarkable (explanatory) discourse'.[1] The book was published in Paris in 1678. One year later it was in the hands of Leibniz, interested in both Maimonides's philosophy and Perrault's architecture; in May of that year Leibniz wrote a letter to Johann Graevius, the eminent classical scholar, drawing his correspondent's attention to this book and its illustrations which, he pointed out, were the work of 'Perrotius Medicus Parisiensis et Architectus insignis'. Leibniz's only other comment on these illustrations was to the effect that 'they are very different from those made by Villalpandus'.[2]

And indeed, the difference is immense (Figs. 1 and 2). Villalpandus makes the Temple the focus of a huge grid of eight courtyards; Perrault places it within the walled-in square of the Temple ground, distinctly out of center. Villalpandus covers the whole ground with various buildings enclosing Temple and courts and even extends the ground on all sides by a further courtyard surrounded by porticoes, whereas Perrault leaves the major part of the ground free so that the built-up area of his design takes up only a tenth of the area filled by the complex buildings planned by Villalpandus. Perrault refrains from making use of a single

column, Villalpandus provides 1,500 of them. Columns, pilasters, entablatures, the whole formal grammar of classical architecture are summoned for the decoration of Villalpandus's elevations, while Perrault's façade of the Temple is a plain, square wall of layers of roughly hewn stones, and only the cornice, the balusters of the parapet and of galleries, and the semi-circular windows give an indication of the age to which these drawings belong (Fig. 3).[3]

Moreover, Villalpandus's and Perrault's viewpoints differed as much as their designs. Villalpandus's chief object in writing the *Explanationes in Ezechielem* was to prove that the Temple of the Prophet's vision was identical with that built by Solomon and that, because this Temple was the model of the Christian Church to come, the symbolical significance of Solomon's Temple far outweighed the reality of its existence in the past. Having been designed by God, it necessarily was a perfect building, and since the only style capable of perfection was the classical one, it was this style, emanating from God, in which the Temple had to be clothed.[4] Perrault, in whose opinion custom constantly changed the standard of beauty, disagreed. Deriding architects for looking upon Greek and Roman monuments with almost religious reverence, he ironically concluded that their attitude would only be consistent if 'they were of Villalpandus's opinion who maintains that God had taught the architects of the Temple of Solomon all these proportions by special inspiration and that the Greeks, who are generally believed to have invented them, have in fact learned them from these architects'.[5]

---

3. Perrault's third plate pictures the Table of Shewbread and the Altar. Since the problems connected with these were far less controversial, and mainly involve questions of ritual, they will not be dealt with in this article. Neither, of course, will it be relevant to examine how far the assertions and conjectures brought forward during the period under review stood up to the results of modern research. For its present position two comprehensive books can be consulted: F. J. Hollis, *The Archaeology of Herod's Temple*, London, 1934, and L. Vincent and M.-A. Steve, *Jérusalem de l'ancien testament*, Paris, 1954.
4. Villalpandus (no. 12), II, pp. 31, 28, 17; for divine origin of classical style see pp. 44 ff., 70, 374, 414 ff.
5. *Ordonnance des cinq espèces de colonnes*, Paris, 1683, p. XVIII. Another biting remark about Villalpandus's irrational belief in the biblical origin of Vitruvian rules already in *Vitruvius*, Paris, 1673, p. 78, n. 2.

---

1. *De Cultu Divino*, Preface. For the full title and other bibliographical data see no. 29 of the appended list of sources. In the following notes the number in brackets behind a title or an author's name refers to this appendix.
2. Gottfried Wilhelm Leibniz, *Sämtliche Schriften und Briefe*, Darmstadt, 1923 ff., 1 Reihe, II, pp. 475 f.

Perrault's remark obviously implied that no architect in his senses could accept this absurd idea. François Blondel too did not believe in the divine origin of the Orders; Solomon's Temple was for him but one of many landmarks in the architectural evolution.[6] French architectural writers of the seventeenth century seem on the whole to have been indifferent to Villalpandus's main argument, even though Fréart published Villalpandus's Solomonic Order and Ouvrard attempted to demonstrate the correctness of his proportional system through the measurements of the Temple of Jerusalem.[7] However, the impression of passive detachment ceases as soon as one passes from architectural to theological writers, and changes into a strong and critical reaction. A review of this reaction seems relevant to the evaluation of Perrault's designs which impress as being singularly independent from the designs of Villalpandus who, one tends to assume, overshadowed and greatly influenced all succeeding interpretations of the seventeenth century. The next few pages will attempt this review; thereafter we shall proceed to a closer examination of Perrault's designs.

*   *   *

Only five years after the *Explanationes* had been published in Rome, there appeared in Milan the *Annales Sacri* by the distinguished member of the Barnabite Order, Agostino Tornielli, a work that went over the next fifty years into many editions.[8] Having reached the reign of Solomon, Tornielli dealt extensively with the first Temple as known through the Scriptures and also, further on in his chronicle, with the testimony of Ezechiel. While he reiterated the orthodox view that the Temple as seen by Ezechiel stood as symbol for the future Christian Church, he emphatically rejected Villalpandus's main postulate that the visionary and the Solomonic Temple were identical. Ezechiel's Temple had for Tornielli no other than a spiritual existence; therefore it was, in his opinion, wrong to infer the appearance of the historical Temple built by Solomon from the image, however detailed, which God had shown to Ezechiel.[9] Furthermore, it was quite improbable, Tornielli argued, that Solomon's Temple was built in the style of the Greeks and Romans. The style in current use in Syria at Solomon's

time must have been as different from that introduced much later by Greeks and Romans as was the style of his, Tornielli's, time from that which had flourished in Northern Europe two hundred years earlier. Time always gave rise to changes, specially in the Arts, progressing from primitive beginnings to ever-increasing perfection. Solomon's Temple was, he proved in detail, of comparatively small size, and therefore Villalpandus's elaborate reconstruction had no historical foundation. The real Temple could not possibly have had the extensive porticoes and buildings surrounding the great number of courts that were such a striking feature of 'the very fine drawings of Villalpandus'.[10] When, later in the *Annales*, he was dealing with Herod's Temple, he once again became critical of Villalpandus. The disagreement arose from Villalpandus's belief that there could be only one model for the Christian Church.[11] For that reason, he not only had to insist on the identity of Solomon's and Ezechiel's Temples, but also had to deny that the Herodian Temple surpassed its predecessors in size and magnificence. He therefore disparaged the veracity of the chief witness, Josephus—in Tornielli's view without any justification—and furthermore argued that it was impossible for the morally weak Herod to surpass the work of the godfearing Solomon.[12] This notion too Tornielli rejected, pointing out that crucifixes made by morally inferior but competent artists were not less venerated than those made by morally good artists, an argument that is rather surprising considering the period and Tornielli's standing.[13]

Tornielli's objections were thus directed against the distortion of historical process. He rejected the application of the classical style from the viewpoint of the historian, and not because he felt outraged about Villalpandus's attempt to reconcile the Bible with Humanism. If this really was Villalpandus's main objective, as it has recently been claimed, no trace of disapproval directed against this conception can be detected among the theological writers.[14] On the contrary, even those who criticized his reconstruction invariably acclaimed the beauty and elegance of the designs. We know of an opposition against Villalpandus's interpretation by a group of men led by Arias

6. *Cours d'architecture*, Paris, 1675, I, part II, chap. I, p. 2.
7. Fréart de Chambray, *Parallèle de l'architecture*, Paris, 1650, p. 70; René Ouvrard, *Architecture harmonique*, Paris, 1679, Dédication and p. 12. Members of the Academy were highly sceptical about the archaeological soundness of Villalpandus's Order (*Procès-verbaux*, III, p. 246 (3 May 1706).
8. Tornielli (no. 14).
9. *Ibid.*, II, p. 12. I quote from the enlarged edition of 1620. The first edition contains already most of these critical remarks. The main biblical passages dealing with the Temple are: I Kings 6, 7 (Vulgata. 3 Kings 6, 7), 2 Chronicles 2–5, Ezechiel 40–43.

10. *Ibid.*, pp. 15 f.
11. *Op. cit.*, pp. 28, 34 f.
12. *Ibid.*, pp. 576 ff., 588 ff. Josephus's account of the Temple is given in his *Antiquities*, XV, 11, and *Jewish War*, V, 5.
13. *Op. cit.*, pp. 551 ff. The last remark on p. 557. Tornielli added this rejection of Villalpandus's attack on Josephus to the edition of 1620.
14. R. C. Taylor, 'El Padre Villalpando (1552–1608) y sus ideas esteticas', *Academia. Anales y Boletin de la Real Academia de San Fernando*, 1952, p. 9.

Montano. Their motive has been thought to stem from their anti-humanistic attitude.[15] Arias himself, a great authority on the exegesis of the Bible, had published several decades earlier his views on the Temple together with a set of designs.[16] Although these are artistically greatly inferior to Villalpandus's competent drawings, they, nevertheless, show that Arias too thought in terms of the classical style.[17] But, more than that, we have his own testimony. As early as 1572 he expressed the opinion that, if the architectural measurements and numbers mentioned in the Bible were carefully examined, one would certainly admit that the style of the Greeks and Romans 'either came to them from [the Bible] or that it is praised and famed just for this reason, namely that it is not unlike [the biblical measurements]'.[18] However, in contrast to Villalpandus, Arias's outlook was historical. Solomon's Temple was, according to him, not the sacrosanct work of God, perfect from the moment of its creation, but had undergone subsequent alterations like any other historical building; the measurements of the second Temple were prescribed by Cyrus and differed in many respects from the first and—most objectionable to Villalpandus—the Temple built anew by Herod surpassed Solomon's in size and magnificence.[19] All this runs counter to everything Villalpandus believed in. Arias, like Tornielli, certainly attacked Villalpandus's unhistorical method, not his aesthetic partiality.[20]

Not only was Villalpandus criticized for his assertion that the form of Solomon's Temple could be deduced from Ezechiel's vision, not only was the classical style judged to be an anachronism, but a number of writers also disapproved of the size he had chosen. Ezechiel uses two units for measuring, the cubit and the calamos, consisting of six cubits. In one instance he vaccilates between the two units and describes the total area as a square of 500 calamos and in the next verse as a square of only 500 cubits which makes the first area 36 times larger than the second, an inconsistency that had puzzled almost every commentator.[21] Villalpandus was here in a particular difficulty. On the one hand, he was convinced that Solomon's Temple had surpassed all the Seven Wonders of the Old World, on the other hand, he insisted that God had presented to Ezechiel the future Christian Church not in a vague vision but in such a detailed image of the particular Temple that had been built by Solomon on a grandiose but nevertheless realistic scale that Ezechiel, so Villalpandus believed, had in fact produced exact drawings. One of the principles that guided Villalpandus was the notion that only by repeating the process, namely by producing accurate drawings, could the true inner meaning of the vision be grasped.[22] He, therefore, had to compromise between the two conflicting units and this he achieved through an ingenious interpretation of the text that allowed him to arrive at a square of just under 800 cubits.[23]

It was hardly surprising that his arguments found little favour. Those who followed the commentaries of the Christian Fathers and medieval writers were chiefly interested in the symbolical significance of the visionary Temple. For them Villalpandus's building was by far not extensive enough. On the other hand there were those who tried to picture the Temple as it existed either in Solomonic or Herodian times. In their view Villalpandus had blundered because his complex buildings exceeded the actual area available on Mount Morion. To the latter group belonged the French Teacher of Hebrew, Louis Cappel, who, after an extensive study of the *Explanationes*, criticized them in detail.[24] Dealing with the *atrium gentium*—the existence of which in Solomonic times he denied—he ridiculed Villalpandus's suspended outer courtyard and porticoes, built as it were 'into the empty Democritical space'. With the *raison d'être* of the *atrium gentium* gone, the gigantic substructures too became

15. The document recording the opposition against Villalpandus was published by Taylor, *op. cit.*, pp. 10 f. It gives as reason for Arias's criticism his belief that Solomon's Temple was not identical with Ezechiel's. Taylor dismisses this as theological sophistry which obscures the real cause, that is his anti-humanism. I believe that it clearly signifies fundamentally conflicting attitudes, that of the historian and that of the mystic, a conflict that is borne out by Arias's own writings (see below).

16. Arias (no. 9).

17. Particularly noticeable on a perspective view added to the reprint of 1593.

18. *Op. cit.*, VIII, p. 3: 'Si enim universa illa mensurarum, figurarum, totiusque structurae, et artificii ratio, quae sacris continetur libris, diligenter et attente consideretur, sine dubio omnem illam aedificationum rationem, quae apud Graecos et Latinos fuit, aut hinc ad ipsos effluxisse, aut certe ob eam potissimum causam, quod huic non sit absimilis, laudatam celebratamque esse fatendum erit.'

19. *Ibid.*, pp. 13 ff.

20. Taylor, *op. cit.*, p. 50, recognizes the emergence of a scientific spirit from the time of Caramuel (no. 30), but it certainly made itself felt much earlier, as the writings of Tornielli (no. 14), Cappel (no. 25) and Lightfoot (no. 24) prove, to name only a few. Taylor, p. 53, is aware of the general critical attitude, but obviously does not attach great importance to it, since the critical remarks he observed are referred to in footnotes only.

21. Vulgata, Ezechiel 42:16–20.

22. *Op. cit.*, pp. 32, 20. Also p. 1, where the title of the book is repeated with the following addition: 'Templum Salomonis ab Ezechiele descriptum imaginibus exprimendum esse.'

23. *Ibid.*, pp. 378 ff.

24. The first part of Cappel's treatise (no. 25) contains abstracts from Villalpandus's *Explanationes*; also his designs, engraved on a small scale by Wenzel Hollar. In this way, Villalpandus's book, which was expensive, became more widely known. In fact, he is sometimes quoted from these abstracts (for instance by Lund (no. 42)).

unnecessary and thus another salient feature of Villalpandus's Temple had been shown to have no historical justification.[25] Cappel's critical review was first published in the Polyglot Bible of 1657, but his views were known before they reached the press. He himself referred to lectures he had given on the subject, and there is also the independent testimony of Hugo Grotius who in 1644 recommended Villalpandus to his readers, praising his conscientiousness, good judgment in architectural matters and mastery of languages, but also expressing the wish that the observations made on Villalpandus's work by Cappel, 'a man of rare erudition', would appear in print.[26]

A few years earlier, John Lightfoot, an authority on the Temple of Jerusalem and acknowledged even today, had published his own reconstruction.[27] His aim was to present a convincing picture of the Herodian Temple, relying thereby mainly on Talmudic sources. He nowhere mentioned Villalpandus, whose work he must have known; evidently it was of no value to his historical research since he dismissed the testimony of Ezechiel altogether criticizing the unrealistic size of his Temple which could only be understood 'spiritually and mystically'.[28] With this view another English writer, Samuel Lee, agreed. He too rejected Ezechiel as a witness for 'the true figure of Solomon's Temple' and wondered 'at the costs and pains of Villalpandus' who had based his reconstruction on nothing more than a vision which 'cannot be a sound foundation for material Temple-building'.[29]

Villalpandus was also reproached for not giving sufficient weight to Jewish tradition. Saubert, a German linguist of repute, believed this to have been the cause that Villalpandus 'omitted much, was led astray and added a few completely alien things', while Johannes Lund, writing in the same year in which Perrault's designs were published, stated categorically that 'where there is no vital necessity to deviate from the traditions of the Jews, there it is only fair to believe them'.[30] It is therefore understandable that Louis Compiègne de Veil in his Preface expressed surprise that Villalpandus, after having spared no expense, time, labour and inconvenience, arrived finally at a picture of the Temple that was not a portrait of historical truth but a pattern of a lavish building. Villalpandus's main aim, in Veil's opinion, had been to show that his Temple conformed to Vitruvian principles and at the same time to prove

that Greeks and Romans received the art of building only through the careful attention given to this monument.

Considering the high quality of Villalpandus's designs, admiration would seem to be the natural reaction; the presence of widespread opposition is more surprising and undoubtedly significant. For that reason, the critical reaction has been stressed in the foregoing pages. Of course, almost unreserved acceptance of the *Explanationes* existed too. Nicolaus Goldmann's *Architectura Sacra*, written before 1665, the year of his death, was never published, but from a chapter in his *Civilbaukunst*, edited by his pupil Leonhard Sturm towards the end of the century, and from Sturm's own book on the Temple, it is obvious that both were basically in agreement with Villalpandus, even if they corrected him in details.[31] The two books made Villalpandus's work known and appreciated in Germany where his design had already appeared in a Bible of 1679.[32] This positive attitude was further strengthened through the powerful support of Fischer von Erlach who included Villalpandus's version of the Temple in his *Historische Architectur*.[33] Nothing comparable to this unreserved admiration can be found among the architectural writers outside Germany.[34] Whole-hearted approval was confined here to a few fellow members of the Jesuit Order, such as Pineda, Salian and Menochio, theological writers who in comparison to scholars of Tornielli's, Lightfoot's and Cappel's standing were only second rate.[35] However, Salian's *Annales* contains a reply to Tornielli's criticism which is interesting. If, he argues, Tornielli's assumption that the form of the Temple had changed throughout the ages were correct, then the Angel would have shown Ezechiel an imperfect building, since it is an indisputable dictum that nothing can be added to or subtracted from an important work of art without affecting the perfection of the whole. Equally absurd is the notion that Solomon could not have employed the classical style for the reason that the then prevailing manner of building was yet imperfect. Since everything, Salian retorts, was measured and designed according to God's command, this view would want us to believe that the worldly wisdom of human architects, living centuries after the construction of the Temple, was greater than the heavenly wisdom at the time of Solomon.[36]

Perrault, as we know, rejected this argument; his ironical remark about Villalpandus's belief in the

25. *Polyglot* (no. 25), I, p. 15, and *Critici Sacri* (no. 25), IX, p. 3746.
26. *Annotata ad Vetus Testamentum*, Paris, 1644, II, p. 402.
27. Lightfoot (no. 24).
28. *Ibid.*, pp. 5 f.
29. Lee (no. 26), Preface.
30. Saubert in Preface to Jacob Jehuda's book (no. 21); Lund (no. 42), p. 287.

31. Goldmann (nos. 31 and 39); Sturm (no. 36).
32. Küsel (no. 33).
33. Fischer von Erlach (no. 46).
34. On Louis Maillet's book on the Temple see no. 37.
35. Pineda (no. 13), Salian (no. 16), Menochio (no. 23).
36. Salian (no. 16), III, pp. 407 f.

divine origin of the Orders must be seen against the background of the manifold critical writings. There is nothing to prove that he knew Tornielli's *Annales*, though it is not impossible. Yet, he must have read Cappel's writings. Veil was, of course, familiar with all the relevant literature, but even without his guiding hand Perrault was no doubt acquainted with the Polyglot Bible of 1657 the fame of which was so great that just at the time when Veil's translation was published, a French writer could claim that 'we have nothing more perfect for the Bible than the Polyglot from London'.[37] Besides, Perrault and his brothers with their leanings towards Jansenism were interested in Bible exegesis.[37a]

*   *   *

Turning now to Perrault's designs, it must be admitted at once that part of the difference between Perrault's and Villalpandus's reconstructions was simply caused by the different literary sources from which they start. Villalpandus extracted the forms of Solomon's Temple from the various measurements mentioned in Ezechiel's chapters; Perrault was asked to reconstruct the Jewish Temple according to Maimonides's codification. Whereas Ezechiel is ambiguous and easily induces the interpreter to make use of his own imagination, Maimonides's account is specific. It was quite impossible for Perrault, reading the fourth and fifth chapters of the first treatise of Maimonides's book, to arrive at a plan even remotely resembling that of Villalpandus.[38] These are the measurements given by Maimonides which he took mainly from the Middoth: the Temple grounds were a square of 500 cubits (Fig. 3: AAAA); the surrounding wall had five gates, one on each side with the exception of the side towards the south which had two. Inside this wall was another partition, the so-called *soreg* (BBBB). A second wall formed an inner court, 187 cubits long and 135 cubits wide; it was entered by seven gates (DDDD). The position of the Temple itself within this second court is clearly specified, while the asymmetrical position of this inner court within the Temple grounds is given in general terms: the greatest distance was towards the south, the least distance towards the west, and the distance towards

the east was greater than towards the north. The overall length and width of the Temple, a hundred cubits in both directions (the vestibule always included), are broken down in detail, as are the overall dimensions of the inner court. Perrault kept strictly to these figures, also to those fixing the exact position of altar and slaughtering place and to the shape of two further courts, parallel strips only eleven cubits deep, one for the people, the other for the priests (PPQQ). Another court for the women was situated outside the main entrance to the inner court; it was a square of 135 cubits and had four square chambers of forty cubits at the four corners (TVXY).[39]

It cannot have been difficult for Perrault to arrive at a satisfactory interpretation of these explicit directions. But he certainly also studied the plans produced by three writers who had based their findings mainly on Jewish tradition: L'Empereur in 1630, Lightfoot in 1650 and Cappel in 1657.[40] On the main features all three agreed, but it is clearly Cappel's plan which Perrault approached most closely (Fig. 4). This is easily explained by the fact that Cappel was alone in differentiating between a plan derived exclusively from the Middoth and Maimonides, and another one, shown at the top of the same plate, based on Josephus (Fig. 5). However, in a few instances Perrault's and Cappel's plans diverge.

Two notable differences were, on Perrault's part, the result of probably purely aesthetic considerations. No indication was given, either in Maimonides or in the Middoth, about the distance between the *soreg* and the outer wall of the Temple Mount. Perrault, determined to keep clear of classical elements whenever possible, reduced the distance to a minimum, thus having no place left for a colonnaded portico, such as planned not only by Cappel, but also by L'Empereur and Lightfoot. The other deviation had to do with the eccentrically placed inner court. L'Empereur, Lightfoot and also Cappel made the distance to the south, as specified in the Talmud, decidedly large, and that to the west decidedly narrow. The resulting lack of balance was too awkward to be acceptable to Perrault. He therefore shifted the inner court as much to the center as was just compatible with Maimonides's instructions into a position where the relation between the two distances, towards south and towards north, complied to the pleasant ratio of 4:3, and the two distances, towards east and towards west, to the equally acceptable one of 5:4.[41]

37. Richard Simon, *Histoire critique du vieux Testament*, Paris, 1678, p. 647.

37a. After completion of the manuscript I found among Perrault's scientific papers a note in his handwriting with excerpts from Ezechiel, Paralegomena and Kings, all relating to the Temple. (Paris, Académie des Sciences, Dossier Perrault, liasse 17.)

38. The first English translation of Maimonides's treatise has recently been published: *The Code of Maimonides, Book eight. The Book of Temple Service* (Yale Judaica Series, vol. XII), New Haven and London 1957; the most recent translation of the Middoth in *The Babylonian Talmud*, ed. I. Epstein, London, 1948.

39. It is not easy to see why Perrault separated the women's court from the wall of the inner court, except that in this way he escaped from the necessity to show it on the side elevation.

40. L'Empereur (no. 19); Lightfoot (no. 24); Cappel (no. 25).

41. In addition Perrault co-ordinates the gates wherever possible.

Perrault's plan contains another feature not to be found on any plan for the Temple of Jerusalem, be it that of Solomon, Ezechiel, the Talmud or Herod. Three narrowly spaced parallel walls are joined to the Temple on the western side (6), and two similar sets of six walls on the southern and northern sides (7, 7). It is a strange structure, recorded only by Maimonides. What purpose these walls should have served is not clear. Cappel called them 'a pure dream of demented Maimonides'.[42] Perrault, faithfully following the text, lines the Temple with these multiple layers of walls.

This, however, brought another difficulty upon him. An arrangement, that was recorded in the Scriptures as well as in the Talmud and by Josephus, had become over the centuries one of the specific features of almost all reconstructions: a row of cells, or chambers, 30 or 38 in all, joined to all walls of the Temple except in the east, in three stories, reaching about half-way up the wall of the Temple. Maimonides too mentions these cells, believing them to have been built on to the last of his set of walls. As Perrault points out in his notes, this was impossible, particularly on the western side where the available space had through Maimonides's set of walls been narrowed to only eleven cubits. L'Empereur, referring to this arrangement, greatly wondered what had come into Maimonides's mind to make a proposition that was ostensibly wrong.[43] Perrault believed he had found a solution to this predicament: he suggested having the cells joined not, as was usual, to the Temple itself, but to the outside of the wall surrounding the inner court (S, S, S, S). In his notes he tried to make out that not only Maimonides had this position in mind, but that support for it could be found in certain passages from the Bible. Needless to say that his arguments are unconvincing. But the solution at which he arrived gave his building, as we shall see, a distinct character.[44]

The idea of placing the cells where he did may again have been suggested to Perrault by Cappel's plan, this time by the plan according to Josephus, where a number of large rooms, or *exhedrae* as they were called, are arranged along the wall surrounding the inner court, separated by steps leading up to the higher level of the court (Fig. 5). This last detail was taken over by Perrault, as the side elevation clearly shows (Fig. 3). These *exhedrae* were, however, distinct from and in

addition to the 38 smaller cells surrounding the Temple.[45] Maimonides too refers to them, but since Perrault had surrounded the Temple by layers of walls, and had shifted the cells to the wall of the court, he had no space left for the *exhedrae* in the vicinity of the Temple where, for reasons of Temple service, they ought to have been placed. The upshot of it was that Perrault did not include them at all in his plan. Yet, he did provide for another building containing four chambers which the other interpreters of Jewish sources had also attached to the wall of the inner court. In this instance, Perrault might have genuinely misunderstood the somewhat ambiguous text of Maimonides, but in any case he had little space for manœuvre and thus had no alternative but to place this building with the four chambers next to the women's court (Z,Θ,Λ,X). This is another feature peculiar only to Perrault's plan. Thus Maimonides's distinct instruction about the layers of walls surrounding the Temple compelled Perrault to two deviations which could not be justified by sound literary evidence. In spite of these unusual features Perrault's plan conforms in its general disposition and essential measurements to the plans based on Jewish tradition and thus stands in striking contrast to the fanciful dreams of those who tried to interpret Ezechiel's vision.

But the contrast is at least as pronounced when comparing Perrault's elevations with those of other reconstructions, a contrast that cannot be said to be due to the difference in the underlying literary sources which accounted so naturally for the different character of the groundplans. None of these sources give more than scanty indication about the external appearance of the Temple, so that the interpreter had either to abandon altogether the idea of designing an elevation, which was the alternative chosen by serious scholars such as L'Empereur, Cappel and also Lightfoot, or he had to embark on the unsafe venture of inventing an elevation.[46] Typical for this second group is Jacob Jehuda Leon, a Jewish scholar from Spain who had settled in Holland. He had made a large wooden model of the Temple which he exhibited in many places and which, incidentally, Perrault might have seen when, in 1671, he paid a visit to his friend Huygens.[47] Jacob Jehuda

42. *Polyglot* (no. 25), 1, p. 33. Sturm (no. 36), p. 30, defends Maimonides's arrangement against Cappel's criticism.
43. L'Empereur (no. 19), p. 147.
44. The section and the side elevation do not quite agree. In order to restore some sort of communication between the cells and the Holy Place Perrault provided a bridge leading from the wall to the southeast corner of the vestibule. He made the doubtful claim that 1 Kings 6:6 could be interpreted in this way.

45. Middoth, v, 3, Maimonides, v, 17.
46. Lightfoot (no. 24) incorporates in his plan outlines of the gates the form of which he apparently adopted from popular illustrations showing the Temple surrounded by fortified walls (see Zev Vilnay, *The Holy Land in Old Prints and Maps*, Jerusalem, 1963, Figs. 34, 49, 50 and p. xxxv).
47. Christian Huygens, *Œuvres complètes*, The Hague, 1888 ff., vii, p. 57. Letter dated April 14, 1671, by Huygens to his brother informing him of the impending visit of Monsieur Perrault.
L. Wolf, *Transactions of the Jewish Historical Society of England*, ii, pp. 157 f., infers from the Dedication of a book pub-

wrote a small guide to the model; the book was soon translated from Spanish into Dutch, French, Hebrew, German and Latin, often with engravings attached. Next to Villalpandus's it was Jacob Jehuda's book that made the wider public acquainted with the image of the Temple of Jerusalem.[48] Since he relied almost exclusively on the Middoth, the Latin translator, Saubert, thought he could do no better than attach to his edition the plan which L'Empereur had drawn a decade earlier. But for the elevation Jacob Jehuda had to provide his own design and in so doing he felt no inhibition in borrowing heavily from Villalpandus: the substructures, though even more elaborate than those of Villalpandus, are almost copied from him; the buildings, in disposition roughly following L'Empereur's plan, present even in this primitive drawing an unmistakingly classical appearance (Fig. 6). Obviously, it was not considered incongruous to restrict the interpretation to the narrow limits set by the Talmud, and yet adopt for its outer appearance what was thought to be the 'perfect' style This is confirmed by the views of the Temple as reproduced, during the seventeenth century, in many Passover-Haggadahs.[49] Even Tornielli, who, as we have seen, rejected the application of the Greek style as an anachronism, was guided in his own version by a pattern belonging to a comparatively recent past: a typical town-palace of the early Renaissance, the rusticated walls of which lacked indeed classical Orders, but had rows of windows with manifestly classical frames, and even the two pillars Boz and Jachem were classical, or romanesque, columns. At the beginning of the next century, a French author, reiterating Tornielli's arguments and wondering how the Jews could possibly 'have come to know of the different architectural Orders which were only invented by the Greeks six hundred years later', nevertheless attached engravings to his treatise, designed by the Lyonnais architect Ferdinand Delamonce, showing the Temple as a typical utilitarian building of that period,

governed by simple, yet classical proportions.[50] Similarly, two other authors who had criticized the Vitruvian character of Villalpandus's designs, the Maurist Auguste Calmet and the Oratorian Bernard Lamy, visualized Solomon's Temple in a severe and forbidding style, probably meant to suggest its Egyptian origin, but they both surrounded the courts with porticoes and arcaded galleries supported by columns and pillars.[51] They all were unable to completely suppress the inborn habit of thinking in terms of classical architecture.

It was hard to break away from customary conception of harmony and order. All the more exceptional is Perrault's design of the façade (Fig. 3). He found in the text submitted to him the following particulars on which to base the design: the Temple was built on a solid foundation six cubits high. Vestibule and Temple were on the same level, that is six cubits above the level of the court. Twelve steps, each of a rise of half a cubit, led to the great entrance door, the dimension of which was given as forty by twenty cubits. Over the entrance were five oak beams, the lowest being two cubits wider than the width of the entrance and each of the remaining beams exceeding the one below by another two cubits. To the left and right of the entrance were two small doors and opposite to it, at the back of the vestibule, was the door, twenty cubits high and ten cubits wide, leading into the Holy Place itself. The overall width of the vestibule was a hundred cubits, its height above the foundation also a hundred cubits. The latter measurement included the area taken up by the roof, consisting of ceiling, pannelling and gutters (five cubits), and a parapet (three cubits).[52] These were the specifications. Perrault kept strictly within their limits. He added nothing to make his façade look more attractive (with the possible exception of the form of the parapet). No string-courses or pilasters, no windows at all or architraves around the doorways, relieve the monotony of the square rugged wall. Those who expected to be shown the most beautiful building in the world must have been shocked; how deeply is clear from Lund's categorical —and contemporaneous—statement that a wall without windows would turn the Temple into 'a great deformity' (eine grosse Ungestalt) while he himself uncritically accepts Jacob Jehuda's uncorroborated assertion that the façade was decorated 'with various columns above each other and next to each other as well as with many windows between the columns'.[53] Moreover, it was tempting, since the text

lished by Jacob Jehuda in 1675 (*A Relation of the most memorable thinges*..., Amsterdam) that he had sold the model in 1643 to Queen Henrietta. But Goeree (no. 41), II, Preface, knows only of Jacob Jehuda's departure for England, not of the dispatch of the model, while Sturm (no. 36), p. 31, mentions that the model was exhibited in Flanders in 1694 or shortly before; this is confirmed by Lamy (no. 45), p. 697. The Dedication probably refers to an engraving not to a wooden model.
Another model, completed in 1694 and commissioned by a man who had studied under Saubert (no. 21), was, before the war, at a museum in Hamburg. It exactly reproduces Villalpandus's Temple (see *Mitteilung des Vereins für Hamburgische Geschichte*, 1910, and *Jahresbericht des Museums für Hamburgische Geschichte für das Jahr 1910*, Hamburg, 1911).
48. Jacob Jehuda (no. 21).
49. Haggadah (no. 18).

50. Desbruslins (no. 44).
51. Calmet (no. 43); Lamy (no. 45).
52. Maimonides, IV, 3, 6, 7, 8.
53. Lund (no. 42), pp. 262, 299.
See also Pineda's description of the façade (no. 13), p. 355:

mentions some kind of carving, to turn the five beams above the entrance door into a beautifully decorated lintel, as Lund proposed, or even into a proper Vitruvian frieze, as L'Empereur suggested.[54] Perrault resisted the temptation and followed the text scrupulously: 'between one beam and the other there was a tier of stones'.[55]

Perrault, it seems, arrived at this primitive piece of architecture by just adhering to a principle that nobody before him had applied so rigidly, namely to confine himself to the information he was able to extract from the text and to be satisfied with having produced an exact or sensible record of the known data, a restraint for which as a scientist he had the necessary training. But although it is true that he did not—or only in a minor detail—add to the information, he disregarded it in one particular instance.

Maimonides mentions tiers of galleries or terraces projecting from the façade of the vestibule. He, no doubt, misinterpreted a passage in the Middoth which more likely refers to the particular arrangement of the twelve steps leading up to the vestibule. Maimonides was therefore alone in describing terraces.[56] This in itself would not have prevented Perrault from incorporating them into his design, just as he was not deterred from incorporating the layers of walls surrounding the Temple although they equally originated from an interpretation peculiar to Maimonides. But in this instance it was really difficult to understand what Maimonides had in mind since he explicitly states that these 'extensions' were built one above the other from the ground level right up to the top of the façade,

'Templi, id est, domus exterioris, vestibulum magnificentissimum fuit.... Quia vero vestibuli facies Orientalis exornabatur turri pulcherrima, atque fortissima ... secundum triplicem columnationem, et columnarum triplicis ordinis proportionem et symmetriam.'

54. Lund (no. 42), p. 298; L'Empereur (no. 19), p. 127.
55. Maimonides, IV, 8.
It is interesting to see how closely a modern writer's views can be related to the appearance of Perrault's façade. Hollis, *op. cit.*, p. 205, writes: 'We may be astonished that no mention whatever is made of windows to the Holy Place, but the very fact that nothing is said may surely mean that there were none ... That the Porch should need windows seems doubtful, seeing that the great opening would have been quite sufficient to admit all the light required. The roof was probably flat ...' Perrault, in fact, brought light into the vestibule by lateral windows, but this did not affect the appearance of the plain stonewall of the façade. From his note in Vitruvius, ed. 1684, p. 80, it is evident that he himself regarded the windowless façade as a primitive state in the architectural evolution. Temples were built with windows, but, he writes, this was done only at a later stage; the earliest temples 'ne prenoient du jour que par la porte'.
56. Maimonides, IV, 9. See editor's note and also note to Middoth, III, 6. Lightfoot (no. 24), p. 59: 'And here we meet with a passage in the Treatise Middoth ... which is exceeding hard to be understood, and the very same also in Maimonides, and in him it is harder.' Lund (no. 42), pp. 299 f., deals in detail with the interpretation of this passage.

separated from each other by either only one cubit, i.e. 18 inches, or three cubits, i.e. $4\frac{1}{2}$ feet. In either case it meant that there were an incredibly great number of galleries (either almost 100 or more than 30), and also that the space between them was so narrow that they could not possibly have served any purpose. Probably for that reason, Perrault decided to disregard this passage altogether. The sensible decision is at the same time revealing. It shows that the design for the façade was not only the result of passive reaction to the scanty information provided by the text, but also the result of a positive will to create a convincing image of a primitive building erected at the time of Solomon, an image he was unwilling to have spoilt by an ambiguous passage based on some misinterpretation.

Perrault was less severe in the design of the remaining parts of the building. The Temple consisted, according to Maimonides and other sources, of two stories of equal height of which the lower one contained the Holy Place and the Holy of Holies, while the upper story served some unknown purpose. But rooms it undoubtedly contained, so that it was only natural to provide windows. This was done in nearly all preceding reconstructions and Perrault, in this instance, conformed. It is this upper part of the Temple, appearing over the top of the surrounding walls, that mainly gives away the date of design. To this we shall return later.

Perrault dealt in his explanatory remarks with two details. One, already discussed, refers to the position of the 38 cells, the other to the puzzling problem of intercommunication between the cells and between the three floors. For the latter purpose the sources mention a single spiral staircase in the northeast corner, reaching up to the roof. This was evidently a primitive arrangement, but nevertheless the one adopted by L'Empereur. As Cappel rightly pointed out, it meant that one would have to pass through every single cell on the northern and western side before those on the opposite side could be reached.[57] Most authors, therefore, provided two spiral staircases, one on each corner of the Temple. This mitigated the inconvenience only slightly since the only communication mentioned in the sources are doors leading directly from one cell to the adjoining ones. Lightfoot, dissatisfied with an interpretation so much at loggerheads with the notion of a perfect building as conceived in the seventeenth century, devised an ingenuous scheme which he thought accommodated both the text and the aesthetic requirements. The main feature of his plan

57. *Polyglot* (no. 25), I, p. 29.
Tirinus (no. 22), III, p. 542, believes one spiral staircase to be sufficient since the cells were interconnected.

were anterooms between each pair of cells with a spiral staircase at the back of them and a corridor in front of the cells from which, on the ground floor, doors opened out into the courtyard.[58]

Perrault, judging from the lengthy comment he made on the subject of the spiral staircase, was equally concerned about the unsatisfactory nature of these arrangements. He, first of all, pointed out—correctly it seems—that it was only due to inaccurate translation that the notion of a spiral staircase had arisen at all. Maimonides, in any case, had apparently in mind a staircase leading up in a straight flight. Cappel understood this to mean that one of the empty spaces between Maimonides's set of six walls was taken up by a staircase and ridiculed such an arrangement because of the complete darkness into which it would have been plunged.[59] Yet, in Perrault's opinion Maimonides's description would be quite consistent with an ordinary staircase where straight flights between landings were built around a square well. Nevertheless, he rejected this form because—and here he took up Cappel's argument—anyone wishing to reach the last cell on the southern side would still be forced to pass first through all intervening cells. Therefore, he provided for easier intercommunication galleries in front of the cells, not Lightfoot's corridors but open balconies. A passage in Ezechiel justified, so he believed, this arrangement.[60] These balconies were interconnected at three corners by straight flights of stairs, thus allowing a free passage from ground floor to roof; at the same time they gave convenient access to each cell. Perrault could rightly claim that this scheme fitted well Maimonides's description.

Whatever its merits, he had achieved a lively and unusual composition. It is feasible that Perrault wished to stress the oriental provenance of the Temple, an aim consistent with the objections voiced against Villalpandus's plea for the classical style. Perhaps he already held the opinion, set forth later by Lamy, that for an understanding of the biblical text one should study Egyptian monuments, since God, when commanding the building of the Temple, had not rejected everything that was typical of Egyptian architecture. Lamy singled out mass and solidity as such typical qualities, the same which certainly mark Perrault's façade.[61] In the seventeenth century, Egyptian and also Turkish architecture was known, though necessarily in a superficial way; but, as far as I can see, no engravings existed at that time of buildings that could have served as models. If it really was Perrault's inten-

tion to give the Temple an oriental look, he would have sought in vain for guidance in the reports of travellers.[62]

But he might have hoped to find models among the vast literature on the Temple. He most certainly had studied the Polyglot Bible and Cappel's engravings, but these were of no help in designing the elevation. Only a few authors gave, in addition to the ground-plan, a complete view of the Temple and its surrounding buildings, and they all followed preconceived ideas. Tornielli, as already mentioned, imagined the Temple in the guise of an Italian palace, while Arias Montano and Hafenreffer gave it the form of a contemporary church with a tall single tower, surrounded by buildings of equally contemporary appearance, which, in the case of Hafenreffer, were indistinguishable from a German castle of the sixteenth century.[63] These designs, basically not at variance with Villalpandus's point of view, were of no value to Perrault. For the same reason he, no doubt, rejected the then most recent attempt, that by Johannes Coccejus, who, in spite of taking exceptions to Villalpandus's 'extraordinary mistakes', obviously accepted his thesis of the perfect style and pictured the Temple in the undiluted form of French—or Dutch—classicism.[64]

Glancing—with the help of Veil—through these books, Perrault must have come across the name of François Vatable, mentioned by almost every writer on the subject. He had been teacher in Hebrew at the *Collège de France* in Paris where he died in 1547. He never published his commentaries, but Robert Estienne, the scholarly publisher, joined them to his editions of the Bible, culling them from students' notes. Estienne has been charged with giving these commentaries a bias reflecting his own inclination towards protestantism, but this charge could hardly be meant to apply to the uncontroversial chapters of Ezechiel nor to the woodcuts of which Estienne specifically acknowledged Vatable's authorship. These woodcuts were published

58. Lightfoot (no. 24), p. 55.
59. *Loc. cit.*
60. Ezechiel 42:3.
61. Lamy (no. 45), pp. 267, 254, 160.

62. On this subject see J. M. Carré, *Voyageurs et écrivains français en Egypte*, Cairo, 1932, and N. Pevsner and S. Lang, 'The Egyptian Revival', *The Architectural Review*, cxix, 1956, pp. 243 ff.
63. Tornielli (no. 14); Arias (no. 9); Hafenreffer (no. 15). The high single tower is the result of another attempt to reconcile conflicting evidence. According to 1 Kings 6:2 Solomon's Temple was only thirty cubits high, while the second Temple, according to Ezra 6:3, reached 60 cubits. This run counter to the firm belief in the superiority of Solomon's Temple. It was therefore argued that the thirty cubits applied only to the height of the first of four stories; but the resulting total height of 120 cubits was then difficult to reconcile with the comparatively narrow width. For that reason, many authors gave the Holy Place itself the low height according to Kings, but transformed the vestibule into a tower of 120 cubits, a dimension also in accordance with 2 Chronicles 3:4.
64. Coccejus (no. 27).

again and again; in many editions of the Bible which Estienne printed after his emigration to Geneva, in Bibles published by René Benoist in Paris, in the splendid Paris *Biblia Sacra* of 1573, in a Frankfurt Bible and in many others. They were still thought interesting enough to be reproduced in a prominent edition of the Bible at the beginning of the next century at Antwerp, that is thirteen years after publication of Villalpandus's engravings. The high esteem in which Vatable's designs were held is also proved by the fact that Hafenreffer used one of them to illustrate his text.[65] Perrault had therefore ample opportunity to get acquainted with these woodcuts.

The similarity between his and Vatable's designs of the façade is remarkable. The plain square wall of stones crowned by a cornice and a parapet in form of a balustrade is common to both, as are the rows of semi-circular windows on the upper part of the side elevations (Figs. 3, 7, 8). Of course, the motif of a semi-circular window was familiar to Perrault; he himself had used it on the Observatoire. Nevertheless, Vatable's woodcut might have provided a welcome confirmation for the propriety of its application on this particular building. Naturally, there are differences. Perrault is far more radical than Vatable. He omits on the façade Vatable's five windows and also the classical frame of the doorway and can ignore the projecting cells, having shifted them to another position. In this way, Perrault achieved a design unique in its almost crude simplicity. Nevertheless, I think it most likely that the initial impetus was due to Vatable. It is more difficult to decide whether the other prominent feature in Perrault's design, the balconies in front of the cells, had its root too in older reconstructions. According to a passage in the Bible, and confirmed by the Talmud, the width of the cells increased by one cubit from one floor to the next.[66] This arrangement can clearly be seen in Vatable's woodcut. It was shown for the first time in the fourteenth century by Nicolaus de Lyra.[67] His illustration contrasted two interpretations of the relevant passage: one according to Jewish sources of cells progressively increasing in width, the other according to Christian scholars who understood the words 'latera in circumitu' to refer not to cells but to balconies. When Lyra's *Glossae*, known in many manuscripts, was printed, the explanatory drawings were more or less accurately reproduced. The woodcut commonly found in the printed editions shows, on the right-hand side, the balconies which, according to Lyra's comment, run along the sidewalls of the Temple

in all three stories (Fig. 9).[68] Another woodcut, evidently designed in the fifteenth century, shows the balconies in a more competent manner (Fig. 10). Lyra's *Glossae* was still widely read in the seventeenth century; an edition, though without illustrations, was published in Paris as late as 1660. It does not seem impossible that it was one of these woodcuts that suggested to Perrault the feature of balconies. On the other hand, one should perhaps look to reconstructions nearer to his own time. Coccejus's attempt preceded his own by only a few years. As mentioned before, his designs are entirely different from Perrault's, yet there is one building, standing apart from the Temple, which Coccejus too imagined with a double tier of balconies and a corresponding balustrade along the flat roof (Fig. 11). The proportions and the whole aspect of the two elevations differ greatly, but the motif itself is so unusual for this period that it yet may have been Coccejus's design that suggested balconies to Perrault.

It would be interesting to learn of the impressions which Perrault's conception of the Temple made on those who came after him. Yet, it is no exaggeration to say that his designs remained almost unknown or at least were, with two exceptions as far as I can see, not commented upon, although they were included in two reprints of Veil's translation; in 1696 in a collection of theological treatises, and again fifty years later in one of the volumes of the similar and well-known collection edited by Blasius Ugolino.[69] Veil's preface, mentioning Perrault's name and referring to his manifold achievements in flattering terms, was included in both reprints.

One of the two writers just referred to, Bernard Lamy, does not name but at least indicates the author's identity; he speaks of him as the same person 'who translated Vitruvius into French and became famous through other books'.[70] The context in which this is said reveals the reason for the otherwise almost unbroken silence. Lamy is speaking of those authors who mainly draw from Jewish sources and finds that all— Jacob Jehuda, L'Empereur, Lightfoot—fail to give an adequate idea of the Temple simply because the Jewish writers, on whom they rely, were inexperienced in the art of building and therefore unable to give a competent and detailed account of the Temple. This

65. Vatable (no. 6); Hafenreffer (no. 15), p. 242.
66. Vulgata 3 Kings 6:6; Middoth, IV, 4.
67. Lyra (no. 4).

68. I was unable to identify the manuscript from which the woodcut has undoubtedly been copied.
69. Maimonides (no. 29).
70. Lamy (no. 45), p. 695.
Veil's translation, but not Perrault's engravings, is cited by Hermann Wits, *Miscellanea Sacra*, Amsterdam, 1692 ff., II, p. 254. Newton, whose *Description of the Temple of Solomon* was posthumously published in 1728, knew Perrault's designs from his own copy of Veil's translation (listed in R. de Villamil, *Newton: The Man*, London, s.d., p. 85).

is, in his opinion, the reason why these authors formed such an imperfect notion of it, not at all worthy of God and in no way reflecting the splendour that Josephus praised and even pagan writers admired. In short, all Jewish discourses on the Temple belittle its glory. This, he concludes, is also the fault of the illustrations which Veil inserted in his book, although they are the work of a man experienced in architectural matters.[71]

The other writer, the Dutch scholar W. Goeree, does not even obliquely refer to Perrault.[72] On the other hand, his reference to Veil's book and its engravings is more specific and far more outspoken than Lamy's general remarks. Goeree belonged, so he says, 'to the party of those who, when describing this beautiful building [the Temple], call to their help the rules of architecture'. He thus looked down on philologists, such as Veil, who disregard these rules and instead listen to the fancies of the Rabbis and who believe that Jewish authors do better than those who follow the teaching of Vitruvius. To realize how wrong this belief is, Goeree advises his readers to look at the illustrations Veil had added to Maimonides's text. At this point he makes the only explicit judgment we have of Perrault's façade, condemning it with this poignant remark: 'It looks more like a prison than a Temple.' In his view, Maimonides's description of the façade is bad enough, but the illustration of it is far worse.[73]

Goeree was a follower of Villalpandus, disagreeing with critics such as Cappel. But partisans as well as most critics agreed on one maxim: that the Temple had been a unique building, if not for size then for splendour. It was unthinkable that this building, commanded by God, could have been as drab and small as the Jews believed. This was one reason why Perrault's designs made no impression and were, when noticed, severely criticized. There were also those who followed the lead given by L'Empereur and Lightfoot and recognized the value of Jewish tradition. Yet, they must have found fault in certain features of Perrault's plan, as for instance the unorthodox placing of the cells, resulting in the omission of a number of important rooms, for all of which the textual evidence submitted by Perrault was glaringly weak and unworthy of the consideration of these scholars steeped in theological and linguistic problems. In any case, those scholars who used Veil's book in their researches were interested in Maimonides, not in Perrault, while the general reader, concerned with the artistic aspect of the Temple, would hardly have looked into a book containing the Latin translation of Maimonides. As it happened, it was Leibniz's short remark to Graevius that in the end delivered Perrault's designs from oblivion.

Measured by the response which these designs called forth among Perrault's contemporaries and succeeding generations, their historical value is negligible. But seen in a different context, they become significant. The present Chapel of Versailles was begun in 1688; in the following year work was interrupted for almost a decade. When it was resumed, the design for the upper part was radically modified: the height was much increased and in the interior a straight entablature resting on free-standing columns took the place of arches resting on pillars. It has always been recognized that the new arrangement of the interior introduced an element akin to the Colonnade of the Louvre, commonly connected with Perrault's name. For that reason and because of Charles Perrault's statement that his brother had worked on plans for Versailles, it has recently been suggested that 'the abrupt change of the plan in 1698 is probably due to an idea of Perrault'.[74] So far this conjecture rested solely on Charles's word, not always to be trusted, and on a stylistic comparison.

But now more tangible evidence can be added (Fig. 12). J.-F. Blondel's engraving shows the contrast between the lofty Chapel and the low buildings in front of it, and a row of semi-circular windows, separated by flying buttresses, appearing over the rooftop of the houses. These are the same basic elements that mark Perrault's lateral elevation of the Temple (Fig. 3). The comparison is obscured by the steep and richly adorned roof, the statuary work and other decorative embellishments of the present Chapel. Yet, these are additions due to a new fashion. The earliest known set of plans,

71. *Op. cit.*, pp. 695, 698, 891.

72. Goeree (no. 41), III, Preface. Goeree is obviously unaware that Perrault was responsible for the designs. Since he himself had written a book on architecture (no. 34), he was, of course, familiar with the name of the translator of Vitruvius. The only possible conclusion is that he did not read Veil's preface.

73. *Ibid.*, 'Ce traducteur voudroit . . . nous persuader que ce Rabbin a très bien réussi dans la description qu'il donne du Temple . . . et qu'il a mieux fait que ceux qui ont suivi les règles de l'Architecture ancienne; telle que Vitruve nous l'enseigne. Mais il se trompe bien fort. Pour en être persuadé, il n'y a qu'à considérer avec attention la description de Maimonides et la figure que cet auteur a fait faire selon les vues de ce Rabbin; cette figure nous représente bien plutôt une prison qu'un Temple aussi magnifique, qu'étoit le Temple de Jérusalem . . . Toutes les descriptions donc, qui donnent une idée de ce Temple, peu convenable à sa beauté et à sa magnificence, doivent passer pour fausses. Quelque sèche et quelque mal en ordre, que soit la description que Maimonides donne du Frontispice du Temple, la figure de l'auteur . . . demeure encore bien au dessous.'

74. Michael Petzet, 'Un projet des Perrault pour l'église de Sainte-Geneviève à Paris', *Bulletin Monumental*, cxv, 1957, p. 90. Also R. Josephson, 'Quelques dessins de Claude Perrault pour le Louvre', *Gazette des Beaux-Arts*, 1927, ii, p. 192.

probably of 1688, have none of it.[75] The roof is flat, or so low that it would not have been noticeable from below, the lower and upper balustrades are without statues and *pots à feu*, the windows are plain without festoons. A plan by Perrault for the Chapel, if it existed, cannot have been later than 1688, the year of his death; it would certainly be stylistically nearer to the designs just mentioned than to the ornamentation of the Chapel as executed between 1698 and 1710. Stripped of its high roof and decorative frills, the Chapel would reveal its similarity to Perrault's design for the Temple, a similarity that, in my opinion, cannot be coincidental.[76]

It could, of course, be assumed that it was not a plan by Perrault that was responsible for the final shape of the Chapel, but that Mansart, or whoever was responsible for the change of 1698, was influenced by the engravings of the Temple. But in view of the little echo that these designs evoked, this is most unlikely. Besides, it would not account for the elements of Perrault's style noticeable in the interior. I think it more plausible to assume that Perrault, when working on a plan for the chapel, made use of a composition he had designed a decade earlier. In fact, he might have thought it appropriate to model Louis le Grand's Castle and Chapel after King Solomon's Palace and Temple. In that case it would have been Perrault's plan of 1688, based on his design for the Temple of 1678, that influenced the final designs of 1698.

Perrault may have regretted the care he had taken over the interpretation of Maimonides's text, seeing that the small engravings in an obscure book remained unnoticed by scholars and architects alike. Yet, if this work should now help to support the claim for his share in the creation of the Chapel of Versailles, all the time he spent on it would, after all, have been worth while.

75. Published by Michael Petzet, 'Quelques projets inédits pour la chapelle de Versailles', *Art de France*, I, 1961, pp. 315 ff. See also Fiske Kimball, 'The Chapels of the Château of Versailles', *Gazette des Beaux-Arts*, II, 1944, pp. 315 ff.

76. This reverses my own view, expressed in *Laugier and Eighteenth Century French Theory*, London, 1962, p. 109, when I thought the then available evidence insufficient to sustain the conjecture of an independent plan by Perrault for the Chapel of Versailles. The prototype for a church dominating the surrounding low buildings is the Escorial which, of course, influenced Villalpandus. In the *Ordonnance*, p. 120, Perrault refers to this particular aspect of the Escorial and points out that in this respect it could serve as model for modern palaces.

SOURCES

The following list contains those major works on the Temple that were known and widely used during the seventeenth and the beginning of the eighteenth centuries. Completeness is not claimed. If that had been the aim, innumerable commentators, both Christian and Jewish, would have had to be included, even if their contribution to the problem of reconstructing the Temple was insignificant.

1. Christian Fathers. They are frequently quoted, specially St. Jerome, *Commentariorum in Ezechielem Prophetam* (Migne, *Patrologiae*, vol. 25) and St. Gregory, *Homiliarum in Ezechielem* (Migne, vol. 76), who, however, were interested in the allegorical meaning of the prophecy, not in the building itself. This is still the case with Bede (673–735), *De Templo Salomonis* (J. A. Giles, *Patres Ecclesiae Anglicanae*, vol. 8) and with Rupert of Deutz (1070–1129), *In Ezechielem Prophetam commentariorum* (Migne, vol. 167). On these and the next see Wilhelm Neuss, *Das Buch Ezechiel in Theologie und Kunst bis zum Ende des XII. Jahrhunderts*, Münster, 1912.

2. Richard of St. Victor (d. 1173), *De Templo Salomonis ad litteram* and *De aedificia Ezechielis* (sometimes called *In visionem Ezechielis*) (Migne, vol. 196, with reproductions of drawings). He was the first to explain the literal sense of the Scriptures, believing an understanding of the primary sense to be necessary for any mystical interpretation. He was therefore also the first to devise explanatory drawings: a plan, one frontal and two lateral views, typical Romanesque buildings with decorative arcading and battlements. Interesting in view of later reconstructions the arcaded substructures over the rocky foundation of the rising mount. Several manuscripts survive; Bibl. Nat. MS. Latin 3848 with illuminated drawings. They were reproduced in the various editions of his *Opera omnia*: Paris 1518, Lyons 1534, Venice 1592 and even in the last edition published as late as 1650 in Rhoan.

3. Hugh of St. Cher (Hugo Cardinalis) (*c.* 1200–1263), *Postillae in sacram scripturam juxta quadruplicem sensum, litteralem, allegoricum, anagogicum et moralem*. Printed in Basle Bible of 1498 (vols. I and V. Ges. Kat. 4285) and in *Biblia Sacra*, Lyons, 1669. Commenting on Ezechiel 41:6, he made the curious suggestion that *latera* meant sixty-six seats placed inside the Temple for the use of the priests. Lyra (see no. 4) made an explanatory drawing, but rejected this interpretation. It was still reiterated by Hector Pinto (see no. 8). The woodcut in vol. I of the Bible of 1498 is a reproduction of one of Lyra's drawings.

4. Nicolaus de Lyra (1270–1349), *Postilla litteralis* and *Postilla mystica seu moralis*. His great and lasting reputation rests on his interpretation of the literal sense, although he too emphasizes that the description of the Temple is not important in itself but only in furthering the understanding of its inner meaning. Some explanations are derived from Richard (see no. 2), such as the three tiers of *deambulatoria*, the flat roofs 'according to Palestinian custom' and the clear distinction between Solomon's and Ezechiel's Temple; but he also relies on Jewish commentaries and often refers to Maimonides and Rashi. He brings the first detailed overall plan of all buildings described by Ezechiel. The Temple itself is pictured as a castle, now with mullioned Gothic windows. See Figs. 9 and 10 and text p. 152. Many illustrated manuscripts survive. Good specimens Bibl. Nat. MS. Latin 358 and 461 and Bibl. Ste Geneviève MS. 35. The *Postillae* were printed with all illustrations in the following editions of the Bible: Nürnberg 1481 (Ges. Kat. 4286), 1485 (Ges. Kat. 4288) and 1493 (Ges. Kat. 4293), Basle 1498 (Ges. Kat. 4284) and 1502, Venice 1489 (Ges. Kat. 4291) and 1588, Lyons 1502.

5. Alfonso Tostado Abulensis (1400–1455), *Commentaria*. These massive and often cited commentaries form the major part of his *Opera omnia* of which several editions were published during the sixteenth century in Venice. Like Richard and Lyra (see nos. 2 and 4) he concentrates on the interpretation of the literal sense (Kings and Chronicles), but refrains from making designs because, he says, the Temple was a solid thing which needs for proper representation not one but six surfaces and which in any case would not differ from a tower of three stories with 'tabulata per gyrum quae nos balcones vulgariter apellamus'.

6. François Vatable (d. 1547). His designs for Solomon's Temple (1 Kings 3:6) were published by Robert Estienne in his Paris Bible of 1540 (see text p. 151). The title-page ends: 'His accesserunt schemata Tabernaculi Mosaici, & Templi Salomonis, quae praeeunte Francisco Vatablo . . . expressa sunt.' These woodcuts were used again by Estienne in his Paris Bibles of 1545 and 1546 and his Geneva Bible of 1557; also by three Bibles in French (Lyons 1551 by Jean de Tournes, and Paris 1566 and 1573 by R. Benoist) and by a Frankfurt Bible of 1571. When Estienne published at Geneva in 1560 his translation of the Bible, he added at the end of the Book Ezechiel a bird's-eye view of the visionary Temple together with explanatory text. Whether this design is also by Vatable is impossible to say. These two sets of woodcuts were reproduced in the same year at Geneva by F. Jacquay, then again in the *Biblia Latino-gallica* (Geneva, 1568), in Ludwig Lavater, *Propheta Ezechiel*, 1571, in a French Bible by Jean Lertout (Lyons, 1580), in the *Biblia Sacra* (Antwerp, 1617) and no doubt in many other Bibles. The overall plans differ: Solomon's Temple has only one paved and one unpaved court, Ezechiel's six paved and three huge unpaved courts. These illustrations displaced those by Lyra (see no. 4) which no doubt looked by then obsolete. Besides a few 'modern' details, the whole arrangement is far more consistent with the text than the older primitive drawings by Lyra and Richard (see no. 2).

7. Sebastien Châteillon (Castalion) (1515–1563). His Latin Bible was published at Basle 1551 and again 1573, his French translation at Basle 1555. All three have plans for Solomon's and Ezechiel's Temple. Of Solomon's buildings only the Temple is shown; for the surrounding courtyards he refers to the chapters in Ezechiel where he illustrates the whole Temple ground, a strictly symmetrical composition with the Temple placed at the intersection of eight courts which form a Greek cross and with four open spaces between the limbs of the cross, 'although they are nowhere mentioned'; the whole, a square of 500 cubits, is surrounded by a wall. At the time this was the most methodical design.

8. Hector Pinto (d. 1584), *In Ezechielem Prophetam commentaria*, Salamanca, 1568. His main concern is the interpretation of the symbolical significance; he, therefore, accepts the unrealistic figure of 3,000 cubits as the size of the Temple square. On p. 650 is a small sketch of the total disposition taken from Richard (see no. 2); he agrees with Hugh of St. Cher (see no. 3) about the sixty-six seats for the priests.

9. Benedictus Arias Montano (1527–1598), *Exemplar, sive, de sacris fabricis liber*, Antwerp, 1572, in vol. VIII of the Antwerp Polyglot Bible (with three plates on the Temple, one of which is also reproduced in *Biblia Sacra*, Antwerp, 1583). Reprinted in: *Antiquitatum Judaicarum libri IX*, Leyden, 1593. Preface by F. Raphelengus (with four plates on the Temple). Also in *Critici Sacri* (ed. J. Pearson), London, 1660, vol. VIII, and in new edition of *Critici Sacri*, Amsterdam, 1698, vol. V (both with all designs). In the general layout Arias was influenced by the Middoth to which he constantly refers; the elevations, on the other hand, represent the first attempt to let the design conform to the standard of contemporary architecture. More important than this is his attitude as commentator. He is the first who considers the descriptions of Solomon's, Zorobabel's and Herod's Temples as those of *real* buildings, and who gives a purely historical account of them without ever referring to Ezechiel's vision.

10. Francisco de Ribera (1537–1591), *De Templo et de iis quae ad templum pertinent*, Antwerp, 1593 (further editions 1602 and 1623). Only one of the five

books deals with the three Temples; much of it is taken up with explanations of the mystical sense.

11. Sebastian Barradas (1558–1615), *Commentariorum in concordiam*, Lisbon, 1605 (Book III, chaps. 10–40, pp. 283–334, 'De Templo Ierosolymitano'). Villalpandus's book is unknown to him. He describes the three Temples, but not Ezechiel's vision, and accepts Josephus's testimony that Herod pulled the second Temple down and rebuilt at great cost a remarkable new building (pp. 325 ff.).

12. Juan Baptista Villalpandus (1552–1608), *In Ezechielem Explanationes et Apparatus Urbis ac Templi Hierosolymitani, commentariis et imaginibus illustratus*, Rome, 1596 ff. (vol. II, 1605). His designs are in quality, consistency and architectural soundness far above anything seen so far. But as an interpreter of the text he tends more towards the past than towards the new scientific spirit noticeable already in Arias Montano (see no. 9). His insistence that Ezechiel's Temple was identical with Solomon's (p. 29) and his denial that there ever was an Herodian Temple as described by Josephus (pp. 570 ff.) is akin to medieval mysticism. But he stresses that in order to grasp the inner meaning of Ezechiel's vision a realistic representation of the Temple is essential; hence he criticizes all preceding attempts of reconstructions, referring in some detail to the Christian Fathers, to Richard, Lyra, Arias and in more general terms to designs in Paris Bibles (Vatable) and other contemporary writers who have no knowledge of Vitruvius and Euclid (pp. 20 f.).

13. Joannes de Pineda (1558–1637), *De Rebus Salomonis Regis libri octo*, Lyons, 1609 (2nd ed. Mainz, 1613). Book V, chap. 5, deals with the Temple. He is in full agreement with Villalpandus, subscribes to his arguments in favour of the classical style and praises his ingenious scheme for arriving at a realistic, but large area for the Temple grounds (pp. 338, 341).

14. Agostino Tornielli (1543–1622), *Annales sacri et profani*, Milan, 1610 (later editions: Frankfurt 1611 and 1616, Antwerp 1620, Cologne 1622, Frankfurt 1640, Antwerp 1649, Lucca 1756) (see text p. 144).

15. Mathias Hafenreffer (1561–1619), *Templum Ezechielis*, Tübingen, 1613. His designs have nothing in common with those by Villalpandus published eight years earlier. Because he rarely refers to contemporary literature, it is impossible to decide whether he was unaware of the *Explicationes* or rejected them.

16. Jacques Salian (1558–1640), *Annales Ecclesiastici veteris Testamenti*, Cologne, 1620 (later editions: Paris 1625, 1635, 1641, Rhoan 1646, Lyons 1664) (see text p. 146).

17. Cornelius a Lapide (Steen) (1567–1637), *Commentaria in quatuor Prophetas majores*, Paris, 1622. This contains his lengthy 'Commentaria in Ezechielem

Prophetam'. He accepts the Vitruvian proportions applied by Villalpandus (p. 230), but proves that he erred in the actual length of the calamos which has the result that 'most dimensions of his Temple are faulty' (p. 234). Since he believes in the mystical character of Ezechiel's Temple, he favours the enormous size of 3,000 cubits and accuses Villalpandus of twisting and turning in order not to be caught (p. 260). The problems of measurements and proportions are, however, too involved for him; he prefers to leave the subject to the architects (p. 254).

18. Passover-Haggadah, Amsterdam, 1629. Perspective view of Temple, reprinted many times (ill. in Zev Vilnay, *The Holy Land in Old Prints and Maps*, Jerusalem, 1963, Fig. 63; identical print from a later Haggadah in *Jewish Encyclopedia*, sub 'Temple'). The three concentric courts recall layouts by medieval writers, such as Richard (no. 2). The Temple itself shows Venetian characteristics; Lamy (no. 45, p. 698) mentions a drawing of the Temple from a Hebrew book sent to him from Venice. It is surprising that in spite of the specifications given in the Talmud the plan is strictly symmetrical.

19. Constantin L'Empereur (1591–1648), *Talmudis Babylonici Codex Middoth sive de Mensuris Templi*, Leyden, 1630. Reprinted in vol. V, pp. 311–82, of *Mishnah*, Amsterdam, 1702 (see no. 40). This is an important annotated Latin translation of the Talmudic treatise. Attached is a plan recording the information derived from Jewish sources. L'Empereur is the first to show the Temple in an asymmetrical position.

20. Louis Cappel (1585–1658), *Historia Apostolica illustrata*, Geneva, 1634. On p. 146 is a large plan of the Temple according to Josephus agreeing in all important points with the one in the *Biblia Polyglotta* (see no. 25). A short account of the Temple on pp. 153 ff.

21. Jacob Jehuda Leon (Aryeh) (1603–after 1675), *Retrato del Templo de Selomoh*, Middleburg, 1642; *Afbeeldinghe van den Tempel Salomonis*, Middleburg, 1642; *Portraict du Temple de Salomon...dont le modelle se trouve après le mesme Autheur, comme chacun peut voir*, Amsterdam, 1643; *Tabnit Hekal*, 1650; *De Templo Hierosolymitano*, Helmstedt, 1665 (transl. by Johann Saubert) (see Fig. 6 and text pp. 148 f.).

22. Jacobus Tirinus (1580–1636), *Biblia magna commentariorum literalium*, Paris, 1643. He believes in the 'mystical' Temple area of 3,000 cubits (p. 545).

23. Giovanni Stefano Menochio (1575–1655), *De Republica Hebraeorum libri octo*, Paris, 1648.

24. John Lightfoot (1602–1675), *The Temple: especially as it stood in the dayes of our Saviour*, London, 1650. Reprinted in *The Works of John Lightfoot,*

London, 1684, and in *J. Lightfooti . . . Opera omnia*, Rotterdam, 1686. As indicated by the title Lightfoot's overriding interest is the historical reality of the Jewish Temple.

25. Louis Cappel (1585–1658), '*Trisagion sive Templi Hierosolymitani triplex delineatio*', published in vol. I of *Biblia Sacra Polyglotta*, ed. Brian Walton, London, 1657 (Taylor, *op. cit.*, p. 49, mentions a first edition of 1643; I have been unable to trace it). Reprinted, but without the plates, in *Biblicus apparatus*, Zürich, 1673. A revised and partly enlarged edition appeared in vol. IX, pp. 3716–3968, of *Critici Sacri*, ed. John Pearson, London, 1660. This edition does not bring the plans according to Josephus and the Talmud. Reprinted in vol. V of the new edition of *Critici Sacri*, Amsterdam, 1698, this time with the Talmud but not the Villalpandus plates.

26. Samuel Lee (1625–1691), *Orbis Miraculum; or, the Temple of Solomon*, London, 1659. With crude drawings: a bird's-eye view, an elevation and a ground-plan covering an area of 400 square cubits according to Josephus.

27. Johannes Coccejus (1603–1669), *Prophetia Ezechielis cum Commentaria illustrata*, Amsterdam, 1669, with nineteen plates of the Temple (see Fig. 11). Reprinted in *Opera omnia*, Amsterdam, 1673, vol. II, and 1701, vol. III. He names a mathematician Samuel Carl Kechel v. Hollenstein, assisted by an unnamed architect, to be responsible for the designs.

28. Jan Leusden (1624–1699), *Philologus Hebraeus*, Utrecht, 1672. Jacob Jehuda's view of the Temple (see no. 21) is shown on the title-page.

29. Maimonides (Moses ben Maimon) (1135–1204), *De Cultu Divino, ex Mosis Majemonidae secunda Lege seu Manu Forti liber VIII. Dividitur in IX tractatus . . . Accesserunt tabulae aere incisae, in quibus exprimitur Hierosolymitani Templi forma accuratissime, et eleganter descripta. Hunc librum ex Hebraeo Latinum fecit . . . Ludovicus de Compiegne de Veil*, Paris, 1678. Reprinted in *Fasciculus sextus Opisculorum quae ad historiam ac philologiam sacram spectant* (ed. Thomas Crenius), Rotterdam, 1696, and in Blasius Ugolinus, *Thesaurus Antiquitatum Sacrarium*, vol. VIII, Venice, 1747.

30. Juan Caramuel v. Lobkowitz (1606–1682), *Architectura civil recta, y obliqua*, Vigeven, 1678. His design (Plate A) is taken over from Jacob Jehuda (see no. 21), not from Villalpandus. This is confirmed by Caramuel's explicit statement in the *Tabla General* that he represented the Temple 'not as P. Juan Bautista Villalpando imagined it but as the Rabbis presented it and as in fact it had been'.

31. Nicolaus Goldmann (1611–1665), *Architectura Sacra*. The manuscript, never published, was in Sturm's possession (no. 36, p. 16); it was also used by Reyher (no. 32, pp. 461, 630, 691) who reproduced one of Goldmann's designs, a plan for the chapel of Solomon's palace.

32. Samuel Reyher (1635–1714), *Mathesis Mosaica*, Kiel, 1679. Chapters XXXV–XXXVIII: 'De Templo Salomonis'.

33. Melchior Küsel, *Icones Biblicae Veteris et Novi Testamenti*, Nürnberg, 1679. Plate 49 of part II shows Villalpandus's Temple.

34. Willem Goeree (1635–1711), *D'Algemeene Bouwkunde*, Amsterdam, 1681; pp. 65–85 on Solomon's Order.

35. Bernard Lamy (1640–1715), *Introduction à la lecture de l'écriture sainte composée en Latin*, Lyons, 1669. The plan of the Temple is similar to those by L'Empereur, Lightfoot and Perrault with the exception of the symmetrical position of the Temple and the additional Court of Gentiles.

36. Leonhard Christoph Sturm (1669–1719), *Sciagraphia Templi Hierosolymitani*, Leipzig, 1694. Although the plan for Ezechiel's Temple is derived from Villalpandus, to some extent their viewpoints differ. In Sturm's opinion Ezechiel's Temple, the mystical model for the Christian Church and the most perfect building, was never built, while the Temple at the time of Christ, of which he brings a plan, was built according to the Talmudic description.

37. Louis Maillet (d. 1720), *Les Figures du Temple et du Palais de Salomon*, Paris, 1695. The only French architect to work independently on the Temple. (Perrault and Delamonce (see no. 44) were commissioned to illustrate a theological treatise.) His approach is similar to Villalpandus's although he pretends not to have made use of his work. Tostado (no. 5) and Lapide (no. 17) are the only authors to whom he refers.

38. Bernard Lamy, *Apparatus Biblicus*, Lyons, 1696 (French translation, 1697). The designs differ greatly from the plan he published ten years earlier (no. 35). Now the whole area is covered with buildings. The elevation, though original in its conception, is clearly classical in character.

39. Nicolaus Goldmann, *Vollständige Anweisung zu der Civilbaukunst* (ed. by L. Chr. Sturm), Wolfenbüttel, 1698. Chapter 7 of Book I and Plates 9–15 may have been taken from his *Architectura Sacra* (no. 31).

40. *Mishnah*, translated into Latin by W. Surenhus, 6 vols., Amsterdam, 1698 ff., with Maimonides's and Obadiah Bertinoro's commentaries. The title-pages and p. 260 of vol. II show the Temple similar in style to Villalpandus's designs. Reprint of L'Empereur's Latin translation in vol. V (see no. 19).

41. Willem Goeree, *La République des Hebreux*,

Amsterdam, 1705, 3 vols. of which vol. I is a translation of Peter Cunaeus, *De Republica Hebraeorum*, Leyden, 1631. The Dutch edition appeared in 1700. The *Biographie Nouvelle* mentions a first edition in 3 vols. of 1685.

42. Johannes Lund (1638–1686), *Die Alten Jüdischen Heiligthümer*, Hamburg, 1704, with a preface by Heinrich Mühl. According to a remark on p. 256 Lund wrote it in 1678. The elevation of the Temple (p. 254), derived from Villalpandus, agrees neither with the plan (p. 302) nor with the text.

43. Augustin Calmet (1672–1757), *Commentaire littéral sur tous les livres de l'ancien et du nouveau Testament*, Paris, 1707 ff. Vol. VI: 'Commentaire littéral sur Ezechiel'. The text mentions engravings; they were missing from the copies I have seen. His criticism of preceding reconstructions and of Villalpandus on p. 558.

44. F. Desbruslins, 'Description du Tabernacle . . . du Temple de Salomon. . . .' Part of vol. III of an eighteenth-century Bible, bound to a British Museum copy of the *Biblia Sacra vulgatae editionis*, Paris, 1662 (B.M. L.12 f.4). Before 1716, the year in which the engraver G. Scotin l'aîné died. The three plates presenting the Temple were designed by Ferdinand Delamonce (1678–1753), a well-known Lyonnais architect. When criticizing reconstructions in Vitruvian style, Desbruslins argues against the notion that the Temple, commanded by God, must have been a perfect masterpiece. In his opinion the meaning is that God's orders were executed without deviation, not that their perfection could not be improved. This copy also contains a plan by Humphrey Prideaux (1648–1724), based on Lightfoot (see no. 24).

45. Bernard Lamy, *De Tabernaculo Foederis, de Sancta Civitate Jerusalem, et de Templo ejus*, Paris,

1720. The preparatory research to this comprehensive work started over twenty years earlier. The prospectus of 1697 (*De Templo Hierosolymitano*, Bibl. Nat. MS. Fond Clairambault 450 fol. 96) not only gives sequence and contents of chapters agreeing with those published in 1720, but contains already the demand for a comparative approach, placing Solomon's Temple next to the contemporary Phoenician and Egyptian architecture. There is also a reference to Maimonides's description of the Temple. Criticism of Villalpandus was still missing in the *Apparatus* of 1696 (no. 38). The change of viewpoint must have taken place during the research for the larger book. The groundplan agrees in all essential parts with that of 1696, but the elevation is now freed of almost any resemblance with the classical style.

46. Johann Bernhard Fischer von Erlach (1656–1723), *Entwurff einer Historischen Architectur*, Vienna, 1721.

47. Augustin Calmet, *Dictionnaire historique, critique, chronologique . . . de la Bible*, Paris, 1722, vol. II (2nd enlarged ed. 1730, vol. III), sub 'Temple'. A number of engravings show the Temple as envisaged by Calmet; another set reproduces Villalpandus's designs. These, in the second edition, Calmet strongly criticizes: their classical style, the multitude of courts and colonnades, the richness of the material. The aim of a reconstruction ought to be, not to produce the most beautiful and sumptious building, but one that conforms best with the sacred text. His own designs, though largely lacking classical forms, are nevertheless almost as fanciful as those produced by Villalpandus. Calmet is equally opposed to reconstructions based on Jewish sources as his comments on a plan designed by Humphrey Prideaux, Dean of Norwich (1648–1724) show (2nd ed., p. 633). Rabbinical writings of the Middle Ages as well as the Talmud are rejected as unreliable.

DOROTHEA NYBERG

La sainte Antiquité

Focus of an Eighteenth-century Architectural Debate

In his convenient *Abrégé* of Vitruvius' architectural treatise published in 1674 for connoisseurs of the building art, Claude Perrault warns his reader that, if through study he would form an accurate and disciplined concept of architecture, 'it is absolutely necessary to be convinced that the taste one follows is better than any other'. Failing this conviction, ideas always remain 'vague and uncertain'.[1] Thirty-five years later there began a publishing event which illustrates, by a dramatic clash between two different concepts of architecture, that taste is usually, in fact, what guides the formation of architectural aesthetics. Between 1709 and 1712 the prestigious *Mémoires de Trévoux*, a monthly journal published by the Jesuits for the insatiably curious Frenchman, printed an exchange of articles which constitute one of the liveliest and most biting arguments preserved in the abundant literature of architectural aesthetics. That the strangely intense and intricate debate which the Abbé de Cordemoy and the engineer Amédée-François Frézier carried on in the pages of a periodical of European-wide circulation was long remembered we know from a reference to it some forty years later in Diderot's and D'Alembert's monumental *Encyclopédie*.[2] Yet the occasion for this outpouring of words was not unusual: the appearance in 1706 of Cordemoy's *Nouveau traité de toute l'architecture*. The unsolicited critique of Cordemoy's treatise by Frézier—for which the editors prudently abjured responsibility—was the engineer's response, specifically, to an anonymous review which the book had received in the September, 1706, issue of the *Mémoires*.[3] For the reviewer not only had juxtaposed quotations from the *Nouveau traité* which seem to favor certain Gothic cathedrals over Michelangelo's St. Peter's in Rome, but had ended by assuring the public that it would find Cordemoy's book both judicious and instructive.[4] To a no-nonsense type of person, such as we know Frézier to have been, this opinion was dangerously ignorant. Frézier was a man

of acknowledged competence, who possessed, moreover, a keen intelligence of the kind which does not easily accept what it considers mere foolishness. His responsibility as a professional engineer was aroused: the public must be warned that the Abbé simply was not competent in architectural matters. However, as it turned out, Cordemoy was not the only non-specialist in the exchange. For the argument quickly became centered on religious architecture, so that in some measure it was Frézier who was the layman, not Cordemoy.[5] Above all, it was this ambiguous situation, so fruitful for polemics, which was responsible for the quality of immense conviction displayed by the participants of the debate.

Unquestionably, the five articles which constitute the exchange[6]—Cordemoy, as it happened, had the final word—make difficult reading today for the student of eighteenth-century architecture. They belong to that class of writing, the 'reply to the reply of M....', which in periods such as our own most authors would prefer to forget. This was not true of the eighteenth century, however. Frézier was still 'arguing' in 1739

1. *Abrégé ... de Vitruve*, Paris, 1674, p. 6.
2. V (1755), pp. 421–2.
3. Pp. 1523–42.
4. 'Le Public sans qu'on l'en prie sera sans doute disposé à pardonner quelques défauts de style à un Ecrivain si judicieux, & si instructif' (*ibid.*, p. 1542). The reviewer was kind to Cordemoy; his French style is even worse than the remark suggests.

5. The best source of information about the colorful, extremely active life of Frézier (1682–1773) is Pierre du Colombier, 'Amédée François Frézier', *Festschrift für Karl Lohmeyer*, ed. K. Schwingel, Saarbrücken, 1954, pp. 159–66 (see also *Biographie universelle*, ed. J. F. Michaud, 2nd ed., Paris, 1880, XV, pp. 185–6); Frézier's engineering treatise, *La theorie et la pratique de la coupe des pierres* (3 vols., Paris, 1737–9) was highly respected in the eighteenth century (J.-F. Blondel, *Discours sur la nécessité de l'étude de l'architecture*, Paris, 1754, p. 87). About Cordemoy's life, by contrast, almost nothing is known; see R. D. Middleton, 'The Abbé de Cordemoy and the Graeco-Gothic Ideal: A Prelude to Romantic Classicism', *Journal of the Warburg and Courtauld Institutes*, XXV (1962), pp. 278–320, XXVI (1963), pp. 90–123; XXV, p. 280 and n. 10. See below, n. 20. On the issue of authority, which at this time was a divisive factor between a professional and a lay approach to architecture, see Dorothea Nyberg, 'The *Mémoires critiques d'architecture* by Michel de Frémin', *Journal of The Society of Architectural Historians*, XXII (1963), pp. 217–24.
6. Frézier, 'Remarques sur le *Nouveau traité de toute l'architecture* de Monsieur de Cordemoy', *Mémoires de Trévoux* (Paris, 1701–75), Sept. 1709, pp. 1618–40; Cordemoy, 'Réponse aux Remarques de Mr. Frézier...', *ibid.*, July–August 1710, pp. 1248–75, 1345–64; Frézier, 'Repliques à la Réponse de Monsieur de Cordemoy aux remarques de Mr. Frézier...', *ibid.*, Sept. 1711, pp. 1569–87; Cordemoy, 'Dissertation sur la maniere dont les Eglises doivent être bâtis, pour être conformes à l'Antiquité & à la belle Architecture, qui peut servir de réponse aux repliques de Mr. Frézier...', *ibid.*, July 1712, pp. 1250–85.

with his then long-dead antagonist in the pages of a formal *Dissertation sur les ordres d'architecture*,[7] and forty-five years after he had first taken up his pen against the Abbé de Cordemoy he again took it in hand, this time in the pages of the *Mercure de France* against the ideas of the man who inherited Cordemoy's intellectual legacy, the Abbé Laugier.[8] The furor which the latter's *Essai sur l'architecture* created in the 1750's and 60's among architects and connoisseurs alike had been prepared for fifty years earlier in the pages of the *Mémoires de Trévoux*. But while Cordemoy's *Nouveau traité* has recently been the subject of an important study by Middleton,[9] the informal debate which it set off has received only passing references from scholars. Thus the purpose of the present essay is limited: to make amends for this neglect by focusing on the debate itself. Such a study is long overdue. For despite the difficulty of unraveling the threads of intertwined issues from the polemical context of journalistic give and take, these issues were to be of the greatest import for architecture throughout the eighteenth century. One of them especially has gone almost unnoticed up to now, and on it this essay will concentrate. To what might be called the Graeco-Gothic equation of church architecture which the Abbé de Cordemoy had presented in his *Nouveau traité*, in the subsequent debate a third factor was added—the Early Christian basilican church of the Constantinian era. Perhaps more than anything else, it was the fourth-century structure—which, be it noted, belongs by right both to Antiquity and the Christian religion—which as an ideal was to act as the catalytic agent in the creation of Neo-classical architecture.

Frézier's original critical onslaught in 1709 was primarily directed against Cordemoy's ideal for contemporary church architecture in the *Nouveau traité*. In Chapter III, Cordemoy had discussed what is appropriate for this highest category of public buildings.[10] Like Frémin in his *Mémoires critiques d'architecture* (1702), he was dissatisfied with modern church design, complaining that it always followed 'the same

model', St. Peter's in Rome, instead of ancient architecture. Both St. Peter's and the Val-de-Grâce in Paris, for example, have massive arcades supported by piers against which pilasters are placed. Moreover, the crossing domes of both churches are sustained by four gigantic arcades—which in Cordemoy's judgment are *porte-à-faux*, faults of the aesthetics of structure. By contrast, what ancient architecture meant to Cordemoy, whose book is manifestly indebted both to Perrault's Vitruvius (1673, 1684) and his *Ordonnance des cinq espèces de colonnes* (1683), was the dignity and grace of free-standing columns supporting a straight entablature. However, his enthusiasm for colonnades was structurally naïve, to say the least. For instance, he believed that instead of 'all these useless and heavy arcades, as well as these great piers that support them' in the Val-de-Grâce, the church would be *infiniment plus belle* if columns were simply substituted, and if colonnades replaced the four arcades supporting the dome.[11] The Abbé made other suggestions for the reformation of church architecture in his *Nouveau traité*. He would like a portico on the façade, which would recall those '*porches* that for a long time Christians liked to place in front of the churches, in order to shelter there the catechumens and penitents'; he would like the High Altar placed in the crossing under the dome, but without a baldacchino; and he would like the side aisles to be covered with flat ceilings 'distributed as they were by the ancients, one for each bay of the porticoes or peristyles—in a word, the way they were made in the portico of the Louvre'.[12] There are hints in this chapter of his book, then, that Cordemoy could well have been thinking of the Early Christian church-type best exemplified by Old St. Peter's of fourth-century Rome.[13] But they are hints merely. The exemplar by which he chose to illustrate his reformed church-structure was built in Paris during his lifetime by Claude Perrault, as well the great defender of the Moderns as the skillful translator-editor of Vitruvius. Of his ideal for church architecture Cordemoy wrote: 'I would indeed consider a church in the taste of the portico of the Louvre

7. Strasbourg, 1738, pp. 32, 33, 36 (bound with *La theorie et la pratique* . . . , III, 1739).

8. 'Remarques sur quelques Livres nouveaux concernant la beauté & le bon goût de l'Architecture', *Mercure de France*, July 1754, pp. 7–59; of the three works reviewed, Laugier's *Essai sur l'architecture* (Paris, 1753) receives the major share of attention (pp. 18–59), perhaps because Frézier is fighting the ideas of *both* Cordemoy and Laugier throughout. For example, he remarks that Cordemoy did not succeed, as he wished, in 'bannir la fâcheuse incertitude qui rend les régles de l'Architecture comme arbitraires' (p. 19).

9. Middleton, *op. cit*; on the Cordemoy-Frézier debate, xxv, pp. 287–8.

10. *Nouveau traité* . . . , 1st ed., 1706, ch. III, sect. i–v, pp. 169–92.

11. *Ibid*., pp. 172–3.

12. *Ibid*., pp. 178, 180 ff., 192.

13. The most often repeated view of the Vatican basilica in the seventeenth century is the engraving by Martino Ferrabosco, first published in 1620 in Costaguti's work on St. Peter's, and reprinted by Ciampini, Carlo Fontana, and Buonanni. See Paul Durrieu, 'Une vue intérieure de l'ancien Saint Pierre de Rome au milieu du XVᵉ siècle peinte par Jean Foucquet', *Mélanges G. B. De Rossi, École Française de Rome, Mémoires*, XII (1892), Suppl., pp. 221–2. It shows the interior in cross-section, as does Foucquet's miniature (*Grandes Chroniques de France*, fol. 89v) now in the Bibliothèque nationale, Paris, MS. fr. 6465). There is no way of knowing whether Cordemoy knew any visual representation of the lost building.

entrance, or of that which was invented by the famous P. de Creil at the Abbey of Sainte Geneviève in Paris, as the most beautiful thing in the world; instead of which I see only ponderousness, little boldness, and much sterility in these churches with arcades such as are made at present.'[14]

Frézier's pen was never gentle. He attacked this thesis at its weakest point, in a literal as well as a figurative sense: the utter impracticality of the Abbé's wish to substitute a column-and-lintel system in St. Peter's and the Val-de-Grâce for the pier-and-arch construction in use. Observing that at least a modicum of knowledge about engineering is necessary if one would be a reformer of architecture, he requested with ironical politeness that Cordemoy 'produce a design according to his taste, and a new manner of cutting stones, which would teach us to make lintels of 40 and 78 feet in span, such as the architraves would have to be that it would be necessary to substitute for the arcades of the size that are seen there [i.e., in St. Peter's]'.[15]

Further, analyzing the modular proportions of the hypothetical St. Peter's according to Cordemoy's *petit module*, he pointed out that the columns would be twelve feet in diameter—that is, like a fairly good-sized tower.[16] Thus even the choice of the narrowest possible intercolumniation of $1\frac{1}{2}$ diameters would produce architraves eighteen feet from column to column. 'But', he exclaimed, 'what an embarrassment to find such masses of columns almost at each step along one's way.'[17] The main altar under the dome would be lost from sight when one was in the aisles. The conclusion was logically inevitable. It is precisely *by means of* the pier-and-arch system that St. Peter's achieves the quality which the Abbé—following Perrault—valued so highly, namely *dégagement*. What is more, Frézier kindly reminded Cordemoy that since he was so fond of columns, the interior of St. Peter's has one hundred and thirty, measuring from twenty-five to thirty feet in height.

Now this single example of Frézier's method of argumentation in the 1709 article may serve to demonstrate the formidable nature of Cordemoy's disputant. Frézier's skillful dialectics have turned Cordemoy's 'ideal' St. Peter's into a ponderous, structurally timid and awkward building, while his ability to reason specifically in terms of the practical exigencies which an architect must control has made Cordemoy appear as an ineffectual dreamer of dreams. Finally, the

engineer's dramatic talent has enabled him to create the polemical flourish that mocks just when it seems to take its object most seriously. We cannot be surprised that in the face of such an attack Cordemoy felt called upon to defend himself against every point Frézier had raised. The Abbé was forced both to amplify and make specific the thesis he had presented so cryptically in his *Nouveau traité*.

In his first reply to Frézier, published in the July, 1710, issue of the *Mémoires*, Cordemoy tackled precisely the point of contention that seemed to offer his own position the least security: 'How does he know that I have not *the slightest notion about construction*?'[18] Pointing out that he knows how to draw—his work has not displeased those with taste—he added that he is not at all bad with *l'ebauchoir & le ciseau*. In fact, he claimed building experience: 'I have directed some architectural work that has been found acceptable enough.'[19] This personal information, which somehow has been overlooked, cannot fail to interest us. Almost nothing has been added by scholars to what we know about the author of the *Nouveau traité* from the book itself, which gives his titles: *Chanoine Regulier de S. Jean de Soissons & Prieur de la Ferté-sous-Joüars*.[20] The mystery surrounding Cordemoy's life is merely confounded by the fact that he wrote a treatise which confidently advocates a dramatic reform of architecture—and then accepted the challenge of a man like Frézier. Clearly, he was indignant at the charge of incompetence. In the light of modern technological sophistication the two antagonists may well appear to be unequally matched—it must be stressed that Frézier has yet to receive his due as one of the most powerful thinkers in eighteenth-century architecture—but from the point of view of history Cordemoy's *belief* that he had irrefutable evidence to support his thesis is the most significant factor in determining the direction the debate was to take.

But what evidence could there possibly be to refute the inexorable structural logic of the engineer? Simply this: Cordemoy thought his ideal church *had already*

---

14. *Op. cit.*, pp. 176–7. See Middleton, *op. cit.*, p. 285, n. 19. C. P. de Creil (1633–1708) designed a façade *c.* 1691 which, as Middleton remarks, 'is a rather naïve paraphrase of the arrangement of Perrault's Louvre façade'.
15. *Mémoires de Trévoux*, Sept. 1709, p. 1621.
16. *Ibid.*, p. 1625.
17. *Ibid.*, p. 1626; see also 1711, p. 1574.

18. *Ibid.*, July 1710, p. 1250.
19. *Ibid*; this provides at least circumstantial support, be it noted, for Middleton's idea (*op. cit.*, p. 285) that Cordemoy may have helped with drawings for a Ste-Geneviève project by the Perrault brothers (see below, pp. 166–7).
20. Given on the title page. In a reference to his dispute with Cordemoy, Frézier claimed in 1738 that he had been prevented from replying again, after his 1711 article, by a $2\frac{1}{2}$-year trip to the South Seas and by the subsequent death of his antagonist (*Dissertation . . .* , p. 63). Cordemoy, therefore, must have died *c.* 1715, which makes the possibility that he can be identified with the Cistercian theologian, Louis Géraud de Cordemoy (1651–1722), even less likely than Middleton has supposed (*op. cit.*, p. 280, n. 10; p. 284, n. 18). Joan Evans accepts the Augustinian designation of his title as Canon at Soissons (*Monastic Architecture in France*, Cambridge, 1964, p. 72, n. 5).

been realized by the first Christians. What he desired for modern church architecture was a return to this lost perfection, as if he had transferred to the sphere of church architecture the sentiment expressed by his contemporary, the Abbé Claude Fleury, who wrote that the Christian religion, since it 'is not an invention of men, but a work of God, . . . had its perfection at the beginning, as also the universe'.[21] In fact, the entire course of the debate was deflected away from modern St. Peter's and contemporary building practice, henceforth to center almost exclusively on the churches of the first Christians[22] when Cordemoy claimed that modern St. Peter's 'would be much more beautiful if it had free-standing columns'. For he left no doubt that, as built, this church did not satisfy him: 'And if one dares to reproach Bramante and Michelangelo, these great men, with anything, it is in not having done everything *in their power* to imitate in St. Peter's of Rome, the principal church of the Christian world, what the first faithful were very careful to observe in theirs, I mean colonnades.'[23] No longer merely a question of two discordant aesthetic judgments about the primary church of Christendom, the exchange had become a Battle of the Ancient Christian and the Modern Christian.

The reader will probably be wondering what evidence about Early Christian architecture was available to Cordemoy and Frézier, and how they made use of it in their debate. Besides Vitruvius—who, with one exception discussed below, was the only source cited for architectural illustrations—they appealed to Early Christian writers: Eusebius of Caesarea (approx. 263–339), Prudentius (348–c. 408) from Saragossa, Sidonius Apollinaris (431–482) of Lyons and Clermont, St. Gregory of Tours (538–594), and Paul the Silentiary (sixth century) of Constantinople. One particular example of how Cordemoy and Frézier used these authors is especially revealing, because a study of Early Christian architecture presented—indeed still presents—complex problems involving the critical evaluation of data. Cordemoy, in order to prove that the ciborium over the altar of early churches 'was properly speaking a dome or cupola', quoted from the panegyric poem on Hagia Sophia by Paul the Silentiary.[24] Noting that the poem describes an *immensa*

turris, rising over the altar *vastum in aïrem* and supported by columns and entablature overlaid with silver, he argued that such a description simply could not apply merely to a baldacchino. Paul the Silentiary's *immensa turris* must be a true dome, part of the building's fabric. He found support, moreover, for his interpretation of the poem in the description of an Auvergne church by Gregory of Tours.[25] Therefore drawing from this evidence 'consequences completely contrary to those of Mr. Frézier', the Abbé enumerated them as follows: '1. That there were neither piers nor arcades in the churches. 2. That the dome was always supported by columns; and that finally the altar was placed there in the center, in order to be seen from all sides.'[26]

Now, from the fact that he cited the contrary interpretation of Paul the Silentiary's poem by the erudite Benedictine scholar, Dom Jean Mabillon, and fully admitted the latter's disagreement,[27] we know that Cordemoy was firmly convinced that he had drawn the correct inference from these early texts. But Frézier's method of dealing with the early texts, and with the Abbé's sweeping conclusions about the early churches, was completely different. Replying that 'hyperbole' is a perfectly legitimate artistic technique for poets who wish 'to give a lofty idea of what they describe', he emphasized that poetic expressions cannot be taken as proof of what a building actually looked like.[28] He inquired bitingly what likelihood there was that the dome of Hagia Sophia 'was carried only by four columns and as many *arcades* of silver, or [even] covered with silver?'[29] And as evidence, he referred to the 'plan and elevation' of Hagia Sophia by 'M. Grelot'.[30]

The Grelot in question is Guillaume-Joseph Grelot, who in 1680 had published a plan and interior view of Hagia Sophia (Fig. 1)—along with three other engravings of the building—in a *Relation nouvelle d'un*

---

21. *Mœurs des Chrétiens*, Paris, 1824, p. 6; it is cited by Frézier (*Mémoires de Trévoux*, Sept. 1711, p. 1580) on the apse disposition in early churches. Besides writing on the history of the early Church, Fleury (1640–1723) wrote a *Discours sur les libertés de l'église gallicane* and an essay on Plato.

22. The only exception is the August 1710 article (*ibid.*, pp. 1345–64) where Cordemoy is concerned with defending his strictures against pediments.

23. *Mémoires de Trévoux*, July 1710, pp. 1251–2 (my italics).

24. *Mémoires de Trévoux*, July 1710, p. 1270.

25. *Ibid.*, pp. 1270–1; the church is not identified.

26. *Ibid.*, pp. 1271–2; see Frézier's answer, *ibid.*, Sept. 1711, pp. 1583–4.

27. 'Le Pere Mabillon croit que ce [terme] *Ciboire* n'étoit que ce que nous nommons à présent *Dias* ou *Baldaquin*. Mais s'il m'est permis de faire des conjectures après ce sçavant Homme, je crois que ce *Ciboire* étoit proprement un dôme ou une coupole' (*ibid.*, July 1710, p. 1270). The Abbé's insistence on his right to make his own judgments is in the same spirit as that shown by Michel de Frémin, when he wrote—in more vivid phraseology, however—that 'comme chacun dans le monde a un droit naturel de penser, je m'imagine par ce titre que je puis aussi bien que Sostrate, Sintare, & Polion enfanter des opinions, . . . je les nourriray de raisons aussi palpables que legitimes' (*Mémoires critiques d'architecture*, Paris, 1702, p. 238).

28. *Mémoires de Trévoux*, Sept. 1711, p. 1577.

29. *Ibid.*; the substitution of the word arcade in the passage is a typical example of Frézier's irony—Cordemoy had, of course, not used it.

30. *Ibid.*

voyage de Constantinople.[31] Grelot's description which accompanies these engravings stresses not only the 'four heavy piers with large arcades which join them together', but also the sheer size of the dome which they support—'eighteen *toises* in diameter'.[32] Having spent weeks studying the building under the hazardous conditions imposed by the Turkish rule of Constantinople, Grelot was nothing if not conscientious—a characteristic to which both his engravings and his text bear witness. Going into the history of Hagia Sophia, he carefully discriminated between fact and legend, in every case checking as far as possible the veracity of what he had been told or had read. Grelot, indeed, was passionately devoted to the task simply of establishing scientific facts. For instance, in his account of the construction of the building's second dome, to replace the one that had fallen, he refers to the claim of several people that cement was used in the second attempt in order to lighten the dome, and here he noted: 'If I could have gone up to the top in order to report the truth about it, I would have done it with all my heart: but in the state of things today, a Christian is not permitted to ascend there.'[33]

We can thus readily appreciate the irony with which Frézier, Grelot's book in hand, dealt with Cordemoy's poetic evidence. The sixth-century poem, considered as a factual building account of the Justinian church, was proved utterly unreliable by modern scientific data. Yet, as Frézier pointed out, Paul the Silentiary lived in the Justinian period. The engineer's meaning is clear. Poetic truth must not be confused with factual accuracy. Paul the Silentiary's *immensa turris* rising high over the altar but supported on only four columns could not possibly be the 'dome or cupola' of Hagia Sophia. On the contrary, its dome 'is supported by *piers and arcades*, on four pendentives, like our modern domes: a fact established by all travellers, for the columns seen there serve only to support galleries'.[34]

First, of course, among modern examples is the dome of St. Peter's in Rome.

Frézier had been fortunate in the ciborium-dome exchange. Modern data were available as a basis for evaluating the textual source, and he made use of them with full awareness of their significance for scientific method. But in the last article of the series Cordemoy stubbornly refused to concede his defeat on the issue and instead noted 'that the Saint Sophia of Mr. Grelot is not that of *Constantine*'.[35] An extraordinary statement!—since Frézier had not claimed that it *was* the Constantinian building.[36] Is this a case, then, of deliberate evasion on Cordemoy's part? A study of the development of their debate does not lend support to such an hypothesis. For it is apparent that from 1710, when he first replied to his critic, Cordemoy had been thinking of the fourth century when the 'first faithful' built colonnades in their churches. 'Constantine the Great had no sooner granted peace to the Christians', he had written, 'than they built churches or basilicas everywhere. Some were in cross form, others completely straight [i.e., longitudinal], and the last round. But all had peristyles.'[37] Indeed, the fourth century was to the Abbé *la sainte Antiquité*.[38] Thus the verses on the 'dome' of Hagia Sophia were introduced by a reference to the Constantinian Holy Sepulchre in Jerusalem, described in a passage of Eusebius' *Life of Constantine* which Cordemoy had already quoted.[39] In the 1712 article his concern was

31. Plan, facing p. 109, and interior view toward apse (Fig. 1), p. 147; exterior from the northwest, facing p. 127, and from the south, p. 143; interior toward the entrance, facing p. 155. Grelot published in his book only a small number of the drawings made during a six-year sojourn in Turkey and Persia; that his reader may have confidence in the accuracy of his engravings, he included 'Attestations des plus celebres et illustres voyageurs' among which is one by the Director of the *Académie Royale d'Architecture*, François Blondel ('Avis au lecteur', and page following).
32. P. 103.
33. *Ibid.*, p. 104. Desgodets exhibited the same attitude in *Les édifices antiques de Rome*, Paris, 1682, as Herrmann has demonstrated; see 'Antoine Desgodets and the Académie Royale d'Architecture', *The Art Bulletin*, XL (1958), pp. 23–53.
34. *Mémoires de Trévoux*, Sept. 1711, p. 1584. Grelot had remarked that 'quelque magnifique qu'ait esté & que soit encore l'Eglise de Sainte Sophie, je ne croy pas qu'elle ait jamais approché de celle du fameux Temple de Salomon, puisque mesme il s'en faut de beaucoup qu'elle ne soit égale, ny en

grandeur, ny en richesse, ny en beauté à l'Eglise de S. Pierre de Rome' (*op. cit.*, p. 100). With the latter part of this sentiment, at least, Frézier would certainly agree.
35. *Mémoires de Trévoux*, July 1712, pp. 1274–5 (my italics).
36. Furthermore, Grelot had been very explicit about the fourth-century plan of Hagia Sophia, comparing it to that of Old St. Peter's and of S. Paolo fuori le mura: 'c'est à dire une Eglise fort longue avec un travers au bout qui faisoit la figure d'une croix, & le tout accompagné de grandes galleries appuyées sur quantité de colonnes' (*op. cit.*, pp. 96–97). Middleton is therefore not accurate when he says that 'Frézier cited Grelot's engravings of Sancta Sophia but Cordemoy correctly refused to believe that the extant building had any formal relationship to the church erected by Constantine' (*op. cit.*, p. 288). Cordemoy was not correcting Frézier, since the latter had made no mistake.
37. *Mémoires de Trévoux*, July 1710, p. 1252. Like the Early Christian writers, Cordemoy used the term 'basilica' in a broadly generic sense. See A. Furetière, *Dictionaire universelle*, 3 vols., The Hague, 1690, I, *sub* Basilique: 'On appelle encore en Italie la *Basilique de St. Pierre*, pour dire, la grande Eglise de St. Pierre, & *Basilique d'or* l'Eglise de St. Sauveur, ou de Latran, à cause de son excellente structure & de ses riches ornements.'
38. *Mémoires de Trévoux*, July 1710, p. 1272, July 1712, p. 1251; Frézier used the phrase in reply, Sept. 1711, pp. 1570, 1582.
39. *Ibid.*, July 1710, p. 1270; the Eusebius passage, from his *Life of Constantine*, Bks. III and IV, is quoted on p. 1254. As Frézier remarked (*Mémoires de Trévoux*, Sept. 1711, p. 1572), Eusebius 'ne dit pas tout ce qu'on lui fait dire'. However, in the light of the profusion of modern reconstructions of the fourth-century Holy Sepulchre based on the Eusebian description, it would be more accurate to say that Cordemoy combined atrium,

still with the age of Constantine: 'I do not really believe that the basilicas of the Saint Sepulchre, and of Saint Sophia, such as they exist today are the same as Constantine had built.'[40] Again he was quite correct, of course. What scholarship has failed to notice, however, is the simple fact that neither participant in the debate had anywhere claimed that the extant buildings *were* Constantinian in date.[41] Thus by his bluntly factual statement that 'Grelot's' Hagia Sophia was not the building constructed by Constantine, the Abbé was merely pointing out that the Justinian work was *irrelevant* to his own concern, which all along had been the Constantinian period. He was not in the least confused that what interested him was *la sainte Antiquité* of the Peace of the Church. This ideal is what he obstinately refused to surrender. On the other hand, Cordemoy had not been at all clear about the Constantinian and Justinian churches of Hagia Sophia when he first introduced the sixth-century poem into the debate as evidence about the former. When a genuine confusion over the building history of the church was inadvertently brought to light by Frézier's use of Grelot's visual material, Cordemoy then assumed that Paul the Silentiary's poem referred to the predecessor of 'Grelot's' Hagia Sophia, destroyed in the Nika Riots of 532 and thus presumably known by the Byzantine official. Certainly we cannot blame Cordemoy for not knowing that this building, too, had been a successor to the Constantinian Hagia Sophia.

This confused and incomplete historical knowledge merely serves to emphasize the fact that the Abbé located his prototype for modern church architecture in the Constantinian period: Old St. Peter's and the churches of Lyons, Limoges and Clermont in the West; the Basilica of Tyre, the Holy Sepulchre, Hagia Sophia and the church of Antioch in the East, were his models. It is understandable, then, that each Early Christian writer was first introduced into the debate by Cordemoy. His antagonist's only concern was to expose a certain absence of technological sophistication in the Abbé's insistence that these buildings provided a viable structural alternative to the one ennobled by modern St. Peter's in Rome. For such is the position that Cordemoy stated in 1710, and that in greater

detail he elaborated in his last article of 1712. In the first reply, for instance, he quoted from a poem by the fifth-century bishop of Clermont, Sidonius Apollinaris, which describes the church of Lyons.[42] Deciding on the basis of this description 'that they were then in agreement with the preference [goût] of the ancients in the matter of the austerity[43] of intercolumniations', his comment was that the nave which 'Sidonius indicates by these words, *campum medium*, was very spacious, and the columns which surrounded it did not at all obstruct it, since they were very far apart, *procul locatus . . . per columnas [sic]*'.[44] The Abbé immediately drew a lesson from the Sidonius text: 'Why then have Bramante and Michelangelo not followed such a beautiful model? Was the execution of it more difficult in their time than in the fourth century?'[45] Frézier's reply was to point out that Sidonius' phrase did not prove that the church of Lyons had lintels rather than arcades; indeed, because of the technical problems then presented by large stone architraves, it seemed 'to favor the latter construction'.[46] But Cordemoy would not admit this. Claiming that Sidonius' poem clearly referred to 'the architraves of this temple with its large vault', he added an analysis of the bishop's Latin to support his thesis.[47] As for the technical problem which the engineer had raised—ancient stone-cutting techniques did not permit lintels of the span envisioned by the Abbé for fourth-century Lyons—he responded bluntly: 'It matters to me neither of what these architraves were made nor how. It is an established fact that the side aisles or porticoes of this temple had them.'[48] Obviously, engineering problems produced in Cordemoy not a little frustration and impatience. He could not agree with Frézier's assumption that stone-cutting had over the course of centuries greatly increased the structural

---

basilica and anastasis into his own reconstruction; the latter, supported by 12 columns with the silver capitals which Constantine had donated (III, 38), he assumed to be the dome over the sanctuary of the basilica. See *The Churches of Constantine at Jerusalem: . . . Translations from Eusebius and The Early Pilgrims*, tr. J. H. Bernard, London, 1896.

40. *Mémoires de Trévoux*, July 1712, pp. 1262–3.

41. Frézier was content to unmask the assumption of his antagonist, namely that the 'peristyles' of the Eusebian description *must* refer to colonnades (*ibid.*, Sept. 1711, p. 1572); with as much justice one could maintain that the columns supported arches since the text is vague on this point.

42. *Ibid.*, July 1710, pp. 1252–3. On the episcopal church of Lyons described in Sidonius' poem, see Jean Hubert, *L'art préroman*, Paris, 1938, pp. 6–7, 46; the original apse of the large basilican church which Bishop Patientius completed between 469–71 was found in 1935 under the pavement of the cathedral of S. Jean in Lyons. Of Sidonius' literary output, which was highly esteemed throughout the Middle Ages, there survive 24 poems and 147 letters describing the life of the period. See Pierre de Labriolle, *Histoire de la littérature latine chrétienne*, 3rd ed., 2 vols., Paris, 1947, II, pp. 736–42.

43. On the term, 'âpreté', see Claude Perrault, *Les dix livres d'architecture . . .*, 1st ed., Paris, 1673, p. 76, n. 3: 'Cette façon de parler est assez significative pour representer l'inegalité de superficie qu'un grand nombre de Colonnes donne aux costez d'un Temple lorsqu'on le regarde par les Angles. L'effet de cet aspect est de faire paroistre les Colonnes serrées l'un contre l'autre, & cette maniere plaisoit grandement aux Anciens.'

44. *Mémoires de Trévoux, loc. cit.*

45. *Ibid.*, p. 1253.

46. *Ibid.*, Sept. 1711, p. 1571.

47. *Ibid.*, July 1712, pp. 1257–8.

48. *Ibid.*, p. 1258.

efficiency of architrave construction, so that its modern inadequacy for large structures must be accepted as fact. For to make such an admission would threaten his ideal of *la sainte Antiquité* by turning it into an impractical idea from which no consequences for contemporary architecture could be drawn. Thus, he presented examples of architraved buildings which predated the church of Lyons: at Fano Vitruvius had used wooden architraves; copper architraves had been discovered at the Pantheon by Bernini, if he remembered correctly; stone architraves were used in the so-called *Piliers de Tutelles* in Bordeaux, where the intercolumniation was seven feet.[49] In the last case, he noted that in each span of the intercolumniation a keystone was used and surmised that architects, following this example, could well have gained the skill to construct architraves of ten or twelve feet since, as he remarked, 'between the end of the first century, when the emperor Claudius lived, to whom this building is attributed, and the fourth, when Bishop Patientius lived who built this church of Lyons, experience could well have perfected the art of building'.[50] Now, as an example of ancient architrave construction Cordemoy's choice of the Bordeaux structure is hardly surprising. Claude Perrault had sketched it on his 1669 trip to that city, and Lepautre later engraved it for Claude's Vitruvius; the keystones to which Cordemoy referred are clearly visible (Fig. 2).[51] Not without relevance for our context is the fact that twenty-five years later Frézier, denied by the Abbé's death the opportunity of replying once again, will write in his treatise on *La theorie et la pratique de la coupe des pierres* that modern architects have tried constructing architraves *de claveaux* but, discovering that stresses are too great, have preferred an arcade construction.[52] Such a comment, appearing in an erudite and highly specialized work on engineering, places the earlier discussion of architrave construction by the layman of engineering in historical perspective. The Abbé believed fully in the vast possibilities of a modern architrave system of construction simply because he believed these very possibilities had already been realized in *la sainte Antiquité*.[53]

While in the *Nouveau traité* Cordemoy had expressed

his concept of ancient architecture more in the form of general precepts for the modern architect than in that of a developed thesis, as his argument with Frézier progressed his ideal gradually became specified in a particular building-type: the basilican churches erected at the time of the Church's triumph under Constantine. If Cordemoy was in favor of 'peristyles' —colonnades rather than arcades—it was on behalf, then, of a larger ideal, which included all those principal characteristics by which we recognize the style of the basilican churches of fourth-century Rome —monumentality, a lavish use of rich materials, and a plan disposition of either longitudinal or cross form, with screens of columns separating the side aisles from the nave. He described the episcopal basilica of Clermont, for example, in the following way: 'That [church] ... which Bishop Namatius of Clermont built there was one hundred and fifty feet long, sixty feet wide and fifty feet high, from the floor of the nave up to the vault. There was between this nave and the *apse* a rotunda, such however that the whole building was arranged in the manner of a cross, and the aisles were embellished with porticoes of an admirable structure. They were supported by *seventy columns*, and the walls which surrounded the sanctuary were incrusted with marble.'[54] The source for this passage is the sixth-century author of the valuable *Historia Francorum*, St. Gregory of Tours.[55] Like this writer, Cordemoy also loved to give the statistics of the buildings he described; we are told that one hundred and twenty columns were used by Bishop Perpetuus in St. Martin in Limoges, and that in Old St. Peter's there were precisely one hundred white marble columns.[56] And just as the Early Christian writers had delighted in prose evocations of the rich materials used in the buildings they described, so the Abbé dwelt on the gilded ceilings and marble-incrusted vault of the church of Lyons.[57] In a letter from which Cordemoy quoted a few phrases, Sidonius Apollinaris described the church of Lyons in terms which could scarcely fail of appeal to the age of the *Roi-Soleil*: 'In the interior the light glitters, and the sun, which attracts the gold of the ceiling, mingles its rays with the tawny reflections of

49. *Ibid.*, pp. 1258–9.

50. *Ibid.*, p. 1259; see above, n. 42, for the date of the Lyons church.

51. The drawing, on which Lepautre's engraving is based, is reproduced in Bonnefon's ed. of Claude's *Voyage à Bordeaux* (published with Charles Perrault's *Mémoires de ma vie*, Paris, 1909), p. 184; Claude's account of the structure (pp. 183–5) makes no reference to the keystones, however.

52. I, p. xvi.

53. For the developing 'architectural laïcism' of this period, observable in Cordemoy as in Frémin, see Nyberg, *op. cit.*, pp. 223–4.

54. *Mémoires de Trévoux*, July 1712, pp. 1263–4. Hubert (*op. cit.*, p. 168) has dated Bishop Namatius' church *c.* 430–40.

55. In the sixteenth century Claude Fauchet had called him the 'Père de nôtre histoire' (Labriolle, *op. cit.*, p. 791); interest in the history of Gaul was, of course, greatly stimulated in the late seventeenth century by the researches of Mabillon, who studied all aspects of the religious history of the Merovingian period and with whose work Cordemoy would have been thoroughly familiar.

56. *Mémoires de Trévoux*, July 1712, p. 1263; the accuracy of Gregory's count of 100 has received an unexpectedly significant confirmation (see Richard Krautheimer, 'Some Drawings of Early Christian Basilicas in Rome: St. Peter's and S. Maria Maggiore', *The Art Bulletin*, XXXI (1949), pp. 212–13).

57. *Mémoires de Trévoux*, July 1712, pp. 1257–8.

the metal. Diverse marbles decorate the vault of the apse, the floor, the windows, and, animated by figures of various colors, the meadow-colored revetment transforms the little stones into sapphires by means of green-colored glass.'[58] Such a description was as contemporary with Cordemoy's own period as the one in which Louis XIV's historiographer, Jean-François Félibien, described in 1706 the shimmering, trophy-strewn golden dome of the Invalides.[59]

Just as contemporary with late seventeenth-century France as this ingenuous delight of the early Christians in materials of a marvelously sensuous appeal, however, was the monumentality of their basilican churches in 'peristyle' form. The characteristics of the ideal which the Abbé projected back to the distant fourth century were factors in the taste of his own time. Thus the examples given in the *Nouveau traité* of how the new St. Peter's *should* have been built were the Louvre colonnade of Perrault and de Creil's derivative portico of Ste-Geneviève. Yet neither the east façade of the Louvre nor the façade of the church has anything in common with the disposition of churches, ancient or modern. When his book was written, Cordemoy had not given his ideal church-form expression in writing. That he may even then have been ruminating on an Early Christian prototype is nevertheless possible. For in the decade of the 1670's, the Perrault brothers had designed a project for the complete rebuilding of Ste-Geneviève in Paris which, if it had been executed, would have provided the city with a monumental basilican church of impressive proportions, with 'peristyles' of marble Corinthian colonnades screening the side aisles from the nave and with an altar placed directly under the crossing dome.[60] With few changes, indeed, Cordemoy's description of the episcopal basilica of Clermont could well describe the disposition of the Perrault church of Ste-Geneviève. Middleton has suggested that the Abbé may have co-operated on the project.[61] Whether this is so or not—there is simply no evidence available to settle the question—Cordemoy certainly knew this project in which the characteristics of an Early Christian basilican plan that he later recommended are so strikingly embodied.

But there is still another element of the Perrault church design which, when studied in conjunction with Cordemoy's final article, helps to clarify the Abbé's formula for the perfect church. The Perraults would have raised on a fourth-century type of basilican plan a tripartite interior elevation, the inspiration of which is the French Gothic cathedral. Petzet's recent observation that the classical structure in late seventeenth-century France is 'Gothic' in character is relevant here.[62] It was this strange commingling of stylistic inspirations in the Perrault project that was later to bear fruit in Cordemoy's concept of ecclesiastical architecture. Just as the Abbé's architectural fundamentalism led him to the source of the Christian church plan in the Constantinian period, so he believed that, as built, churches had long remained faithful to this form, turning against it only in modern times. Thus he claimed that the churches built 'up to the time of Bramante and Michelangelo have been constructed almost on the same model'—that of the Christian Antiquity of the fourth century.[63] Understanding the basilican plan and the monumental scale of medieval churches as part of an ongoing tradition established definitively by the 'first faithful', Cordemoy fashioned in his Early Christian ideal the link between Antiquity and the Gothic period. As a modern scholar has noted, 'the fact that the cathedral of Amiens has nave, aisles, and a transept; that in its elevation arcades, triforium and clearstory succeed each other; that the walls seem to consist of translucent screens: all this would seem to be rooted in the tradition of the fourth-century basilicas'.[64] Unquestionably the Perraults would have agreed. The peculiarly French concept of church architecture in the late seventeenth century, with its combination of classical and Gothic elements into what Middleton, for want of

58. *Epist.*, II, 10, 44 (quoted from Hubert, *op. cit.*, pp. 6–7 and p. 7, n. 1); the two phrases which Cordemoy quoted, but without a citation, occur in the 1712 article, p. 1257.

59. *Description de l'Eglise Royale des Invalides*, Paris, 1706, pp. 24–25.

60. The six drawings were first identified by Michael Petzet ('Un projet des Perrault pour l'église Sainte-Geneviève à Paris', *Bulletin monumentale*, CXV (1957), pp. 81–96) who, more recently, has discussed them in relationship to Cordemoy's theory in the *Nouveau traité*: see *Soufflots Sainte-Geneviève und das französische Kirchenbau des 18. Jahrhunderts*, Berlin, 1961, pp. 74–80 and Figs. 49–55.

61. See above, n. 19.

62. 'Im Kampf gegen die barocke Pilasterarkade verbünden sich der "ordre classique" mit dem "ordre gothique"—die "klassichste" Kirche der Zeit, die Kirche über Kolonnaden, ist ihrer Struktur nach die "gotischste"' (*op. cit.*, p. 78).

63. *Mémoires de Trévoux*, July 1712, p. 1264. Cordemoy's belief in the continuity of this tradition for a thousand years, and his desire for a return to its source in the fourth century, is related to the intense interest taken in late seventeenth-century France in the early history and traditions of the country (see above, n. 55). As for his advocacy of a reform of church design along the lines of a specifically Christian prototype of the Late Antique period, such a renaissance would not be unique. In his study of the Carolingian Renaissance, Richard Krautheimer has observed that 'the evidence seems to show that in the design of a church, preference among the prototypes of Antiquity was given to edifices of Christian Antiquity of the fourth and fifth century'. 'The Carolingian Revival of Early Christian Architecture', *The Art Bulletin*, XXIV (1942), pp. 1–38, p. 30. Cordemoy's reform must be seen as one manifestation of the pro-French mood around 1700 to which the remark by Petzet (see above, n. 62) must also be referred.

64. Krautheimer, *op. cit.*, p. 29.

a better term, has called a 'Graeco-Gothic' ideal, received unique expression in the Ste-Geneviève project. But it is to the polemical Cordemoy of the debate that we are indebted for the first formulation of the reconciling 'middle term' in this combination: the Christian basilica of Late Antiquity.

The thesis which Cordemoy presented on the origin of the fourth-century church of basilican form is particularly interesting in the light of modern theories. His 1710 article makes a few points that bear on the origin of the building-type of the 'first churches which the great Constantine had built',[65] while the last presents an explicit view of how the Christian basilica-form originated. Consisting of two main parts—on the one hand the nave, on the other the sanctuary and choir— these churches were always terminated at the east end by a semi-circular apse.[66] It was in the apse that the ecclesiastics and clerics sat, with the bishop in their midst on a raised throne. The altar—already discussed above—was placed under a dome-ciborium. Now Cordemoy cited as precedent for the latter the *bienséance* of pagan temples. Noting that the pagans had placed their idols in the center of rotundas—their offerings they suspended from the keystone of the vault 'which they named *tholus*'—he claimed that 'since the time when peace was given to the Church, the Christians not only did not hesitate to avail themselves of most of these temples, but they found too that it was *de la Majesté* to place the altar in the spot where formerly the idol was [placed] and to suspend in a golden or silver dove the Eucharist, their unique Offering, as well as the principal object of their cult, at the very spot where the pagans had attached their presents'.[67] The architectural 'model' of the Christian basilica itself Cordemoy believed to be the judicial basilica of Antiquity, which he described as 'a large rectangular structure, according to Vitruvius, always supported by a peristyle on each side along its length, sometimes even by two, and terminated in a semi-circle, in the middle of which was the tribunal where in the first times the kings, and since then the magistrates in their stead, rendered justice'.[68] Not un-

expectedly, the judicial basilica which Cordemoy cited as an example is the one built at Fano by Vitruvius, known to him in Claude Perrault's reconstruction (Fig. 3).[69]

This theory, which in its general outline has found support among modern scholars, can be traced to a certain amount of speculation on the source of the Christian church structure in seventeenth-century France. Henri Sauval, for instance, had attributed its origin to the judicial basilicas of Greece and Rome.[70] Arguing against a theory proposed by Adrien de Valois *le jeune*, who had evidently written a *Traité des basiliques*,[71] Sauval had promised to demonstrate that 'the churches which the Christians called basilicas resembled the basilicas and tribunals where the Greeks and Romans rendered justice. For . . . they consisted in a nave which extended between two counter-naves; further, [which was] bordered with columns, and terminated by a tribunal rounded in semi-circle, and . . . *this is the form of most of our churches*.'[72] Apparently, then, there was considerable support for the interpretation which, immediately following Sauval's death in 1670, is implied in the Perrault design for Ste-Geneviève, with its fusion of Late Antique and Gothic elements. But to this period, as well, belongs Claude Perrault's reconstruction of the Vitruvian Basilica at Fano. We are not as well informed as we would like to be about whatever free play of ideas may then have taken place concerning the relationship between the structure of the Christian church on the one hand, and the Antique basilica and the Gothic cathedral on the other. One thing we do know, however. Some forty years later this triple liaison was to be revived and, in the process, receive explicit formulation by Cordemoy. In this task he will be aided—as in all his architectural ideas—by his chief mentors in the building art: Vitruvius and Claude Perrault.

To the identification of the prototype of the fourth-century Christian basilica, Cordemoy added an explanation for its choice by the early Christians which

65. *Mémoires de Trévoux*, July 1710, p. 1269.
66. *Ibid.*, p. 1267.
67. *Ibid.*, pp. 1272–3. A Eucharistic tabernacle in the shape of a dove was used by the ancient Greeks according to the church historian, Jean Baptiste Thiers. See the anonymous review of his *Dissertations ecclésiastiques sur les principaux autels des églises . . .*, Paris, 1688, in *Histoires des Ouvrages des Scavans*, June 1688, p. 230. Regarding the choir of the church-form, the reviewer claims that Thiers believed that 'cette séparation [of laïcs from the clergy in the choir] ne se fit que sous le regne de Constantin, & lors que l'Eglise se trouva dans le repos & dans sa splendour' (*ibid.*, p. 236). Apparently Thiers was at least as devoted to the building-forms 'consacrées par la tradition' of the Early Church as was Cordemoy.
68. *Mémoires de Trévoux*, July 1712, pp. 1264–5.

69. *Ibid.*, p. 1265 (his description of the plan of the Basilica at Fano is quite accurate, mentioning the 'tribunal' apse of the Temple of Augustus, the roof of which is visible (L) at the right edge of the cross-section (Fig. 3).
70. *Histoire et recherches des antiquités de la ville de Paris*, 3 vols., Paris, 1724, I, p. 291. At his death in 1670, Sauval left a MS. filling nine folio volumes, the result of twenty years' labor; it was widely read, especially by the circle to which Claude and Charles Perrault belonged. In its final form, the MS. was completed before 1700, but the result is haphazard and disorganized. Lenglet-Dufresnoy correctly estimated the first volume to be good, with the second and third ranging from undistinguished to terrible (see *Biographie universelle*, XXXVIII, pp. 87–88).
71. It is mentioned by Jean-François Pommeraye (*Histoire de l'église cathedrale de Rouen*, Rouen, 1686, p. 5).
72. *Op. cit.* (my italics).

reveals a hitherto unsuspected reason for the interest taken in Louis XIV's reign in the church architecture of the Constantinian period. For the Abbé saw a parallel of functions between the classical judicial, and the Christian church basilica. Claiming that by the term 'apse' interpreters mean 'a structure within the church built in the manner of a tribunal, in short to serve as the seat of the bishop', he concluded that the apse had referred solely to the bishop's *throne* which is 'the throne or tribunal of Jesus Christ'.[73] With this explanation in hand, we can finally understand the vehemence with which Cordemoy insisted on the *convenance* of the dome-ciborium location for the altar —contrary to the more usual custom defended by Frézier, of placing it in the apse. For if the altar sits directly under a crossing dome, the bishop's throne can then be placed in the 'tribunal' position in the apse, an arrangement which the Abbé not only believed followed the invariable practice of fourth-century churches, but the one described for a structure such as the Basilica at Fano as well.[74] It was in order to conform to this dual tradition, then, that he recommended that the more common disposition in modern churches be radically changed; the altar *must* be placed under a dome, with the bishop's throne at the head of the apse. Now, such a commensurate relationship of function between the tribunals of emperor and bishop implies a concept of justice that was as much at home in the France of Louis XIV as it had been in the empires of Constantine and Charlemagne. Briefly stated, this concept maintains the doctrine of the two vicars of Christ: as the bishop is Christ's delegate in religious matters, rendering judgments in his name and by his authority, so the sovereign is also Christ's delegate, from whose rule of secular affairs there is no appeal and whose person is clothed in a semi-divine majesty. It is hardly surprising that Cordemoy should advocate a return to an 'ideal' church-form which he believed not only belonged to the age of the first Christian emperor, but also embodied the continuing tradition of imperial justice. As a churchman he, with many prominent members of the clergy, found the absolutism of Louis XIV's reign congruous with his belief in religious authority.[75]

Another related factor in the timeliness of Cordemoy's Early Christian ideal for church architecture must be mentioned, perhaps the most curious and the most telling of them all. In his program for the reformation of contemporary ecclesiastical architecture, the Abbé considered the ancient theoretician, Vitruvius, to be the powerful 'ally' of his fourth-century 'ideal' church. To understand how this could come about, and its meaning for French architecture, the fluctuation of Vitruvius' reputation in France must be indicated. By 1709, when Frézier launched the debate, the ancient theoretician no longer 'belonged' almost exclusively to the professional architect. As Herrmann has pointed out, the status of the ancient had been reduced to that of a popularizer, one among many writers for the general public on the subject of architecture.[76] The emphasis that Cordemoy gave to Vitruvius' Basilica at Fano, as an example of the model which he thought the fourth-century Christians had followed in their churches, therefore deserves special notice. He did not equally favor all ancient buildings, as he more than once remarked, and his preferences were necessarily those of a layman in architectural matters. That is, they were strongly guided by both the theory and the practice of Antiquity's only surviving witness. And Cordemoy could not help but be vividly aware of Vitruvius' only contribution to architectural practice. The reconstruction of the Basilica at Fano, published by his other mentor, Perrault, made all conjecture about the appearance of the Augustan building unnecessary for the Abbé. To the rigorous follower of Vitruvian doctrine, the architect-theorist of Augustus was the oracular voice of the ancients, whose single construction, a judicial basilica, represented the purest stream of ancient architecture—as opposed to the one represented by pier-and-arch buildings like the Colosseum and the Basilica of Maxentius, which he disliked.[77] More than an appreciation of one particular building is involved. For just as Perrault's Louvre colonnade meant the triumph of modern 'peristyle' architecture to Cordemoy, so Vitruvius' Basilica at Fano *à la Perrault* epitomized

73. *Mémoires de Trévoux*, July 1712, pp. 1268-9; the bishops, he added, 'sont sur la terre les Juges des hommes'. Although Cordemoy cites Furetière for support, the latter explicitly disagrees: 'Dans les vieux titres on a appellé *absides*, la partie interieure de l'Eglise où est le maistre autel, qui avoit ordinairement une voute particuliere & separée' (*op. cit.*, *sub* 'Absides').
74. Modern St. Peter's in this regard is praised by Cordemoy (see *Mémoires de Trévoux*, July 1710, p. 1272; July 1712, p. 1271). The excavated apse of the church at Lyons, described by Sidonius Apollinaris, shows the arrangement Cordemoy advocated. See Hubert, *op. cit.*, p. 46 and Fig. 15.
75. The most outspoken and definitive expression of the political

absolutism which first emerged in Louis' reign in the decade of the 1660's occurs in Bossuet's *Politique tirée des propres paroles de l'Écriture sainte* of 1677, which is concerned primarily with a practical—and fundamentally secular—context, scripture being used as support for a developed political thesis (see Stephan Skalweit, 'Political Thought', *New Cambridge Modern History: Volume V, the Ascendancy of France 1648–88*, ed. F. L. Carsten, Cambridge, 1961, pp. 99–102). The Jesuit Claude-François Menestrier went almost to the point of divinizing Louis in his incredible work on the *Histoire du regne de Louis le Grand par les medailles, emblemes, devisis . . .* , Paris, 1700. He was truly 'épris de symbolique', as Louis Hautecœur has remarked.
76. *Op. cit.*, p. 42.
77. *Mémoires de Trévoux*, July 1712, p. 1263.

for him the grace and clarity of 'peristyle' construction in ancient architecture. As the renown of the ancient architect and that of the modern were linked, so also the renown of both buildings was inextricably knotted together, since the issue for the Abbé was the same in either case—the victory of aesthetic truth. His faith in the supreme achievement of the Louvre façade required belief, as well, in an extraordinary accomplishment at Fano. In much the same way, his precepts on church architecture in the *Nouveau traité* required, in strictly logical terms, the kind of defense he provided in the *Mémoires de Trévoux*. It was with such an attitude that Cordemoy looked at Perrault's small vignette in which Vitruvius, the ancient Perrault, is shown presenting the design of his building to Augustus, the ancient Louis XIV (Fig. 4).[78] In the right background stands the as yet 'unbuilt' Colosseum, a reminder that—like the modern period—Antiquity had also strayed from the aesthetic truth of peristyle architecture. Like the early Christians of the fourth century, however, Cordemoy would once again return architecture to its ancient and splendid tradition.

78. See the last line of Charpentier's sonnet, with which Perrault had prefaced the dedication to the king of his 1673 edition of Vitruvius: 'Sous un nouvel Auguste un Vitruve nouveau'.

Peter II Thumb and German Rococo Architecture

Thumb's architectural career opened in the first decade of the eighteenth century (Fig. 1) and ended a half-century later with the building of his library in the Benedictine monastery at St.-Gallen (Figs. 38–39) in Switzerland, designed in 1757 and completed without his supervision in 1767, the year after his death.[1] He began practice some years before French Rococo influence first reached Germany[2] and then continued as a Baroque architect for twenty years and more. His finest work, however, the pilgrimage church in Baden at Birnau on the Bodensee (Figs. 16–26) of 1746–1750, is a superb example of truly Rococo architecture with an interior, at least, from which almost all inheritance from the Baroque has been purged or melted away. One may leave unsettled for the present the degree of his responsibility for the vast abbey church at St.-Gallen in Switzerland (Figs. 33–37). That looks back in some respects to the German Baroque of 1700; yet it may also be thought to look forward towards the Neo-classicism of the later eighteenth century. This is not altogether surprising, since construction of the church began only in 1755, and much of the decoration throughout and even the actual structure of the eastern arm—not by Thumb—

date from after 1760. Thus his career, stylistically, is characteristic of the general modulation of German architecture from the Baroque towards the Rococo and then away from the Rococo during the half-century that extends from 1710 to the 1760's.[3]

Certain questions of attribution in eighteenth-century Germany are probably unanswerable, since the thoroughly-studied archives in the monasteries have not as yet provided the information. Weingarten, for example, is much less convincingly assignable to any one architect than St.-Gallen; Wiblingen, Maria Steinbach, and Frauenzell are usually assigned either to no namable designer or, hypothetically, to rather too many alternative ones. Dating, moreover, is not always absolutely certain, particularly for the stucco decoration which is so important a part of the interior architecture of this period. (Frescoes, on the other hand, are quite often signed and dated.) Yet the general historical picture is less affected by gaps in documentation than in most other periods. This is especially true as regards Thumb—there is, goodness knows, no lack of dates for St.-Gallen. Those before 1715, however, for the initiation of work at two of his earliest churches, St.-Trudpert in Baden and Ebersmunster (Haut-Rhin) in Alsace, are not very significant for the buildings, largely carried out later, that survive today. Moreover, in the case of his library at St.-Peter in Baden there were two campaigns separated by more than a decade, one of construction and a second for the decoration.

The unsettled questions that most concern Thumb might be considered psychological. How did it come about that an artist capable of three or four of the finest interiors of his period also produced so much

1. The latest list of Thumb's work, at least of his 'wichtigsten Bauten', is that given by P.-H. Boerlin in *Die Stiftskirche St. Gallen*, Bern, [1964], pp. 83–84 (henceforth cited merely as Boerlin), a list that includes nineteen commissions only; this author discusses Thumb's career before St.-Gallen at some length on pp. 84–89. J. L. Wohleb in 'Peter Thumb oder Thum?', *Schau ins Land*, 1956, pp. 141–7, and N. Lieb and F. Dieth in *Vorarlberger Barockbaumeister*, Munich, [1960], pp. 118–19 (henceforth cited as Lieb-Dieth), offer many more works in their lists, including supervision of buildings designed by others, some unexecuted projects, and even a few attributions. Lieb-Dieth also make many references to details of Thumb's life and to particular buildings and projects in their introductory text (pp. 7, 10–13, 16–22, 24–27, 33–38, 40, 52–57, 62–65, 67). Their treatment of the subject, being the latest except for Boerlin's more restricted account, supersedes Wohleb's as well as that in Thieme-Becker, especially as so many of Thumb's minor as well as major works are there illustrated by Dieth's—unfortunately unprocurable—photographs.

2. This may be considered to have been in 1716–19 when the Elector Max Emanuel of Bavaria employed his French-trained architect Joseph Effner (1687–1745) and various craftsmen whom he had called from Paris upon his return from exile in 1715 after the ending of the War of the Spanish Succession to design and decorate the Pagodenburg at Nymphenburg. In these same years Max Emanuel's brother, Josef Clemens, archbishop and elector of Cologne, was obtaining designs for the Buen Retiro wing of the Residenz at Bonn from Robert de Cotte and even from Oppenord.

3. For a rather verbalistic summary of this stylistic modulation in Germany as arbitrarily periodized by various scholars in the last fifty years, see my article 'The Brothers Asam and the Beginnings of Bavarian Rococo Architecture', *JSAH*, Oct., 1965, pp. 192–4 (henceforth cited as 'Asam' 1). Obviously the particular development of individual artists of distinction such as the Asams or Thumb and the intrinsic qualities of their major works are more interesting and significant than the hypothetical presentation of any abstract stylistic sequence. Yet it may be noted here that Thumb played no part in the earliest stage of formulation of a German Rococo interior architecture to which the Asams contributed so much in the 1720's and early 1730's. As regards the Rococo, he was a late-comer; but this does not diminish the value of his major works, which are contemporary with the highest point of florescence of the German Rococo in the years between 1735 and 1755.

mediocre or at least very conventional work? and why were these masterpieces all designed late in his career? The library at St.-Peter was begun in the mid-1730's, when he was 56, and not completed for fifteen years or more; he was 64 when he started to build Birnau, and he was 77 when he designed the St.-Gallen library. One may think of Frank Lloyd Wright, hardly uninventive in his early years, who was—if anything—still more inventive in his 70's and 80's though relatively unproductive in his 50's and 60's. But Wright's reputation hardly rests on a mere three or four works. More comparable are certain of Thumb's close German contemporaries: Dominikus Zimmermann, born in 1685 four years after Thumb, began his first great church, that at Steinhausen, when he was 41; but his other masterpiece, Die Wies, in a range of production considerably smaller than Thumb's, was built at the same time as Birnau, so that he was 70 when it reached completion in the mid-1750's.[4] Joseph Schmuzer (1683–1752), like Dominikus Zimmermann a stuccator-architect from Wessobrunn, undertook his greatest work, the transformation of the big circular Gothic church at Ettal, in 1745 when he was 62. For this notable achievement only his remodelling of the medieval church at Rottenbuch, undertaken in his 50's, and up to a point, the modest new parish church at Oberammergau of 1737–1742, offer any persuasive premonition.[5] The career of J. G. Fischer (1673–1747) offers similar problems, since his major works are as few as the Schmuzers' and the finest of them (unless he can be credited with Maria Steinbach, begun in 1746 just before his death), St.-Katherine at Wolfegg and the Franziskanerinnen at Dillingen, were built, respectively, in 1733–1735 and 1736–1737 when he was in his 60's. The contrary situation, as regards their age at the time of their finest production, exists with the Asam brothers: Cosmas Damian was only 30 when he was commissioned to build Weltenburg in 1716 and Egid Quirin a year younger when, in 1721, he executed the great high altar compositions there and at Rohr, where he had actually designed and begun the church three or four years earlier.[6]

However impossible the satisfactory explanation of such situations may be, it is still worthwhile to examine the works that preceded the rare masterpieces of artists like Thumb in order to see if the former may not, after all, have led up in some significant respects to the latter. At the very least such an examination exposes the matrix in which the jewel took form and throws some light on the differing contexts that conditioned the masterpieces and the run-of-the-mill work the same men produced.

Peter Thumb, called 'II' to distinguish him from his grandfather of the same name, was born into one of the leading builder-families of the Austrian Vorarlberg.[7] From that district, after about 1650, many masons who later became architects had set out to work throughout southern Germany, Switzerland, and Austria, dominating the field particularly in the lands around the Bodensee. Thumb's grandmother, Barbara Beer, belonged to another such family, and various relatives of his mother, Christiana Feuerstein, were architects or stuccators. Peter's father Michael (c. 1640–1690) was a prominent architect. But he died at the age of 50, leaving his greatest works, Obermarchtal and Hofen (Friedrichshafen), to be completed by his brother Christian (c. 1640–1726) and their cousin Franz II Beer (1660–1726), the leading South-German architect of his generation.[7a] Born at Bregau in 1681, Peter Thumb became an apprentice at Au in 1697 under Michael Herbig, a mason and stone-carver, for the usual term of three years. In 1709 he was taken into the famous Au Zunft (masons' guild). But he had already begun to work in architecture under other men. Moreover, in that year 1709 he was actually commissioned by the Benedictines of St.-Trudpert in Baden—and possibly also by those of Ebersmunster in Alsace—and the following year he vaulted the surviving Gothic choir there.[8]

In 1707 Thumb married Anna Maria Beer, the daughter of his cousin, Franz II, and between 1704 and 1711 he supervised the construction of Beer's big Benedictine church at Rheinau in Canton Zürich just as, a decade later, Joseph Schmuzer would supervise Beer's Heilig Kreuz at Donauwörth[9] in Bavaria at the opening of his architectural career. Unlike Schmuzer and his brother Franz Xaver I (1676–1741)—who were already being employed by Beer to execute *stucchi* in the opening years of the century after their father

4. See Hitchcock, *German Rococo: The Brothers Zimmermann*, London, 1967 (henceforth cited as *Zimmermann*).
5. See Hitchcock, 'The Schmuzers and the Rococo Transformation of Mediaeval Churches in Bavaria', *Art Bulletin*, June, 1966, pp. 159–76, Figs. 18–23, 29–35 (henceforth cited as 'Schmuzers').
6. 'Asam' I, pp. 197–202, 211–15, 222–7. The 1721 date of E. Q. Asam's high altar composition at Weltenburg has been disputed on iconographic grounds by Gerhard Hojer in an unpublished Munich doctoral dissertation. He would associate it with the founding of the Bavarian Order of St. George by the Elector Karl Albrecht in 1729 and assign it the still later date of the fresco of Tassilo's Founding of the Monastery, painted on the vault of the choir in front of the altar.

7. This brief account of Thumb's life is largely based on Lieb-Dieth. See note 1.
7a. Beer was knighted by the Emperor Karl VI in 1722.
8. See W. Sebert, *Die Klosterkirche St. Trudpert* [Freiburg], n.d., p. 6; F. Piel, *Baden-Württemberg* (Handbuch der deutschen Kunstdenkmäler), [Munich], 1964, pp. 418–19 (henceforth cited as Piel).
9. 'Schmuzers', pp. 164–5; Fig. 6.

Johann's death in 1701—Thumb was not a stuccator. Indeed, the stucco-decoration at Rheinau[10] was executed by Franz Schmuzer, as may have been that at St.-Urban in Canton Lucerne,[11] another major Beer commission which Thumb supervised from 1711 to 1715. In 1707–1711 he was also engaged, together with his considerably older brother Gabriel (1671–?), in carrying out a project initiated in 1703 by Caspar Moosbrugger (1656–1723), a member of a third great family of Vorarlberg architects, for the parish church at Lachen in Canton Schwyz. In Thumb's later career the great majority of his churches would be built in southern Germany, particularly in the region around the Austrian-ruled city of Freiburg-im-Breisgau and in contiguous Baden. These districts north of the Bodensee were in easy reach of Konstanz, where he settled in 1720 and was made a citizen in 1726.[11a] He was perhaps fortunate in these years (1704–1714) of the War of the Spanish Succession to be so largely employed in Switzerland and across the Rhine in Alsace.[12] The earliest work of his own design carried to completion after the church at Ebersmunster, built c. 1710–1715 but rebuilt 1719–1727, was probably the modest tower of the church at Erstein, also in Alsace, dating from 1715–1716.[12a] Next, doubtless, came the execution of the nave of St.-Trudpert over the years 1715–1722.[13] A four-bayed wall-pillar church with galleries (Figs. 6–8), the interior of St.-Trudpert is chiefly appealing because of the *stucchi*, reputedly executed in 1716 by the Italians Carpoforo Orsati and Michelangelo de Prevostis, which surround rather large frescoes by F. A. Giorgioli (c. 1655–1725), a painter from Mendrisiotto in the Ticino, that were completed in 1722. Thumb had worked earlier with Giorgioli when he was supervising Rheinau for Franz Beer, but the frescoes at St.-Trudpert play a far more important part in the decoration. If the stucco-work that surrounds them is indeed of 1716, the large size of the areas provided for the frescoes overhead, made possible by the continuous surface of the un-ribbed barrel vault, and the scalloped framing of the big cartouche-like frescoes at the sides of the vault must be considered quite advanced in character. In the narrow choir, on the vault Thumb had built in 1710, the principal fresco extends over two of the narrow bays in the manner of C. D. Asam's fresco of 1720 in the choir of Aldersbach.[14] That in the middle of the nave is even longer since it extends through three of the wider bays of the new construction (Fig. 7). The shapes of these frescoes, however, remain relatively simple compared to Asam's and the *stucchi* include no proto-Rococo elements. Moreover, the flanking sections of the eastern wall, made necessary by the disparity in width between the inherited choir and the new nave, break the interior space into two unrelated parts; moreover, the richly colored stucco drapery over the choir arch, against which light-toned figures in high relief are set, visually separates rather than joins these parts.

A more considerable opportunity came to Thumb before St.-Trudpert was completed,[15] when the Benedictines of Ebersmunster called him back across the Rhine to rebuild the church he had completed for them in 1715 (Fig. 1) after it had been largely destroyed in a fire set by a stroke of lightning in 1717.[16] Into the new church he incorporated several important surviving elements of the earlier one (Figs. 2–5): the choir with its seven-sided apse, of which the shape and the plain external buttresses recall the church consecrated in 1155 whose foundations were retained; the square crossing, of the same width as the choir, with its wide transeptal arms; and the tall shafts, at least, of the three towers, two flanking the west front, conventionally enough, and a third at the rear of the apse. Thus the remarkable external composition, recalling Carolingian churches, belongs to the church of c. 1710–1715, though the crowning elements of the towers,

10. 'Schmuzers', pp. 161–2, Fig. 8.
11. 'Schmuzers', pp. 162–3, Fig. 9.
11a. In that year he bought the 'Haus zur Leithern' for 2,370 gulden: Lieb-Dieth, p. 21.
12. In the ten years after the battle of Blenheim and before the Treaty of Rastatt, Bavaria was occupied by the Austrians; it is not clear just what the situation was to the west in the Austrian enclave around Freiburg and in French Alsace. Evidently this area cannot have been too much disturbed by the war if the Benedictines of St.-Trudpert and of Ebersmunster were able to begin the renewal of their medieval churches at that time.
12a. See W. Holtz, *Handbuch der Kunstdenkmäler in Elsass*, [Munich, 1965], pp. 40–42: Ebersmunster; p. 4: Erstein. The tower was replaced in 1861.
13. Piel, *loc. cit.* Foundation stone of nave laid 1715; core of west tower probably tenth century; terminal octagon and spire 1720–2. The monastery building was built after 1737 by Thumb. The frescoes offer legends of SS. Peter and Paul and of St. Margaret as well as the story of St. Trudpert. The high altar of 1780–4 is by F. J. Christian, a brother of the then abbot.

14. 'Asam' I, pp. 217–18, Figs. 25–27.
15. The large monastery, also in Baden, that Thumb built over the years 1718–31 and enlarged in 1738–40 for the Benedictine abbey of Ettenheimmünster near Freiburg was demolished in the nineteenth century. Several handsome Rococo doorways from the abbey buildings survive in various locations in nearby Lahr, Riegel, and Ettenheimweiler. The surviving church was altered and enlarged by F. J. Salzmann in 1765. See *Ettenheimmünster Wallfahrtskirche und ehemaliges Kloster*, Stuttgart [1963], pp. 3, 16.
16. G. Metken, *Ebermünster* (Kunstführer Nr. 821), [Munich, 1965], p. 6; X. Ohresser, *Eglise et abbaye d'Ebersmunster*, Sélestat, 1961, pp. 18–20; idem, *Histoire de l'abbaye d'Ebersmunster*, Sélestat, 1963, p. 48. Abbot Bernard Roethlin undertook the building of the church that was completed in 1715; according to Boerlin, p. 83, the abbot started this as early as 1708, but that seems unlikely. See Note 12a. Abbot Jean V Sengler began the new church in 1719 and Prior Ildefonse Beck carried it nearly to completion before his death in 1730.

particularly that to the east, were elaborated in the rebuilding (Fig. 3).

That rebuilding began in 1719 and Thumb brought with him no less than 200 assistants and workmen to carry out his design under the direction of two *Palier*, his brother Gabriel and J. G. I Feuerstein, probably a relative of their mother. In 1728 Heinrich Kohler and another Feuerstein, Leopold, took charge. Caspar Wöllfel was the master carpenter in 1727 by which date, according to an inscription behind the organ, the structural work in the church was complete and the decoration already begun. In 1731, after the stucco-work and many of the frescoes were finished, Johann Vogel was called in to build the spiral stairs leading up to the organ. In 1727 Georg Machoff (or Machauff) received 300 livres for the *stucchi* in the nave and forty-five for those in the choir. He had two assistants, Peter N. (?) and Anton Blanck. The fresco-painters active in 1728–1729 were Joseph Matter, Joseph Sibert or Siffert, and (?) Collet, the first two, at least, coming from Strassburg. They executed, respectively, the frescoes in the first, second, and third bays of the nave. The fresco over the crossing is by Joseph Magges from the Tyrol and was not executed until 1759. The furnishing of the church with altars, confessionals, and organ was effectively completed in 1733–1735 with the gilding by Edmond 'der Fasser' of the high altar; but for the sculpture in the composition Leonard Meyer of Sélestat had already received fifteen livres on account in 1728. The work of other minor craftsmen need not be itemized here.[17]

In most respects a typical Vorarlberg church of its slightly uncertain date,[18] Ebersmunster is exceptionally romantic as seen from a distance (Fig. 3), not because of its site, which is not remarkable, but for its silhouette. Seen in varied relation to the two conventional west towers with their solid octagonal belfry stages and lantern-crowned onion roofs covered with green glazed tiles, the centrally located eastern tower, taller and more varied in shape, always dominates.

The interior rivals in size and grandeur not only the Swiss churches Thumb had supervised for Beer, Rheinau and St.-Urban, but also Beer's Weissenau of 1717–1723 and even Weingarten, which had been begun in 1715 and was approaching completion internally in 1719[19] when the rebuilding of Ebersmunster

started. Like Weingarten, Ebersmunster (Fig. 5) has handkerchief vaults over the broad oblong bays of the nave as well as a flat dome over the square crossing like Weissenau. The grand effect is actually enhanced by the way the pilasters on the pillars here in Alsace are painted to look like ashlar masonry[20]—irregularly banded in two colours, moreover—although the vaults are treated in the German manner with stucco-work and large frescoes.

The contrast with a great church in northeastern France, St.-Jacques at Lunéville, is striking.[21] This was begun in 1730 by a French architect, Romain, probably to the designs of a more distinguished one much employed by German clients—Germain Boffrand—and completed by Héré de Corny in 1747. St.-Jacques follows the medieval hall-church scheme, at this time little used in Germany but very popular in the eighteenth century in northern France. For all its size and fine masonry, inside as well as out, however, it quite fails to match either the still truly Baroque scale and tectonic vigor of Thumb's interior or the more advanced sort of richness, already approaching the Early Rococo, of that interior's stuccoes and frescoed vaults. It is notable, nonetheless, that the vaults of the narrow bays of the long nave of St.-Jacques, as well as those of the aisles, are of the handkerchief type even though only that of the square dome over the crossing carries any Rococo decoration. Héré's towers, on the other hand, above a lower stage based on Borromini's at S. Agnese in Agone in Rome, are of an elaboration and a Rococo fantasy never rivalled by the western towers of German eighteenth-century churches, even those of as late a date as these must be.

Considered in relation to contemporary South-German architecture, however, Ebersmunster is not advanced, for it has little[22] of the over-all Early Rococo character of the Asams' church interiors of the mid-1720's at Freising Cathedral, redecorated 1723–1724, and at Einsiedeln, where they worked in 1724–1726,[23] much

17. Metken, *op. cit.*, pp. 6–7; Ohresser, *op. cit.* (1961), pp. 20–22.

18. Some have wondered if the church completed in 1727 was that designed and begun in 1719. Actually the campaign of 1719–27 would have been only a little longer than that of 1715–1722 for the construction of St.-Trudpert.

19. 1719 was actually the peak year for the employment of Vorarlberg architects; thenceforth their relative importance, high since the 1680's and with an earlier peak around 1700, dropped to such an extent that they are hardly recognizable as

a significant group by 1760. See Lieb-Dieth (graph on unnumbered page).

20. Actually, except for the incorporation of some medieval stone masonry in the lower walls of the choir, the church is almost entirely built of bricks made by the monks on the site. However, the base courses of the piers and the decorative trim of the exterior are in sandstone from the Vosges, some of it beige but mostly pink. The external brickwork, like that inside, is entirely covered with stucco. See Ohresser, *op. cit.* (1961), p. 22. The stiff Ionic pilasters in the choir, all of beige stone, contrast with the later and more elegant Corinthian pilaster order of the nave.

21. [Pourel and Gérardin] *L'Eglise Saint-Jacques de Lunéville*, [Lunéville?], n.d. See also Hitchcock, 'The Brothers Asam and the Beginnings of Bavarian Rococo Church Architecture', pt. II, *JSAH*, March, 1966, p. 11, n. 18 (henceforth cited as 'Asam' II).

22. The statement, 'Asam' II, *loc. cit.*, that Ebersmunster is 'not at all Rococo' is perhaps too categorical.

23. 'Asam' II, pp. 8–14, 14–21.

less of Osterhofen[24] or Steinhausen,[25] with which the Ebersmunster stucco-work and frescoes of 1727–1729 are more closely contemporary. Nonetheless the frescoes[26] in the four bays of the nave are very large and airy in composition even if no larger than C. D. Asam's at Weingarten of ten years before. Their frames, moreover, if hardly to be considered scalloped, are of distinctly varied outline, especially that of the one above the organ. If Machoff's *stucchi* have quite lost the Italianate fullness of those which Orsati and De Prevostis executed at St.-Trudpert over a decade earlier, there is in the dry and rather sparse bandwork no evidence as yet of any awareness of J. B. Zimmermann's French-derived ceiling decorations of 1723 and 1725 at Schleissheim and Benediktbeuern.[27] If hardly even faintly transitional, the interior of Ebersmunster, like its far more exceptional exterior, is nonetheless truly impressive, carrying the characteristics of the Vorarlberg masters' mature style farther westward than it had ever been seen before. It provides a Late Baroque monument unique in French territory and complete down to the side altars, executed by Mathias Wurtzer and Antoine Kettler with paintings by André von Will, and the church doors, the ten confessionals, and the frames of the altarpieces carved by Rupert Haagel.[28]

Unfortunately at St.-Peter in Baden, where Thumb was commissioned on May 1, 1724, to build the new church of the Benedictine monastery, he seems not to have had the same opportunities as in Alsace. This church, begun in 1724, was completed and consecrated in 1727.[29] The somewhat later altars, with rich sculpture by J. A. Feuchtmayr (1696–1770), only serve to emphasize its otherwise rather barren appearance so awkwardly do those at the east end of the nave overlap the pilastered piers supporting the arch at the entrance to the narrower choir (Fig. 12). Even so, in certain respects this interior approaches the Early

Rococo architecturally in ways that Ebersmunster does not, if with a rather unhappy result—as is also true of Schmuzer's somewhat comparable St.-Martin at Garmisch of 1730–1732.[30] As at St.-Trudpert, a continuous barrel vault unifies the three bays of the nave and the slightly wider crossing bay (Fig. 10); indeed a similar vault carries on the vista through the two bays of the deep choir and the terminal square sanctuary, interrupted only by the range of frescoed medallions surrounding the choir arch. As later at Garmisch, however, the effect of spatial continuity is weakened visually by the ribs, here of fairly vigorous profile, between the bays of both nave and choir (Fig. 12). The pilaster clusters are less tectonic in effect, thanks both to their conjunction with the segmental arches carrying the balconies and, theoretically at least, to the panelling and the dry proto-Rococo ornamentation, in the tradition of St.-Urban,[31] on their shafts. This stucco-work by the Swiss G. B. Clerici from Mendrisiotto in the Ticino and the relatively small and tightly-framed frescoes by F. J. Spiegler (1691–1757) overhead—which were very roughly treated in the nineteenth century—do little to complement the relative novelty of the spatial organization.[32] Fortunately a later interior by Thumb in the monastery at St.-Peter and the way the group of buildings crowns this romantically rural site make up for the marked inferiority of the interior of the church (Figs. 9, 11).

The west front is very tall and strong, following closely but improving upon that of Ebersmunster. The belfry stage of the towers is shorter and the double-onion terminals, small above large, are at once more boldly and more gracefully curved. The arcade at the base between the towers is blind since there is no porch as on the Alsatian church, and statues fill three niches in the crowning storey below a double-curved central pediment and flanking scrolls. The result is far more

24. 'Asam' II, pp. 25–26.
25. *Zimmermann.*
26. The frescoes, whitewashed during the French Revolution, were cleaned in 1866.
27. *Zimmermann.*
28. '... Aidé', Ohresser, *op. cit.* (1961), p. 21, notes: 'de trois compagnons dont la conduite donna lieu à des plaintes pour des fréquentes escapades nocturnes et qui se virent infligés des retenues de salaires. . . .' One wonders whether these lively wood-carvers were Swiss, Tyrolian, or natives of Alsace. Will, like Meyer, came from nearby Sélestat; Matter and Siffert were from Strassburg; Kettler came from Colmar; but Magges was a Tyrolian.
29. H. Ginter, *St. Peter/Schwarzwald* (Kunstführer Nr. 561), 6th ed. (Munich, 1966), pp. 3–6. Abbot Ulrich Bürgli was responsible for the rebuilding of the church, the surviving medieval edifice having been merely repaired after a bad fire in 1678. Jakob Felger supervised the construction in a short campaign of three years that included the execution of much of the decoration.

30. 'Schmuzers', pp. 166–7, Figs. 16, 17.
31. See Note 11.
32. Spiegler's frescoes were twice whitewashed, once in 1824 and again in 1874–5. Their present poor condition is not surprising. The restoration of 1964–5, moreover, has exaggerated the contrast between the very pale stucco-work and the dark hard tones of the frescoes. The result is today the least attractive of Thumb's larger works. In detail, however, Clerici's thin and wiry *stucchi* approach the Early Rococo somewhat more closely than Mackoff's of perhaps a year or two later at Ebersmunster. In addition to Clerici, Spiegler, and Feuchtmayer, Christian Wenzinger (1710–97), later responsible for both the frescoes and the *stucchi* at St.-Gallen, worked at St.-Peter, providing the sculpture on the baptismal font in 1733; and J. C. Stoner, Gossmann, and Pellandella painted the altarpieces. The choir gates by Michael Reinhardt from St.-Trudpert are dated 1728, the pulpit 1729, the organ 1730, and the choirstalls as late as 1770.
The monastery buildings at Schwarzach near Bühl in Baden, also begun by Thumb in 1724, were completed in 1736 but little remains of them today.

Baroque than the rather flat and dry arrangement of the comparable elements at Ebersmunster. The small onion-topped belfry over the sanctuary to the east, however, is no rival to the splendid terminal tower in Alsace (Figs. 3, 11).

Franz II Beer died in 1726 and henceforth for the next thirty years his son-in-law's architectural services were almost as much in demand as his had been, even if the earlier results were not comparable to Beer's best works in size and in quality. In the following ten years before Bürgi, the abbot who had commissioned St.-Peter, called on Thumb to build the library—completed and decorated only under the next abbot, P. J. Steyrer, who succeeded Bürgi in 1749—he built the church and the Cistercian nunnery at Friedenweiler near Freiburg (1725–1731); the church and a wing of the Benedictine nunnery at Frauenalb near Karlsruhe (1726–1731)—largely erected from 1704 on by Franz Beer; subsidiary buildings at Rheinau (1726) carried out in association with his brother-in-law Johann Michael II Beer (1700–1767); the Cistercian monastery at Tennenbach near Freiburg, begun in 1726; work in Cistercian nunneries and churches at Günsterstal near Freiburg (1728) and Lichtental at Baden-Baden (1724; 1728–1734); the remodelling of the church and the buildings of the Cistercian nunnery at Königsbrück in Alsace (1728),[32a] the parish church at Biengen near Freiburg (1730); the priory at Wipperskirch (1731–1732); the Augustinian church and priory at Waldkirch (1732–1734); and the choir and tower of the parish church at Rust (1733), all four near Freiburg; and the remodelling of the Rhine Mill at Konstanz, a work of engineering rather than architecture (1737). From 1732 he was architect of the medieval Münster in Konstanz and responsible for the maintenance of the fabric, but this entailed no new construction in his day.

Such a volume of production was rivalled in the period only by that of J. M. Fischer (1692–1766) in Bavaria and Franconia, and it is not surprising that Thumb had little chance to develop stylistically when his clients were content with—in fact, may even have dictated—familiar solutions of the monastery-and-church problem when he was building or rebuilding for them.

Friedenweiler is small and has little decoration, but for Frauenalb, commissioned in 1725, a very interesting scheme was evolved. There the church was placed across one end of a quadrangle and had a 2½-bay choir and a 2½-bay nave to left and right of a domed crossing (Fig. 14). Toward the quadrangle a bowed aisle, which served as a vestibule inside the main entrance, was flanked by two towers that composed with the dome somewhat as at S. Agnese in Agone in Rome. This arrangement is clearly premonitory of St.-Gallen (Fig. 28) as actually built, though even Thumb's earliest project dates from some twenty-five years later. But the Frauenalb church is a ruin today having been burned, together with the convent, in 1853. The Tennenbach monastery was demolished in 1807. Extant is the church (now serving the parish) at Waldkirch, notable for its rich decoration including a fine ceiling fresco by F. B. Altenburger and a sculptured high altar of 1738–1741 by J. M. Winterhalter. It is unnecessary here to deal further with these minor works beyond noting the exceptional amount of monastic construction of which St.-Peter offers the largest and most impressive surviving example. Most of this is very plain in character, though often surprisingly monumental in bulk, even at minor foundations such as St.-Trudpert (Fig. 6).

The libraries in monasteries of the eighteenth century in Germany, Austria, and Switzerland are among the most striking architectural interiors of their day, rivalling the churches in richness of decoration, if not in size, and the great halls of palaces in the variety of their spatial composition. The Austrian monasteries set the pace in Thumb's day, Jakob Prandtauer's at Melk, completed after his death in 1726 by Josef Munggenast (1680–1741) and frescoed by Paul Troger (1698–1762), and Munggenast's at Altenburg, begun in 1740, and at St.-Florian, carried out by Gothart Hayberger in 1744–1750. But the early eighteenth century saw some fine ones built and decorated in southern Germany such as those that J. B. Zimmermann stuccoed at Ottobeuren (1715–1718) and Benediktbeuern (1725).[33] The libraries at Ottobeuren, at Melk, and at St.-Florian all had galleries around the walls, and so do both of those that Thumb built, the earlier one at St.-Peter (Fig. 13) and the later one at St.-Gallen (Fig. 38). Of the two, the earlier is the more interesting architecturally though much less well known or readily accessible. It is, moreover, the first example of interior architecture by Thumb that can be considered to be at all consistently Rococo. His churches had continued hitherto to be Baroque, even though with more and more decoration that approached the Early Rococo in character.

Since the libraries usually occupied portions of the monastery complex[34]—though that at Benediktbeuern

32a. See Holtz, *op. cit.*, p. 88. The buildings were destroyed in the French Revolution.

33. *Zimmermann.*

34. At St.-Peter the library occupies the central portion of the wing separating the west and east courts of the extensive monastery buildings (Fig. 11). It was probably always incorporated in such a range, but the rest of the monastery was rebuilt 1752–7 for Bürgi's successor Steyrer by the minor Vorarlberger Hans VI

is free-standing—they were almost necessarily rectangular in basic plan. In order to provide as much space as possible for books they were two storeys tall, except for Benediktbeuern which is relatively low. The ceilings in the more elaborate examples were always vaulted and decorated, like those in the churches, with *stucchi* and frescoes. As with the churches, the furnishings are frequently later than the architecture and not always harmonious or worthy of their setting, as is unfortunately true of that at St.-Peter.

The date of construction of the St.-Peter library is given by the authorities of the present-day seminary there as 1734–1739. But the plan was not formally accepted until 1737,[35] and the decoration was executed only after 1750. Although the architectural design belongs to the mid-1730's, the large fresco overhead by Benedikt Gamb is signed and dated 1751 and the Rococo stucco-work is by J. G. Gigl (?–1765), who also worked in the Fürstensaal and the House Chapel when the monastery was rebuilt—all except the library— from 1752 on.[36]

To a greater extent than in most churches of the day, the rectangular shape of the St.-Peter library was 'ovalized' spatially by Thumb (Fig. 13), partly by his ingenious treatment of the vaulting and partly by the waving outline of the gallery, so different from the straight lines of the galleries in most other libraries. The vault is very flat at the crown and Gamb's big fresco that now extends across it echoes the ellipsoid spatial effect in its scalloped shape, a shape that in southern Germany goes back at least to C. D. Asam's fresco of 1720 in the nave of Aldersbach.[37]

The vault rises from ten vaulting conoids. Those at the corners are minimized, as in Wren's St. Stephen's Walbrook or the crossing of St. Paul's, while the single ones at the middle of the ends and the pairs in the middle of either side, though they are triangular continuations downwards of the main vault surface,

are so masked by their decoration with large frescoed and stucco-framed 'cartouches'[38] that they hardly appear to constitute tectonic elements in the composition overhead. As in Early Gothic vaulting, the severies over the cross-bays, which are wider in the middle of the sides than at the corners, vary in curvature in order to keep their crowns of the same height. But the still usual pointed intersections of such cross-vaults with the main handkerchief vault are here indicated by only the slightest of mouldings on the arrises. Similar arrises rise from each of the corners though the observer's eye is drawn rather to the stronger arched mouldings that cross the corners diagonally. These correspond very closely in length, and even approximate in curvature, the arrises with which the broader cross-vaults above the central bays of the sides meet the main vault. The latter are, however, pushed far outward in effect by the bulging sides of the frame of the main fresco: The nearly flat surface of the fresco, indeed, actually distorts the underlying handkerchief vault at these points, as was presumably already intended by Thumb in his original design of the 1730's. The result, one may claim, is almost the most exemplary, as it is one of the most extreme, examples of Rococo vaulting, even if the memory of certain of Borromini's vaults, ribbed though most of those are, must for us hover in the background. These could probably have been known only at third or fourth remove, if indeed at all, to Thumb. Certainly he never saw the ceiling of the refectory, now sacristy, at S. Carlo alle Quattro Fontane in Rome Borromini built a hundred years earlier, which comes closest to this vault in spirit.

The gallery bends in and out, loosely following the shape of the overhead fresco. Bold convex bulges, crowned with pairs of wooden figures of the Arts and Sciences by Christian Wenzinger, marbled to look like alabaster, mark the centers of the two ends and flank the middle bays at the sides, with deep concave curves at the corners. The swinging Rococo rhythm is further enhanced by the slighter bulges in front of the first and third bays on the sides, as also by the absence of articulated supports below. In the two most nearly comparable libraries, the one by the Wiedemans at Wiblingen built just before this in the early 1730's, and that carried out by Jakob Emele in the 1750's at Schussenried following, to a considerable extent at least, a design of Dominikus Zimmermann's of 1748, the surrounding galleries are carried on columns.[38a] These clutter the

---

Willam (1702–*c.* 1765). This forms today a long and, though very simply detailed, impressive pile as seen from the southeast, with the roof of the church and Thumb's two west towers rising above it (Figs. 9, 11). The more approachable west façade is considerably less attractive since its stuccoed walls and tiled roofs are overshadowed by the tall west front of the church, entirely executed in the red sandstone that in the monastery buildings and on the sides and rear of the church is used only for window-framing and so forth. According to Boerlin, p. 84, Thumb initiated the monastery buildings in 1728; whether any portion of them other than the library survives is not clear, but the detailing of the west front suggests an early date.

35. Lieb-Dieth, p. 118.

36. Piel, p. 418.

37. 'Asam' I, pp. 217–18. Still earlier is the even more closely comparable ceiling of the Weissenstein Schlosskapelle at Pommersfelden in Franconia, designed presumably by Johann Dientzenhofer (1665–1726), with *stucchi* by Daniel Schenk (?–1737) surrounding a fresco by Jakob Gebhardt, dated 1714, set in a heavy but boldly scalloped frame.

38. It is surprising to note the close similarity of the fresco-filled cartouches of a good generation earlier on the nave vault of St.-Trudpert to these thoroughly Rococo features in the St.-Peter library.

38a. *Zimmermann.*

edges of the interior space in the lower storey. Since they serve a structural purpose, moreover, they introduce tectonic elements that may be considered alien to the spirit of the mature Rococo of these decades in southern Germany. It should be noted, however, that Thumb returned to the use of columns in the library at St.-Gallen (Fig. 38).

One can hardly suppose that any of the detailing executed in stucco is an integral part of the design of the late 1730's. Certainly the predominant coloring, so delicate in its very slight contrast of creamy off-white against white as to appear monochromatic in photographs, dates from the 1750's. But the emphasis that the space-defining balcony receives thanks to the blue-grey scagliola of its balustrade, as also the contrast provided by the curious panels that take the place of pilasters below the bulges in the cove under the balcony, also of deep-toned scagliola, may well have been intended from the first. These vertical elements rather recall the equally curious scagliola panels against which the tapered pilasters on the upper wall of E. Q. Asam's church of St.-Johann-Nepomuk in Munich are set; indeed, the winding cove-supported balcony might equally have been suggested by that in Munich, for the balusters are of similar shape here, though not so richly decorated, and the swings only exaggerate the slight curvatures in plan of the balcony in the Asamkirche.[39] Following the original designing and the beginning of the construction of the St.-Peter library, Thumb, though then only in his 50's, was somewhat less active than earlier during the twenty years that intervened before the construction of the great church of St.-Gallen finally got under way in 1756. But in the middle of this period came his masterpiece, the pilgrimage church and summer residence of the abbots of Salem at Birnau, on the north side of the Bodensee east of Überlingen, which occupied him over the years 1745–1750.

In 1738–1739 he built the monastery beside his early church at St.-Trudpert (Fig. 6). In 1738 he also pro-

vided the designs for the Piaristenkolleg (now the Gymnasium) founded by Margrave Ludwig Georg of Baden-Baden in 1731 at Rastatt. This was executed in 1739–1745 by the local architect J. P. L. Rohrer (1683–1732). In addition he advised Rohrer on his project of 1740 for the Stadtkirche at Rastatt which was erected much later in 1756–1764.[40] In 1739–1742 he built the very modest church and priory at St.-Ulrich near Freiburg, a dependency of the abbey of St.-Peter, and in 1739–1742 he worked in the parish church at Mengen near Sigmaringen in southern Württemberg. His slight connection with the execution of St.-Peter at Bruchsal in Baden in 1742, a church designed by J. B. Neumann for Hugo Damian Cardinal von Schönborn, prince-bishop of Speyer and Konstanz, and his related activity at the Neues Schloss at Meersburg on the Bodensee in 1743, also for the cardinal, can be ignored;[41] while at St.-Ulrich the *stucchi* and the frescoes by F. L. Hermann (1710–1797) in the church date from 1767, after Thumb's death. The Mengen parish church is Gothic and his work there only a remodelling and redecoration as a setting for frescoes executed in 1740 by G. W. Vollmer and Joseph Sautter. Even less than what he had carried out in the late 1720's and early 1730's does any of this compare in interest with the library of St.-Peter or the church at Ebersmunster (Figs. 5, 38). The church of the Petershausen Priory at Mengen, built in 1741–1746 but destroyed by fire in 1810, was apparently of considerably greater interest.[41a]

Eighteenth-century monastery and pilgrimage churches, the most characteristic architectural monuments of the age in Germany exceeding in number the palaces of secular and religious princes, are usually impressive externally because of their bulk, dominating by their great height the massive ranges of monastery buildings or residential quarters for the attached priests. These churches are very often picturesque as well as bulky, thanks to their double towers, their occasional tall domes—rare after 1720—their gables, and their heavy roofs. Thus Ebersmunster, though the monastery buildings are small and plain, profits from its striking cluster of onion-topped towers, an unexpectedly Middle-European sight on the French side of the Rhine (Fig. 3). Many churches, unlike Ebersmunster, have superb hilltop or valley-bottom sites, backed with broad cultivated fields and dark, well-maintained forests, as in the case of St.-Peter (Fig. 9). Sometimes, moreover, a single tower

---

39. As construction of the Asamkirche began in 1733, features of its interior could have been known to Thumb when he designed the St.-Peter library ('Asam' II, pp. 43–46). The unusually long period over which in both cases construction and decoration continued makes it difficult to date precisely particular elements of the interiors. By the 1750's, of course, one may suppose that the interior of the Asamkirche was well known to Gigl, if the balusters of the St.-Peter balcony and the scagliola panels below are, in fact, of his design rather than Thumb's. Whether or not influenced by E. Q. Asam's church in Munich, the cove-supported balcony and its curved plan must almost certainly be integral to the original design of the middle of the 1730's. The vaulting in Willam's modest Abtskapelle (now Hauskapelle) of the 1750's at St.-Peter, with fine Rococo *stucchi* by Gigl and frescoes by F. L. Hermann (1710–97), is very similar to that in the library, but this interior has little spatial interest because of its crypt-like proportions in contrast to the two-storey height of the library.

40. Lieb-Dieth, p. 118. Piel, p. 382, does not mention Thumb in connection with these works of Rohrer.
41. Both at Bruchsal and at Meersburg J. G. Stahl (1687–1755) rather than Thumb was responsible for executing Neumann's designs: Piel, pp. 69–70, 314.
41a. See Note 49.

takes the place of the more usual pair at the west front. When, as at St.-Ulrich (Fig. 15), this occupies a transeptal position—usually because it has, so to say, medieval roots if not a medieval trunk—the composition can be picturesquely asymmetrical almost in the High Victorian way. When the tower is centered on the west front as it is (to take an especially distinguished example) at J. B. Neumann's St.-Paulin in Trier, designed in the 1730's and completed in the 1740's, the great height of the tower usually overshadows the church behind. Even Neumann's great plastic ingenuity hardly achieved at St.-Paulin a satisfactory relationship between the very narrow portions of the west front of the nave extending to left and right and the central projecting shaft of the tower above the main entrance.

It is in this connection that Birnau[42] deserves more comment than most of Thumb's earlier exteriors (Fig. 16). Taking his cue, doubtless, from the largest monasteries—though here the residential element, being only summer quarters for the abbot and the monks of Salem, is relatively small as at Zimmermann's contemporary Die Wies[43]—such as Weingarten and Einsiedeln, where a two-towered church façade is set between long monastery blocks to left and right, he flanked his single west tower by massive three-storeyed square blocks, setting back slightly the plain elements between, but without attempting otherwise than by the greater richness of treatment of the front of the tower to indicate that the central portion is actually the façade of a church. To the rear the taller roof of the nave of the church extends backwards behind the middle stage of the tower while the double roofs of the segmental 'transepts' at either side echo those of the corner blocks in front.

From the rear (Fig. 17), also, it is the handling of the roof that provides the major plastic interest rather than the thin pilaster order with its entablature bent upward in segmental curves over the gallery windows. The choir roof is higher than those of the transepts and

the front corner blocks because this portion of the church, though narrower than the nave, is still quite wide; behind that the even narrower apse is again crowned with a double roof the upper portion of which is a continuation of that of the choir. Such thorough and unconventional study of the plastic composition of a church exterior was rare at the time and contrasts happily with the episodic fashion in which Dominikus Zimmermann, for example, strung out the comparable elements of his great church and its adjuncts at Die Wies.

Whether Thumb's achievement in the design of the exterior of Birnau should be considered Rococo is not easy to say. The upper stage of his tower (Fig. 16), with its diagonally-set pilasters and its curved capping above and below the tiny lantern, is certainly unusually rich for the period yet hardly Rococo in the sense of the tops of Héré's towers on St.-Jacques at Lunéville. The exotic window shapes and painted bandwork on the flanks of Die Wies are certainly a good deal less academic than the pilaster order and the two ranges of windows, one above the other, consistently used for both the front and the sides of Birnau (Figs. 16, 17). All of this is really more in continuity with Baroque principles, and even international Baroque practice, than consistent with the originality of his interior here or that of the earlier St.-Peter library. But the Rococo in the Germany of the mid-eighteenth century, as from its beginnings in France, was an interior style or mode, not one ever formulated and elaborated for exteriors.

The Birnau pilgrimage dates from the fifteenth century, unlike Die Wies, Birnau's contemporary architectural rival, which was built to house a new object of devotion. The cult object here was a medieval Madonna, and the original church where it was enshrined at 'Old' Birnau, burned in the Thirty Years War, had been rebuilt in the late seventeenth century. The shrine was an appanage of the Cistercian abbey of Salem to the north, to which land had been given at Birnau by the lords of Bodman in 1241. But in the eighteenth century, when the popularity of the pilgrimage began to increase, the monks had difficulties with the neighboring city of Überlingen and so decided to build further to the east along the north shore of the Bodensee on their own property, combining with the new church a summer residence as was being done at the same time by the abbey of Steingaden when building Die Wies.[44] A natural terrace well above the level of the lake provided a superb site[45] to which, as has been noted, Thumb responded most worthily.

42. Birnau is sometimes called Neubirnau, but writers seem to prefer the simpler form as do map-makers. See Mauritius Linder and Leodegar Walter, *Birnau das barock Juwel am Bodensee*, Birnau, n.d.; H. Ginter, *Birnau am Bodensee* (Kunstführer Nr. 435), Farbdruckausgabe, [Munich, 1962], (henceforth cited as Ginter); and H. Schnell, *Birnau am Bodensee Marien-Wallfahrtskirche* (Grosse Kunstführer Nr. 10), 2nd ed., [Munich, 1955], (henceforth cited as Schnell). Linder-Walter as well as Ginter provide many color plates both of the exterior and the interior, but these are now outdated thanks to a restoration that was still proceeding in the summer of 1966. Externally only the belfry stage of the tower has been repainted, with the wall surface pink and the pilasters stone color. Internally the first three bays of the nave are finished, but the scaffolding is still in place in the eastern half of the nave. This situation makes description of the coloring of the interior difficult at present (July, 1966).
43. *Zimmermann*.

44. Ginter, pp. 2–5.
45. Thumb intended to build a wide staircase leading to the lake. He also proposed a generous circular landing around an

In 1741 the monastery had obtained plans from Stahl, the architect of Cardinal Schönborn, whose seat nearby at Meersburg has been mentioned. At Meersburg Stahl, with considerable advice from Neumann if not from Neumann's actual designs, was building the stair-hall of the Neues Schloss. Nothing came of Stahl's project for Birnau. But it will be recalled that Thumb was architect of the Münster of Konstanz and was even being consulted by the cardinal at this point about the work at Meersburg and in connection also with the execution by Stahl of Neumann's church of St.-Peter at Bruchsal. It was not surprising that in 1745 the new Salem abbot, Stephan Euroth, who actually came from Meersburg, should call in Thumb who had already done a great deal of work for Cistercians in Switzerland, in Baden, and in Alsace, beginning with his supervision of St.-Urban for Franz Beer thirty years before.

On March 17 of that year there was what would today be called a design-conference at Salem, and five days later the exact site was fixed. The next year, on March 4, the old church was given up and, on April 12, the cornerstone of the new one was laid. Then, on June 17, an agreement with Thumb was signed by Euroth's successor as abbot of Salem, Anselm II Schwab,[46] elected only eleven days earlier, including a rather low estimate of 7,800 gulden, and in August of that year the cornerstone of the priests' house at the front was laid. The structural work went forward with no breaks so that already on March 10, 1748, the first payment, not covered by the contract with Thumb, was being made to the stuccator

J. A. Feuchtmayr (1696–1770). He was a son of J. F. Feuchtmayr (1659–1718), who had worked with Franz Beer at Salem on the stucco decoration of the Kaisersaal there in 1708–1710,[47] and had himself provided the altars for Thumb's church at St.-Peter shortly after its consecration in 1727. The payments made in 1748 were for two pairs of side altars, sixty-one stucco capitals and, on November 23, for a design for the high altar.[47a] In 1749 (July 13) he was further paid for eighty-eight carved keystones used on the exterior of the church and three window-frames on the tower. The Augsburg painter G. B. Goez (1708–1774), who like Feuchtmayr had worked in the chapel of the Neues Schloss at Meersburg in 1741, was commissioned to execute the frescoes in this year 1748, and they were carried out in 1749.[48] On September 20–21, 1750, the church, by then effectively complete, was consecrated. Feuchtmayr, however, continued to provide various fittings. In this year 1750 he was asked to provide six confessionals and the Stations of the Cross, of which only eight survive, and was paid for ninety-six pew ends as also for already-executed stucchi and gilding on the galleries. Payment for his other work came later, so that his last bill, for the statues of Sts. Windelin and Blasius on the side altars, is dated as late as June 1, 1758. But despite the late date of some of the payments to Feuchtmayr—for the sculpture on the organ, April 7, 1752; for the confessionals and the Stations of the Cross commissioned in 1750, May 17 and December 1, 1753; and for the busts, putti and flower vases on the gallery, April 20, 1757—the interior, with the exception of these last on which he had the assistance of F. A. Dirr, must have been completely finished and furnished within a year or two after the consecration. Fortunately very few changes have occurred since. But the present high altar is not as Feuchtmayr and Dirr designed it since it was modified by J. G. Wieland in 1790; the small lantern that originally rode the ridge of the apse roof was removed in 1810; and the original organ, removed in 1824, was replaced with the present one only in 1950.

The interior of Birnau is so original that it is very possibly unique in church architecture (Fig. 20); certainly there are no close parallels in eighteenth-century

elaborate fountain halfway down that would be fenced with a tall iron fence between stone posts carrying urns (Fig. 18). In *Barock am Bodensee/Architektur*, Bregenz, 1962, No. 156, the drawing reproduced here, which is now in the Generallandes-archiv, Stuttgart, is attributed to J. A. Feuchtmayr, who was responsible for the *stucchi* in the church. In this same exposition catalogue pl. 26 illustrates a contemporary portrait of Thumb.

46. Certain notations by Schwab dated August 26, 1746, on this agreement have led Boerlin, pp. 86–87, to query Thumb's responsibility for the design of Birnau as executed. But the fact that the executed church does not follow the scheme described in the agreement on which the abbot then noted that it should be 'cassirt und ein neuer errichtet worden' certainly does not seem to exclude the probability that a new agreement was made with Thumb before the construction of the church was carried forward. Boerlin, however, suggests J. C. Bagnato (1696–1757) from the Palatinate as the designer of the existing church, noting certain stylistic resemblances to his Deutschordenschloss church at Mainau of 1733–9 and his parish church of 1738–41 at Merdingen. Neither the fact that Bagnato may have been associated in some capacity with work of the 1740's at Meersburg, as was also true of Thumb, nor his later employment by Schwab at Salem on the remodelling of the choir in 1752–7 seems to strengthen much this rather surprising attribution. Neither Schnell, *op. cit.*, nor N. Lieb in his account of Birnau in *Barockkirchen zwischen Donau und Alpen*, 2nd ed., Munich [1958], pp. 128–35, 163–4, 173, mentions Bagnato's name in connection with Birnau.

47. The elder Feuchtmayr spent most of his life working for the Salem monastery and the son was brought up in a nearby village so that he was well known to the monks.

47a. Drawings for various elements of the stucco decoration by Feuchtmayr survive in the library at St.-Gallen as well as for the altars: *Barock am Bodensee/Architektur*, Nos. 148, 150–4, pl. 29, 30. No. 149 is a drawing by F. A. Dirr for the high altar signed and dated 1757. This was developed from Feuchtmayr's earlier design, No. 148.

48. It is worth underlining that the initiation of the decoration of Birnau by Feuchtmayr and Goez antedates by three years the comparable work in the St.-Peter library by Gigl and Gambs.

Germany before this time and what leads up to it is the library at St.-Peter (Fig. 13) rather than any of Thumb's extant churches.[49] The nave is neither basilican nor yet of the wall-pillar type that Thumb had inherited from Franz Beer and used so far for all his larger churches (Figs. 5, 8, 12, 19). The nave approaches most closely such a 'praying-hall' as S. Maria de Victoria in Ingolstadt, probably built and certainly decorated by the Asams in the mid-1730's.[50] Yet it is unlike this in its generous dimensions, especially that of height, and is perhaps almost as closely related to the deep choirs of such churches as Polling, Vilgertshofen, and Günzburg.[51] The quadrantal corners at the east end, balanced by a narrower diagonal truncation of the corners at the west end, have a long history in eighteenth-century Germany, and had been closely associated with the development of the Rococo church interior ever since the Krippkirche of 1717–1719 in Füssen, designed by J. J. Herkomer (1652–1717) and executed after his death by his nephew J. G. Fischer (1673–1747).[51a]

The transeptal chapels of curved outline, placed not midway of the nave nor at its east end but in the fourth of the five bays of the nave as at Waldkirch and Mengen, might have been suggested by the half-round side chapels at St.-Urban. But by carrying these chapels up the full two-storey height of the interior, Thumb made of them important features of the space-composition, echoing here the broader but equally tall spaces of the choir and the sanctuary to the east. The vault is very much flattened to an elliptical curve,[52] which the choir arch conspicuously repeats, and the vaulting conoids below its crown barely have independent existence visually so far does the vast ceiling fresco extend down into them (Figs. 20, 22) as in the St.-Peter library (Fig. 13).

Beyond the nave to the east the plan is telescopic as the exterior massing clearly indicates (Fig. 17). The square choir is somewhat narrower than the nave and the apse still narrower. The circle of the shallow dome of the choir, therefore, which is filled with a large round fresco in the fashion common since H. G. Asam painted the dome at Tegernsee sixty years earlier, rests not on four equal pendentives as usual but on six (Fig. 24). These are unevenly disposed around the sides between the wide elliptical opening of the choir arch to the west and the narrower opening, also elliptical, of the sanctuary arch to the east. The handling of the vault elements here is thus as free (not to say freehand) as in the St.-Peter library (Fig. 13). The wall membering in the eastern corners of the choir repeats effectively that in the curved eastern corners of the nave even though the vault segments above them are quite different. Finally, over the small horseshoe-shaped sanctuary, which the open edicule of the high altar completely fills spatially, there is not another dome but instead a handkerchief vault. This is penetrated at its sides by the severies of the sub-vaults above the flanking windows in much the same way as the severies over the arches and the side windows of the choir fit between the pendentives below the dome. Thus there is overhead along the central axis a sequential development from the broad, practically flat, ceiling of the nave, flanked though it is by rather boldly pointed intersecting vaulting elements above the side and corner bays, through the shallow-domed choir with its pendentives, to the tighter and more confining curvature of the vault that crowns the easternmost compartment (Figs. 20, 21). This is Rococo space-composition at its richest and most subtle in contrast to the effectively unbroken rectangle of S. Maria de Victoria with which the nave, if considered by itself, may not improperly be compared.

Galleries were constituent features of the wall-pillar type of church and occasionally, as for example at Einsiedeln in the 1720's, they had constituted important elements in the total spatial effect. Such galleries,

49. The nave of Mengen-Petershausen, built by Thumb in 1741–6 and destroyed by fire in 1810 as has been mentioned, was evidently quite similar as regards the surrounding gallery, continued there at the sides of the deep rectangular choir, and the placing and shape of the quasi-transeptal chapels. The corners of the nave were not rounded, however, nor the choir domed. Two plans by Thumb of *c.* 1741 survive in the Generallandesarchiv, Karlsruhe: *Barock am Bodensee/Architektur*, Nos. 142, 143, pl. 27. This is not included by Lieb-Dieth in their 1960 list of Thumb's works.

50. See 'Asam' II, pp. 38–43. Thumb, of course, had built several modest aisle-less churches. That of 1732–4 at Waldkirch, with its transeptal chapels, as well as Mengen, is already somewhat premonitory of the Birnau nave.

51. *Zimmermann.*

51a. M. Petzet, *Stadt und Landkreis Füssen*, Munich [1960], pp. 50–53, with plan and elevation.

52. The barrel vault of St.-Trudpert was already oval in section, but not as wide or as much flattened in the center. Once more the resemblance to the quite flat frescoed ceiling of S. Maria de Victoria is notable. In the St.-Peter library the vaulting rises much higher than here and the frescoed area is more restricted and by no means so flat. But Goez's fresco in the chapel of the

Meersburg Schloss occupies an even flatter ceiling, provided by Stahl in 1741.

53. The gallery at Birnau, carried on a cove, recalls even more distinctly than that of the St.-Peter library the similar feature in E. Q. Asam's St. Johann Nepomuk in Munich where the pilasters of the lower storey are also without entablature ('Asam' II, pp. 43–47). Even the rib-like curved members over Asam's pilasters that break the surface of the cove are omitted by Thumb, while the continuity of the cove is interrupted in each bay above the lower range of windows by shallow transverse severies corresponding, in a more delicate and less structural way, with those above the upper range of windows. The closest prototypes in Munich of the spreading elements above the pilasters at Birnau are the warped three-dimensional facets of Asam's cove that flank the entrance to the choir of St. Johann Nepomuk.

however, had almost always been subordinated hitherto to a giant order or its equivalent except in libraries (Figs. 5, 8, 12). Here, however, there are no continuous vertical elements of structure. The balcony continues unbroken around nave and choir and even passes, diminished in breadth, behind the tops of the altars in the transeptal projections (Figs. 20, 22). The gallery provides, moreover, the only continuous horizontal below the plane of the nave fresco overhead, for entablatures and even entablature-blocks are consistently omitted except in the edicule of the altar which is not of Thumb's period. Yet, surprisingly enough, pilasters are used in great profusion (Figs. 23, 25). Clusters of them below the balcony separate all the bays, both longitudinal and oblique, and upon them rest the bases of the coved elements, similar to those supporting the balcony at St.-Peter and echoing at smaller scale the vaulting conoids that rise from an upper order of pilaster-clusters.[53] But these pilasters, with their very freely designed capitals, can hardly be considered tectonic elements, at least not in the Baroque sense. Rather they articulate the wall surface in the manner of the tall panels which so often, but by no means always, replace pilasters in the *boiseries* of French Rococo interiors; while the flanking elements of the clusters are associated with the 'wall-arches', so to call them, that outline the bays above the concentric segmental heads of the windows.

Of the profuse but delicate stucco-work, here incidental yet complementary to Thumb's architecture, it is hardly necessary to speak in detail. This is neither the 'constructed decoration' of Dominikus Zimmermann's precisely contemporary choir at Die Wies[54]—a total substitution of *rocaille* elements for inherited architectural forms—nor yet the almost unrelated overgrowth which, for all its high intrinsic quality, seems to submerge and confuse the architectonic values of many of J. M. Fischer's grandest churches, and most notably Ottobeuren—he took over responsibility there for the completion of the abbey church at just this point, but the interior was decorated only in the mid-1750's by J. M. Feuchtmayr (1709–1772). The interior of Birnau is generally white though varied here and there by pale pastel tones; even the accents in this interior, provided by the somewhat stronger pink and blue marbling of the posts in the balcony railing, are high in key and restricted in quantity.[55] The altars, more-

over, are also of a relatively light pink and blue despite the hard shining surface of their scagliola. The statuary, here of the highest quality, is also mostly white, with stronger color on the draperies in some cases—for example, the famous *Honigschlecker*, a putto holding a beehive and licking honey from his finger. Only the small figures in the Stations of the Cross are fully and naturalistically polychromed.

All the more curious and unfortunate, therefore, in this interior that otherwise represents the highest Rococo accomplishment of the mid-century, is the retardataire character of Goez's frescoes. Despite the greater freedom of its painted architecture, that of the Woman of the Apocalypse in the dome of the choir still follows the Pozzo-derived formula of C. D. Asam's choir fresco of 1718–1720 at Weingarten (Fig. 24). This is not a serious anachronism, since it affects very little the total spatial composition of the interior and the tonality of the whole is light and even gay.[56] But in the nave, where one might have expected an open aerial composition such as J. B. Zimmermann had used as early as 1731 over the oval nave of Steinhausen and was providing at this very point again for his brother at Die Wies,[57] Goez started out by breaking the ceiling into two areas: one, occupying the western two bays of the nave, that is almost square; and a second more extensive one, centered on the transeptal axis, filling the other three bays (Fig. 22). Fortunately his broad painted rib, though darker in tone than the largely white architecture below, is so closely related to the tonality of the fresco as a whole that it is not conspicuous. But the two independent systems of perspective in the two parts of the fresco tend to break up the spatial unity of the nave and work against the carefully graded succession of spaces Thumb had provided in his architecture. Finally, the brownish parapet which Goez stretched across the

54. *Zimmermann.*

55. It is difficult to speak altogether accurately of the coloring of the *stucchi* at Birnau since at the time of writing the repainting of the interior, as has been noted, is still under way. There is no assurance, moreover, that the decisions controlling the choice of tones are correct. However that may be, where the repainting has been completed the walls remain white, the upper pilaster shafts are marbled in pale pink, and those below are of a medium to light grey, a sort of putty color. The raised

ornament is creamy, with some fields of very pale blue, pale pink, or pale green. Gold is introduced only for the highlights of the white scrollwork of the balcony railings, but the solider elements of this balustrade that line up with the pilasters above and below are marbled in blue and pink. Elsewhere equally strong tones are used only in the severies above the upper windows, evidently as a transition to the deeper tones of the *quadratura* elements that frame the ceiling fresco. One may assume that the high key of the tonality throughout is proper for *c.* 1750. He may query, however, whether modern taste has not reduced the liveliness of the general effect by making the relatively stronger notes of blue and pink and green too pale, if not the beige of the raised ornaments. The livelier contrasts at S. Maria de Victoria seem closer to Rococo coloring as it has survived unfaded in porcelain.

56. In Feuchtmayr's contract of 1741 for the decoration of the Schlosskapelle at Meersburg, Cardinal Schönborn included the recommendation that in deciding on the coloring Feuchtmayr should reach an agreement with Goez, there also the painter, and that in his estimation 'sweet colors are always the best': Boeck, *Joseph Anton Feuchtmayr*, Tübingen, 1948.

57. *Zimmermann.*

vaulting conoids (Figs. 20, 22), of heavy painted *quadratura* architecture somewhat in the manner of Michelangelo's Sistine ceiling, made impossible that easy freehand grace in the handling of vault-intersections which is such a notable example of the Rococo transformation of an inherited Baroque architectural device in the library at St.-Peter (Fig. 13).

Following once more the manner of C. D. Asam—in this case that of his ceiling fresco in the nave of Oster-hofen of twenty years earlier[58]—the principal fresco over the eastern bays of the nave (which is devoted to the Glorification of the Virgin as Queen of Heaven) has conspicuous *quadratura* architecture so handled perspectively that it seems to extend upward a Baroque nave of a sort which has no physical existence below, thus providing only a minimal area of open sky in the center (Figs. 20, 22). The architectural elements are, however, so organized as to suggest an ovalized rectangle at the base rising to the circle of sky in the center; while in the western half of the nave the clouds that carry the trumpeting angels largely obscure the simpler architectural setting.

So great, however, is Thumb's achievement here as a Rococo architect, so happy the embellishment provided by his other collaborators, the sculptor and stuccator Feuchtmayr and his assistant Dirr, that one can only be surprised he never again produced anything at all similar to this interior in the way that the nave of Birnau is similar to his library at St.-Peter.[59] Younger architects, particularly the Dossenbergers,[60] would move in this direction in the 1750's and 1760's, but Thumb did not, even in his latest work, the St.-Gallen library (Fig. 38), designed a decade later than Birnau. Although the degree of Specht's responsibility for the church at Wiblingen, which he began to execute in 1771, is much disputed,[61] it is perhaps not

irrelevant to note, despite the ambiguity of that curious church stylistically, that J. G. Specht (1721–1803) was associated with Thumb at Birnau.

Although Thumb was even less active after the completion of Birnau than just before, his association with one of the largest and grandest churches of the second half of the eighteenth century, that of the Benedictine abbey of St.-Gallen, and his designing of the library there fill the last years of his productive career with major interest down to his retirement in 1758. The story of the design and construction of St.-Gallen is as complicated as that of Weingarten or Wiblingen, but from that story can be deduced more conclusive evidence for assigning it to Thumb than Weingarten to either Franz Beer or Caspar Moosbrugger or Wiblingen to J. M. Fischer or Specht.[62] As at Weingarten and at Einsiedeln, the Benedictine lay-brother Caspar Moosbrugger's name appears early in the sequence at St.-Gallen, he having already provided projects for a new church in 1720–1721. Next came, a few years later, projects by a local Benedictine lay-brother, Gabriel Hecht (1664–1745), for a partial reconstruction of the medieval church or, more accurately, churches. Then, in 1730, Thumb's brother-in-law, Johann Michael II Beer, made a report on the state of the old edifice, the medieval successor to that of which the famous pre-Romanesque plan is still preserved in Thumb's library.

In 1749, on February 27, Thumb first offered a project for the church. This had presumably been prepared the previous year just after Birnau was structurally complete. On April 14 he, together with another Beer, Johann Michael I (1696–1780), and J. C. Bagnato, made another report on the old church, as did also J. M. II Beer on September 13. In 1749–1750 another Vorarlberger, Johann IV Rüf (1686–1750) who—together with his brother Michael II (1667–1726), Moosbrugger's brother-in-law—had been in charge of the construction of Einsiedeln from Moosbrugger's designs since 1720 and who had himself designed and built in 1746 the north wing of that monastery, provided a project, as did Bagnato again in 1750. The following year Thumb once more prepared a project and, probably the year after that, a younger Benedictine lay-brother, Gabriel Looser, who was employed as a cabinetmaker at St.-Gallen, constructed a handsome

58. 'Asam' II, pp. 26–27.

59. The St.-Peter library is of a distinctly bolder and more Rococo character: This is more, I suspect, because J. G. Gigl was from Wessobrunn and probably younger than J. A. Feuchtmayr—though his birth date is not known—than because the stucco-work there was initiated at least three years later than at Birnau. Contrary to the usual situation in churches of the mid-century, the architecture of Birnau, for which Thumb was responsible, is more Rococo than the *stucchi*, which are here distinctly subordinate to the handling of the architectonic elements. One can imagine this interior as existing as an effective spatial entity without Feuchtmayr's stucco or Goez's frescoes. This is, of course, not the case at Die Wies (see *Zimmermann*) where architect and stuccator were the same man and the fresco painter his brother. Curiously enough it is closer to the situation in J. M. Fischer's churches of the mid-century—Zwiefalten and Ottobeuren especially—where the ebullient Rococo *stucchi* by J. M. Feuchtmayr of the late 1740's and 1750's seem irrelevant to the still, in Fischer's case, essentially Baroque architecture.

60. A. Wohlhaupter, *Die Brüder Hans Adam und Joseph Dossenberger*, Munich (1950).

61. Lieb, *Barockkirchen . . . Munich*, [1958], pp. 136–44, 164–5, 173–4.

62. Boerlin identifies and illustrates fourteen different projects produced by various architects before the reconstruction of the church at last actually began. It is impossible here to do more than summarize Boerlin's thirty pages (35–65) of discussion of these successive projects of 1720–55. Shorter accounts of the history of the church as rebuilt in 1756–64 by Thumb and J. M. I Beer are provided by J. Duft, *Kathedrale St. Gallen* (Kunstführer Nr. 550), 7th ed., [Munich, 1962], pp. 3–14; and by H. Landolt, *Schweizer Barockkirchen*, Frauenfeld, [1948], pp. 74–81.

wooden model that happily survives. It largely follows Thumb's ideas, though to some extent those of Bagnato.

In 1752, however, the chapter of the abbey decided definitely to keep the old eastern church as their choir, rebuilding only the western one as a nave. Two years later further projects were offered by J. M. I Beer and by J. J. Rüscher (1662–1755), a Vorarlberger active in the Palatinate. Finally in 1755, after Thumb had further modified his design of 1751, the demolition of the old western church of Carolingian origin began. At that point Thumb was finally commissioned by Abbot Coelestin Gugger von Standach to build the present nave and central domed area, though the eastern church on the site of the present choir was still to be kept.

Before proceeding further with this account of St.-Gallen something should be said about Thumb's responsibility for the design, since P.-H. Boerlin, in discussing the question at length,[63] refuses to give full credit to him as most scholars have hitherto done. First the evidence provided by the surviving plans I–XIV,[64] most of them preserved at St.-Gallen, should be noted. The earliest, the Moosbrugger projects of 1720–1721 (I and II),[65] both include *two* domed crossings but nothing approaching a central rotunda. His next project (III),[66] which retains the medieval church to the east, has a more or less centrally planned nave with a heavily framed ovalizing fresco indicated over the crossing. Nothing at all relevant is to be found in the plans of Hecht, Rüf, or the earliest of J. M. I Beer's (IV, V, VI).[67] Beer's next projects (VII, VIII, IX, X),[68] however, propose a domed crossing where the new nave joins the choir, but with no attempt at symmetry in the treatment of the eastern and western arms. What is perhaps significant in these schemes, however, are the bulging façades on the transept ends as at Thumb's Frauenalb. In VII[69] this is even flanked by towers on the north side. If the project belongs to the year when Beer's name is first mentioned in the records as making a report on the condition of the old church, 1749, it is later by nearly twenty-five years than Frauenalb and contemporary with Thumb's first project for St.-Gallen.

The surviving projects most relevant to the design of the church as finally built are those numbered XII, XIII, and XIV.[70] Of equal relevance is Looser's model

of 1752.[71] Closest of all to the church as built is a plan found in Lucerne by Adolf Reinle in 1950 (Fig. 31).

Project XII (Fig. 29), with a rotunda as wide as the nave and aisles and slightly projecting transepts with central bulges, Boerlin attributes to Moosbrugger on the basis of the resemblance of the eastern pair of towers to those in Moosbrugger's project (III) of 1721[72] and details of the north elevation that resemble elements of the west front of Einsiedeln. The attribution is not persuasive, both because of Moosbrugger's death two years after his earlier project (III) was submitted and because of the marked superiority of the draftsmanship to his other surviving drawings. Lieb and Dieth[72a] propose more plausibly Thumb's brother-in-law J. M. II Beer as the author and a date not earlier than 1730 for this crucial project which once more suggests, though not so definitely, influence from Thumb's Frauenalb plan, as in the case of J. M. I Beer's projects (VII and VIII).

Project XIII, of 1750 and by Bagnato,[73] is much less similar to the church as executed, although the diagonally placed eastern towers may well have provided the model for those finally executed by J. M. I Beer. But Thumb's project, XIV (Fig. 27), incorporates similar towers, as does the Looser model.[74] The model, however, is closer in plan[75] to project XII, since nave and choir each have only two bays instead of three as in the executed church. The scalloped plan of the transepts, moreover, corresponds to Thumb's project of 1751 (XIV) rather than to the plain bulges of the Lucerne plan (assigned to Thumb by Lieb-Dieth as well as by Reinle)[76] and the executed church (Figs. 27, 28, 31). But the surviving plan that is closest to the nave and rotunda Thumb actually built, since it shows the medieval choir retained, is one found at Au (Fig. 30) by Franz Dieth in 1956 that must certainly be by Thumb. The model, however, has an internal elevation in two storeys with, as shown on the southern side,[77] no entablature above the lower order of coupled pilasters but rather a cove supporting a shallow balcony that is very similar to the one at Birnau. Despite the abbot's close relations with Bagnato, of which Boerlin makes much in his 'Conclusio',[78] there seems to be little more reason at St.-Gallen than at Birnau to transfer the major credit for the design of the nave and rotunda as executed from Thumb to Bagnato. Nor do

63. Boerlin, pp. 79–114.
64. Boerlin, Figs. 1–44. The Roman numerals are those used both by Lieb-Dieth and by Boerlin.
65. Boerlin, Figs. 1–3.
66. Boerlin, Figs. 4–7.
67. Boerlin, Figs. 9–14.
68. Boerlin, Figs. 15–22.
69. Boerlin, Fig. 15.
70. Boerlin, Figs. 27–35.

71. Boerlin, Figs. 36–42.
72. Boerlin, Figs. 7, 8.
72a. Lieb-Dieth, p. 51.
73. Boerlin, Figs. 31–34.
74. Boerlin, Fig. 36.
75. Boerlin, Fig. 38.
76. Lieb-Dieth, p. 53.
77. Boerlin, Figs. 37, 41.
78. Boerlin, p. 117.

Lieb and Dieth,[79] who were familiar with Boerlin's contentions from an article,[80] give his attributions as much attention as I have done here.

What is really significant, regardless of variant attributions of surviving projects, is that the basic idea of a church with a central domed area flanked by matching nave and choir goes back some thirty years before the construction of St.-Gallen actually began in 1755 to Thumb's Frauenalb. Thus in German lands, as often elsewhere, such an architect as Thumb can be seen to have taken up again, in the third quarter of the century, certain formal aspects of the pre-Rococo decades early in the century when the Baroque, which had reached full maturity only belatedly in the north, came almost full circle within the lifetime of a generation.

Work on the foundations at St.-Gallen began in 1755 and on August 29, 1756, the cornerstone was laid. The following year the raw construction was complete and the stucco and fresco decoration begun by Christian Wenzinger whom Thumb had known at St.-Peter thirty years before. The work was completed by 1760 when the church was consecrated on November 15.

Peter Thumb had retired to Konstanz on October 26, 1758, his career already ended. When the decision was finally made to reconstruct the east end of the church, apparently about the time of the consecration in 1760, the chapter therefore turned to J. M. I Beer, then over 60, who provided on December 20 a two-towered project with a shallow segmental apse. The following February 19 the changes he was proposing in the existing designs of 1750–1751 for the east end by Bagnato and by Thumb (as represented in Looser's model of 1751) were accepted, and very soon demolition of the old eastern church made possible the building of the new choir. This was probably completed structurally by 1764 when the stuccators, in this case J. G. Gigl who had been working at St.-Peter in the 1750's and his brother Mathias, began to execute the *stucchi* inside.

In some respects St.-Gallen must be accepted as a culminating point in eighteenth-century Germanic architecture. Behind it lay the line of great churches that had begun in the 1680's and 1690's with Obermarchtal in Swabia by Peter Thumb's father and his uncle Christian, and in Switzerland with the Jesuit church at Solothurn, sometimes attributed to a member of another Vorarlberg building family, H. G. Kuen (1641–1691); ahead lay international Neo-classicism, initiated in this part of Europe at St.-Blasien in Baden by the French architect P.-M. d'Ixnard shortly after the old church there burned in 1768 just as the

decoration of the choir of St.-Gallen was coming to completion. More than that, because of its great size and the particular character of its plan and spatial organization, St.-Gallen has an almost equally prominent place in the international sequence of great post-Reformation churches that began almost two hundred years earlier in Milan and Rome. Yet, paradoxically, it does not represent the culminating point in Thumb's architectural career, much less a culminating example of Rococo architecture, as does the church at Birnau.

The long history of the commission for St.-Gallen helps to make its position in Thumb's *œuvre* clear. One cannot say that St.-Gallen was actually the result of committee-design, notoriously a method only too likely to produce weak solutions; but the sequence of projects by so many different men over thirty-five years, the six years of study in successive projects by Thumb intended to meet the objections of the abbot and the monks, and the decision—eventually negated —to retain the medieval eastern church (which can hardly have been sympathetic to any of the architects involved, but which they had to take into account even in making projects for a totally new church) set up limitations that were more often thwarting than stimulating.

All the same the church that was finally produced after the old eastern church was eventually replaced in the 1760's by Beer's new choir does represent essentially what Thumb had all along been working towards. That was a church dominated spatially by a rotunda so placed, as earlier in 1726–1731 at Frauenalb, that the nave and the choir extended symmetrically to east and west on either side (Fig. 14). Such a plan, probably first seriously proposed for St.-Gallen in project XII (Fig. 29), whatever its precise date and whoever its designer, was arrived at conceptually by moving the characteristic crossing-dome of the post-Reformation church-formula westward. This had in fact already been done quite early in the seventeenth century by Jacques Le Mercier in designing his Eglise de la Sorbonne in Paris, presumably because that church, like Frauenalb, lay across the end of a quadrangle and therefore required a major entrance on the cross-axis.

Le Mercier's domed crossing, however, being very little wider than his nave and his choir, is no rotunda. This was also true of Frauenalb, except that the end of the transept there was bowed outward to make the existence of the circular *pièce centrale* apparent from the exterior and to provide a cross-axial element in which the main entrance could be appropriately set. This tower-flanked bulge could hardly be more different from Le Mercier's temple portico in Paris. An earlier German approach to such planning is found in

79. Lieb-Dieth, pp. 51–53.
80. *Schweizerische Zeitschrift für Archäologie und Kunstgeschichte*, 1953, pp. 223 ff.

the church of Stift Haug in Würzburg built in 1670–1691 by Antonio Petrini (?–1701).

The closest any architect had come to the St.-Gallen scheme in a major executed work was, curiously enough, Christopher Wren's St. Paul's in London as finally designed in 1675 and completed in 1710. After a characteristic struggle, of the sort that goes back to Bramante's difficulties in planning St. Peter's, between an architect set on creating an edifice of a central type and a clergy determined, partly for functional reasons and partly out of respect for local tradition, to have a church with a longitudinal axis, the moderately long nave to contain the worshipping public was balanced against what is, for the period, a very deep choir, respecting the tradition of that of the pre-existing medieval church. Thus Wren arrived at a plan that was effectively symmetrical on the cross-axis. However, the pair of towers at his west end—at St.-Gallen they were eventually provided at the east end—and the paired chapels behind them (not to speak of the relative unimportance of the transeptal entrances, compared at least to Le Mercier's temple-fronted north façade at the Sorbonne) diminished the external effect of symmetry on the transverse axis. All the same, the high-drummed dome over the crossing of St. Paul's clearly revealed the centrality of the rotunda underneath it. Moreover, the broadening of the core-space internally beyond the width of the nave and choir so that the aisles run into the rotunda through diagonal bays, while the dome as a result rises over not four but eight pendentives, insured that the rotunda would dominate the spatial composition of the interior.

In the long struggle between centralized and longitudinal church plans, some of the most interesting Baroque examples had been those in which the two conceptions were merged into a space that was roughly, rather than precisely, oval in shape—as, probably for the first time, in Borromini's S. Carlo alle Quattro Fontane in the 1630's. Such merging in eighteenth-century German architecture had, in several characteristic works from as early as the 1720's, taken either the form of an oval more or less rectangularized or of a rectangle more or less ovalized. At the mid-century the nave of Zimmermann's Die Wies[81] is an example of the first, that of Thumb's Birnau of the second (Fig. 23), and both are climactic examples of Rococo interior architecture. Other German architects were working along rather different lines.

Josef Greising (1664–1721), a Vorarlberger active in Franconia who built a great deal for the Schönborns, had provided in 1711–1721 at the west end of the Neumünster in Würzburg an octagon the full width

of the surviving Romanesque nave and aisles that followed beyond though this was masked externally by a typical Roman Baroque façade of concave rather than convex plan. After producing several projects for Einsiedeln that included an oval choir with an annular aisle, Caspar Moosbrugger eventually worked out a quite different plan with a western octagon centered on the existing small shrine of the Madonna, and this is what was finally executed by the Rüfs in the 1720's.[82] The curious and confused sequence of interrelated spaces at Einsiedeln could hardly be expected to appeal to Thumb or to any other well-trained and experienced architect and hardly supports the theory that the crucial project XII for St.-Gallen (Fig. 29) is by Moosbrugger. Yet familiarity with Benedictine Einsiedeln may have helped to make the idea of a rotunda acceptable to the Benedictines of St.-Gallen from the first. The preoccupation of another architect family not of Vorarlberg origin, the Dientzenhofers, who were from Bavaria but chiefly active in Bohemia, with longitudinal plans made up of intersecting ovals—as suggested by many of Guarini's published projects and more especially that of 1679 for the church of Our Lady of Altötting in Prague—was represented in southern Germany by Johann Dientzenhofer's Banz at the opening of the century. This line of plan-development reached a climax in J. B. Neumann's Vierzehnheiligen across the Main from Banz, a great church that was projected a few years earlier than Thumb's design of 1749 for St.-Gallen though carried out over an even longer period.[83] In this the nave was widened and enlarged to provide the setting for the shrine of the fourteen *Nothilfer*, but this hardly constitutes a definite rotunda. Neumann's church at Neresheim, designed in the late 1740's but executed by his son only after his death in 1753, is probably even less relevant to Thumb and St.-Gallen because of its later date, although the rotunda-like dominance of the principal oval element of the interior is carried considerably further than at Vierzehnheiligen. But the interest of the most productive of Bavarian church-architects among Thumb's close contemporaries, J. M. Fischer, in flanking a round, or more accurately an octagonal, *pièce centrale* with longitudinal elements to west and east certainly is.[84]

This recurrent scheme of Fischer's found notable expression first in 1736–1739 at Aufhausen, although

---

81. See *Zimmermann*.

82. 'Asam' ii, pp. 15–16.
83. Neumann's design was developed in the mid-1740's; the church was structurally complete and ready to receive the stucco decoration provided by J. M. Feuchtmayr only in 1763. The decoration, therefore, is contemporary with the work of the Gigls in the choir of St.-Gallen.
84. See F. Hagen-Dempf, *Der Zentralbaugedanke bei Johann Michael Fischer*, Munich [1954].

neither nave nor choir there is more than a single, rather narrow square bay. This is very like project XII for St.-Gallen (Fig. 29) but without the half-bays extending the arms in that to east and to west. Furthermore Fischer was content in such important churches as Berg-am-Laim and the Franziskanerinnen at Ingolstadt which followed at the end of the decade shortly after Aufhausen to let his broad octagons serve as the naves, lengthening the plan longitudinally only eastward, somewhat as Greising and Moosbrugger had done at Neumünster and at Einsiedeln, respectively. Despite the increasing importance given to domed crossings, the conditions under which several of Fischer's largest and richest churches were erected: Fürstenzell in 1740–1745; Zwiefalten in 1741–1752; and Ottobeuren in 1749–1766, required that he continue to provide long naves to the west as well as shorter choirs to the east. At Rott-am-Inn, however, designed in 1759, a decade later than Thumb's earliest project for St.-Gallen, Fischer was finally able to enlarge the Aufhausen scheme dimensionally. Even so, the main subsidiary spaces of nave and choir to east and west of the very big octagon there remained single dome-covered bays of square plan, not the three-bayed arms of Thumb's nave and Beer's choir.

Thumb's solution, which is even larger dimensionally than Fischer's, was also more traditional than that and most of the others that have been mentioned. His nave (Fig. 32), at the outer end of which is a galleried western apse,[85] remained of the wall-pillar type so long a favorite of the Vorarlbergers, and each of the three oblong bays that replaced the two proposed in project XIV and in the Looser model is covered by a handkerchief vault, as in his nave at Ebersmunster thirty years before (Fig. 5). So large are the arches behind the pilaster clusters, so open the subsidiary spaces between them, thanks to the absence of side galleries, that the effect is notably multi-spatial and tectonic in the Baroque rather than in the Rococo tradition of a unified and decoratively walled space. The frescoes executed by Wenzinger,[86] begun in 1757 just before

Thumb left St.-Gallen, are extraordinarily aerial and open, especially that over the rotunda (Figs. 32, 33)— just the sort one would have liked to see at Birnau (Figs. 20, 22). Yet the nave vaults, here separated by rather plain and quite tectonic ribs, might more appropriately have carried frescoes of the Pozzo-like order of C. D. Asam's of forty years earlier at Weingarten.

The *stucchi* in the nave of St.-Gallen, also by Wenzinger, are extremely bold and plastic, with more use of figures than is usual in Rococo decoration (Fig. 35). Yet they seem almost as much an afterthought as those J. M. Feuchtmayr was executing at this point in Fischer's Ottobeuren, with none of the inevitability of the *stucchi* at Birnau which resulted, one may presume, from close collaboration between the architect and the stuccator there (Figs. 21, 25). This is especially true in the rotunda where the pendentives are almost as firmly articulated tectonically as Viscardi's at Freystadt a half-century earlier and carry groups of stucco figures in relief (Fig. 33). They rise, moreover, above alternate half-round and stilted arches, quite as at Freystadt or Borromini's S. Agnese in Agone, so that there is here none of that freehand curvature of vaulting surfaces characteristic of the St.-Peter library and Birnau. Indeed the rotunda is not altogether improperly considered proto-Neo-classic by some scholars. How truly Baroque it really is, all the same, if academically and traditionally so, the advanced Neo-classicism of the high altar to the east, of 1810 and by J. S. Moosbrugger, makes evident by contrast (Fig. 33).

The Rococo character of the Wenzinger stuccoes in the nave and the rotunda was maintained in those executed a decade later in the choir by the Gigls, but the frescoes there by A. O. Moretti of 1819–1821 naturally have nothing in common with the original style of the rest of the church, whether that be considered Baroque, Rococo, or even proto-Neo-classic. Happily, however, Thumb's able collaborators at Birnau, J. A. Feuchtmayr and his associate F. A. Dirr, had been called on in the 1760's to carve the confessionals in the aisles of the church and the magnificent organ-crowned choir stalls to the east so that the church is not without rich furnishings appropriate to a Rococo interior despite the rather late date of their execution.

A not altogether irrelevant point about St.-Gallen used to be that, despite the light from the tall side windows,

---

85. This is the final shrunken survival of the church associated with Otmar, the eighth-century abbot who founded St.-Gallen. Most of the early projects (I–VIII) for the reconstruction of the abbey retained this, while the designer of project XII proposed instead to substitute a small chapel to the south of the western apse. Such a chapel, this time larger and more nearly detached, also appears in Bagnato's project (XIII) of 1750 and even in Thumb's of 1751. It is significant that neither the Lucerne nor the Au plan provides any such chapel, but in the latter three altars are indicated in the western apse which is there semicircular rather than flattened as in the executed church (Figs. 29, 30).

86. Wenzinger had studied in Rome in 1731 and after that in Paris from 1737 on; indeed, he even received an award from the Académie. Because of this foreign training he seems to have responded early to the international currents leading towards

Neo-classicism in the 1750's. This hardly explains the extreme openness of his composition on the dome of the rotunda which seems rather an attempt to emulate Tiepolo's fresco, completed in 1753, over the stairhall in the Würzburg Residenz or, more probably, J. J. Zeiller's on the dome at Ettal, painted in 1752. Fortunately the stiffening of the figures in the fresco was not echoed in those executed in stucco, not altogether unworthy rivals of J. A. Feuchtmayr's more famous ones at Birnau, and no premonition of Neo-classicism restrained the exuberance of the *rocaille* elements in the decoration (Fig. 35).

the interior appeared slightly dingy in comparison with Birnau and with most great interiors of the mid-eighteenth century. This doubtless meant no more than that the restoration of 1866–1867, which altered the original color scheme—white walls with light green stucco decoration and gold highlights—to near-monochrome, should have been followed by a new and more accurate restoration of the interior at the time the exterior was renewed in 1928–1938. It is pleasant to report that such a restoration has been under way since 1964, though in the summer of 1966 it was not yet complete.[87]

As the imposing two-towered east façade (Fig. 37), which still recalls Moosbrugger's project III of 1721, is definitely not by Thumb, it seems unnecessary to discuss it here in detail. Thumb's project XIV of the early 1750's shows towers placed diagonally (Fig. 27), as earlier proposed by Bagnato in his project XIII of 1750 and as seen in the Looser model. That provided, however, no side entrance directly into the rotunda. Such an entrance in the center of the bulge appeared first in the plan surviving at Au (Fig. 30). The executed north façade gives a rather different sort of emphasis to the rotunda externally than Thumb proposed in project XIV (Fig. 27). Instead of a two-pitched roof, like those over the transepts and apse of Birnau, rising above a continuous entablature related as at Birnau to a continuous pilaster order, and with a blocking course and a pediment to give emphasis to the cross-axis, there are in the executed church long ranges of plain wall broken only by very tall arched windows (Figs. 36, 37). Over the bulge of the rotunda, however, the cornice line is considerably raised. Even on this bulge there is no order, only flat projections with plain sunken panels and niches between the three still larger and taller windows. The center is accented by a modest portal below and a freely curved gable rising against the roof which, though still two-pitched, is somewhat less boldly modelled than in the project. The statues in the niches are by Wenzinger, as is presumably also the scroll-surrounded armorial achievement in the gable. This portion of the façade was evidently erected from the amended design of Thumb as represented by the Au plan (Fig. 30). The comparable feature of the Looser model differs both from project

XIV and from the executed work since it follows externally the scalloped plan of the interior and thus recalls slightly Bagnato's project XIII of 1750. Beer reverted to a far richer treatment in executing the east front though he continued the design of Thumb's nave along the side walls of the choir (Fig. 37).

If Thumb left St.-Gallen in 1758 and retired to Konstanz with the largest architectural work of his long career still far from finished and, stylistically, more Baroque than Rococo, he did not leave before initiating the previous year, in the latest of all his productions, the monastery library,[88] a Late Rococo interior of very high quality. This, like the church, was carried out and decorated only in his absence and over the next ten years, although the raw construction was complete by 1758. At the least, however, we may assume that the ceiling paintings of the early 1760's by Joseph Wannenmacher (1722–1780), dark though they have become, and the delicate stucco decoration by the Gigls, which vignettes them, who were working here in these years as well as in the choir of the church, (not to speak of Looser's rich cabinet work and marquetry floor) would have met with his approval. His second son, Michael Peter Franz Xaver (1725–1769), supervised the completion of the library as also of the nave and rotunda of the church.

The library (Figs. 38, 39) is considerably longer than that at St.-Peter (Fig. 13) so that it appears lower, especially as the vaults, carried on the solid cores of broad book stacks that function like wall-pillars in churches, are so low-pitched as to be nearly flat. The continuous gallery, supported by red scagliola columns and entablature blocks set diagonally at the corners of the stacks in the lower storey, winds in and out. With its alternating curves and straight sections, however, this feature is less continuously flowing, and hence less truly Rococo, than that at St.-Peter. In part because of the coloring of the St.-Gallen interior, all reddish and golden in tone below the vaults in contrast to the predominant white of St.-Peter, this is, indeed, distinctly less characteristic of the Rococo. Here, as more strongly in the rotunda of the church, one senses not so much the beginnings of proto-Neo-classicism as a slightly bored reaction against the light-hearted exuberance of the High Rococo.

Thus the conclusion, like the early stages of Thumb's career, leaves still a mystery the sources of the originality and the assurance of the major Rococo achievements of his middle years in the library at St.-Peter and at Birnau. But the late works at St.-Gallen round out a picture distinctly characteristic of the stylistic ebb and flow of the forty years between the years

87. Since the church has been filled with scaffolding for the last two years and the repainted interior has been revealed as yet only in the nave, it would be premature to attempt to describe in detail the present coloring of the *stucchi*. Glimpsed here and there, the green of the raised decoration appears rather too pale, though this may well be correct, providing further evidence of Wenzinger's somewhat academic taste. On the other hand it appears that much stronger colors are being introduced around the figural groups on the pendentives of the rotunda, entrance to which is still difficult.

88. Duft, *op. cit.*, pp. 16–23.

around 1720, when Thumb was building his first considerable churches at St.-Trudpert and Ebersmunster, and the mid-1760's when he died. He had been the most prolific major architect of his generation in the lands around the Bodensee. No other Vorarlberger, moreover, had mastered so fully as he the Rococo mode introduced into Germany in his early youth that first matured in Bavaria in the 1720's and early 1730's. He and several of his contemporaries then developed the Rococo into a consistent style of monumental interior architecture that flourished into the 1750's. Like most of his contemporaries, however, Thumb seems to have worked quite without theory, following for a while whole-heartedly a stylistic current that more famous architects such as J. M. Fischer and J. B. Neumann accepted only occasionally and with considerable diffidence and then returning to the main international stream of mid-eighteenth-century evolution towards Neo-classicism.[89]

89. This development, perhaps most evident in the career of A. J. Gabriel, underlines the curious fact that certain of the more original artistic manifestations of the eighteenth century, such as Chinoiserie and the Rococo, were historically *culs-de-sac* without relevant succession in the following period. The course of architectural theory in the early and mid-eighteenth century helps to explain this phenomenon, for contemporary theorists seem never to have concerned themselves positively with the Rococo, but rather to have condemned it consistently, while not disdaining, if they were themselves designers, to employ it freely in decoration.

JOHN HARRIS

Le Geay, Piranesi and International Neo-classicism in Rome 1740–1750

Seen in the light of our current knowledge of neo-classic architecture, the designs made by Sir William Chambers (1723–1796) in 1751–1752 for the Mausoleum of Frederick Prince of Wales (Figs. 33–36) are in such an advanced neo-classic style that it seems impossible for them to anticipate by over ten years such designs as Marie-Joseph Peyre's in his *Œuvres d'Architecture* (1765), a book that rightly represents the mainstream of Parisian neo-classicism. Yet because architectural history has a very long way to go before it can even begin to approach the depths to which studies of eighteenth-century literature and aesthetics have been carried, and because we are in receipt of so few neo-classic designs of the seventeen-forties and fifties, it may be that Chambers' designs, rather than being precursors, are in fact the product of fairly current advanced thought. If we wish to prove this the case, then it is necessary to probe into architectural design in Rome between 1740 and 1750, a decade wherein we may discover the genesis of international neo-classicism as that style is known from the seventeen-sixties onwards, or as has been said, the style of the mature Peyre.[1]

A clarification of the term neo-classicism is perhaps not necessary in this context so long as one bears in mind Professor Wittkower's fundamental distinction between Lord Burlington's classicism, with its reliance upon Palladio and other interpreters of antiquity, and mid-eighteenth-century neo-classicism with its empirical approach to the monuments themselves—a distinction which is, of course, essential in an effort to build up some coherent picture of neo-classicism in the vital decade 1740–1750.[2] It is also necessary to attempt an evaluation of a now obscure French architect reputed to have been in his day the genius of French architecture. His name was Jean Laurent Le Geay, who seems

not only to have influenced the greater Piranesi, but to have possibly been the father of a style of design that can be followed through the seventeen-forties to Chambers, Peyre, and French neo-classicism in its maturity.[3]

A few dates will help to clarify any potential relationships between Le Geay and Piranesi. The former's birth date is unknown, but on the basis of his Grand Prix at the French Academy in Paris in 1732, it may be presumed that, like his contemporaries there,[4] he would have been born around 1710. For some reason he did not take up his Rome prize until 1737, when we may presume he would have been nearing the age of thirty. Because there is no record of Le Geay's Parisian activities during this interim period it is impossible to evaluate any pre-Rome influences upon his later work. Yet even Rome is a negative moment, for although he spent five years there until early 1742, only during his last months do we hear that he had acquired considerable status among his fellow students at the French Academy. But what is perhaps more important, his work during this latter period might have attracted the attention of Piranesi.

In comparison with Le Geay, what is most surprising about Piranesi is that despite his greatness our knowledge of his early years consists only of a few brief facts. He was born in Venice in 1720, served an apprenticeship under Matteo Lucchesi, who was not only his uncle, but was also a noted Venetian architect and engineer, and seems to have studied architecture with Giovanni Antonio Scalfurotto and perspective with Carlo Zucchi. We also know that he departed for Rome as a draughtsman under the patronage of

---

1. The hypotheses put forward in this article were first disseminated as a paper titled *Piranesi and International Neo-Classicism in Rome*, delivered in December 1963 to the Graduate Art History Association of Columbia University. In March 1964 it was given again in a more detailed form to a professorial seminar on the eighteenth century, and in March 1966 as a public lecture at the Courtauld Institute of Art. I benefited immensely from the discussions that followed this second reading.

2. Wittkower expounds this in F. Saxl and R. Wittkower, *British Art and the Mediterranean*, Oxford, 1948, 71.

3. The bibliography of Le Geay is small and is summarized in the only account of his Rome career by Emil Kaufmann in 'Three Revolutionary Architects, Boullee, Ledoux and Lequeu', *Transactions of the American Philosophical Society*, N.S., 42, pt. 3 (1952), 450–3, an expansion of what he wrote in *Architecture in the Age of Reason*, published posthumously in 1955. Pierre du Columbier has discussed Le Geay's work at Sans Souci and Berlin in his *L'Architecture Français En Allemagne Au XVIIIe Siècle*, Traveaux Et Mémoires Des Instituts Français En Allemagne, 5, Paris, 1956; and cf. also L. Réau, *Histoire De L'Expansion De L'Art Français*, vol. 2, Paris, 1928, 182–3.

4. On 12th May 1732 *equisses* were received by the Academy from Haneuse, Rousset, Laurent, Payen, Méres, Labadye, Nivelet, Mariaud, Lange and Le Franc. Cf. *Procés—Verbaux de L'Academie Royale ...*, ed. Lemonnier, v (1727–43), 1918, 98.

Marco Foscarini, the Venetian Ambassador to Pope Benedict XIV. In Rome he lived in the Palazzo Venezia and seems to have attached himself to the studio of Giuseppe Vasi the topographical artist and cartographer. He also learnt etching from Felice Polanzani, one of his first Roman friends and the author of the romantic etched portrait in the 1750 *Opera Varie*.[5] Yet although armed with these facts, what makes a judgment of the youthful Piranesi difficult is the absence of any reliable drawing before his first publication, the *Prima Parte di Architetture e Prospettive*, a book dedicated not, as might have been expected, to some noble patron, but to Nicola Giobbe, an obscure Roman builder.

Rome in 1740 therefore would have seen Le Geay, a French architect of about thirty years of age, in residence since 1737, and Piranesi aged twenty and newly arrived from Venice. The younger man could hardly have been unaware of what was happening at the French Academy, where, unlike any other academies in Italy, could be found the vortex of new architectural ideas and theories that were to change the patterns of European architecture.

What is known about Le Geay's activities is contained in a number of eulogies made at various times, but supported only by three suites of etchings published in the seventeen-sixties and a few precious designs, mostly copies made by Sir William Chambers. The thrill of excitement caused by Le Geay and his designs provoked praises from François de Troy, Director of the French Academy in Rome; from C. N. Cochin, the acolyte of neo-classicism; from Andrieux, Secretary of the Academy of Architecture in Paris; and from Joseph Lavallée the painter. The earliest was by de Troy, who when announcing Le Geay's departure from Rome for Paris on 9th January, said, 'il emporte une quantité de fort beaux desseins, tant des études qu'il a fait d'après les edifices publics que de sa propre compositions; dans ces derniers; il y a du feu et du génie'.[6] Then possibly in the sixties Cochin made this remarkable statement: 'On peut donner pour première époque du retour d'un meilleur goust, l'arrivée de Legeay architecte, qui avoit été pensionnaire à Rome. C'étoit un des plus beaux génies en architecture qu'il y ait eu; mais d'ailleurs, sans frein, et, pour ainsi dire, sans raison. Il ne pouvoit jamais se borner à la

demands qu'on lui faisoit, et le grand Mogel d'auroit pas été assés riche pour élever les bâtimens qu'il projettoit.... Quoiqu'il en soit, comme le gousts de Legeay étoit excellent, il ouvrit les yeaux a beaucoup de gens. Les jeunes architects le saisirent autant qu'ils purent, peut etre plutost parce qu'il leur parut nouveau que par un véritable sentiment de ses beautés. On vit changer sensiblement l'ecole d'architecture au grand étonnement de tous les architects anciens de l'Academie.'[7] So Le Geay's reputation is pervasive through to 1760 or 1770. But even as late as 1799 and 1801, following the death of de Wailly, both Andrieux and Lavallée in their obituaries could be in awe of Le Geay's influence upon de Wailly and his generation. Lavallée thought that de Wailly had discovered in Le Geay's drawings some idea of the true perfection of architecture: 'ce ne fut que chez l'architecte le J'ai qu'il parvint à decouvrir, à travers les exaggérations de ce nouveau maître, le véritable point de perfection dans l'architecture dont il avait le pressentiment'.[8] And Andrieux is even more fulsome in his praises: 'On peut fixer à Lejay la renaissance du bon goût dans cet art; il a commencé à donner a la composition des plans une disposition plus grande que l'architecture n'avait plus depuis longtemps; d'ailleurs il dessinait avec de goût que de précision. Ce maître forme une nouvelle école d'où sont sortis plusieurs des architectes les plus célèbres de notre temps, Boullée, Moreau, Peyre l'ainé et de Wailly ... autrefois et jusqu'au de L'école de Lejeay les architectes se continaient de fixer des lignes et tout au plus de tracer des plans, mais ne dessinaient ni les contours, ni les corps avancés, ni les ornements; ils ne savaient pour ainsi dire pas leur langue tout entière.'[9]

In the absence of designs by Le Geay nothing could be more provocative than these praises, nor can one but be impressed by them. Fortunately we can judge and assess Le Geay from three principal sources: the etchings, *Vasi* (n.d.), *Fontane* (1767), *Tombeaux* (1768), and *Rovine* (1768); from the valuable interest of Sir William Chambers; and from Le Geay's designs for a church dedicated to the Trinity and published in 1767. There is also the enigmatic problem of his responsibility for the Berlin Hedwigskirche and for the 'Communs' building at Sans Souci, Potsdam.[10] It

5. The catalogue of the exhibition held at the Smith College Museum of Art, Northampton, Mass., in 1961 is the most useful and recent scholarly assessment of Piranesi, with contributions from Hofer, Lehmann, Parks, and Wittkower. But the basic study of Piranesi as an architect is still Werner Korte's 'Giovanni Battista Piranesi als praktischer Architekt', in *Zeitschrift für Kunstgeschichte*, II, 1933, 16 ff.
6. *Correspondence des Directeurs de l'Académie de France a Rome*, ed. Montaiglon, x, pt. 1, 1900.

7. Cochin, C. N., *Mémoires Inédits*, ed. C. Henry, 1880, 141–2.
8. Lavallée, Joseph, *Notice historique sur Ch. Dewailly*, Paris, 1799, 7.
9. Paris, *Mémoires de L'Institut national des Sciences et des Arts*, 1801, 36.
10. Because these two buildings are not central to the hypothesis put forward in this article, they are not discussed here. The columnar nature of the 'Communs' building at Sans Souci is, however, undeniable, and would appear to have been Le Geay's contribution rather than Gontard's. This will form the substance of a forthcoming article.

might be said that the printed material is too late in date to use as evidence in assessing an architect supposed to have been a formative influence upon his contemporaries from as early as 1740. But if this is studied in conjunction with the drawings by Chambers, the hypothesis for the early dating of the etchings can almost be proved, and because of this, Le Geay's influence upon Piranesi may therefore be better judged.

An association between Chambers and Le Geay may at first seem improbable. Yet on at least one occasion their paths crossed. Although we know little about Le Geay's activities upon his return to Paris in 1742, he possibly attached himself to J.-F. Blondel's newly-established *Ecole des Arts*. Le Geay may even have taught here in some capacity. If he did belong to Blondel's circle, then his drawings could have been available to Chambers between the autumn of 1749 and the winter of 1750. But because Le Geay became *Baumeister* to the Duke Christian II-Louis de Mecklenburg-Schwerin in 1748, he is, I suppose, unlikely to have met Chambers, although there is no reason why he could not have returned to Paris. It is also known that Le Geay came to England to seek work in 1767–1768, at which time he probably composed the view of the Casino at Marino, now in Miss Lambart John's Collection (Fig. 39). Another important souvenir from this London period may be the complete set of etchings inscribed anonymously 'this Book Given to me by M. Chambers anno Dom 1770 in sheets',[11] perhaps a present from Le Geay to Chambers upon his return to Paris. It is tantalizing not to know who could have been interested in their subject matter to receive them in 1770.

Kauffman wanted these fantastic etchings to precede the better-known engravings in Piranesi's *Prima Parte di Architetture* published in 1743. As he rightly pointed out, despite the publication of Le Geay's etchings in Paris, they were titled in Italian (Figs. 1–2). Why, he asked, should Le Geay, who had not been in Italy since 1742, suddenly take to using Italian even if his subjects were Roman? We also know that in the seventeen-sixties Le Geay was desperate for work, and surely it would have been unwise for a Frenchman in those circumstances to adopt foreign airs. It is also significant that the few other surviving etchings by Le Geay are inscribed in French.[12] Chambers fortunately provides us with a very satisfactory answer to this problem, for he must have had access to Le Geay's designs and compositions at least as early as 1749–1754, the years he passed in Italy and France. In what we call his *Franco-Italian* album of sketches made whilst on the Grand Tour, are five drawings after Le Geay,[13] including (no. 460) portions of two columnar plans; an interior elevation, also of a niched columnar nature; and a temple with a dome terminated by an obelisk (no. 499). On another sheet is a perspective of a monumental pier of a church decoratively treated in an advanced neo-classic manner (Fig. 3); and on another (no. 500) an unpublished tomb project with supporting sphinxes facing each other and carrying the tomb upon their heads, a perverse reversal of the normal manner (Fig. 4). Finally, as a crux of the hypothesis for an early dating of the etchings is a copy (no. 499) (Fig. 5) from one of the *Tombeaux* not published until 1768 (Fig. 6). If these compositions by Le Geay were therefore available, most likely in 1750, then it is surely not unreasonable to suppose they represent some part at least of the 'beaux desseins...du feu et du génie' commented upon by de Troy in 1742. If so, then Piranesi could well have been aware of their content and interest.

The first important publishing event in Piranesi's career was his *Prima Parte di Architetture e Prospettive*, where we have both a consolidation of older influences and premonitions for the future. We shall find among the engravings fairly standard designs in the manner of Pozzo or of the Galli-Bibiena; of Marco Ricci (Fig. 7); or of Pannini and Juvarra. But there is already a bigness of scale, and a dwarfing of the human figure within the architectural framework, as in the *Gruppo di Colonne* (Fig. 8), or the *Tempio antico*, and *Ponte Magnifico* published in the *Opera Varie* of 1750, but dated 1743. The *Carcere oscura* (Fig. 9) has as yet none of the tortuosity of the *c.* 1745 etchings titled *Invenzioni Capricci di Carceri*, but here in any event Juvarra must have been laid under tribute for the general style and feeling of the composition.[14]

But to discover Piranesi's first design that carries absolute conviction as a neo-classic compilation we must turn to the *Mausoleo antico* from the *Opera Varie*

---

11. Victoria and Albert Museum, 27737, A.I. 24. Location 93. 3.134.
12. These etchings are in the Cooper Union Museum, New York. They are also undated and were shown to me by the kindness of Dr. Richard Wunder, now of the Smithsonian Institution, Washington.

13. The album now in the Victoria and Albert Museum, 5712, location 93. B. 21. The relevant drawings are numbers 460, 499, 500. The binding of the album is titled *Recueil de Divers Dessein D'Architecture and other ornaments*, and was obviously made-up in Paris or soon after Chambers' return to London. In only a few instances have later drawings been interpolated, an intrusion that is quite noticeable. Otherwise the whole album has a consistent character, of draughtsmanship, size and type of paper, and of mounting or pasting-in.
14. For precursors to the *Carceri*, cf. Juvarra's stage designs in the Biblioteca Nazionale, Turin, two of which are reproduced in Viale, V., Rovere, L., and Brinckmann, A. E., *Filipo Juvarra*, 1937, pls. 248–9.

(Fig. 18). There is unfortunately no certainty that it *does* belong to the original *Prima Parte* group of etchings. Its early date has always been presumed. As a columnar compilation this may I believe be fathered upon Le Geay, who shares with the great Piranesi the characteristics of an overwhelming heroic monumentality, an archaeological interest in reconstructions, and a passion for the incorporation of antique fragments into the general conspectus of embellishment. Piranesi's *Pianta di ampio magnifico collegio*, again from the 1750 publication (Fig. 20), may also be grouped in this columnar family; as may also his *Ponte Magnifico*. Their importance lies in their position as lodestones for the Grand Prix fantasies of the coming half a century. If Piranesi saw the drawings for Le Geay's etched compositions at the French Academy he would have been fascinated by the perverse dissolution of the Vitruvian vocabulary. If we examine examples from the *Rovine* or *Tombeaux* (Figs. 10–11), we shall see that the architectural structures are clearly anti-classical, as are some of the more extreme examples of sixteenth-century mannerism. Le Geay, however, composes in a fertile manner that verges close to the lunatic fringe. His forms are weird, his human beings are overwhelmed by nature and antiquity, and there is a horrific quality in the animals that seem guardians of an unhappy dream world. Piranesi would have been sympathetic to all this, especially when he was advocating his own anti-classical, anti-Vitruvian theory of design in his *Parere su l'Architettura*, that part of the *Osservazione . . . sopra la lettre di M. Mariette* issued in 1765 as a polemic in the famous Roman-Greek controversy. Here (Figs. 12–13) is evident the supreme genius of Piranesi's mind, following a path of novelty where he reverses the meaning of architectural structure and pleads for an ornate sculptural, quasi-archaeological embellishment. For precedent, first one must return to Le Geay's Roman studies between 1737 and 1742, then to the sixteenth-century world of Giulio Romano.

The etchings are not, however, the most important souvenir of Le Geay, for among Chambers' drawings in the R.I.B.A. is none other than one of Cochin's 'exaggerations bizarres', a copy in Chambers' hand and inscribed by him 'A plan composed by Monsr Legay'[15] (Fig. 15). Here at last then is concrete evidence of those praises, and of de Troy's comment 'fait d'apres les edifices publics', for Le Geay has taken the Peruzzian plan of St. Peter's from Serlio,[16] and elaborated it in a fantastic columnar way, paying considerable respect to the Roman Baths. But to the basic St. Peter's shape he has added lateral rotundas, joined to the main body in a way that may also be Serlian.[17] This type of peripteral rotunda with an internal colonnade follows the patterns of Santa Costanza, another ancient Roman monument. Looking at this megalomaniac plan one can appreciate why Cochin and company chose such epithets of surprise or astonishment, and why Le Geay was highly regarded as a perspectivist. It is also clearly apparent that he has an obsessive fascination for columns, an obsession that well accords with Dr. Middleton's succinct observations upon the French Neo-Classicists' love for columnar articulation.[18]

Ancient and modern Rome is again the theme of Le Geay's *Plan d'une Rotunde, ou Eglise Dédiée a La Ste Trinité* (Fig. 16), published by de Petity[19] in 1767, the year, we should remember, that saw the appearance of the *Fontane* suite of etchings. Here in this rotunda plan are combined, on the antique side, Santa Costanza and the Baths of Agrippa (Pantheon), and on the modern, Borromini's San Ivo. Like so many of Le Geay's designs, this rotunda is undated, but it belongs clearly, however, to the family of the lateral rotundas of the fantastic plan.[20]

Having examined these two plans and shown Le Geay's method of composition it now remains to parallel them with a similar attitude in the Renaissance, by a follower of Palladio. A plan (Fig. 19) in the Burlington-Devonshire Collection of the R.I.B.A.[21] has been attributed to Scamozzi. This is for a somewhat puzzling building, a colossal circular church either within an amphitheatre, or on top of a hill or mount. I believe we may here discover another compilation from ancient and modern Rome. The external ring is an expansion of Bramante's dome plan of St. Peter's found in Serlio,[22] whilst the internal ring is composed of those columnar-screened shapes taken from the

15. Royal Institute of British Architects, E3/9a. The drawing measures 33½ × 23 inches and is on paper similar to that used by Chambers when in Paris or Rome, as testified by the drawings in the Victoria and Albert Museum. The manner of washing-in with yellow was also used at this time, and although not, of course, uncommon, compares favourably with Chambers' measured plans of the Château de Belleville (made *c.* 1750), now R.I.B.A. E3/9B¹⁻⁴.

16. Serlio, *Tutta l'opera d'Architettura di Sebastiano Serlio*, 1584, lib. III, 65 v.

17. Serlio, *op. cit.*, lib. V, 211 v.

18. Cf. Middleton's articles under the title 'The Abbé de Cordemoy and the Graeco-Gothic Ideal: A Prelude to Romantic Classicism', in *Jn. Warburg & Courtauld Institutes*, XXV, nos. 3–4, 1962, 278–320; and XXVI, 1963, 70–123.

19. L'Abbé Jean Raymond de Petity, *Encyclopédie Elémentaire ou Introduction a L'Etude des Lettres, des Science, et des Arts*, II, pt. I, Paris, 1767, pls. 400 *bis* (plan) and 402 *bis* (elevation and section).

20. The church is also related to Le Geay's plans of 1747 for the Berlin Hedwigskirche. Cf. Schmitz, H., *Berliner Baumeister*, Berlin, 1925, 20.

21. R.I.B.A. Burlington-Devonshire Collection, Palladio, XV, 5.

22. Serlio, *loc. cit.*, 66.

Roman Baths and so beloved by Palladio. It will be of interest when discussing a mausoleum plan by Chambers. Although Renaissance architects had always been fascinated by the Baths, Palladio represents the vortex of that interest, and was the cynosure of Lord Burlington's eye in early eighteenth-century England. His Lordship published his influential *Fabbriche antiche disegnate da Andrea Palladio* in 1730, a year that marks a general revival of interest in this aspect of antiquity. It precedes the movement that gained momentum in the thirties and forties that began to insist upon the verification of the rules of antiquity and the statements of the Renaissance theorists by first-hand knowledge of antiquity through travel, archaeology and measured drawings.

Filippo Juvarra is, however, another figure who looms potently large as a precursor to Le Geay and his period. His project for the church of San Raffaele,[23] conceived about 1718, combines the Santa Costanza theme (perhaps via Sammicheli's Madonna di Campagna, Verona) with echoes from the axial and spatial planning of Palladio's Venetian churches; and also relevant is his project[24] of *c.* 1709 for Carl Landgrave of Hesse-Cassel, which is conceived on such a colossal, impractical scale that it outbids Le Geay or Piranesi. But even more interesting is his project for a Royal Mausoleum, almost certainly that intended for the French kings, and engraved by Vasi in 1739, four years after Juvarra's death.[25] Here the plan (Fig. 14) and most of the main structure may be accepted as by Juvarra, but the surprisingly advanced neo-classic embellishment of the obelisks (Fig. 17) suggests that this design may have been altered by Vasi. If this is so, then we have here, not only a valuable document from Le Geay's Roman period, but an indication of Vasi's capabilities as a designer.

An inheritance of ideas from Juvarra to Le Geay is, therefore, very probable, and potently so for Piranesi, who may well have arrived in Rome from Venice with a knowledge of Juvarra's architectural designs. By reason of Piranesi's undoubted association with the French Academy in Rome he is unlikely not to have noticed Le Geay's designs, if they were composed with 'feu et du génie'. Once we accept Le Geay's fantastic columnar plan as a typical product of those that aroused such praises, then it is certainly a companion to Piranesi's *Mausoleo antico*, which is also a columnar essay displaying a similar, if more muted, method of incorporating antique elements into the decorative composition (Fig. 18).

From this moment the idea of the mausoleum as a neo-classic exercise is born. Le Geay had proposed several monumental tombs in his suite of *Tombeaux*, but the only circular domed structure known apart from the Trinity church and the Berlin Hedwigkirche is the severe, proto-Boullée style one in the undated composition in the author's own collection[26] (Fig. 21). Throughout the forties we shall find the architectural students of the French Academy displaying a predilection for the mausoleum and the columnar style. They are Louis-Joseph Le Lorrain (1715–1759), Charles Michel-Ange Challe (1718–1778), Nicholas-Henri Jardin (1720–1799), Gabriel-Pierre Martin Dumont (1720–1790), and Ennemond-Alexandre Petitot (1727–1801). To follow their designs through this decade is to build a bridge to the mausoleums of Sir William Chambers and Marie-Joseph Peyre in the following one.

Although Le Lorrain is relatively unknown in the history of French art, Mr. Svend Erikson has reinstated him as an important neo-classic designer of fête and firework decorations, of furniture and of painted interiors.[27] He was the author, for example, of some of the earliest neo-classic furniture, designed in 1756 for the French collector Lalive de Jully, or of an early scheme of neo-classic decorative painting, at Åkerö in Sweden, designed for C. G. Tessin in 1754. But undoubtedly Le Lorrain's most interesting contribution to the history of neo-classicism was three (out of four) temporary monuments made for the *Festa della Chinea*, held biannually on 28th June (Feast of Sts. Peter and Paul), and 8th September (Feast of Birth of the Virgin).[28] Each festival was accompanied by a

26. This drawing is signed in the same precise, miniaturist's hand as the etchings, although its size, $5\frac{1}{4} \times 9$ inches, is larger. The red chalk seems to have been deliberately rubbed to give the effect of impermanence. That Le Geay worked in other mediums is shown by the signed ruin study in the collection of Dr. Richard Wunder.

27. Erikson's researches have been published in *Sartryck Ur Konsthistorisk Tidskrift*, 1963, 'Om Salon pas Åkerö og dens Kunstner Louis-Joseph Le Lorrain', 94–100; *Burlington Magazine*, August 1961, 'Lalive de Jully's Furniture "a la grecque"'; *Burlington Magazine*, March 1962 'Marigny and "Le Gout Grec"'; and *Apollo*, November 1963, 'Early Neo-classicism in French Furniture'. Reference must also be made to D. Elling's valuable study, *Jardin i Rom*, Copenhagen, 1943. I have not discussed in this article the part played by certain sculptors and painters, but my conclusions that the first *neo-grec* furniture in France may also have been inspired in this 'critical' decade of the seventeen-forties is proposed in my article 'Early Neo-Classical Furniture', *Jnl Furniture Hist. Soc.*, II 1966. I point out that Le Lorrain was, yet again, a principal innovator; that Saly the sculptor was in Rome 1740–8; Vien the painter from 1744 to 1750; and for events in London, Gavin Hamilton, the neo-classic history painter, was there in the forties, as was James Stuart who made the first drawings for English neo-classic furniture; and, of course, Chambers, as the designer of the first executed neo-classic chair, arrived in 1750.

28. The *Festa della Chinea* as an architectural manifestation has

23. Viale, Rovere, and Brinckmann, *op. cit.*, pl. 43.
24. Viale, Rovere and Brinckmann, *loc. cit.*, pl. 146.
25. For this illustration I am indebted to Dr. Richard Pommer, and to him for permission to publish it.

temporary structure or painted backcloth and until about the middle of the eighteenth century was held outside the Palazzo Colonna, and after this, generally outside the Palazzo Farnese, which site gave rise to the name *fuochi Farnesiani*. The *macchine* of these *fuochi* provide a chronological survey of Roman design over a period when actual building in Rome was at a low ebb.[29]

If we survey the festival engravings from *c.* 1730 to *c.* 1760 one most typical of the series would be Francesco Preziado's *Macchina*, erected in September 1746 in the Late Baroque Classical style of Ferdinando Fuga (Fig. 22). This is typical of the conservative Italian contributions in the Late Baroque Classical, or Baroque-Rococo styles. After Le Lorrain arrived in Rome in December 1742 his first *Macchina* of 1744, a decorative backcloth executed in a traditional type of rococo-laced classicism, is what we would expect from a painter. But in 1745 occurs a remarkable change, for Le Lorrain now presents (Fig. 24) a triumphal arch of undigested neo-classic form, with a rotunda paying tribute to the Bibiena scenographers, and garlanded panels and 'Capitoline' openings to Michelangelo, whose compositions were to be a constantly-used quarry for the neo-classicists. The breath of change can be seen in the way the oval panels with ropy garlands, and the bas-reliefs above the Capitoline openings, are consciously placed with deference to the bare areas of wall around them. In any context this design would be remarkable for 1745. Yet in 1746 and 1747 Le Lorrain's two further displays were of outstanding and singular neo-classic form, adumbrating almost everything we shall find in the mainstream of Parisian style in the seventeen-fifties or sixties.

Certain decorative motifs in 1746 (Fig. 23) are taken over from the previous year. But the new device is the conversion of the dome into a smoking altar with an encircling bas-relief[30] based upon a sacrificial theme.

This manner of using the bas-relief, like the ropy swag motif, was to become an accepted part of the neo-classic vocabulary. Yet what surprise we may express in 1746 changes to incredulity the following year when Le Lorrain presents a mausoleum with all its neo-classic accompaniments: peripherally-placed obelisks, flaming altars, creating an impression of antique severity (Fig. 25). In our knowledge of its context it is unexplainable. But what is certain is its place in the midst of the ideas and theories emanating from the French Academy. If we knew more about Piranesi's designs between 1743 and 1750 we could perhaps suggest he was laid under tribute for these ideas. But unfortunately any associable designs by him are conspicuous by their absence. Piranesi was not, of course, a practicing architect; Le Lorrain was a painter; and it is perhaps not surprising to discover that Challe was also a painter. Challe had arrived at the Rome Academy in November 1742 and displays his style in the 'Roman Composition' dated 1746 and now in Mrs. Phyllis Lambert's collection (Fig. 26). Bigness of scale and neo-classic motifs are, however, mixed with a baroque liveliness that reflects something of Challe's masters, Lemoyne and Boucher.[31] But again we are at a loss to compare it with dated examples by Piranesi from this period. In terms of grandeur and sweep of design the closest parallel is to his *Parte di ampio magnifico porto* from the *Opera Varie*. Yet I believe Le Lorrain to have been as decisive an influence upon this group, far more perhaps than Dumont, who was Piranesi's age, and arrived at the French Academy the same month as Le Lorrain. Dumont is perhaps a follower rather than leader of fashion. His *Temple des Arts* offered as his *Morceau de Reception* to the *Accademia di San Luca* in 1746 (Figs. 28 and 29) borrows Le Lorrain's Capitoline openings but has an interesting triangular columnar plan. He must also have known Le Geay, for in his *Recueil De Plusieurs parties d'Architecture De Differents Maîtres Tant d'Italie Que De France*, published in 1768 and containing the designs for the *Temple des Arts*, there are a number of title-pieces and vignettes by Le Geay, one of which is a circular temple with a bas-relief encircling the dome.

As much as Dumont is influenced by Le Lorrain, so

hardly been treated. But cf. Ferrari, G., *Bellezze Architettoniche Per le Feste Delle Chinea in Rom Nei Secoli XVII e XVIII*, Turin; and Tintelot, H., *Barocktheater und barocke Kunst*, 1939. I am grateful to Mr. Erikson for providing me with a complete microfilm of the engraved *Chinea* subjects from the set in the Library of the Copenhagen Kunstindustri Museum; and to Dr. Richard Wunder who has been tracing the original drawings for these engravings

29. This period in Rome is best treated by R. Wittkower in *Art and Architecture in Italy, 1600–1750*, 1958, chapter 16, although he does not refer to the manifestation of the *Chinea*. Caroll Meeks' *Italian Architecture 1750–1914* had not appeared when this article went to press.

30. Both Piranesi and Peyre are fond of the bas-relief frieze used in this manner. But one must go to England to discover the more monumental expositions of the theme; as an interior feature, in the Oval Hall at Stowe (Bucks.), designed by Georges François Blondel before 1769, and executed by Vincenze Valdrè. This is of remarkably early date (cf. Harris, J., 'Blondel

at Stowe', in *The Connoisseur*, March 1964; and Croft-Murray, E., 'Un Decoratore Faentino in Inghilterra: Vincenzo Valdrati O Valdre' (1742–1814), in *Studi Romagnoli*, VIII (1957). And as an exterior feature, at Ickworth after 1800 where the great frieze is by the Carabelli brothers and the Coade factory, after Flaxman models.

31. Compare this with the architectural fantasy signed and dated by Challe 1747 in the Pierpont Morgan Library (exhib. 'A Century of Mozart', Nelson Art Gallery, Kansas City, 1956. Cat. no. B2, Fig. 28).

are our two other *pensionnaires*: Jardin and Petitot. Jardin arrived in Rome December 1744 and his *Pont Triomphale* (Fig. 27) and *Chapelle Sepulchrale*[32] (Fig. 30) are redolent, not only of Le Lorrain's *macchine* of 1746 and 1747, but also of Challe and Piranesi. Similarly Petitot, an arrival of 1746, engraved, like Jardin, a *projet d'un pont triomphale inventé et gravé par E. A. Petitot a rome* (Fig. 32), that must surely be a contemporary of Jardin's engraved bridge of 1748 and probably initiated under the same auspices. Here again is an indebtedness to Le Lorrain's 1745 designs (oval draped panels), to his 1746 one (bas-relief to dome), and the ships' prows echo those on Challe's 1746 composition. His contribution to the *Chinea* of 1749 is a splendid Grand Prix mausoleum (Fig. 31) in the most advanced Peyre style. But both Jardin and Petitot are, I think, conveyors of ideas rather than initiators like Le Geay, Piranesi and Le Lorrain.

Seen in perspective, these neo-classic designs form a chain of events whose genesis may be located in the late seventeen-thirties where stands the enigmatic Le Geay, obviously attracting attention by 1741 or 1742. The young Piranesi had arrived in Rome in 1740 and would hardly have missed an opportunity of seeing designs composed with such *feu et génie*. If we are to believe Cochin (and there is no reason not to), when Le Geay returned to Paris in 1742 his designs marked a turn in the tides of taste, and were particularly influential upon architects of the generation of Jardin and Le Lorrain. We have seen that Piranesi, in the compositions of his *Prima Parte* of 1743, displays a wavering attitude, a middle-of-the-road course between conservative and advanced design. But if certain etchings in his 1750 *Opera Varie* were drawn earlier, then his importance is much increased. Piranesi may have found in common with Le Geay a bigness of scale, a grandeur of conception, a fascination for the manipulation of columns, a certain lunatic-fringe attitude, and an ability as a perspectivist. There is also Le Geay's

obviously perverse delight in pursuing an anti-Vitruvian, mannerist, method of composition. After Le Lorrain arrived in Rome in 1742, he had formulated within a few years a canon of neo-classic taste with his *Chinea* decorations of 1746 and 1747. Another *pensionnaire* of Le Lorrain's year was Challe, who in 1746 partakes so intimately of Piranesi's vocabulary and sweep of draughtsmanship, that one can only presume him to have had direct knowledge of Piranesi's drawings made between the appearance of the *Prima Parte* and *Opera Varie*. I do not think the debt can be the other way round. We have then seen that Dumont keeps just behind the vanguard of neo-classic ideas, and that Jardin and Petitot, with their projects around 1748, bring to fruition in the late forties what had been instigated over the past decade. Jardin returned to Paris in November 1748, Le Lorrain left in March the following year, Challe followed him six months later, and Petitot in 1750. So by the autumn of 1749 most of the French participants in this neo-classic episode reassembled in Paris, where there can be little doubt that they had contact with the circle of students and general *bonhomie* at J.-F. Blondel's *Ecole des Arts*. There at this time was William Chambers.

Only by reviewing the events of this critical decade in the history of neo-classicism is it possible to comprehend the remarkable mausoleum designed by Chambers in 1751–1752 when he was in Rome, and projected for Frederick Prince of Wales who had died in March 1751.[33] There are four designs, a plan and elevation dated 1751 (Figs. 33 and 35), a section of February 1752 (Fig. 34), and an undated elevation (Fig. 36).[34] Like Le Geay, Chambers is here composing in a spirit of ancient and modern Rome. His complex columnar plan is an exercise drawing upon Le Geay's fantastic plan, and expressing an identity of style with the inner circle of the Scamozzian fantasy (Fig. 19). For the elevation to his plan Chambers is obviously reliant upon Le Lorrain's *Chinea* of 1747, and sets his mausoleum in an imaginary landscape, a proto-picturesque move that may be cradled in the tutelage of the ubiquitously

---

32. Both engravings are reproduced by Elling, *op. cit.*, pls. 6 and 7. They were published by Jardin as a suite of engravings often attached to his *Plans, Coupes et Elévations De L'Eglise Royale De Frederic V . . . 1765*, under the title *Description De Sujet Der Quatre Estampes Suivantes Representant des Projets en perspective . . . ont été faits pour études en 1747 et 1748, pendant qu'il étoit Pensionnaire du Roi, a l'Académie de France à Rome*. Apart from these theoretical designs, Jardin is best remembered as the architect of the *Eglise Royale Fréderik* in Copenhagen. His designs of 1755 were advancedly neo-classic, drawing much upon his Roman studies. They are illustrated in Elling and Fisker, *Monumenta Architecturae Danicae*, Copenhagen, 1961, pl. 59. This interesting scheme was sadly superseded by the more mundane one finally published by Jardin in 1765. It is perhaps worth mentioning that when the *Académie royale d'architecture* in Paris decided in 1762 to create honorary corresponding members, Jardin and Chambers were among the first to be selected.

33. The question has been asked: why should Chambers, an ex-merchant, an Anglo-Swede in Rome, have taken it upon himself to make such designs, when as far as we know the death of the Prince did not prompt the making of any other funeral projects? The reasons are given in my 'Exoticism at Kew', *Apollo*, August 1963, where the circumstantial evidence is collected for the hypothesis that Chambers may have designed the House of Confucius at Kew, built in 1749 and then called the 'India House'. In other words, Chambers could boast some previous connection with the Kew ménage, one that must surely have contributed to his acquiring in 1757 the post of tutor in architecture to George Prince of Wales.

34. The plan of 1751 is Victoria and Albert Museum 3341; elevation of 1751 is Sir John Soane's Museum, 718; section of 1752 is Victoria and Albert Museum 3339; and undated elevation is Victoria and Albert Museum 3340.

puzzling Charles-Louis Clérisseau.[35] The section dated February 1752 to this plan and elevation dated 1751, is even more picturesquely treated, for it is a ruin that could hardly have been intended as such.[36] With his elevation for the second project (Fig. 36) probably drawn in 1752, Chambers has captured the spirit of an ideal antique monument, conceived in terms of gravity and monumentality, yet essentially of a practicality that had not been present in the earlier mauso-

leums under discussion. Chambers here pays homage to the tomb of Caecilia Metella, to the interior screened elevations of the Pantheon, and for his details to Vignola, whose works he greatly admired. Chambers provides a direct link to that fully developed French neo-classicism published by Marie-Joseph Peyre in his *Œuvres d'Architecture* (1765), containing his Roman designs from 1753 until 1757. His book is often regarded as a work in the forefront of the style, but if his mausoleum (Fig. 37) is compared with Chambers' one, it can be seen as the logical culmination of a series of neo-classic projects that begin with the fantastic ideas of Le Geay in Rome in the late seventeen-thirties.

Chambers' neo-classic episode ended when he returned to London in 1755. His loss of the commission to rebuild Harewood in 1756 because his design was in Franco-Italian style,[37] taught him that English patrons immured to conservative second-generation Palladianism were not attracted by any advanced neo-classic ideas. But in the Earl of Charlemont at Marino near Dublin, Chambers found a patron and friend who was prepared to implicitly accept his designs and execute them. The result was that exquisite neo-classic Casino built, from 1758, upon a columnar plan (Fig. 38). It may have been just its columnar novelty that attracted Le Geay to draw it in 1767 or 1768 (Fig. 39).[38]

35. For the evidence that Clérisseau taught Chambers draughtsmanship, cf. John Fleming, *Robert Adam and His Circle*, 1962; and for further information, Thomas J. McCormick, 'Virginia's Gallic Godfather' in *Arts in Virginia*, vol. 4, no. 2, Winter 1964; and also his 'An Unknown Collection of Drawings by Charles-Louis Clérisseau' in *Jnl. of the Society of Architectural Historians*, October 1963. In the history of architectural draughtsmanship this mausoleum design is important, for it may be one of the earliest examples of presentation in a manner that within a decade had become fairly commonplace. Only slightly later, Adam also significantly draws in this style, and he had also been a pupil of Clerisseau. Earlier designs had never been depicted in a landscape, although my wife points out the engraving of an 'Adytum' in Robert Morris' *Rural Architecture* of 1750, where Morris states that his friend Daniel Garrett 'was pleased jocosely to intimate, that my Title Rural Architecture, was not justly appropriated, because I had not anywhere introduced trees'. Morris' attitude, however, implies some theory of association, whilst both Chambers and Adam are using landscape and trees only to improve the presentation of their design. The ultimate in this direction would be the designs of the Victorian age, like those by Edward Blore, where a house placed in a landscape is, to the uninitiated, no different from a topographical watercolour.

36. I have been unable to find precedents for treating a design or section as a ruin when not really intended as one. A smaller version of this Kew design is R.I.B.A. J4/25, where the medallion portrait is drawn to a larger scale in the Victoria and Albert Museum Franco-Italian Album, no. 144. This picturesque mode of presentation had become commonplace with Chambers and Adam by 1761, the year the former exhibited at the Society of Artists his unexecuted design (1759) for York House, whose section (R.I.B.A. J4/26) is made more attractive by having a ruined and grass-strewn cornice.

37. Two plans and an elevation are in the Harewood archives.
38. In this article I have not attempted to even remotely suggest what influence Carlo Lodoli (1690–1761) might have exercised upon the young Piranesi. The two could have met in Venice, and Piranesi might have listened to the lectures of this monk. I think Wolfgang Herrmann's suggestion that the *Carceri* 'are like a vision of the autonomous architecture in stone which formed the centre of Lodoli's theory' should be treated with caution until we know more about Piranesi's early life (cf. W. Herrmann, *Laugier and Eighteenth Century French Theory*, 1962, 190).

DAMIE STILLMAN

Robert Adam and Piranesi

Among the most interesting and most fruitful relationships between eighteenth-century artists was that of Robert Adam and Giovanni Battista Piranesi. Their acquaintance began in Rome in the mid-1750's at the moment when the Neo-classicism to which they both contributed so much was bursting into flower, and it lasted for over twenty years. Though the two men complimented and praised each other all through this period, the artistic influence was largely one-sided. It was the Italian who served as inspiration for the Britisher, not only during Adam's sojourn in Rome but many years later, as well. For Piranesi supplied the only major new source for the Adam style after its maturation in the mid-1760's. Though Adam's style was altered substantially after the mid-1760's, the change was largely one of greater refinement, elegance, and delicacy. The principal ingredients had already been brought together; only their character was modified. The two major exceptions to this—the introduction of Adam's Etruscan rooms and the addition of a whole new group of chimney-pieces—were directly inspired by Piranesi's *Diverse maniere d'adornare i cammini* of 1769. As both a continuing influence and a formative one, Piranesi played a vital role in the development of the Adam style. In other ways, too, Piranesi served as an inspiration to Adam. He encouraged Robert's taste for 'the grand', he inspired him with archaeological zeal, and he contributed to the development of Adam's theoretical concepts. If Piranesi's influence was the stronger and the more significant, Adam, on the other hand, provided illustration of much of what Piranesi proposed. Adam also offers us new insights into Piranesi's personality and his role in the efflorescence of Neo-classicism. The interplay of two individuals, not merely the one-sided influence, is the crux of their relationship.

When Robert Adam embarked on his Grand Tour in the autumn of 1754, he was, for all practical purposes, a professional architect. Trained by his father in Scotland and experienced through work with his older brother John, he came to Italy in order to put the finishing touches to his education and to add luster to his reputation. He arrived in Rome on February 24, 1755, already imbued with the spirit of antiquity and a sense of grandeur. As he wrote to his sister a few days later, 'In short, I am antique Mad, or what they woud Call in Scotland an Antick, But antique here

antique there, P'haps to be capable to invent a great thing; if I should never, be able to execute one, and thats my ambition'.[1] This heartfelt expression of the twenty-six-year-old Scottish architect went hand-in-hand with his enthusiasm for Rome, which he called in the same letter 'the most glorious place in the Universal World'.

These sentiments expressed on his arrival in Rome were to be important aspects of Adam's creed through his entire career, but they also set the stage for his study in Rome. He spent two years there examining antique ruins and Renaissance buildings, sketching and collecting drawings, mastering a free type of drawing and 'all these Knacks, so necessary to us Architects'.[2] His principal teacher, but also both his confidant and employee, was the French architect and delineator of architectural ruins, Charles-Louis Clérisseau. From Clérisseau, Adam learned a new method of drawing and something of the character of the emerging Neo-classicism. From his instructor in anatomical drawing, Laurent Pécheux, he learned to draw figures, a step which he considered 'absolutely requisite ... without which an Architect cannot ornament a building, Draw a Basrelievo or a Statue'.[3] In addition to his more formal instruction from Pécheux and Clérisseau, Adam absorbed a great deal from the Roman *milieu* and the various figures in it. Of these, probably the most interesting and certainly the most influential was Piranesi.

Even before their meeting, Adam and Piranesi shared an enthusiasm for antiquity, a feeling for grandeur, and a love of Rome. All of these things were heightened in Adam by his acquaintance with the Italian engraver, archaeologist, and architect, whom Adam described as 'the most extraordinary fellow I ever saw'.[4] Piranesi had known Clérisseau since the Frenchman's arrival in Rome at the end of the 1740's,[5] and it was probably through Clérisseau that Adam met Piranesi. Occasionally accompanying Adam and Clérisseau on their

1. Letter to Margaret Adam, Mar. 5, 1755 (Register House, Edinburgh, Clerk of Penicuik Papers no. 4766).
2. Letter from Robt. to Jas. Adam, Oct. 19, 1755 (Register House, Edinburgh, Clerk of Penicuik Papers no. 4789).
3. Letter from Robt. to Margaret Adam and the family, June 18, 1755 (misdated 1754; Register House, Edinburgh, Clerk of Penicuik Papers no. 4776).
4. *Ibid.*
5. Henri Focillon, *Giovanni-Battista Piranesi, 1720–1778* (Paris, 1918), p. 56.

sketching expeditions in Rome, Piranesi developed an interest in the young Scotsman, eight years his junior. As early as June 18, 1755, Adam wrote that Piranesi

> is become immensely intimate with me & as he imagined at first that I was like the other Englishes who had love for Antiques without knowledge, upon seeing some of my Sketches, & Drawings, was So highly delighted that he almost ran quite distracted, & says I have more genius for the true noble Architecture than any Englishman ever was in Italy.[6]

As if this were not enough, Adam added that Piranesi 'threatens' to dedicate to him his next plan of ancient Rome. The various vicissitudes of this dedication, first mentioned in June, 1755, served almost as a *leitmotif* of the Adam-Piranesi relationship during Adam's two years in Rome and, indeed, until 1762, when it finally appeared in the *Campo Marzio* in a truly grand and generous manner. Every so often in his letters home, Adam commented upon the progress—or lack of it— of the proposed dedication. Finally, a month before his departure in the spring of 1757, Robert told his sister Helen of a visit to Piranesi's studio where he had seen the frontispiece dedicated to him and then described it more or less as it was eventually to appear.[7] The last statement in Italy on the subject occurred on May 16, 1757, when he informed his mother in a letter from Florence that he had left Rome as a good friend of Piranesi, who was turning the plan of Rome into a book.[8] Hardly was he back in London when his mind turned again to this topic, for on January 25, 1758 (only a week after his arrival), he wrote to his Italian banker Barazzi concerning the *Campo Marzio* dedication.[9]

Although this magnificent accolade did not appear in print until Adam had established himself in London as one of the principal architects of the day, Piranesi did pay honor to his friend in a volume that was issued in the midst of Adam's stay in Rome. On the second frontispiece of Volume II of *Le antichità romane*, published in May, 1756, there exists among the monuments of the Appian Way a prominent inscription to 'ROBERTI ADAMS SCOT ARCHITECTI'. Perhaps in payment to Piranesi for this publicity—and perhaps also to give wider currency to this publicity—Adam

sent five four-volume sets of the *Antichità romane* to London, three of them to be forwarded to Scotland and two to be sold by a bookseller in order to recoup Robert's expense.[10] Along with them he sent two volumes of *vedute*.

Lurking suspicions concerning Piranesi's motives, a Scotsman's natural distrust of financial dealings with foreigners, the uncertainties of the *Campo Marzio* dedication, and the Italian's personality so different from his own all affected the course of Adam's friendship with Piranesi. Along with his delight at Piranesi's interest in him, Adam was somewhat put off by Piranesi's nature. Thus we find Adam in the autumn of 1755 telling his brother James that Piranesi was of 'such dispositions as barrs all Instruction; His Ideas in locution so ill ranged, His expressions so furious & fantastick. That a Venetian hint is all can be got from him, never anything fixt, or well digested. So that a quarter of an hour makes you Sick of his Company.'[11] Yet, in this same letter Robert acknowledged Piranesi as the only Italian at the time 'to breath the Antient Air'. This appreciation of Piranesi's devotion to classical antiquity and the Italian's feeling for grandeur are, of course, far more significant than Adam's pique at Piranesi's character or diction or even the delay of the proposed dedication. Piranesi's enthusiasm for archaeology, his breadth of spirit, and his sense of magnificence were essential to Adam's development as a Neo-classicist; they were an indispensable aspect of his Roman education. While these qualities were also conveyed to Adam by Clérisseau, they could be found much more strikingly in the works and words of Piranesi. Piranesi's formative influence on Adam, on the Scotsman's 'Love for the Grand',[12] his infatuation with the art of antiquity, and his sense of mass and scale, was only part of the Roman *milieu* and its effect on Adam; but it was an important and powerful part. This influence is readily apparent when one compares the grandiose sketches and designs of Adam's Roman period with Piranesi's compositions of the earlier part of the 1750's. Both the piling up of masses and the assemblage of various architectural elements in such Adam sketches as that shown in Fig. 1 demonstrate an affinity to Piranesi.[13] Here Adam has combined a myriad of antique forms, ranging from triumphal arches and saucer domes to obelisks and pyramids,

6. Letter from Robt. to Margaret Adam and the family, June 18, 1755 (misdated 1754; Register House, Edinburgh, Clerk of Penicuik Papers no. 4776).

7. Letter dated Apr. 9, 1757 (Register House, Edinburgh, Clerk of Penicuik Papers no. 4834).

8. Register House, Edinburgh, Clerk of Penicuik Papers no. 4837.

9. Sir John Soane's Museum, London, Adam Drawings, vol. IX, no. 147 (note on back).

10. He first announced this plan to his London bankers, Innes & Clerk, in a letter dated May 8, 1756 (MS. at Royal Institute of British Architects). On July 16, 1756, he informed them that the volumes had been sent (Guildhall Library, London, MS. 3070, p. 20).

11. Letter dated Oct. 19, 1755 (Register House, Edinburgh, Clerk of Penicuik Papers no. 4789).

12. *Ibid.*

13. Soane Museum, Adam Drawings, vol. X, no. 18.

into a swelling conglomeration that reveals both his archaeological and his picturesque bent. Though there is a world of difference in style and execution, it is related to a number of Piranesi designs, as, for example, the drawing in Fig. 2, which Piranesi apparently gave to Adam.[14] This magnificent red chalk and brown ink drawing exhibits a similar crescendo and combination of various forms. The spirit, the fluency, and the drama set it apart from the Adam sketch, but the relationship is none the less real. From such Piranesi designs, Adam learned to compose and to display his archaeological erudition. In scale, too, he is indebted to Piranesi, for both have the same cyclopean proportions.

Sketches such as this one of *c.* 1756–1757 also served as preliminary studies for the elaborate palaces that Robert conceived toward the end of his study in Rome. Fig. 4 illustrates only a part—one-third—of a nine-foot design that he created in the first few months of 1757.[15] Here we see again the massing, the gigantic scale, and the proliferation of antique elements that characterized the sketch. Combining the Arch of Constantine, the Vatican Belvedere, the Tempietto, the Pantheon, the Column of Trajan, the Trophies of Octavianus Augustus, and scores of other Roman monuments and architectural details into a fantastic composition, Adam openly acknowledged his indebtedness to Piranesi.

Shortly after completing this design, Adam left Rome on the start of his rather circuitous journey home. During his twenty-six months in Rome, he had absorbed a tremendous amount. His earlier style and predilection for Palladianism, the Rococo, and a fanciful form of Gothic had been overlaid by a wealth of new materials and a new attitude toward art and antiquity. The influence of Piranesi was an important factor in this change, but his influence did not end then or there. Although Robert Adam never again saw Piranesi after the spring of 1757, their relationship persisted for the rest of Piranesi's life, and the Italian remained a significant influence on the Adam style.

The continuation of their mutual friendship and admiration was expressed in a series of published tributes issued by one or the other during the 1760's and 1770's, beginning with the appearance of the *Campo Marzio dell'antica Roma* in 1762. The single plan which Piranesi had first mentioned to Adam in the spring of 1755 reached fruition seven years later in a sumptuous volume that announced to the world Piranesi's admiration for the British—note no longer only Scottish as on the 1756 *Antichità romane* frontispiece—architect. On both the first title page and the

large scenographic view that is Plate II, Adam's name appears prominently—'ROBERTO ADAM BRITANNO ARCHITECTO CELEBERRIMO' on a shaft on the former and 'ROBERTO ADAM ARCH' on the remnant of a frieze on the latter. But much more impressive is Plate V with its large dedicatory plaque inscribed:

ROBERTO · ADAM · BRITANNO
AR·CHITECTVRAE · CVLTORI
ICHNOGRAPHIAM
CAMPI · MARTII
ANTIQVAE · VRBIS
IOANNES · BAPTISTA · PIRANESIVS
IN · SVI · AMORIS · ARGVMENTVM
D · D · D

Scattered around the large panel are Roman fragments, while above the plaque is placed a long classical frieze with a medallion superimposed on both ends. On the left one appears a goddess holding an architectural plan, surrounded by still another tribute: 'R · ADAM · ACADEMIAR · DIVI · LVCAE · FLORENT · BONONIEN · SOCIVS' and the date 'ROMAE MDCCLVII'. The medallion at the other end features Adam's head overlapping that of Piranesi, both rather Romanized, and their names: 'IO · BAPT · PIRANESIVS—ROBERTVS ADAM—ARCHITECTI'.

Adam had seen this dedicatory sheet in Piranesi's studio during his last visit there, and it appeared as he described it, though with a few minor changes.[16] Piranesi also praised him in the introductory text. In total, the *Campo Marzio* is both a striking testimonial to Piranesi's friendship with Adam and the most handsome and effective advertisement that could be imagined, even by so calculating and ambitious an individual as Robert Adam.

Twice again in the 1760's, Piranesi cited Adam in his writings, both times as support for his own arguments. In the *Parere su l'architettura* of 1765, Piranesi, in advocating both ornament and variety, brings Adam into the discussion as evidence of his contentions. As the principal mention of Adam concerns a grandiose parliament house and learned society complex, the reference may be to James Adam, though it may also be to Robert.[17] Again, four years later in the *Diverse maniere* (1769), Piranesi used Adam to illustrate his ideas, comparing two capitals with sphinxes—one in the Villa Borghese and the other 'in Inghilterra presso

14. *Ibid.*, vol. XXVI, no. 163.
15. *Ibid.*, vol. X, no. 1.

16. Letter to Helen Adam, Apr. 9, 1757 (Register House, Edinburgh, Clerk of Penicuik Papers no. 4834).
17. P. 13 in the original ed., p. 47 in the Paris, 1836 ed. As James Adam created a large series of designs for a parliament house during his study in Rome in the early 1760's (see Soane Museum, Adam Drawings, vol. VII), the reference may be to this, though this is not certain.

il Signor Adams architetto celebre'—in order to demonstrate the beauty, variety, and richness possible through the effective and original use of the wealth of ancient forms.[18]

Piranesi also demonstrated his friendship by subscribing to both of Adam's major publications, the *Ruins of the Palace of the Emperor Diocletian at Spalatro in Dalmatia* (1764) and *The Works in Architecture of Robert and James Adam* (1773–1778), and by engraving four of the plates for the *Works*. As early as 1760, Robert had thought of using Piranesi as an engraver for the *Ruins of Spalatro*. On July 24 he wrote to James, then in Venice supervising the completion of the plates, that 'if the Frontispiece Could be done by Piranesi it Would be showy & make a puff here'.[19] This scheme came to naught, but Piranesi did engrave four large plates of the hall and ante-room at Syon for the second volume of the *Works*. These plates, 'the largest he has ever attempted in regular architecture', were published in 1778, though the designs are signed and dated by Adam in 1761.[20] In crediting him with this work, the Adam brothers paid tribute to Piranesi and to his repeated compliments to them: 'we owe [it] to that friendship we contracted with him during our long residence at Rome, and which he has since taken every occasion to testify in the most handsome manner.'[21]

Still another tangible illustration of the continued interest of Adam and Piranesi in one another is furnished by a drawing of the façade of Sta. Maria del Priorato (Fig. 3) which exists in the Adam collection.[22] That Adam owned a view of Piranesi's only executed architectural commission (built 1764–1766) again confirms their mutual tastes, though unfortunately neither the date of the drawing nor that of its acquisition by Adam can be ascertained.

It is appropriate that this design was part of Adam's collection, as it demonstrates so well the artistic theory that Piranesi was evolving in the mid-1760's, a theory that was exceedingly important for Adam's own. For while the various dedications and compliments of the 1760's and 1770's are interesting manifestations of the relationship of the two men, it is the artistic influence that is more significant for an understanding of eighteenth-century art. After Adam left Italy, he not only maintained a personal friendship with Piranesi, but he also continued to derive inspiration, more

specific inspiration, as a matter of fact, than was true of the period of his Roman study. Piranesi's theoretical concepts of the mid-1760's and the designs published in 1769 that were the logical result of this theory were highly influential on Adam and form the most important new influences on him after his style had matured. In the period when Adam was in Rome, Piranesi had not as yet evolved a conscious aesthetic theory nor was he especially concerned with purely theoretical concepts. He was, as we have seen, passionately devoted to Roman antiquity and full of archaeological zeal and a sense of grandeur, all of which he passed on to Adam. But his involvement in theoretical controversy and his development of an artistic theory date only from the end of the 1750's. This new interest was manifested in 1761, when Piranesi published his first polemical treatise, his *Della magnificenza ed architettura de' Romani*, in which he fervently defended the virtues of Rome over Greece. That Piranesi was not violently anti-Greek in the mid-1750's is indicated by his friendship in 1756 with Allan Ramsay, who had published an anonymous essay the preceding year emphasizing the primacy and superiority of Greek architecture.[23] This friendship is reported by Adam, their mutual friend, and is reinforced by the inclusion of Ramsay's name and accomplishments on the same frontispiece of Volume II of the *Antichità romane* as that on which Piranesi had first honored Adam.[24] By 1761, however, the Roman engraver had become the most active supporter of Roman art, attacking both J.-D. LeRoy's *Les ruines des plus beaux monuments de la Grèce* and the essay by Ramsay. Using LeRoy's own rationalistic criteria, Piranesi advanced the thesis that Roman art was derived from the Etruscan, finer, simpler than that of the Greeks, and that Roman art was not debased Greek art.[25]

Four years later Piranesi had moved away from a strict rationalist stance and from the criterion of simplicity. Provoked by a letter from P.-J. Mariette published in the *Gazette Littéraire de l'Europe*, Piranesi in his *Osservatore* and especially in the *Parere*

18. P. 3 (in the 1836 ed.).
19. Register House, Edinburgh, Clerk of Penicuik Papers no. 4866.
20. Adam's description of them is in the preface to vol. II, part iv. The plates are 1, 3, 4 and 5 of this part.
21. *Works*, vol. II, part iv.
22. Soane Museum, Adam Drawings, vol. XXVII, no. 48.

23. The essay, 'A Dialogue on Taste', appeared in the *Investigator*, no. 332, 1755. It was republished as a separate pamphlet (London, 1762), and Ramsay's pro-Greek statements appear on pp. 37–38 of this edition. For Ramsay's authorship of the essay, see his letter to Sir Alex. Dick, Bt., Jan. 31, 1762, printed in Mrs. Atholl Forbes, ed., *Curiosities of a Scots Charta Chest, 1600–1800* (Edinburgh, 1897), p. 199.
24. In addition to the frontispiece, see letter from Robt. to Jenny Adam, Apr. 23, 1756 (Register House, Edinburgh, Clerk of Penicuik Papers no. 4805).
25. For an excellent and a more thorough account of Piranesi's theoretical concepts, as summarized here and in the following paragraphs, see Rudolf Wittkower, 'Piranesi's "Parere su l'architettura"', *Journal of the Warburg Institute*, II (1938–39), 147–58. For my discussion of this material, I am greatly indebted to this article and to conversations with Professor Wittkower.

su l'architettura of 1765 advocated ornament and variety, as well as the imaginative adaptation of ancient art in place of the servile copying of it. These ideas he expressed not only in his text but also in his plates, which were compositions characterized by complex superimpositions, variety, framed ornament, and ingenious combinations of forms. These same themes are also illustrated in Sta. Maria del Priorato in Rome upon which he was engaged at exactly the same time (see Fig. 3).[26] It is thus especially significant that Adam should have owned a drawing of this church, for these new ideas, though not the actual designs, are very close to the ones he himself espoused in the 1770's in the *Works in Architecture*. Various concepts advanced by Piranesi in the *Parere su l'architettura* and expanded and more fully developed in the *Diverse maniere d'adornare i cammini* of 1769 are thus crucial to Adam's theories and also to his style.

Among these concepts are those of novelty, of the proper and necessary use of ornament, of the imaginative use of antiquity, and of genius and freedom from rule. These are summed up by Piranesi in a passage from the *Diverse maniere* that almost sounds like the Adam creed:

> An artist, who would do himself honour, and acquire a name, must not content himself with copying faithfully the ancients, but studying their works he ought to shew himself of an inventive, and, I had almost said, of a creating Genius; And by prudently combining the Grecian, the Tuscan, and the Egyptian together, he ought to open himself a road to the finding out of new ornaments and new manners. The human understanding is not so short and limited, as to be unable to add new graces, and embellishments to the works of architecture, if to an attentive and profound study of nature one would likewise join that of the ancient monuments.[27]

These words of Piranesi's aptly describe the Adam style and epitomize the aims and theories expressed four years later in the *Works in Architecture*. In the preface to the earliest part of the *Works* to appear, the first eight plates of Syon, the Adam brothers struck a keynote that reads very much as if they had taken the advice of Piranesi to heart:

> . . . if we have any claim to approbation, we found it on this alone: That, we flatter ourselves, we have been able to seize, with some degree of success, the beautiful spirit of antiquity, and to transfuse it, with novelty and variety, through all our numerous works.[28]

Novelty and variety are, indeed, the cornerstones of the Adam style, and both the Adam brothers and Piranesi frequently fall back on these qualities in their writings. They go hand-in-hand with the condemnation of slavish imitation and the advocacy of freedom from absolute rule. Piranesi expressed this view in the passage quoted above, as he had done earlier in the *Parere* and in the dedication to Adam in the *Campo Marzio*. Even ancient architects, he argued, did not adhere rigidly to the rules,[29] and he need only cite the enormous variety of Roman capitals to prove his point. Similarly, the Adams criticized 'architects destitute of genius and incapable of venturing into the great line of their art' for their minute and frivolous attention to rules and proportions. The ancient masters, said Robert and James, 'varied their proportions as the general spirit of their compositions required, clearly perceiving, that however necessary these rules may be to form the taste and to correct the licentiousness of the scholar, they often cramp the genius and circumscribe the ideas of the master'.[30]

Like Piranesi, too, the Adams would mix original invention with study of the ancients, though they tended to lay somewhat more stress on study. Yet they felt that an artist of genius would move on after a thorough study of the best of the past to an imaginative use of that past, characterized, of course, by novelty and variety. Having emphasized genius and freedom from rule elsewhere in the *Works*, they also expounded on the virtues of study:

> Architecture has not, like some other arts, an immediate standard in nature, to which the artist can always refer, and which would enable the skilful instantly to decide with respect to the degree of excellence attained in any work. In architecture, it must be formed and improved by a correct taste, and diligent study of the beauties exhibited by great masters in their productions; and it is only by profound meditation upon these, that one becomes capable of distinguishing between what is graceful and what is inelegant; between that which possesses, and that which is destitute of harmony.[31]

The advocacy of ornament derived from a variety of sources is another point of similarity between Piranesi and the Adams. It is manifested in Piranesi's writings,

---

26. For the *Parere* and Sta. Maria del Priorato, see Wittkower, *Warburg Journal*, II, 147–58; and Rudolf Wittkower, 'Piranesi as Architect', in *Piranesi*, ed. Robert O. Parks (Northampton, Mass., 1961), pp. 99–109.
27. P. 33 (in the original 1769 ed.).
28. I, i, 6.
29. For these, see Wittkower, *Warburg Journal*, II, 155–56.
30. *Works*, I, i, 6–7.
31. I, ii, 3.

illustrations, and architecture of the 1760's and all through Adam architecture. From his earliest sketches in Rome to his most highly developed style in the 1770's and later, Robert Adam demonstrated his enjoyment of ornament and decoration and his skillful and judicious use of them. As in Piranesi's support of ornamentation, it is the framed ornament, rather than the untamed flow, that is most often employed by Adam. There are, of course, exceptions, but generally Adam's decorative ornament is found within panels or friezes. It is highly organized, not free-flowing.

With respect to the Greek-Roman controversy that had excited Piranesi and a great many others, Adam basically charted a middle course. On the one hand he supported the Etruscan-Roman argument, on the other he attacked the Tuscan and Composite orders. With Piranesi, he and James praised the Italians:

> Long before their acquaintance with the Greeks, the Romans had derived from Etruria such information as enabled them to make a very considerable progress in many branches of architecture. This accounts for the great and masterly style in which they planned and constructed their public works from the most early period.[32]

Yet, in a footnote they attacked the Tuscan order as so much inferior to the Doric 'that we have refused it a place in our list of Orders'.[33]

As exemplified by this comment, Adam and Piranesi did not always agree. Adam's support of the three Greek orders and his criticism of 'the two mongrel orders The Composite & Tuscan' was expressed at least as early as 1763,[34] at the height of Piranesi's anti-Greek outbursts, as well as in 1778, when the footnote quoted above was published. And even when the two men did agree, as was usually the case, it was not necessarily a matter of Piranesi's influence on an impressionable Adam. Before his arrival in Rome and his encounter with Piranesi, Adam was already excited by antiquity and grandeur; Piranesi heightened this excitement, but he did not create it. Similarly, a number of the ideas propounded by Piranesi in the mid-1760's were anticipated by Adam or were developed concurrently. The effective use of ornament and decoration, for example, was characteristic of the Adam style long before Piranesi advocated their use in the *Parere*, and, as a matter of fact, he there cited Adam as evidence, as we have seen. The concept of study coupled with freedom from rigid formulae had also been suggested in Adam's 1763 letter to Lord

Kames. Speaking of his brother James's Italian tour, Robert told of James's 'Love & Enthusiasm of Architecture which no one could feel that has not formed very Extensive Ideas of it. It is easy to tame, & bring under proper management those large views, & the Detail of our profession comes naturally, But the Architect who begins with minutiae, will never rise above the Race of the Reptile Architects who have infested & Crawled about this Country for these many Years.'[35]

Adam's concern for the large view and freedom from rule, demonstrated in 1763 as well as a decade later in the *Works*, is thus contemporary with Piranesi's similar sentiments. On the other hand, these ideas had been put forth ten years earlier by Laugier and were shortly thereafter taken up in England by Isaac Ware.[36] Clérisseau, too, shared this belief, though his published attack on servile copying appeared only in 1778.[37] Adam could therefore have derived his ideas from any or all of these sources. Piranesi was in this case, as in others, a corroborating force rather than a direct influence.[38]

In terms of both artistic theory and artistic style, Piranesi's publications of the 1760's served three functions for Adam. In the first place, they gave legitimacy and public approval to stylistic tendencies already evident in Adam's work. Among these were the use of ornament, the delight in variety, and the utilization of a wide variety of sources. Some of this, it is true, was inspired by Adam's study in Rome and his acquaintance with Piranesi, but this inspiration had already been absorbed into the Adam style by the time of Piranesi's public advocacy of them in the mid-1760's. In the second place, the Piranesi volumes of the 1760's expressed ideas with which Adam may already have been familiar but which contributed to the development of his own artistic theory. These ideas, such as the concepts of novelty, freedom from absolute rule, and genius, Adam in turn published in the 1770's. Finally, Piranesi in the 1760's provided Adam with new concepts and, even more important, new sources

32. *Works*, II, i, 1.
33. *Ibid.*
34. Letter to Lord Kames, Mar. 31, 1763 (Register House, Edinburgh, Abercairny Papers no. 564).
35. Register House, Edinburgh, Abercairny Papers no. 564.
36. See Laugier, *Essai sur l'architecture* (Paris, 1753), pp. v–vi; and Ware, *Complete Body of Architecture* (London, 1756), p. 131.
37. *Antiquités de la France: Monumens de Nismes* (Paris, 1778), p. xii.
38. The background of the question of ornament illustrates how complex can be the forces involved in the development of Neo-classical theory. Although Piranesi, in the *Parere*, advocated its use more effectively than had anyone previously, it had already been demonstrated by Adam and proposed by Winckelmann. In his *Anmerkungen über die Baukunst der Alten* (Leipzig, 1762), p. 50, Winckelmann had equated a building without ornament with both monotony in architecture and a sick body; and this may well have been Piranesi's source. See also Wittkower, *Warburg Journal*, II, 147–58.

of design. Piranesi's advocacy and use of previously unknown or little-known models and his recommendation of antique urns as sources for wall decoration Adam found especially appealing, while Piranesi's designs in the *Diverse maniere* were an invaluable fount of new designs for the British architect. This volume, published by Piranesi in 1769, furnished Adam with the idea for his Etruscan rooms and with designs to follow, as well as with the inspiration for a whole new type of chimney-piece. In doing so, the *Diverse maniere* provided Adam with his most significant innovations of the 1770's and '80's.

The decoration of interiors was a subject that attracted a great deal of Adam's attention, due both to circumstances and to his own predilections. While a substantial number of his commissions were concerned with additions to and remodeling and redecoration of existing country seats and London town houses, Adam seems to have relished this side of his work. It was in this sphere that he and James claimed that they had wrought 'an almost total change'.[39] And they felt, as Robert's would-be biographer wrote,

> that their art must ever remain extremely deficient, untill they should be able to supply some new & undiscovered resources for the internal decoration of private apartments, by introducing elegance, gayity, & variety, instead of that dull & elaborate floridity which universally prevailed in the buildings of this Island, till the time of M[r]. Adam's return from abroad.[40]

Adam supplied this new and different type of decoration in his grotesque and arabesque panels, inset decorative paintings, and other wall treatments of the 1760's and later. But in the 1770's he was able to add a still newer form of interior decoration—the Etruscan room. In a way these rooms with their flat, linear, elegant, and delicate decoration epitomize Adam's style of the 1770's. He designed at least eight of them, all dating between *c.* 1773 and *c.* 1780, but only one— that at Osterley—survives virtually in its original condition.[41] As one would expect with Adam, they were by no means identical, though they all shared the same character, certain similar motifs and arrangements,

and the use of black and terracotta coloring, usually on a pale green or pale blue background.

The Etruscan dressing room at Osterley (Fig. 5) of 1775–1777 is both a very fine and a typical example. The conception of the ceiling, the chimney-piece, and the frieze were Adam's contribution, as was the idea of designing the entire room *en suite*, even to the chairs. So, too, were the elongation and spirit. But the stylistic inspiration was Piranesi's. Though Adam said in the *Works* that this type of decoration was used by him for the first time in Europe,[42] the rationale had been provided in the *Diverse maniere* about four years before Adam's first Etruscan room and six years before the Osterley example. In his volume, Piranesi defended his use of urns, bases, and the like as motifs and sources for wall decoration and, of even greater significance, illustrated three examples.[43] Adam appears to have seen these plates and read the justification, looked at antique vases and at such publications on them as d'Hancarville, and then evolved his own scheme of decoration. Lighter and more ordered than Piranesi's, it is nevertheless dependent on his designs. A comparison of the Osterley room with Plate 2 of the *Diverse maniere* bears this out (cf. Figs. 5 and 6). Adam's version has a good deal more open space; it is more fragile and delicate; the figures are more elongated; and the whole is much less lively and vibrant. In addition, many of the motifs and forms at Osterley are not to be found in the Piranesi design and are actually highly characteristic of much of Adam's decorative work; and, of course, the colored decoration at Osterley creates a very different effect than the black-and-white engraving. Despite all of these differences, the relationship is still strong. The trellis-like network of delicate foliage rising from sphinxes and the scale and pose of the female figures, as well as the general arrangement, are common to both. When one combines this with Piranesi's specific mention of urns as sources for wall decoration, there can be little doubt of Piranesi's influence on Adam's Etruscan rooms. Yet it is typical of Adam that what he took was absorbed into his own style. He here demonstrated the ingenious adaptation of various sources that was so highly recommended by both himself and Piranesi.

Just as the *Diverse maniere* suggested to Adam a new kind of wall decoration, so too it provided him with a new type of chimney-piece. Whereas almost all of Adam's chimney-pieces during the last half of the 1760's were basically refinements and modifications of kinds that he had been using in his first six or seven years in London and even in his Scottish work before

39. *Works*, I, i, 3.
40. Draft notes for a life of Robert Adam, probably by John Clerk (Register House, Edinburgh, Clerk of Penicuik Papers no. 4981).
41. Others were at Derby House, Grosvenor Square; Apsley House; Home House; Cumberland House; 'M[r]. Adamson's Parlor', probably in the Adelphi; Osterley (a small room under the stairs of the garden façade); and Byram, Yorks. The first three are mentioned in the *Works*, vol. II, part i; the others are documented through Soane Museum, Adam Drawings, vol. XIV, nos. 138–40; 136–37; and 54; and vol. L, no. 70, respectively.

42. Vol. II, part i, preface.
43. P. 9 (in the original 1769 ed.) and pls. 2, 3 and 55.

the Grand Tour, the 1770's saw the introduction of a new variety. Generally with wider and more complex stiles, they appear to owe their ultimate inspiration to Piranesi's 1769 volume. Many of Adam's designs have no specific relationship to Piranesi's plates, but this publication seems to have awakened Adam's fertile imagination to all sorts of new possibilities in chimney-piece design. As is typical of Adam, even his designs that are directly derived from the plates of the *Diverse maniere* have been substantially modified. Usually he took only a part, for the Piranesi conceptions were on the whole too wild and complex for Adam's taste, but what he borrowed was transformed into the Adam spirit.

Although Adam had employed rather heavy, three-dimensional caryatid chimney-pieces in his first projects in England, his return to a variation on this theme in the early 1770's was not a throwback to his previous practice. On the contrary, these flatter, more refined, and more classicistic chimney-pieces with figures in low relief on the stiles were inspired by the *Diverse maniere*. The first drawing room of Wynn House (20 St. James's Square) features such a chimney-piece, which was executed as Adam designed it in 1772 (Fig. 7).[44] The pensive maidens playing horns were derived from Plate 9A of Piranesi's volume of three years earlier (Fig. 8). Adam placed his figures on classical bases and made a few minor alterations, including the musical instruments; but the subject, the poses, and even the nature of the drapery folds were obviously taken from the Piranesi plate. The frieze, too, is probably due to Piranesi, though the resemblance is not quite so striking. While the idea of a long subject panel replacing the more typical decorative frieze may have been inspired by this plate from the *Diverse maniere* or by one that is even closer,[45] Adam chose to use a different classical subject. Instead of the assembly of classical figures within a giant swag here or the chariot race employed in the other Piranesi design, Adam preferred the theme of Aurora. Yet while he borrowed the stile and frieze treatments from his Italian friend of long-standing, he placed them in a more typical Adam context. The flutes and paterae on the corners, as well as the various moldings and the general spacing, are all characteristic of Adam and are not related to the Piranesi designs.

The low-relief maidens on the stiles that Adam derived from the *Diverse maniere* for Wynn House, he also used in other designs, though again varying the context. They appeared, for example, on the chimney-piece of the second drawing room at Derby House

(1774), but there the pose was slightly different, the pipes or horns were missing, and the rest of the chimney-piece was not at all Piranesian.[46] In addition to this executed piece, Adam had at one stage conceived another chimney-piece for Derby House with somewhat similar stiles, though he eventually discarded it in favor of a different design.[47] This was for the third—or great—drawing room and had the horn-blowing maidens facing frontally, rather than toward the side, as in Piranesi and the Wynn House chimney. Like the Wynn House chimney-piece, this one also would have had a long classical panel as the frieze, as well as paterae on the corners.

Another type of Adam chimney-piece stile inspired by the *Diverse maniere* is that illustrated in Fig. 9.[48] Designed in 1777 for Drummond's Bank at Charing Cross and still extant, this piece features the wide stiles with relatively complex decoration that Adam often employed from about 1770 on. Plate 25 of the *Diverse maniere* (Fig. 10) may have been Adam's source, as the chimney-piece shown on the 'superimposed' sheet of this engraving also includes the addorsed griffins supporting a panel with rams' heads at the top. The actual contents of the panels are different, and Piranesi employed ambiguous overlapping parts, while Adam did not. The remainder of the two chimney-pieces differs substantially, though both friezes have central motifs composed of a classical form flanked by two confronting elements. As is usual, Adam's design is both more elegant and more refined.

While the Drummond's Bank chimney-piece seems related to this particular Piranesi plate, there is another Adam chimney-piece whose stile is even closer to Piranesi's. For the first drawing room at Apsley House (Fig. 12),[49] Adam, *c.* 1774, sketched a form that uses not only the rams' heads and the addorsed griffins, but even the base rising up between the griffins to support the large loop in the main panel. The bases between the griffins vary, though both employ a medallion, and the contents of the large loops are also quite different. So, too, are the corners and the central frieze motifs, yet blank friezes are employed in both. This sketch was elaborated into a finished drawing,[50] which

---

44. Soane Museum, Adam Drawings, vol. XXIII, no. 10.
45. Pl. 8A.

46. Although the house has been destroyed, the chimney-piece design can be seen in Adam, *Works*, vol. II, part i, pl. 3. This follows closely Soane Museum, Adam Drawings, vol. XXIII, no. 46. Earlier, slightly different versions are Soane Museum, Adam Drawings, vol. XXIV, nos. 59 and 162a, the latter a sketch showing an alternate stile design.
47. See Soane Museum, Adam Drawings, vol. XXIV, nos. 172 and 58. The former is a sketch which also includes an alternate stile, much closer to the executed version; the latter drawing is a finished rendering.
48. Soane Museum, Adam Drawings, vol. XXIII, no. 90.
49. *Ibid.*, vol. XXIV, no. 165 (top).
50. *Ibid.*, vol. XXIII, no. 60.

was then executed, though with some of the detailed decoration eliminated.

Addorsed griffins figure in another chimney-piece design that Adam derived from Piranesi. The stile on the right half of Fig. 14 has its source in Plate 4A of the *Diverse maniere* (Fig. 11). Adam's griffins are more elegant; the whole stile is somewhat less complex; and in place of Piranesi's Greek-key frieze, Adam has substituted a band of rosettes and a band of decorated flutes.[51] The left half of the sketch is also Piranesi-inspired, and, interestingly, its model appears on the same page of the *Diverse maniere* as the source for the other part of the sketch (cf. Figs. 13 and 14).[52] Here, Adam has simplified his prototype and added his own delicate decorative detail; but he has retained the inverted L-shaped guilloche band, the rams' heads, the central swag, the skull, and the leafy base. Differences include a change in the lower part of the panel and the addition of an upper frieze, as well, of course, as a greater delicacy and refinement.

Just as Adam borrowed only elements of Piranesi's designs, so, too, he might combine part of one Piranesi design with part of another. The two chimney-pieces on Plate 4 of the *Diverse maniere* that Adam had used separately were in turn models for different sections of another design. For the sketch illustrated in Fig. 15, he adapted the stile and frieze treatment of Piranesi's Plate 4B (Fig. 13) and the central motif of the frieze of Plate 4A (Fig. 11).[53] The stile treatment here is even closer to Piranesi's than was the design shown on the left half of Fig. 14. Adam preserved the patera and skull, the rams' heads and swag, the foliage base, and even the urn, though he used only one of Piranesi's, not two. The inverted L-shaped band was also employed, but the decoration within it was altered. Instead of the uninterrupted frieze of Fig. 14 or the central motif of the Piranesi frieze of Fig. 13, Adam substituted the animal heads flanking a wreathed patera featured by Piranesi in the chimney-piece of Fig. 11. Significantly, however, he set the motif within a frame, which Piranesi had not done. The sketch, probably a third—and unexecuted—alternative for the chimney-piece in the second drawing room at Derby House, was created *c.* 1774 and then worked up

into a much more finished version (Fig. 16).[54] The only major change from the sketch was in the stiles, which were elongated, thus providing more space for decoration on the panel below the swag. This Adam filled with a lamp, patera, bow, and bell-flowers.

A comparison of the finished rendering with the Piranesi plates that were its sources reveals both the degree of Adam's indebtedness and the divergence between his interpretation and that of Piranesi. While the similarities, as noted above, are both obvious and striking, the differences are equally pronounced. In place of Piranesi's sculptural flow, Adam has substituted a series of discrete elements, albeit within a highly organized pattern. He has reduced Piranesi's heavy superimpositions to one almost innocuous example, the swag on the stiles. The enframement of the central frieze motif is still another point of divergence. Finally, of course, both the Adam piece as a whole and all of its details are much crisper and more delicate than its prototypes.

As so often in his art, Adam here demonstrated the theoretical precept expressed by both himself and Piranesi, the judicious and ingenious adaptation and combination of a variety of sources. In the same way as Piranesi's designs of Sta. Maria del Priorato and his engravings in the *Parere su l'architettura* and the *Diverse maniere* illustrate the theories propounded in the books, so, too, Adam's decorative designs exemplify the theoretical concepts that he published in the *Works in Architecture*.

Piranesi was of vital importance to Adam. In the formative years of Adam's sojourn in Rome, Piranesi encouraged and guided him in an appreciation of the wonders of antiquity and in the utilization of those wonders. In the years of Adam's maturity and artistic efflorescence, Piranesi was a colleague who gave international currency to many of the ideas and attitudes that the two men shared, but he was also a source of new inspiration to Adam, both theoretical and artistic. Through the plates of the *Diverse maniere*, he provided Adam with the springboard for enriching the variety of his decorative style. Yet this was possible only because Adam's ideas and those of Piranesi were in general agreement. To someone who was antipathetic to the new theories of Piranesi, the designs that he published in 1769 would have been wild and strange and an anathema. To Adam, who subscribed to many of the same beliefs as his Italian friend, these designs offered exciting possibilities for elaborating and refreshing his style. As he had done with all

51. The sketch and a finished rendering that conforms quite closely to it are in Soane Museum, Adam Drawings, vol. XXIV, nos. 205 and 63, respectively. Although neither is dated, the designs can probably be assigned to *c.* 1777, as the finished drawing for the left side of the sketch bears that date. The project for which this chimney-piece was intended is not known.

52. Cf. Soane Museum, Adam Drawings, vol. XXIV, no. 205, and *Diverse maniere*, pl. 4B. The finished drawing worked up from this sketch (Soane Museum, Adam Drawings, vol. XXIV, no. 64) is dated 1777, but it is not identified as to client or location.

53. The Adam sketch is Soane Museum, Adam Drawings, vol. XXIV, no. 162.

54. Soane Museum, Adam Drawings, vol. XXIV, no. 61. There is also a pencil drawing intermediate between the rendering and the rough sketch (vol. XXIII, no. 196 in the same collection).

previous influences, he absorbed them into his manner, stamping them with his own brand of Neo-classicism.

Yet if Adam was the beneficiary of Piranesi's influence, he was also important to Piranesi. For Adam was a practicing—and highly successful—architect whose work demonstrated the merit of a good part of Piranesi's theory. In this way, they were complementary. Although Piranesi's theories and engraved designs of the 1760's and Adam's decorative work and theoretical concepts of the 1760's and 1770's can be appreciated and understood on their own, they are even more effectively studied in the context of the other. Together, these two friends, through their mutual interests and the specific nature of their artistic relationship, proclaimed and illustrated many of the tenets and characteristics of eighteenth-century Neo-classicism. Their friendship was one of equals, marked by a certain amount of dissension and friction but also by a good deal of respect and admiration. Each played his part in what was, indeed, a lively, fertile, and complementary relationship.

EILEEN HARRIS

Burke and Chambers on the Sublime and Beautiful

Burke's *Philosophical Enquiry into the Origin of our Ideas of the Sublime and Beautiful* roused most eighteenth-century readers to reweigh their own thoughts, and to react in favour or against. Sir William Chambers was no exception. In fact, the *Enquiry* seems to have left upon him a virtually indelible impression. Throughout his professional life, from the first edition of his *Treatise on Civil Architecture* in 1759, to the third in 1791, he returned again and again to Burke's challenging ideas, sometimes with approving interest, but most often with a gnawing desire to find more satisfactory explanations of our aesthetic experiences.

The first edition of the *Enquiry* was published anonymously in 1757. In 1759 we find Chambers using and acknowledging some of its ideas in his *Treatise*.[1] Several years later, in 1770 and 1771, lectures on architecture,[2] prepared in the event that he might be called upon to replace the ailing Thomas Sandby as Professor to the newly established Royal Academy, brought him back to Burke, and to questions of beauty—this time with more intense and vigorous interest. Although the opportunity to address the Academy students never

arose, Chambers persevered with his lectures, completing two and collecting notes for others, which he hoped eventually to publish, in emulation, no doubt, of Reynolds' *Discourses*.[3] With this and his earlier promise to provide a second volume of the *Treatise*[4] in mind, he continued making notes, and recording his thoughts on anything that applied to architecture—the beautiful and sublime included. Although neither of his projects was ever completed, some of his notes were incorporated in the third edition of the *Treatise*.

Before we examine Chambers' views on the sublime and beautiful, it must be understood that he did not attempt to formulate anything like a complete or systematic theory of his own, but simply jotted down ideas as they occurred. His notes are rough, unconnected, and often fragmentary, varying in length from a fully covered foolscap page, to a sentence or two hastily written on a scrap of paper no bigger than four inches by six inches. They are the fresh, unpolished workings of his mind. Yet, disordered as they may appear at first, they soon fall into place, and are fortunately numerous enough to furnish, along with his publications, a clear picture of what his ideas were.

(i) The Sublime

In May 1757, one month after the appearance of Burke's *Enquiry*, Chambers published his *Designs for Chinese Buildings* in which he included a short essay on 'The Art of Laying Out Gardens'. Here he provides what purports to be an authoritative account of the Chinese methods of imitating nature 'in all her beautiful irregularities'. Chinese gardeners, he tells us, 'distinguish three different species of scenes . . . pleasing, horrid, and enchanted'.[5] In the 'enchanted' or 'surprising' scenes, the spectator is confronted not only with exotic plants and flowers, and monstrous birds

---

1. William Chambers, *Treatise on Civil Architecture* (London, 1759), p. 28. In a large composition the roses in the soffit of a composite order may be of two kinds, but should be similar in outline and dimension, '. . . for then, the images succeed each other so rapidly, and are from their similitude, so instantaneously comprehended; that the third impression takes place, before the first is in any degree obliterated: so that nearly the same effect is produced, as by a continued succession of the same object'. Cf. Edmund Burke, *Philosophical Enquiry into the Origin of our Ideas of the Sublime and Beautiful*, ed. J. T. Boulton (London, 1958), pp. 74, 141–2; p. 34. To explain why, contrary to the laws of optics, the shaft of an undiminished pilaster should appear larger at the top than at the base, Chambers offers the observation of 'A late ingenious writer of our own country . . . that the senses, strongly affected in some one manner, cannot quickly change their tenour, or adapt themselves to other things; but continue in their own channel, untill the strength of the first mover decays.' This is an exact quote from Burke, *op. cit.*, p. 76. Although Chambers footnotes the *Enquiry*, he does not mention Burke as author until the third edition of the *Treatise*. William Chambers, *Treatise on the Decorative Part of Civil Architecture* (3rd ed., London, 1791), p. 67; p. 58. 'Beauty and fitness are qualities that have very little connection with each other. . . .' Cf. Burke, *op. cit.*, pp. 104–7. Chambers uses Burke to oppose Laugier who he accuses of concentrating 'perfection in propriety'.

2. The manuscripts of the lectures are now in the Royal Institute of British Architects, and the Royal Academy (ex Professor A. E. Richardson's collection, Ampthill). They came, through Chambers' daughter, from Halnaby Hall, Yorks., were arbitrarily split into two parts, and have now been reunited in London.

3. Historical Manuscripts Commission, *The Manuscripts and Correspondence of James First Earl of Charlemont* (London, 1891), I, 304–5. Letter from Chambers, 30 January 1771: 'Sir Joshua Reynolds is now with me . . . He purposes [*sic*] sending you a copy of his dissertations or discourses . . . I have also an intention of making discourses on architecture. One I have finished, which I have shown to a friend or two who tell me it is very well and encourage me to go on; but I am going on so many ways at once that God knows when I shall get to the end of any of them.'

4. Chambers, *Treatise* (1759), p. 84.

5. William Chambers, *Designs of Chinese Buildings* (London, 1757), p. 15.

and animals, but also with strange, disturbing sounds that he can neither identify nor locate—sounds of a turbulent stream hidden underground; of wind whistling through artfully disposed rocks, buildings, or other contrivances; and of 'artificial and complicated ecchoes'. Elsewhere emotions of horror or terror are aroused by the introduction of fallen and distorted trees, ruined buildings, impetuous cataracts, dark caverns, and other devices suggesting ruthless power or impending danger. These terrifying scenes are employed not for their own sake, but to heighten pleasing and beautiful objects; for the Chinese well know 'how powerfully contrast operates on the mind'.

In his use of the terrible as an emotional stimulus, as a source of variety, and as an essential factor in a reproduction of Nature as she really is, Chambers comes closer to Thomson and the so-called 'graveyard' poets than to Burke, for whom pain had an aesthetic value all its own. Although, as Professor Monk points out,[6] the presence of terror in later eighteenth-century literature is not always synonymous with the sublime, in Chambers' essay, the relationship, whether or not intentional, does exist, or at least did to contemporary readers, among them Burke who recognized it immediately.

In 1758, Burke reprinted the whole of 'The Art of Laying Out Gardens' in the initial volume of the Annual Register,[7] a new periodical of which he was both editor and author until 1766. Although he considered the piece to be 'much the best which has ever been written on this subject', that was only part of his motive for reprinting it. The reviews in the Annual Register are known to have been used on certain occasions to endorse principles set forth in the Enquiry,[8] and the present case is no exception. It can be no mere coincidence that Chambers' essay is followed by abstracts from three other books describing astonishing landscapes or mysterious buildings.[9] The Chinese garden has doubtlessly been invoked for the relation of its terrible scenes to the sublime, this relationship being one of the subjects of Burke's Enquiry most criticized by his reviewers.

If it was possible for Burke to find hints of his sublime

in the very brief sketch of 'horrid' and 'enchanted' scenes in Chambers' essay of 1757, what would he have thought of the considerably enlarged Dissertation on Oriental Gardening published in 1772? The same scenes, appropriately renamed 'terrible' and 'surprizing',[10] now teem with a multitude of new horrors, howling jackals, gibbets, apparatus of torture, poisonous weeds, foundries belching large volumes of flame and smoke, shocks of electrical impulse, serpents, lizards, apes, and parrots,[11] all so dreadful and obnoxious that the earlier descriptions seem almost pleasing by comparison. Interestingly enough, this unbridled flight into the phantasmagoric was ridiculed by Richard Payne Knight,[12] in one of his frequent attacks on Burke, as one of the most far-fetched and unsuccessful imitations of the Enquiry. Indeed, Chambers was familiar with the Enquiry in 1772, but Payne Knight has overlooked his first excursion into the terrible, which was simply magnified in the Dissertation. While the scenes of terror are independent of Burke, there are, nevertheless, other details that do reveal his influence: the use of the term 'sublime' (which did not appear at all in the earlier essay) to describe one of the desirable ends to be gained by a conversion of England's wastelands into entertaining scenes of terror;[13] the recommendation of 'straight roads' which, by their 'exact order and symmetry', or what Burke would call 'Uniformity and Succession', are 'productive of grandeur',[14] and 'give[s] birth to many sublime and pleasing reflections';[15] the analysis of the invigorating effects of abrupt change, frequent repetition, incertitude, and anxiety, that may arise from extensive road works 'composed of repeated straight lines, altering their direction at certain points';[16] and no doubt some of the other ideas on gardening that Chambers fostered upon the Chinese.

For a fuller and more definite picture of Chambers' response to Burke's theories of the sublime, especially as they apply to architecture, we must turn to his manuscript notes.[17] His basic premise, that 'grandeur',

6. Samuel H. Monk, The Sublime: A Study of Critical Theories in XVIII-Century England (MLA, New York, 1935), n. 1, pp. 164–5.

7. Annual Register (1758), pp. 319–23.

8. Burke, op. cit., pp. xxv–xxvi.

9. 'Description of Lough-lane, or the lake of Killarny, in the barony of Magunihy, in the county of Kerry, in Ireland. From Mr. Smith's ingenious account of that county, lately published at Dublin'; 'The natural history of Hertz Forest, in his Majesty's German dominions. Written in German by H. Ebrens, M.D. Of the cavern at Scharzfeld'; 'From Mr. Grosse's voyage to the East-Indies. Account of a very remarkable Island near Bombay in the East-Indies'. Annual Register, op. cit., pp. 323–37.

10. William Chambers, Dissertation on Oriental Gardening (2nd ed., London, 1773), p. 39.

11. Ibid., pp. 40–44, 131.

12. Richard Payne Knight, An Analytical Inquiry into the Principles of Taste (2nd ed., London, 1805), pp. 378–9.

13. Chambers, Dissertation, p. 131. In a letter (Cornell University) dated May 13, 1772 to an anonymous gentleman who had objected to certain parts of his Dissertation, Chambers defends his objects of terror as being 'of a nature to produce the Sublime in the highest degree'. This letter forms the basis of the 'Explanatory Discourse by Tan Chet-Qua' added to the second edition of the Dissertation.

14. Chambers, Dissertation, p. 17.

15. Ibid., p. 57.

16. Ibid., pp. 50–51.

17. R.I.B.A., Chambers MSS. All the notes on grandeur or the sublime that are quoted below are in the R.I.B.A.

or the sublime, 'excites in the mind of the Spectator the most violent Sensation', and is, therefore, the most essential and powerful ingredient of perfection in architecture, is in perfect agreement with Burke. When he comes, however, to the sources of the sublime, he begins to have some reservations. To Burke, one of the primary requisites of the sublime, particularly in building, is magnitude, or greatness of dimension, for which 'no greatness of manner can effectually compensate'.[18] Chambers admits that 'the specific dimensions of bodys, will on most occasions produce the Sublime', but not, he argues, on all occasions, for the largest dimension may easily be rendered trifling by being divided into too many parts excessively varied in form, colour, and arrangement. Likewise, 'an able artist may give dignity to trifles' where real grandeur is lacking. Grandeur, then, 'depends in some measure upon the specific dimensions of the object but chiefly upon the form and its subdivisions'. Even unity of colour may be more conducive to the sublime than mere bulk, as witnessed by a comparison of St. Peter's, where 'ten thousand colours . . . divide the attention by confusing the form', and the very much smaller church of S. Maria di Carignano at Genoa, which being 'all of one colour the form is instantaneously convey'd to the mind and fixes it in a state of astonishment'. This analysis is thoroughly Burkeian, in spite of the fact that it is intended to qualify Burke, who does incidentally mention diversity of colour as 'prejudicial to the idea of infinity',[19] and hence to the idea of the sublime, but does not either discuss the positive effects of unity of colour, or evaluate this particular factor in the same way. Although Burke clearly attaches more importance to size than Chambers does, he also includes uniformity as a source of the sublime, observing that excessive changes, as they constantly check the imagination with new ideas, prevent the reception of a single strong impression. 'Uniformity' together with 'Succession' (a continuation of parts causing 'frequent impulses on the senses') constitute what he calls the 'artificial infinite', and it is this that raises ideas of the sublime.[20] Burke's 'artificial infinite' had a particular appeal to Chambers who used it in 1759 in the first edition of his *Treatise*,[21] and again in his lecture notes. Also from Burke come brief and scattered references to difficulty, the marks of distant times, or of ancient customs and ceremonies, mystery, and gloom as causes of the sublime.

In addition to making his own comments upon Burke's *Enquiry*, Chambers copied out a large section of the review of the book by Arthur Murphey, published anonymously in the *Literary Magazine* in May 1757.[22] His choice of the part of the review pertaining to terror, uniformity, succession, and the 'artificial infinite' is a significant echo of what we have already observed, indicating that it was these particular aspects of the sublime that interested him most. Equally significant is the heading of his abstract, 'Johnson's review of a Philosophical Enquiry'. As the review was only included in the first edition of Johnson's *Works* published in 1787,[23] this establishes a *post-quem* date for Chambers' manuscript—three decades after his initial acquaintance with the *Enquiry*.

(ii) The Beautiful

While Burke's analysis of the sublime elicited a mild mixture of approving and qualifying remarks, his theories of beauty, on the other hand, threw Chambers headlong into a lengthy, albeit fractured, philosophical and psychological debate, not so much over *what* is beautiful, which was his main concern with the sublime, but over the more fundamental question of *why* certain things arouse ideas of beauty, and *how* our impressions of beauty are formed. The challenge was Burke's definition of beauty as 'some quality in bodies, acting mechanically upon the human mind by the intervention of the senses'; without any assistance from reason or will, from which it followed that as long as the organs of sense are normal, there must be a uniformity of response among all men.[24] To Chambers, neither the uncompromising sensationism, nor the idea of a standard were at all acceptable. Taking a relativist point of view, he argues that our responses are by and large not uniform, but diverse; that the pleasure derived from objects of sight, unlike sound, does not depend upon the senses alone, but is primarily the result of association of ideas, and reasoning; and that since the preparation and 'turn' of the mind, and hence the ideas which it associates, vary from one individual to another, so the impressions received from the same object may also vary. In his own words:

> There are particular qualities in Visible Objects that Act immediately upon the organs of Vision & exact Sensations of pain or Pleasure according to the greater or Smaller degree of tension in these organs; but far the most powerful impressions made by Visible objects are those which act upon the mind, which are the result of reasoning, & arise from an Association of Ideas. Whatever relates to dimension, to Quantity of light & to brilliancy of Colour

18. Burke, *op. cit.*, pp. 76–77.
19. *Ibid.*, pp. 75, 142.
20. *Ibid.*, pp. 74–76.
21. Chambers, *Treatise* (1759), p. 28. Also *supra*, note 1.

22. Royal Academy, Chambers MSS., Richardson Coll.
23. Samuel Johnson, *Works* (London, 1787), X, 207–11.
24. Burke, *op. cit.*, pp. 112, 92.

is in a great meas[ure] though not totally reducible [*sic*] to the first of these Classes & is felt nearly in the same manner by all persons whose Organ of Vision is Perfect.

But whatever relates to Propriety, Proportion, Symetry [*sic*], local Colours, Grace, dignity, imitation, Accuracy, or neatness of Execution, materials, fitness, perfection, distance may be ranged under the Second of these Classes, and owe their power Chiefly to the Ideas which we connect with them, and excite in different minds differ[ent] feelings. According as the minds are prepared for their reception.[25]

The same ideas are repeated in a passage first worked out in the lecture notes, and inserted in the third edition of the *Treatise*.

Sounds operate very differently from visible objects; the former of which affect all, and always in the same manner. The operation being merely mechanical, the same sort of vibration, produces at all times the same effect; as equal strokes upon a bell, produce the same sounds. But visible objects act differently. Their effect is not alone produced by the image on the organ of sight; but by a series of reasoning and association of ideas, impressed, and guiding the mind in its decision. Hence it is that the same object pleases one, and is disliked by another; or delights today, is seen with indifference, or disgust tomorrow. For if the object seen, had alone the power of affecting; as is the case with sounds; it must affect all men alike, and at all times in the same manner, which by long and repeated experience, we know is not the case.[26]

Chambers was not the first to take exception to these particular aspects of Burke's theory. Similar objections had been voiced first by an anonymous reviewer of the *Enquiry* in the *Critical Review*, who pointed out that if beauty was a sensible quality acting mechanically on the mind by the intervention of the senses, it 'would be the same in every eye; and would have an effect upon infants as well as adults';[27] and again by Reynolds in his third letter to the *Idler*, from which Chambers made several notes. Reynolds, having attri-

buted aesthetic preference to 'habit and custom', goes on to attack Burke's implicit faith in the efficacy of the senses: 'It is absurd to say that beauty is possessed of attractive powers, which irresistably seize the corresponding mind with love and admiration, since that argument is equally conclusive in favour of the white and the black philosophers',[28] who, as he had explained earlier, have very different concepts of beauty.

As an advocate of association and reason as the major causes of our ideas of beauty, Chambers falls in line with Perrault, and even more closely with Alexander Gerard, whose *Essay on Taste* appeared in 1759. Perrault, in his *Ordonnance des Cinq Especes de Colonnes*, 1683, distinguishes two kinds of beauties: 'positive' beauties founded on 'solid convincing Reasons ['Richness of Materials, the Grandeur and Magnificence of the Structure, the Exactness and Neatness of the Performance', etc.] which please every one'; and 'arbitrary' beauties (like proportions) which 'are not agreeable for Reasons of which everyone is a Judge, but only through Custom, and a Connexion which the Mind makes of two Things of a different Nature, for by this Connexion, it comes to pass that the Esteem wherewith the Mind is prepossess'd, for some things whose Value it knows, insinuates an Esteem, also, for others, whose Worth it knows not, and insensibly engages it to respect them like'.[29] By the mid-eighteenth century the theory of association had been scrutinized by most English aestheticians.[30] Locke, Hutcheson, Kames, and even Burke recognized its power to effect ideas and diversify opinion. Nevertheless, they did not consider it to be a *cause* of our ideas—that being the prerogative of the senses—and, in fact, were inclined to charge it with distorting and modifying sense perceptions. Gerard, influenced to some extent by Hume, departs from this point of view. Like Chambers, he differentiates between the pleasures produced by the effect that certain qualities have on the senses, and those resulting from associated ideas, concluding that most of the pleasures derived from visible objects are attributable to association. The term 'beauty', he believes, can be precisely applied 'to every pleasure which is conveyed by the eye, and which has not got a proper and peculiar name; to the pleasure we receive, either when an object of sight suggests pleasant ideas of other senses; or when the ideas suggested are agreeable ones formed from the

25. R.I.B.A., Chambers MSS. The first sentence depends upon Burke, *op. cit.*, pt. IV, *passim*.
26. Chambers, *Treatise* (1791), p. 108. Chambers' analysis of the operation of sounds compares with Burke, *op. cit.*, pp. 139–40. But his distinction between sounds and visible objects is probably derived from Claude Perrault, *A Treatise of the Five Orders of Columns in Architecture*, trans. John James (London, 1708), pp. iv–v.
27. *Critical Review*, III (April 1757), p. 367. There is a note by Chambers in the R.I.B.A., presenting virtually the same argument.

28. Sir Joshua Reynolds, *Idler*, no. 82 (Nov. 10, 1759), *Works*, ed. Edmond Malone (London, 1798), II, 240.
29. Perrault, *op. cit.*, p. vi.
30. Martin Kallich, 'The Association of Ideas and Critical Theory: Hobbes, Locke, and Addison', *English Literary History*, XII (December, 1945), 290–315.

sensations of sight; or when both of these circumstances occur. In all cases, beauty is, at least in part, resolvable into association.'[31] Colours, for instance, in so far as they are 'nothing else than various degrees and modifications of light', may be more or less 'hurtfull to the organs of sight', and consequently more or less beautiful; but in most instances their beauty is 'resolvable into association, those being approved which either by a natural resemblance, or by custom, or opinion, introduce and are connected with agreeable ideas of any sort'.[32] Here is an obvious parallel to Chambers' distinction between 'quantity of light and brilliancy of colour' as qualities that act immediately upon the organs of vision, causing sensations of pain or pleasure; and 'local colours' that act more powerfully on the mind by reasoning, and association of ideas. Inspired perhaps by Gerard, Chambers goes much further than Perrault in tracing virtually everything, including 'dignity, Accuracy and neatness of Execution, and materials', qualities that Perrault regarded as positive beauties, to association.

Association, in Chambers' discussions of aesthetic experience, is always accompanied by 'reasoning'. But, while the function of the former is explicity defined, that of the latter remains relatively obscure. It is only from an isolated comment on this subject alone that the part he assigns to reason in the perception of beauty can be deduced. 'Our approbation our love for beauty is involuntary but what then does that prove that it has no dependence on reason? Surely no. We do not love a thing til [sic] we discover it & find out its properties & when we have found it lovely we love it and cannot help loving it.'[33] This is clearly a retort to Burke's radical rejection of reason in his effort to isolate the immediate causes of aesthetic judgment. According to Burke, 'it is not by the force of long attention and inquiry that we find any object to be beautiful; beauty demands no assistance from our reasoning; even the will is unconcerned; the appearance of beauty as effectually causes some degree of love in us, as the application of ice or fire produces the ideas of heat or cold'.[34] Although he does include judgment or 'the reasoning faculty' in his analysis of taste,[35] he relegates it to an inferior position dependent upon sense perception and imagination from which it is to draw conclusions. The pleasures that might be derived from correct judgment are far fewer and weaker than those offered by the senses and the imagination. In fact, judgment is, to Burke, a 'dis-

agreeable yoke' that restrains the imagination, preventing it from making free use of the senses.[36] Chambers' brief defense of reason as a guide to the senses links him, once again, with Hume and Gerard. According to Hume, 'Some species of beauty, especially the natural kinds, on their first appearance, command our affection and approbation; and where they fail of this effect, it is impossible for any reasoning to redress their influence, or adapt them better to our taste and sentiment. But in many orders of beauty, particularly those of the finer arts, it is requisite to employ much reasoning, in order to feel the proper sentiment, and a false relish may frequently be corrected by argument and reflection.'[37] Reason, by discovering all the parts of an object, comparing and relating them, and drawing appropriate conclusions, enables us to perceive the 'beauties and blemishes' of 'nobler productions of genius',[38] and 'paves the way' for agreeable sentiment.[39] A similar part is assigned to reason in Gerard's Essay on Taste, which was a much more likely source for Chambers than the voluminous writings of Hume. Gerard's 'internal or reflex senses', which are responsible for aesthetic perceptions, 'do not operate, till certain qualities in objects have been perceived, discriminated from others similar, compared and compounded',[40] and this is the task of judgment. Once these qualities have been revealed, 'it is sense, which is pleased or displeased ... but judgment alone can determine them, and present to sense the object of its perception'.[41] This seems to be what Chambers is hinting at when he replies to Burke that 'we do not love a thing til [sic] we discover it & find out its properties', or when he speaks of reasoning, and association of ideas as 'guiding the mind in its decision'.

If Chambers could be provoked by Burke's definition of beauty to the extent of devising his own theory of aesthetic response, he could hardly have avoided commenting upon Burke's invasion of subjects much closer to his own professional interests—proportion and fitness. In order to arrive at the primary causes of aesthetic experience, Burke begins by thoroughly and systematically demolishing the traditional theories connecting beauty with proportion and fitness which he insists are non-aesthetic qualities that appeal to the

31. Alexander Gerard, Essay on Taste (London, 1759), p. 45.
32. Ibid., pp. 42–43.
33. R.I.B.A., Chambers MSS.
34. Burke, op. cit., p. 92.
35. Ibid., p. 23.

36. Ibid., p. 25.
37. David Hume, An Enquiry Concerning the Principles of Morals, Sect. I, in The Philosophical Works, ed. T. H. Green and T. H. Grose (London, 1875), IV, 172.
38. David Hume, 'Of the Standard of Taste', The Philosophical Works, op. cit., III, 277.
39. Hume, An Enquiry Concerning the Principles of Morals, op. cit., IV, 172.
40. Gerard, op. cit., p. 90.
41. Ibid., p. 94.

understanding rather than to the senses or the imagination, and therefore cannot be constituents of beauty.[42] The fact that there is no certain proportion that is invariably and universally pleasing had been recognized long before Burke by Perrault,[43] and was fully accepted by Chambers.[44] What Chambers could not accept, however, was the total exclusion of proportions in Burke's rigorous sensationism: ' . . . it doth not follow because there is an infinite number of proportions diametrically opposite to each other which nevertheless are equally beautiful that proportion is not necessary to the Essence of beauty, any more than that proportion is Superfluous in Music because these proportions may be combined in ten thousand different ways & yet all of them produce harmony . . .'.[45] At this point one would expect him to defend the relative beauty of proportions, as he does in his *Treatise*, and as Perrault had done before him, by custom, habit, or association of ideas. But no—this explanation hardly enters his debate with Burke at all. Instead he embarks on arguments that are peculiarly long-winded, unresolved, and often negative. Hard as he tries to disprove Burke's conclusions, he fails to provide any positive or convincing proof of his own that proportions are essential to beauty.

In answer to Burke's use of the swan and the peacock to demonstrate that proportion is not the cause of beauty in animals,[46] Chambers argues:

> We do indeed as the Author observes admire b[ot]h a Swan & a peacock, two birds whose proportions differ as much as possible, but I do not apprehend it is either the form of the one or the other that Strikes us. The majestic Grandeur with which the Swan Glides upon the Surface of the Water, the beautiful form of his neck & the dazling [*sic*] Whiteness of his plumage are what we admire and are Instantaneously Struck with, but take him out of the Water & Se[e] him move and our Admiration Ceases. The regularity & Splendor of the peacocks tail, the rich colour of his plumage & the Statelyness of his pace are what we are struck with at first Sight. Our admiration abates the moment we perceive his diminutive form & little head, & thus it may be laid down that unless Some other powerful quality makes us overlook the want of proportion we are disgusted with it.[47]

But this reasoning leads nowhere, for, as Burke points out,[48] it is an error to presume that because the absence of proportion disgusts, its presence necessarily pleases. When writing this note, Chambers may have had in mind Reynolds' attack on Burke in the *Idler*, where he contends that our preference for one species to another —in this case, a swan to a dove—has nothing to do with form. 'When we apply the word Beauty, we do not mean always by it a more beautiful form, but something valuable on account of its rarity, usefulness, colour, or any other property.'[49] The similarity, however, ends there.

To prove that proportion, in spite of its apparent diversity, is essential to beauty, Chambers introduces fitness. The several different proportions observable among horses, for instance, may be 'all accounted equally beautiful and they are so because they render the Animal more fit for his destination . . .', whether it be the 'Turf, the Chace, the Manege, or the Draught'.[50] Of course, for Burke, the very fact that proportion does depend upon the end for which an object is designed, and therefore cannot be judged before the end is known, is evidence that it is not a cause of beauty[51] which is perceived immediately by the senses. To this Chambers replies that a man skilled or experienced in horses instantly sees what the horse is intended for, and immediately pronounces it beautiful for that end. Indeed, even the ignorant 'seldom admire a horse if they admire it at all that is not fit for Some of the above mentioned purposes or remarkably unfit'. This argument, however, gets him no further than the first one did. Firstly, it is illogical to conclude that because, in things intended for use, unfitness is never admired, that fitness therefore is always admired. Secondly, all that he has proved is that those, like himself, who have special knowledge or long experience find immediate pleasure in proportions and fitness. He does not account for the vast majority who may admire a horse, or any other form without knowing for what it is best suited. In addition, Burke would have found him guilty of the sophism 'which makes us take that for a cause which is only a concomitant . . . the sophism of the fly; who imagined he raised a great dust, because he stood upon the chariot that really raised it'.[52] Nevertheless, he does partly redeem himself by compromise. Although he holds fitness to be one of the causes of the diversity and beauty of proportions, and a 'primary concern in things intended for use',[53] he also maintains, along with Burke, that 'there

42. Burke, *op. cit.*, pt. III, secs. ii–v.
43. Perrault, *op. cit.*, p. v *et passim*.
44. Chambers, *Treatise* (1759), p. 64.
45. R.I.B.A., Chambers MSS.
46. Burke, *op. cit.*, p. 95.
47. R.I.B.A., Chambers MSS.

48. Burke, *op. cit.*, p. 104.
49. Reynolds, *op. cit.*, pp. 239, 241.
50. R.I.B.A., Chambers MSS.
51. Burke, *op. cit.*, p. 108.
52. *Ibid.*, pp. 106–7.
53. Chambers, *Treatise* (1759), p. 59.

are many things [like the Corinthian capital] . . . which, though beautiful in the highest degree, yet in their application, carry with them an evident absurdity . . .'; and thus, 'in objects merely ornamental, which are designed to captivate the sense, rather than to satisfy the understanding. It seems unreasonable to sacrifice other qualities much more efficacious to Fitness alone.'[54] Even in his theory of proportions, fitness, it would appear, bows to 'convenience, custom, prejudice, or to the habit of connecting other ideas with these figures'[55] as the major sources of the pleasures we derive.

To Chambers, then, whatever we call beautiful in visible objects, whether it be proportion, fitness, colour, materials, workmanship, or any other quality, owes its merit not to anything positive that automatically captivates the mind, and excites the same sensations in all, but to the ideas we associate with it, to custom, habit, or education. Although the logical outcome of this theory should be complete subjectivity of aesthetic judgment, the idea of no standard whatsoever was as inconceivable to Chambers as it was to his contemporaries. In the end, those who seek the source of beauty in positive qualities are happily reconciled with their opponents who find it in association or custom, 'the maintainers of harmonick proportions, proving their system by the measures observed in the most esteemed buildings of antiquity; and the supporters of the opposite doctrine allowing, that as both artists and criticks, form their ideas of perfection upon these same buildings of antiquity; there cannot be a more infallible way of pleasing, than by imitating that, which is so universally approved'.[56]

54. *Ibid.*, pp. 58–59.
55. *Ibid.*, p. 64.

56. Chambers, *Treatise* (1791), p. 107. For similar conclusions in French architectural literature see Wolfgang Herrmann, *Laugier and 18th Century French Theory* (London, 1962) pp. 39–40.

HANS HUTH

Chambers and Potsdam

Many years ago, while Rudolf Wittkower was still in Rome planning the new edition of Ernst Steinmann's Michelangelo bibliography, I was in charge of the inventory of the royal palaces in Prussia. In the library of Frederick the Great in the New Palace at Potsdam, I discovered, stuck behind a glass pane in one of the book cupboards, a drawing of a Chinese bridge signed by William Chambers. How did it get there, and what did it mean?

The so-called New Palace was built between 1763 and 1769. There had been no particular need for it and the King once called it a 'fanfaronade' but besides the suite for the King himself, in which he never stayed for any length of time, the guest suites were occupied by his nieces and nephews when they came to visit, and the handsome little theatre was used for their entertainment. The King once told Voltaire, 'I must give them a chance to go to the theatre, as a compensation for the tedium I am sure they must feel in the company of an old man. One should not be deceived about oneself and one has to try to be bearable to youth.' The façade of the palace was done after the model of Sir John Vanbrugh's Castle Howard completed in 1714 which was illustrated in *Vitruvius Britannicus* (1715), a book among those in the King's library. There were, of course, differences, one being that the entire New Palace was built of brick with only the quoins of stone. It is known that the King's architects, J. G. Büring and H. L. Manger, designed the façade from a sketch given them by the King. Manger mentions in a report that this sketch was not quite clear enough to guide an architect though it had been drawn by the hand of a master. Where this sketch came from is unknown but it is certain that the King on a visit to Holland and Westphalia in 1755 had been impressed by the brick and sandstone façades he had seen, and it is quite possible that he procured the sketch on his travels. It is equally possible that the sketch may not have shown anything except a plan for brick and sandstone construction (prints of Castle Howard were available in the King's library). These somewhat detailed indications are only given to dispose of any idea that Chambers might have provided the sketch in question. Certainly out of respect for the King, he would not have delivered a drawing so inadequate that it could not be interpreted by an architect.

As to Chambers' drawing, it is quite possible that it

had been in the book cupboard since it was put there, perhaps by the King himself. Unless there are sudden upheavals, objects in palaces are not arbitrarily removed, especially from locked cupboards. Since all the King's libraries contained similar sets of books and since revisions made in 1918 showed that almost no losses had occurred, it is likely that the drawing was never disturbed. After the death of the King in 1786, the palace was not used as a dwelling until 1888 when Empress Victoria and later Emperor Wilhelm II occupied it until 1918. One can assume that nobody ever bothered to remove the drawing, if ever it was noticed. Mr. Sydney Kitson in 1935 gave Sir William Chambers' papers to the Royal Institute of British Architects[1] and shortly thereafter an inquiry as to whether there was anything in the documents concerning Chambers' relations with Prussia, produced a letter from a John Forbes to William Chambers, dated Emden, February 3, 1752. The letter dealt with Chambers' application to enter the service of Frederick the Great. The writer could not have been the John Forbes who was appointed admiral in 1749, for the writer speaks of 'our king' meaning the Prussian king, also the further content of the letter makes it unlikely. The fact that the letter is dated Emden might permit the assumption that the writer had a connection with the Prussian fleet which was stationed in Emden, even if Forbes was an English subject, since many foreigners served in government positions. But Forbes may also have been a representative of English shipping interests, stationed in Rotterdam and only temporarily staying in Emden. In his attempt to have Chambers appointed 'Architect du Roy' Forbes had induced the Earl Marishal of Scotland, George Keith who resided in Potsdam and was a close friend of the King, to act as intermediary. Keith had come to Berlin as a Jacobite refugee after being condemned to death by an English court. The same fate had been meted out to his brother James who also came to Berlin and received the rank of field-marshal in the Prussian army. James was killed on the battlefield of Hochkirch in 1758.

At the time the letter was written Keith was Prussian

1. I am much indebted to Mr. Edward Carter, Librarian Editor of the Royal Institute of British Architects, who found the letter by John Forbes in 1937, and to Mr. John Harris, at present Curator of the Drawing Collection of the same Institute, for kindly providing information.

ambassador in Paris (1750–1754) and may possibly have met Chambers there though in reading the letter this does not seem likely. As Forbes tells Chambers, the Earl Marishal had been asked, undoubtedly by the King, whether if Chambers was appointed he would settle in Prussia. This is a strange question and could mean that it was not certain whether Chambers wanted to serve the King or merely wished to receive a title. The Earl Marishal also wished to know where Chambers had studied and had practiced his art and advised Chambers to forward 'some pretty thing' of his doing, and stated that he would do everything in his power 'to get him his patent as soon as possible'. The rest of the letter has no bearing on the present matter.

The reason the Earl Marishal thought this a propitious moment for Chambers to enter the King's service may have been based on the fact that at the time the King was greatly in need of an architect. Georg Wenceslaus von Knobelsdorf had been in charge of all the buildings the King had planned since he had been the crown prince. Von Knobelsdorf was suddenly dismissed, supposedly after some disputes on aesthetic matters, and the result was that the King's residences at Potsdam were completed by competent but by no means architects of great genius. In 1752 though no major projects were contemplated, the park at Sans Souci still needed some features to make its buildings balance each other in a better way. One of the buildings, erected between 1745 and 1757, was the charming Chinese pavilion inspired by one built by Héré in Lunéville for King Stanislaus Lescinsky. Though plans for a building of this type might have been in the wind in 1752, Chambers would not have been especially desirable for this Chinoiserie since his *Designs of Chinese Buildings* was not published until 1757. Thus it would seem that the Earl Marishal's interest in Chambers was nothing more than that of one Scotchman trying to help another and the apparent need of the King to find an architect versed in what was up-to-date. How serious Chambers' application was is somewhat dubious for we know that his plans in 1752 would not have lent themselves very well to the acceptance of a position in Berlin. For reasons unknown, the application failed and in the same year in which the letters were exchanged, we find Chambers on his way to Italy to study architecture.

After his return to England in 1755 and the publication of his Chinese designs in 1757 Chambers' name headed the list of fashionable architects, and there could be no discussion of Chinese taste without his name being mentioned. The unknown young man of 1752 had become a celebrity. Though by this time Chambers may no longer have thought of his old business with the King of Prussia, he seems to have kept up some relationship with Prussian authorities. Research in the former Hohenzollern Archives in Berlin yielded a receipt dated London, June 6, 1763, signed by Chambers. This document with others had been stolen from the archives by a discerning man named Hauck in the 1920's but by good luck was retrieved and received the ominous stamp, 'Furtum Hauckianum'.

In the paper Chambers testifies to having received fifteen guineas from 'Monsieur Michel, Ministre de Sa Majestee le Roy de Prusse' for three drawings and three plans for bridges 'a la Chinoise', but not knowing how large they were to be he had attached no scale. Further instructions are given on how to execute the design; the bridge was to be executed in stone, brick or wood, but the building was to be carried out in wood, painted or lacquered. The roof might be covered with linen, enameled brick, or very thin tin sheets painted and lacquered. In the substruction the drawing shows some relationship to buildings on Plates II and III of Chambers' *Chinese Designs*, otherwise it represents an original idea. This time Chambers' signature as 'Architecte du Roy de la Grande Bretagne' testifies to the fact that he was now in a secure position, and with this drawing was giving service to a king entertaining good relations with his own. The Prussian ambassador from whom he received payment was Louis Abraham Michel, who resided in London from 1753 to 1766, and was constantly in difficulties with the government to which he was accredited because he had to protest incessantly against the harassment of Prussian commercial vessels by the British fleet.

There remains the question as to why Chambers was asked for designs for Chinese bridges. Apparently this was done shortly after the Seven Years War when peace made it possible to build the New Palace as well as a small temple to house the collection of Roman antiquities the King had purchased. None of these buildings nor any situation in the park called for a bridge. On the contrary, anything which had to do with water, pumps, or fountains was not to be mentioned in the presence of the King. Unfortunately all efforts to make the fountains work had been unsuccessful and in 1780 all endeavors in this direction were given up. Yet it is quite possible that at one time there had existed a plan to build a pond with the bridge as a Chinese motif and Chambers was asked for a design. If there ever had been such an idea, it must have been rather vague since Chambers was not given any dimensions. With so much difficulty in providing water for existing installations, any project requiring more water would necessarily have been discarded.

In 1770 the King decided to build a small tower on an eminence which offered a good view. For this building, later called *Drachenhaus* (Dragon House) a Chinese design was selected. Though only three stories high the tower was supposed to reflect the Pagoda at Kew which Chambers built shortly before in 1763. Thus after all one of Chambers' creations did find an echo in the park of Sans Souci.[2]

Letter by John Forbes to William Chambers

(Published by permission of the Royal Institute of British Architects, London)

Embden, 3rd Fbry
1752

To William Chambers

Sir:

I had yours of the past which I could have answered sooner only waited to give you some light into my progress into getting the Character of Architect du Roy for you from Our King for that End I send you here copy of a letter I had from Marishall Keith last post date 22nd Jan.

2. For sources and literature see Hans Huth, *Der Park von Sans Souci*, Berlin, 1929; photographs of the present condition of the park in Georg Piltz, *Sans Souci*, Dresden, 1954, as well as in Willy Kurth, *Sans Souci*, Berlin 1957. (New and larger version 1964.) Arno Krause, *Das chinesische Teehaus im Park von Sanssouci*, Potsdam, 1963. While Dr. Kurth (now deceased) expresses some strange and controversial points of view in his book, the care he took of the park during his period of office as Director of the Administration of Palaces and Parks from the end of the war to 1964, has been most exemplary, so that the park, buildings and their inventory are now in an excellent state of preservation.

'I had the honour to write you some posts ago that 'there was two Questions asked me about Mr. Cham-'bers, wether on Receiving the title he designed to 'settle in any part of the Kings Dominions, & where 'he studyed & practiced his Art. these two questions 'be pleased to make him answer & at the same time if 'send something of his designing it would not be amiss, 'After which you may depend on it I shall use all my 'interest to get him what he desires etc.'
It seems the former letter he mentions has gone to Rottdm however if you'll answer these send me some pretty thing of your doing I'll forward them & use my interest to get you the Patent so the sooner you can do this the better address all to Rottdm—.
As to what you mention of Könings acepting its not yet known to us & till the we cant say anything nor have I mentioned your Brother as yet because he's not at home & its proper before he be engaged that at least he appears & when he does he shall be sure of my interest, what you say as to goods might be made easy by a particular leave tho its ag^t our Rules & then as to the having it in writing of your being employed you know that already in our books & you cant have it stronger if you desire I can get you an Extract but its needless since such is never altered & I've only further to add that

I am Sir your most obdtly
John Forbes

our first ship has been ready now several days but is detained by frost in the River so that I believe both will go together [name of the ship indecipherable but it could be read as] 'The Tiger' being arrived long ago.

WINSLOW AMES

The Completion of Stafford House

The architectural history of what is now called Lancaster House has been confused by the considerable number of distinguished architects who worked upon it, by the need of the later ones to conform more or less to the palace style initiated in its interiors for the Duke of York by Benjamin Dean Wyatt, and by some misunderstanding of dates.

In *Early Victorian Architecture in Britain* (1954), Henry-Russell Hitchcock dealt admirably with the style of the building and with the problem of the additional storey by Sir Robert Smirke. It is typical of the confusion that in older editions of Muirhead's Blue Guide, *London and Its Environs*, the architectural information in which came from W. R. Lethaby, the top storey was attributed to Sir Charles Barry. In *Georgian London* (1946), Sir John Summerson dated this additional storey and the grand staircase 'after 1841' in his captions to plates LXVIII and LXIX because of his assumption that all this work was done only after York House 'was bought by the Sutherland family in 1841'. He may have taken this date 1841 from the younger Barry's life of his father (Hitchcock also depended on the rather casual Alfred Barry); or from the verifiable date when Pennethorne invested the proceeds of the sale of York House in the site of Victoria Park in East London. There are also confusions in the article on the Dukes of Sutherland in the *Dictionary of National Biography*, in which it is said that the first duke, while still Marquess of Stafford, gave the house in 1827 to his eldest son plus £30,000 to complete it with. The present Duke (in *Looking Back*, 1957, p. 40) gives Disraeli as authority for the statement that the Marquess of Stafford had lent the Duke of York '£60,000 towards the building costs and never saw his loan redeemed!' Summerson begins the story by saying (*op. cit.*, p. 234), '... in 1825 ... the Duke of York ... was granted a site in St. James's on a 999 years' lease. He borrowed money from the Marquis of Stafford to build the house, and employed Benjamin Dean Wyatt as architect.' The present Sutherland says it was a 99 years' lease, but never mind that. The Duke of York, at any rate, died deep in debt on 7 January 1827, the house unfinished and his creditors clamoring. He had built in anticipation of succeeding his brother George IV, whose health was already shaky.

What follows is hardly architectural history, but it may facilitate a clearing up of the York-Stafford-Lancaster House story. The sources which supply evidence for the earliness of work by Barry and Smirke there are as follows:

Stafford House Letters, edited by Lord Ronald Gower, 1891; *Three Howard Sisters*, edited by Lady Leconfield and completed by John Gore, 1955; and Queen Victoria's diary, which by gracious permission of Her Majesty Queen Elizabeth II has been made available to me for research on Prince Albert's activities in the arts. The Stafford House letters are largely letters from the second Duke of Sutherland to his mother; the three Howard sisters were Harriet, who in 1823 married the second Marquess of Stafford's heir, twenty years older than herself, who bore the courtesy title of Earl Gower; Georgiana, later Lady Dover; and Caroline, later Countess of Harewood. They were daughters of the Earl of Carlisle.

Caroline's diary in March 1827 (*Three Howard Sisters*, p. 67) says, 'I went with Georgiana, Mr. Ellis [the future Lord Dover], Mr. F. Byng, and Mr. Luttrell, to see York House.' This was eight to ten weeks after the Duke of York died. In the second half of June her diary (*Sisters*, p. 75) says: 'Lord Stafford intends, if he can, to buy York House for the Gowers, which is certainly *magnifique de sa part*.' And on 30 June 1827 (*Sisters*, p. 76): 'In the evening I dined with the Gowers and met Papa, Mr. Trench, and Mr. Loch. They had all the plans of York House.' Loch was agent to Stafford, and managed both his land and the enormous property of his wife, who was Countess of Sutherland in her own right.

Lady Leconfield in her connective text (*Sisters*, p. 81) says, 'Harriet ... must have been overjoyed at the prospect of possessing York House. No sooner was it his, however, than Lord Stafford decided to keep it for himself'; she goes on to quote Harriet as writing to Caroline about this time, 'Lord Stafford has decided to employ the Wyatts, which gives us very great pleasure.' This will have meant B. D. Wyatt and his brother Philip. On 23 August 1828 Harriet Gower, writing to her mother-in-law from Silesia after having seen Dresden (*Stafford House Letters*, p. 160), says, 'I have often felt glad to think Lord Stafford has rejected for York House a style whose ornaments and decorations so nearly approach this [modern] German taste.'

[217]

By 1830 the building was being called Stafford House and the Marquess was living in it; on 26 October 1830 (*Sisters*, p. 158) Harriet writes that Lady Stafford has had 'a visit from all the French in London, who came to see Stafford House'; and on 1 November she reports (p. 152) from Hamilton Place, 'We dined yesterday at Stafford House.' The French of course were the refugees surrounding Charles X; in mid-November Georgiana is writing to Caroline (p. 163) that 'we met [Talleyrand] at Stafford House. The rooms looked beautiful and the dinner did very well.'

In the last year of his life, 1833, the second Marquess of Stafford was created Duke of Sutherland. At his death, the Bridgewater estate that had been his for thirty years went to his second son Francis, who later built Bridgewater House as a rival to Stafford House and very near it, while the Gowers took over Stafford House.

In John Gore's postscript to Lady Leconfield (*Sisters*, p. 284), 'The "improvements" to Stafford House' in 1834 are said to have caused difficulties. '"Was it," Lady Wharncliffe had asked, "*really* true that the Sutherlands are *obliged* to add a storey to Stafford House?" It was quite true. "We have had little annoyances lately about the works at Stafford House"', Gore quotes Harriet, now Duchess, as saying. The reason was that the workmen's noise woke up William IV and Queen Adelaide as early as five in the morning (the Palace was not more than a thousand feet away); and Sir Robert Smirke had to apologize. And on 11 August 1834 Harriet wrote, 'We came here [West-hill near Putney] last night. There is no sleep at Stafford House after 6. The last time we went over the Upper part we were struck with the less agreeable looks of some of the men, and we hear there is to be a general strike on Friday.' Perhaps the men's working hours had been shortened with a loss of pay. But the Duchess had written a few days earlier to the dowager her mother-in-law, 'The upper rooms at Stafford House are delightful' (*Letters*, p. 187, 3 August 1834). From all this it seems reasonably plain that Smirke's top storey must have been complete by the end of 1834, and this will have allowed Barry to proceed with the splendid stair court. On 6 July 1835 the Duke writes his mother (*Letters*, p. 189) about a great musical party given the night before to unveil the stairs: '. . . gas lighting from the outside of the lantern did beautifully for the upper part of the staircase.' Thenceforward there were enrichments such as the Duke mentions to his mother in writing from Paris on 3 January 1836 (*Letters*, p. 201): 'Mr. Westmacott's son [Richard Westmacott was not knighted until 1837] is making a valuable chimney-piece for Stafford House, with two statues.' Again from Paris on 3 April

1837 (*Letters*, p. 217) he reports that Thiers told him and Harriet that he could arrange to have bronze casts made for them from plasters of Ghiberti's Baptistery gates which Thiers had—'I think it might have not a bad effect at the north end of the gallery, to be a false door.'

In 1838, the year in which the Duke gave out that he was somewhat 'reduced by building' expenses, Queen Victoria went, as godmother to a new Leveson-Gower child, to a christening party at Stafford House (the Duchess was her Mistress of the Robes whenever there was a Liberal government). On the fourth of July she found the house 'beautifully fitted up'. Two seasons later she wrote on 18 July 1840 that the picture gallery was 'quite beautiful now'; on 1 July 1841 the Sutherlands were opening their new dining-room, and this time invited not only the Queen and Prince Albert but visiting Belgian royalties. On 1 August 1843 the Queen, in whose eyes the Duchess could do no wrong, took other Coburg relatives to see the perfect taste of some new Stafford House furniture, and on 22 June 1844 she mentioned again 'the Dining Room, with its splendid lustre . . . *everything* is *so* beautiful in that house, that one does not know which way to turn'.

Lady Leconfield says (*Sisters*, p. 81) that the remainder of the lease cost the Marquess of Stafford £72,000; the present Duke of Sutherland (*op. cit.*, p. 40) confirms this and adds that the ground rent was £758 per year. Whether or not there were thirty thousand in cash in 1827 for completion of the house, it may be suspected that the seventy-two thousand were paid closer to 1841 than to 1827; the improvements to properties in Sutherland, Staffordshire, and the Bridgewater canal enterprise cost a great deal over the whole tenure of the second Marquess; it was not until the next generation that tremendous income gushed from the mines and potteries and waterways to adorn Stafford and Bridgewater Houses.

But, though the second Duke of Sutherland and his tastemaking Duchess were certainly continuing to enrich their house after 1841, it was obviously in good condition to receive the Queen in the season of 1838. The Wyatts (Philip died in 1836) must have been working largely on interior decoration over the years from, say, 1828 to perhaps 1833; Smirke will have added his attic to Wyatt's lower storeys 1833–1834; and Barry's stair court was evidently ready by the middle of 1835; thereafter, more decoration.

As an epilogue to the remark attributed to the Queen ('I have come from my house to your palace'), it may be interesting to add that Nathaniel Hawthorne thought Stafford House much more beautiful than Buckingham Palace (*English Notes*, 1902 edition, ii, p. 94).

ENRICO CASTELNUOVO

Una disputa ottocentesca sull' "Architettura Simbolica"

Il 26 settembre 1826 l'Ateneo di Brescia proponeva questo programma per il consueto premio biennale: "Determinare lo stato dell'architettura adoperata in Italia all'epoca della dominazione longobarda. Investigare se questa architettura abbia un'origine particolare. Stabilire i caratteri peculiari che la distinguono, principalmente nella costruzione de'templi tanto in riguardo alla costruzione interna che esterna di essi, come nella distribuzione della pianta; e nella scelta e uso dei materiali per fabbricarli. Notare finalmente i principali edifizi di tale architettura in Italia."
Che accademie e istituti di cultura proponessero pubblici concorsi su determinati temi era ben radicato costume settecentesco, che questi temi poi vertessero sull'epoca che segna la fine del mondo classico e l'inizio di quello medioevale era cosa che già da qualche decina d'anni si andava con minore o maggiore frequenza producendo; nel 1808 l'Institut de France non aveva forse premiato una memoria[1] di Georg Friedrich Cristoph Sartorius von Waltershausen, professore all'Università di Tubinga, in risposta al quesito "Quale fu sotto il governo dei Goti lo stato civile e politico dei popoli d'Italia? Quali furono i principî fondamentali della legislazione di Teodorico e dei suoi successori, e soprattutto quali furono le distinzioni che essa stabilì tra vincitori e popoli vinti?"
Nell'Italia di quegli anni la questione longobarda era al centro di una vasta, appassionata discussione. Senza voler scendere a esaminarne i precedenti, dal Machiavelli al Baronio al Muratori, al Maffei e via via alle "Antichità longobardico-milanesi" del Fumagalli e alla storia di Como del marchese Giuseppe Rovelli, basterà ricordare che nel 1822 Alessandro Manzoni aveva pubblicato il suo "Discorso su alcuni punti della storia longobarda in Italia" a commento dell'Adelchi. La posizione del Manzoni è nota. E' una confutazione recisa delle tesi settecentesche favorevoli ai Longobardi, una serrata polemica contro gli antichi dominatori d'Italia, una giustificazione e una difesa della condotta del papato e della chiamata dei Franchi, un invito infine a studiare e a ricercare "la storia patria di quei secoli". "Rispose all'invito—scrive Giorgio

Falco[2]—non qualche acuto ed insistente ingegno, ma un intero esercito di studiosi". Un esempio tra i tanti: nello stesso anno 1826 in cui l'ateneo bresciano poneva il suo quesito, usciva a Udine una traduzione della "Historia Langobardorum" di Paolo Diacono, curata dal professore Q. Viviani. Per citare ancora una volta il Falco; "Con un tantino di esagerazione si può affermare che fra il '22 e il '50, è compito quasi disperato trovare fra gli storici italiani chi non si sia occupato, non si occupi, non intenda occuparsi della questione longobarda".
E' in questa cornice che va visto il concorso bresciano. La novità, ed è quella che qui ci interessa, sta nell'aver impostato il programma su un problema di storia della architettura, già affrontato, ma di sfuggita, dal d'Agincourt in un capitolo della sua storia.[3]
I risultati del concorso vennero resi noti nel 1828: vincente era giudicato il saggio del cavaliere Giulio Cordero dei Conti di San Quintino, che vedeva la luce l'anno successivo in appendice al volume del 1828 dei "Commentari" dell'Ateneo (Brescia, 1829), mentre una "onorevole menzione" otteneva uno scritto dei cugini Defendente e Giuseppe Sacchi, pubblicato nel 1828 a Milano presso Antonio Fortunato Stella e Figli, sotto il titolo suggestivo di "Antichità romantiche in Italia" e con il sottotitolo: "Della condizione economica, morale e politica degli italiani nei bassi tempi. Saggio I, Intorno alla architettura simbolica, civile e militare usata in Italia nei secoli VI, VII, VIII e intorno all'origine de'Longobardi, alla loro dominazione in Italia; alla divisione dei due popoli ed ai loro usi, culto e costumi".[4]

2. G. Falco, "La questione longobarda e la moderna storiografia italiana", in *Rivista Storica italiana*, anno LXIII (1951), pp. 265 segg.
3. J. B. Séroux d'Agincourt, "Histoire de l'art par les monumens", I, Paris, 1823, capitolo X; "Règne des rois lombards en Italie". "Tableau de la situation de Rome, de Naples, de Venise, et de l'exarchat de Ravenne. Etat des arts sous le gouvernement des lombards au VIe et VIIe siècle, jusqu'à sa destruction vers la fin du VIIIe siècle", pp. 30–35 del "Tableau Historique". Cfr. anche le pp. 38–40 della seconda parte ("Architecture"), dello stesso volume e la tavola XXIV del IV volume.
4. Il termine "romantico" usato per l'architettura altomedioevale segue, dopo non molti anni, l'impiego di "roman" fatto dallo Gerville e costituisce un fatto non privo d' interesse per la storiografia artistica italiana dell'ottocento. Eccone la giustificazione datane dai Sacchi: "Tutto il medioevo poi ci sembrò

1. Pubblicata a Parigi nel 1811 col titolo: "Essai sur l'état civil et politique des peuples de l'Italia sous le gouvernement des Goths". Una traduzione italiana ne uscì a Milano nel 1820.

[219]

Le due opere hanno caratteristiche molto diverse, diseguale valore, ma offrono entrambe più di un motivo di interesse, anche per la polemica che ne seguì e in cui fu implicato il filosofo Gian Domenico Romagnosi.

L'unico risultato comune cui approdarono le due indagini, e che ben si accorda alla polemica anti-longobarda del Manzoni, fu che questo popolo non aveva apportato niente di nuovo e di originale alla storia dell'architettura italiana, e che gli edifici eretti in quel tempo avevano continuato le tradizioni e i metodi costruttivi dell'età precedente. Ma quali erano questi edifici? Quali le loro caratteristiche? e che criterio occorreva usare per darne una soddisfacente lettura? Qui le due trattazioni divergono radicalmente, come divergono le personalità dei loro autori.

Il Cavaliere Giulio Paolo Cordero dei conti di San Quintino era un gentiluomo all'antica; nato sotto l'ancien régime a Mondovì il 30 gennaio del 1778,[5] aveva avuto, come molti cadetti di famiglie patrizie, un'educazione religiosa che non si era però conclusa con i voti sacerdotali. La sua vita fu quella di un nobile di mediocre agiatezza: erudito, curioso, buon viaggiatore in Italia e all'estero, si era occupato di numismatica, di agricoltura, di antichità egizie. Al momento del concorso bresciano era conservatore del Museo Egiziano testè fondato a Torino grazie all'acquisto da parte del re Carlo Felice delle collezioni di Bernardo Drovetti, ma in questo campo la sua notorietà ebbe breve durata essendosi egli opposto, con scarsi argomenti e minore fortuna, a un avversario della forza di uno Champollion-le-Jeune. La sua grande passione era da molti anni la storia dell'architettura medioevale e il concorso bresciano fu per lui la occasione di portare a compimento un progetto che da anni aveva in mente, quello di un *trattatello* sulla architettura dei bassi tempi, per cui già nel 1819 scriveva di aver "messo insieme tutti i materiali".[6] Un "dilettante" settecentesco insomma il Cordero, legato

alla generazione del Lanzi e del d'Agincourt, e ce ne fa fede il ritrattino con cui si conclude un suo necrologio: "compito e socievole gentiluomo, prestante della persona, lento e lungo nel conversare, quasi sempre alludendo ai suoi studi. Modesto di carattere e di costumi; parco con sè, liberale con i bisognosi, non avareggiava che col tempo e per isgomentare gli oziosi e gli importuni aveva fatto scrivere sull'uscio del suo quartiere: Si ter pulsanti tibi non aperitur, abito. Non sum, non possum, non placet esse domi".

Di una ventina d'anni più giovane del Cordero, Defendente Sacchi (chè a lui più che al minore cugino Giuseppe—1804-1891—si deve la impostazione delle "Antichità romantiche", era nato presso Pavia nel 1796.[7]

Discepolo devotissimo e amico di Gian Domenico Romagnosi, si occupò dapprima di filosofia classica, ma le sue curiosità inclinarono poi verso la storia e specialmente verso la storia dell'arte. Scrittore assai fecondo, saggista, annotatore, recensore, polemista collaborò a diverse riviste, principalmente agli *Annali Universali di Statistica*, alla *Gazzetta privilegiata di Milano*, all'*Album*, al *Cosmorama pittorico*, ecc., scrisse anche romanzi. Un abisso insomma divide i due personaggi; lento, dotto, metodico il primo, parco amministratore dei propri scritti che voleva pubblicati su atti e su memorie di accademie e di società erudite, ferace poligrafo, turbinoso divulgatore, pubblicista, collaboratore dei fogli più diffusi e discussi l'altro. Inoltre se il Cordero era arrivato alla storia dell'architettura dalla numismatica, il Sacchi ci era arrivato dagli studi di filosofia, il che spiega il diverso punto di partenza nella "lettura" delle opere; se l'uno analizzava minutamente i monumenti, applicando, con buoni risultati come si vedrà, il metodo di esame stilistico del d'Agincourt,[8] fondando sui risultati di questa indagine la loro sistemazione cronologica, l'altro tenta un esame iconologico e iconografico, cerca di stabilire il significato liturgico degli edifici, di metterli in rapporto con determinate forme di pensiero, con specifici assetti culturali.

Sul metodo usato dal Sacchi verso una lettura più "concettuale" che formale qualche lume viene fin dal motto prescelto a contrassegnare il lavoro:

> "... In testimonio ai vivi
> Il ver legge Polinnia entro le scritte
> Cifre, dal tempo ancorchè infrante e guaste".

con titolo più moderno denominare "romantico", e tali le antichità che vi appartengono; perchè come fra le altre cose v'ebbe pure in que' tempi una lingua di mezzo che stette fra la latina corrotta e l'italiana che risorse, ed era il dialetto romano degenerato, o la lingua romangia, o come per vezzo l'appellano taluni romantica, quindi credemmo si potessero così denominare anche le storiche indagini intorno a tal epoca, massime che tal nome fu adoperato allo stesso oggetto in Francia e in Inghilterra, per denotare le antichità della Normandia e della Scozia dei secoli di mezzo" (Antichità romantiche, 1°, p. 6).

5. Sul Cordero vedasi particolarmente A. Bertacchi, "Storia dell'Accademia lucchese" in "Memorie e documenti per servire alla storia di Lucca", Tomo XIII, p. 1, Lucca, 1881, pp. CXXII-CLI e S. Samek-Lodovici, "Storici e teorici e critici delle arti figurative". "Enciclopedia Biografica e Bibliografica Italiana", serie VI, Roma, 1942, pp. 113-14.

6. A. Bertacchi, "Storia dell'Accademia lucchese", cit. p. CXXXIV.

7. Su D. Sacchi vedasi l'articolo di G. Chiappa sulla "Biografia degli Italiani illustri", del De Tipaldo, vol. IX, pp. 337-42.

8. Nella nota 2 a p. 47 di "Dell'Italiana Architettura durante la dominazione Longobarda. Ragionamento del cav. Giulio Cordero", Brescia, 1829, si cita il giudizio del d'Agincourt: "Le style de l'architecture est le moyen le plus sûr de juger de l'époque des monumens". (d'Agincourt, "Histoire", cit. vol. I, Paris, 1833. Parte II, "Architecture", p. 15.)

Questo metodo era quello illustrato dal Romagnosi in un articolo apparso nel 1827 sul volume XXVII° della *Antologia Italiana* di Firenze, dal titolo "Discorso sulle ricerche da instituirsi intorno la scienza simbolica degli antichi e dei sussidi necessari per intraprenderle". L'interesse del Romagnosi verso i problemi della espressione simbolica rientrava nella sua vastissima curiosità per l' etnologia, era un punto del suo grande disegno di ridurre a unità il corso vario della antica storia umana, si inquadrava nella sua "Dottrina della Umanità" in cui intendeva comprendere tutti gli scritti "riguardanti l'Archeologia, le diverse relazioni dei costumi, della coltura e della posizione dei diversi popoli".

All'inizio del suo "Discorso" il Romagnosi, compiacendosi dello sviluppo e del progresso delle ricerche storiche in tempi di cui altri scorgevano solo l'aspetto "stazionario e finanche retrogrado" lamentava che "incominciando dalla metà del passato secolo e venendo ai giorni nostri due maniere hanno dirò così predominato la mente degli archeologi". Da un lato "un misticismo astronomico assorbente e forzato", dall'altro "un misticismo psicologico trascendentale il quale a furia dei nomi di naturalismo, di dualismo, di panteismo, di individualismo... tenta di sciferare la filosofia ed i monumenti antichi". L'attacco del Romagnosi sembra dunque muovere verso quell'astrocentrismo settecentesco che culmina ne "L'origine de toutes les cultures ou la réligion universelle" di C. F. Dupuis (1794) da un lato, e dall'altro verso l'idealismo tedesco e verso Schelling e i suoi seguaci in particolare. Autentico metodo archeologico sarebbe stato quello in grado di intendere compiutamente il linguaggio degli antichi monumenti chiarendone le origini e i significati simbolici.[9] Perciò il Romagnosi si preoccupava innanzitutto di definire, rifacendosi al Condillac, segno e simbolo, per avvertire quindi che i segni "ermetici o enigmatici" potevano venire espressi "con monumenti mitici sia dipinti sia scolpiti, sia costruiti a modo di edificio" e tentare infine una distinzione tra "scienza" ed "erudizione" simbolica che prelude in certo modo a quella celebre del Panofsky tra iconografia e iconologia: "Benchè questa (l'erudizione simbolica) non possa andare disgiunta da quella (la scienza simbolica) come i fatti materiali e positivi non possono essere scompagnati dalle teorie, ciò non ostante io voglio indicare che la mira da me proposta si è di considerare i fatti dell'erudizione come altrettanti fenomeni dei quali vogliamo scoprire le cause naturali, sia per la loro originaria creazione, sia

per le loro variate modificazioni, sia finalmente per il successivo loro andamento". Nella seconda parte, dedicata ai "sussidi per bene interpretare le suddette ricerche" premessa una distinzione tra "simbolica naturale o volgare", e "simbolica artificiale e riservata" si definivano le forme della seconda come quelle "dettate da un tipo razionale e dirò così studiate; come sono quelle derivate dall'aritmetica e dalla geometria" e che, "suggerite da certe figure geometriche, le quali all'indigrosso si potevano assomigliare ad esseri viventi e specialmente all'uomo, e racchiuderne le grandi proporzioni esterne, furono assunte come leggi della divina economia sulla natura vivente e sull'uomo in particolare". Queste forme—secondo il Romagnosi— non potevano essere nate contemporaneamente e per caso in diverse società ma dovevano avere avuto una origine comune: "non si possono presumere che positivamente comunicate dagli inventori e propagate da popolo a popolo"—Per chiarire i significati di questa "simbolica artifiziale e riservata" occorreva delucidare non soltanto le caratteristiche analogiche e allusive delle forme, non solo il loro significato aritmetico-geometrico, ma valersi altresì nel modo più largo della storia naturale e culturale del paese e del tempo in cui il simbolo era stato creato: "una statistica pertanto positiva ed accertata, dirò così, del dato popolo, del quale si vogliono spiegare i simboli, venir deve in sussidio di colui che brama di addurre spiegazioni soddisfacenti di simboli degli antichi". E la cosa potrebbe apparire impossibile per la mancanza di testimonianze scritte per lunghi periodi e per interi popoli, o perchè laddove delle storie esistono, in esse "si teneva come regola non di descrivere lo stato dei popoli, ma solamente di tener conto della successione dei regnanti, e di ricordare qualche strepitosa impresa di personaggi"; tuttavia "la tenacità e la costanza di mantenere nelle forme e nelle pratiche religiose gli usi e lo stile introdotto" permettono di risalire con fiducia "dallo stato moderno... in ordine retrogrado, all'antico tutte le volte che non si frappongano quelle strepitose riforme le quali bandiscono gli usi e le opinioni precedenti".

Per arrivare alla completa decifrazione del linguaggio simbolico occorreva infine una "chiave maestra", "indispensabile a sciferare gli enigmi che ci furono trasmessi". A questo punto il discorso del Romagnosi fa ricorso a una sorta di neo-pitagorismo: "Ora per possedere questa chiave, questo alfabeto e questo dizionario che cosa si esige? Conoscere e possedere quella che noi chiamiamo scienza pitagorica e che pochi secoli fa appellavasi aritmetica formale".

Risulterà chiaro pure da questo succinto esame quanto la problematica del Romagnosi risenta di quell'interesse entusiastico che aveva spinto eruditi e filosofi del Settecento alla ricerca di una spiegazione unitaria

---

9. Cfr. F. Venturi, "L'Antichità svelata e l'idea di progresso in N. A. Boulanger", Bari, 1947, A. Momigliano, "Ancient History and the Antiquarians", in *Journal of the Warburg and Courtauld Institutes*, XIII, 1950, pp. 285 segg.

e simbolica dell'antichità[10] e aveva avuto uno dei suoi prodotti più caratteristici nei nove volumi del "Monde Primitif", di Antoine Court de Gébelin.[11] In questa opera, per tanti versi singolare, si trova fin dalle prime pagine propugnata la necessità di una dottrina atta a spiegare i simboli e le allegorie dell'antichità, in quanto "l'Allégorie donna le ton à l'antiquité entière... elle présida à ses Symboles... tout porta son empreinte: ce fut en quelque sort l'unique language de l'antiquité primitive. C'est celui de tous les anciens peuples dont il nous reste quelque monumens: celui des Celtes, des Scythes des Etrusques, des Phéniciens, des Indiens, des Chinois, des Chaldéens...". Una volta che di essa si sia perduto il senso riposto "les Monumens que l'on nous en a trasmis et qui ont échapé aux ravages du tems, dénués de tout ce qui y mettoit du sens, et qui en faisoit la beauté, nous paraissent ou des fables absurdes et fastidieuses, ou des récits d'histoires incroyables, et de faits qui ne purent jamais avoir lieu...", una volta dimenticato il suo alfabeto "les monumens allégoriques sont totalement perdus pour nous: car ne pouvant nous élever au sens le plus sublime qu'ils renferment, ils sont morts en quelque façon pour nous, ils sont sans âme, sans beauté, sans force, sans intérêt...".

Le esigenze che furono proprie al Court de Gébelin e a tanti altri ingegni del Settecento, l'aspirazione a trovare una "chiave", un modo unitario di interpretazione per intendere le testimonianze del passato, si fondono, nell'opera del Romagnosi, con una sorta di neo-pitagorismo, di "furor mathematicus" non privo di qualche punta di esoterismo, che aveva qualcosa in comune con quello del polacco Wronsky, la cui metafisica aritmetica aveva pur suscitato l'aspra polemica del Romagnosi.[12]

L'articolo del Romagnosi rappresenta insomma la sintesi da un lato delle sue larghissime curiosità per la storia degli antichi popoli, dall'altra dei suoi profondi interessi matematici, già espressi nel suo "Dello insegnamento primitivo delle matematiche", scritto in carcere nel '21 e pubblicato a Milano nel '22. Punto fondamentale di quest'opera è la critica del metodo analitico nella matematica e il tentativo di ritornare, su una base geometrica, ai metodi sintetici dell'antichità. Si postula in essa la necessità di un ritorno ai metodi di calcolo "primitivi e naturali". "Universalità di una stessa legge segreta che presiede al calcolo", si intitola uno dei suoi paragrafi.[13] Lo stesso linguaggio e in parte gli stessi problemi che si ritrovano nell'articolo del '27. A più riprese il Romagnosi tornerà su queste questioni che lo assillano: "In questo secolo—scrive nella recensione al volume sulla Astronomia solare di Ipparco di J. B. P. Marcoz[14]—nel quale si vanno rivilicando le origini coll'affrontare la folta ed immensa caligine della vetustà e col sorpassare le rovine del tempo, sarebbe certamente prezzo dell'opera, lo strappare il segreto dell'asiatico algoritmo, il quale per la culta Europa diverrebbe un'acquisizione di valore inestimabile, onde anche scifferare una folla di enigmi e di allegorie che avvolgono nella oscurità e nel mistero tanti antichi monumenti, tante leggende e dottrine ascose, frutto della antica sapienza e fondamento di tanti ulteriori progressi dello spirito umano". Quanto all'applicazione alla "simbolica cristiana" e di converso ai monumenti medioevali del metodo proposto per lo studio dell'antichità, uno spunto se ne trova già nelle "Osservazioni su la Scienza Nuova di Vico" pubblicate dal Romagnosi su *L'Ape Italiana* del 1822;[15] si accenna qui a questa "disciplina dell'arcano... per la quale disciplina le vere idee delle cose parte si tacevano e parte non si rivelavano che involte dal velo dell'allegoria.... Questo allegorismo nasceva spontaneamente dal modo stesso col quale si generava la scienza... così... nasceva un linguaggio simbolico e quindi un tessuto veramente allegorico generato dal modo stesso di ricavare la dottrina. Fu poi detto che la scienza fu in primo essenzialmente simbolica; e ciò... consta pure da tutti i monumenti religiosi di tutte le nazioni incivilite o che l'hanno avuto da altre anteriori. Ciò consta perfino anche presso i Cristiani, come si verde dall'opera attribuita a San Dionigi l'Areopagita, e da quelle di San Ireneo e dalla storia medesima delle prime eresie. I monumenti stessi cristiani, anteriori al secolo XVI, ne offrono ancora le tracce nelle nostre chiese e perfino nelle facciate."

Fu questa per i Sacchi la pietra angolare su cui imbastire la loro costruzione.

10. A. Court de Gébelin: "Le Monde Primitif analysé et comparé avec le monde moderne; consideré dans son génie allégorique et dans les allégories auxquelles conduisit ce génie". Paris, 1773–1781, Cfr. F. Venturi, *op. cit.*

11. J. M. Wronsky, "Introduction à la philosophie des mathematiques et tecnique de l'algorithme", Paris, 1811; G. D. Romagnosi, "Dell'Insegnamento primitivo delle matematiche", Milano, 1822. Su Romagnosi matematico cfr. F. Tonelli: "G. D. Romagnosi e la matematica", in *Annuario del Liceo Romagnosi di Parma*, 1926–7, Parma, 1927.

12. G. D. Romagnosi, "Dell'insegnamento ecc.", cit. ed. delle opere complete a cura di A. De Giorgi, vol. I, parte II, p. 1181, paragr. 69, Milano, 1841.

13. Pubblicata nel volume XIX degli *Annali Universali di Statistica*, pp. 95–108, vedi in particolare pp. 105–6; ripubblicata in G. D. Romagnosi, "Dottrina dell'Umanità", 2 ed., Prato, 1836, pp. 98 segg.

14. *L'Ape Italiana*, 1822, I, pp. 81 segg., II, pp. 3 segg. Pubblicate poi in "Scritti scelti o rari di G. D. Romagnosi", Pavia, Bizzoni, 1826, pp. 37 segg. e successivamente nella edizione delle opere complete di G. D. Romagnosi a cura di A. De Giorgi, vol. III, parte I, Milano, 1844, pp. 297 segg.

15. Cfr. F. D. Romagnosi, "Dottrina dell'Umanità", II ed., Prato, 1836, pp. 77 segg.

Rispondeva essa alle premesse metodologiche del Romagnosi? Apparentemente si, se questi in un articolo apparso sul 18° volume (pp. 95–97) degli *Annali Universali di Statistica*[16] ne riferiva come di "un lavoro che a parere nostro può servire di modello ad opere di questo genere" e ne lodava il metodo sostenendo che "alto, nuovo, e di universale influenza fu il criterio onde giudicare della architettura sacra... tratto dai tipi della simbolica cristiana, impiegata... fino da principio nelle basiliche e ne'battisteri".

In realtà la teoria del Romagnosi era del tutto inadatta a fungere da pietra angolare per qualsiasi costruzione, e ciò in primo luogo perchè non era che un'ipotesi appena abbozzata, una proposta di lavoro. Di questa famosa "chiave maestra" atta ad esplicare i più diversi linguaggi figurativi il filosofo parmense non era ovviamente in possesso: finora si era limitato ad auspicarne la ricerca e ad indicare le direzioni in cui tale ricerca doveva essere condotta. Ora nell'opera dei Sacchi gli spunti romagnosiani non vengono approfonditi o discussi, ma solo enunciati come postulati di validità universale per comprendere ogni edificio religioso: "Dai misteriosi sacrarj elevati nelle regioni abitate dagli Hindus a'magnifici templi dell'antica Grecia... alle rustiche incavature praticate negli alpestri massi delle isole dell'Occidente".

I capitoli iniziali delle "Antichità Romantiche" sono i più importanti per intendere l'impostazione dell'opera; il primo contiene una sommaria trattazione sullo stato dell'architettura sacra in Italia prima dell'arrivo dei Longobardi, vanno in questo periodo riconosciute, secondo gli autori, le origini della nuova architettura, in quanto "al propagarsi della nuova e vera rigenerazione religiosa, sentissi forte il bisogno di staccarsi affatto dalle sozze pratiche gentilesche, persino nell'edificazione delle case consacrate all'adorazione, e fu quindi all'uopo trascelto un nuovo marchio architettonico tratto dai dettati della simbolica cristiana"; l'espressione "un nuovo marchio architettonico" indicando, evidentemente, l'emergere di un nuovo stile. Nel secondo capitolo gli autori danno un lungo elenco ragionato delle costruzioni che ritengono spettare all'età longobarda; il terzo è dedicato alle caratteristiche architettoniche degli edifici, alle piante, alle elevazioni, alle sezioni, alla distribuzione esterna delle masse ecc., mentre il quarto, come si avverte sin dal titolo, "Della simbolica cristiana applicata all'architettura delle chiese e loro decorazione", dovrebbe rappresentare il nucleo del discorso. Tuttavia proprio in questo capitolo si trova un brano che bene scopre l'approssimativa ingenuità del metodo seguito, ed è quel paragrafo che, dati gli assunti, avrebbe dovuto costituire il pilastro maestro di tutta l'opera, quello cioè dedicato alla

"Simbolica cristiana ermetica", che "reggeva la struttura e la configurazione delle piante ne'sacri edifici". Dopo una trattazione quanto mei esile esso si conclude in questo modo: "... oltre non ci estenderemo su tale materia che per noi fu ora solo accennata, occorrendo alla sua completa soluzione uno infaticabile studio in quella scienza numerica e geometrica ad un tempo, della quale quanto prima un sommo italiano ha divisato sciferarne i più intricati problemi." E in nota: "Egli è questi Gian Domenico Romagnosi. Il discorso che venne da lui pubblicato nell'anno 1827 nell'*Antologia di Firenze*... ha porto i primi cardini di criterio logico onde dar nuove basi assegnate a questa materia di studi, senza di cui il ramo più rilevante dell'archeologia non avrebbe scintille di vita. Noi quindi ci attenemmo alle classificazioni generali tracciate in quella preziosissima dissertazione: ma per quanto toccava la simbolica ermetica, ci sentimmo immaturi di addentrarci ne'suoi più riposti penetrali, onde poter esporla in un diffuso trattato. Lo stesso rigeneratore però di tale scienza, che noi veneriamo qual maestro e padre, si piacque, non ha guari, impartircene le prime nozioni, e noi andiamo lieti di poter annunciare che sotto la sua direzione ci darem cura di chiarire quanto prima anche quest'ardua parte dell'antica sapienza per ciò che concerne l'architettura cristiana...."

L'applicazione del nuovo metodo vien dunque rimandata a una prossima occasione (che però non si presenterà) e per questa volta rimane allo stato di intenzione. Ove si abbandoni la difficile ricerca dell' "algoritmo" la novità della dottrina Romagnosi-Sacchi consisteva soprattutto nel definir "simbolica" l'architettura dell'alto medio-evo, facendo di questo aggettivo addirittura l'elemento distintivo di una stile, il quale stile, "Introdotto una volta... e venerato come augusto e solutore perchè rappresentava i misteri e le speranze dei fedeli... recava seco il principio della sua conservazione anche nelle età consecutive; talchè non poteva soffrire

---

16. Sempre seguendo il d'Agincourt, e verisimilmente basandosi sulle sole sue illustrazioni e senza una diretta conoscenza dei monumenti, i Sacchi discutono tra l'altro due chiesette lombarde: Santa Giulia di Bonate di Sotto e la rotonda di San Tommaso in Limine in Almenno San Salvatore, accettando per la prima un'origine longobarda e proponendo per la seconda una datazione addirittura anteriore. I due edifici sono peraltro ambedue romanici e la loro notorietà, sugli inizi dell'Ottocento (il d'Agincourt accanto a San Michele di Pavia cita solo questi due esempi a illustrare l'architettura longobarda) è dovuta alla pubblicazione (Bergamo, 1784) del "Codex diplomaticus civitatis et ecclesiae bergomatis" di Mario Lupo che ne dava ottime incisioni. Cfr. anche F. Osten, "Die Bauwerke in der Lombardei...", Darmstadt, S. D., ma 1846–1847, tav. XLI–XLVI e F. De Dartein, "Etude sur l'architecture lombarde", Paris, 1865–82, II, p. 305.

altro deterioramento che quello che nell'esecuzione dell'arte derivò dalla forza invincibile dell'asiatica dominazione. E siccome dai conquistatori fu bel bello adottata la religione dei vinti, così, con lo scorrere degli anni, lungi dallo scemare fu vieppiù affrancata la conservazione dell'antica architettura".

Romagnosi e Sacchi accentuano dunque l'aspetto conservatore dello "stile simbolico", i cui caratteri d'altronde sono definiti in modo così vago che possono essere applicati senza urto a edifici dei secoli più diversi. Vengono enumerati infatti come esempi di architettura simbolica dell'età longobarda edifici quali Santa Maria Maggiore di Bergamo, San Michele di Pavia (sulla scia del d'Agincourt), la Rotonda o Duomo Vecchio di Brescia, San Pietro di Civate, la cattedrale di Verona ecc.[16] I criteri di questa sistemazione sono assai spicci; basta una testimonianza anche incerta sulla data di fondazione, e il riscontrare che l'edificio per qualche suo carattere possa essere annoverato tra gli esempi della cosidetta "architettura simbolica", termine questo in egual misura applicabile alla architettura paleocristiana, bizantina, preromanica e romanica. In assenza di un attento esame formale nonchè di un'analisi iconografica meno generica la dottrina dell'architettura simbolica si rivela quindi inutilizzabile ai fini di una attendibile ricostruzione storica.

Arnaldo Momigliano ha opportunamente segnalato, a proposito degli antiquari settecenteschi che si proponevano di spiegare la storia antica attraverso la esplicazione delle allegorie e dei simboli, quale divario si presentasse tra la complessità dei problemi che essi si ponevano e le loro assai scarne conoscenze dei dati archeologici.[17] Il fatto che questa osservazione possa applicarsi in modo tanto calzante alla dottrina archeologica del Romagnosi e dei Sacchi ne sottolinea l'aspetto settecentesco che curiosamente si fonde alla più antica tradizione della antiquaria cattolica di un Bosio, di un Severano, o di un Ciampini.[18] Chiari dunque i limiti del libro dei Sacchi che tuttavia non manca di interesse per quel suo appassionato rivendicare l'importanza del "contenuto" nella storia della architettura medioevale. Di ben maggior rigore scientifico, di più moderno impianto, di più serrata e logica costruzione è il saggio del Cordero, che i giudici di Brescia prescelsero.

L'opera del patrizio piemontese è genialmente congegnata. Tutta la prima parte, che rappresenta circa

due terzi dell'insieme, è centrata sulla datazione della chiesa di San Michele a Pavia che il d'Agincourt— come faranno poi i Sacchi—aveva considerato "come il miglior modello di quella qualità d'architettura che incominciò a introdursi in Italia nel sesto secolo e generale vi divenne nel secolo settimo e nell'ottavo". La dimostrazione impeccabile è condotta per più vie che vengono infine a convergere, affrontata in primo luogo da un punto di vista storico—documentario, "perciocchè il voler affermare che una chiesa od altro edificio qualunque, appartenga veramente ad una determinata età per la sola ragione che in quella età appunto, comecchè remotissima, era una chiesa nella medesima città intitolata del medesimo nome, ella è questa una maniera troppo fallace di ragionare"—si stringe e diviene incalzante quando si affrontano i temi stilistici. Qui l'argomentazione è ricchissima e involge, onde permettere un confronto tra i caratteri della chiesa pavese e quelli propri ad un determinato momento stilistico, una personale e suggestiva ricostruzione della storia dell'architettura medioevale. Due radici vengono poste a questa: da un lato la tradizione romana, dall'altro il nuovo stile bizantino, caratterizzato da una maggiore abbondanza di apporti orientali. Una serrata dialettica si instaura tra questi due elementi, una dialettica che continua ad agire per tutto il corso del medioevo, ravvivata sempre da nuove influenze, tra le quali non secondaria per il Cordero quella araba. L'architettura islamica, derivata dapprima da quella bizantina, si modifica quindi a sua volta dopo il XII secolo per apporti indiani e dell'Oriente più lontano. L'arco pressochè intero dell'architettura medioevale è chiamato dal Cordero con il nome di "gotico", con questo termine egli abbraccia l'architettura di circa sette secoli, dalla fine dell'ottavo a quella del quattordicesimo e alla "restaurazione della antica architettura greca".

"Gotico" chiama dunque il Cordero il periodo più originale dell'architettura europea dell'età di mezzo, e il "gotico" egli fa iniziare dalla restaurazione carolingia, perchè precedentemente non scorge nell'architettura occidentale caratteri francamente innovatori rispetto a quella romana e bizantina. All'interno di questo termine vengono distinti un "gotico anteriore" —o "antico"—(dalla fine dell'ottavo a quella del dodicesimo secolo), e uno "posteriore"—o "moderno" —(dalla fine del dodicesimo a quella del quattordicesimo secolo), il "gotico posteriore" coincidendo dunque con il nostro "gotico". Il "gotico anteriore" è diviso a sua volta in due periodi, detti del primo (ottavo-decimo secolo) e del secondo stile (fine decimo-fine dodicesimo). Il "primo stile" del "gotico anteriore" comprende l'età carolingia e quella post-carolingia, mentre il "secondo stile" coincide con il

17. A. Momigliano, "Ancient History and the Antiquarians", cit. p. 310.
18. Cfr. R. Krautheimer, "Introduction to an Iconography of Medieval Architecture". In *Journal of the Warburg and Courtauld Institutes*, v, 1942, 1 ss. G. Previtali, "La fortuna dei Primitivi", Torino, 1964.

romanico. La terminologia del Cordero può essere macchinosa e poco elegante, ma ciò non toglie che le sue partizioni cronologiche si giustifichino perfettamente. All'interno di queste partizioni singoli monumenti particolarmente significativi vengono analizzati con esemplare rigore (si veda a pp. 73–88 il caso della cappella palatina di Aquisgrana), mentre vengono messe a frutto le ampie conoscenze che l'autore, attraverso numerosi viaggi ed ampie letture aveva acquistato dei monumenti medioevali europei.[19]

Questo rapido disegno è condotto con un piglio schivo ma personale e con una tale potenza di persuasione da suggestionare profondamente il lettore. "Imaginez—scriveva nel 1874 Adolphe Thiers a Federico Sclopis—que dans ma jeunesse après avoir déjà bien voyagé et vu beaucoup de monuments chrétiens du IIIème au Xème siècle et ne trouvant rien d'exact, de raisonnable dans ce que je lisais dans les écrivains français ou italiens, je tombais sur un écrit de 200 à 300 pages da M. de San Quintino sur Saint Michel da Pavie, je fu saisi de lumière".

In effetti un'altra lettera del Thiers, scritta da Como il 24 settembre 1838 al visconte de Grouchy, segretario dell'ambasciata francese a Torino, fornisce una testimonianza diretta di questo "saisissement": "je viens de lire avec une attention particulière l'ouvrage de Monsieur San-Quintino, et en outre ceux qu'ont concouru avec le sien à l'Athénée de Brescia. Non seulement Monsieur San-Quintino est supérieur aux autres, mais il peut être considéré comme auteur du meilleur ouvrage qu'on ait écrit sur l'architecture du Moyen Age. Il a démontré parfaitement que jusqu'au dizième siècle, à peu près, l'architecture des anciennes basiliques de Constantin avait dominée seule, quel les lombards n'avaient rien fait; qu'en neuf cent, ou mille, une architecture nouvelle, qu'il appelle "gotico anteriore" avait pris naissance . . . Je suis l'appréciateur le plus sincère de son ouvrage. On n'a rien fait de comparable, on n'a surtout pas encore écrit d'une manière, plus compétante et moins pédantesque tout à la fois sur ce sujet, qui est fort grave, plus grave qu'on ne le croit pour l'histoire. Il y a bien longtemps que je l'étudie, j'ai beaucoup lu et beaucoup vu, et je crois que je puis donner à Monsieur San-Quintino un suffrage éclairé".[20]

Uno dei punti di maggior interesse del "Ragionamento" del Cordero riguarda la Normandia; egli avverte (p. 138) come "si andò preparando presso i Normanni, prima forse che per tutto altrove, il passaggio dall'antico al moderno stile del gotico"— il passaggio, in altri termini, dal sistema costruttivo romanico a quello gotico—e come presso i Normanni sorgesse "quel nuovo sistema di costruzioni leggiero e gigantesco ad un tempo, debole in apparenza ma in realtà robustissimo, avente per norma nelle sue opere la figura piramidale, il triangolo equilatero e l'arco acuto, . . . al quale sistema fu data dagli oltramontani la denominazione impropria di "gottica architettura" (p. 56). Se riconosce l'importanza delle esperienze normanne per l'elaborazione della architettura gotica il Cordero mette altresì in rilievo il valore fondamentale che per la Normandia ebbero i contatti con la Lombardia, specialmente attraverso l'abate-costruttore Guglielmo da Volpiano, e ciò gli valse di essere acclamato membro della Société des Antiquaires de Normandie, retta allora da Arcisse de Caumont, il fondatore della archeologia medioevale francese, per aver mostrato: "que c'est aux abbées, aux prélats, à la colonie des savants que la Lombardie nous a fourni au XI siècle, que nous devons probablement la résurrection de l'architecture ecclésiastique, aussi bien que de toutes les autres branches alors cultivées du savoir et de l'industrie humaine" e per aver introdotto "le flambeau de la critique dans l'étude de nos vieux monuments".[21]

Tutte le analisi, storico-documentaria, stilistica, paleografica vengono a confermare che la chiesa pavese di San Michele, nella sua ultima forma, non poteva risalire all'età longobarda, ma si collocava invece "nè prima della metà del secolo del mille, nè dopo la metà del duodecimo nel "secondo stile" del "gotico anteriore". L'espunzione di San Michele di Pavia dal catalogo delle costruzioni di età longobarda ebbe come conseguenza tutta una serie di rettifiche cronologiche

19. La bibliografia del Cordero comprende le "Ruins of Spalatro" dello Adam, le "Antiquities of India" del Daniell, i "Monumens anciens et modernes de l'Hindoustan" del Langles, la grande "Description de l'Egypte" degli accademici francesi, il "Voyage en Levant" del De Forbin, la "Histoire et description de la Cathédrale de Cologne" del Boisserée, la Storia della architettura del Wiebekind, la monografia del Britten sulla cattedrale di Winchester, il saggio sulle chiese sassoni del Bentham, le "Architectural antiquities of Normandy" del Cotman, e gli scritti degli eruditi normanni da Arcisse de Caumont a Gérville, da Le Prevost a Deshayes.

20. La lettera del Thiers allo Sclopis fu da questi resa nota nella commemorazione del Thiers tenuta all'accademia delle Scienze di Torino il 9 Dicembre 1877 (pubblicata negli *Atti della R. Accademia delle Scienze di Torino*, XIII, pp. 210–11; quella al de Grouchy fu pubblicata dall'Odorici, "Antichità cristiane di Brescia", Brescia, 1845, p. 42, nota 209.
Lo studio del Cordero fu introdotto in Francia da una lunga recensione di L. Vitet, che sulla *Revue Française* del 1830 (n. 16, luglio, pp. 151–73) analizzò partitamente il "Ragionamento" dello studioso piemontese e le "Antichità romantiche" dei Sacchi, schierandosi incondizionatamente con il Cordero. Il testo venne poi ripubblicato dal Vitet nei suoi "Etudes sur l'Histoire de l'art" (Paris, 1866, II, pp. 291–315).

21. Cfr. la lettera del 27 febbraio 1830 del Cordero al Marchese Cesare Lucchesini, pubblicata in A. Bertacchi, *op. cit.*, p. CXXXV, nota 2.

che rivoluzionarono la storia dell'architettura alto-medioevale.

Malgrado la rigorosa potatura effettuata nell'orto fin ad allora incolto della cosidetta architettura longobarda il Cordero vi lasciò vegetare ancora più di un elemento estraneo, le chiese di San Michele e di San Frediano a Lucca[22] per esempio, o le Porte Palatine di Torino. Tuttavia l'importanza storica del "ragionamento" "sull'italiana architettura durante la dominazione longobarda" non può essere sottovalutata come ben vide sul finire dell'Ottocento, Raffaele Cattaneo, che, nella prefazione a un fondamentale studio sui monumenti preromanici, ebbe a scrivere "... fra tutti quegli scrittori però ve ne ha uno al quale gli eruditi devono assai più che agli altri, perchè fu il primo che incominciasse ad abbattere le pregiudicate opinioni che si erano fatte strada circa la storia dei monumenti dell'età longobardica. Come è noto prima che il conte Cordero di San Quintino desse alla luce il suo interessante studio sull'architettura italiana durante la dominazione dei longobardi, grandi errori correvano fra gli archeologi e i cultori della storia dell'arte intorno alle origini dell'architettura lombarda e romanica e al periodo di tempo in cui questa tenne il campo".[23]

Se l'opera del Cordero fu accolta con vivo interesse al suo apparire, non solo in Italia e in Francia, ma anche in Germania,[24] essa incorse tuttavia immediatamente nei fulmini del Romagnosi e dei Sacchi.

Recensendo nel 1828 l'opera dei Sacchi, apparsa poco prima della pubblicazione del "Ragionamento" del Cordero sui *Commentari dell'Ateneo di Brescia*, il Romagnosi stesso dà un ambiguo avvio alla polemica: "Il pubblico intelligente—scriveva a chiusura del suo articolo—dopo la lettura del lavoro degno di menzione onorevole diverrà certamente ansioso di conoscere la mozione coronata. Se cotanto esimio è il merito dello scritto giudicato sol degno di mezione onorevole, sommo ed eminentemente sommo esser dovrà il merito dell'opera coronata. L'Italia potrà essere grata verso il Bresciano Ateneo per aver dato occasione a lavori sì eccellenti in un ramo di studj da tanti anni trascurato, e che serve ad illustrare le memorie, contuttochè in-

fauste, pur sempre conservatrici delle tracce della Italiana civiltà. La repubblica letteraria poi tributerà all'accademico consesso quella considerazione che egli si sarà meritata col suo giudizio".[25] Il peggio deve ancora sopraggiungere, il volume dei "Commentari" è appena uscito che Gaetano Sacchi cerca di liquidare speditamente il Cordero nel corso di una recensione alla Storia di Como di Cesare Cantù, esaltando il metodo delle ricerche simboliche (". . . In un' epoca in cui tutto si esamina, tutto si dicifra, questo fervore di indagini merita una particolare attenzione. Mentre Champollion, Younk e Rosellini ne dispiegano le arcane cifre degli Egizi noi vorremmo che altri dotti ne disvelassero quelle che gli stessi nostri padri ne sculsero su i monumenti di quel culto che tuttora ne regge le mistiche speranze della vita") e ridicolizzando le partizioni cronologiche e stilistiche del Cordero ("le nuove illustrazioni . . . proveranno . . . abbastanza come l'architettura cristiana usata da'primi secoli dell'era volgare sino al mille, non sia stata punto una degenerazione del greco e del romano stile, degenerazione qualificata da un poveretto coi nomi veramente barbarici di gusto gotico anteriore e posteriore del primo e secondo stile con qualche carattere bizantino e persino indostanico e mussulmanico, ma sibbene una architettura di un genere tutto suo particolare, la quale con un nome forse più proprio di quello per noi già usato dovrebbe dirsi *architettura rituale*").[26] La polemica verte principalmente su di un punto: la architettura europea dell'alto medioevo deriva originariamente da quella classica e attraversa varie fasi stilistiche con caratteri distinti, oppure è un fenomeno del tutto nuovo da giudicare nel suo insieme come un autentico blocco storico, senza partizione cronologico-stilistica alcuna, sotto la nuova etichetta di architettura simbolica (o rituale)?[27]

Sulla *Minerva Ticinese* del '30 è Defendente Sacchi che emula il cugino nell'asprezza della critica; seguono quasi due anni di requie, quindi l'attacco si ripete, e questa volta si estende su ben trentun facciate degli *Annali Universali di Statistica*, prendendo lo spunto da un libro di storia pavese di Giuseppe

---

22. La datazione di San Frediano al XII secolo spetta a Michele Ridolfi che la sostenne nel 1853 all'Accademia Lucchese, dopo gli scavi praticati a partire dal 1840. Cfr. F. de Dartein, *op. cit.*, II, pp. 513 sgg.
23. R. Cattaneo, "L'architettura in Italia dal secolo VI al mille circa", Venezia, 1889, pp. 10–11. Anni prima il de Dartein aveva scritto: "Au comte Cordero di San Quintino revient l'honneur d'avoir le premier, en 1828, hardiment combattu ces préjugés, et posé les vrais principes de l'archéologie pour les monuments italiens du haut Moyen-Age", *op. cit.*, I, p. 91.
24. Cfr. F. Kugler in "Museum", 1834, n. 6–7, e in "Kleine Schriften und Studien zur Kunstgeschichte", Stuttgart, 1853-4, I, pp. 204 sgg.

25. *Annali Universali di Statistica*, vol. XVIII, 1828, p. 97.
26. C. Cantù, "Storia della città e della diocesi di Como", Como, 1829, recensita da G. Sacchi nel vol. XXII degli *Annali Universali di Statistica*, 1829, pp. 301–17.
27. Scrive G. D. Romagnosi sul vol. XXXI (1832) e p. 43 degli *Annali Universali di Statistica*: "Abbandonando ogni discussione locale e di particolare interesse, ripetiamo di nuovo che l'architettura dei templj cristiani eretti da' fondamenti, fu di stile interamente rituale avente caratteri così proprj e così distinti da ogni altro stile architettonico conosciuto, che non si può dire essere nè una imitazione nè una depravazione, nè del Greco, nè del Romano, nè dell'Arabico, nè dell'Indiano, ma bensì un sistema tutto suo, solidale, e ricavato da un tipo distinto, sottoposto ad una rigorosa unità".

Robolini.[28] La novità è data questa volta da un viaggio a Venezia e a Lucca intrapreso dai Sacchi che offre loro l'occasione di contestare veementemente e di nuovo l'intera ricostruzione del Cordero, in primis la datazione di San Michele di Pavia. Inoltre la datazione delle chiese lucchesi che il Cordero aveva creduto (a torto) poter far risalire all'età longobarda viene discussa con argomenti per la verità poco probanti e con un tono piuttosto minaccioso, come svela questo brano: "In seguito alla visita fatta sul luogo dai Sacchi è loro risultato: . . . che l'altra chiesa detta di San Michele in Lucca è stata intieramente ricostrutta dopo il mille, e di questo fatto esiste nel coro della chiesa medesima una lapide latina, nella quale è precisato l'anno in cui ebbe luogo questo integrale rifacimento: l'architettura del tempio così ricostrutto, appartiene alla scuola dei fratelli Pisani. I Sacchi posseggono i documenti ed i disegni ritratti sul sito che giustificano queste risultanze di fatto. Tutte le osservazioni e le deduzioni pertanto che trasse il signore di San Quintino da questi due edifici sono basate a due monumenti architettonici che non appartengono più alla epoca longobardica: cadono quindi del tutto le teorie che egli ne dedusse come unico sostegno della sua Opera". Il Cordero ingiustamente accusato di aver trascurato un elemento così essenziale quale la data fornita da una lapide si rammarica con l'amico Lucchesini degli attacchi di cui è oggetto e lo prega di intervenire a sua difesa nella polemica.[29] Finalmente scrive di persona una lettera agli *Annali Universali di Statistica*[30] in cui molto urbanamente difende le proprie tesi, si dichiara pronto a modificarle ove nuovi elementi vengano alla luce e per questo chiede ulteriori chiarimenti sul documento che i Sacchi sostenevano di

aver scoperto in San Michele di Lucca. La pubblicazione della lettera del Cordero sugli *Annali* e la mancanza di una qualsiasi risposta da parte dei Sacchi segna la fine, invero in tono minore, dell'annosa polemica sull'architettura simbolica.

Si erano affrontati in essa due metodi diversi di analisi architettonica: da una parte l'esame formale che il Cordero aveva derivato sì dal d'Agincourt e dai "connoisseurs" settecenteschi, ma che aveva impiegato con tale originalità e ricchezza di riferimenti da collocare il suo "Ragionamento" tra i primi grandi testi della critica stilistica in architettura, dall'altra la ricerca iconografica del Romagnosi e dei Sacchi appassionante ma complicata e appesantita da singolari bizzarrie, quali l'ipotizzazione dell'algoritmo universalmente risolutivo, e dalla caparbia tenacia nel postulare la unicità e la non riducibilità ad altre esperienze della "architettura simbolica". Di questi due metodi il più moderno, per l'epoca è, finalmente, il primo, ed è quello destinato ad avere maggiori sviluppi nel futuro; il secondo, impedito dalle eccessive sedimentazioni di una problematica quasi dimenticata, manda un suono più arcaico e avrà bisogno di molto tempo ancora, e di radicali trasformazioni, per divenire veramente operante. Dietro ai metodi due uomini: un patrizio piemontese conservatore, un patriota liberale lombardo. Che il metodo e la ricerca del primo siano in realtà più moderni e avanzati di quelli del secondo può trovare una spiegazione nella tradizione settecentesca dei grandi "dilettanti", nel fatto cioè che gli studi di archeologia e storia dell'arte fossero particolarmente coltivati nel settecento in determinati ambienti aristocratici, ma svela anche purtroppo una certa confusione e precipitazione culturale, fomentata anche dalla disinvoltura propria della pubblicistica, nella corrente più progressiva.

Lo scontro, nel corso del terzo e del quarto decennio dell'Ottocento, sullo sfondo di un'Italia mortificata dalla Restaurazione, tra critica formalistica e critica contenutistica, a proposito di un problema di storia della architettura medioevale, non manca di indicare suggestivamente alcune direzioni della futura ricerca.

---

28. "Nuove questioni intorno all'architettura rituale usata in Italia nei bassi tempi in relazione alle. "Notizie appartenenti alla storia della sua patria" raccolte ed illustrate da Giuseppe Robolini, gentiluomo pavese", in *Annali Universali di Statistica*, vol. XXXI, 1832, pp. 17 sgg.

29. Lettera pubblicata da A. Bertacchi, *op. cit.*, p. CXXXVI, nota.

30. "Lettera del Signor G. di San Quintino al Signor D. Sacchi intorno all'architettura rituale", in *Annali Universali di Statistica*, 1832, vol. XXXII.

EDUARD F. SEKLER

The Stoclet House by Josef Hoffmann

'Dans l'histoire de l'architecture contemporaine, dans la marche vers une esthétique contemporaine, le Prof. Hoffmann, occupe l'une des places les plus lumineuses.'

Le Corbusier 1929

'Dass das Stoclet Palais in Brüssel einen Markstein in der Geschichte der modernen Baukunst bezeichnet, steht ausser Zweifel.'[1] These emphatic words were written in 1914 by the critic A. S. Levetus about a building that had been finished in 1911. They betray an enthusiasm that was shared by others as the following incident shows. When a board meeting of the *Deutscher Werkbund* happened to coincide with an historic event, Italy's declaration of war against Turkey in 1911, all members of the board were understandably concerned with so momentous a political happening. They could not make up their minds to turn the discussion to their own regular agenda. Finally Osthaus, of Folkwang-museum fame, remarked that for members of the *Werkbund* a more important fact than the problem of Italy and Turkey had to be recorded: the Stoclet House in Brussels had just been taken over by the client—'ein Werk von solcher Reife und künstlerischer Hoheit wie kein zweites in Europa seit den Tagen des Barock . . .'[2]

More than half a century has passed since the pre-World War I days of Levetus and Osthaus—enough time to warrant a reassessment of the Stoclet House in its historic and artistic significance. Fortunately it still stands, very much as it was finished in 1911,[3] at 281 Avenue de Tervueren in the *Commune de Woluwe St. Pierre*, a suburb of Brussels.

1. 'There can be no doubt that the Stoclet Palace in Brussels represents a landmark in the history of modern architecture.' A. S. Levetus, 'Das Stoclethaus in Brüssel', *Moderne Bauformen*, XIII/1 (Jan. 1914), 1. For a shortened version of the same article in English see *The Studio*, LXI (1914), 189 ff.
2. '. . . a work of such maturity and artistic grandeur as had not originated in Europe since the days of the Baroque . . .'. The incident was related by Dr. Adolf Vetter and published by Leopold W. Rochowanski, *Ein Führer durch das österreichische Kunstgewerbe* (Vienna, 1930), however with the wrong date of 1912 for the declaration of war.
3. Some of the changes which occurred are: the original copper roof was removed during the war and has been replaced by a non-metallic covering; white glass has been used to repair some of the soffits in the entrance corridor and over the entrance to the garage courtyard; the car entrance from the avenue has been enlarged; the neighboring building on the right-hand side was pulled down and its site added to the garden which necessitated an extension of the fence along the Avenue de Tervueren.

I

When the site for the Stoclet House was selected, at a point where the Avenue de Tervueren widens into an oval as it changes both its direction and its gradient, the situation must have appeared ideal from many points of view. The piece of property was virtually at the end of the built-up area, on an avenue and promenade (Fig. 1) that had only been finished a few years earlier in 1899 and that carried a good deal of social prestige, both owing to its being a continuation of the important *Rue de la Loi* past the lavish *Palais du Cinquantenaire*, and to its imposing scale in size and planting.

With a fine view towards south and east over wooded deeper-lying areas, partly developed as landscaped parks, the Stoclet site promised the amenities of country life and a fairly undisturbed privacy without sacrificing relative proximity to the center of the city. Any design for a building on this site obviously would have had to take into account all of this but specially the fact that the site is not rectangular (see plot plan, Fig. 17) and that it follows the light slope of the Avenue which runs past it on the NE and begins to descend here towards the parks which have just been mentioned.

The earliest reference to a design for the Stoclet House was published in November 1905, by Ludwig Hevesi[4] who saw drawings and a model at the premises of the *Wiener Werkstätte*. This model and some drawings were later exhibited at Miethke's, an art gallery that had just opened its doors to *avant-garde* artists, at the Graben, Vienna.

The model does not seem to have survived, but photographs of it, a few drawings and a written progress-report have.[5] From the report we can gather that on

On the inside, modern technical amenities necessitated certain changes. A number of carpets and textile coverings of upholstery had to be replaced. Paintings and sculptures were removed from their original places of display, or replaced by other pieces.
4. Ludwig Hevesi, *Altkunst-Neukunst* (Vienna, 1909), 220.
5. Material in the estate of Josef Hoffmann. Both J. A. Lux, *Hohe Warte*, II (1905–6), 69, and A. S. Levetus, *The Studio*, XXXVII (1906), 166, illustrated the model.

6 August 1906 drawings of the façades to a scale of
1:100 had been sent to three firms for glass and marble,
and to François, the building contractor in Brussels, for
a preliminary estimate; work was also going ahead on
more detailed façade drawings, scale 1:20.

The application for a building permit which is on
deposit at the communal archives of Woluwé-St.
Lambert, is accompanied by a plan dated 2 April
1906 and by sections and façades dated 15 May 1906.
There are some slight discrepancies between plan and
sections.

Drawings of the long elevations, scale 1:100, were
published at a reduced scale by A. S. Levetus[6] and by
Hans Ankwicz-Kleehoven.[7] There are, in addition,
two sketches of preliminary plans, scale 1:200 (Figs.
2, 3), a plan, scale 1:100 (Fig. 16), a plan of the upper
floor, scale 1:200, a drawing of the garden façade,
scale 1:200 (Figs. 7, 8) and two perspective drawings
of the garden façade (Figs. 9, 10), one drawn in ink
and one rendered in water color.[8] Five perspective
drawings for different interiors are also known (Figs.
11–15);[9] they differ sufficiently from the actual rooms
which they represent to show that a good deal of
modification went on in the course of more detailed
design and final execution. There must have been
more drawings, including working drawings and
details (Fig. 32), but they have not come to light.[10]

With the aid of the existing evidence, scanty as it is,
the main steps in the evolution of the Stoclet design
may be traced.

The earliest known version of a *preliminary design*,
presumably the first one, is represented by two sketches
of plans (Figs. 2, 3), both drawn in Hoffmann's typical
manner—free hand with a soft pencil on squared
paper; one of them is initialled JH. They show
ground floor and second floor of the same scheme and
they differ drastically from later solutions; yet the

guiding ideas of the programme are clearly recognizable. As in the later version, a central hall with a
gallery is the chief organizing element of the plan, and
in it a place is designated for the fountain by Minne
(marked *Minnebr.*) which obviously was intended
from the very beginning roughly at the same place
near the entrance where it finally came to stand. But
while dining-hall and music-room at least relate in an
approximately similar fashion to the central hall as in
the final design, this cannot be said of the study. The
staircase, too, is in a completely different and not very
happy location. There are two projections towards the
garden but they are square-ended, not angular.

The exact plan from which the model was built has
not turned up, but it must have been much closer to
the final plan than to the preliminary design which
has just been discussed. The *model design* (Figs. 4, 6)
differs from the final one in several ways. Most striking
is the simple, not to say timid manner in which the
tower is handled. The central portion of the garden
front has a straight recess on the second floor instead
of the curved one which is so effective in the final
version. The two lateral projections of the garden
front have straight ends but they carry wedge-shaped
balconies. The fenestration shows different rhythms
and proportions and finally, apart from other minor
changes, there is a most important variation in façade
treatment: the white surfaces of the façades are not
delimited by metal bands but by black lines which
were meant to be carried out in black Swedish granite.
Accordingly, the model design has the kind of contrast
between white and black which by that time had become typical for Hoffmann's personal style and was
considered a trademark of the *Wiener Werkstätte*.

The perspective of the garden front rendered in water
color (Fig. 10) corresponds closely to the model except
that the two lateral projections no longer carry wedge-
shaped balconies; instead, the solution with angular
projections on the ground floor which support the
balcony-terraces has been adopted. This solution is
also shown in the second perspective drawing (Fig. 9)
which goes together with a preliminary façade sketch,
scale 1:200 (Fig. 7). The tower now has some indication of a crowning feature which was not shown on the
model, but the central projection of the garden front
is still straight, and the east façade differs from the
one carried out both in the way the staircase is handled
and by having a segmental instead of a semicylindrical
shape at the end of the music-room.

There is still some hesitation about the termination of
this room in a plan, scale 1:100, on squared paper and
partly inked in (Fig. 16), which otherwise in general
disposition comes close to the *final design* (Fig. 17), in
spite of some differences in detail. Notable among

6. *Moderne Bauformen* XIII/1 (Jan. 1914), 7. Perhaps these
elevations are derived from those on deposit with the application for the building permit which, unfortunately, the author
was not permitted to see. One ozalid print of the rear elevation,
coming from the estate of Josef Hoffmann, is in the collection of
the Bauhaus Archives, Darmstadt.

7. Hans Ankwicz-Kleehoven, 'Josef Hoffmann, Das Palais Stoclet etc.', *Alte und Moderne Kunst*, VI (Jan. 1961), 7.

8. Estate of Josef Hoffmann, collection of the author and
Museum des XX. Jahrhunderts, Vienna.

9. Unidentified photographs of three of these were acquired by
the author from the estate of the late Hans Ankwicz-Kleehoven.
The two other perspective drawings for interiors are in the
Museum des XX. Jahrhunderts, Vienna.

10. The author has only been able to identify one drawing for a
detail, a coat-hook for the cloakroom of the Stoclet House,
among the many drawings from the archives of the *Wiener
Werkstätte* which are now in the library of the *Österreichisches Museum für angewandte Kunst*, Vienna. Unfortunately
Josef Hoffmann lost a great deal of material, including drawings and photographs, during World War II.

them is a different solution for the entrance group with square, apse-ended vestibule, and a different indication for the juncture of study and music-room. The initialled perspective of an interior (Fig. 12) which shows a wash-room with three basins and, in the background, a single toilet, must belong to this plan. It is interesting to observe that in the plan a central axis is indicated in pencil and that almost perfect bilateral symmetry has been achieved with regard to it. In this as in the final plan (Fig. 17) all elements are linked in an extremely straightforward and convincing manner, and a maximum of order is imposed.

When glancing at a plan of the ground floor in the final version (Fig. 17), the discipline of regularity and axial coordination is not so apparent because on this level the buildings around the service courtyard to the west form an irregular group with the main building. The plan of the next higher floor, however, clearly shows how the main block of the building is extremely regular and almost—not quite—bilaterally symmetrical around an axis that runs through the middle of the bay-window. The square, preferred shape in so many of Josef Hoffmann's designs, determines in a simple manner the overall scheme of proportions in plan. One square (c. 12 × 12 m)[11] corresponds to the size of the great hall on the second floor; three squares of the same size form the rectangle of the total second floor, exclusive of the thickness of the outside walls. In details of the plans and in elevation too, the square asserts itself in many places, notably in the size of windows and visually important areas.

The elevation which was published by Hans Ankwicz-Kleehoven[12] proves that for a while the architect considered having a small diamond-shaped element in the center of every slab of façade-cladding, and breaking up the long staircase window into several parts—both devices which would have interfered seriously with the integrity of uninterrupted interlocking planes that is so characteristic for the building as it was finally built.

II

Normally a visitor will approach the Stoclet House coming from the center of the city, and he will catch his first view of the building, rather unexpectedly, between the trees of the avenue (Fig. 18). Probably the strongest first impression is that of a building which not only looks different from anything around it—an impression which must have been much stronger in 1911—but which in many ways eludes even a rapid search for immediate comparisons with any other

building one has seen. It takes some effort to overcome this impact of unfamiliarity and to proceed to a more detailed inspection of the façade.

The long street façade of the building is not immediately seen in its full extension but its recessed western portion with the long staircase window and the dominating tower assume the greatest importance. Their verticality is in contrast to the horizontality of the covered entrance approach which stretches between the street-line with its elaborate metal and stone fence and the main block. Next to this, the polygonal projection of the bow-window with its adjoining small precinct of privacy created by means of screening parapet walls, appears of minor importance. It assumes greater visual weight, however, when the street façade is viewed from the lower, eastern end of the site (Fig. 19). Seen from here, the bow-window, together with the projecting volumes of the east façade, tends to balance the richness of the distant west-part with its tower. The total impression along the Avenue de Tervueren is so varied by means of asymmetrically placed elements that it comes as a surprise to discover that the entrance is placed almost in the exact middle of the total façade—a very plausible location, incidentally, from a functional point of view. Owing to the lower service wing which is seen as a direct extension of the main block in this façade, the building appears impressive even through its sheer extension.

Most observers would probably agree that in all façades the single most striking feature is the moulding of gilt and darkened metal which frames all edges (Figs. 21, 22). A strongly linear element is introduced by these articulated metal bands but it has nothing to do with 'lines of force' the way linear elements did in the architecture of Victor Horta. At the Stoclet House we have lines which occur equally along horizontal and vertical edges—they are tectonically neutral. At the corners or any other places of juncture where two or more of these parallel mouldings come together, the effect tends towards a negation of the solidity of the built volumes. A feeling persists as if the walls had not been built up in a heavy construction but consisted of large sheets of a thin material, joined at the corners with metal bands to protect the edges.

Naturally a justification could be given for this treatment by explaining that the brick-built walls were actually clad with thin slabs of Norwegian white marble and that this fact has been expressed in the formal treatment, just as Otto Wagner at the Vienna Postal Savings Bank (1904–1906) expressed his stone cladding as an applied veneer that had nothing to carry except its own load.

With or without such justification, the visual result is very striking and atectonic to the extreme. 'Atectonic'

11. Measurements during construction, from wall to wall prior to marble sheathing.
12. See note 7.

is used here to describe a manner in which the expressive interaction of load and support in architecture is visually negated or obscured. The metal mouldings which appear as if they had been formed by joining many identical elements like beads in a necklace, or flowers in a garland, are most effective as atectonic devices when they are seen repeated side by side, forming bundles as alongside the tower (Fig. 48), or when they are carried around an opening the way a rope would be hung.[13]

There are many other atectonic details at the Stoclet House. Heavy piers have nothing of adequate visual weight to support but carry a thin, flat roof as at the entrance and over the loggia on the roof terrace (Fig. 24). No visual distinction is made between what is a load-bearing wall in a façade and what a parapet in front of a terrace (Fig. 26). The transition between low and high parts in a façade occurs without any distinction or articulation in one plane (Figs. 19, 20) in such a way that the character of the façade as a purely two-dimensional surface is stressed at the expense of its quality as part of a volume with implications of mass and weight. In this connection it is equally significant that windows are set flush into the façades, even slightly protruding, not in recesses which would betray the thickness of the wall,[14] and that they cut into the tops of the cornice-less façades.[15] Since the windows are treated as defined planes much as the stone surfaces next to them, an effect of interlocking planes rather than of a plane with holes is created which counteracts any feeling of heaviness that otherwise might have gone with the prevailing planarity. Finally there are many elements which visually seem to slide past each other or at least appear ready to do so.

Across the driveway to the garage-court a bridgelike element is thrown (Fig. 24). It has no visible supports and, towards the street, its lateral lines of juncture are treated with the typical metal moulding: the effect is that of an element slid into place—almost ready to slide out again. Another comparable 'bridge' is created by the curved central portion of the garden front (Fig. 26). Here, as at the other 'bridge', the effect of a hovering element is enhanced by the formal treatment of the visible soffit; in both cases it has a lattice of thin metal bands which seem to tie it together. If these 'bridges' seem slid into place, the tower (Fig. 48) with its receding stages provides another instance of elements that seem to have glided past each other, with a veritable cascading of profiles, especially at the long staircase window.

It appears almost like a symbol of the atectonic attitude that prevails when the shape which is placed in the most important position in the garden, in the central fountain (Fig. 26), is made to resemble vaguely an archaic Doric column with considerable entasis but at closer inspection turns out to be something entirely different: something in the nature of a very elongated vase-shape with a top that does not end in a square abacus in a gesture of support but houses a small spout from which water may flow into the basin below.

The garden with its various areas and features is rigorously treated in a formal manner akin to that which prevails in the architecture. There are many ways in which garden and façades are tied together, actually through walks and pergolas and virtually through the creation of vistas. From certain points in the garden an impression of complete bilateral symmetry is created for the garden façade, with a main axis leading into the central hall of the building.

In actual fact the garden front is not symmetrical. The western service wing extends its sheltering bulk along the weather-side of the site, a tall chimney and the tower with its striking monumental termination remain much in evidence, and on the eastern extremity there is the low, cylindrical extension which corresponds to the end of the music-room on the inside, and which makes an easy transition to the east façade (Fig. 20).

Today, because the adjacent trees have grown so much, it is hard to appreciate the simple, bold composition of this façade with its large unbroken rectangular surface on the upper level and its contrast of cylinder and rectilinear volume on the ground floor. The apse-like shape at the east end and the tower on the west combine, in the model at least, to give a curious churchlike aspect when seen from certain angles (Fig. 4); the effect can also be observed when looking at geometrical drawings of the street façade.

A stair leads from the music-room wing directly into the garden. It runs parallel to the façade and has a parapet which, significantly, does not follow the rake of the stairs but is carried up to a continuous horizontal ending at a uniform height. Thus it becomes another predominantly planar element, a plane parallel to and in front of the façade. It served as a backdrop for a small sculpture of Ganesha, the elephant-headed

13. Actual cable mouldings around windows were not unknown in Belgian architecture as proved by a house on the market-place of Louvain.
14. Such treatment of the windows was later repeated by Le Corbusier in his early houses as Henry-Russell Hitchcock has pointed out, in *Architecture 19th & 20th Centuries* (Baltimore, 1958), 369.
15. Robert Schmutzler, *Art Nouveau-Jugendstil* (Stuttgart, 1962), 246, rightly points out that Mackintosh used the motif of windows which interrupt the cornice line. Hill House, Helensburgh (1902–3), is an example which Hoffmann may have known. The side-elevation of Berlage's Amsterdam Stock Exchange has a somewhat similar arrangement.

deity, but today it is completely overgrown by a vine. Works of sculpture were also incorporated at other strategic points of the exterior composition, as on the side towards the avenue where a Romanesque lion is conspicuous guarding the entrance to the sheltered terrace near the bow-window (Fig. 27).

The southern or garden façade (Fig. 26) in its three-dimensional treatment mirrors the close relationship between garden and building, and the potential presence of strong sunlight: it is much more strongly modelled than the northern or street façade. The center portion, two stories high with a terrace on top in front of the three-storied main block, extends considerably into the garden with two prow-like polygonal projections on the ground floor.

The top of each projection forms a terrace, protected by solid parapets and entered from the room behind it through a door which sits between two windows in such a way that a framed group is formed. This reads as one visual unit from the eye-level of a person standing in the garden because his line of vision is intersected by the unbroken parapets. The view from all terraces, especially the higher ones, is beautiful, over the garden towards the open country which stretches south and east.

Between the wedge-shaped projections an open but sheltered area (Fig. 26) forms a transition from the open garden terrace on the ground floor to the enclosed central hall. This area is covered by an upper story which recedes in a gentle curve. Obviously a strong interplay takes place between the receding or hollowed-out center and the flat or advancing sides, and one is tempted to describe it empathetically as gestures of reaching out and welcoming in.

A similar employment of contrasting yet unified compositional devices can be observed when analyzing the second important approach to the central hall which is from the street side. The carefully considered manner in which the core of the building is reached from the garden has its parallel in the elaborate sequence of preparatory and transitional zones that lead to it from the Avenue de Tervueren.

The main entrance on the avenue (Fig. 27) is part of an overall arrangement that forms a screen between street and front-garden of the building and that includes a stone parapet and stone uprights with richly curving black wrought-iron grilles set in between. The fence is simpler in front of the service wing than where it faces the main block. In its eastern sections it is higher than eye-height owing to the slope of the street. It plays an important part in giving the building a dignified setting.

The outer gate is protected by a black iron canopy supported on metal cantilevers which with their flow-

ing lines are as typically Art Nouveau as the shapes of the original lettering for the street number (303) (Fig. 27). The gate sits between coupled stone piers which are carried up to a considerable height above the canopy, framing a simple grille between them. They form the front supports of a square pavilion (Fig. 29), open except for a low sculptured parapet, which marks the first zone into which one enters once the outer door has opened. The pavilion is wider than the corridor that follows it and its special character and importance are underscored by its severe, almost Soanesque monumentality and by the fact that it is crowned by a sculpture of Pallas Athene.

From the pavilion one proceeds into a bay of equal height and depth but smaller width which is completely open on the sides. This is followed by a corridor which not only shares the smaller width but in addition is enclosed by a high parapet, by densely spaced stone piers and by glazing. A flight of seven easy steps inside this corridor makes the transition to the higher level of the inner gate which in its two high wings echoes the feeling of dignity if not of severity that is already conveyed by the proportions of the corridor and by its effective articulation of space into areas of increasing enclosure. The higher level of the entrance combines with the length of the formal approach to impress a visitor with the importance of the place he is about to enter.

III

The elaborate approach from the outside has its parallel inside the house. Immediately behind the doors a white but completely windowless small zone of transition to a second set of doors helps to give a strong feeling of penetration through something deep and solid before one emerges into a room that presents itself as a space very definitely confined and disciplined in shape and measure. It is a *vestibule* or anteroom which owes its particular atmosphere to a number of devices that work together to create an interior which is at the same time solemn and subdued (Fig. 28).

The room is not very brightly lit and the prevailing wall color is that of *verde antico* marble, a dark green tending towards black. The white ceiling seems to billow up gently into its segmental shape as if hollowed out by the same impulse that carved segmental niches into the upper part of the walls. They recall the motif of a segmental recess from the central part of the garden façade just as the moulding under the vault recalls the mouldings from outside. The niches house gilt vases, lit from above. These and the small mosaic by Leopold Forstner together with thin gold strips which articulate the ceiling impart an aura of festivity, or rather of festive dignity that helps to heighten that general tension of anticipation which began at the street gate. In a preliminary design (Fig. 11) the billowing, velarium-like character of the ceiling was even more pronounced and one plan (Fig. 16) shows that originally the room was to have been square with a great segmental niche opposite the entrance—a room shape strongly in the classical tradition.

The floor of the anteroom is of whitish veined marble with a simple pattern of black which marks the two main axes of the room and their intersection. In this way the impression is heightened that nothing is left to coincidence once this room is entered. The furniture, the sculptures which flank the doors on built-in pedestals (Fig. 30), and the paintings in gilt frames had to go into their predestined positions much as the visitor has to follow a path firmly outlined for him.

Exactly on axis with the black marble line in the floor two glass doors open to the right and left of the visitor. One opens into the great hall, the other into a cloakroom (Fig. 31) from which one can reach a corridor that gives access to secondary staircase and service quarters, and to the toilet facilities. In this whole area a totality of white and simple rectilinear shapes forms a strong contrast to the vestibule.

To come from the vestibule into the *great hall* (Figs. 33, 34) is a subtle and yet dramatic change. The two rooms have enough in common to leave no doubt about their being members of the same family—both as far as the general atmosphere and the careful handling in detail of kindred materials are concerned. But their contrast is equally unequivocal—in size, height, in the prevailing hue which is much lighter and warmer in the hall, and in spatial articulation.

The hall runs through the entire depth of the building and, in its central part, through the full height of two stories. This central part is defined by slender marble-clad piers which run from floor to ceiling. They form a rectangle four bays by three except that on the shorter side towards the garden terrace the piers have been omitted. On the second floor a gallery runs all the way around the central space giving access to the master-bedroom suite on the one side and to the children's quarters on the other. This gallery runs across in unbroken sweep on the garden side; on the opposite short side and on the long side towards the staircase it is supported by the piers. On the other long side it rests directly on the solid walls below; these, however, are articulated by the piers set into them.

It is understandable that the space of the central hall with its many extensions tends to be elusive because its defining boundaries are so varied and its profile

changes in section—it is obviously wider on the second floor where it forms a square in plan than on the ground floor.[16]

The center of the great bow-window on the street side of the hall is occupied by a marble fountain with a small sculpture by Georges Minne. In front of some of the piers dark marble pedestals are placed for pieces of sculpture from the owner's collection and there are transparent showcases for smaller items at right angles to the short sides of the hall. Their panes of crystal glass together with the glass of the chandeliers, the polished marble surfaces and the polished wood of furniture and inlaid floor all help together to make the room come to life in a particularly exciting fashion when artificial light is used, as it was during most of the social functions which took place here.

The space of the great hall has its elusive aspects, but it remains securely a part of a thoroughly ordered total composition where nothing is left vague: vistas are created in all main axes (Fig. 33) and every juxtaposition of two materials is completely thought out and formalized. This, of course, includes the device of framing surfaces by mouldings which creates a similar atectonic effect on the inside as it does on the outside. The stuccoed compartments of the balcony in the central hall seem to hover between the piers and walls much as the various 'bridges' do on the outside. The atectonic effect would have been even stronger had the original intention been carried out to frame all four sides of every pier by mouldings, as is shown on a perspective drawing (Fig. 14).

The open *main staircase* (Fig. 33) of three flights is handled in the same vocabulary as the hall proper (Fig. 34) of which it is at the same time an extension and an integral part. Between its slender piers of polished marble the grillework of the balustrades becomes a design feature of importance. Under its upper flight a small sitting-room, in the tradition of the Anglo-Saxon inglenook, has been fitted (Fig. 35). Two upholstered built-in benches face each other on either side of an open fireplace in the outside wall. The glow of the flames is echoed by the rich glow from one vast piece of translucent onyx which forms the mantel and is illuminated from behind. No wonder that during a visit in 1955 the architect remarked about this *tour de force*: 'Man sieht, dass ich jung war, wie ich das gemacht habe, und vor nichts Angst hatte.'[17]

All rooms which on the ground floor are accessible from the great hall are kept darker in general tone than the central space. This is as true of the study, of

16. Similar fusions of high and low spaces were later exploited to the full by Le Corbusier in many designs.
17. 'One can see that I was young when I did this, and that I was afraid of nothing.'

the music-room and of the large dining-room, as it was of the vestibule.

The *study*, which is situated in one of the two wings that jut out into the garden, has at its inner end an inglenook and is panelled and furnished in blackened oak. The surfaces here are not glossy and the total quality of the room is very quiet if not a little sombre, although it is amply lit owing to the big windows in the angled end-walls. In the cabinets of this room many of the most precious small objects from the owner's collection were kept.

The theater or *music-room* (Fig. 36) is on a level four steps below the hall and its stage is shaped like a half-round into which, originally, an organ was placed. A gallery opens into the auditorium opposite the window-wall. Since the walls are covered by highly polished black Portovenere marble while the floor is in teak and coralwood, the predominating hue is black. It sets off to best advantage the purplish red of upholstery, carpet and curtains, and the glitter of inlaid enamel and glass panels and of gold in carvings and mouldings. Particularly an altar-like many-layered *aedicula* (Fig. 15) not far from the entrance strikes the eye as a most precious setting for one of Fernand Khnopff's esoteric works, a version of his *I lock my door upon myself*.

The gallery which has just been mentioned as permitting a view into the theater room from a higher level is reached in a very ingenious simple fashion over the first flight of the main stairs. It is also used to give access to a small room off-stage and to an intimate polygonal salon or ladies' parlor, which has very rich multicolored wall coverings and elaborately carved gilt furniture with black embroidered upholstery. The built-in display cases in this room are a later addition.

Directly opposite to the entrance of the music-room, across the central hall, are the glazed double doors which open into the *large dining-room* (Fig. 37). Gustav Klimt's mosaics[18] have made this room deservedly the most famous interior of the building and one of the best known ones of the period. With its only source of natural light at the far end of some fourteen meters' length, the room appears dark compared to the adjacent hall, in spite of the fact that the same honey-colored Paonazzo marble is used for the walls. But here it is combined with very dark Porto-venere marble and with Macassar wood for table and chairs, upholstered in black morocco leather with gold tooling.

18. The mosaics were carried out by Leopold Forstner under Klimt's direct supervision. Literature about the frieze is given in Johannes Dobai, 'Gustav Klimt', in: *Gustav Klimt and Egon Schiele*, Catalogue of the Guggenheim Museum (New York, 1965), 39.

Because of its subdued natural illumination the interior provides an ideal setting for the glow of mosaics and precious metals. There are a few gold plaques on the walls and silver goes not only on the table but also on the sideboards where a tower-shaped candle-holder in silver recalls the tower motif from the outside.

Spatially the room consists of three segments though one's first impression is one of an entirely unified whole. At one end of the room two great angled windows form a wedge of light; between them a small high window is placed above a marble fountain and the three windows together provide an area of luminous transparency during the daytime.

At the opposite end of the room where one enters from the great hall there is again a slight wedge-shape created, this time, by walls which are angled and house glazed, built-in display cupboards which can be illuminated artificially. In addition, the walls are recessed: the lateral ones to receive the doors, the end wall to provide a frame for the central panel of Klimt's mosaic frieze which is strongly colored and an entirely non-figurative composition. It is given a very particular, almost hieratic quality by its placement in a recess which is twice stepped back from the frontal plane of reference.

Piers clad in marble delimit both the entrance- and the window-zone. Between them the two great lateral mosaics, *Expectation* and *Fulfilment*, extend the whole length of the wall. They protrude slightly over the strip of marble which separates them from the sideboards below. In these, square wooden doors alternate with open marble shelving. The square is stressed by a gilt moulded framing strip and its dimension relates to that of the mosaic; their heights are approximately in a ratio of $1:2$.

It is striking how in spite of the powerful presence of the mosaics the rest of the room holds its own. All elements from the black and white squares of the marble floor and its olive-colored carpet to the row of chandeliers on the ceiling are coordinated to enhance each other and all surface finishes have a high lustre throughout, appropriate to create, together with the mosaics, that atmosphere of festive brilliance that was desired. As with so many other rooms in the building that were designed primarily for use at formal occasions in the evening, the large dining-room takes on an additional fascination when seen in artificial light.

In contrast to the courtly formality of the great dining-room the contiguous *breakfast room* (Figs. 38, 39) is characterized by a more intimate atmosphere of brightness and happy domesticity. It has a compact octagonal shape with niches in the oblique sides and is amply illuminated. There is a cheerful floral wall-decoration carved in a very low relief in wood and painted in white and yellow against a black background. White in the shape of dots on a background predominantly black with yellow at the margin are also the colors of the carpet—supposedly chosen so that crumbs dropped during a meal would not show up on the pattern.[19] The upper parts of the walls, the ceiling and the built-in corner cupboards are in an unbroken white which contrasts as happily with the highly polished black round table that forms the focus of the room as does the whiteness of fresh linen placed on it.

For obvious practical reasons only the most important rooms, those on the ground floor, have been discussed. There would be many more which deserve description: on the ground floor the service rooms and the second staircase which has a striking cylindrical telephone booth standing in its open center; on the two upper floors many elaborately equipped and lavishly dimensioned rooms including the master bedroom (c. 9.50 m × 5.70 m) (Fig. 40) and its bathroom (Fig. 41) which covers an area equal to that of the study below, i.e. approximately 5.80 m × 5.90 m (!), and which is treated in marble with inlays of malachite and has its own balcony-terrace overlooking the garden. But enough has been said without going into further detail to show where the strength and character of the Stoclet interiors lie.

These rooms were clearly conceived as a sequence of experiences in space, enhanced by every possible device in the use of light, color and texture in contrapuntal arrangement. The rooms, especially on the ground floor, are at the same time in harmony and in contrast with each other and enhance their complementary qualities through highly sophisticated juxtapositions, while at the same time no opportunity is missed to tie together the ensemble by repeating and recalling forms, mouldings, proportions and other elements of composition.

A visitor may not be aware consciously of the manner in which his reactions are affected, but he will react—whether he evaluates his impressions positively or negatively. Even today it is not rare to observe how visitors who have a chance to see the great hall for the first time tend to lower their voices upon entering as if awed by the experience.

On closer inspection one finds that an incredible care was taken with every material, every juncture, and every detail, true to the ideals of the *Wiener Werkstätte* where all the interiors had been produced. Above all, behind the successful coordination of all efforts of design a sense of purpose is felt which seems to have been shared with equal clarity and conviction by architect and client.

IV

At the Stoclet House the relation between client and architect was very happy indeed, a fact clearly mirrored in the consistent character and quality of the building which shows that no compromises were forced onto it. A fundamental agreement must have existed between the taste and predilections of Adolphe and Suzanne Stoclet and the artistic intentions and capacities of Josef Hoffmann. The creations of the *Wiener Werkstätte*, which had been founded while Mr. Stoclet with his family lived in Vienna, so completely captured his sympathy that many years later in his testament he expressed the wish to take on his last journey a handkerchief of silk designed in black and white by Hoffmann. The Stoclets held Hoffmann in the highest possible esteem and he, in turn, was challenged to the utmost by the well-defined demands of people who were connoisseurs and amateurs of the arts in the best possible sense of these words.

The Stoclet guestbook—designed by Hoffmann—between its silver covers preserves names which represent many aspects of excellence in cultural life: Paderewsky, Diaghilev, Strawinsky, Cocteau, Anatole France, Sacha Guitry, and a contemporary eyewitness describes how 'on many occasions a handpicked audience would be invited to their theatre, . . . to discover an artist as yet unknown—an Indian dancer, a Russian pianist, a French composer or actor. . . .'[20] At times there must have been assembled at the house a group of artists and intellectuals fully as brilliant as any found in one of those famous late nineteenth-century Parisian salons which Suzanne Stoclet had known well during the years immediately preceding her marriage. Her father, the art critic and dealer Arthur Stevens, was one of three brothers who played an important rôle in the art world of Paris; best known among them was Alfred Stevens, the much sought-after painter of ladies of the high society.

Adolphe Stoclet came from a different kind of background. His family was well established in banking and the high finances of Belgian economy which at the time went through a phase of great expansion owing to the operations in the Congo. He married the beautiful young *Parisienne* against the wishes of his family, it seems, and consequently went abroad, first to Milan, then to Vienna where in 1903 his third child, a son, was born.

He and his wife had started their art collection by

19. Edmond de Bruyn, 'Adieu à Monsieur Adolphe Stoclet', reprint from *Le Flambeau*, no. 6 (1949), 2.

20. George A. Salles in his preface to *Adolphe Stoclet Collection* (Brussels, 1956), xv.

then; they must have taken an interest in the art life of Vienna, in such events as the exhibitions in the *Sezession* building. But they also explored the city and its surroundings, and it was on the occasion of such a trip that they met Hoffmann under circumstances which were flattering for the young architect.

The Belgian couple had gone for a morning walk to the Hohe Warte, a hill of gardens and parks at the outskirts of Vienna, with vineyards close by and fine views especially towards the Viennese woods. One of a group of brand-new residences attracted their attention and they entered its garden. They were promptly discovered by the owner, the painter Carl Moll who had been one of the founders of the Vienna *Sezession*. When Moll and his wife learned that admiration had been the reason for the intrusion, they offered to show their new house to the visitors and to introduce them to the architect who was to come to the site the same afternoon—it was Josef Hoffmann.[21]

Since Mr. Stoclet expected to stay in Vienna for some time, he actually went as far as to commission a house-design from Hoffmann. It was for a site on the Hohe Warte—later utilized for the Ast House—which shared with the Brussels site characteristics with regard to view, location on a slope and distance from the center of town. The Vienna site was not utilized by the Belgian visitor because in 1904 his father died and he was called back to Brussels. He now had considerable means at his disposal—he never disclosed to his family what had been the cost of his house[22]—and could call on Hoffmann for a design on a palatial scale.

When in 1949 Adolphe and Suzanne Stoclet both died within one month, after half a century of shared love for the arts, they left behind a unique house and an outstanding art collection. With its stress on highest quality and remoteness in time and place—the archaic and the exotic—the collection expresses as much as the house about the character and taste of the two people who were responsible for both. The house cannot be understood fully without the collection nor the collection without its splendid container; both, for the Stoclets, demanded a continuous living up to self-imposed exacting standards.

Edmond de Bruyn described Monsieur and Madame Stoclet, on the occasion of a social event, descending the great staircase . . . 'la maîtresse de maison lamée d'or par Poiret et coiffee d'aigrettes, au coté d'Adolphe Stoclet, droit dans sa barbe symmétrique et lustrée d'Assurbanipal. . . .'[23] The image can be supplemented

from the recollections of Georges A. Salles[24] about Adolphe Stoclet: 'His black beard threaded with silver, his manner—charming with just a hint of pomposity—and his distinguished presence gave him a remarkable affinity of style with the objects in his collection, with which he seemed to be quite naturally in contact. In fact the polished surfaces of the marble in the great entrance hall applied equally well to him as to the carvings displayed against the background of the decoration: Buddhist deities, Egyptian kings, a head of Darius, a Khmer torso, a golden bear or a green dragon. In this monumental company he was perfectly at ease.'

One understands how much the Stoclets were one with the framework they had created for their lives. Nothing was left to coincidence, as in the design of the house, and 'les fleurs—toujours d'un seul ton—sur la table et la cravate de M. Stoclet s'assortissaient sur la toilette de Madame'. 'La bâtisse se manifestait incompatible avec quoi ce soit de banal, de provisoire ou de mediocre.'[25]

The building was a very personal setting for a way of life based on a profound respect for beauty and the transfiguring power of art, but worked out by a man who was a realist capable of running a big bank and of enjoying a bathroom of Roman thermal scale and luxury. Pride in this building is tempered by the reticence of a highly cultured individualist for whom aesthetic perfection assumes almost metaphysical significance. This, in my opinion, accounts for the somewhat hieratic character in some parts of the building which so struck contemporaries that they made comparisons with Egypt and Byzantium.

It is not difficult to understand why Pallas Athene should have been placed over the gate (Fig. 27). As militant protectress of wisdom and the arts she had been one of the favorite symbols of the Vienna *Sezession* and such artists as Gustav Klimt and Kolo Moser had represented her. At the Stoclet House she shares pride of place with another tutelary deity of wisdom, the elephant-headed Ganesha at the east end.

It is equally simple to understand why in a panel above the long staircase window (Figs. 18, 24) heads should have been put which form a perpetual look-out. But it is less easy to interpret the four herculean figures which are placed on the four sides of the tower (Fig.

---

heron's feathers in her coiffure, on the side of Adolphe Stoclet, straight in his symmetrical lustrous beard of Assurbanipal...', Edmond de Bruyn, *op. cit.*, 2.

24. Salles, *op. cit.*, IX.

25. 'The flowers on the table—always of one tone only—and the tie of Mr. Stoclet were in perfect accord with the dress of the lady.' 'The building manifested itself incompatible with anything banal, provisional or mediocre.' Edmond de Bruyn, *op. cit.*, 3.

---

21. This and several other details of a personal nature were kindly related to the author by the late Jacques Stoclet.

22. Christian M. Nebehay, preface to his catalogue 92, *Die Wiener Werkstätte und die Kunst um 1900* (Vienna, 1965).

23. 'The mistress of the house in gold lamé by Poiret and with

48). They may have been a direct suggestion of the sculptor who did them; Franz Metzner, from 1903 to 1906 Hoffmann's colleague as a teacher, was fond of a rather heavy-handed monumentality. He could indulge it to the full in his many years of collaboration with Bruno Schmitz: their monument to the *Völkerschlacht* at Leipzig best illustrates the way their ambitions went. There is, at any rate, something Nietzschean or Wagnerian about the way in which these four figures stand underneath and around the crowning feature of the whole design—a metal dome of flowers, perhaps reminiscent of the Vienna *Sezession* building. Flowers—age old as decoration and as symbol of a dedication to beauty—occur again on the four corners of the tower at a lower level and in the square sculptural panel below the staircase window (Fig. 21). Here two female figures in sacrificial attitude carry a basket of them. From the floral cupola on top, the metal mouldings cascade down, several of them side by side, until they reach the sides of the building which they encircle like so many garlands.

The profile used in these mouldings somewhat recalls the one in the wreaths which female figures, modelled by Bacher, were carrying in Hoffmann's setting for Klinger's Beethoven at the XIV *Sezession* exhibition of 1902.[26] Moreover, Hoffmann used an avowedly floral motif in the design of encircling mouldings at the Ast House (Fig. 23), a building that was finished about the same time as the Stoclet House. The Stoclet profiles, which are often carried around a window in something of a garland or cable fashion, may well owe their particular and unique shape to a merging, in the architect's mind, of several formal concepts: last reminiscences from the world of classical mouldings,[27] far-eastern lotus leaf patterns, and the idea of treating an encircling profile like a floral garland (Fig. 22).

During the years when Hoffmann was engaged on the Stoclet designs his other work shows clearly how intensively he was concerned with them, and how he had recourse to certain basic ideas more than once. The motif of a hall with a white balcony and slender piers[28] occurs in his *Cabaret Fledermaus* of 1907 and in the exhibition *Kunstschau* of 1908. In the *Fledermaus* he also employed a multicolored ceramic mosaic that anticipates parts of Klimt's mosaic frieze at the Stoclet which was begun in 1909. Hoffmann also kept experimenting with the use of delimiting repetitive mouldings.

A very striking incidence of this occurs on a table which he designed for the sumptuous hunting lodge of Dr. Wittgenstein at Hochreith, in 1906.[29] Here parallel mouldings meeting at the corners of the legs create a similar impression of dematerializing the volume as they do at the Stoclet. Similar relations between designs for tables and architectural designs can be pointed out at other moments in Hoffmann's career[30] and a striking parallel between a design motif in furniture and in architecture can be found by comparing a little wedge-shaped wall case, designed in 1901 (Fig. 5),[31] with the wedge-shaped balconies on the Stoclet model design (Fig. 6). There is not necessarily a direct connection between these two designs but they provide a useful reminder that for Hoffmann there was no fundamental difference between the design of forms for furniture and objects and that for architecture.

V

It is patently impossible to establish all influences on the process of design with Hoffmann prior and during his work on the Brussels building, which means during the most important formative years of his creative career. But three very relevant factors at least can be singled out for discussion: his education and study; his relation to England and Scotland; his personal creative development and reaction to changes of taste and attitude around him.

More than once during the discussion of the Stoclet design it was necessary to talk of bilateral symmetry, of axiality and of similar devices which impart the discipline of a classical tradition and a sense of monumentality. They remind us that at the beginning of Hoffmann's career he underwent the influence of two teachers entirely steeped in the classical tradition of monumental composition: Karl von Hasenauer and Otto Wagner. If both of them shared a flair for the great gesture in architecture, Wagner alone went definitely beyond it in his work and thought. He did

---

26. *Deutsche Kunst und Dekoration*, x (1902), 487.
27. It is interesting in this connection to note how Otto Wagner uses a classical moulding to frame windows at the house Stadiongasse 6–8, Vienna.
28. Giulia Veronesi, *Josef Hoffmann* (Milan, 1956), 86, has correctly compared the screen of pier-like elements in the House Henneberg to the Stoclet hall but she has reversed their relationship. The Henneberg designs antedate the Stoclet House by three to four years.
29. *Deutsche Kunst und Dekoration*, xix (1906–7), 443 ff.
30. The table illustrated in Leopold Kleiner, *Josef Hoffmann* (Berlin, 1927), 40, anticipates or at least parallels one of the basic design features of the Austrian pavilion at the Werkbund exhibition of 1914, the placing of a slab that has three steps at the sides on top of grooved supports. In a similar manner the table illustrated in *Moderne Bauformen*, xiii (Nov. 1914), 512, repeats architectural features of the Ast House.
Even the total form of the Stoclet House has been compared to a precious piece of furniture, a box that holds valuables, by Arthur Graf Strachwitz, *Alte und Moderne Kunst*, vii (July–Aug. 1962), 22 ff., a statement that was anticipated by Mrs. Erich Mendelsohn in 1914 (see note 73).
31. *Das Interieur*, ii (1901), pl. 91.

so partly at least under the influence of Semper who had been called to Vienna to work with Hasenauer. Semper probably made his greatest impact in Austria not through his architecture but through the way in which his rationalism and seriousness affected the thinking of Otto Wagner and in turn Wagner's pupils. When Hoffmann in a programmatic statement of 1901 wrote 'Ich meine, dass man vor allem den jeweiligen Zweck und das Material berücksichtigen sollte',[32] so is this a direct echo from Semper by way of Otto Wagner, for in Wagner's book *Moderne Architektur* the architecture of the future is characterized as being based on fulfilment of purpose and happy selection of material and construction. The book, which was intended as a guide for Wagner's students at the Academy, came out in 1895, the same year in which young Hoffmann graduated with a Rome prize for a grandiose composition *Forum Orbis - Insula Pacis* (Fig. 42) and went to Italy, in the footsteps of Olbrich who had won the same prize two years earlier, the year when Hoffmann entered Hasenauer's class. Olbrich not only went to Italy but also to North Africa, and the significance of such Mediterranean trips for the two young architects must have been great.

Hoffmann had been to the Adriatic before, and from there and the next extended trip south he brought back a great number of sketches (Figs. 43, 44). They show an interest not only in what might be called canonical objects of a young architect's interest such as Palladio's *Villa Rotonda* and antique remains but also in what today would be called anonymous architecture. Hoffmann showed an interest in the direct, often bold way in which architectural forms are born from meeting simple needs by simple means in anonymous buildings, whether in town or country. In this he can be compared to Le Corbusier who some ten years later came to show Hoffmann sketches made on a similar trip[33] and to Charles Mackintosh in his studies of Scottish folk architecture.[34] One cannot help but won-

der whether for Hoffmann these studies of white-washed buildings in simple cubical forms with large unbroken expanses of wall and irregularly placed openings do not indicate one of the roots of his capacity later to simplify drastically and to compose freely with white, stereometric forms, as, indeed, in the volumetric treatment of the Stoclet House. On more than one occasion he indicated how a direct transposition could be made from anonymous architecture to his own designs (Fig. 43).

After his return from Italy, however, it was not at first a question of simplicity for Josef Hoffmann but of joining full-heartedly and in emulation of Olbrich in the formal exuberance that had come to Vienna from Belgium, perhaps by way of Munich. By 1898 the *Vereinigung Bildender Künstler*, better known as *Sezession*, had been founded, Olbrich built its exhibition hall, and a series of splendid *avant-garde* exhibitions began. Hoffmann was responsible for many of the installations and here he learned what it means to integrate works of art with their setting—an experience that later stood him in such good stead when faced with the task of making a coherent entity of an art collection and his architecture at the Stoclet House. To think in terms of a totality which consciously includes works of art, furniture and every little detail of equipment in an interior was, of course, largely a legacy from the English Arts and Crafts and later related aesthetic movements.[35] Hoffmann's relationship to these has several distinct though interconnected aspects, all of them important as factors in the formation of his own, unmistakably personal style.

First of all there was an acceptance of basic assumptions and principles which became a lasting source of spiritual inspiration as for other European architects of the time. Secondly, there was a simple practical interest in technical and organizational models and prototypes. Finally, a direct connection through formal dependence existed at times, particularly at the outset of Hoffmann's career when individual manners and mannerisms of formal treatment were closely studied and followed.

All of this has to be seen not as isolated phenomena but against a background of many links between the architectural revolution in Austria of which Hoffmann formed a part and concomitant British developments. Both the *Österreichische Museum für Kunst und Industrie* and the school attached to it where Hoffmann began teaching in 1899 were inspired by and modelled after the South Kensington Museum and its organization. Arthur von Scala, the newly appointed

32. 'I am of the opinion that one should consider above all the purpose in each case and the material.' *Ibid.*, 201.

33. Le Corbusier came to Vienna with a portfolio of drawings in 1907 after his first tour of study to Italy. He had an opportunity to show his travel sketches to Alfred Roller who wanted to buy some and to Hoffmann who got so impressed by them that he hired the young man to help him—as far as Le Corbusier remembers—with the arrangement of a fête in the Hofburg. Le Corbusier came to Hoffmann because he had been impressed by what he had seen of his *œuvre* in periodicals. He was, however, disappointed by the architecture he saw in Vienna and decided to go back to Paris, having been finally moved to do so by the nostalgic feelings evoked through a performance of *La Bohème* in the Vienna Opera. He never took up his position in Hoffmann's studio, but his earliest houses in La Chaux-de-Fonds may owe something to Hoffmann's early houses in Vienna.

34. Thomas Howarth, *Charles Rennie Mackintosh* (London, 1952), 7.

35. Nikolaus Pevsner, *Pioneers of Modern Design* (New York, 1949); Robert Schmutzler, *Art Nouveau-Jugendstil* (Stuttgart, 1962).

director (1897) at the Austrian museum, introduced many English and American pieces in his furniture exhibitions and Felician Freiherr von Myrbach who was entrusted with a reorganization of the school was familiar with Western Europe from years of personal experience.

Hoffmann acknowledged his awareness of the English aims and achievements already in his first published statement of 1897 when he wrote: 'Hoffentlich wird auch bei uns einmal die Stunde schlagen, wo man die Tapete, die Deckenmalerei, wie die Möbel und Nutz-gegenstände nicht beim Händler, sondern beim Künstler bestellen wird. England geht uns hierin weit voran. . . .'[36] Three years later we have another piece of evidence for his strong interest in the English work-shop movement. On 20 April 1900 he wrote to Myrbach who then prepared a trip to England: 'Gewiss haben Herr Baron die Absicht, in London die Guild of Handicraft im Essex-House . . . zu besuchen. Dort arbeitet C. B. Aschbee [sic] . . . Es müsste sehr interessant sein, die Werkstätten zu besuchen. . . .'[37]

Half a year later Ashbee was exhibiting in Vienna, in the eighth exhibition of the Sezession, and Hevesi re-marked about his furniture that it looked 'als käme sie von einem viereckigen Planeten, der von vier-schrötigen Bauern bewohnt ist . . .' (as if it came from a foursquare planet which is inhabited by square-built peasants). In the same exhibition, the Glasgow group, the Mackintoshes and MacNairs, had an entire room. 'Eines der Interieurs,' as Hevesi put it, 'ganz jenseits von Gut und Böse' (One of the interiors . . . quite beyond good and evil).[38]

1900 was also the year in which Ruskin's *The Seven Lamps of Architecture* came out in a German edition, translated by W. Schoelermann who, one year earlier, had published an extensive article in *The Studio* on 'Modern fine and applied arts in Vienna'. Volumes of the German edition of Ruskin's works still remain in Josef Hoffmann's library and many of his program-matic pronouncements have a strongly Ruskinian flavor. The periodical *Hohe Warte* which had Hoff-mann on the editorial board not only published illus-trations of British buildings but lengthy quotations from Ruskin and Morris and when, a quarter of a century after the foundation of the *Wiener Werk-stätte*, a book about it was published under Hoffmann's

guidance and supervision it again is full of quotations from the two great English reformers. Even in a state-ment connected with controversies inside the Austrian Werkbund in 1933 Hoffmann still referred to England: 'Aber ebenso wie in England eine beginnende Bewe-gung um Makintosch [sic] interesselos verhallte, und ein so hochstehendes Land auf diesem Gebiet ins Hintertreffen brachte. . . .'[39]

As an artistic personality Mackintosh seems to have made the deepest impression on Hoffmann who not only knew the Scotsman from the *Sezession* exhibition but also shared two clients with him: Hugo Henne-berg[40] and Fritz Wärndorfer. Both of them acquired furniture designed by Mackintosh as well as pieces designed by Hoffmann. They were typical representa-tives of the liberal bourgeoisie which still provided much of the support for what was progressive in the arts in Vienna, and both had ties to England, Henne-berg through his interest in artistic experimental photography and Wärndorfer, who later translated letters by Beardsley, through business and personal connections. Wärndorfer undertook frequent trips across the Channel from which he would send or bring picture postcards or photographs to Hoffmann,[41] and he may well have been helpful in preparing finally a personal visit of Hoffmann to the British Isles.

Two letters from Hermann Muthesius to Hoffmann survive from which we learn that they met in London at the end of 1902, that Hoffmann had been to the South Kensington Museum and that he had been slightly disappointed in what he had seen in England; it is doubtful whether he also went to Scotland.[42]

---

36. 'It is to be hoped that with us too the hour will strike when wallpaper, ceiling-painting, just as the furniture and utensils will be ordered from the artist, not from the dealer. England in this leads us by far . . .' *Der Architekt*, III (1897), 13.

37. I owe knowledge of this letter to the late Hans Ankwicz-Kleehoven who owned it and kindly sent me an excerpt of the relevant passages.

38. Ludwig Hevesi, *Acht Jahre Sezession* (Vienna, 1906), 289.

39. 'But just as in England a beginning movement around Makintosch [sic] died away without interest, and brought a country so advanced in this area into a losing position . . .' About the events in 1933 see Eduard F. Sekler, 'The Archi-tectural Reaction in Austria', *Journal of the Society of Archi-tectural Historians*, XXIV (March, 1965), 67.

40. Dr. Hugo Henneberg's study in the house designed by Hoff-mann contained a dark cabinet by Mackintosh which had been part of his exhibit at the *Sezession*. *Das Interieur*, IV (1903), 139.

41. Nikolaus Pevsner, *Charles R. Mackintosh* (Milan, 1950), 29, and Howarth, *op. cit.*, 151 ff., both discuss the Wärndorfer-Mackintosh relationship. The following evidence further clarifies the problem. A letter by Wärndorfer, dated 29 April 1902, in the estate of Josef Hoffmann, states: 'Die Zeichnungen in Natur-grösse für alle festen Holzteile hat mir Macksh [sic] ge-schickt . . .' (Macksh has sent to me the drawings in natural size for all fixed wooden parts.) On 15 September 1902 Wärn-dorfer sent Hoffmann a postcard from Glasgow.

42. Hoffmann is said to have stated that he 'traveled all over Europe' before he designed the Stoclet House. There are in his estate some amateur photographs which might be construed as evidence for a trip to Scotland; they show details of a cottage (gatehouse) at Auchenbothie, Kilmalcolm, 1901, by Mackintosh (the photograph was kindly identified for me by Dr. Thomas Howarth) and of the White House, Helensburgh, by Baillie Scott. These photographs which were later published in *Hohe Warte*, I (1904–5), 179, may, however, have been from Wärndorfer, who could have taken them during his Scottish trip in 1902.

It is not unlikely that one of the main reasons for Hoffmann's trip was a desire to study personally methods and achievements of British designers and craftsmen in preparation for an undertaking that was beginning to take concrete shape in his mind: an Austrian parallel to something like the 'Guild of Handicraft'. In March 1903 Wärndorfer was busy in this matter and reported to Hoffmann: 'Macksh [sic], dem ich unter strenger Diskretion von unserem Metallwerkstätten Projekt schrieb . . . gibt mir heute folgende [positive] Antwort . . . Ich fahre nächste Woche zu Muthesius. . . .'[43] Less than two months later the *Wiener Werkstätte* was founded with Hoffmann and Kolo Moser as chief designers and Wärndorfer as the commercial director and supporter.[44] The practical framework for carrying out design commissions of considerable magnitude now existed and there was a span of some two years to gain practical experience with it before work on the Stoclet House began.

As far as direct formal dependence on British prototypes was concerned, it was frequent but never lasted long with Hoffmann owing to his own strong capacity for the invention and modification of form. It is sufficient to mention a few examples here.

His first houses on the Hohe Warte (Moll-Moser, Spitzer, Henneberg) were all built for artists or people closely related to the arts. Accordingly there was an obvious parallelism in programme to the British 'artist's cottages' so often found in illustrated periodicals of the time. The one which Voysey built for J. W. Forster

at Bedford Park[45] was even discussed by Hevesi in one of his newspaper articles in 1898.[46] It is not surprising, therefore, to find that Hoffmann in his early studio houses of 1901–1902 included such Voysey-like features as thin metal brackets under the eaves troughs and white roughcast. The use of applied half timber in the upper stories together with very steeply gabled projections, however, recalls work of British architects other than Voysey. It may be compared to Rowantreehill by J. Salmon and Son, Glasgow.[47]

Inside these early houses there are some strikingly simple staircase halls, comparable to Voysey's at the Orchard and of a kind that first occurs in Hoffmann's *œuvre* in a sketch published in *Ver Sacrum*, III, 1900, 71, where it stands in surprising contrast to his earlier extremely florid and exuberant sketches.

Similar parallels could be pointed out between early Hoffmann furniture[48] and typical arts and crafts furniture with its box-like shapes and with the uprights topped by a horizontal slab that go back to Mackmurdo.[49] Even Hoffmann's favorite device of carrying the stringers all the way around at the bottom of a chair, thus creating a cubical shape, can be found in furniture by Baillie Scott who also provided in his community hall for Onchan[50] a likely source of inspiration for Hoffmann's simple country church in Hohenberg, N.O., of 1903.

The strong impression made by Mackintosh has been mentioned; for a while his influence is unmistakable, as in decorative designs which Hoffmann made[51] and in pieces of furniture such as the one illustrated by Fernand Khnopff, the Belgian symbolist, in his article on Josef Hoffmann.[52] A comparison of two works of architecture, however, by Hoffmann and by Mackintosh, may serve to illustrate how differently they had developed by the time the Stoclet designs were worked out.

When Charles R. Mackintosh had to solve a problem akin to Hoffmann's at the Stoclet House, for the

43. 'Macksh, to whom I wrote in a strictly confidential manner about our project of a metal workshop . . . today gives me the following [positive] answer . . . Next week I travel to Muthesius. . . .' Letter in the estate of Josef Hoffmann.

44. Hoffmann's own version of the story about the events which directly preceded the foundation of the *Wiener Werkstätte* exists in the *Wiener Stadtbibliothek, Handschriftensammlung,* I. Nr. 151370. 'Es war im Sommer 1903. Wir sassen mittags im Caffe Heinrichshof mit Otto Wagner, Kolo Moser, einigen Freunden und mit Fritz Wärndorfer. Moser und ich resonierten [sic] heftig über die Kunstzustände in Wien. Nichts wollte vorwärts gehen . . . Wir redeten uns immer tiefer in Vorwürfe für die stumpfe Zeit und alle Unmöglichkeiten. Endlich sagte einer der Herren, die wir nur flüchtig kannten und welcher eben nach längerem Aufenthalt von London nach Wien zurückgekehrt war, dass es doch kein Haus kosten würde, wenn wir etwas derartiges versuchen wollten.' (It was in the summer of 1903. We sat at noon in the Caffe Heinrichshof with Otto Wagner, Kolo Moser, some friends and with Fritz Wärndorfer. Moser and I grumbled strongly about the conditions of art in Vienna. Nothing wanted to go forward . . . We talked ourselves more and more deeply into reproaches for the dull time and all the impossibilities. Finally one of the gentlemen whom we knew superficially only and who had just returned to Vienna from an extended stay in London, said that it surely would not cost a house if we wanted to try something of the kind.) Here the MS. ends but oral tradition has it that Wärndorfer pulled out his wallet on the spot and provided the 500 *Kronen* deemed necessary for a start.

45. *The Studio,* XI (1897), 20.
46. Hevesi, *Acht Jahre Sezession,* 6.
47. *Dekorative Kunst,* V (1900), 97.
48. *Das Interieur,* II (1901), 197.
49. Schmutzler, *op. cit.,* 103.
50. A table by Baillie Scott with stringers carried all the way around at the floor was illustrated in *Hohe Warte,* II (1905–6), 52. The community hall for Onchan appeared in *Dekorative Kunst,* V (1900), 46.
51. The title panel to his programmatic essay on furniture in *Das Interieur,* II (1901), 193, is a case in point. When Gabriel Mourey, *The Studio,* XXI (1900–1), 113, wrote about the Austrian interiors at the Paris exhibition of 1900 he praised Hoffmann's room but remarked: 'In the mural decoration there is perhaps somewhat too strong a suggestion of the familiar motif of the Glasgow school . . . ' Stephan Tschudi Madsen, *Sources of Art Nouveau* (New York, 1956), 403, also discusses the relation between Mackintosh and Hoffmann.
52. *The Studio,* XXII (1901), 261.

'House of a Lover of Art' competition of 1901[53] (Figs. 45, 46), the organization of the plan shows a departure from similar premises as Hoffmann's first project for Brussels (Fig. 2). There is a hall parallel to the long axis of the building two stories high, in close connection with a stair of two flights. There is a terrace near the elaborate entrance and an articulation of the outside by numerous breaks and protrusions. But Hoffmann's final plan (Fig. 17) goes beyond that of Mackintosh in the creation of a tightly knit, axially integrated whole. It is significant in this connection how several of the most important rooms which were parallel to the long axis of the building in Hoffmann's first version, are at right angles to it in his final one, which permits a closer grouping of elements.

In a similar fashion Hoffmann's model design (Figs. 4, 6) shows an outside which is much more tightly organized and classicistically tranquil than the 'House for a Lover of Art' (Fig. 45). Where the Scotsman still has the loose grouping of superbly modelled volumes that is a heritage from the nineteenth-century interest in medieval informal planning, the Viennese has the rigorous axiality of a classical composition. Where Mackintosh handled his surfaces as the modelled boundaries of a sculptural volume into which an opening like the long staircase window is slit, Hoffmann treated his like so many clearly defined, framed surfaces in their own right, underplaying the sculptural qualities of the volume.

Hoffmann did not seem to have any interest in medieval prototypes and in strongly sculptural treatment owing to his earlier training which had been disciplined by classical tradition and rationalism. At the same time, he remained extremely aware of the importance of the unbroken, clearly delimited plane as a compositional element. What his teacher Otto Wagner had predicted came true in Hoffmann's architecture: 'die tafelförmige Ausbildung der Fläche' (the planar handling of the surface) became the leitmotiv of a new architecture.

It is an impressive symbol for this concern with the rectangular sharply defined slablike plane, and a tribute to the power of Hoffmann's creative imagination, that in 1902 he created an abstract stucco relief (Fig. 47)[54] as part of his interior for the exhibition of Klinger's Beethoven in the *Sezession* which anticipates, in a breathtaking fashion, developments that were only to mature some fifteen years later, in neoplasticism, suprematism and related movements.

The authentically revolutionary character of this completely abstract, asymmetrical composition with rectangles in our context is sufficient guarantee that comparable occurrences in the composition of the Stoclet House, specially in its side-elevations (Fig. 48), may not be dismissed as purely fortuitous. It also introduces in a quite dramatic manner the third and most important factor that was influential in Hoffmann's design process: his own creative development in reaction to changes of taste and attitude around him.

Hoffmann only for a short period of time worked in a manner directly related to international Art Nouveau —in the narrow sense of that term—the Art Nouveau of the Belgians and their direct followers and parallels.[55] Then, encouraged no doubt by Lichtwark and Muthesius in their call for '*Sachlichkeit*', and following what soon was a general trend, he became critical about it and remembered the more rational roots of his art, and the discipline of tradition; in 1901 already he wrote: 'Auch die Moderne leidet unter unerträglichen Fehlern ... Man nimmt nicht Rücksicht auf die gerade Faserung des Holzes und macht Curven über Curven. ...'[56]

Hoffmann at first set out to find his own creative solution for overcoming Art Nouveau by turning to simple elementary forms: the square and the cube, in white and black. No doubt he was partly inspired to do so by British prototypes but he went further than most of them in a radical elan that was characteristic for the early years of his career and the young *Sezession* movement. The *Sanatorium Purkersdorf* and the Stoclet House mark his most advanced solutions with the introduction of cube and square and sharply defined white planes into architecture.

But the square and cube have this in common that they are inherently non-directional, static. And something of a feeling that static elements have been put together in an additive manner remains as typical for the Stoclet House as its patent negation of tectonic expression. A turning away from tectonic expression at that particular moment in history might simply be a reaction to the way in which, a short while ago, flowing lines and twisting surfaces had forcibly engaged a beholder's empathy; the reinstatement of the plain surface in architecture can also be seen as a particular case of the more general return to a respect of the unbroken plane, including the picture plane— a phenomenon that was characteristic for the whole period, as has been pointed out frequently. But the

53. Howarth, *op. cit.*, 157.
54. *Deutsche Kunst und Dekoration*, x (1902), 486.

55. I am not convinced that it is very useful to stretch the term Art Nouveau too far in an attempt to create artifically a new overly comprehensive label for stylistic categorization.
56. 'The modern movement too suffers from insufferable faults ... one does not respect the straight grain of the wood and makes curves over curves ...' *Das Interieur*, II (1901), 201.

Stoclet House goes beyond all this in one important respect.

There are many places in the building where visually a separation of contiguous planes seems the obvious next step according to the inner logic of the design. This has been mentioned when the various bridgelike elements were discussed, or the two angular prow-like projections where a virtual movement of the angled planes is implied, as of two door wings about to open.

Otto Wagner indicated a similar direction in the way he handled the corners of the Postal Savings Bank, 1904–1905, where two façades are expressed as independent slabs which do not meet but are separated by a short, oblique surface which is slightly set back. But neither in his œuvre nor in Hoffmann's was the last step taken that would have liberated space through an actual separation of the confining planes, setting at work a process of 'active dematerialization' that was to be so characteristic for the 'New Architecture' of the twenties. This was only achieved by Frank Lloyd Wright[57] and later by others.

With Hoffmann where any virtual movement occurs, it is not in the nature of a clearly defined dynamism, but of a passive motion; a sliding and gliding past each other of elements which leads to an effect of 'passive dematerialization' and recalls a similar tendency in many paintings by Gustav Klimt.[58] In them forms and bodies seem to float past each other not driven by their own volition but as in a trance. With all due caution in making comparisons from one field of creativity to another, one is also reminded of the glissando effects so typical for the *avant-garde* music of the period, and perhaps even of Hugo von Hofmannsthal's attempt at a characterization of the whole epoch, written in 1905, the year when the Stoclet House was begun: '. . . das Wesen unserer Epoche ist Vieldeutigkeit und Unbestimmtheit. Sie kann nur auf Gleitendem ausruhen und ist sich bewusst, dass es Gleitendes ist, wo andere Generationen an das Feste glaubten.'[59]

In the face of such uncertainty one of the few points of departure that supposedly remained firm beyond dispute was a return to the roots of a nationally oriented tradition. All around Hoffmann the pressure was building up towards traditionalism and nationalism, a pressure which was hard to resist since it was closely linked to people and attitudes—including those coming from England—which had been his valued guides in the past.

It began with Herrmann Muthesius who already in 1901, in his *Stilarchitektur und Baukunst*, p. 61, wrote: '. . . die Wiederaufnahme örtlich-bürgerlicher und ländlicher Baumotive verspricht uns aber gerade in Deutschland die reichste Ernte . . . so haben wir bald wieder nicht nur eine vernünftige, sondern auch eine nationale bürgerliche Baukunst.'[60]

Writers like Hevesi and J. A. Lux followed suit, praising the Biedermeier as the period when a sound national tradition had still existed in Austria and Germany. Lux joined Hoffmann in 1904 on the editorial board of a new periodical *Hohe Warte* which read and looked very different from *Ver Sacrum* that had just ceased to appear. *Heimatschutz* and *heimatliches Bauen* were greatly stressed, Schultze-Naumburg appeared as one of the collaborators, and it does not come as a surprise under these circumstances to discover that even the Stoclet House was provided with a 'respectable' ancestry. Its forms, so we read, were to be related to ancient Flemish prototypes: castles and mansion houses.[61]

By 1905 Karl Widmer could boast: '. . . man hat über die Grundlagen der historischen Stile nicht hinausgekonnt. Aber man fusst auf sie in einem anderen, freieren Geiste. Man hängt nicht mehr so zäh an Einzelheiten der äusseren historischen Richtigkeit . . . hier haben wir die Quellen des neuen Stils zu suchen.'[62] The same idea was expressed five years later in different words: '. . . man sah wieder die feinen Fäden, die uns mit der Vergangenheit verknüpfen . . . Man greift irgend eine Anregung auf, gleichgültig in welcher Zeit man sie findet, entkleidet sie ihrer zeitlichen

57. In Wright's early work there are some striking parallels to Hoffmann's, cf. Eduard F. Sekler, 'Frank Lloyd Wright zum Gedächtnis', *Der Aufbau*, XIV (Aug. 1959), 299.

58. A contemporary observer remarked about Klimt's overriding influence in Vienna: 'So glaube ich in Klimt den zu sehen, der die Verschiedenheiten der Wiener Meister in jene eigentümliche Gemeinsamkeit bringt, die man Stil der Wiener Werkstätte nennt.' (So I believe to see in Klimt the one who brings the diversities of the Viennese masters into that peculiar rapport which one calls style of the *Wiener Werkstätte*.) Franz Blei, *Deutsche Kunst und Dekoration*, XIX (1906–7), 45.

59. '. . . the essence of our epoch is ambiguity and uncertainty. It can only rest on that which is gliding and it is aware of the fact that gliding is what other generations believed firm', quoted by Carl E. Schorske, 'Schnitzler und Hofmannsthal', *Wort und Wahrheit*, XVII (May 1962), 378.

60. '. . . but to take up again local-civil and rural architectural motifs promises us the richest harvest particularly in Germany . . . thus we have soon again not only a reasonable but also a national civil architecture.'

61. *Hohe Warte*, II (1905–6), 68. Hoffmann must have approved of this article since he was on the editorial board. Photographs from his possession indicate that he did take an interest in the historic architecture of Belgium, particularly in anonymous ensembles such as old warehouses along a canal, or a beguinage.

62. '. . . one has not been capable of going beyond the bases of the historical styles. But one is based on them in a different, freer spirit. One is no longer so tightly attached to details of external historical correctness . . . here we have to look for the sources of the new style.' *Moderne Bauformen*, IV (1905), 2nd issue.

Nüancen und fügt sie der neuen Schöpfung ein, als neues Stilelement. . . .'[63]

When J. A. Lux resigned as an editor of the *Hohe Warte* in 1908, his last printed words were a strong plea against exaggerated '*Bodenständigkeit*' and '*Heimatkunst*'.[64] But considering the greater political forces at work all over Europe, it is not surprising that his words went unheeded. After a brief lull during Ernst von Koerber's government, 1900–1904, the forces of nationalism gathered momentum again in the Austro-Hungarian Monarchy and architectural developments here and in Germany prior to World War I with a few exceptions were strongly traditional and often nationalistic. In 1908 the severely classicistic House Feinhals was built by Olbrich, Hoffmann's admired former companion in revolutionary Art Nouveau exuberance, and in 1911 the German Embassy in St. Petersburg by Peter Behrens was equally classicistic and monumental. Many comparable examples by less important contemporaneous architects could be added and even Adolf Loos wrote in 1913: 'Im Anfang des 19. Jahrhunderts haben wir die Tradition verlassen, dort will ich wieder anknüpfen.'[65] A kindred attitude had already been expressed by Hoffmann in 1901 when he stated: 'Wo also . . . sollen wir . . . die Tradition finden? Möglich wäre eine Anknüpfung nur dort, wo bei uns das Selbstschöpferische aufgehört hat.'[66]

With all this it was to be expected that Hoffmann should have turned to a re-examination of such elements of the classical tradition as grooving, tympana and heavy cornices. The Ast House (Fig. 23), finished almost simultaneously with the Stoclet House, the Primavesi-Skywa House, and the Austrian pavilion at the Werkbund exhibition of 1914 indicate how he transformed the ancient vocabulary, usually contradicting its original tectonic meaning but imbuing it with a grace of his own.

Hoffmann by talent, temperament and background was not the man to pursue a course of lonely opposition. His strength was to design from an unfailing capacity to invent forms, not from a rigorously formulated and maintained revolutionary position. He was not fascinated by new technological developments and does not seem to have had any particular interest in the great forces at work behind the scenes of his time. But he was always happy to support young talent and new ideas[67] in the younger generation of architects to whom he left the task of following up the architectural implications of the Stoclet House, chief among them the definition of space by isolated planes. In retrospect this feat seems clearly adumbrated at the Stoclet House, and when it happened, it marked the well-known new stage in architectural history[68] which is dramatically represented by such famous buildings as Rietveld's Schröder House and the Barcelona Pavilion by Mies van der Rohe.

Both Rietveld and Mies are very likely to have known the Stoclet House, not only from having worked in close geographic proximity but also from publications about Hoffmann such as the special issue which *Wendingen*, the Dutch periodical, dedicated to Hoffmann in 1920. Rietveld must have had a particular professional interest in Hoffman's furniture and Mies has even been described as a pupil of Hoffmann's by Morton Shand who knew the period well from personal experience.[69] Of Theo van Doesburg, we know that he was impressed by the completely non-figurative passages in Klimt's mosaic frieze at the Stoclet House[70] and Robert Mallet Stevens often admired the building in his youth; he was a relative of the family on the mother's side. Especially some of his designs for exhibition pavilions are strongly reminiscent of what he saw at the Stoclet House.

Other architects and artists visited the house at some time, among them Peter Behrens who praised it highly,[71] Max Bill, Richard Neutra and Le Corbusier. Some relevant remarks were made about it by critics,[72] but on the whole it did not attract a great deal of professional comment. Partly this was due to the historical circumstances. Three years after its completion

---

63. ' . . . one saw again the delicate threads which link us with the past . . . one takes up some suggestion, no matter in which period it is found, disrobes it of its time-bound peculiarities and fits it into the new creation, as a new element of style . . . ' Introduction to *Architektur des XX. Jahrhunderts*, 7th special issue (Berlin, 1910).

64. See note 39 for a reference to a more detailed discussion of the events around the *Hohe Warte* and its editor.

65. 'At the beginning of the nineteenth century we have left the tradition, there I want to link up again.' Adolf Loos, *Sämtliche Schriften*, edited by Franz Glück, I (Vienna, 1962), 323.

66. 'Where then . . . should we . . . find the tradition? A linking up would only be possible where, with us, the autonomously creative has ceased.' *Das Interieur*, II (1901), 201.

67. Hoffmann was on the council of the 'Friends of the Bauhaus' and it is well known that he voted for Le Corbusier's design as a juror at the famous competition for a Palace of the League of Nations in Geneva, 1927.

68. Sigfried Giedion, *Space, Time and Architecture* (Cambridge, Mass., 1952), especially pt. VI.

69. P. Morton Shand, 'Van de Velde, Hoffmann, etc.', *Architectural Association Journal*, LXXV (Jan. 1959), 170.

70. Dobai, *op. cit.*, 21.

71. *Journal of the American Institute of Architects*, XII (Oct. 1924), 422.

72. H. S. Goodhart-Rendel, *How Architecture is Made* (London, 1947), 57, ' . . . an example of the architecture that wears no mask but whose natural face is distinctly made up . . . ' Emil Kaufmann, *Architecture in the Age of Reason* (Cambridge, Mass., 1955), 59, 'The spirit which created the Dulwich Gallery (1811–14), was revived in buildings like Josef Hoffmann's Palais Stoclet . . . '

the First World War broke out and dramatically marked the end of an era for which the Stoclet House had been a characteristic and leading monument. The post-war years had other interests than the house of an art-lover. But partly the reason must be sought in the direction Hoffmann's career as a designer had taken after the Stoclet House, a direction not likely to attract the attention of the *avant-garde*.

Erich Mendelsohn, in a letter of 14 March 1914, evaluated the Stoclet House, at that time still new and topical, from his point of view: '... Was grosszügig daran ist, ist der neue Wille, vieles von dem was ich ausführte. Nur noch nicht vollendet, noch nicht das Werk, noch nicht Stil. Noch sind es Flächen von Innenwänden und nicht Gesichter der Struktur und der tektonischen Notwendigkeit.'[73]

Some twenty years later E. Persico could be more detached when he assessed the value of the Stoclet House for his generation in an article in *Casabella* entitled 'Trent'anni dopo il Palazzo Stoclet'. His words were recently quoted again, significantly to conclude the first volume of a history of modern architecture[74]—the volume that brings the story to the

threshold of the Modern Movement. What follows is an excerpt from Persico's essay, in translation:

> We are not talking of the Stoclet Palace here in order to present it as a model of the architecture of today; it is judged as a part of its environment, and from this some lessons are to be drawn. First that it was in tune with its time ... in the relation of the style to the most vital ideas of its time. Measured by this standard the Stoclet Palace is an outstanding example ... will the architects of today be able to realize in art a comparable totality of life? To resist the temptations of rhetoric and to retain the tradition of European architecture without deviations? These questions ... let the Stoclet Palace appear as the monument of an epoch that was glorious for the destinies of art.

In retrospect, it appears indeed that the Stoclet House marked the high-point internally and externally in Hoffmann's entire *œuvre*.[75] It remained an achievement in scope, quality and significance which he did not surpass during the rest of a long and fruitful career. He had been 35 when he began the Stoclet designs and he died, aged 86, in 1956.

73. '...what is great about it is the new will, much of what I have explained. Only not yet finished, not yet the work, not yet style. These are still surfaces of inner walls and not faces of structure and of tectonic necessity.' Erich Mendelsohn, *Briefe eines Architekten* (Munich, 1961), 27.
74. Leonardo Benevolo, *Storia dell'architettura moderna* (Bari,

1960), 429, quoting from E. Persico, *Scritti critici e polemici* (Milan, 1947), 183.
75. The most comprehensive recent summary of Hoffmann's *œuvre* was given by Hans Ankwicz-Kleehoven in his article for *Neue Österreichische Biographie*, x (Vienna, 1957).

ACKNOWLEDGMENTS

The author wishes to express his appreciation to the Council of the Harvard Foundation for two grants which materially aided his research for this paper. The late Mr. Jacques Stoclet and his widow permitted several visits to their house and provided information otherwise unobtainable. Mrs. Karla Hoffmann, widow of the late Josef Hoffmann, very kindly made material available from the estate of her husband and extended every possible help. Without her full-hearted cooperation this paper could not

have been written. Many other individuals have helped by answering enquiries and providing valuable indications for which I am deeply grateful. They include DDr. Gerhart Egger, Mlle Mina Martens, Mr. Pierre Genlet, Prof. Thomas Howarth, Prof. Victor G. Martiny, Mr. Adolph K. Placzek, Dr. Arthur Graf Strachwitz, Prof. Herbert Thurner, Mr. Erich Vencour and Dr. Hans M. Wingler. Last but not least my wife has been a patient and helpful critic and aide.

ILLUSTRATIONS

1. Seventy-First Regiment Armory, 1905. Clinton and Russel Architects (New York Convention and Visitors Bureau).
From the files of R. Koch, gratefully acknowledged

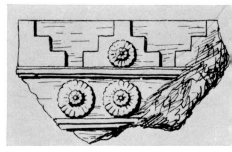

4. The top of an altar from Carchemish (9 or 8th century B.C.). C. L. Woolley, *Carchemish* Pt. II, *The Town Defences*. London, British Museum, 1921, p. 151, Fig. 56

5. Cylinder seal impression from Assur showing turreted and battlemented walls of a town (probably 13th or 12th century B.C. O. Weber, 'Altorientalische Siegelbilder', *Der Alte Orient* 17 and 18. Leipzig, 1920, p. 105, No. 531

2. Reconstruction of the walls and the high gate of Medinet Habu (Ramesses III, 1182–1151 B.C.), U. Hölscher, *Das hohe Tor von Medinet Habu* (12. Wissenschaftliche Veröffentlichung der Deutschen Orient-Gesellschaft), Leipzig, 1910, Frontispiece (Pl. 1)

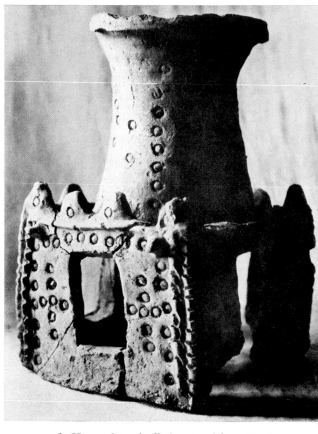

3. Rim of a Hittite vase from Boghazköy with battlemented wall and tower (15th century B.C.). E. Akurgal and M. Hirmer, *The Art of the Hittites*, New York, 1962, Pl. 46

6. House-shaped offering stand from Nuzi (15th or 14th century B.C.) R. F. S. Starr, *Nuzi*, Vol. II, Cambridge, 1937, Pl. 113 A

Wall painting from palace at Nuzi (15th or 14th century B.C.). Starr, *Nuzi*, Vol. II, Pl. 128 H

9. Fragment of bone inlay from Ziwiye, Northwest Iran (late 8th or 7th century B.C.). Length 2.6 cm., height 1.1 cm. The Metropolitan Museum of Art, Gift of Khalil Rabenou, 1958. Acc. No. 58.131.5. Hitherto unpublished

8. Seal impressions from Assur showing temples (12th century B.C.). A. Moortgat, 'Assyrische Glyptik des 12. Jahrhunderts', *Zeitschrift für Assyriologie* 48 (N.F. 14), 1944, p. 43, Figs. 46 and 45 b

a–d. Statue base from Susa (late 8th or 7th century B.C.). Musée du Louvre, Antiquités orientales, Sb 5641. Greenish, black stone, badly burnt. Each side measures 7.5 cm. on top, height 4.7 cm. Photographs: Musée du Louvre. Hitherto unpublished

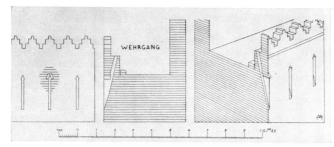

11. Parapet walk of the Late Assyrian period from Assur (late 8th to 7th century B.C.). W. Andrae, *Die Festungswerke von Assur* (23. Wissenschaftliche Veröffentlichung der Deutschen Orient-Gesellschaft), Leipzig, 1913, p. 115, Fig. 186

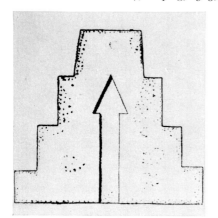

12. A sandstone merlon from Susa (Achaemenid period, 5th–4th centuries B.C.). R. de Mecquenem et G. Contenau, *Mémoires de la mission archéologique en Iran* XXX, Paris, 1947, p. 45, Fig. 21

15

15. Model of a tower from Toprak Kale, near Van (late 8th to 7th century B.C.). London, British Museum. R. D. Barnett, 'The Excavations of the British Museum at Toprak Kale, near Van', *Iraq* XII, 1950, Pl. I: 1

13. Surrender of an Anatolian town. Fragment of a relief from the reign of Tiglathpileser III (745–727 B.C.). Musée du Louvre, Antiquités orientales, No. 19855. Photograph: Musée du Louvre. The same photograph was published in R. D. Barnett and M. Falkner, *The Sculptures of Tiglath-pileser III...* British Museum, 1962, pl. XLVI

14a, b. Models of towns brought as tribute to the Assyrian king. Details of relief from the reign of Sargon II (721–705 B.C.). Musée du Louvre, Antiquités orientales, No. 19887. Photographs: Musée du Louvre

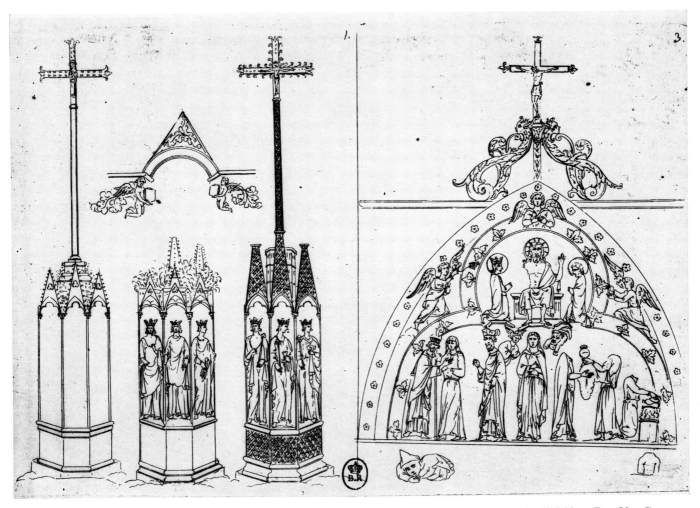

1. The St. Louis Montjoies and the tympanum of the church at St.-Denis de la Chapelle. (Paris, Bibl. Nat., Est., Vx 16)

2. The St. Louis Montjoies. (Paris, Bibl. Nat., Est., Vx 16)

4. The cross at La Chapelle (Prudhomme, 1791)

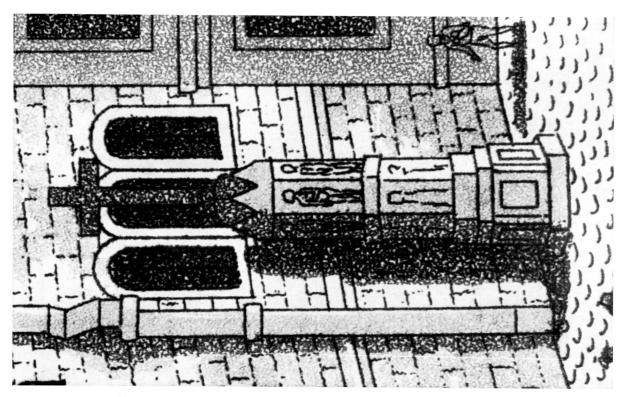

3. The cross by St.-Lazare (Saint-Victor, ca. 1808)

1. Fragmentary model of a building, in lead; side view. Enlargement. The Hague, Gemeente-Museum

2. Fragmentary model of a building, in lead; rear view. Enlargement. The Hague, Gemeente-Museum

3. Three complete models, in lead. Paris, Musée de Cluny

4. Hans Sebald Beham: Saint Sebaldus of Nürnberg. Engraving.
Amsterdam, Rijksmuseum, Printroom

5. Fourteenth-century fragmentary Pilgrimage Ensign, in lead.
Amsterdam, Historisch Museum

6. The Resurrection, on a fifth-century Ampulla.
Monza, Duomo. After Grabar

7. Romanesque turret, Christchurch Church, Hampshire.
After a drawing by Sir Thomas Graham Jackson, Bart

8. Apse of Nôtre-Dame-de-Rioux (Charente-Maritime)

9. Sarcophagus of Saint Aguilberte, Crypts of Jouarre

10. The Holy Sepulchre on a twelfth-century Seal of the Canons
of the Holy Sepulchre. After Formigé

11. The Holy Sepulchre. Detail of a woodcut of 1538. Utrecht, Central Museum

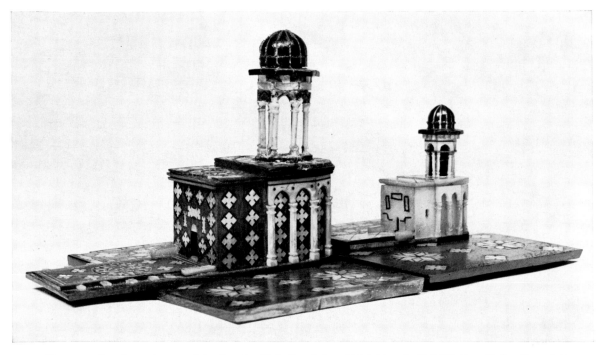

12. Two seventeenth-century models after the Holy Sepulchre. Zeist, Van de Poll-Wolters-Quina Foundation

1–2. Paolo Romano: Statues of St. Paul and St. Peter at the foot of the steps. Vatican Palace, Papal Apartments

3. Anonymous Italian mid-sixteenth-century drawing: View of the Vatican. London. Collection of Sir Anthony Blunt

4. Detail of Fig. 1

5. Attributed to Ventura Salimbeni: Pius II receiving St. Andrew's head at the Ponte Molle. Pen and ink drawing. Florence, Museo Horne, no. 5876

6–8. Marble reliefs with two angels supporting St. Andrew's head. Rome, Grotte Vaticane.
6: by Isaia da Pisa; 7: by Paolo Romano; 8: by Paolo Romano

9. Greek silver-gilt reliquary for St. Andrew's head. Patras, Church of St. Andrew

10. Simone di Giovanni da Firenze: Silver-gilt reliquary for St. Andrew's head. 1463–64. Pienza, Museo del Duomo

11. Paolo Romano: Statue of St. Andrew. Rome, Ponte Molle

12. Attributed to Paolo Romano: Marble relief from the tomb of Pius II. Rome, S. Andrea della Valle

1. Disegno del 'perticatore' Lorenzo Mazzi. Padova, Museo, Archivio di Stato (tomo 320, c. 9)

2. La Casa Cornaro a Padova come è oggi. Facciata

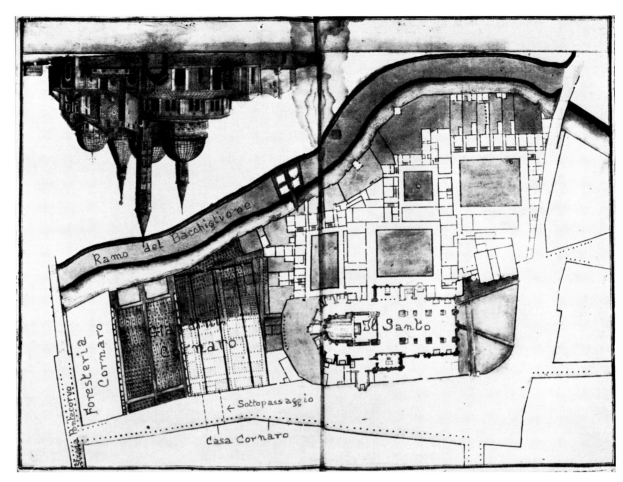

3. La Casa Cornaro da disegno di Lorenzo Mazzi, 1735. Facciata

4. Gianmaria Falconetto: Loggia del Palazzo Cornaro, Padova. 1524

5. Gianmaria Falconetto: Soffitto della Capella del Santo, Basilica di S. Antonio, Padova

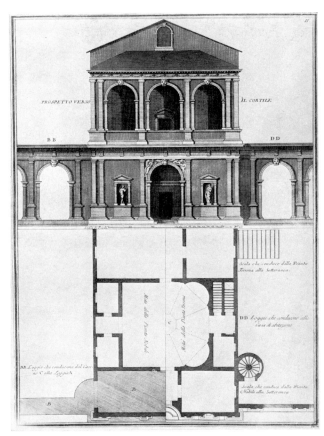

6. Odeo Cornaro

7. Gianmaria Falconetto: Porta di Ca'Farsetti, Este

8. Vincenzo M. Coronelli: La Scala Farsetti, Este

9. Il Cortile del Palazzo Cornaro (da stampa di G. Valle, 1784)

10. Gianmaria Falconetto: Monumento
di Camilla Tedolda, 1533. Parrocchiale (Annunciata),
Arzergrande presso Codenigo (Padova)

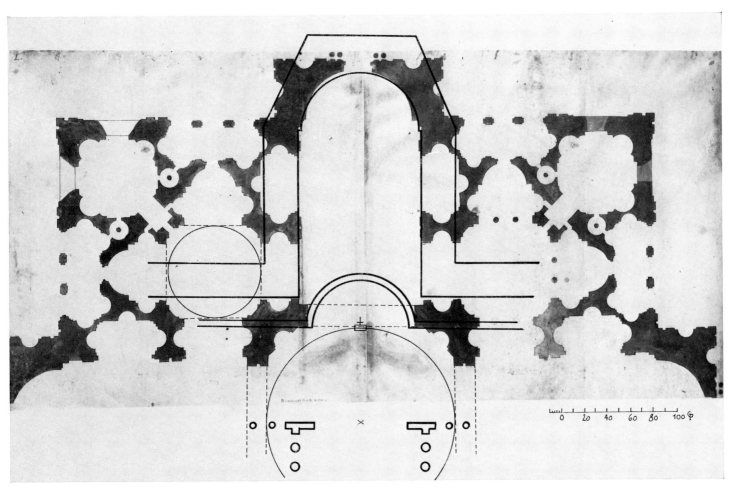

1. Der erste Plan Bramantes für St. Peter mit den Fundamentansätzen der konstantinischen Basilika und Nikolaus V.

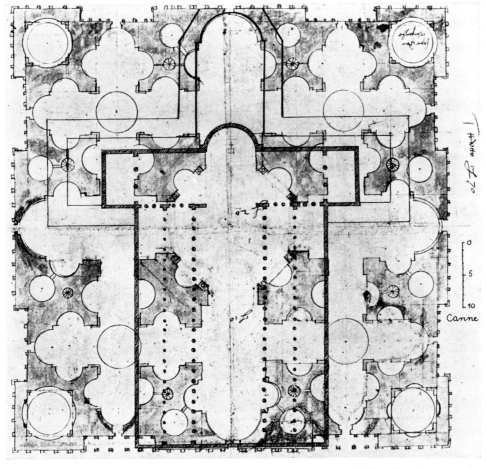

2. Der Entwurf Giulianos da Sangallo für St. Peter, Uff. 8A recto, mit den Fundamenten der konstantinischen Basilika und dem Erweiterungsplan Nikolaus V.

4. Die Rötelzeichnung, Uff. 8 A verso, Deutungsversuch der Alternativvorschläge für das Langhaus

3. Die Rötelzeichnung, Uff. 8 A verso, mit den Fundamenten der konstantinischen Basilika und dem Erweiterungsbau Nikolaus V.

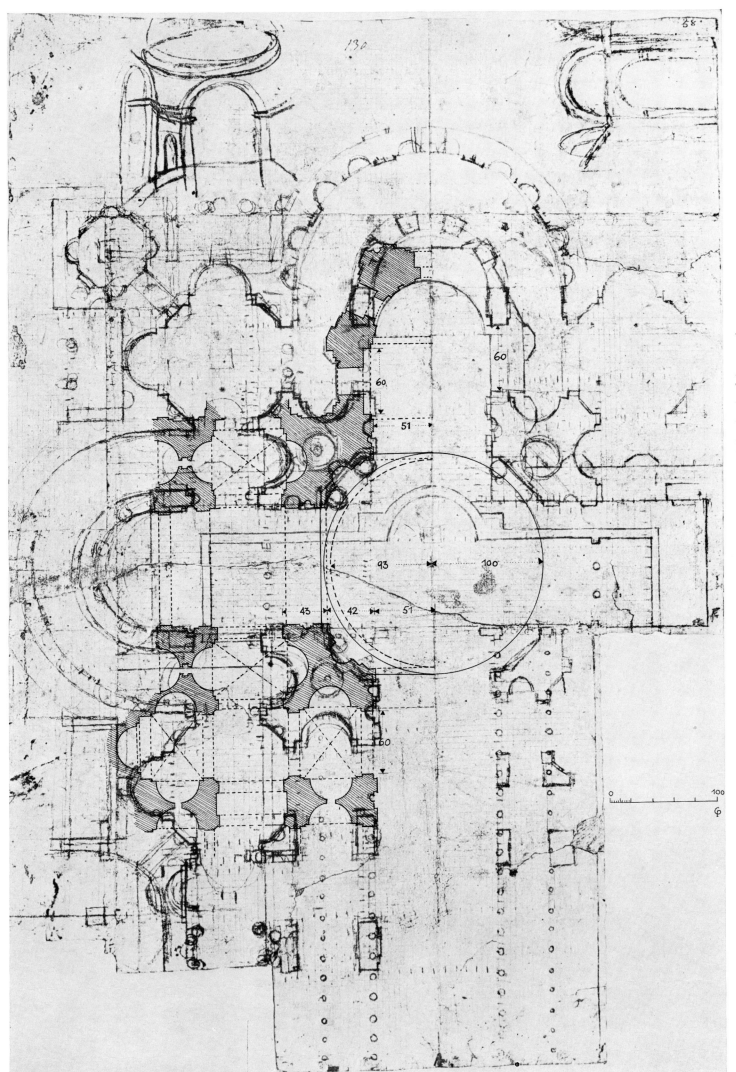

5. Der Grundriss für St. Peter, Uff. 20 A, mit Eintragung der Pfeiler des Ausführungsplanes

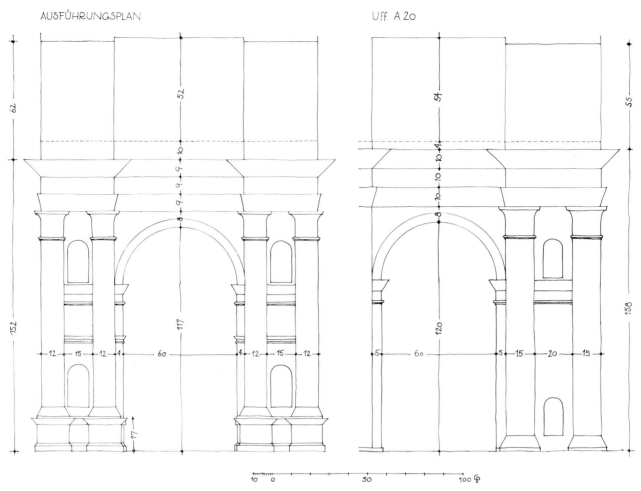

AUSFÜHRUNGSPLAN   Uff. A 20

6. Aufrisse der Pilasterordnungen des Entwurfes Uff. 20 A, und des Ausführungsplanes

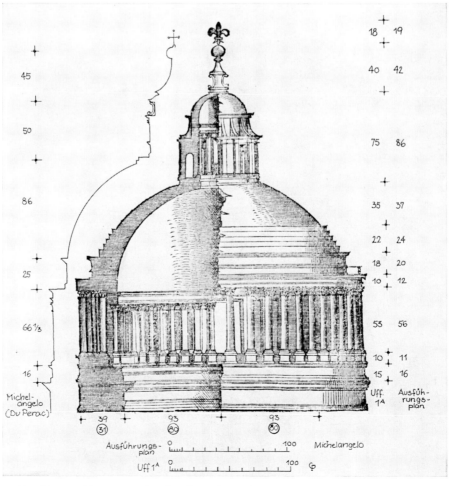

7. Der Entwurf Bramantes für die Kuppel von St. Peter (nach Serlio) mit den vergleichenden Grössenangaben und der Umrisslinie der Michelangelokuppel (nach du Pérac)

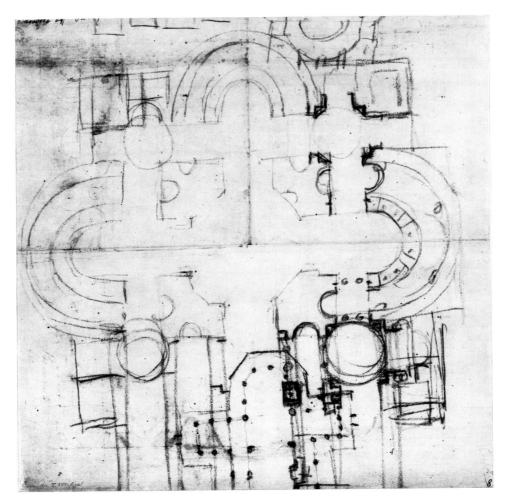

1. Studie für St. Peter. Uff. arch. 8 verso

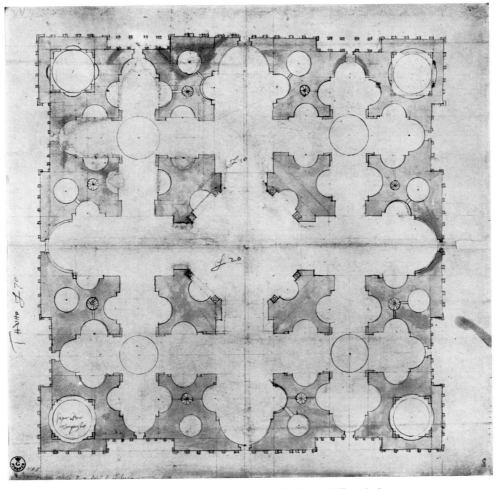

2. Giuliano da Sangallo: Studie für St. Peter. Uff. arch. 8 recto

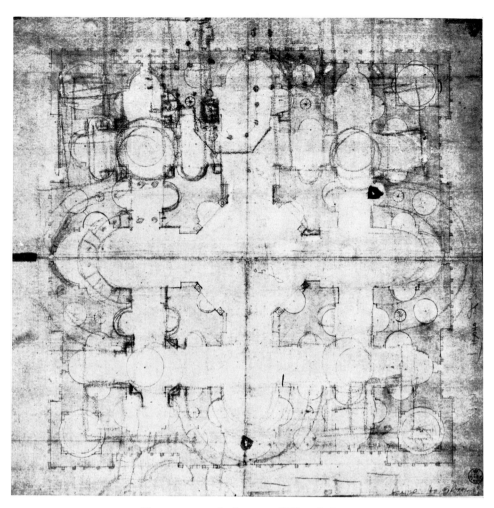

3. Transparenzaufnahme von Uff. arch. 8 verso

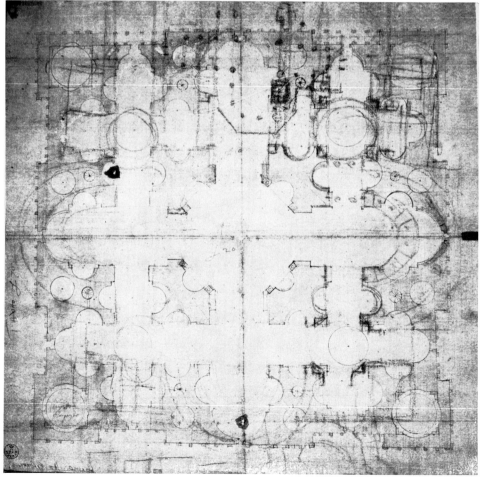

4. Transparenzaufnahme von Uff. arch. 8 recto

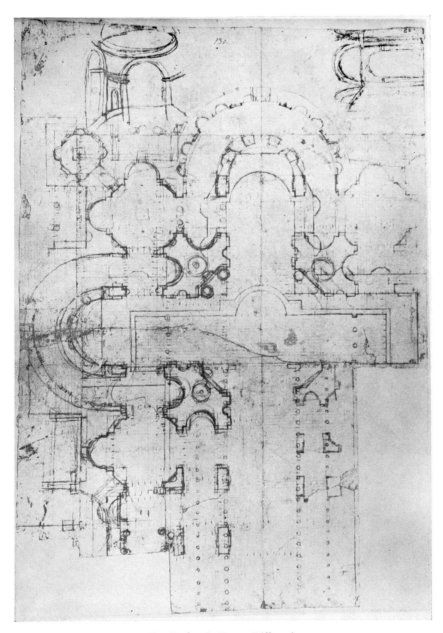

5. Studie für St. Peter. Uff. arch. 20

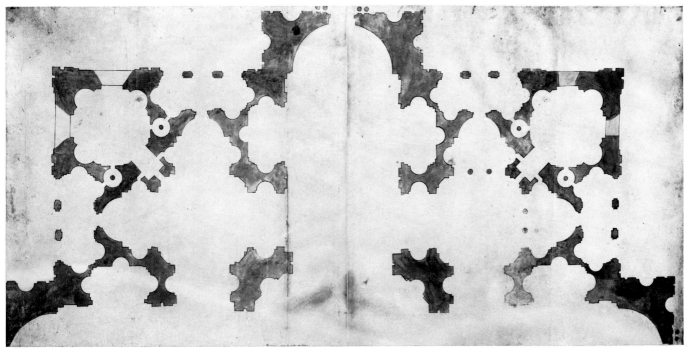

6. Der sogenannte Pergamentplan Bramante's. Uff. arch. 1

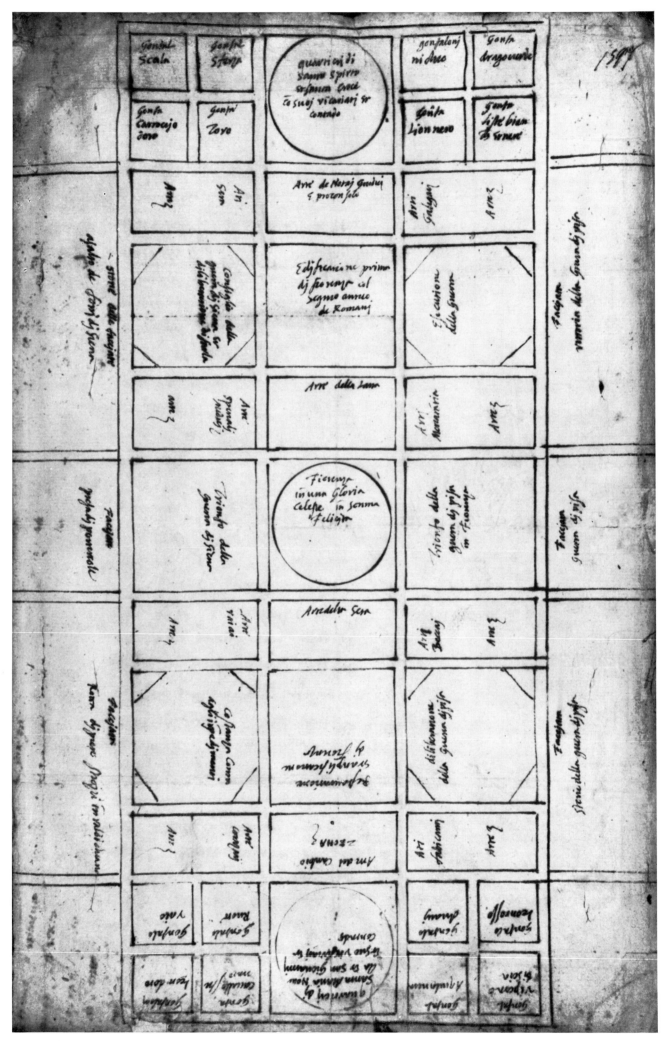

1. Vasari: Scheme for the ceiling of the Salone del Cinquecento in the Palazzo Vecchio, Florence. Florence, Archivio di Stato, Mediceo del Principato, Carteggio universale 497 a, fol. 1597

2. Vasari: Scheme for the ceiling of the Salone del Cinquecento. Florence, Archivio di Stato, Carte Strozziane, 1ª serie, CXXXIII, fol. 141

3. Vasari: Design for the ceiling of the Salone del Cinquecento. Cambridge, Mass., Fogg Art Museum, no. 1932.157

4. Vasari: The Building of the third *cerchio*. Florence, Palazzo Vecchio, Salone del Cinquecento

5. Vasari: The Foundation of Florence. Florence, Palazzo Vecchio, Salone del Cinquecento

6. Detail of Fig. 5

7. Detail of Fig. 5

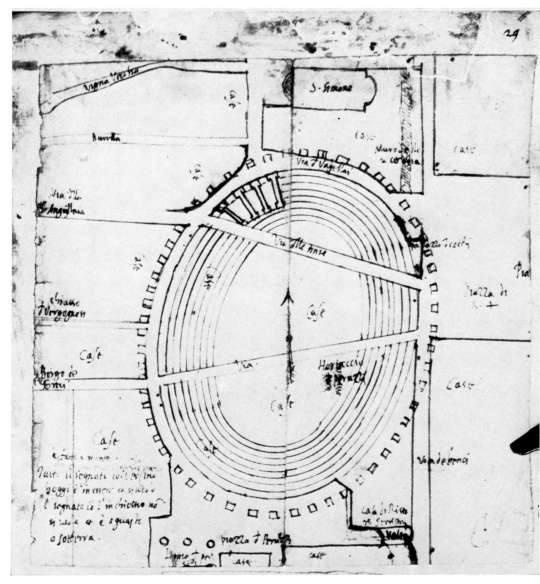

9 a–b. Roman coins of the Temple of Mars Ultor in Rome. London, British Museum, Department of Coins and Medals

8. Borghini: Drawing of a reconstruction of the Roman amphitheatre in Florence.
Florence, Biblioteca Nazionale, MS. Magl. xxv. 551, fol. 29 r

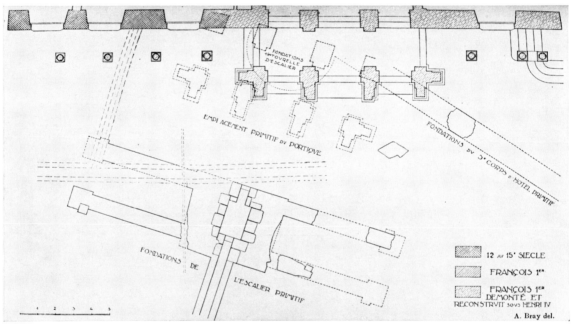

1. Ducerceau, *Les plus excellents Bâtiments de France*, plan de la Cour Ovale

2. Plan des fouilles de A. Bray, op. cit., note 15

3. Photo des fouilles de A. Bray (Archives des Monuments Historiques)

Photo des fouilles de A. Bray (Archives des Monuments Historiques)

5. Restitution de l'escalier par A. Bray, ibid.

6. Escalier d'après Serlio (Livre II, voir note 17)

7. Le Portique, état au XIXe siècle, relevé de Pfnor avant les réfections
de 1894, Paris, 1863

8. La Chapelle Saint Saturnin, relevé de Pfnor, Paris, 1863

9. La Porte Dorée, relevé de Pfnor, Paris, 1863

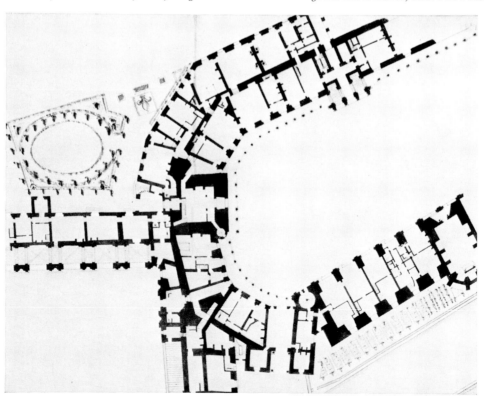

10. Relevé de Robert de Cotte (B.N. Est. Va. 340) 1729 (Rez-de-chaussée)

1. Luca Cambiaso: Detail of fresco on vault over upper choir of Escorial

2. Tibaldi: Sketch for bay dedicated to *Gramatica* in the Escorial library. British Museum

Escorial library. Frescoes by Tibaldi and Carducci: 3. The Egyptian priests. – 4. The Gymnosophists. –
5. Orpheus and Eurydice. – 6. Hercules Gallicus. – 7. The Tower of Babel

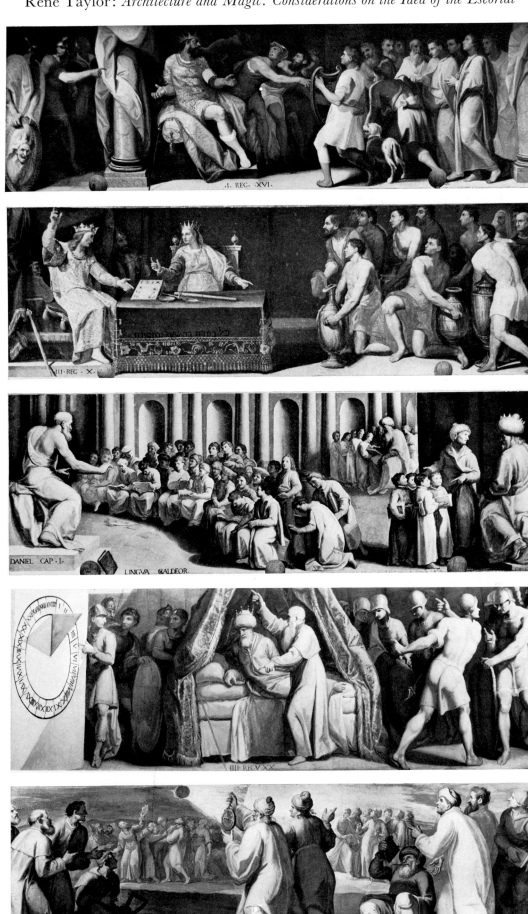

Escorial library. Frescoes by Tibaldi and Carducci: 8. David exorcising Saul by means of his music. –
9. The Queen of Sheba questioning Solomon. – 10. Daniel and his companions instructed by the Chaldean
Magi. – 11. King Hezekiah watching the retrogression of the sun's shadow. – 12. Dionysius the Areopagite observing the eclipse at Christ's Passion.

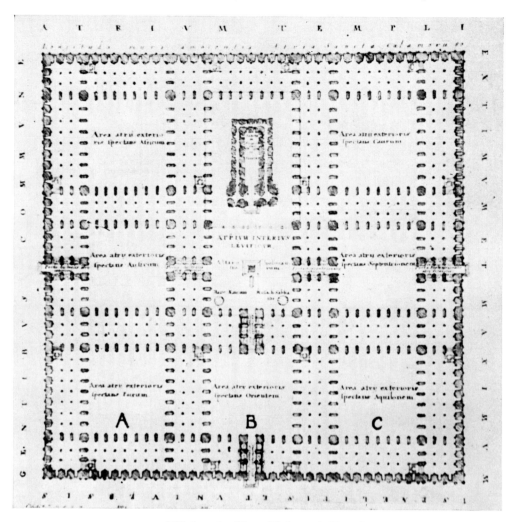

13. Villalpando: Plan of Solomon's Temple

14. Villalpando: The Tabernacle of Moses

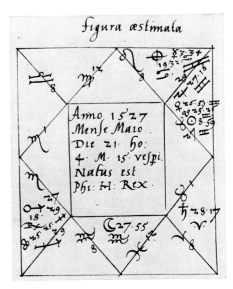

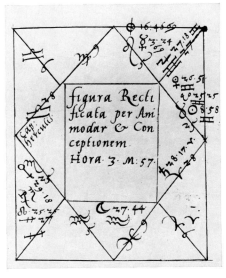

15–16. Matthias Hacus Sumbergius: *Prognosticon*. Estimated and rectified charts of Philip II's birth

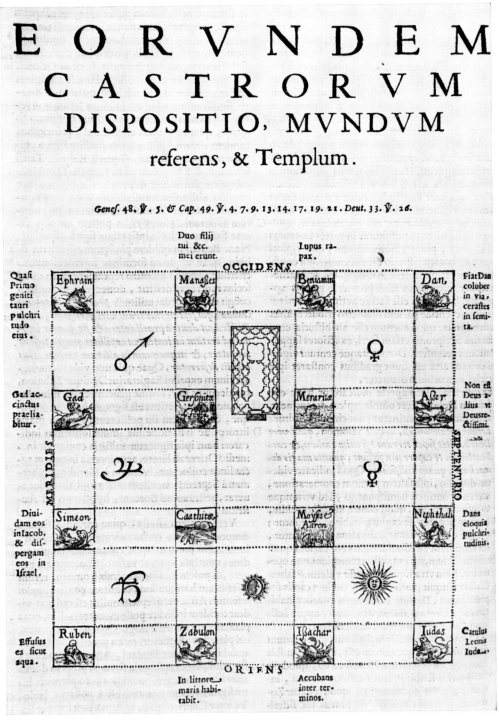

17. Villalpando: The astrological organization of Solomon's Temple

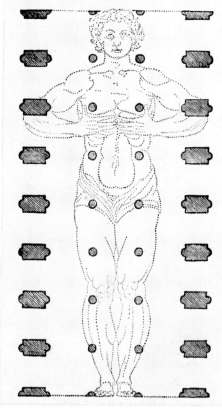

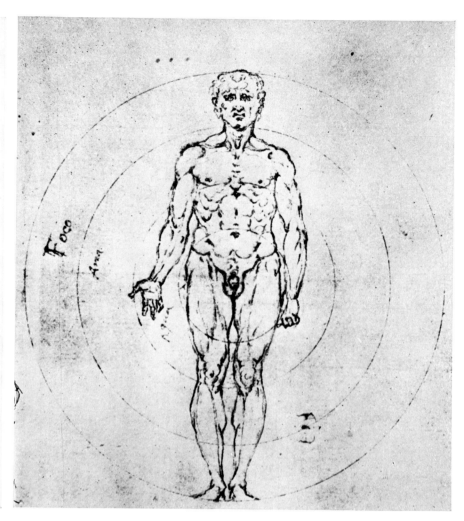

18. Villalpando. Anthropomorphic organisation of the porticoes of the Temple

19. Codex Huygens: The cosmological man

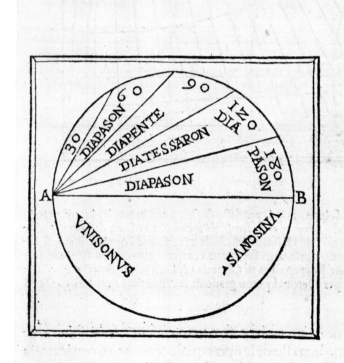

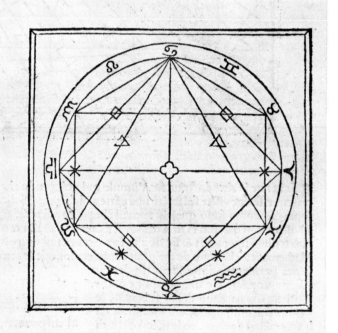

20. Illustration from Cesariano's and Caporali's editions of Vitruvius

21. Escorial Library: Euclid

22. Escorial Library: The astrologer Alchabitius

23. Escorial Church: Alonso Sanchez Coello: St. Augustine (detail)

24. Escorial Library: King Alfonso the Wise

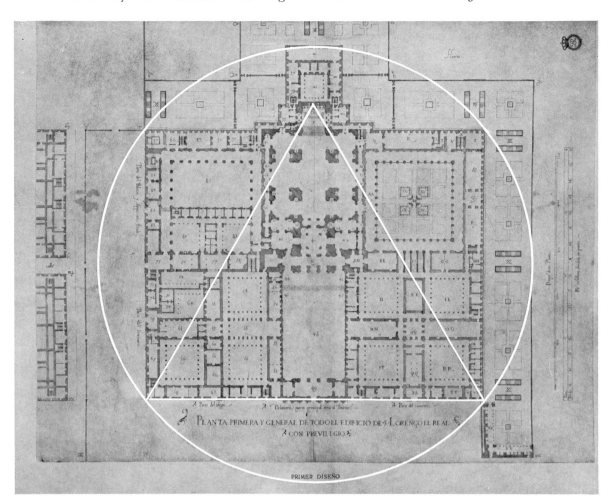

25. Plan of the Escorial in relation to the triangle and the circle

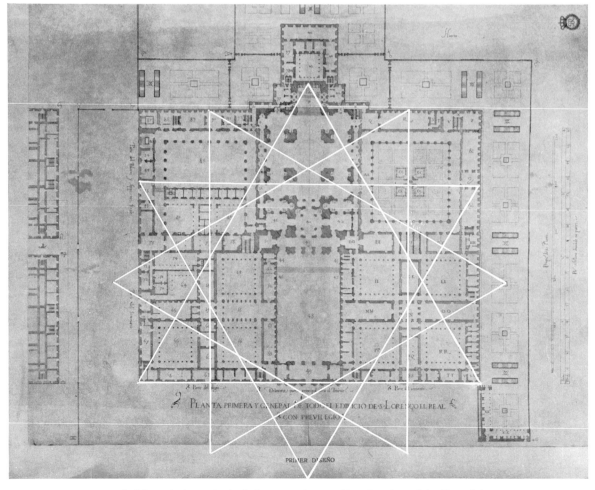

26. Vitruvius' astrological plan superimposed on the plan of the Escorial

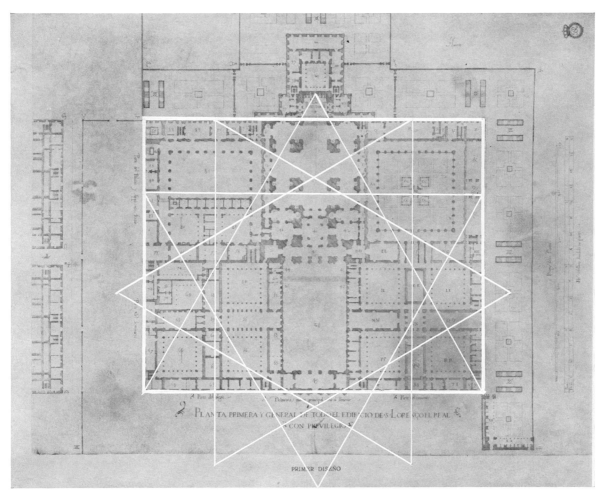

27. The *quadro* of the Escorial in relation to Vitruvius' astrological plan

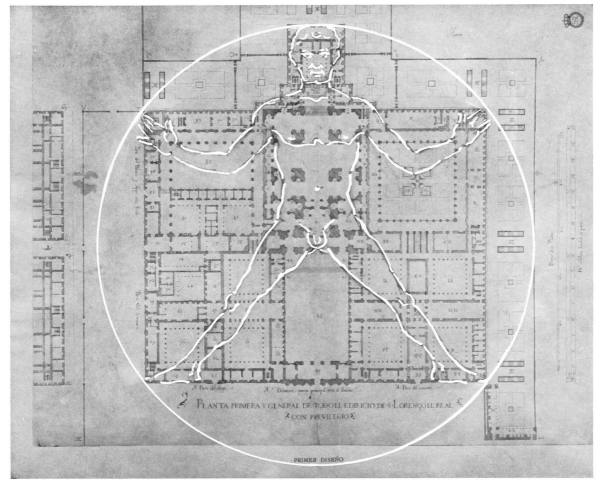

28. The cosmological man superimposed on the plan of the Escorial

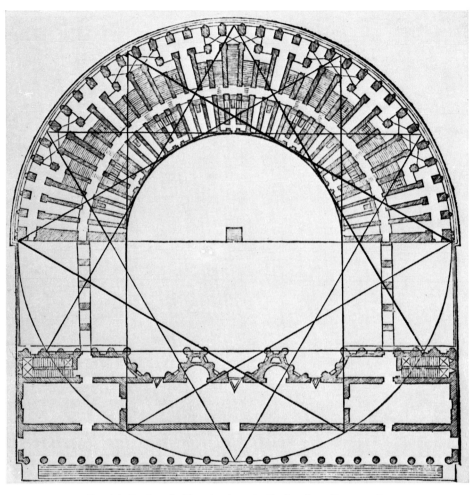

29. Daniele Barbaro's *Vitruvius* (1557): Design for a Roman theater

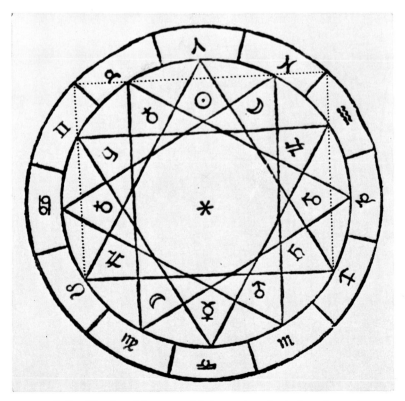

30. Julius Firmicus Maternus, *Matheseos*, Astrological configuration

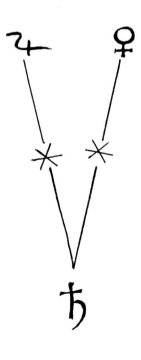

31. Escorial library. Matthias Hacus Sumbergius: *Prognosticon* of Philip II

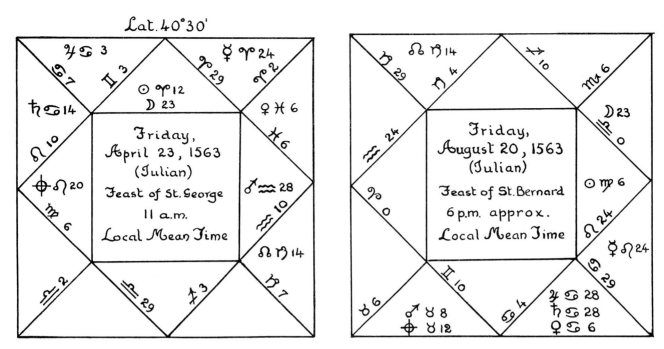

32–33. Horoscopes of the laying of the foundation-stones of the building and the church

34. Escorial. Medal of Jacopo da Trezzo

1. Bologna, San Petronio. Façade

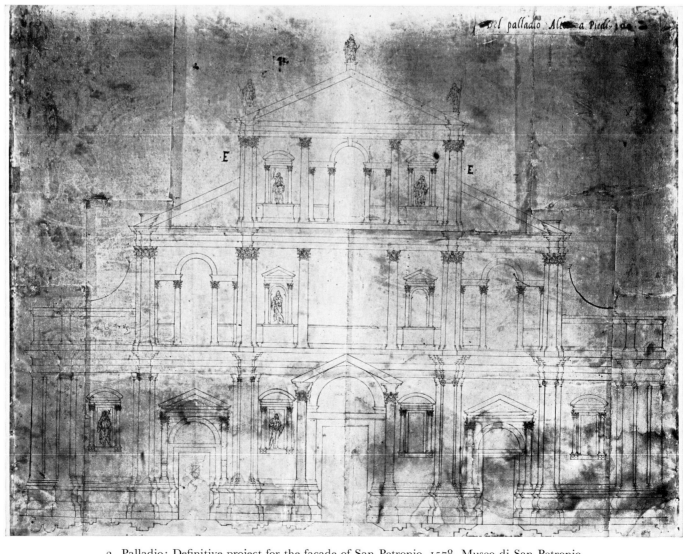

2. Palladio: Definitive project for the façade of San Petronio. 1578. Museo di San Petronio

3. After Palladio: Portico project for San Petronio. 1579. Chicago/New York, Lambert Collection

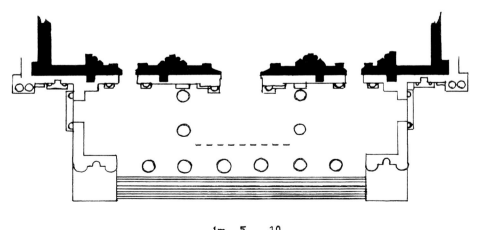

4. Reconstructed plan of Palladio's portico project. (Black portion indicates
existing Gothic walls; dotted line indicates top of existing stairs)

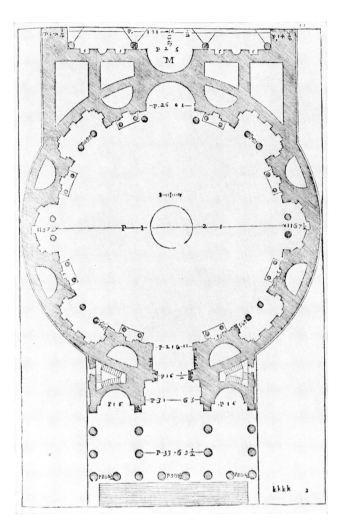

5a–b. Rome, Pantheon (from Palladio's *Quattro Libri*, 1570): plan and longitudinal section

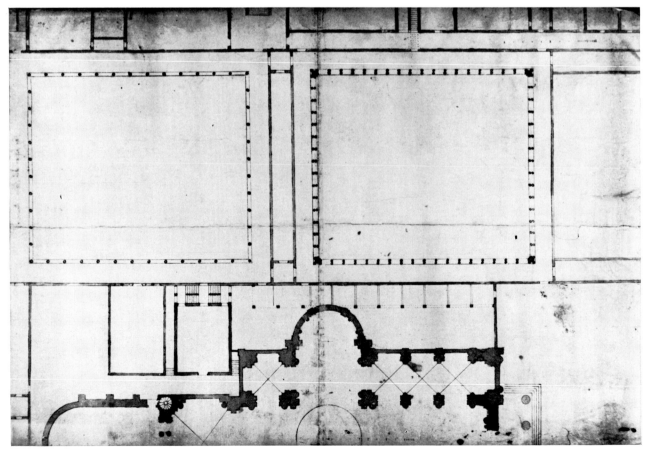

6. Palladio shop: Plan of the Church and Cloister of S. Giorgio Maggiore, Venice. 1577–80

1. A. Palladio: Loggia Bernarda. Prospetto su Piazza dei Signori, Vicenza

3. A. Palladio: Strutture del primo ordine della Basilica, Vicenza

2. A. Palladio: Basilica, lato ovest, Vicenza

5. A. Palladio: I piedistalli delle semicolonne giganti di Palazzo Da Porto Breganze

4. A. Palladio: Palazzo Da Porto Breganze, Vicenza

6. A. Palladio: Palazzo Chiericati, Vicenza

7. A. Palladio: Il portico di Palazzo Chiericati, Vicenza

8. A. Palladio: Cortile di Palazzo Thiene, ora Banca Popolare, Vicenza

9. A. Palladio: Particolare del piano nobile di Palazzo Thiene, ora Banca Popolare, Vicenza

10. A. Palladio: Palazzo Barbaran Da Porto, Vicenza

11. A. Palladio: Teatro Olimpico, Vicenza

12. A. Palladio: Navata sinistra di S. Giorgio Maggiore, Venezia

13. A. Palladio: Villa Barbaro, Masèr (Treviso)

14. A. Palladio: Interno di S. Giorgio Maggiore, Venezia

1. Chapel of the Beato Amedeo, Cathedral of Vercelli, main altar

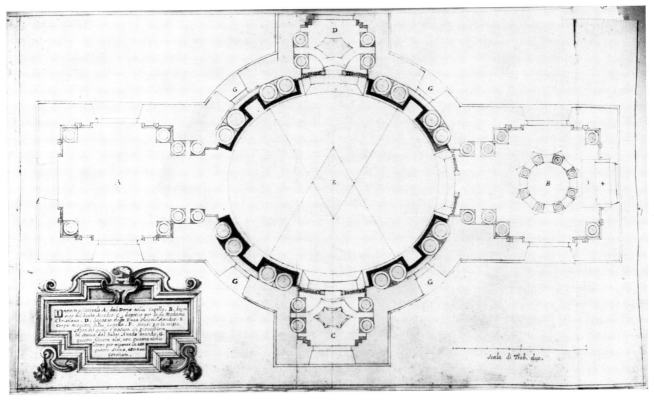

2. Attributed to Andrea Valperga: Chapel of the Beato Amedeo, Cathedral of Vercelli, plan. Turin, Biblioteca Nazionale,
Volume Q . I . 64, f. 12

3. Attributed to Andrea Valperga: Chapel of the Beato Amedeo, Cathedral of Vercelli, section. Turin, Biblioteca Nazionale, Volume Q. I. 64, f. 13

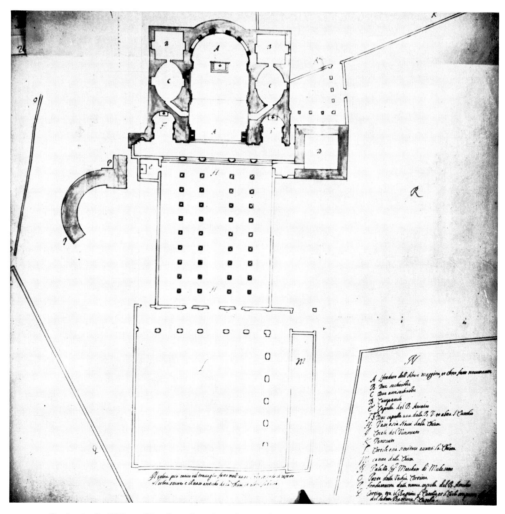

4. Cathedral of Vercelli, plan showing sixteenth century apse and early Christian nave and atrium. Turin, Biblioteca Nazionale, Volume Q. I. 64, f. 25

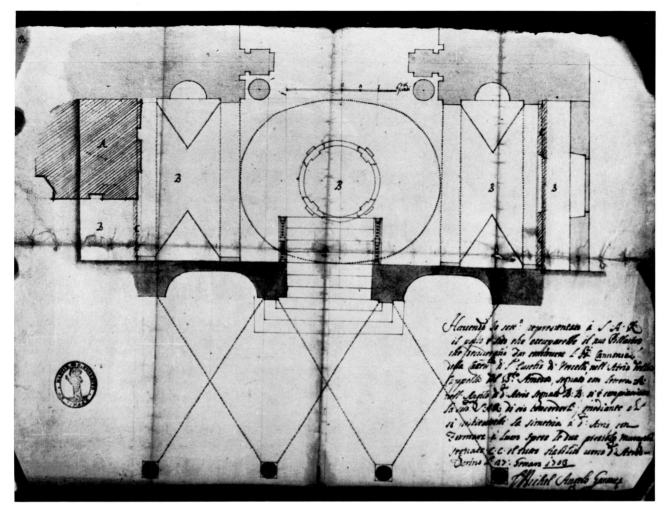

5. Michelangelo Garove: Chapel of the Beato Amedeo, entrance atrium, plan. Archivio Capitolare, Duomo di Vercelli

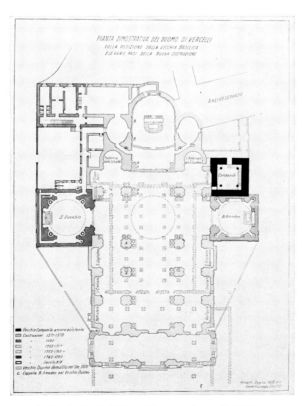

6. Cathedral of Vercelli, plan (from G. Chicco,
Memorie del Vecchio Duomo di Vercelli, Vercelli, 1943)

7. Chapel of the Beato Amedeo, Cathedral of Vercelli, exterior from the south

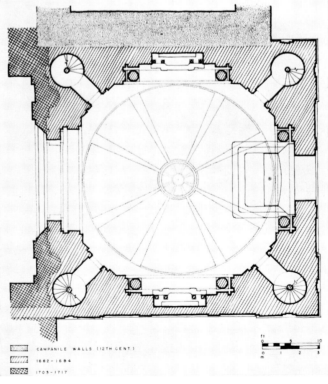

8. Chapel of the Beato Amedeo, Cathedral of Vercelli, plan

10. Chapel of the Beato Amedeo, Cathedral of Vercelli, east tomb-niche *(deposito)*

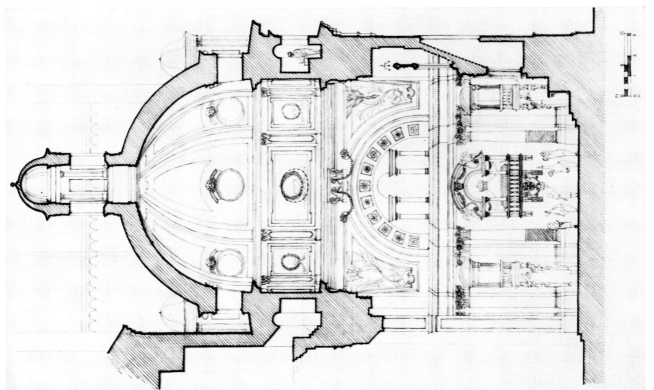

9. Chapel of the Beato Amedeo, Cathedral of Vercelli, section

11. Chapel of the Beato Amedeo, Cathedral of Vercelli, dome interior

12. Palazzo Asinari di San Marzano, Turin, atrium (photo courtesy Carpano)

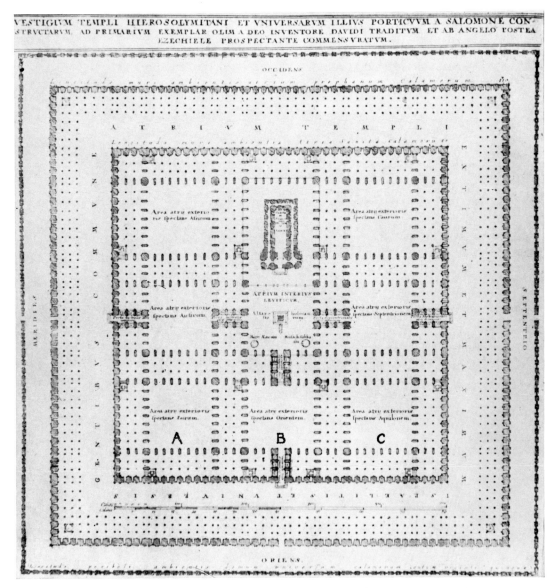

1. Villalpandus: Plan of Temple. 1605

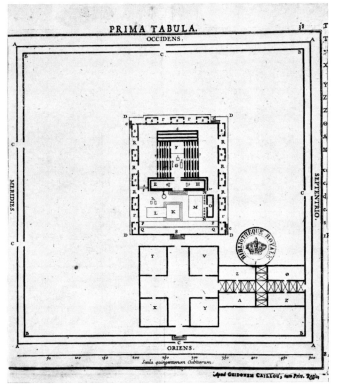

2. Claude Perrault: Plan of Temple. 1678

3. Claude Perrault: Elevations from East and from North

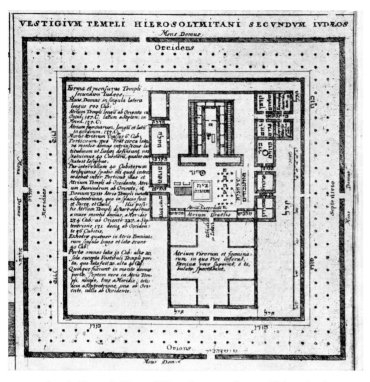

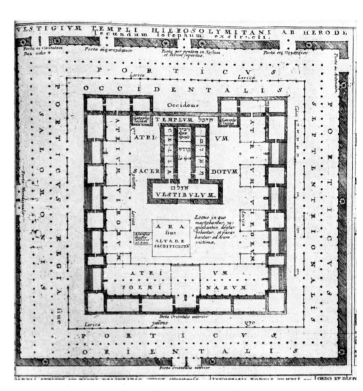

4. Louis Cappel: Plan of Temple according to Talmud. 1657

5. Louis Cappel: Plan of Temple according to Josephus. 1657

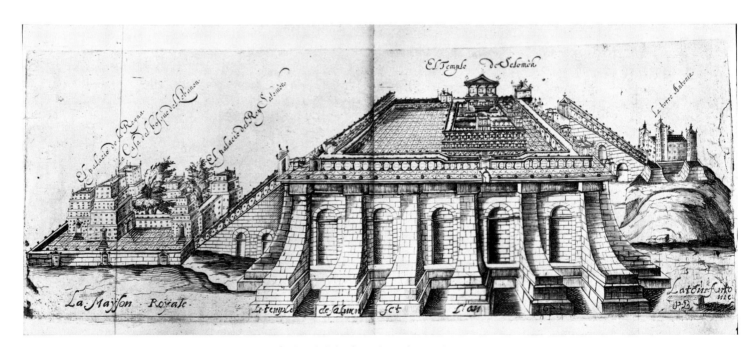

6. Jacob Jehuda: View of Temple. 1642

7. François Vatable: Façade of Temple. 1540

8. François Vatable: Interior of Temple. 1540

9. Nicolaus de Lyra: Elevations of Temple with cells and deambulatoria. 1588 (after drawings in medieval manuscripts)

10. Nicolaus de Lyra: Elevations of Temple with deambulatoria and cells. 1489

11. Johannes Coccejus: Elevation of House for Priests. 1669

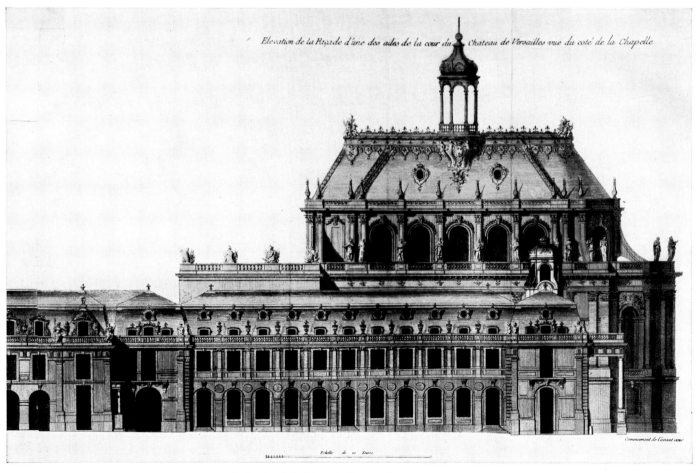

12. J.-F. Blondel: Chapel of Versailles seen from South

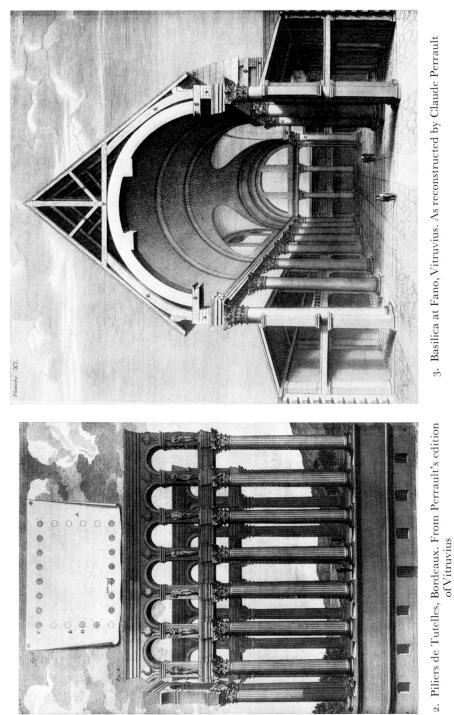

3. Basilica at Fano, Vitruvius. As reconstructed by Claude Perrault

4. Vignette. From Perrault's edition of Vitruvius

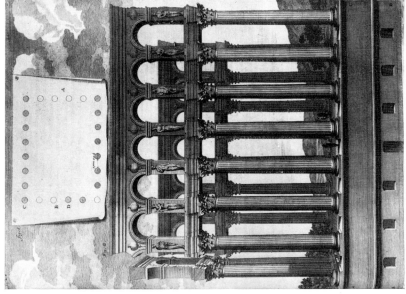

2. Piliers de Tutelles, Bordeaux. From Perrault's edition of Vitruvius

1. Grelot: Engraving of Hagia Sophia, Constantinople

1. Ebersmunster I, completed by 1712, burned 1717. Exterior
(from *Zodiacus Coelestis*, Strassburg, 1712)

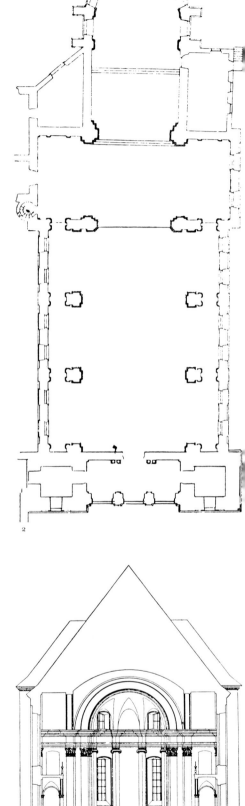

3. Ebersmunster II, 1719–27. Exterior from East (photo: Schmitt)

2, 4. Ebersmunster II, 1719–27.
Plan and Section (from Ohresser,
Eglise et abbaye d'Ebersmunster)

5. Ebersmunster II, 1719–27. Interior (photo: Steiner)

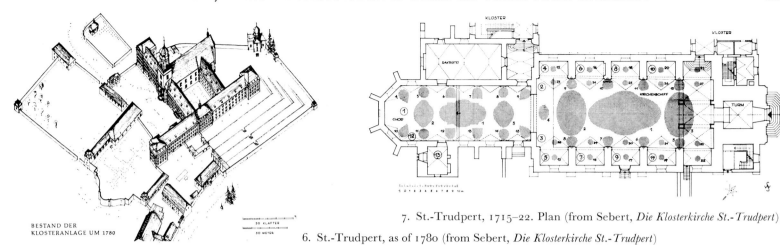

BESTAND DER
KLOSTERANLAGE UM 1780

7. St.-Trudpert, 1715–22. Plan (from Sebert, *Die Klosterkirche St.-Trudpert*)

6. St.-Trudpert, as of 1780 (from Sebert, *Die Klosterkirche St.-Trudpert*)

8. St.-Trudpert, 1715–22. Interior to East (photo: Pöppel)

9. St.-Peter, 1725–27. Exterior in landscape (photo: Burda)

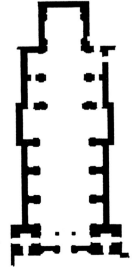

10. St.-Peter, 1725–27. Plan
(from Kunstführer Nr. 561)

11. St.-Peter, as of 1758 (from engraving by Peter Mayr)

12. St.-Peter, 1725–27. Interior to East (photo: Schnell)

13. St.-Peter, Library, 1737–50 (photo: Le Brun)

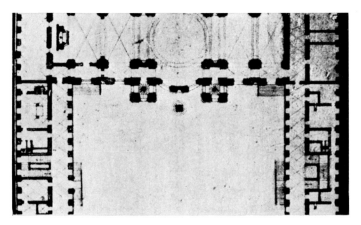

14. Frauenalb, 1726–31. Plan
(from Lieb-Dieth, *Vorarlberger Barockbaumeister*)

15. St.-Ulrich, 1739–40. Exterior (photo: Calig)

16. Birnau, 1746–50. Exterior from Southwest (photo: Steiner)

17. Birnau, 1746–50. Exterior from North (photo: Eckener)

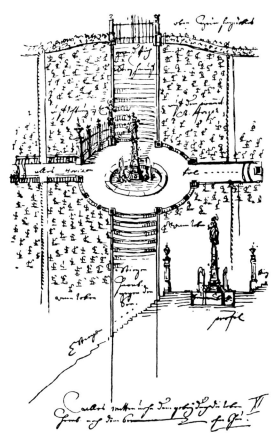

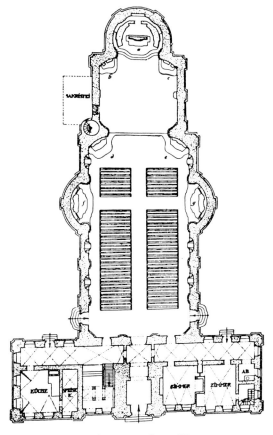

18. Birnau. Project for stairway to lake
(from Grosser Kunstführer Nr. 10)

19. Birnau, 1746–50. Plan
(from Grosser Kunstführer Nr. 10)

20. Birnau, 1746–50. Interior to North (photo: Steiner)

21. Birnau, 1746–50. Choir and apse (photo: Andrews)

22. Birnau, 1746–50. Interior to South (photo: Aufsberg)

23. Birnau, 1746–50. Interior to Northwest (photo: Steiner)

24. Birnau, 1746–50. Fresco in choir (photo: Steiner)

25. Birnau, 1746–50. Pilaster capitals and cove (photo: Aufsberg)

26. Birnau, 1746–50. Side altar and pulpit (photo: Anger)

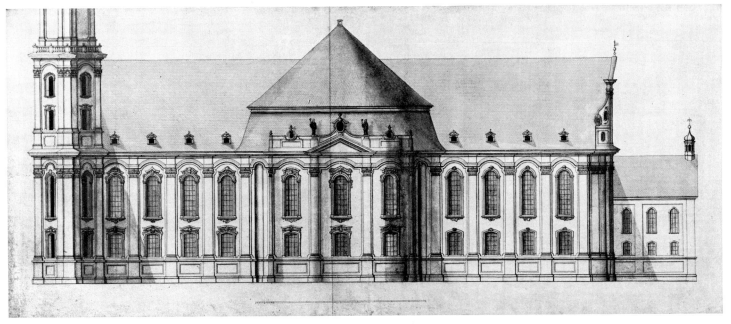

27. Thumb's project for St.-Gallen, 1751 (photo courtesy of Schweizerisches Landesmuseum)

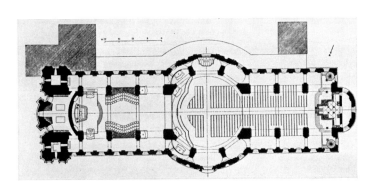

28. St.-Gallen, 1755–65. Plan (from Landolt, *Schweizer Barockkirchen*)

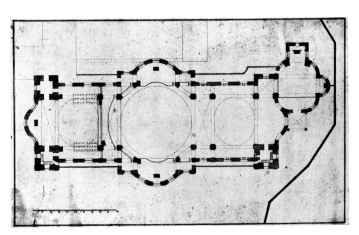

29. Anonymous project for St.-Gallen
(photo courtesy of Schweizerisches Landesmuseum)

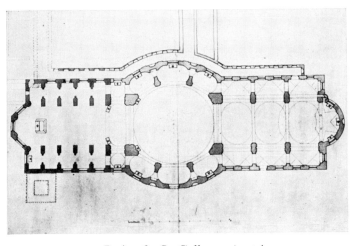

30. Project for St.-Gallen, now at Au
(from Lieb-Dieth, *Vorarlberger Barockbaumeister*)

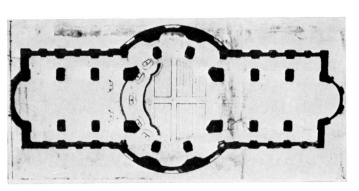

31. Final plan for St.-Gallen, now at Lucerne
(photo courtesy of Schweizerisches Landesmuseum)

32. St.-Gallen, 1755–60. Interior of nave to East (photo: Schnell)

33. St.-Gallen, 1755–60. Rotunda (photo: Seeger)

35. St.-Gallen, 1755–60. *Stucchi* in south transept (photo: Seeger)

34. St.-Gallen, 1755–60. Interior of nave to West (photo: Seeger)

37. St.-Gallen, 1760–65. East end by J.M.II Beer (photo: Gross)

36. St.-Gallen, 1755–65. Exterior from Northwest (photo: Gross)

38. St.-Gallen, Library, 1757–67 (photo: Seeger)

39. St.-Gallen, Library, 1757–67 (photo: Seeger)

1. J.L. Le Geay: Title page to *Rovine*, 1768

2. J. L. Le Geay: Title page to *Tombeaux*, 1768

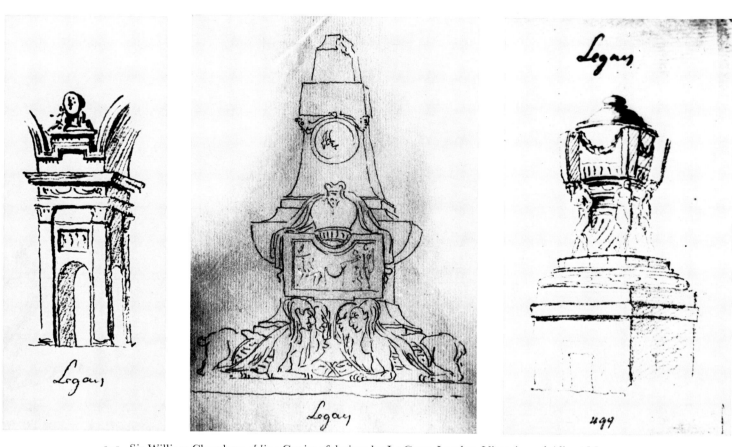

3–5. Sir William Chambers, *delin.:* Copies of designs by Le Geay. London, Victoria and Albert Museum

6. J. L. Le Geay: Etching from *Tombeaux*, 1768

7. G. B. Piranesi: Engraving from
Prima Parte di Architetture e Prospettive, 1743

8. G.B. Piranesi: *Gruppo di Colonne*, 1743.
From *Opera Varie*, 1750

9. G.B. Piranesi: *Capricci de Carceri*
from *Prima Parte di Architetture e Prospettive*, 1743

10. J.L. Le Geay: Etching from *Tombeaux*, 1768

11. J.L. Le Geay: Etching from *Rovine*, 1768

12. G.B. Piranesi: Composition from *Parere su l'architettura*, 1765

13. G.B. Piranesi: Composition from *Parere su l'architettura*, 1765

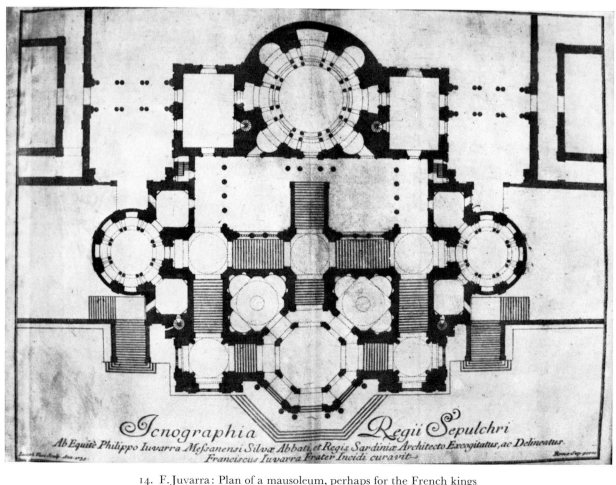

14. F. Juvarra: Plan of a mausoleum, perhaps for the French kings

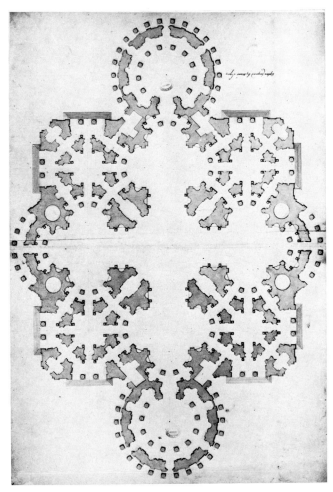

15. Sir William Chambers, *delin.*: Copy of a design by Le Geay. London, Royal Institute of British Architects

16. J.L. Le Geay: Plan of a church dedicated to the Trinity, 1767

17. F. Juvarra: Perspective of a mausoleum, perhaps for the French kings

18. G.B. Piranesi: *Mausoleo antico*, from the *Opera Varie*, 1750

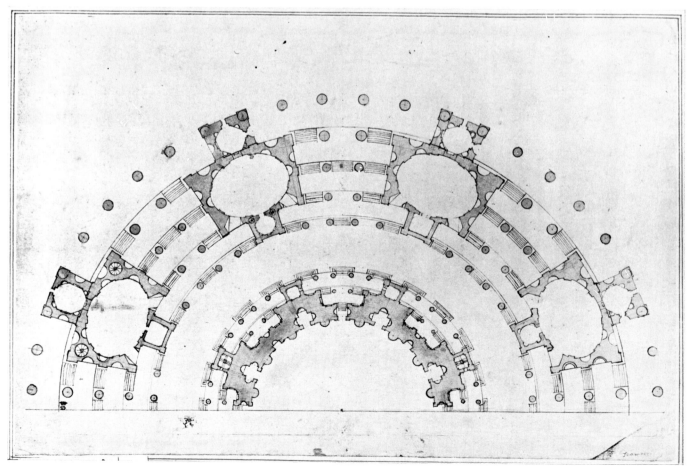

19. Studio of Palladio or Scamozzi: Plan for a monumental church. London, Royal Institute of British Architects

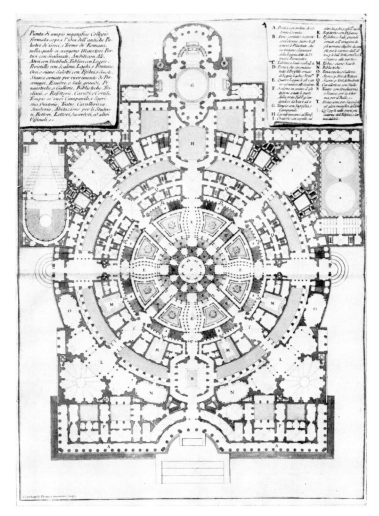

20. G. B. Piranesi: *Pianta di ampio magnifico Collegio*, from *Opera Varie*, 1750

21. J. L. Le Geay: Composition. London, John Harris Collection

22. Francesco Preziado: *Macchina* for Festival of the Chinea, 1746

23. J.L. Le Lorrain: *Macchina* for Festival of the Chinea, 1746

24. J.L.Le Lorrain: *Macchina* for Festival of the Chinea, 1745

25. J.L.Le Lorrain: *Macchina* for Festival of the Chinea, 1747

26. M.A. Challe: Imaginary Composition, 1746. Chicago, Mrs Phyllis Lambert Collection

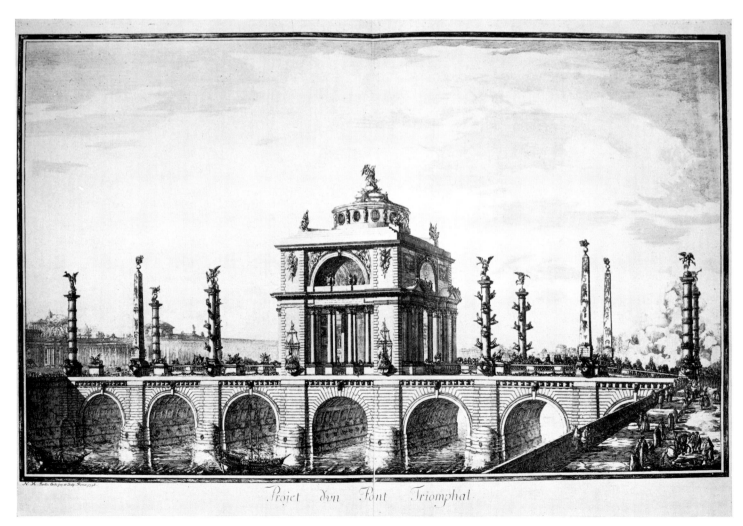

27. N.H. Jardin: *Projet d'un Pont Triomphal*, 1748

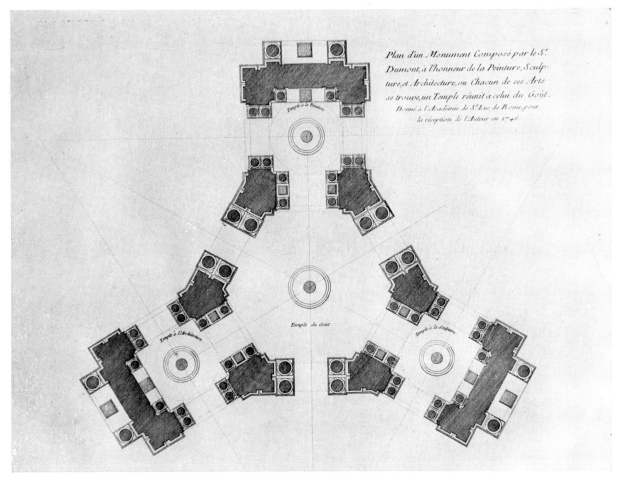

28. G. P. M. Dumont: Plan of *Temple des Arts*, 1746

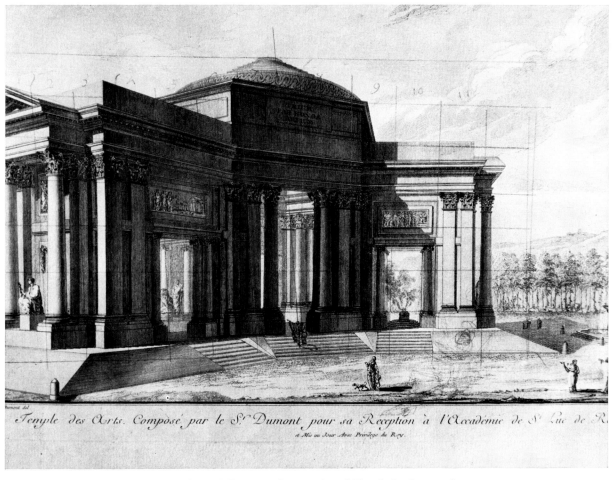

29. G. P. M. Dumont: Perspective of *Temple des Arts*, 1746

30. N.H. Jardin: Perspective of *Chapelle Sepulcrale*, 1748

31. E.A. Petitot: *Macchina* for Festival of the Chinea, 1749

32. E. A. Petitot: Triumphal bridge, *c.* 1748

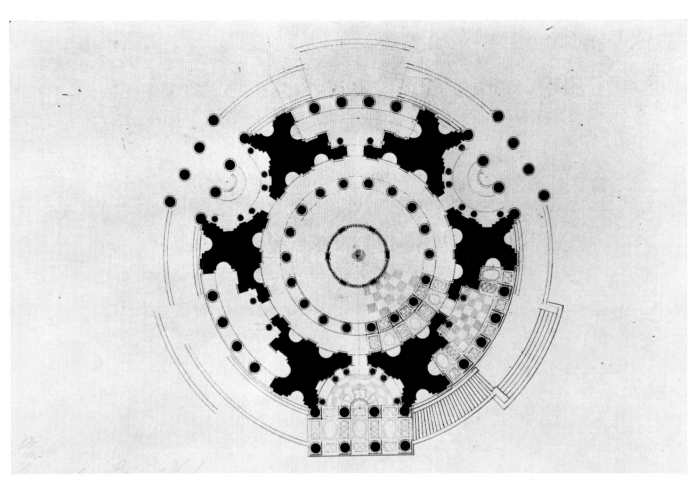

33. Sir William Chambers: Plan of Mausoleum to Frederick Prince of Wales, 1751. London, Victoria and Albert Museum

34. Sir William Chambers: Sectional perspective of Mausoleum to Frederick Prince of Wales, 1752.
London, Victoria and Albert Museum

35. Sir William Chambers: Perspective of Mausoleum to Frederick Prince of Wales, 1751.
London, Sir John Soane's Museum

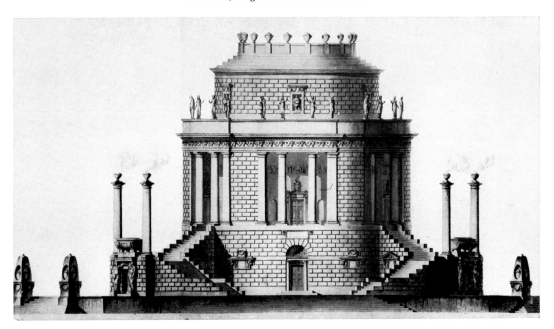

36. Sir William Chambers: Perspective of Mausoleum to Frederick Prince of Wales, 1752.
London, Victoria and Albert Museum

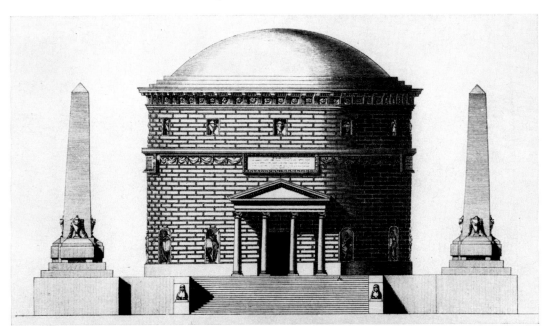

37. J. M. Peyre: *Chapelle Sepulcrale, c.* 1756, from *Œuvres d'Architecture*, 1765

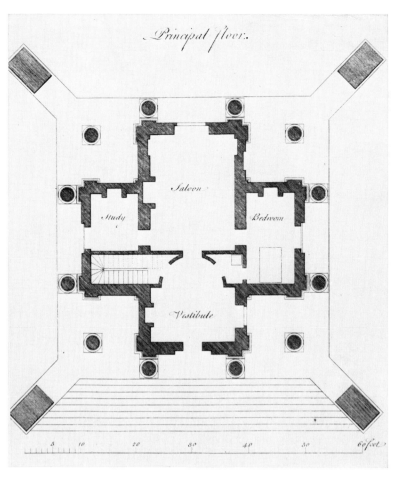

38. Sir William Chambers: Plan of the Casino at Marino, Dublin, *c.* 1758.
From Treatise on *Civil Architecture*, 1759

39. J.L. Le Geay: Drawing of Casino at Marino in a neo-classic frame designed, probably,
by Sir William Chambers, *c.* 1767. London, Miss Lambert John Collection

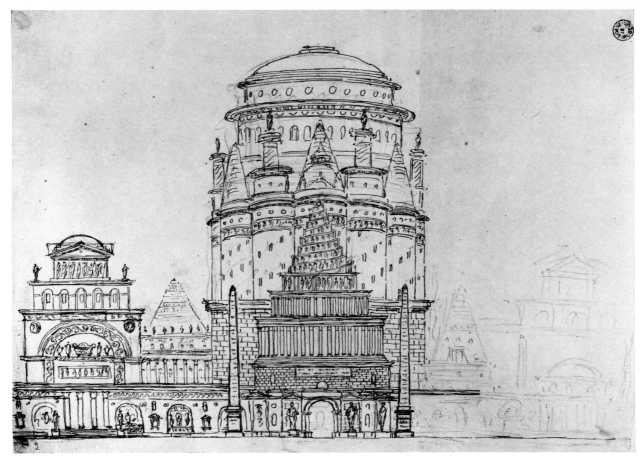

1. Robert Adam: Imaginary Design, *c.* 1756–57. London, Sir John Soane's Museum

2. G.B. Piranesi: Imaginary Design. London, Sir John Soane's Museum

3. Anonymous drawing of S. Maria del Priorato, Rome, after G. B. Piranesi. Detail.
London, Sir John Soane's Museum

4. Robert Adam: Imaginary Design for a Palace, 1757. Detail. London, Sir John Soane's Museum

5. Robert Adam: Etruscan Room, Osterley Park, Middlesex, 1775–77 (courtesy Victoria and Albert Museum, London. Crown Copyright)

6. G.B. Piranesi: *Diverse maniere*, 1769, Pl. 2 (courtesy Sir John Soane's Museum, London)

7. Robert Adam: Design for a Chimney-Piece for the First Drawing
Room, Wynn House, London, 1772. London, Sir John Soane's Museum

8. G.B. Piranesi: *Diverse maniere*, 1769, Pl. 9 A
(courtesy Sir John Soane's Museum, London)

9. Robert Adam: Design for a Chimney-Piece for Drummond's
Bank, London, 1777. London, Sir John Soane's Museum

10. G.B. Piranesi: *Diverse maniere*, 1769, Pl. 25
(courtesy Sir John Soane's Museum, London)

11. G.B. Piranesi: *Diverse maniere*, 1769, Pl. 4 A (courtesy Sir John Soane's Museum, London)

12. Robert Adam: Sketch Design for a Chimney-Piece for the First Drawing Room, Apsley House, London, *c.* 1774. London, Sir John Soane's Museum

13. G. B. Piranesi: *Diverse maniere*, 1769, Pl. 4 B (courtesy Sir John Soane's Museum, London)

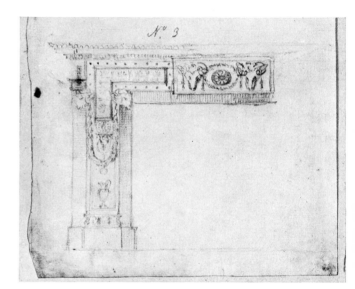

14. Robert Adam: Sketch Designs for Chimney-Pieces, *c.* 1777. London, Sir John Soane's Museum

15. Robert Adam: Sketch Design for a Chimney-Piece, probably for the Second Drawing Room, Derby House, London, *c.* 1774. London, Sir John Soane's Museum

16. Robert Adam: Unexecuted Design for a Chimney-Piece, probably for the Second Drawing Room, Derby House, London, *c.* 1774. London, Sir John Soane's Museum

Furtum Hauckianum   1.
N.º 497

Je Soussigné reconnois avoir reçu de Monsieur Michel
Ministre de Sa Majestée le Roy de Prusse la Somme de Quinze
Guinées pour trois Elevations et trois Plans de Ponts à
la Chinoise, aux quels Je n'ai point mis des Echelles
ne Sachant pas de quelle grandeur Sa Majestée les
voudra faire executer, la Grandeur Generale etant
un fois Determinée, l'on pourra construire l'Echelle, et
executer toutes les Parties selon les proportions qui se
trouvent dans les desseins, à l'exception, des gardefoux
et des marches les quels ne doivent point exceder de
beaucoup les hauteurs ordinaires, tel grandeur qui ait
le reste de l'Ouvrage.

        Les Ponts se peuvent construire de pierre, de
Brique, ou de bois, les Bâtiments qui les couronnent
doivent etre de bois, peint et Vernissé, les couvertures des
Toits se font de toile, de tuilles Emaillés, ou de plaques
de fer, fort mince peint et Vernissé. fait à Londres ce 6 Juin
1763.

                    W Chambers. Architecte du Roy de
                    la Grande Bretagne.

1. Receipt signed by Chambers in 1763 (In 1937 Hohenzollern Haus-Archiv, Berlin)

2. Drawing by William Chambers, 1763 (In 1937 Neues Palais, Potsdam)

3. The 'Dragon House', built in 1763. Park of Sanssouci (photo Marta Huth)

1. Sir Richard Westmacott, R.A. (1775–1856): Court yard of Stafford House; pen and ink and watercolor.
Formerly collection of the Duke of Sutherland, 1958 (now on the art market)

2. Stafford House (now Lancaster House), from a photograph of about 1910

1. The Avenue de Tervueren at the Stoclet House, around 1911 (from a photograph in the estate of Josef Hoffmann)

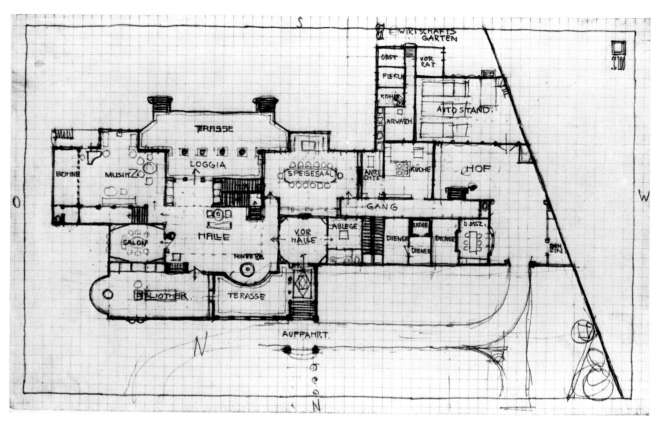

2. Preliminary Design, plan of ground floor, pencil and crayon (Collection of the author)

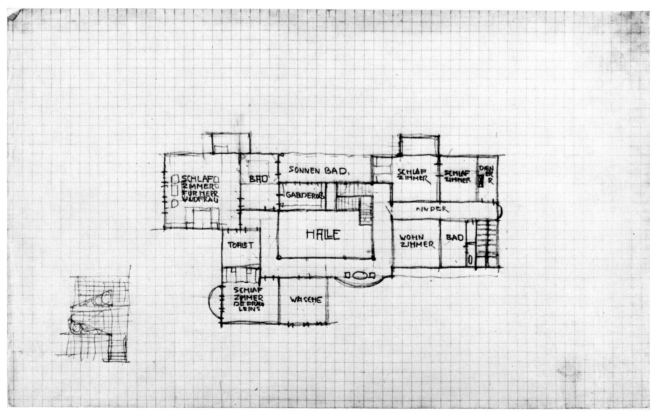

3. Preliminary Design, plan of upper floor, pencil (Collection of the author)

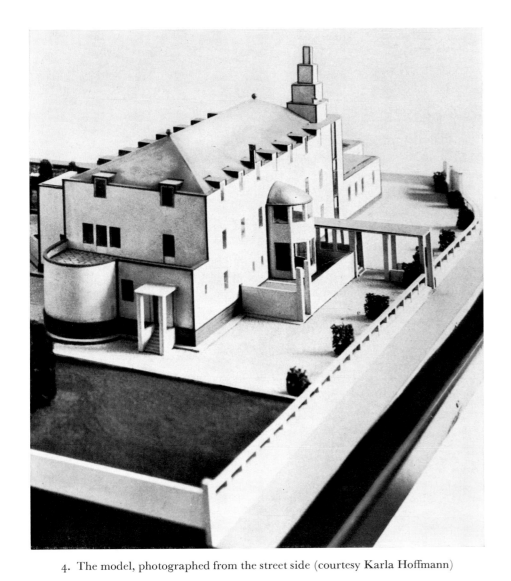

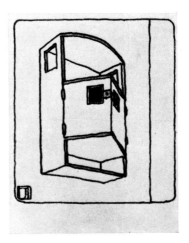

5. Design by Josef Hoffmann for a small wedge-shaped wall cabinet (from *Das Interieur*, II, 1901)

4. The model, photographed from the street side (courtesy Karla Hoffmann)

6. The model, photographed from the garden side (courtesy Karla Hoffmann)

7. Drawing of the garden façade, an early version (courtesy *Museum des XX. Jahrhunderts*, Vienna)

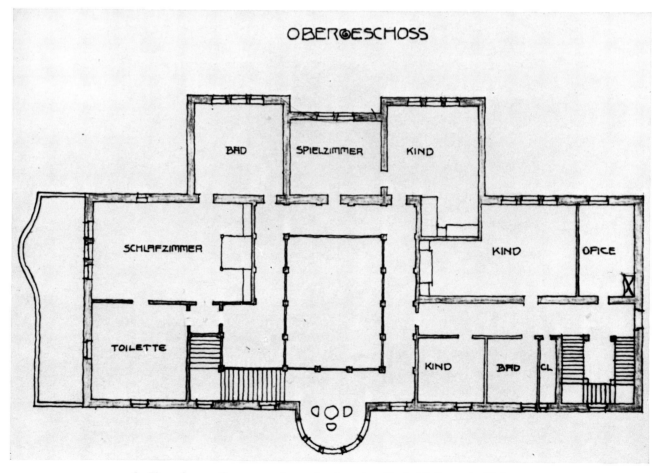

8. Plan of upper floor, an early version (courtesy Karla Hoffmann). Cf. fig. 7

9. The garden façade, an early version; perspective drawing in ink (courtesy *Museum des XX. Jahrhunderts*, Vienna).
Cf. figs. 7, 8, 10

10. The garden façade, an early version; perspective drawing in water color (courtesy *Museum des XX. Jahrhunderts*, Vienna).
Cf. figs. 7–9

11. Design for the vestibule, initialed J. H.
(from a photograph in the author's collection)

12. Design for washroom and toilet facilities, initialed J. H.
(from a photograph in the author's collection)

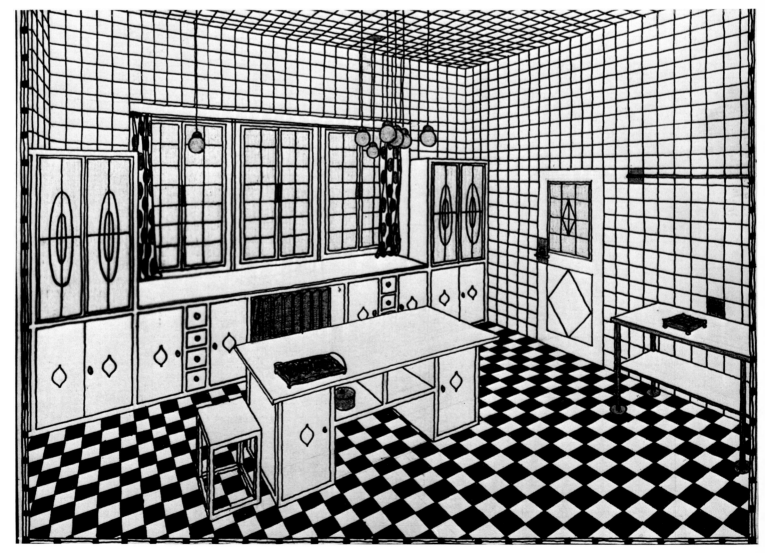

13. Design for the kitchen (from a photograph in the author's collection)

14. Design for the great hall, pencil, pen and crayon
(courtesy *Museum des XX. Jahrhunderts*, Vienna)

15. Design for the music- or theater room, pencil, pen, crayon and wash (courtesy *Museum des XX. Jahrhunderts*, Vienna)

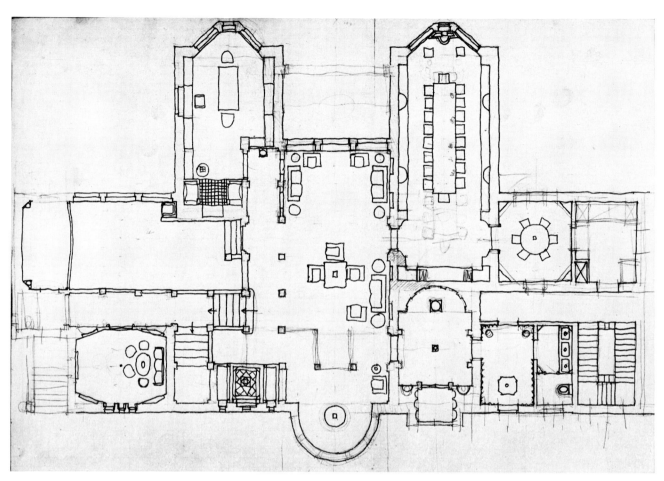

16. Plan of ground floor, pencil and pen (courtesy *Museum des XX. Jahrhunderts*, Vienna)

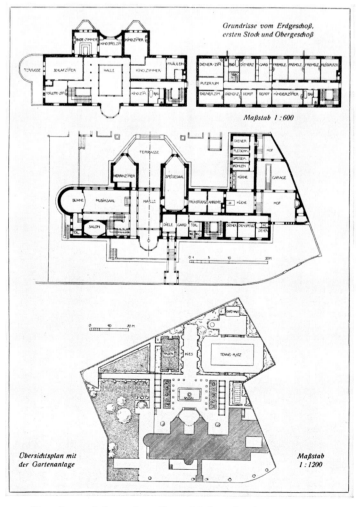

17. Site plan and floor plans (from *Moderne Bauformen*, XIII, 1914)

18. The Stoclet House, Brussels, street façade seen from NW, 1965 (photo: author)

19. The Stoclet House, Brussels, street façade seen from NE, around 1911 (from a photograph, retouched at the upper right, in the estate of Josef Hoffmann)

20. East end of garden façade (photo: Vencour)

21. Detail from the large staircase window, street façade
(photo: author)

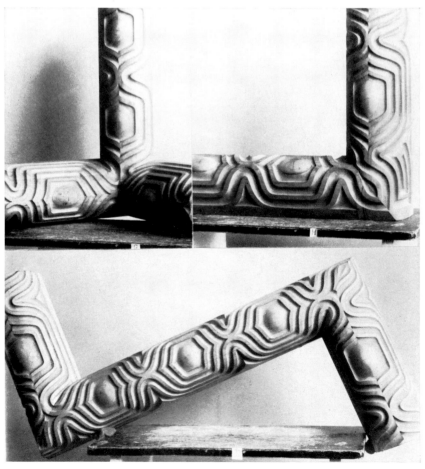

22. Wooden models for the metal mouldings of the façade
(courtesy Karla Hoffmann)

23. The Ast House, Vienna, Hohe Warte, 1910–11, by Josef Hoffmann; detail of garden façade with framing floreal mouldings
(photo: Kudrnofsky)

24. The Stoclet House, bridge over entrance to service courtyard and garage (photo: author)

25. Sheltered area under bridge-like curved central portion of garden façade (photo: Hubmann)

26. Partial view of garden façade with fountain in foreground (photo: Ritter)

27. The entrance from the Avenue de Tervueren
(photo: author)

28. The vestibule (photo: Minders, Genk)

29. Entrance pavilion seen from the house
(photo: Vencour)

30. View from the vestibule into the great hall
(from *Moderne Bauformen*, XIII, 1914)

31. The cloakroom (photo: Minders, Genk)

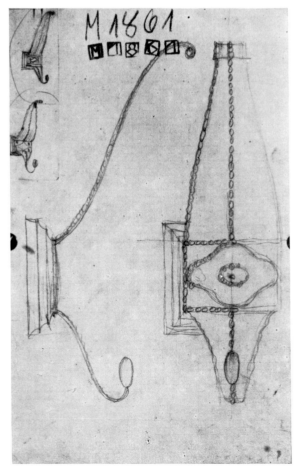

32. Detail drawing for a coat hook, from the archives of the *Wiener Werkstätte* (courtesy Österreichisches Museum für angewandte Kunst; I. Nr. 12173/1). Cf. fig. 31

33. The great hall, looking towards the staircase (from a photograph in the estate of Josef Hoffmann)

34. The great hall, looking towards the bow window (photo: Minders, Genk)

35. Small sitting room under the stairs (photo: Minders, Genk)

36. The music- or theater room (photo: Minders, Genk)

37. The large dining room with mosaics by Gustav Klimt (photo: Ritter)

38. The breakfast room; the carpet is not the original one (photo: Hubmann)

39. Josef Hoffmann at lunch in the breakfast room, 1955 (photo: Ritter)

40. The master bedroom (photo: Minders, Genk)

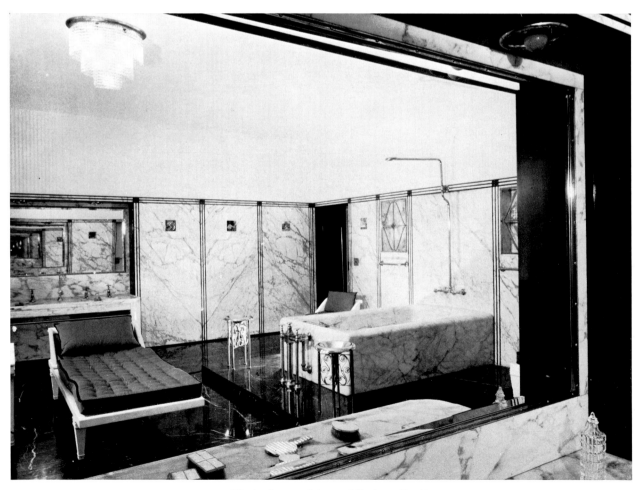

41. The bathroom (photo: Minders, Genk)

42. '*Forum Orbis – insula pacis*'; Josef Hoffmann's project for the Rome Prize at the Vienna Academy (from *Der Architekt*, I, 1895)

43. Travel sketch by Josef Hoffmann from Pozzuoli, 1896. In the lower left a direct transposition of the motif is shown (collection of the author, photo: Balack)

44. Travel sketch by Josef Hoffmann from southern Italy, 1896 (courtesy Karla Hoffmann)

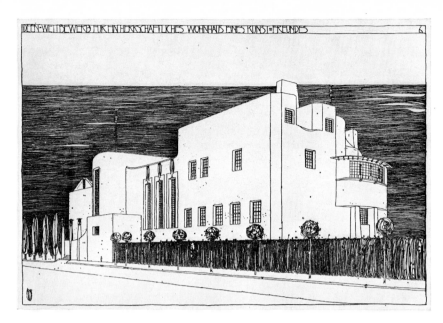

45. Charles Rennie Mackintosh:
'The House of a Lover of Art', street façade
(from *Meister der Innenkunst*, Darmstadt, 1902)

46. Charles Rennie Mackintosh:
'The House of a Lover of Art', floor plans
(from *Meister der Innenkunst*, Darmstadt, 1902)

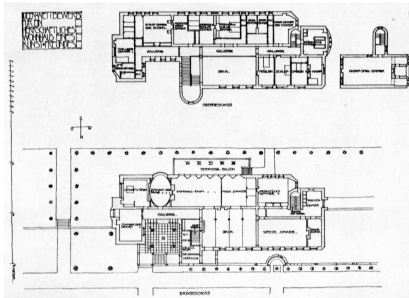

47. Josef Hoffmann: stucco relief, from the XIVth exhibition of the *Sezession*,
Vienna 1902 (courtesy *Bildarchiv der Österreichischen Nationalbibliothek*)

48. The Stoclet House, detail of West-elevation and tower
(photo: author)

THE WRITINGS OF RUDOLF WITTKOWER

The Writings of Rudolf Wittkower

Note: The following is a complete list of Professor Wittkower's major publications up to June 22, 1966, omitting detailed notice of such work as the entries in Thieme-Becker (1925–1934), revisions of the 16th edition of Baedeker's *Rome and Central Italy* (Leipzig, 1930), entries in *Chambers's Encyclopedia* (1950) and the *Encyclopedia Britannica* (1953, 1956), and obituaries (e.g., those of Fritz Saxl and Ludwig Schudt). The periodical literature has been grouped according to content although there are, of course, some conflicts of classification. Within each group the listing is chronological.

BOOKS

Michelangelo-Bibliographie, 1510–1926 (Römische Forschungen der Bibliotheca Hertziana, vol. I). In collaboration with Ernst Steinmann. Leipzig, 1927.

Die Zeichnungen des Gianlorenzo Bernini (Römische Forschungen der Bibliotheca Hertziana, vols. IX–X). In collaboration with Heinrich Brauer. 2 vols. Berlin, 1931.

Catalogue of the Collection of Drawings by the Old Masters, Formed by Sir Robert Mond. In collaboration with Tancred Borenius. London, 1937.

The Drawings of Nicolas Poussin. Edited by Walter Friedlaender in collaboration with Rudolf Wittkower and Anthony Blunt. Vol. I, London, 1938. Vol. II, London, 1949.

British Art and the Mediterranean. In collaboration with Fritz Saxl. London, 1948.

Architectural Principles in the Age of Humanism. London, 1949. 2nd ed., London, 1952. 3rd ed., London, 1962. Spanish ed., Buenos Aires, 1958. Italian ed., Milan, 1964. American ed. (Columbia Studies in Art History and Archaeology, vol. I), New York, 1965.

The Drawings of the Carracci in the Collection of Her Majesty the Queen at Windsor Castle. London, 1952. American ed., Garden City, L.I., 1953.

Gian Lorenzo Bernini, the Sculptor of the Roman Baroque. London, 1955. 2nd ed., London, 1966.

Art and Architecture in Italy, 1600–1750 (The Pelican History of Art). Harmondsworth and Baltimore, 1958. 2nd ed., Harmondsworth and Baltimore, 1965.

Born under Saturn: The Character and Conduct of Artists; A Documented History from Antiquity to the French Revolution. In collaboration with Margot Wittkower. London, 1963. German ed. under the title *Künstler—Aussenseiter der Gesellschaft*, Stuttgart, 1965.

Dupérac, Disegni de le ruine di Roma e come anticamente erono. Facsimile ed. with Introduction by Rudolf Wittkower. Milan, 1963.

The Divine Michelangelo: The Florentine Academy's Homage on his Death in 1564. Introduced, translated, and annotated in collaboration with Margot Wittkower. London, 1964.

La cupola di San Pietro di Michelangelo. Florence, 1964.

PAMPHLETS

Exhibition of Architectural and Decorative Drawings at London University, the Courtauld Institute of Art. In collaboration with Anthony Blunt. London, 1941.

The Earl of Burlington and William Kent. York Georgian Society Occasional Papers, no. 5, 1948.

Bernini's Bust of Louis XIV. London, 1951.

The Artist and the Liberal Arts. An inaugural lecture delivered at University College, London, January 30, 1950. London, 1952.

The History of the York Assembly Rooms. Compiled for and on behalf of the York Corporation, York, 1952.

ARTICLES

I. MIGRATION AND INTERPRETATION OF SYMBOLS

'Miraculous Birds. 1. "Physiologus" in Beatus Manuscripts. 2. "Roc": an Eastern Prodigy in a Dutch Engraving', *Journal of the Warburg and Courtauld Institutes*, I (1937–8), pp. 253–7.

'Eagle and Serpent: a Study in the Migration of Symbols', *Journal of the Warburg and Courtauld Institutes*, II (1938–9), pp. 293–325.

'Interpretation of Visual Symbols in the Arts', in *Studies in Communication* (London University, Communications Research Centre), London, 1955, pp. 109–24.

'Introduction', *East-West in Art, Patterns of Cultural and Aesthetic Relationships* (ed. Theodore Bowie), Bloomington and London, 1966, pp. 13–19.

II. STUDIES IN PROPORTION AND PERSPECTIVE

'Some Observations on Medieval and Renaissance Proportion', *Festschrift in Honor of Johannes Wilde* (unpublished typescript), 1951.

'International Congress on Proportion in the Arts', *Burlington Magazine*, XCIV (1952), pp. 52–5.

'Systems of Proportion', in *Architect's Yearbook*, V (1953), pp. 9–18.

'Brunelleschi and "Proportion in Perspective"', *Journal of the Warburg and Courtauld Institutes*, XVI (1953), pp. 275–91.

'The Perspective of Piero della Francesca's "Flagellation"', *Journal of the Warburg and Courtauld Institutes*, XVI (1953), pp. 292–302 (with B. A. R. Carter).

'The Changing Concept of Proportion', *Daedalus* (Winter, 1960), pp. 199–215.

III. ICONOGRAPHY

'Patience and Chance: The Story of a Political Emblem', *Journal of the Warburg and Courtauld Institutes*, I (1937–8), pp. 171–7.

'A Symbol of Platonic Love in a Portrait Bust of Donatello', *Journal of the Warburg and Courtauld Institutes*, I (1937–8), pp. 260–1.

'Chance, Time and Virtue', *Journal of the Warburg and Courtauld Institutes*, I (1937–8), pp. 313–21.

'"Grammatica": From Martianus Capella to Hogarth', *Journal of the Warburg and Courtauld Institutes*, II (1938–9), pp. 82–4.

'Transformations of Minerva in Renaissance Imagery', *Journal of the Warburg and Courtauld Institutes*, II (1938–9), pp. 194–205.

'Titian's Allegory of "Religion succoured by Spain"', *Journal of the Warburg and Courtauld Institutes*, III (1939–40), pp. 138–40.

'Death and Resurrection in a Picture by Marten de Vos', in *Miscellanea Leo van Puyvelde*, Brussels (1949), pp. 117–23.

IV. MEDIEVAL ART

'Marvels of the East: a Study in the History of Monsters', *Journal of the Warburg and Courtauld Institutes*, V (1942), pp. 159–97.

'Marco Polo and the Pictorial Tradition of the Marvels of the East', in *Oriente Poliano* (Istituto Italiano per il medio ed estremo oriente), Rome, 1957, pp. 155–72.

V. RENAISSANCE AND MANNERIST ART AND ARCHITECTURE

'Studien zur Geschichte der Malerei in Verona. I and II: Domenico Morone. III: Die Schüler des Domenico Morone', *Jahrbuch für Kunstwissenschaft* (1924–5), pp. 269–89; (1927), pp. 185–222.

'Ein Selbstporträt Michelangelos im Jüngsten Gericht', *Kunstchronik*, LIX, n.f. XXXV (1925–6), pp. 366–7.

'Das Problem der Bewegung innerhalb der manieristischen Architektur', *Festschrift für Walter Friedländer zum 60. Geburtstag am 10.3.1933* (unpublished typescript), pp. 192 ff.

'Zur Peterskuppel Michelangelos', *Zeitschrift für Kunstgeschichte*, II (1933), pp. 348–70.

'Michelangelo's Biblioteca Laurenziana', *Art Bulletin*, XVI (1934), pp. 123–218.

'Sculpture in the Mellon Collection', *Apollo*, XXVI (1937), pp. 79–84.

'Physiognomical Experiments by Michelangelo and his Pupils', *Journal of the Warburg and Courtauld Institutes*, I (1937–8), pp. 183–4.

'A Note on Michelangelo's Pietà in St. Peter's', *Journal of the Warburg and Courtauld Institutes*, II (1938–9), p. 80.

'Alberti's Approach to Antiquity in Architecture', *Journal of the Warburg and Courtauld Institutes*, IV (1940–1), pp. 1–18.

'A Newly Discovered Drawing by Michelangelo', *Burlington Magazine*, LXXVIII (1941), pp. 159–60.

'Federico Zuccari and John Wood of Bath', *Journal of the Warburg and Courtauld Institutes*, VI (1943), pp. 220–2.

'Holbein und England', *Die Auslese*, I (1945), pp. 55 ff.

'El Greco's Language of Gestures', *Art News*, LVI (1957), pp. 44–49 and 53–54.

'The Arts in Western Europe: Italy', in *The New Cambridge Modern History*, vol. I: 1493–1520, Cambridge, 1957, pp. 127–53.

'L'architettura del Rinascimento e la tradizione classica', *Casabella*, no. 234 (1959), pp. 43–9.

'Montagnes sacrées', *L'Œil*, no. 59 (1959), pp. 54–61 and p. 92.

'Individualism in Art and Artists: A Renaissance Problem', *Journal of the History of Ideas*, XXII (1961), pp. 291–302.

'La cupola di San Pietro di Michelangelo', *Arte antica e moderna* (no. 20) (1962), pp. 390–437 (revised and enlarged translation of 'Zur Peterskuppel Michelangelos', 1933).

'L'arcadia e il Giorgionismo', in *Umanesimo europeo e umanesimo veneziano*, Florence, 1963, pp. 473–84.

'The Young Raphael', *Allen Memorial Art Museum Bulletin*, xx (1963), pp. 150–68.

VI. PALLADIO, PALLADIANISM AND ENGLISH ARCHITECTURE

'Pseudo-Palladian Elements in English Neo-classical Architecture', *Journal of the Warburg and Courtauld Institutes*, VI (1943), pp. 154–64. (This paper appeared in a revised and improved form in a volume published by the Oxford Press.)

'Principles of Palladio's Architecture', *Journal of the Warburg and Courtauld Institutes*, VII (1944), pt. I, pp. 102–22; VIII (1945), pt. 2, pp. 68–106.

'Lord Burlington and William Kent', *The Archaeological Journal*, CII (1945), pp. 151–64.

'Inigo Jones—Puritanissimo Fiero', *Burlington Magazine*, XC (1948), pp. 50–1.

'Palladianism in England', *The Listener*, XLIII (May 18, 1950), pp. 866–8 and p. 879.

'Lord Burlington and the York Assembly Rooms', *York Georgian Society, Reports*, 1950–1, pp. 42–54.

'That Great Luminary of Architecture', *The Listener*, L (December 24, 1953), pp. 1080–1.

'Inigo Jones, Architect and Man of Letters', *Royal Institute of British Architects Journal*, LX (1953), pp. 83–90.

'The Influence of Palladio's Villas', *Country Life*, CXV (February 25, 1954), pp. 516–7.

'Burlington and his Work in York', *Studies in Architectural History*, ed. W. A. Singleton, London and York, 1954, I, pp. 47–66.

'Giacomo Leoni's Edition of Palladio's *Quattro Libri dell'Architettura*', *Arte Veneta*, VIII (1954), pp. 310–6.

I: 'Sviluppo stilistico dell'architettura palladiana'; and II: 'Diffusione dei modi palladiani in Inghilterra', *Bollettino del Centro Internazionale di Studi di Architettura Andrea Palladio*, I (1959), pp. 61–9.

I: 'Il "Pre-Neopalladianesimo" in Inghilterra'; II: 'I principii informativi del nuovo movimento'; and III: 'L'architettura di Lord Burlington e il suo ambiente', *Bollettino del Centro Internazionale di Studi di Architettura Andrea Palladio*, II (1960), pp. 77–87.

'L'influenza del Palladio sullo sviluppo dell'architettura religiosa veneziana nel sei e settecento', *Bollettino del Centro Internazionale di Studi di Architettura Andrea Palladio*, V (1963), pp. 61–72.

'Le chiese di Andrea Palladio e l'architettura barocca veneta', in *Barocco europeo e barocco veneziano* (ed. V. Branca). Florence, 1963, pp. 77–87.

'Palladio nel mondo anglosassone', *Rotary Club Vicenza*, December 1965, pp. 7–8.

VII. BAROQUE ART AND ARCHITECTURE

'Die vier Apostelstatuen des Camillo Rusconi im Mittelschiff von S. Giovanni in Laterano in Rom, Stilkritische Beiträge zur römischen Plastik des Spätbarock', *Zeitschrift für bildende Kunst*, LX (1926–7), pp. 9–20 and 43–9.

'Die Rolle des Modells in der römischen Barockplastik', *Sitzungsberichte der kunstgeschichtlichen Gesellschaft Berlin*, Oktober–Mai 1928, pp. 5–7.

'Un bronzo dell'Algardi a Urbino', *Rassegna Marchigiana*, VII (1928), pp. 41–4.

'Ein Werk des Stefano Maderno in Dresden', *Zeitschrift für bildende Kunst*, LXII (1928–9), pp. 26–8.

'Eine Bronzegruppe des Melchiorre Cafà', *Zeitschrift für bildende Kunst*, LXII (1928–9), pp. 227–31.

'Ein Bozzetto des Bildhauers Lorenzo Ottoni im Museo Petriano zu Rom', *Repertorium für Kunstwissenschaft*, L (1929), pp. 6–15.

'Die Taufe Christi von Francesco Mochi', *Zeitschrift für bildende Kunst*, LXIV (1930–1), pp. 158–60.

'Zu Hans Sedlmayrs Besprechung von E. Coudenhove-Erthal: *Carlo Fontana*', *Kritische Berichte zur Kunstgeschichtlichen Literatur*, IV (1931–2), pp. 142–5.

'Le Bernin e le Baroque romain', *Gazette des Beaux-Arts*, s. 6, XI (1934), pp. 327–41.

'Pietro da Cortonas Ergänzungsprojekt des Tempels in Palestrina', *Festschrift für Adolph Goldschmidt zu seinem siebenzigsten Geburtstag am 15. Januar 1933*, Berlin, 1935, pp. 137–43.

'Carlo Rainaldi and the Roman Architecture of the Full Baroque', *Art Bulletin*, XIX (1937), pp. 242–313.

'Piranesi's "Parere su l'Architettura"', *Journal of the Warburg and Courtauld Institutes*, II (1938–9), pp. 147–58.

'Domenico Guidi and French Classicism', *Journal of the Warburg and Courtauld Institutes*, II (1938–9), pp. 188–90.

'A Counter-Project to Bernini's "Piazza di S. Pietro"', *Journal of the Warburg and Courtauld Institutes*, III (1939–40), pp. 88–106.

'Domenichino's Madonna della Rosa', *Burlington Magazine*, XC (1948), pp. 220–2.

'Un libro di schizzi di Filippo Juvarra a Chatsworth', *Bollettino Società Piemontese d'archeologia e di belle arti*, III (1949), pp. 94–118.

'Documenti sui modelli per la Sacrestia di S. Pietro a Roma', *Bollettino Società Piemontese d'archeologia e di belle arti*, III (1949), pp. 158–61.

'Il Terzo Braccio del Bernini in Piazza S. Pietro', *Bollettino d'Arte*, XXXIV (1949), pp. 129–34.

'Bernini's Famous Marble Group "Neptune and

Glaucus"', *Illustrated London News*, II (1950), p. 129.

'Works by Bernini at the Royal Academy', *Burlington Magazine*, XCIII (1951), pp. 51–6.

'Bernini Studies I. The Group of Neptune and Triton', *Burlington Magazine*, XCIV (1952), pp. 68–76.

'Bernini Studies II. The Bust of Mr. Baker', *Burlington Magazine*, XCV (1953), pp. 19–22.

'Bernin', in *Les sculpteurs célèbres* (ed. Lucien Mazenod), Paris, 1954, pp. 246–9.

'S. Maria della Salute: Scenographic Architecture and the Venetian Baroque', *Journal of the Society of Architectural Historians*, XVI (1957), pp. 3–10.

'Melchiorre Cafà's Bust of Alexander VII', *The Metropolitan Museum of Art Bulletin*, n.s. XVII (1959), pp. 197–204.

'Impressioni di Varallo', *Atti e memorie del terzo congresso piemontese di antichità ed arte, Congresso di Varallo Sesia* (Sept. 1960), Turin, 1962, pp. xxx–xxxiii.

'Algardi's Relief of Pope Liberius Baptizing Neophytes', *The Minneapolis Institute of Arts Bulletin*, XLIX (1960), pp. 28–42.

'Cornacchinis Reiterstatue Karls des Grossen in St. Peter', *Miscellanea Bibliothecae Hertzianae zu Ehren von Leo Bruhns* (Römische Forschungen der Bibliotheca Hertziana, XV). Munich, 1961, pp. 464–73.

'The Vicissitudes of a Dynastic Monument: Bernini's Equestrian Statue of Louis XIV', in: *De Artibus Opuscula XL, Essays in Honor of Erwin Panofsky*, New York, 1961, pp. 497–531.

'Art and Architecture', in *The New Cambridge Modern History*, V: The Ascendancy of France 1648–88. Cambridge, 1961, pp. 149–75.

'Piranesi as Architect', in *Piranesi* (Exhibition at Smith College Museum of Art, Northampton, Mass.), 1961, pp. 99–109.

'Il barocco in Italia', in *Manierismo, Barocco, Rococò: Concetti e Termini* (Convegno Internazionale, Rome, April 21–24, 1960, Problemi attuali di scienza e di cultura, Accademia Nazionale dei Lincei), Anno CCCLIX, ser. 8, XVII, no. 52 (1962), pp. 319–27.

'S. Maria della Salute', *Saggi e memorie di storia dell'arte*, III (1963), pp. 33–54.

'The Role of Classical Models in Bernini's and Poussin's Preparatory Work', in *Studies in Western Art* (20th International Congress of the History of Art), 1963, III, pp. 41–50.

'Imitation, Eclecticism and Genius', in *Aspects of the Eighteenth Century* (ed. Earl Wasserman). Baltimore, 1965, pp. 143–61.

'Introduction', *Art in Italy, 1600–1700* (ed. Frederick Cummings), The Detroit Institute of Arts, 1965, pp. 11–21.

'La teoria classica e la nuova sensibilità', *Lettere italiane*, XVIII (1966), pp. 194–206.

VIII. CONTEMPORARY PROBLEMS AND MODERN ARCHITECTURE

'Die Eröffnung des Museo di San Pietro in Rom', *Kunstchronik*, LIX, n.f. XXXV (1925–6), pp. 83–5.

'Die dritte Römische Biennale', *Kunstchronik*, LIX, n.f. XXXV (1925–6), pp. 138–9.

'Jahresausstellung der "Accademia di Francia" in Rom', *Kunstchronik*, LIX, n.f. XXXV (1925–6), p. 180.

'Die städtebauliche Zukunft Roms im 20. Jahrhundert', *Kunstchronik*, LIX, n.f. XXXV (1925–6), pp. 673–7.

'Ankauf der Villa Aldobrandini durch den Staat', *Kunstchronik*, LIX, n.f. XXXV (1925–6), pp. 690 f.

'Museumspolitik in Russland', *Die Weltkunst*, Dezember 1931, p. 1.

'Camillo Sitte's *Art of Building Cities* in an American Translation', *Town Planning Review*, XIX (1947), pp. 164–9.

'An Exhibition of American Art at Chicago', *Burlington Magazine*, XCI (1949), p. 254.

'Restoration of Italian Monuments', *Burlington Magazine*, XCI (1949), pp. 141–2.

'Art History as a Discipline', *Winterthur Seminar on Museum Operation and Connoisseurship*, 1959. Winterthur, Delaware, 1961, pp. 55–69.

'Le Corbusier's Modulor', in *Four Great Makers of Modern Architecture* (Symposium from March to May, 1961, School of Architecture, Columbia University). New York, 1963, pp. 196–204.

IX. BOOK REVIEWS

From among the host of reviews—published over the course of the years in such publications as the *Burlington Magazine, Bibliography on the Survival of the Classics* (Warburg Institute, 1931), *Kunstchronik, Zeitschrift für Kunstgeschichte, Kunstgeschichtliche Anzeigen, Architectural Review, The Listener, Review of English Studies, Erasmus*, etc.—the following have been selected for their length, importance, or interest.

'Ernst Heimeran: *Michelangelo und das Porträt*', *Repertorium für Kunstwissenschaft*, XLV (1925), p. 44.

'Leopold Zahn: *Caravaggio*', *Zeitschrift für bildende Kunst*, LXII (1929), p. 96.

'*Notizen und Nachrichten*', *Zeitschrift für Kunstgeschichte*, I (1932), pp. 177–82.

'Josef Weingartner: *Römische Barockkirchen*', *Deutsche Literaturzeitung*, LIII (September 25, 1932), pp. 1854–8.

'A. E. Richardson: *An Introduction to Georgian Architecture*', *Burlington Magazine*, XCII (1950), pp. 331–2.

'C. H. C. and M. Baker: *The Life and Circumstances of James Brydges, First Duke of Chandos, Patron of the Liberal Arts*', *Review of English Studies*, n.s. II (1951), pp. 184–6.

'M. Borissavliévitsch: *Les théories de l'architecture*', *Architectural Review*, CXI (1952), p. 265.

'F. Barbieri: *Vincenzo Scamozzi*', *Burlington Magazine*, XCV (1953), p. 171.

'A proposito dei *Disegni inediti di G. L. Bernini e di L. Vanvitelli* di A. Schiavo', *Palladio*, n.s. IV (1954), p. 89.

'E. Wüsten: *Die Architektur des Manierismus in England*', *Erasmus*, VII (1954), pp. 614–7.